Learning Disabilities

For Churchill Livingstone

Editorial Director: Mary Law
Project Development Manager: Ellen Green
Project Editor: Valerie Bain
Production Controller: Mark Sanderson/Neil Dickson
Sales Promotion Executive: Hilary Brown

Learning Disabilities

A Handbook of Care

Edited by

Eamon Shanley PhD MSc BA(Hons) RMN RNMH CPN RNT
Senior Lecturer, Department of Nursing Studies, University of Glasgow, Glasgow, UK

Thomas A. Starrs MSc RGN RNMH RCNT RNT
Vice Principal, Forth Valley College of Nursing and Midwifery, Falkirk, UK

SECOND EDITION

CHURCHILL LIVINGSTONE
EDINBURGH LONDON MADRID MELBOURNE NEW YORK AND TOKYO 1993

CHURCHILL LIVINGSTONE
Medical Division of Longman Group UK Limited

Distributed in the United States of America by Churchill
Livingstone Inc., 650 Avenue of the Americas, New York,
N.Y. 10011, and by associated companies, branches and
representatives throughout the world.

First edition 1986
   Reprinted 1989 (twice), 1990, 1991
Second edition 1993

ISBN 0-443-04326-4

British Library Cataloguing in Publication Data
A catalogue record for this book is available from the British
Library.

Library of Congress Cataloging in Publication Data
A catalog record for this book is available from the Library of
Congress.

The
publisher's
policy is to use
**paper manufactured
from sustainable forests**

Produced by Longman Singapore Publishers Pte Ltd
Printed in Singapore

Contents

SECTION 1 Perspectives on service provision   1

1. View of the family   3
   I. Allan, A. Owen

2. Evolution of services   19
   M. Bannerman, M. Lindsay

3. Quality of care   41
   A. Chisholm

SECTION 2 Promotion of skills   59

4. Physical causes and conditions   61
   G. Petrie

5. Social causes   83
   G. Petrie

6. Associated conditions   93
   F. Quinn, A. Mathieson

7. Helping with learning difficulties   119
   G. MacKay

8. Helping with sensory impairments   135
   G. Morbey

9. Helping with behavioural problems   149
   M. McCue

10. Helping with social issues   211
    A. Kay

11. Helping with multiple handicap   229
    P. Bradley, P. Darbyshire

12. Helping with communication through movement   269
    B. Burford

SECTION 3 Context for decision-making   291

13. Ethical issues   293
    I. Hessler, B. Kay

14. Helping agencies   307
    H. Stewart

Index   317

Contributors

Isobel Allan Parent of Susan Allan (see ch. 1)
Founder and President, National Rett Syndrome
Association, Glasgow, UK; Bereavement
Counsellor, Cruse, Glasgow, UK

Mamie Bannerman
Assistant District Officer (Adult Care), Glasgow,
UK

Patrick Bradley RNMH CPN RNT
Nurse Teacher (Mental Handicap), Forth Valley
College of Nursing and Midwifery, Falkirk, UK

Bronwen Burford BA
Research Associate, Edinburgh Centre for Research
in Child Development, Department of Psychology,
University of Edinburgh, Edinburgh, UK

W. Alisdair Chisholm RMN RNMH
Divisional General Manager, Mental Health
Services, Grampian Healthcare, Aberdeen, UK

Philip Darbyshire PhD RNMH RSCN DipNurs(Lond)
RNT
Lecturer, Department of Health and Nursing
Studies, Glasgow Caledonian University, Glasgow,
UK

Isabella Hessler RGN RNMD DCNE RNT
Formerly Nurse Tutor (Mental Handicap),
St Joseph's, Rosewell, Midlothian, UK

Alan Kay
Lecturer, Department of Health and Nursing
Studies, Glasgow Caledonian University, Glasgow,
UK

Brian Kay RNMH CertEd(FE) DipPhil&HealthCare RNT
Specialist Lecturer in Mental Handicap Nursing,
Institute of Advanced Nursing Education, Royal
College of Nursing, London, UK

Meg Lindsay MA(Hons) DipAppSocStuds
Freelance Consultant in Community Care,
Glasgow, UK

Alex Mathieson RGN RNMH
Clinical Editor, Nursing Standard, Harrow, UK

Michael McCue RNMH CertBTN
Clinical Nurse Specialist (Behaviour Therapy),
Lennox Castle Hospital, Glasgow, UK

Gilbert MacKay PhD MA DEP
Research Coordinator, Jordanhill College,
Glasgow, UK

Gillian Morbey BA(Hons) SRN
Director, Sense Scotland, Glasgow, UK

Agnes Owen Parent of Elaine Owen (see ch. 1)
Larbert, Stirlingshire, UK

George Petrie BA RGN RNMH DipNurs(ClinTeaching)
RNT
Coordinator (Recruitment and Staff Development),
Lothian College of Nursing and Midwifery,
Edinburgh, UK

Frank Quinn RGN RMN RNMH DipNurs(Lond) RNT
Deputy Director of Services for People with a
Mental Handicap, St Joseph's, Rosewell,
Midlothian, UK

Hugh W. L. Stewart
Deputy Director, Scottish Society for the Mentally
Handicapped, Glasgow, UK

Preface

This book has been written by carers for carers. The contributors include parents, nurses, members of voluntary organisations, therapists and social workers, each of them with knowledge, skills and competence in their subject areas. Their different perspectives should convey a comprehensive understanding of the subject and should militate against the development of narrow professional tribalism.

Since the first edition of this book was published in 1986, there have been wide-ranging changes in the philosophy of care and in the provision of services for people with learning disabilities. This second edition has been radically revised to take account of these developments. It describes the practical means by which the quality of life of those with learning disabilities can be enhanced. The book's style reflects the emphasis on the promotion of self-help; its central theme is about helping change behaviour so that the person is better able to exercise control over his or her activities of daily living. These activities range from the development of communication skills, such as social skills and movement, to the growth of cognitive, emotional and behavioural skills.

The education of those who help people with learning disabilities has also undergone radical revision and alteration since the late 1980s. In many institutions social workers and nurses have shared training. In all educational centres, the philosophy which underpins learning reflects a much greater emphasis on the team approach to care, with the family being acknowledged as vital members of that team.

This new edition reflects these changes in the philosophy of education of carers and the book should be particularly helpful to students, especially nursing students on Project 2000 courses, as well as social work and other nursing students on diploma and degree courses.

The preface to the first edition acknowledged the controversy over terminology in this field. Since the 1980s, there has been increasing use of the term 'learning disabilities' hence our decision to change the title of this book from *Mental Handicap* to *Learning Disabilities*. However, within the text itself, we have chosen to employ a variety of terms in current use. Our position on this contentious issue is stated in full in the Note on Terminology which follows.

1993   E.S. & T.S.

Note on Terminology

For many years a search has been underway for a definitive, stigma-free term to describe people with 'mental handicap'. Unfortunately, the quest for such a term has proved elusive and the history of mental handicap is littered with discarded terms including:

- moron, feebleminded, imbecile, idiot
- mentally subnormal
- mentally retarded
- mentally impaired patients
- mentally handicapped people.

Many professionals feel that the challenge is to identify a term which is both precise in its meaning and stigma-free. However, our observations have led us to conclude that any term — no matter how neutral — will eventually become unsuitable because of its association with a group of people who, unfortunately, continue to be stigmatized by society at large. In other words, until we succeed in changing the public's perception of people with learning disabilities, the terms used to descibe them will continue to come and go. In our view, this preoccupation with terminology distracts attention from this much more important and damaging issue of society's failure towards this group: it is analogous to rearranging the deck chairs on the Titanic and ignoring the real problem.

Having reached this conclusion, we are reluctant, as editors, to enter into this unproductive debate about the relative merits of one term over another. Therefore, throughout this book no one term has been used to the exlusion of all others. Instead, a variety has been employed, namely mental handicap, learning difficulties and learning disabilities. In adopting this approach we are trying to avoid being prescriptive by simply allowing the contributions of each author to reflect current usage.

1993   E.S. & T.S.

Perspectives on service provision

SECTION CONTENTS

1. View of the family   3

2. Evolution of services   19

3. Quality of care   41

Section 1 provides three differing accounts of the interaction between the affected person and his family and the service providers.

The first chapter examines difficulties encountered by the family. The second looks closely at the nature of shortcomings within the service. The third chapter presents a more optimistic outlook in identifying ways that the services can be managed to meet the needs of both the person with learning disabilities and the family through social role valorization.

Chapter 1, written by parents, gives a firsthand account of the experiences of having a child with learning disabilities. The experiences of the two families were quite different, but their common problem was in coming to terms with the knowledge that their children would require some form of care for the rest of their lives.

In Chapter 2, Bannerman and Lindsay outline the social context within which those with learning disabilities have been dealt with in the past. It contains details of changes in attitude and patterns of service provision. It focuses on the underlying philosophy of society today towards people with learning disabilities and examines how this philosophy is expressed in the nature of service provision. In addition, it pursues an issue raised in Chapter 1 by discussing a major cause of the helplessness of parents, that is, the view of professionals that only they, as professionals, are appropriately qualified and sufficiently objective to make decisions for the person with learning disabilities and his or her family.

In Chapter 3, Chisholm describes in detail the issues surrounding the principles and application of quality assurance. These principles are expressed through the framework of social role valorization which attempts to create a role in society for the client, a role which is seen as being of value to him and to society, putting him or her on an equal footing with other people.

CHAPTER CONTENTS

Introduction   3

Elaine's story   4

The first year   4
Family life with Elaine   5
Elaine in hospital   7
Early days   7
Recent years   9

Living with Susan   10

Introduction   10
Awareness of handicap   10
Living with handicap   12
The importance of attitude   14
Acceptance of the individual   17

Mrs Owen with Elaine

Mrs Allan with Susan

1

View of the family

I. Allan   A. Owen

Key points
- Failure of professionals to offer support to parents at the time it was realised that their child was mentally handicapped
- Inadequate support was received from health and social support services, ranging from practical help to support during the grieving process
- The distress of one set of parents seeing their child becoming institutionalized was difficult to bear
- Parents have to learn to deal with emotional problems, often on their own
- More benefit was derived from personal relationships with professionals than from the help given through the professional's formal role
- Parents want a greater degree of involvement in decisions taken about their children

INTRODUCTION

This chapter presents two accounts by mothers of the lives of their children with learning disabilities, born over a decade apart. Elaine was born in 1969 and Susan was born in 1980. The accounts of their lives give the reader some insight into the experience of the arrival of a child with learning disabilities into a family and the family's experience with the services they encountered. There are similarities in the ways both parents were first informed about their child's handicap and in the inadequacy of support and advice given, both during and after the time they were informed of their child's condition.

Elaine's mother, Agnes, in particular, was informed in an extremely insensitive manner, while Susan's mother, Isobel, felt considerable distress.

There is currently no nationally accepted system of providing support and advice for parents and family at the time they are told of the diagnosis. The problem is exacerbated by the lack of coordination among the large number of professionals and agencies involved in the provision of care. Agencies and individuals often assume others are providing the necessary services while the person falls through the net. From the parents' perspective it may be difficult to identify what help is available and how to access it – this point is particularly well illustrated in *Living with Susan*.

The descriptions of the involvement of the parents in decision-making are an important aspect of the chapter. In Isobel's case, there were attempts to involve her in discussion about Susan's needs. However, in one instance, when she was invited to attend a meeting to decide on Susan's educational future she was excluded from major discussions in the meeting. Only towards the end of the meeting was she asked to join in. The experience of being excluded is not unusual for many parents. With the increased emphasis on the rights of the consumers of services, parents should no longer be subjected to the same level of disregard but be seen by professionals as central figures in deciding the future of their children.

ELAINE'S STORY
A. Owen

THE FIRST YEAR

When I broke the news of my third pregnancy in 3 years to my husband and family they were not pleased. We already had a 4-year-old daughter and an infant son, and I had suffered a 7-month miscarriage in between their births.

My pregnancy was normal, but I worried quite a bit about how we would cope with two infants. On 25 December 1969, after filling Christmas stockings for our two children, I went into labour

at 3 a.m. and Elaine was born in the local maternity hospital at 6.40 a.m. by normal delivery. She was the hospital's 'Christmas baby'. Elaine progressed normally. She was a very good baby and she slept a lot, which was a great help in giving me time for our other children.

When Elaine was 3 months old she suddenly went into a kind of spasm of her hands and body. We immediately sent for our family doctor. The doctor was most reassuring. Elaine was having small fits caused by her having a slight head cold. He said that it was not unusual for infants to fit when their temperature was raised and prescribed a small dose of phenobarbitone until the fits stopped. When the fits did not stop after several weeks Elaine was referred to the paediatrician. He too was very reassuring and admitted Elaine to hospital for tests. She was then 4 months old. I was very upset and asked about the tests but was simply told not to worry.

We collected Elaine from hospital 2 weeks later. She had been given a series of injections which had left her whole body puffy, with the drastic side effect of a constant raging thirst. (I discovered years later that she had been given steroids.) She had turned into a screaming, shrieking baby who hated to be touched and required constant attention. When the effects of the injections wore off the fits began to get very bad and she became very hyperactive.

In the middle of this nightmare a semblance of normal life carried on. Our elder daughter started school, our son started to walk and my husband went to work. The doctor at the baby clinic advised against Elaine having the whooping cough vaccination, but she had all the rest of the recommended inoculations and sugar lumps.

Every month the ambulance came to take us to the outpatients' department at the hospital. Elaine was weighed and examined and I was asked how she was. I would then ask what was wrong with her but never received an answer. Then came the magic words, 'I will give a diagnosis when Elaine is 1 year old'. The paediatrician decided to give Elaine another series of injections and the district nurse called every day for 2 weeks to administer them. We were never informed what the injections were for. Again, Elaine had to suffer a puffy body and raging thirst, and the whole family suffered with her. One evening in desperation, after she had screamed for 4 solid hours, I asked our GP to call. He gave Elaine an injection to make her sleep and waited a few minutes until it took effect. She was awake and screaming 5 minutes later. This was the beginning of the discovery that Elaine's body did not recognise time. A 5-minute snooze and it was though she had been asleep for hours.

Elaine's body continued to develop normally during this time. She had very fast reflexes but showed no sign of talking or sitting on her own. We used to surround her with cushions, toys and members of the family, but there was little response apart from her occasional smile. We knew that Elaine was ill as every day we watched her take fit after fit, but there was always the hope that she would get better. I don't know how we survived the next few months. The worry and stress affected all of us. My own life became very narrow; my time and energy went to Elaine first then the rest of the family. I also made a point of going out socially one night a week and my husband went out on another night. I think this escape was very important to both of us as a reminder that there was still a normal life outside our home.

Elaine's first birthday arrived and the most important appointment in her life. The paediatrician broke the good news first: the series of injections had saved Elaine's life. Then came the diagnosis: 'Elaine is epileptic and brain damaged. Keep her clean and fed and ignore her. She will never sit up, walk or talk. Do not waste time on looking after her. She will get a residential place in a hospital for the mentally handicapped. Until then bring her to see me every month.'

I was so angry I could not even be civil to him. What right had this man to decide our daughter's future with no more emotion than if she was a piece of wood? I could accept that Elaine was mentally handicapped, indeed I think we already knew this, but that she would be little more than a vegetable I could not accept.

FAMILY LIFE WITH ELAINE

Relatives and friends had very mixed reactions to the news. One close relation kept suggesting that Elaine could have an operation. We could not make her understand that there was no operation. Most people tried to be understanding, but Elaine could not be left with anyone as they appeared nervous about coping with her fits. One odd reaction that some people had was that it was a waste of time to talk to Elaine because she would not understand. We have come up against this attitude several times. From the start we never tried to hide Elaine away or disguise the fact that she was handicapped. When people commented on her slowness in, for example, sitting up, we explained about her fits. I think this helped us enormously in accepting Elaine as she is. We never played the game of 'If only she was all right' as some of our relatives did.

Our GP was very supportive and helpful through all the months of worry. He advised using maximum doses of the drugs Mogadon and Valium and made constant house calls during the months that Elaine suffered with whooping cough, which of course she took. She also had measles, mumps, bronchitis and pneumonia, all of which I nursed her through. Our doctor even arranged a caravan holiday for us through a local charity. We never received any counselling or advice on dealing with epileptic fits or mental handicap. We learned by trial and error. Our elder daughter, although very young, was a great help. She fetched and carried, looked after her brother and helped look after Elaine.

Elaine eventually sat up on her own and we spent hours walking her by holding her up until she walked on her own. When she walks she has no sense of direction so the end result is a kind of aimless wandering. But she does walk. Elaine had to have her movement restricted as it was dangerous for her to walk around unsupervised because she banged into furniture, overbalanced and had no awareness of danger. She learned to tip the pram over so we obtained a wheelchair. Because she could relax her body completely she could escape from any kind of restraint. She would be harnessed into her chair with a belt round her middle and still escape. She also escaped from her clothes, either by taking them off or by biting through them.

I had requested a second opinion about Elaine's condition and she was admitted to a specialized children's hospital for an assessment. There was a hint of a suggestion by the admitting doctor that Elaine had been abused as she had several bruises. These had been caused when she was allowed to walk about freely for a short time each day and I explained this, but I could see his uncertainty. When we visited the following week we were horrified by the way she had deteriorated. She was in a cot beside children's drawings on the wall and had been eating them. Her leg was badly bruised where it was caught between the spars on the cot. Her drugs had been withdrawn all at once so tests could be done and she was extremely distressed. We were once again given the same advice – wait for the residential place in hospital. (It is now commonly known that sudden withdrawal of Valium has drastic side effects yet this was done to our daughter before she was 2 years old.)

When Elaine was 2 years old a place was obtained for her at a nursery for disabled children. She went every weekday, which made a big difference to her life and gave me a break. She was not capable of taking part in the activities, but the change of environment and people seemed to help her. The couple who ran the nursery offered to take Elaine for a week so we could have a family holiday. We spent the whole week worrying about her. When we returned we were informed that she did not sleep. Elaine continued to attend the nursery for the next 2 years and appeared to be quite happy. During this time we were awarded an attendance allowance for Elaine and this helped our financial situation.

We found that a small tin filled with pennies was a toy that kept Elaine amused for 10 minutes at a time. We also discovered that if Elaine cried she did not know how to stop so we tried to prevent her crying. She loved to eat and small cheese savouries spread over her tray kept her occupied for a while because she would pick them up and eat them one at a time. Bathtime followed by supper, was a very happy time of

day before the nightly trauma of bedtime. If Elaine was put in a cot awake she simply toppled out, placing herself in danger. We wrapped her in a blanket and took turns trying to get her to sleep. If this was successful she was then placed in her cot for her sleep of one hour. If we did not get her to sleep she was put in our bed and we went to sleep with Elaine jumping around between us.

The staff at the day nursery were no longer keen to have Elaine. They did not have the facilities for such a profoundly handicapped child. When Elaine chewed a new pair of curtains at the nursery it was suggested that all her teeth should be extracted to stop her being destructive. This had seemingly been normal treatment years before, but we would never have agreed to this. Elaine stayed at home but eventually went back to the nursery, with her teeth intact.

When I became ill this caused a major problem. My husband took unpaid leave, but we were already living on a small income and could not live without any money. The doctor and social work department arranged for Elaine to go into a home for people with a handicap. As this was a private concern we had to find the money to pay for it. When I recovered Elaine came home and we were assigned a social worker. Unfortunately, our social worker had no knowledge of living with a handicapped child and a long discussion was necessary to inform her of our problems. A month later, when the social worker was due to visit, she was transferred and we were assigned a new one. We felt that any help the social workers could give was not worth the effort on our part. The only advantage gained in our dealings with the social work department was the home use of a high-sided hospital cot.

A strange part of living with Elaine was the silence. She made a noise when she banged her toys but apart from crying she never made a sound. When she took a fit there was no warning noise so she had to be watched all the time. We talked to her constantly saying 'baby talk' phrases over and over again in the hope of stimulating some kind of speech. She still hated to be cuddled or touched, but we continued to try to show her visible affection. Her physical growth continued normally and apart from the hyperactivity she still looked like an ordinary child.

I had approached our GP on several occasions about our son who had reached the age of 4 and was still not talking. I began to be very worried about this and panicked when he started going to the nursery because he could not speak, was very withdrawn and would not mix with the other children. An IQ test and hearing assessment was arranged. The tests showed that he had a very high IQ and his hearing was perfect. It was discovered that he was copying Elaine as she did not speak and his elder sister was inadvertently doing his talking for him so he had no need to learn. Several years of speech therapy were required to correct this. Finding that he was all right was one less worry.

A breakthrough came on a family day out to the seaside. When we arrived Elaine had a massive fit and fell into a deep sleep. When she woke up she suddenly started screaming, but this was different to anything that had happened before. This screaming was a sound of pure joy. Anyone seeing us that day must have thought we were mad. Two adults and two children all smiling and laughing with a third shrieking child in a wheelchair. It did not last, but we remember it as the day there was two-way contact with Elaine.

ELAINE IN HOSPITAL
Early days

It was the health visitor who brought us the news that Elaine had been given a residential place in hospital and on 7 March 1974, we put our 4-year-old daughter into hospital as an informal patient. We still have the receipt.

We were advised not to visit for the first weeks to give Elaine a chance to settle down so I went from caring 23 hours a day to nothing. During Elaine's 4 years I had developed an awareness of her needs that was almost like an extra sense. Because she could not communicate I had to know if she was ill, going to fit, happy, tired, hungry or thirsty. Without Elaine

I became very depressed. I also could not cope with the feeling of guilt that I had given my child away when she needed me. I still had two children who were dependent on me and they were well cared for, but nothing could replace my missing daughter. We had no offer of advice or counselling from any direction on how to manage. In hospital, Elaine had been reassessed and placed in a high-dependency ward. Elaine was very bouncy and energetic compared to the other patients in the ward, but the hospital doctor advised us that she was on the same mental level as them. In fact, he said that Elaine would never recognise us and it made no difference to her where she lived or who looked after her.

At that time, patients in the hospital did not have their own clothes and when we started to visit Elaine every weekend it was very distressing to see her becoming institutionalized. The patients were all dressed the same, had the same hair cuts and the smell of the hospital clung to everything. The nurse in charge referred to the patients as her 'children'. When she started to call Elaine her child I became very annoyed and slightly jealous. It was hard enough trying to cope with Elaine being in hospital without being made to feel inadequate whenever I visited.

There was at this time no therapy for the highly dependent patient and with only three or four staff to 30 patients there was not much play time. We lived only 15 miles from the hospital, but using public transport involved catching four buses and 3 hours of travelling. I did this journey every weekend for over 6 years. I lived with my other children every day – Saturday was Elaine's time.

Over the years the hospital staff had some problems in looking after Elaine. She had to be bathed last every night because she loves water and could be very difficult about getting out of it. As Elaine toppled out of her cot a canvas lid was tied over the top of it. One evening a nurse heard a noise from the dormitory. When she went to check there was Elaine bouncing happily on top of the lid. One of the ties had been loose and she climbed out. Another nurse was very badly bruised when she was sitting near Elaine.

The nurse rose from her chair for a second then sat back down, but Elaine had whipped the chair away. This has happened several times. Elaine sometimes appears to have extending arms. When in her wheelchair she has to be placed away from anything moveable by 2 arms' lengths as she can reach by stretching her arms and body.

During all this time Elaine still had a tendency to rip her clothing. This was obviously due in part to boredom so we were very pleased when the law that every child has a right to an education was implemented and Elaine was accepted into the hospital school. The school made a great difference to Elaine and she became much happier and more alert. During school holidays she seemed to revert to not paying as much attention. We still took Elaine home for regular holidays and it was always very difficult to take her back to the hospital. We were upset, but Elaine was always happy in either place.

One year, when I arrived for the Christmas party I found that Elaine had been transferred to another unit for medical treatment. The sister in charge said that it looked like Elaine had been burnt even though this was not possible. I went to the other unit and found that Elaine was unconscious and had several large blisters on her arms. The blisters looked like burns. The doctor said enquiries would be made and one helpful worker said I could sue. It turned out that Elaine had been given an antibiotic by her GP and the 'burns' were a side effect of this drug. It was a drug that was commonly used and Elaine had been unlucky because she was allergic to it. After a worrying week she started to get better but she still has the scars of the blisters on her arm and hand today.

In 1980 we moved house to within 3 miles of the hospital so visiting Elaine became easier. We had to stop taking Elaine home on overnight visits because she had matured into an adult at a very young age (I believe this is a side effect of all the drugs). Because of arthritis I could no longer bath Elaine on my own and her father felt he could not help as she was no longer a child. So Elaine was brought home every weekend for an afternoon visit.

On one home visit, when Elaine was 17, she discovered how to open doors. Our excitement was almost as great as her delight when she spent the whole afternoon turning the door handle and banging the door back against the wall. I contacted the school headmistress with the news of this development and when they tested Elaine she opened a door in the school. It seems silly that we were so happy about such a small thing, but it was a major step forward for Elaine. Unfortunately, this was as far as the learning process went.

When Elaine reached 18 years of age she was due to leave school. I had to attend an interview with a representative of the education authority on two occasions with reasons why she should be allowed an extension at school. I managed to have her kept on at school until her 19th birthday. After the progress Elaine had maintained in school I was very worried about her being in the ward all day, with very little stimulation. Indeed, I had visions of her just sitting there for years on end. The staff on the ward were excellent, but they did not have time for the one-to-one contact that Elaine required. I requested through the senior nurse manager and Elaine's social worker that they apply for a place for her in a day centre. I felt that just because she was an inpatient there was no reason why she could not attend a centre even for 2 or 3 days a week. Unfortunately, after a considerable time, the day centre supervisor turned Elaine down, but I am hopeful that a place in a new unit can be obtained for her in the future.

At the moment Elaine has several different therapies. She uses the ball pool in a neighbouring ward with great enthusiasm. She has a touch therapy session with an occupational therapist once a week and three 45-minute sessions with a school teacher who visits the ward. While we are very pleased that this is happening it still leaves a great many hours for her to sit in the ward. On a good day Elaine is very bright and happy and on two occasions that I know of this has caused hospital staff to overestimate her capabilities. She was twice left in an unsupervised situation when out of her wheelchair. We were very worried about this and had to seek reassurance from the nursing management that this would not happen again. It was very difficult to complain about this as we had always put our trust implicitly in her carers, but Elaine's welfare and safety is our primary concern at all times. I suppose two complaints in 16 years is an excellent record, but I would be far happier if there had been none. However, over the years a great many people have been involved in caring for Elaine and we are very grateful for this.

In 1989 we moved house again to within 5 minutes' walk of the hospital. Due to a breakdown in my health I have given up work and can now visit Elaine more often.

Thanks to an idea by one of the nursing staff the problem of Elaine tearing and eating her clothes has been solved. A local firm contributed denim material and the hospital sewing team made the material up into one piece suits fastened down the back with Velcro. Elaine has so far been unable to rip her way through them. It took 20 years but we've been successful at last. It is also a weight off my mind as I used to worry a great deal about the materials she swallowed causing an obstruction.

Recent years

Over the years we have maintained close contact with Elaine and as her personality has emerged she has become a very happy, boisterous person. She has never been subjected to anger or unkindness and has no fear. She still loves to eat and play. We have remained a constant factor in her life and she recognises us the minute we walk into the ward. She also screams her delight when taken home. We have learned to, if not live with, accept the guilt and worry that has been an integral part of our lives for so long. Her elder sister is a staff nurse in mental handicap nursing, her brother is a design engineer and they are both at present raising their own families. When I asked them if having Elaine for a sister had detracted from their own childhood they both assured me that they only have happy memories of a united family. We recently introduced Elaine to her 7-week-old nephew and were delighted by her reaction to

him. She smiled for several minutes and stared, then her hand flashed out and grabbed his blue fluffy slippers. We shall have to wait and see if she will eventually notice the baby.

We were very interested when the hospital implemented the Crosby Report (HMSO 1985) and were happy to take part in discussions. As Elaine received a noncontributory pension and mobility allowance she has built up a substantial amount in the bank. We arranged with her senior nurse manager that in future I should purchase all Elaine's clothing. I receive a basic amount and when I return receipts to the hospital I am reimbursed for the amount spent. When Elaine needs anything to wear the charge nurse advises me and I purchase what is required. This seems to work very well and saves the staff on the ward time. We also hope to take Elaine on holiday some time in the future using some of her money to take a nurse to assist. She also has an occasional take-away meal in the evening as a change from the hospital diet.

In all the years that Elaine has been in hospital we have never once been invited to any meeting about her, apart from the one about the Crosby Report. We have always had day-to-day reports from the on-the-spot nursing staff. I have had one or two meetings with her doctor, always at my request, about her levels of toxicity. We have never received any official reports about her abilities, treatments, therapies or anything else. We have never been invited to participate in any joint activity, although we are joint carers and we are Elaine's legal guardians. We were delighted when a relatives' association was formed recently and it has been a pleasure to meet other relatives of residents at the hospital, and to discuss common problems.

There has been a sameness about all the years of visiting Elaine because of her limited learning abilities. There are worrying days when she is taking fits and is miserable, and happy days when we have good eye contact and there is great pleasure to be gained from her simple joy of life. Life with her consists of extremes as there are no half-way measures with Elaine. I have sung the same nursery tunes over and over again for nearly 21 years and it still remains a challenge to get her to react to us each time we see her. Our family has on occasion been isolated by our problems, but we have all gained patience and a wealth of understanding through knowing Elaine and the worries and miseries are far outweighed by the happiness she gives. Our child will never grow up and leave us.

REFERENCE

The Crosby Report 1985 Report of the working party on incapax patients' funds, Chairman: Crosby W S. HMSO, London

LIVING WITH SUSAN
I. Allan

INTRODUCTION

The welcoming news of my fourth pregnancy was greeted with great excitement within our family. Sheer delight at having another child was only marred by the strong medical advice that this child should be our last child. The loss of my first child due to a miscarriage, a difficult birth with my second child, followed by a caesarean section, dictated that this child be a planned caesarean section.

As with my two fine sons, this new baby decided to make an early entrance into the world. During my 38th week I was delivered of a healthy baby daughter. Susan was born on 8 May 1980, weighing 5½ lbs. As our last child she was precious and as a girl she was an added bonus to our now complete family. Her brothers of 5 and 10 years and her proud dad ensured that Susan had constant attention, love and care. Susan was a perfectly healthy little girl and developed well during her first year of life. She crawled, cut her first tooth, spoke her first word and gave us endless joy at her decorative attempts in finger feeding. She adored company and we quite unashamedly indulged and spoiled her.

When Susan was about 1 year old I had an uneasy feeling that 'something was not quite right' with my precious daughter. She seemed to ignore sounds and would not reach out and grasp her favourite toys as she had done so often in the past. She seemed distant and unresponsive when I tried to cuddle and play with her. Her favourite songs no longer held her interest. It was not that she ceased to acquire new skills that concerned me but that she was 'forgetting' the skills she had already learned. My instincts told me that something was seriously wrong with my daughter. Close family and friends tried to reassure me that my concerns were unfounded; after all my child looked so perfectly 'normal'. Numerous visits to my local baby clinic heightened my anxiety and frustration when it was subtly suggested that I was perhaps over-anxious and unduly concerned about her welfare. It seemed everyone felt I had imagined fears about Susan's development and I soon began to question my own ability as a mother. The behaviour and attitude of others towards my concerns seemed almost dismissive and I began to feel embarrassed at voicing my concerns for fear of being labelled a neurotic mother.

AWARENESS OF HANDICAP

Within a few months, however, it became apparent to others that Susan *did* have some underlying problem. My happy, loving daughter became more and more withdrawn and isolated. She screamed incessantly and would sleep for only a few hours daily. I felt helpless when my daughter lost the constructive use of her hands and devastated to discover she no longer recognised or responded to any of her close family. Being an observer to a loved one's suffering, combined with a feeling of helplessness, is an almost unbearable situation to endure.

I felt almost relief at having my concerns believed when my family doctor referred Susan to hospital for further investigations, although I now prayed that my fears were unfounded. During the weeks and months that followed endless tests were made to discover what was wrong with Susan. During this time she continued to deteriorate both physically and mentally. At one of our hospital visits my husband and I were gently informed that our daughter had some serious unknown neurological disorder.

Figure 1.1   Grieving for loss.

We were totally devastated; our worst nightmare became a reality. We had entered a new world: a world of uncertainty, fear and isolation. Although we were grateful for the efforts made in attempting to diagnose Susan's problem, no support was offered to us as a family. We were grieving – not only for what our child had lost but also for what we had lost (Fig. 1.1).

I recalled how supportive it had been to receive a visit, within my home, from a trained professional 24 hours after leaving hospital following the birth of my children. In contrast, having been informed that my only daughter was mentally and physically handicapped, I felt abandoned to cope with my own despair. I was offered no opportunity to share my fears and confused emotions during those critical initial weeks following diagnosis with a skilled experienced counsellor or knowledgeable person in the field of handicap. I now firmly believe that many emotional difficulties in coping with handicap (Fig. 1.2) experienced by families in later years, stem from the lack of immediate and on-going support following the diagnosis of handicap.

The reaction within our close family was akin to that for a bereavement. We were suffering a great loss, not of our child but of our expectations for our child. Some friends avoided us, not quite knowing what to say or do. Our only support came from one or two close family friends and a compassionate family doctor. Susan's health

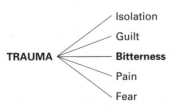

Figure 1.2   Coping with feelings.

visitor became my mentor, offering me the most precious gift – her time and ability to listen to my fears with sensitivity and without judgement. However, no statutory arrangements appear to exist to offer a similar service and families may often have to rely upon the goodwill or availability of their family doctor or local health centre.

It came as some curious relief when my daughter's disorder was eventually identified. She was suffering from a rare and then relatively unknown disorder called Rett syndrome (Kerr & Stephenson 1985). This disorder strikes only *female* children (at least 1–12 000) resulting in profound mental and physical handicap. As the syndrome is confined to girls, the X chromosome must play a vital role. Simply having a name to give the disorder strangely took the edge off my grief. I felt at least I now had something constructive to learn about which may, in time, offer me opportunities to help my child.

Discovering information about Rett syndrome proved difficult, however, as the disorder had only recently been diagnosed worldwide. My love for my child, combined with my concern for her future, motivated me to write countless letters to physicians and organizations, both in this country and abroad, seeking any details on the prognosis of this unheard of disorder. My first supportive feedback and information came, not from this country, but from a doctor in Sweden (Hagberg 1985). Encouraged by this doctor's response to a mother's letter I became determined to discover other families who had a daughter with this disorder. In 1985, an organization was born, the National Rett Syndrome Association, aimed at offering support and information to families and other interested parties.

A handicapped child lives within a handicapped family. The disorder a child suffers from can be equalled by the disorder parents suffer from, that of isolation. No problem within itself may destroy an individual: what can destroy is when we feel that no one cares.

Attempting to understand the system and what could be done to help my child also proved difficult. I quickly discovered that seeking information and support within the statutory system is both frustrating and confusing. Many people are highly trained and knowledgeable in their own particular field, but there appears to be no adequate liaison between skills, no continuity of information and support that could guide families through the maze of services that may be available. I found the most reliable and useful information about statutory services came from other families who had similarly learned from others.

LIVING WITH HANDICAP

As time progresses, families can learn to live and cope with their feelings of despair at *having* a child with a handicap. However, no family can truly 'get used to' handicap; this is impossible when dealing with a nonstatic situation. As the child grows older new difficulties (for both child and carer) have to be faced and dealt with.

Partly due to the course of the disorder and partly due to suffering from a profound handicap, Susan continued to show – sometimes subtle – signs of deterioration. She developed seizures, contractures in her feet and sadly lost her ability to stand or walk. Adding to her difficulties were the signs of early scoliosis (curvature of the spine). These inevitable and distressing problems were, at least in part, offset by my feelings of great joy as Susan began to respond to her family and enjoy once again being hugged and loved. Although she continued to suffer sudden, unexplained and sometimes prolonged outbursts of deep distress, I realised I had entered a new dimension in coping (Fig. 1.3). By being aware and acknowledging Susan's positive responses and attempts I was appreciating the *value of the child within the handicap*. Although she had no pur-

Figure 1.3 Living with handicap.

poseful use of her hands and could not speak, my daughter's enchanting smile spoke volumes. Within the burden of the disease is the blessing of the child and I knew if I were to *live* rather than *exist* with her disabilities I must strive constantly to view the positive, as well as the negative aspects of her handicap. This fine balancing act is the most difficult and long-term challenging problem families will encounter, throughout their own and their child's lifetime.

Within handicap we all tend to fall into one of two categories: we are either observers or sufferers. The true sufferers of handicap are the holders of the handicap; everyone else is but an observer. However, observers can have different roles, that of the parent or full-time carer, or others associated with the handicapped person. As Susan's mother, I quickly found that through *living, loving and caring* for my child, I too became a sufferer – not by *having* the handicap but by living with the consequences of the handicap. This can impose tremendous stress on the parent. A parent with this dual role requires sometimes impossible abilities and talents to combat and offset distress, not only within her child but also within herself and other members of the close family. As her child grows older so too does the parent who may become self-critical when emotional or physical stress seems unrelenting and lifelong.

Many parents may fear or resent the opinions and reactions of others to their distress and may dread being thought of as no longer capable or even unstable. Lack of understanding and awareness can lead others to assume that the parent has not accepted the fact that they have a child with a handicap. Although this may be true of some parents, especially those who lacked support and were denied opportunities to share their hurt feelings following the diagnosis of handicap, I feel it is not true of the majority of families. It is not the fact that the child has a handicap that causes later problems but rather that new challenges and difficulties are constantly being encountered throughout the life of their child.

The continuous yet changing demands imposed by handicap may create tremendous physical, mental, social and emotional strains for the full-time carer. Parents require practical, social and emotional support and encouragement which identify their needs. Too often, we fail to react to the problem as it truly is but respond on the basis of our impression of the problem. Realistic interpretation of a parent's concerns, difficulties and needs are *essential* prerequisites for effective support.

Parents seldom give themselves credit for their own worth, even though the majority of parents (in time) become highly skilled in the care, understanding and management of their own child. It should be mentioned that this knowledge and experience can prove an invaluable resource if incorporated within the training procedures of those who choose to work with the handicapped. A highly skilled (not rote) trained professional will value and respect the opinion and contribution parents can offer towards the development of their child. A need to be sensitive, without being intrusive, and an ability to accept rather than judge parents, offer a professional solid ground on which to build a stable and trusting relationship with the family.

Many parents may resent or be suspicious of professional involvement. This may, in part, be due to some unpleasant past experience or insensitive handling in their past dealings with individuals within the statutory services. This hostility, whether justified or not, often hinders firm relationships being established; parents may become defensive or overprotective of their role. However, if an element of mutual trust can be established support offered and received is often meaningful rather than superficial.

My own greatest support has come from those who could empathize with my own thoughts and feelings. I consider myself *fortunate* to be involved with those who invite me to offer my *thoughts* regarding Susan's health, welfare and educational needs – I consider it *unique* when I am invited to share my *feelings* about Susan. What a person thinks and how a person feels may offer different yet both honest views.

When my daughter was fitted with a splint and boots to help correct contractures in her feet, I was duly shown the correct procedure in fitting these items. I appreciated the fitter's explanation that they were necessary and agreed with the view that white boots are more attractive than the black boots apparently issued in past years. Yet on the return journey home from the fitting I had the most overwhelming feeling of deep sadness. My logic informed me that these items were necessary to help Susan, but my feelings experienced the pain of a mother's helplessness and lack of control over yet another new aspect and deterioration as a result of her handicap. Although my thoughts and feelings differed, they were both nevertheless true.

It is heartwarming when a parent's opinions are invited, yet the most beneficial support can be offered when a parent's feelings are invited, accepted and understood. The opinions of a hurt parent may be honest, perhaps sometimes superficial, whereas the feelings of a hurt parent hold a deeper and more accurate truth.

A milestone in any child's life is when he or she starts school. As with my sons, I viewed Susan's departure to school with a mixture of emotions. The inevitable pangs of concern at sharing your child's upbringing with another are balanced by a sense of excitement at the new challenges they will meet. Prior to Susan starting school, I learned that the Warnock Report (HMSO 1978) had been instrumental in offering every child the right to education. This facility was denied profoundly handicapped children until recent years. A carefully compiled record of needs was recorded about Susan and I was delighted when informed that my contribution and understanding about my daughter's needs, difficulties and abilities were a vital component in its construction. My enthusiasm, however, turned to despair at the final meeting which would formulate my daughter's record of needs. I arrived on time for the meeting and looked forward eagerly to the group discussions that had been arranged. I was impressed at the people arriving for this meeting: Susan's instructress, room teacher, school nurse, school doctor, child psychologist and head of the school. I duly waited and viewed all of the above being invited into a room for the meeting which would involve final group discussions about my child's future educational needs. Over 1 hour passed before I was invited to join the group. During that time, I felt horror, anger and deep distress, knowing *my* child's welfare and future well-being were being discussed by others, while I waited alone in another room. When I was invited to join the group, the participants all showed genuine surprise at my now apparent distress. The most alarming and deeply concerning aspect of that situation focused on the inability of trained professionals to view the contribution of the full-time carer as necessary. Ironically, the information on Rett syndrome which was necessary to formulate the construction of the record of needs was provided by myself from a variety of contacts I had established in the UK and other countries. To conduct any meeting in such a fashion is both insensitive and deeply discourteous, although I do not believe that this unpleasant experience was due to unkindness by anyone involved. However, I firmly believe a lack of awareness of the needs of the family and a position of peer status *did* exist.

I believe the parent or full-time carer is *the* main educator in the life of his or her child, particularly if that child has special needs. A disregard of the parent's role causes unnecessary anxiety and frustration which add to the strain of caring for a handicapped child and can create voids in the parent/professional relationship. Parents who show an interest and desire should be encouraged to become more involved with their child's well-being. It has been my experience that some parents are made to feel somehow indebted to others for their child's deserved right to education. Some professionals and parents may view the educational time given to a profoundly handicapped child as an ideal opportunity to offer the family a break; this attitude reinforces the concept that somehow parents of a handicapped child are offered some sort of special favour. Although I certainly do appreciate the time Susan is at school (and do welcome the break from the 24-hour-a-day commitment) I view this aspect as an added bonus. As with my sons, my daughter has a right to education. No one presumes that the children at mainstream schools are there to give their parents some respite; they attend school to learn *to the fullest of their own abilities*. I wish no less for my daughter than I do for my sons.

There is a richness in a service offered to an individual in contrast to a training applied. The former tends to offer a skill which adapts to the person's needs thus viewing the child within the handicap. The latter may fail to observe the merits of the individual, seeking only to impart knowledge on a one-sided basis. Our attitude towards a mentally handicapped person determines our degree of giving not our degree of success, which is of secondary value. Those who serve with skill and those who apply training only may offer very different views regarding their thoughts and feelings about mental handicap.

The importance of attitude

Parents are often eager to receive support towards the care, management and education of their child. However, support given should be the support needed. Too often, parents may be offered advice when they are faced with a difficulty. This seldom solves the situation, as advice is normally someone else's opinion or solution to another person's problem. Advice without understanding is seldom helpful as it is impossible to *experience* another person's life. A compassionate, skilful person who can supply information needed and offer selfless support can empathize with another's needs. Both the handicapped and nonhandicapped would benefit greatly from this approach.

I believe our thoughts, feelings, communications and actions are governed by one of three things – fear, power or love. Where there is hostility, poor communication or defensiveness on the part of the professional *or* the parent, perhaps fear or power plays a major role. Parents should never feel guilty or inadequate when new challenges arise and seem insurmountable, or if their coping level cannot meet the new difficulty. Realistically, these feelings can occur on numerous occasions and in particular when the balance of responsibility is disproportionate within families, or when emotional exhaustion hinders personal growth. When the child becomes an adult, it is no reflection on the love and care given if a parent feels he or she can no longer continue to cope due to their own advancing years.

The physical care and management problems in dealing with the growing child (Allan 1987) create difficulties not fully appreciated until experienced. Susan is a passive partner in dressing and changing procedures and her lack of co-operation, even in the simplest act of changing clothing, can be exhausting for the carer. The fact that she is doubly incontinent and requires enemas on a regular basis creates difficulties, not only with hygiene but also with privacy. Our social life and family plans can be disrupted when her bodily requirements have to be met. The simple act of bathing Susan is a planned strategy which often requires assistance.

Family mealtimes can be great fun for all the family. We feel it is vital that Susan not only sits with her family at the table at the same level but also that she eats her meal with her family, not before or after them. Having no constructive hand use dictates that Susan requires to be fed at all times by another person. I could not possibly count how many times, over the years, I have eaten a meal on my own without feeding another person. Indeed, when dining out without my daughter I have to make a conscious effort *not* to feed the person on my left-hand side!

Providing adequate safety for Susan in her bed still causes concern, as she tends to kick or unintentionally move (due to her involuntary body movements) the safety rail which we provided for her. Sleepless nights for the family are a common occurrence when Susan awakes in the middle of the night crying. This can occur often during the winter months as she can kick off or manoeuvre out of her bed coverings. Her vulnerability and dependence on others are then painfully obvious as her cries inform us that she is feeling the cold and has no ability to perform the simple act of covering herself. Lengthy delays in providing suitable equipment for a handicapped child, or installing specific adaptations to the home, may cause needless frustration and fail to serve the best interests of the child. The adaptations to a wheelchair provided for Susan

took over 1 year and when finally completed proved inadequate as Susan had outgrown the wheelchair.

Difficulties experienced by families in coping with the newly diagnosed young handicapped child are dominated initially by the need to adjust emotionally to the situation. In later years, although emotional problems may still be experienced, the physical demands of management impose *real* limitations, particularly if the person is wheelchair bound. Some of my own physical problems are a direct result of incorrect procedures in lifting Susan in the past. Although, given time, emotional wounds may heal, it is impossible to repair physical damage to joints and muscles, especially when management problems can only increase with age. Perhaps guidance given in earlier years may have offset present problems and offered me some preparation for the enormity of the physical management difficulties that are a consequence of living with profound mental and physical handicap.

Having a large home can mask the suitability of that home for the handicapped child. Faced with moving house, or adding an extension to our home to provide a downstairs bedroom and bathroom for Susan, we decided choosing the latter course caused less disruption to the lifestyle of other members within our family. Problems in understanding the complicated procedures in building an extension were added to by numerous delays associated with protocol and finance. We discovered there is a ceiling level on grants available with no automatic right of increase for the building of an extension for a disabled person.

The many frustrations and difficulties encountered in coping with handicap are often compensated by supportive intervention from a variety of sources. Support may be offered by the family, community, friends, voluntary or statutory services. Sharing the care of the child with other members of the family not only benefits the main carer but also permits the partner and siblings to display their own feelings and talents towards the child. Occasionally, carers may deny other family members shared involvement or responsibility. This may be due to feelings of supremacy which unwittingly assume their view is best. Other carers may mistakenly believe that shared responsibility would be a burden on other family members, especially the siblings. Such misguided actions are counterproductive and may create voids in relationships which adversely affect family life. Although a balance of responsibility must be achieved, my sons are as competent in coping with Susan (and their own feelings about Susan) as my husband or myself. By involving them from an early stage with all aspects of Susan's development and condition the boys have developed a natural rapport with her that allows them to express, without embarrassment or guilt, their closeness or annoyance with her, depending on her temperament. I find it heartwarming that my sons can freely demonstrate their negative and positive feelings in a natural brother/sister relationship. Being handicapped only produces restrictions and limitations for both sufferer and observer – personality and character offer limitless opportunities for growth.

Susan is well known in her community and she has been directly responsible (simply by her visual presence) in creating changes in her local area, both on a structural and personal level. Her regular attendance at our local church has initiated structural alterations which now make life easier for wheelchair users. Considering our church, prior to Susan's appearance, had made no special adaptations for the nonambulant user since it was built over 100 years ago, *she* has achieved remarkable changes.

Uninvolved people may assume profound handicap prohibits joyful or amusing experiences. Our family experiences totally dismiss this myth. A wonderful event some years ago still brings a smile when recalled. I have always enjoyed dining out with my family (Susan's inclusion only makes such ventures more decorative as her involuntary hand movements tend to send food some considerable distance). As I fed Susan her lunch one day in a local café, I was very aware of the little boy and his mother seated near us. While he was having difficulty concealing his puzzled expression at the sight of Susan in her wheelchair, his mother was obvi-

ously embarrassed by her young son's bulging eyes and gaping mouth fixed firmly on Susan's strange mannerisms and curious appearance. Unable to contain his curiosity, he loudly asked what was wrong with Susan. At his honest and natural question, there descended an instant stillness in the café and it was obvious to me that this young boy had asked what everyone else was thinking. I had to stifle a smile at the reaction of his startled mother when she subtly nudged her son under the table. I welcomed this boy's natural interest and curiosity and told him as simply as possible that Susan was sick and could not walk. The silence grew as he considered my answer and exchanged investigative glances at the sameness of his own and Susan's lunch. After he had compared meals he exclaimed loudly, 'No wonder she's sick – the food was awful.' The laughter echoed about the café as everyone (save the boy's mother and perhaps the proprietor) shared the humour and joy of his remarks. The uneasiness that may have prevailed in the presence of someone with profound handicap had been lessened by a young boy's genuine interest and curiosity, unmarred by embarrassment, and a carer's easiness and delight at being with her handicapped child. There *is* joy in involvement with handicap when barriers can be removed which obstruct insight and understanding. The building of genuine relationships can only occur when the carer and observer find common ground which permits good communication.

Within the professional sector of health and education, although I have sadly encountered complacency, apathy and dictatorial attitudes over the degree and extent of the professional's role and function, I have been greatly supported and encouraged by many professionals who display remarkable talents and commitment towards the handicapped person and his or her family. Such professionals appreciate their role differs from that of a full-time carer; they understand their involvement is by choice and acknowledge that their function is limited and should not invade or dictate coping levels for individuals or their families. Such awareness appreciates their function and role are but a small part of another person's lifetime. A skilful professional who can evaluate and correctly interpret feedback will usually define the true needs of the individual. I consider it a privilege to be involved with a growing number of persons who, by insight and skilful training are establishing mutual links with the handicapped person and his or her family.

By far the most meaningful support I have received in coping with Susan and my own feelings about her handicap has not come from any group (be it a parent group, or one from the voluntary or statutory services) but from the *individual* within each. To generalize or label any group as being more helpful than another suggests one is better equipped than the other to see to the needs of the child and her family.

Acceptance of the individual

Support offered can be meaningful or limited depending on the attitude of the giver. The full-time carer who loves and *accepts* the handicapped person views their role as a partnership. I am striving to accept Susan as she is *and now* realise that I have challenging opportunities to help her develop her potential, not dictate her future. By accepting Susan's weaknesses, acknowledging her abilities and striving to recognise her needs, I offer respect and dignity to my daughter. As Susan's mother I am faced with two challenges – the handicap itself and my reaction towards the handicap. Her profound mental and physical disability is a fact over which I had no choice or control; however, I *do* have choice and control *over my own* reactions towards her handicap. Realistically, I am aware that external forces often influence actions taken, just as past experiences and future doubts may create areas of bias in our dealings with others. My bonding with my precious daughter can take me to the depths of despair on occasions yet permits an appreciation of her tremendous value as an *individual* in her own right. The future for Susan depends greatly on the *quality* not *quantity* of care and help offered (Fig. 1.4).

We do not react to another person as he or

Communication is possible by everyone
Advice without understanding is rarely helpful
Resolve to be optimistic and enthusiastic
Encouragement promotes learning opportunities

Attitudes determine degree of giving
Need to be sensitive without being intrusive
Dignity offered enhances quality of life

Handicap offers restrictions — life offers hope
Expressions of skills should adapt to the individual
Listening is a skill — hearing is a function
Privileged position of a carer

Figure 1.4 Suggestions for care and help.

she truly is – we respond on the basis of our impression of that person. Therefore superficial understanding influences our perception, should our interactions *only* be based on knowledge of the handicap itself:

- Understanding of a *disorder* permits superficial, basic understanding
- Understanding of a *person* permits deeper understanding which *accepts a person for what he or she is* – not what we think they ought to be.

This acceptance of a person is an *essential* prerequisite of genuine love and care. Time may not permit this depth of relationship therefore we should accept our role in *relation to our involvement*. By doing this we can appreciate the merits and value of the individual within the handicap and acknowledge the holder of the handicap as an *equal* who has *abilities, needs and limitations* – we too have these. In simple terms, handicap *only* offers limitations for both holder and observer. With respectful acceptance of 'where a person is' much can be received as well as given. Providing increased, improved training techniques and adequate financing are important elements but may be ineffective without improved individual attitudes towards the handicapped person. The greatest barrier in handicap lies not with the sufferer but with the observer. I believe overcoming our own fears breaks down these barriers and permits the value of learning and the need for improved understanding. Perhaps then we may truly believe that nothing is lost in handicap, it is simply not yet found.

REFERENCES

Allan I 1987 Rett syndrome: a view on care and
management. Personal communication
Committee of Enquiry 1978 Special educational needs
(the Warnock Report). HMSO, London

Hagberg B 1985 Rett syndrome: prevalence and impact on
progressive severe mental retardation in girls. Acta
Paediatrica Scandinavica 74: 405–408
Kerr A M, Stephenson J B P 1985 Rett's syndrome in the west
of Scotland. British Medical Journal 291: 579–582

USEFUL ADDRESS

National Rett Syndrome Association
15 Tanzieknowe Drive
Glasgow G72 8RG
Scotland

CHAPTER CONTENTS

Introduction   19

Early treatment methods   20
The York Retreat   23

**Legislative approaches up to the 20th
    century   24**
The Eugenics movement   25

**Legislative approaches during the 20th
    century   25**

Social changes during the 20th century   28

The service providers   29
The National Health Service   29
Social work   30
Education   30
Voluntary organizations   31
The private sector   31

**The effects of the multiplicity of service
    providers   32**
Route of entry   32
Planning and coordination of services   33

Professionals   34
Style of response   34
Training   35

The need for better coordinated services   36
Community mental handicap teams   37
Case conferences   37

Conclusion   38

Questions   39

2

Evolution of services

M. Bannerman   M. Lindsay

Key points
- There is a danger of people in each era feeling they have the right approach i.e. the myth of the 'Golden Age'
- Legislation is a reflection of society's values and throughout history we have regarded people with learning disabilities as not being entitled to the same rights as those without learning disabilities
- Social and occupational changes made it increasingly difficult for people with learning disabilities to be supported by their community
- The current provision for people with learning disabilities is a patchwork of services with the likelihood of duplication, lack of coordination and, worse still, large gaps in the network of services

INTRODUCTION

Why do we hold the attitudes we do to people who have learning disabilities? Why are our services designed and delivered the way they are in Britain today? Often, we act and speak as if our views are self-evident, that the way we see the world is the only way it can be seen or ever has been seen. When we do encounter differing views held in earlier generations we consider them with pity or contempt and even attribute ulterior motives to those who held them. But all our ideas are the product of a slow evolution of thought and attitude down the generations. Nor has that evolution ended – we have yet to reach the 'Golden Age' when we will for a certainty have 'got it right'.

The crux of the problem is that each generation believes it has already arrived at that 'Golden Age' of certainty. This applied to those who believed people with learning disabilities should be chained up because they were possessed; who saw them as a risk to the genetic purity of the race or who saw them as holy innocents requiring protection. What grounds can we produce to prove that it does not apply to us today: is normalization really the 'Golden Age' of certainty at last? What is clear is that we cannot and must not try to understand our approach to these issues today in ignorance of what has gone before. History can make sense of so much which is otherwise confused. What follows is a glimpse at what society believed about, i.e. did for and to, people with learning disabilities in the centuries leading up to ours. Thereafter, using this perspective, we shall consider the complexity and confusion of the scene today.

As we look back we can see that the blanket term 'insanity' covers all groups until the late 19th and early 20th centuries. The confusion of 'mental handicap' and 'mental illness' is not a recent problem. Indeed, no separate histories of services to people with mental illness and those with learning disabilities can really be produced. In terms of social attitudes 1000 years is a very short span of time and, as we shall see, in each era people were very sure of values which were later held in contempt by the next, a point to bear in mind when we plan future services.

It is an accepted part of nature that birds and animals will destroy one of their kind if it shows features very different from the others; an albino crow, for example, is likely to be pecked to death by other crows. We humans credit ourselves with superiority of reasoning over other animals yet for hundreds of years we have tortured and locked away those we perceived as being different from the norm. We have at times referred to them as 'God's children' or 'beloved of God', but for the most part we have relegated them to the level of the subhuman, unworthy of the most basic respect. Throughout history we have displayed a deep-rooted fear demonstrated by our insistence that those whom we now refer to as having learning disabilities and those who are mentally ill be treated in ways which distinguish them from us, the normal ones in society.

EARLY TREATMENT METHODS

In Saxon times the treatment of insanity or lunacy (among whom those with a mental handicap were classified) was a strange mix of pharmacy, superstition and castigation. For example, holy wells, which were probably pre-Christian in origin, abounded throughout the British Isles and may have been the original source of the use of cold baths, a treatment continued until fairly recent times. Some holy wells were famous for lunacy healing and there are many stories describing miraculous cures. One of these was St Fillan's well in Perthshire, Scotland. Much was written about it and it was recorded in the early 1700s that about 200 people a year were treated there. Patients were first made to walk three times round a cairn on which were placed offerings of flowers and clothing. They were then immersed three times in the pool and left overnight bound hand and foot in the nearby chapel. If found unbound next morning there was said to be a good chance of recovery. If still bound, the cure was in some doubt. It was stated in the same record that 'many were relieved by death of their troubles in the night'.

Holy wells were only one of many methods of treatment most of which were both complicated and bizarre. The writings of the time give many and detailed instructions which had to be carefully adhered to if the desired results were to be obtained. Some were described as particularly efficacious, for instance, 'a clove of wort to be tied round the lunatic's neck with a red thread when the moon is on the wane in the month of April or in the early part of October and he will be healed'. Rarely were such prescriptions considered sufficient in themselves and most had to be accompanied by religious ritual, prayers and incantations. This necessitated the involvement of priests or monks and, from earliest times, linked the Church with the practice of healing.

There were numerous monasteries in existence

around this time, many with quite extensive libraries and cultivated gardens where medicinal herbs were grown, monks being the chief dispensers of medicine available. The local populace were accustomed to turn to the monasteries for assistance on matters both religious and secular. Indeed, many monks were local men who had taken religious orders and were well versed in the customs of the people they served. Demonic possession was believed to be the cause of mental disorder and the harsh treatments administered to the poor sufferers was not considered as punishment but as treatment for the condition, i.e. driving out the devil. Powerful purgatives and emetics were deemed essential along with herbal baths, fomentations and poultices. Mandrake and periwinkle were noted as being powerful for this purpose in conjunction with holy incantation and exorcism.

It was around the 10th century that the influence of the moon was recognised as producing lunacy but long before that it was attributed to Saint Matthew that 'those who were called lunatics are called such, not because their madness comes from the moon, but because the Devil who causes insanity avails himself of the phases of the moon'. The importance of the Church was so intrinsically woven into the treatment of madness that there was no question of its monopoly right up to the dissolution of the monasteries in England by Henry VIII when all medical matters moved into the hands of laymen. However, several hundreds of years were to pass before then, during which a number of hospitals were founded, the most well known and infamous being Bethlehem, better known as Bedlam.

In the year 1247 the order of Mary of Bethlehem was granted some land by Simon Fitzmary on the site where Liverpool Street station, London, now stands and it was here that the hospital was founded. It was originally known as Bethlehem Prison House, the patients actually being called 'prisoners'.

In the year 1330, 83 years after its foundation it matured as a hospital when King Edward III granted it a licence to collect alms in England, Ireland and Wales. However, the word 'hospital' did not denote a place for the sick but described

then, and for long afterwards, a place of shelter and entertainment. If the king had hoped that the collection of alms would earn the hospital enough to maintain it, this was a false hope, as within a few short years it was so miserably poor that application was made to the mayor, aldermen and citizens of London to be received into their protection. This was agreed and thereafter it was governed by the mayor and two aldermen, but the next momentous happening was that it was seized by the crown! This occurred in 1375, still in the reign of Edward III, and presumably was done on the pretext that it was a foreign priory, Simon Fitzmary being a Norman. This explains why Bethlehem Hospital survived the dissolution of the monasteries by Henry VIII – it already belonged to the crown.

It is known that lunatics were admitted to the hospital from the year 1400. Treatment consisted of chaining and whipping and throughout its history its fearful reputation was maintained. Indeed, 50 years after the death of Henry VIII, conditions were said to be so loathsome as to be unfit for anyone to enter. Records show accounts for the purchase of fetters and straw and reveal that the patients were so difficult to manage that local flax dressers were employed to help the keepers in their duties. Patients who were fit to do so were allowed to go out to beg alms and were granted the badge of a horn worn around the neck, which they blew to attract the attention of citizens. They were declared to be a great nuisance as it was common for vagrants to steal their horns and pretend to be lunatics singing and dancing in their attempts to collect alms.

By the 16th century the conviction of demonic possession had by no means diminished, but after the dissolution of the monasteries we find writings by the early lay medics. Borde recommended in 1542 that the insane should 'be kept in a closed chamber with little light and should have a keeper whom he fears'. However, this is followed by the kindlier instruction that 'he shall have no knives or shears and no girdle lest he destroy himself, no pictures of man or woman lest he have fantasies. He is to be shaved once a month, to drink no wine or strong beer but to have a warm sponge down three times a day and a little warm meat. Few words were to be used except for reprehension and gentle reformation' (Borde 1542, in Tuke 1882).

The same Dr Borde became so upset that he could not bear to wait to see the outcome when he describes a visit to Rome where he observed a woman patient being treated for possession by the devil. She was tied to a post and treated so violently that Dr Borde said he 'could not write the words to describe it as men would not believe it but say it were a foul lien'. That he did not doubt the diagnosis of the woman's possession is confirmed in his statement that he was fearful that the demon might leave her and enter himself. Witchcraft was considered to have an undeniable connection with madness although it was debated at length as to whether it was just to burn at the stake those who were said to be possessed by demons as this was not the same as a person practising witchcraft because those possessed had no choice in the matter of consorting with the Devil.

The opposing points of view were expressed in the writings of Sir Thomas Brown, a famous medic, and Reginald Scott (quoted in Tuke 1882). Sir Thomas wrote that 'many deny witches altogether or say if there be any assert that they can do no harm' but he adds 'this is contrary to the opinion of most lawyers, physicians and philosophers'. On the other hand, Reginald Scott was brave enough to write in his *Discovery of Witchcraft*, published in 1584, 'alas I am sorry and ashamed to see how many die who being said to be witches only seek for cures by magic whom wholesome diet and good medicines would have recovered'. Reginald Scott continued to write about melancholy and delusion being symptoms of mental ill health while maintaining his opposition to the burning of lunatics. However, in spite of his deep compassion and understanding his views were overwhelmed by the thinking of the majority, who agreed with Sir Thomas Brown. The insane continued to be persecuted until the laws against witchcraft were abolished in 1736, the last recorded judicial murder of a witch being in 1722, in Sutherland.

The most outstanding feature of this period of history is the helplessness and vulnerability of so many to withstand the power of the authorities over them. Notwithstanding the harshness of life for most people at this time, decimated as they were by poverty and disease, the miseries of the insane appear to have been particularly hard. The lack of sympathy or pity for their state by those who condemned them demonstrates that they were no closer to attaining recognition as human beings with any emotions or feelings than they had been 7 centuries earlier. The rights of an individual had never been given consideration once it had been decided that he or she was mad, and the practice of locking him or her away was unquestioned. Several cases had been made public where innocent individuals had been incarcerated in madhouses as a means of getting rid of them to clear the way for other members of the family to inherit property and wealth. It was also quite common for men to send their wives to Houses of Correction for scolding or nagging. Virtually nothing had been done to prevent the innocent from incarceration or to protect lunatics once they had been committed.

The only legislative changes to have taken place where lunatics were even mentioned was in an Act of 1744 which separated them for the first time from vagrants and paupers, and this was only because the begging laws forbade the latter two from begging beyond their own parish boundaries. Lunatics wandered from one parish to another, being unable to distinguish boundaries, and the change in the law came about because the punishment for crossing parish frontiers was imprisonment. The law was introduced merely to alleviate the cost of imprisoning lunatics for their offence. The Act of 1744 also authorized any two justices to apprehend madmen and have them locked up, but this had been purely to protect society from 'those so far disordered in their senses that they may be too dangerous to be permitted to go abroad'.

Public attention was also drawn to the advertising of madhouse owners making claims about their kind treatment of patients compared to the treatment of rival establishments. Dr Newton, a herbalist, claimed that he could cure the maddest person within 3 months and that some could be cured by his methods in 3 weeks. About the same time another of his contemporaries, Dr Fellows, published a work on insanity claiming wonderful cures by means of herbal medicines and with descriptions of 'black vapours of the brain' which were dispersed by his brew. This was also said to 'confirm the texture (of the brain) strengthen the vessels and give a freedom to the blood and spirit in closing them'. He also boasted of his kind treatment of patients, claiming never to use violent means and providing them with good food and entertainment. Whether his patients were treated as humanely as he said is not known. What is clear is that it was very easy to have a person committed to such places and it was this fact becoming public knowledge which created the demand for legislation.

A committee of the House of Commons was convened in 1763 to enquire into the state of madhouses. Its report aroused great public concern as it confirmed people's worst fears and carried lurid descriptions of atrocities committed against inmates. However, it was a further 10 years before a bill was passed for the regulation of madhouses. Incredibly, it was thrown out by the House of Lords and replaced a year later by another which merely decreed that licences had to be obtained by madhouse owners, not stipulating any minimum standards or conditions but stating that licences would be granted to all who desired them. Reports of abuses were made to the colleges of physicians, but the colleges had no power to take action against the perpetrators so the reports were worthless. Also, the issuing of licences was nonsense as, if they ever were withdrawn, they could be reapplied for and granted the next day.

The good points of the bill for the Regulation of Madhouses were contained in three main aims:

- to secure all persons against unnecessary confinement
- to better the chance of recovery of all such persons confined as being insane, as much by moral treatment as by the use of medicines

- to ensure the restoration of all who might become of sound mind again to society.

However, the bill had very limited success as it failed to empower the commissioners to discharge patients. Moreover, its scope did not extend beyond private madhouses where an order and medical certificate at least were demanded. Even less protection was afforded to pauper lunatics who were sent to public asylums on the authority of parish officers and without the need of a medical certificate.

By the end of the 18th century, several high profile works had been published including *Select Cases on Insanity*, in 1787, and *Perfect methods of cure in some particular cases of insanity*, in 1788, giving many topics for discussion, although those treatments still focused on the use of bleeding, emetics, digitalis and electricity, the combination of which was guaranteed to weaken the most violent of patients to the state whereupon a cure might be declared (Tuke 1882). It was into this climate that a totally radical concept was introduced.

The York Retreat

The York Retreat was an institution founded by the Society of Friends, or Quakers, after a group of them had made a visit to St Luke's Hospital, which was similar to Bethlehem, and had been most distressed by what they saw there. The venture was proposed by one of their number, William Tuke. His ideas were full of common sense and he could not understand why no one had thought of them before. Their basis was simple humanity and he stated from the outset that the Retreat would be a place where 'no frightful treatments would be used, no concealment, and patients treated with kindness'. As may have been expected, such a concept was treated with scorn and outrage by the experts of the day, but Tuke was sure that he was on the right path and took as his role model the Swiss physician Pinel, who had been practising similar ideas for 5 years before him and had many case histories to prove that his theories worked.

Violent patients were taken to the York Retreat to illustrate that they would become quiet after their manacles were removed and they were treated with kindness. Added to this, patients were kept in constant employment. Females sewed, knitted and engaged in domestic tasks. Men were encouraged to take part in activities agreeable to them, gardening and such like, but whatever the activities they had to be the opposite to the illusions of their illness. They were to spend time walking in the garden, listening to soft music, contemplating paintings and eating wholesome food. In many cases they were said to have recovered from their illnesses. William Tuke's wife was one of the first to disagree with him when he first proposed his ideas but she was won round and it was her idea to call the establishment the York Retreat rather than an asylum, a retreat being a haven and a place of safety.

LEGISLATIVE APPROACHES UP TO THE 20TH CENTURY

Concern about the state of madhouses continued to be expressed and yet another committee was set up in 1814. History repeated itself when the House of Lords rejected its report just as it had that of 1763. In 1815, the report was presented again to parliament and, as 51 years earlier, the focus was still on the abuses being perpetrated in madhouses, quoting patients who were chained to the ground although they had been declared harmless. Other revelations of a horrifying nature followed, causing great scandals concerning the York Asylum (not to be confused with the Retreat), St Luke's and Bethlehem Hospitals. The main concerns were about chaining people in conditions of such cold and filth that many of them died.

The conclusions of the report were summarized as:

1. Too many patients in too confined a space thus retarding recovery.
2. Insufficient numbers of attendants resulting in the unnecessary use of force.
3. Mixing of acute and nonacute patients.
4. Absence of medical attention.
5. Insufficient supervision.

The York Retreat was upheld as a model of care which provided a successful alternative method of treatment.

In spite of the evidence it provided, the bill based on the report was thrown out and remained in limbo for another 9 years. It was not until 1828 that efforts to reintroduce the bill succeeded and it was finally passed as the Lunatic Asylum Regulation Act.

In 1842, a motion was brought forward urging the inspection of asylums, pointing out that great numbers of patients were not covered by the 1828 Act, i.e. those confined in their own houses, in lodgings, in public institutions and in the hospitals of St Luke and Bethlehem. The object of this motion was to extend the system of inspection. It was suggested that barristers be appointed to inspect, to the great indignation of the medical profession, and this idea was upheld on the grounds that 'a man of common sense could give as good an opinion as a medical man'. The final agreement was for two medical men and two barristers to be appointed for the task. This meant that the purpose of the Lunacy Commission was at last being clearly defined as having to set minimum standards of care and to encourage improvements. Most importantly, its scope was extended to cover public as well as private institutions, although it still had a huge task ahead of it as many of the insane were still held in prisons and workhouses in appalling conditions.

Along with the new administrative procedures progress was also being made in treatment, the medical profession in general rising in public esteem due to advances in its field. One reason for this was the development of newspapers resulting in the public being better informed than ever before. Doctors working in the mental health field still had some way to go to match the increasing respect for physicians and surgeons, but the new professions of psychology and psychiatry were just beginning to realise the need to separate the 'retarded' from the mentally ill.

Hopes were raised that a new era of compassionate care was about to dawn with the passing of the Lunacy Act of 1890, after years of activity by pressure groups. However, it proved to be a disappointment. It was long winded with detailed concentration on matters of detention, care and release from care, and with little scope for development. It still focused on the avoidance of the illegal detention of the sane and unfortunately made no distinction between the mentally ill and the mentally retarded. This was so in spite of a permissive Idiots' Act which had been passed 4 years previously allowing local authorities to build special asylums for 'idiots'.

The Eugenics movement

Until the time of the Industrial Revolution in the mid-18th century there was little or no established provision of facilities for mentally handicapped people. In fact, there was little or no provision for *any* special group. Reliance was placed on the social network of family, friends and neighbours with any outside help coming from religious organizations. This social network was disrupted and put under great strain with the change from a rural-based society to an urban society. Expanding towns were barely able to cope with the developing industrial labour force let alone the associated social problems. Separation of the able-bodied from the sick and destitute was the solution adopted so those unable to support themselves were segregated from the productive labour force and accommodated in workhouses.

During the 19th century the policy of segregation continued and the idea developed that as the less intelligent and those with other 'undesirable' characteristics (mainly the working class) had more children than the more favourably endowed (the aristocracy, landowners and factory owners) there would eventually be a deterioration in the intelligence and 'fitness' of the general population. Selective breeding in animals had been pioneered during the agricultural revolution and had resulted in better quality, more valuable livestock. The theory was considered equally applicable to humans. People with low intelligence mixing with others of low intelligence were likely to marry one another and produce children of low intelligence. These children were more likely to remain and marry within

this culture thus creating a population with low intelligence. Darwin's theory, as presented in his book *Origin of Species* (1859), added weight to the fear of a deterioration of the intelligence of the general population by stating that it is a natural law that only the fittest of the species survive to produce offspring thus passing on genes with a greater likelihood of survival. It was felt that in the case of human beings the most unfit were procreating faster than the fittest. In 1909, Tredgold stated that it was 'imperative . . . to devise such social laws as will ensure that those unfit do not propagate their kind' (Tuke 1882). An organization called the Eugenics Society had been formed in the mid-19th century to seek ways of preventing degeneration of the human species and the issue of controlling genetic factors in humans has been with us since that time.

The Eugenics Society declared its theories scientific, citing in support a number of works showing evidence that mental deficiency was a key factor in the cause of crime, pauperism, illegitimacy and alcoholism. These pronouncements were made with no scientific proof but had a very powerful effect on public opinion and, in fact, totally negated the 1899 Elementary Education Act (Defective and Epileptic Children) which empowered authorities to set up special schools for these children and raised their school leaving age to 16. It allowed for transport to be provided for them and boarding out if necessary. These provisions, however, were only recommended and, in the face of the powerful advocates for total care, were overwhelmed.

LEGISLATIVE APPROACHES DURING THE 20TH CENTURY

The theory of genetics caught the public imagination and its influence .continued into the 20th century. For example, in the 1930s, a government committee on sterilization considered the feasibility of compulsory sterilization in Britain. During this decade the theory of genetic control was taken to its logical conclusion in Nazi Germany. Extermination of individuals with undesirable characteristics – mentally ill, mentally handicapped and the aged among others – was undertaken on a massive scale. After the Second World War, in 1951, Butler in the USA reported that in 21 states sterilization of mentally handicapped people was practised on the basis of IQ score. Thankfully, less drastic and more humane ways of preventing the transmission of undesirable characteristics from one generation to another have become possible, based mainly on genetic counselling and methods of birth control. In the future, genetic engineering may play a part. Unfortunately, each one of these methods is accompanied by ethical problems which become increasingly difficult to resolve with advancing technical knowledge.

Meanwhile, back in the early years of the 20th century, a royal commission was given the task of looking at the needs of 'defectives'. The Royal Commission on the Care of the Feebleminded (1904–1908) amassed a great deal of information confirming that the genetic school offered an acceptable perspective on the problem presented to society by people with learning disabilities. The royal commission recommended the following:

- Mental defectives needed protection from the worst elements of society and from their own instinctual responses which declared them unfit to take part in life's struggles.
- Absence of social condemnation was sought because 'the mental condition of these persons and not their poverty or their crime is the real ground of their claim for help from the state'.
- It was thought vital that all mental defectives be ascertained and brought into contact with public services.
- A central authority was necessary to work in conjunction with powerful local bodies which would assume responsibility for individual cases.

They therefore recommended the formation of a central board consisting of legal and medical members and at least one woman. Segregation was endorsed although there was scope by way of guardianship for future community care to be developed. The report received a mixed reception due to its liberal elements. It did not go far enough for the Eugenic school

and too far for the opponents of compulsory detention.

Following the royal commission recommendations, the Mental Deficiency Bill was formulated and became law in 1913. There were to be three main divisions made on a rising scale of intelligence beginning at the lower end with idiots, then imbeciles and lastly feebleminded. 'Idiots' were said to be unable to guard themselves from common danger; 'feebleminded' being trainable but unable to protect themselves from moral danger. The middle category, while having a higher degree of intelligence than idiots, were incapable of managing their affairs or incapable of being taught to do so. The fourth grade included was that of 'moral defective' and it differed from the others in kind, not degree. They were persons who displayed 'some permanent mental defect coupled with strong vicious or criminal propensities in which punishment had little or no effect'. (Interestingly, there was general agreement from all sides to the suggestion that prostitutes should be sent to houses for the feebleminded on the grounds that this would save mankind from infection!)

The 1913 Act took cognisance of the impracticality of lifetime institutionalization for the large numbers of people who could fall into its classification framework so it stipulated that being categorized was not sufficient to bring a person into the orbit of the authorities. It decreed that a sympathetic guardian and favourable environment, offering the individual something approaching a normal life, was desirable, and possible, for the vast majority. The decision whether or not to petition for institutionalization was left to the carer and the person with learning disabilities had no control over it. This explains how many who were defined as feebleminded came to be placed in institutions as carers must have felt that their stated inability to guard against moral danger militated against them remaining at home. There were many known cases of young women being placed in institutions because they had given birth to an illegitimate child, whether or not they had been categorized as morally defective before this. By becoming pregnant they had become 'subject to be dealt with' in terms of the Act and the authorities were obliged to petition for institutional care to protect them from themselves. Others became 'subject to be dealt with' if they were destitute, neglected, cruelly treated or without visible means of support.

Part of the Act required that each local authority was required to set up Mental Deficiency Committees responsible for the ascertainment of all 'subjects to be dealt with' and the provision of suitable institutions. They also had the responsibility of appointing officers for the supervision of the care of those in the community. These duties covered a wide range of activities, from conveying patients to and from institutions to visiting guardianship cases in their homes. The committees' duties concerning the ascertainment of children for admission to special schools were later linked with the Education Act (Defective and Epileptic Children) (1914).

The effect of the 1913 Act was to enable local authorities to incorporate or finance the work of voluntary organizations thereby developing services for mental defectives. The most radical feature of the Act was that it was about mental defectives as distinct from psychiatric patients. Also, in spite of the demand for segregation the 1913 Act, by the introduction of guardianship and a system of licence from institutional care, made it possible for many to remain in the community while still receiving a degree of care and control.

Despite increasing provision for those with learning disabilities by the state through education services, health boards, local authorities and the Home Office, the services provided were considered inadequate. The situation was equally bad whether resources for children or adults were concerned and the vast majority were still not receiving services. A survey showed that 10% of those said to require residential care were in mental deficiency institutions, 25% were in mental hospitals and 39% in workhouses, albeit in special sections within them. The total number of cases dealt with by the Mental Deficiency Authority by admission to institution, by licence, voluntary or statutory supervision only amounted to 40 000 out of a known total of 175 000. The

overriding reason for institutional care remained social rather than intellectual and many considered most in need of this type of care were young women who might be considered at moral risk of producing children or those of either sex who showed criminal tendencies.

For those who had remained in the care of their families community life was severely restricted. Parents were impressed upon that their children would 'always be children' and required close supervision. They lived in real fear that their growing sons, and more particularly daughters, would be locked up if they showed the slightest interest in sex. Parents formed associations to support each other and friendships were allowed for people with learning disabilities only within the parameters of those carefully defined boundaries.

The next major piece of legislation affecting those with learning disabilities was the Mental Health Act (1959) in England and similar acts in other parts of the UK. There was a great deal in the 1959 Act about admissions to hospital, the protection of the rights of the patient and various sections dealing with compulsory and voluntary admissions. Guardianship was still very important, with supervision by Responsible Medical Officers and Mental Health Officers given high priority. One very important point made in the Act was that it was unlawful for any man to have sexual intercourse with a woman who was mentally defective. If this was in order to protect them from exploitation, it surely gave scope for interpretation to cover any eventuality!

Later, the Mental Health Act (1983) was passed, which still concentrated upon details of much the same type as the 1959 Act. The term 'mental deficiency' had changed to 'mental handicap', but the section regarding sexual rights, or lack of them, as described above was unchanged. By 1984, many hospitals were discharging people with mental handicaps to care in the community. Hospitals were becoming smaller and less institutional; small group homes and independent living programmes were well underway. Many had married and were living with support in their own homes, but the legacies of the past were still apparent in the fearful reactions of the public to having these people living in their midst. It was not unusual for public meetings to be held to protest against proposals to discharge patients, the general feeling being 'not in my street'. The best recipe for success seems to have been when people were quietly established without any fanfare; once they became known to their neighbours as simply neighbours the handicap ceased to be of consequence, in most cases.

SOCIAL CHANGES DURING THE 20TH CENTURY

It can be seen that the services provided for people with learning disabilities depend far more upon the era in which those people find themselves than upon the difficulties being experienced. Society's definition of what a learning disability is, and its ideas about what causes it, determine who cares for the learning disabled and the sort of care they will receive. This is just as true today as it was in the past. Likewise, the services which exist in any one time will depend heavily on the legacy of previous systems which were established according to different philosophies and in different societal situations. This is very obvious when looking at the situation in the 1990s. We shall do this in several ways.

Firstly, we shall consider some of the changes that have taken place in 20th-century society and how these have affected the lifestyles of people with disabilities. Secondly, the underlying philosophies of today's society will be outlined. Then, taking all this as the backdrop, we will look at who provides services for people with disabilities in the 1990s and the effects of the current situation on the users of these services. After considering the role of professionals we shall lastly consider some of the problems inherent in the structures of service provision which exist today and some of the attempts being made to solve them. If we take a bird's-eye view of society in the 1990s what major changes have occurred in the way we live since the 1890s? Obvious landmarks must surely be the change in the role of women, the rise of the nuclear family, the changes in family patterns and employment

patterns, improved and more widely available medical services and the rise in the expectations of the state as a provider. Women's drive towards equal status with men is a marked trend of the Western 20th-century world. Girls are now educated along with and in the same way as boys, usually work after marriage and increasingly also work after the birth of their children. In previous generations women were the homemakers. It was common for adult daughters, married or single, to retain close links with and responsibility for, their family of origin, as well as for their own husbands and children. The extended family, where grandparents, aunts and uncles shared a couple's life, and sometimes home, and the women stayed at home sharing the caring role for numerous children and elderly and infirm family members, has largely been replaced by the nuclear family (mother, father and children), in which both parents often share the roles of breadwinner and homemaker.

Clearly, this has meant that the arrival of a child with a disability in a family throws particular stresses on the modern family, where the increased and prolonged care needs of that family member cannot be shared among so many adults (see Chapter 1). The responsibility for children and the problems they may have or create is seen as belonging to the parents only, and is not a communal responsibility which the whole family must share. The change in lifestyle necessary is also great, as alternative care arrangements may be hard to make and the employment of one or both parents may have to be sacrificed.

Employment patterns have also changed. The concept of 'going to work' – in which the breadwinner leaves home and neighbourhood and joins another social group at work for a set number of hours per week – is also largely a 20th-century development. Whereas in the 19th century rural communities largely lived and worked together, now the two are separated. This further reduces the support available to the family with a member with a disability. It also makes it more difficult for the adult with a disability to find a role in employment which matches that of his nondisabled counterparts, as employment is largely an individual, skill-based activity rather than being communal and task-oriented.

Improved medical services have led to lower infant mortality and this, coupled with birth control, has resulted in the desire for smaller families. A family's investment in and expectation of their children is often very high and the arrival of a child with a disability may be the end of dearly held dreams about what that child would achieve in life.

All of these changes mean that in many ways the social supports which existed in earlier generations are less and the aspirations of families are greater than they were in earlier generations when the standard of living for most people was markedly lower. For people who have disabilities to approach the standard of life deemed acceptable in 20th-century Britain they now need considerable help from outside their family and local community and this matches the growing expectation that the state is responsible for under-pinning the quality of life of all of the population of the countries which make up the United Kingdom. The belief that the state should see itself as ultimately responsible for providing and overseeing welfare services to everyone is a newer one than we often realize – the National Health Service, one embodiment of this type of thinking, only dates back to 1948. The philosophies that guide our thinking have also changed. Often these are not analysed or even recognized, but they are the unnoticed sea swell of opinion that shapes our lives as well as our legislation and our services. It is true that compared with the 19th century, we now live in a society which is much more varied in its texture. It is a multifaith and multicultural society and this has developed a trend of thought towards the concept that 'every man must go his own way' and no one else has the right to say what is right for another. Another strand of thinking – a philosophical 'buzz' phrase – is that of 'equal opportunities'. This belief states that all people should have equal chances in life regardless of their race, sex or creed.

The seductive thing about underlying philosophies like these is that they appear self-evident and to disagree with them is seen as some form of heresy. But they are trends of thought, just as those described in earlier parts of this chapter were, and they will change and alter and even seem to be outlandish ideas within a few decades or centuries, as did earlier 'self-evident truths' in previously self-proclaimed 'Golden Ages'. For people with disabilities, the theory or philosophy of normalization ties these two strands together. It measures quality of life not by religious or other absolute standards but by what is valued within the society in which the person lives. It is in one sense a philosophy based on relativity and conformity but if this is how most 20th-century British people handle their lives why should people with disabilities be expected to live according to other values?

THE SERVICE PROVIDERS

The providers of the variety of care services for people with disabilities fall into five main groups: firstly, health services; secondly, social work services; thirdly, education services; fourthly, voluntary organizations, and fifthly, private organizations who are to a small but increasing extent also beginning to enter into the provision of care services. These five main providers are not offering neatly segregated services which cope with specific areas of need and slot in a planned and organized way into each other's fields of influence. Rather, as we noted earlier, they have arisen from the social structures and beliefs of previous generations and from the history of social institutions in this country. In looking more closely at this situation it will be helpful to take each of these groups separately and to consider briefly what is the underlying approach (i.e. ' What problem are they trying to solve?') to see how this leads on into the service that they provide, who they choose to provide it for and how the service is resourced.

The National Health Service

As we have seen, the National Health Service had a large role in the provision of care in the latter half of this century. The 'problem' which this type of service is attempting to 'solve' has its origins in the medical model – the definition of mental handicap as a medical problem which needs a high input from medical staff to 'resolve' it. The result of this has been the type of service which can primarily be seen in large institutions, classified as hospitals, which became the main method of residential care for people with mental handicaps from the 1930s onwards. Following the medical definition of the problem these institutions were equipped as hospitals and staffed with medical and nursing staff (often, particularly in days gone by, appropriately uniformed and with training which originated from the pure medical training of medicine and nursing and other paramedical services). Usually, the whole management style and organizational background to these institutions parallel that of general hospitals or other medical provisions, as do the referral route and patterns of contact with families of 'patients'.

In recent years, the movement towards care in the community has put much pressure for change on such institutions, in some cases resulting in their total closure. This has clearly led also to pressure on staff to change their roles and to become more responsive to the changing place of people with learning disabilities in society. Many changes in how staff are recruited, trained and in the expectations of them in their jobs have occurred in order to attempt to adapt to this. The resourcing of these services comes through the National Health Service budget, allocated through health boards or health authorities, with their particular decision-making structure and interplay between clinical and administrative hierarchies.

Social work

Social work services have arisen from a different route and from a different guiding philosophy. Throughout the 20th century there has been increasing recognition of the effect of social problems on people and the need for some form of support, assistance and guidance to be offered to them at different stages in their lives and in the different situations in which they find them-selves. Much of the thinking about social work originated from the old welfare and probation services. The unification of these in 1968 was a result of the Social Work Scotland Act and the Local Authority Social Services Act (1970), and their equivalent acts elsewhere in the UK which resulted in the development of social work and social services departments having a range of responsibilities for all people who have problems or difficulties with which these departments can help. The development of this 'one door' policy meant searching to some extent for a commonality of approach across a range of different age groups, social groupings and issues.

At the risk of oversimplifying things, it might be said that the underlying philosophy was that individuals and families at times in their lives have difficulties which can be helped by the intervention of someone from outside the family or neighbourhood who has skills in enabling the people concerned to look at and understand their own problems and take decisions about these, and who can also access resources for the people or enable them to access these themselves. The type of services offered therefore tend to be counselling and advisory, and the resources of residential services mainly in hostels and day care services. The staff employed to operate these services have come from a background in social work training, tending to have a historical bias towards traditional styles of caring from child care and elderly care.

The resourcing of these services comes from local authority budgets raised by local taxation and central government grant and the decision-making process will rest with the officers of the local authorities under the ultimate power of elected members, either regional or district councillors in their social work or social services committees.

Education

Education services have a clear remit to provide education and training to the country's youth. Their role in the education of children who have learning disabilities came in 1973 when it was recognized that children with learning disabilities were entitled to education rather than occupation. Their entry into the education system at that time was an extremely significant move in terms of providing children with disabilities with an equal experience to that of their peers who did not have such difficulties. However, in many areas provision was, and still is, made by a system of separate schools so that while education is provided it is provided in different buildings with different staffing. In some authorities this educational subdivision can lead to the creation of two or three different types of school targeted at different degrees of disability. Staff may have mixed training, some being instructors from the original occupational centre system and some being teachers with special qualifications in special needs education.

The resourcing of these services is again from the local authority budget controlled through the education committees.

Voluntary organizations

In the case of voluntary organizations it is sometimes less clear which philosophy underpins their services as these can be many and various. It has often been noted with interest by people from other nations that British people are very fond of their voluntary organizations. Many of these organizations have a history substantially longer than that of their statutory counterparts and some voluntary organizations have offered services to people with learning disabilities for many hundreds of years. Each voluntary organization exists as a result of particular values which it exemplifies in the implementation of its services. For example, Dr Thomas Barnardo began his services because of the tremendous deprivation and death that he noticed amongst the street urchins of London. To a large extent society regarded these children as a problem and was inclined to see many of their difficulties as being of the children's own making. As a result of his Christian faith, Barnardo believed that each one of these children had a value equal to

that of any other citizen and he sought to implement this belief by caring for them. Voluntary organizations like Barnado's, thus tend to exist in order to implement certain philosophies of care which may or may not accord with those held by society as a whole. The result is that the provision of care by voluntary organizations is usually, but not exclusively, local and extremely varied in type and style. Everything from a parents' self-help group to a major national voluntary organization such as MENCAP or the Scottish Society for Mentally Handicapped is part of the voluntary sector.

The resourcing of the voluntary sector comes by various routes. It is commonly thought that all voluntary organizations are funded solely by donation, by private individuals and various fund-raising events designed to assist in this. This is not the case. For a long time now most voluntary organizations have depended partially or, in many cases, totally upon funding accessed from local authorities, health services, central government or businesses and industries. This money is usually targeted on the development of a particular very specific service or comes to the organization as a result of per capita payment for residents in a particular hostel or home. In addition to this, central government funding comes to voluntary organizations as a result of the rights of their residents to claim DSS allowances. These allowances can be substantial and are designed to allow individuals to pay for the residential care that they receive. Voluntary income by fundraising, if it exists at all, will usually form quite a small percentage of the total outlay of the organization.

The private sector

The last and still growing provider of care is the private sector. Coming from a background of longstanding and fairly substantial provision of care for people who are elderly, interest is now being shown by the private sector in providing care for people with disabilities. These services are by definition responsive to demand in the 'market place' and therefore tend to borrow their philosophy from what is prevalent and acceptable in society, tied to business concepts such as consumer choices and profit margins. Unlike care for elderly people, who may have their own means to invest in care of their choice if this is available, people with learning disabilities rarely have income of their own. The services will thus be funded as for voluntary organizations by statutory money of one kind or another, i.e. from local authorities, central government or the health service. The result of this will be that the type of private care which is developed will be a reflection of that which is deemed acceptable by the organizations who will pay the bill, i.e. the 'customer' who is 'buying' the service from the provider.

To sum up, at the risk of oversimplifying, it is possible in one sense to see services coming from the health service as originating from the concept of medical need and those coming from social work and social services departments as originating from the idea that there is a problem to be solved and needy people to be assisted. Insofar as people with learning disabilities fall into both these categories they become users of both sets of services. Even although the service they require to meet the particular needs that they have may be the same, it will be met differently depending upon which services they approach. This may be less so in the case of the education system as children enter this now as a result of their status as a child. But again, in most places, their experience of the sort of education offered will vary substantially with how the disability is defined by other professionals with backgrounds not necessarily in education. In the case of the voluntary and private sector the service that people will receive will depend to some extent on whether these services exist in their area and how the service offered is funded.

Overall, it can be seen that history has led to the growth of a variety of different types and styles of services which have different philosophies and historical pedigrees, different types of staffing and styles of service and different routes for resourcing those services, and different decision-making structures about how and what services should be developed and linked together.

THE EFFECTS OF THE MULTIPLICITY OF SERVICE PROVIDERS

Clearly, all this represents an array of different organizations and services which must be approached by people who have learning disabilities. To select two effects, let us consider the effect of the route of entry of the person to the service and the coordination and planning of the various services.

Route of entry

It is undeniable that often when one doorway of service has been opened it is difficult to get back out of the doorway and into an alternative one which may be more suitable. The records department of any large mental handicap hospital is a fascinating, if tragic, litany of examples of this. In one case, a young girl aged about 13 had been causing her parents considerable problems and anxiety. She was rowing constantly with her younger sister, was frequently very insolent to both parents, especially her mother, and regularly ran away from home. It may be considered that this is not a particularly unusual pattern of behaviour and many parents of teenagers could sympathize with the parents of this young girl. In the case of a teenager without a disability, if such problems become severe it might be thought appropriate to involve a psychologist or a social worker, a minister or priest, or perhaps to take advice from a doctor. If the problem became particularly extreme it might even be necessary for parents and child to part company through some residential or other establishment run for this purpose. If this occurred, regular contact with home would be assured and the long-term aim of any reputable child care organization would ultimately be the return of the girl home. However, in this particular case it so happened that this young girl also had Down syndrome. When the parents approached the doctor he suggested that she be assessed in a mental handicap hospital and following the assessment it was suggested that she remain there on a permanent basis. In this example it is fairly clear that the definition of 'learning disability' led to a set of steps being taken to deal with the problem which would not have been taken had the learning disability not been present. By entering the doorway to health services, the medical model took precedence over the child care model and it was not possible to reverse that trend and adopt other solutions. Happily, in this case, as a result of a community care programme a child care organization did become involved with the hospital in which the young girl was staying and came across her situation. As a result of this by adopting methods appropriate to her problems, which were emotional and family based, it was possible to work with the family and the girl to overcome the problem and she has successfully returned home. The fact that she was able to reenter the child care system was atypical. How many adults do we meet whose history in long-stay hospital started in a similar way?

A further example is of a young man who had a learning disability and also acute behavioural difficulties which seemed to be psychiatric in origin. Repeated attempts were made to get him admitted to a psychiatric hospital for treatment, without success. The reason given was that he 'had a mental handicap' and therefore should utilize learning disability services. In these two cases, the definition of the problem centred on the learning disability and therefore entry to and retention in learning disability services became the solution.

On other occasions the reverse may apply. People with learning disabilities may, for example, commit offences and as a result end up within the prison service. The learning disability in that case will often be overlooked in favour of the definition of 'offender', whether or not it was relevant in causing the offence. In these cases and many others it can be seen that the sort of service or treatment or approach which will be utilized to solve a particular problem depends very much upon which professional is approached first and which aspect of the problem facing the professional is identified as the main area needing attention. More often than not it seems that the terms 'mental handicap' or 'learning difficulties'

are definitions which may obscure other ways of thinking.

Planning and coordination of services

Another effect of the multiplicity of service providers and their different styles is that the coordination and planning of services can be extremely difficult to achieve, both in providing those services and in taking decisions to access the funding to be able to do so. Looking at it from the outside it is obvious that services should be as comprehensive as possible, consistent with some kind of overall philosophy of care, well distributed across all areas and matched to local needs and requirements. This, however, is difficult to achieve when the objectives of different organizations may be very different. In areas where there are, or were large long-stay hospitals, health service priorities may be heavily related to creating services which will provide alternative accommodation for the people who are, or were, patients in the hospital. These services may not necessarily be linked to the needs of local residents who also require services and these will be seen as the responsibility of the local authorities. Depending on the relationship between the health board or authority and the social work or social services department, these problems may be handled in a cooperative or competitive way, and the placing of services both geographically and in terms of the need they are designed to meet may be well planned or ad hoc. Also, the priority placed upon services to people with a learning disability by the particular funding agency will determine the amount and range of services that are available in any area and these priorities, at least partly, can be determined by the political will within the statutory organization. The effectiveness of local lobbies on behalf of learning disability or other client groups who may be competing for resources, and also the effectiveness and commitment of employed persons in the health and social work areas who are designing and seeking funding for services, will have a major impact on the development of services in particular areas. In the case of voluntary and private organizations, their ability to flourish, or otherwise, in an area will depend heavily upon which organizations are working in the area, their ability to negotiate and cooperate with the statutory organization, and the power base, financial or otherwise, they have succeeded in achieving. The development of private organizations will depend heavily on the attitude, particularly of the local authority towards their development in a particular area and also on their ability to run services which are acceptable to the funders.

To summarize, what all this teaches is that the services available to people with learning disabilities in the 1990s are a complex combination of historical legacy and political reality. This is not to suggest that services are not moving towards meeting need. It is clear from the historical analysis that they are doing so but that 'need' is redefined by every generation of professionals and by every era of society; it is not an absolute term. When that 'need' is defined in any particular age, how it is met is the result of an interplay of all sorts of different factors and this is true no less in the 1990s than it was in the study of the centuries gone by with which we began this chapter.

PROFESSIONALS

Once people cross the 'threshold' into the service that they are to utilize, the experience they have of that service will be profoundly affected by the people who are employed there to deliver the service to them – what then about these professionals themselves?

Style of response

There are many groups of professionals working directly within services for people with learning disabilities and also large numbers of staff who are not formally qualified but who have long experience of working in one field or another in relation to learning disability. In each case, the professional background and the experience of the people concerned mean that they will tend to

approach problems in a particular way and interpret situations in that light. The system on which their own profession is organized and the training which they have been given will also tend to back up that approach. Let us consider two particular professions in this light – nursing and social work. Nursing is a profession with a considerable history of providing care and nurturing to those who have some kind of medical need; social work, on the other hand, is seen as coping with problems both possessed by and caused by certain groups within society.

In each profession certain people have specialized in developing their skills to work with people who have learning disabilities. This may simply be because they have come across large numbers of such people in their workload and have developed an interest in them and an affinity for them or it may be through particular choice and further training. Nonetheless, their original profession in many ways will dictate their style of response.

When receiving referrals of people with disabilities for residential facilities it is often possible to tell which profession the writer of a particular report came from without any knowledge other than the report itself. Nursing based personnel will tend to write a report which specifies medical history, definition of the particular type of disability, analysis of skills and recommendations based on the individual need and potential of the person concerned. Often, although the reports are otherwise excellent, little attention may be paid to family background or social systems surrounding the person. Other reports, however, coming from those with a social work background are often lengthy in their description of family history and family dynamics. A detailed analysis of the effects on the person of certain events which have occurred in their lives is given and recommendations will be based upon these factors. Often, essential medical and skills information will be totally or largely missing. It is a common experience on the receipt of such reports to have to phone the writer with the nursing background and ask if there are any living relatives or what their views about a particular plan may be, whereas with writers who are social workers it may be necessary to ask such basic facts as 'Can he climb stairs?' or 'Can he speak?' This portrays more than a different approach to writing reports, it portrays that different problems are actually being perceived by each profession. Again, at the risk of oversimplification, one may say that at one level, those using the medical approach tend to be developing the underlying idea that the person is an individual who requires a cure or a mitigation of the effects of their illness, whereas to those using a sociological model the view may be that this is a family malfunction which would be solved either by the solution of the problem or the removal of the cause.

Fundamentally, the two professionals may be in danger of trying to solve a different problem and while the reports they write may be excellent in terms of what they do convey, both may be very lacking in terms of what they do *not* convey. This is not to suggest that many excellent reports are not written by both social workers and mental handicap nurses, nor that they do not work together harmoniously in many instances and provide excellent solutions to the problems that face them and those people they are attempting to help. Nonetheless, it is true that they do come from different 'stables' professionally and tend to see things in slightly different lights as a result of their training, backgrounds and approach. For example, again in the case of nurse and social worker, the mental handicap nurse has a professional skill base which is targeted directly on people who have learning disabilities, and thus knowledge of learning disability is likely to be in much greater depth than that of their social work colleague and the nurse will have a caseload which comprises only people who have learning disabilities. In most cases, the social worker will be handling people with disabilities as part of a generic caseload which will cover all sorts of other client groups and his or her knowledge of learning disability is unlikely to be in such depth as that of their nursing colleague, but they are likely to have a much wider understanding of family groupings and of social pressures on families as a whole. Unfortunately, the failure to understand these

different pressures may mean that both workers become territorial in their approach to their case and deal with those aspects of the case which relate to their own particular skills, finding difficulty in understanding the other pressures operating on their colleague in the different profession. However, as mentioned above, there are tremendous advantages if their skills can be brought together. The indepth knowledge of the nurse, married to the wider knowledge of what would happen in a particular situation if the person did not have a disability which the social worker can provide, give a much richer approach to the solution of the problems facing them. In ideal situations each is able to complement and enhance the other's work. Unfortunately, in all too common situations they misunderstand each other's approach and criticize those in the other profession for not having the skills appropriate to their own profession. At the end of the day, many of the problems between nurses and social workers are because nurses expect social workers to be good nurses and social workers want nurses to be good social workers. Perhaps what is needed is a little more enthusiasm for the view 'Vive la différence'!

Training

Looking at the whole professional scene, and also that of the different agencies which exist, it is true that if we were starting with a 'clean slate' in the design of services to be used by people who have mental handicaps we would not start from the current position. It is obvious that the roles of mental handicap nurse and social worker often cross over and yet in many ways are the same. This applies to many other professions, too. The meticulous attempt made by both professions to justify their professional differences may have as much to do with their desire to keep a clear identity within that profession for themselves as it has to do with their view on how the problems and needs of people with learning disabilities can be met. Looking at the discussion in the related field of cerebral palsy concerning the Peto Institute it can be argued that the difference there is not so much in the content of the training programme for the children but in the different professional boundaries which exist in our situation. In the Hungarian situation skills from a number of professions, and from no profession in particular, have been gathered together into one role and targeted at solving a very difficult problem.

It is clear, that as people from different professions increasingly find themselves meeting and spending more time in each other's company in their attempts to solve the same problem, the confusion and difficulties so often encountered are being given more and more attention. One of the keys to this situation will be the sort of training people will have in future in order to work in services for people with disabilities. It is becoming clearer that there needs to be some analysis of skills people actually require to work in these services and an examination of how these can be provided, rather than a continual modification of other methods of training which were designed primarily for other groups of people. In the case of community care, and residential care in particular, it has become very apparent that many professions can bring skills to bear which are very necessary in this form of work. It has also become apparent that all professions have large gaps in their training which have to be filled later through direct experience and in-service training. Furthermore, all professions have large amounts of information given to them in their training which are not strictly relevant to the care of people with learning disabilities in the settings in which they will work.

What is needed is a clearly thought out statement of where and on what basis we wish services for people with a disability to develop. Much of the necessary thinking has already been done. As this is agreed upon, clearer research into which skills are necessary to bring that about in the different settings in which people will work is leading to the design of training which is relevant to achieving those ends. If we believe that people with disabilities are people like any others, and if we hold to the view therefore that the object of services is to attempt to equalize the opportunity of people with disabili-

ties to live within society as other people do, then we must go on from there to ask which skills are required by staff who work with them to enable them to achieve these opportunities and access these rights.

One approach to this is to glory in the individuality of the people for whom we provide services and accept that, as every individual will be different one from the other, the training that staff receive at one level should be as general as possible, allowing them to specialize in the particular needs of the actual individuals for whom they are caring. In a community house, additional training could be given to staff once they are in a post which will enable them to cope with the particular needs of the small group of residents with whom they are directly involved. For example, if one of the residents in a particular house has a hearing loss then staff in that house should be trained as fully as possible in all matters relating to this, whereas in another house if one of the residents has spina bifida then staff should be trained as fully as possible in all aspects of this condition. Ideally, therefore, staff would have a general training which would enable them to tune in to the type of care being offered and additional training then for the particular needs of the people they will care for. Perhaps, in years to come, development will be away from the desire to tie together existing professions which are very different in origin and philosophy, and more towards the attempt to identify a new profession which will have particular skills in enabling people who have disabilities to be people first and to equalize their opportunities within the society in which they live.

THE NEED FOR BETTER COORDINATED SERVICES

As we have observed, there are a multiplicity of providers and agencies working in services for people who have learning disabilities. It is sometimes argued that multiplicity is a good thing because it provides variety and a range of skills which can operate in any situation. There may certainly be benefits in this but very often it is not possible to convey those benefits to the users of the services because the services themselves are so poorly coordinated. An example of this was a young mother who was informed by paediatricians that her newborn baby had a profound learning disability. The doctor spoke to her for some time in his office and then allowed her to leave. She was completely devastated and depressed. Some months later, through a voluntary organization, she was referred back to the hospital concerned to be seen by a social worker who was able to put her in touch with all the relevant services which were on offer to her. The social worker's office was only three doors down the same corridor from the doctor who had originally told her of her child's disability. Examples such as this, showing the poor coordination of services, are all too common. As a result a number of mechanisms have been designed to improve coordination within the system.

Community Mental Handicap Teams

The problem of poor coordination of services has been recognized for some time and attempts have been made to draw together the various skills which are scattered amongst professional groupings and to use them more productively. One method which has been tried has been the Community Mental Handicap Team. Representatives of a number of professions are placed together in a building with a defined role to perform. Teams usually comprise such professions as medicine, nursing, social work, physiotherapy, speech therapy and occupational therapy. Referrals to the Community Mental Handicap Team lead to a discussion between team members about which services and skills are particularly required in the situation identified and how to target these effectively and in a way which makes sense to the people concerned. Community Mental Handicap Teams have been established in many areas of the country and are working well. They have clearly been a boon to local families who have a member with a learning disability and have previously been confused about the multiplicity of the agencies they should approach and the infinite potential to 'fall between stools'.

However, Community Mental Handicap Teams are as prone to problems of team morale as any other team. Also, there are often built-in stresses about which particular profession should take the lead in the team and how the team itself should take decisions and tie into other bodies which are working alongside them in the area. Further difficulties can be caused by misunderstandings between professional groupings of the role each has in practice.

What is clear is that the original notion of Community Mental Handicap Teams is an eminently sensible one and one which solves problems for the users of services by ensuring that they get access to correct professional advice and that no stone is left unturned on their behalf for the accessing of services which are local and suitable. The problems which Community Mental Handicap Teams have are more often related to the collision between professions, particularly their different managerial and decision-making structures which have caused problems in enabling these teams to flourish and develop as they could do.

Case conferences

Clearly there can be many kinds of difficulties for the users of the services. Parents may not understand the different structure systems and professions which are arrayed to meet them when they first discover that they have a child with a disability. People with disabilities themselves, who often have associated problems in communicating, may find it particularly difficult to understand the different types of professional jargon or be faced in meetings with representatives from all the different groups. The confusion between the services is obvious enough and that confusion cannot fail to be passed on to the people who are attempting to use the services. On top of this, awareness of the need to coordinate services has led to a proliferation of methods for attempting to do this which, while they may have helped in many ways, have also actually made extra demands on the parents of children with disabilities and on the people with disabilities themselves.

One of the main ways in which people have attempted to overcome the problem of poor communication has been the case conference and review system. This system ensures that regular meetings occur between all the professionals involved in providing care or other services to a particular person. Careful minutes are kept and circulated to all concerned and decisions about the way forward in a particular situation are agreed upon. Until recently, and still in many cases, such case conferences were not open to the people concerned. Clearly, therefore, this leaves problems regarding their access to information that is rightfully theirs about themselves or about their child.

However, access to the case conferences also has its problems. It can lead to increased expectations for, for example, parents of a child with a disability to attend a large number of meetings at which they may often feel they are surrounded by professionals who appear to know more about their child than they do. Such meetings can be threatening and intimidating, particularly for a person with a disability who may have difficulty communicating even in simple language and who may find himself faced with very complex language and words which he does not understand. Also, every organization involved with the person may feel it necessary to carry out their obligations to that person by holding reviews. Therefore, in some cases there are multiple reviews held by the school, the residential establishment in which the person may be living and by a social worker who may be visiting the family. In some cases it may be requested that reviews be held within the family home. This may make it easier for parents who do not need therefore to trek out to so many meetings (and possibly they are already having regular outpatient appointments at hospitals and meetings with psychologists, involving more travelling). However, it can mean that parents find themselves attending or even hosting reviews on a very regular basis. The number of different professionals who will visit their homes can be dizzying, including social workers, psychologists, nurses, occupational therapists, physiotherapists and doctors. Each professional may be

doing their professional best, both in concert with other professionals and individually to meet the needs of the particular person concerned. But the logistics for the family or the individual in supporting these number of meetings, even in practical terms, can be very difficult and the feeling of exhaustion and frustration expressed by parents as they are handed from person to person can be very intense.

The confusion of experiencing the different professional methods used by different people can also be frustrating. Parents wish the best assessment and treatment plan to be identified but it can be confusing when different assessment tools are used, for example, by the school and a residential unit used by their child for short-stay breaks. For adults with disabilities, reviews can be helpful in allowing them to feel involved in their own futures and to develop skills of self-advocacy, but they may also be terrifying experiences where they are faced with 12 or more people in a formal setting with which they are unfamiliar and who wish to discuss the most personal aspects of their lives with them. All these things work best when a considerable amount of work has gone into developing good relationships between different professionals in a particular area so that reviews and case conferences can be shared, and assessment methods streamlined and decisions taken about which one will be used in a particular case. To do this, however, involves a degree of trust and a willingness to use an assessment system which would not be the personal choice of the particular professional concerned and a willingness to accept as valid the reports of other professionals so that there is no need for repetition. Therefore, coordination of services is a necessity, not a luxury. It is a necessity much preached but little practised. To practise it involves commitment, determination, trust and a dose of humility by all concerned, at all levels in an organization.

CONCLUSION

We have seen in this section that society, continuing its cycle of change and reorientation of both philosophies and systems, has produced a complex pattern of services from which people with mental handicaps and their families can gain support in the 1990s. We have also seen how this variety in services, service providers and professionals who staff them, can have a bewildering effect on people, and we have considered some of the attempts which have been made to mitigate this bewilderment. The challenge for all professionals in the decades to come will be how to turn this confused hub-bub of services into an organized variety, which can meet individuals at their point of need, without either regimenting or neglecting them.

This chapter has attempted to clarify the current confusing situation of the 1990s by looking back over the previous 10 centuries at the development of services to people with mental handicaps and the relationship of this to the attitudes held by society towards these people. The belief is that by understanding the historical origins of our attitudes and our systems we will better be able to clarify our thinking to understand the problems they may encounter today and to take forward services which are appropriate to the 1990s. It is for tomorrow's professionals to do this by nurturing in themselves open minds and a willingness to learn from each other.

QUESTIONS

1. What modern attitudes can you trace back to attitudes of the past?
2. How would you resolve some of the problems caused by the multiplicity of services and service providers in the 1990s?
3. You visit a family with a teenage daughter. She is pregnant and she has a mental handicap. Which services would be of use to her and the family? How would you expect the family and neighbourhood to react to this situation?

REFERENCE

Jones K 1961 Mental health and social policy 1845-1959. Routledge & Kegan Paul, London
O'Brien J, Tyne A 1981 The principle of normalization – a foundation for effective services. Adapted from a paper for the Georgia Advocacy Office, Atlanta. CMH, London
Tuke D H 1882 History of the treatment of the insane. Kegan Paul & Toench, London

CHAPTER CONTENTS

Normalization 41
The development of social role valorization 41
The role of values in normalization 42
    The role of consciousness and unconsciousness in
        services 42
    The relevance of role expectancy and role
        circularity 43
    The conservatism corollary 43
    The developmental model 44
    The power of imitation 44
    The dynamics and relevance of social imagery 44
    The importance of social integration 44

The vicious circle 45

**The application of the principles of
    normalization 46**
The individual in the service 46
The service as it seeks to support those who use
        it 47
Work 47
A social life 48
Accommodation 49

Image and competency – a dilemma 51

Misunderstandings about normalization 51
Normalization and social role valorization – what is
        the difference? 52

**Quality assurance – other systems and
    measures 52**
What does 'quality' mean? 53
The dimensions of quality 53
Frameworks for quality assurance in nursing 53
    Structure 54
    Process 55
    Outcome 55
    Standards 55
    Problem-solving 55
    Cause and effect analysis 55
    Quality assurance audits 56

Total quality management 56

3

Quality of care

A. Chisholm

Key points
- Social role valorization (normalization) is accepted as the universal principle on which services for those with learning disabilities are based
- Normalization is about being treated in a way that you and I would be happy to accept and is not about 'being made normal'
- Services reflect the attitudes and values of society and as such may be guilty of regarding people with learning disabilities as devalued people
- Quality assurance may be achieved either by using the structure/process/outcome approach or the problem-solving method
- Total quality management is a corporate approach that involves every aspect of the organization in meeting customer needs

NORMALIZATION

The development of social role valorization

The principle of normalization as it is understood and practised today owes most of its development to the work of Wolfensberger (1972) in North America. The idea itself is not new, originating in Scandinavia in the 1960s before being developed in America in the late 60s. What is new is the marriage of philosophies which related to the strategies to improve the lot of individuals and the outcomes which flowed from these strategies. In Britain, the spread of the normalization principle has been largely coordinated, and to a considerable extent promoted and taught, by the Community and Mental Handicap Education and Research Association and the Campaign for Mentally Handicapped – now known as Values Into Action (VIA).

The first statement of the developed idea was published in 1972 by Wolfensberger, followed by the publication of Program Analysis of Service Systems (PASS) (Wolfensberger & Glenn 1987) which is a method used in the evaluation of services. Further developments resulted in the production of Program Analysis of Service Systems Implementation of Normalization Goals (PASSING) (Wolfensberger & Thomas 1983). Both PASS and PASSING are quality assurance tools evaluating the service against the desirable level. PASS has 50 separate 'ratings', and evaluates outcomes for service users using the principle of normalization, other service-oriented ideologies and administrative considerations e.g. financial support. PASSING has 42 ratings and is concerned only with issues relating to the normalization principle. Of the 50 ratings in PASS, 34 are concerned solely with the normalization principle. PASS and PASSING as quality assurance instruments are designed to be applied over a wide range of services though the main users of the evaluation tools to date have been those professionals working in the field of mental handicap.

Although the principles of social role valorization have been applied in many situations for many years under different guises, they have only relatively recently been clearly formulated and accepted as the universal principles on which to deal with those with learning difficulties. Normalization principles as a distinct entity have, to a greater or lesser extent, been applied in Britain since 1975 and the core value – that people with learning difficulties have the same human value as everyone else – is now written into virtually every service statement regarding planning and delivery of services in this country. Normalization is not about 'being normal' or about providing services of a standard typical in our society. On the contrary, normalization theory challenges us to provide services, support, help, encouragement and reward of a standard you and I would be happy to accept. Simply put, the question is (for each discrete part of a theory): If a service or practice was viewed by an ordinary member of the community would he or she consider the service or practice to be acceptable (Fig. 3.1)?

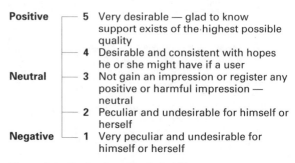

Figure 3.1   Scale of service desirability.

The role of values in normalization

Social value lies at the heart of normalization theory and finds expression in the seven core themes of normalization:

1. The role of consciousness and unconsciousness in services.
2. The relevance of role expectancy and role circularity.
3. The conservatism corollary.
4. The developmental model.
5. The power of imitation.
6. The dynamics and relevance of social imagery.
7. The importance of social integration and participation.

Let us examine each of the core themes one at a time:

The role of consciousness and unconsciousness in services

Much of what we do in our day-to-day lives we do without consciously examining our reasoning, including our activities in our working lives. In any labour intensive service the unconscious motives or assumptions held by staff employed in the organization are likely to have a major impact on the work done.

In services for people with learning difficulties, these unconscious assumptions play a large part in the quality of care. The carer may be unaware of the impact of the values of the culture he or she is part of. Ask any group of people about the terms they used as a child to describe people with learning difficulty, or about the language used to describe people with learning difficulty which they commonly encounter in the community, and you will discover wide use of derogatory (or negatively valued) terms, i.e. 'idiot', 'moron', 'simple' or 'not the full shilling'. Normalization theory argues that these terms are part of our language because people tend to think of those with learning difficulties as having less value than people without learning difficulties. In consequence, it may be considered that the services to those people with difficulties in learning need not be of as high a standard as for others who are not so affected.

Similar examples, though on the face of it more benevolent, may be found that reflect the underlying beliefs prevalent in the community and expressed in service provision – even by professional people who claim to know the belief to be unsound! Consider the widely held social view that people with learning difficulties are children all of their lives. Many services encourage this view by various means; firstly, by providing games and pastimes normally associated with children for people who are very obviously adult, thus reinforcing the societal viewpoint; secondly, by dressing adults in clothing more suited to children; thirdly, by using age inappropriate teaching methods that contrast with the methods of teaching others in the community who have Adult Basic Education needs.

The relevance of role expectancy and role circularity

The second core theme may be simply expressed as the self-fulfilling prophecy. In short, if we hold a low expectation of someone it is likely that we will create a situation in which anything greater than our expected low outcome will be improbable. In the workplace, if we were expected to provide the highest quality service, we could

legitimately expect in turn to be given the best physical environment in which to work and the best tools with which to do the job. Similarly if the expectation is to produce substantial growth and development in a person, a high level of skills and adequate resources are required to meet these expectations. Excellent results will not be achieved in an impoverished environment by people with inadequate resources and skills.

Normalization argues that whenever a service is in a position to influence the dynamic of role expectancy it should do so positively, i.e. expect much of the service user; create the situations in which success is likely; and assist people to acquire the 'badges of social status' like tenant, householder or worker which in turn will raise the expectation of the individual and provoke a positive response to the responsibility of the role.

The conservatism corollary

The conservatism corollary simply means that when a person has a characteristic which is not generally valued in society everything possible should be done to minimize that characteristic. Nothing should be done to exacerbate the characteristic by drawing attention to the person through the addition of other odd or unusual features.

The conservatism corollary has relevance when considered in terms of the individual outwith group situations. Someone who has a learning difficulty but who is well dressed and groomed is likely to be accepted, on appearance at least, as being able and competent. On the other hand, a person who is able and competent but who is badly dressed, unkempt, dirty and in torn clothes may be assumed to have a learning difficulty or mental illness by conforming to the societal stereotype for such a person. Normalization argues that whenever a service has a potential impact on the conservatism corollary, either by assisting the individual to improve his personal impression impact or by minimalizing or maximizing the transference of lesser or greater ability through association, it should work toward the best possible outcome for the individual or group.

The developmental model

The developmental model requires that individual ability to grow and develop be recognized and nurtured if the potential for that growth is to be realized. This assumes that everyone is expected to learn, grow and develop. In practical terms, we are concerned here with provision and support for greater and greater skill acquisition, particularly for people who may be perceived as less able. One example might be the worthwhile and continuing trend towards computer-assisted learning in many training establishments for people with mental handicaps. The provision and use of these sophisticated tools (assuming the programmes on them are relevant and challenging), enable the individual to acquire skills in computer operation, whatever the programme sets out to assist with and at a pace comfortable for the student. Another less positive example is the often observed practice of giving adults with a mental handicap 'toy' adult possessions and experiences, such as children's tape recorders and computers or play shopping. Clearly, there is little expectation of growth present when such practices continue and little in the way of provision and support in practice to enable growth to occur. Failure to reach set goals is often attributed to the learner's inability to learn rather than the teacher's inability to teach! The developmental model also requires that techniques used when working and coping with people should be directed towards an expected and worthwhile goal and be intense and relevant. Equipment necessary to enable people with handicaps (particularly physical handicaps) to access the widest possible range of stimulating and demanding activities and opportunities should be available and should itself be challenging for the individual, encouraging ever greater ranges of mobility and access.

The power of imitation

Imitation or modelling is one of the most powerful learning mechanisms known (Bandura 1977). Who amongst us has not witnessed the child imitate the parent with alarming accuracy –

sometimes for the good and sometimes for the bad! Everyone is influenced heavily by the power of imitation, in fashion, behaviour, language, in fact, in almost every area of our lives. Thus, people with handicaps may benefit from mixing with non-handicapped people who may offer a wide range of positive models.

Of course, the power of imitation can, and often does, work negatively. Care should be taken therefore not to encourage or expose people with handicaps, particularly mental handicap, to role models who, if imitated, would further devalue the individual.

The dynamics and relevance of social imagery

The practice of imaging people, particularly people who are 'different', as objects of dread, pity, criminality, illness, weakness or triviality is common. Often passed on from one generation to another through schools and families, stereotypes are created occasionally so forcefully that even when we have not met an individual with certain handicaps, an image is formed of the likely appearance and characteristics of the individual whose handicaps have been described to us. The result is frequently stigmatization of the individual.

Normalization requires that, wherever possible, services should recognize the prevalent negative imagery, or stigma, associated with the people who use the service and work against these images by conveying messages, through appearance, behaviour, setting and design, which create a more positive picture.

The importance of social integration

People with a mental handicap are at risk of being devalued by remaining apart from other nonhandicapped individuals in their day-to-day lives. However, physically moving people into locally based facilities does not ensure that the person with learning disabilities will interact with neighbours. Discharging people from institutions can result in the person becoming more rather than less isolated and in a strengthening of stereotype.

Normalization requires that, wherever possible, people at risk of being devalued should be housed with, employed beside and taught with people without learning disabilities and should be assisted to spend their time *as* members of the community *with* members of the community.

There are some important points worth noting when considering the core themes:

- While it may be relatively easy to discuss core themes as abstract concepts in practice they do not exist as distinct entities nor do all of them have the same value.
- The importance of certain themes may vary depending on the service in question and the people who use it. Thus, some issues may be very relevant in a residential setting but be less relevant in an educational setting.
- Careful consideration should be given to the relative merits of each theme before deciding on the priorities for each person in specific settings. In practice, issues often conflict and decisions may involve making compromises.
- Normalization is often criticized as being impractical or too idealistic. However, application of the core themes is likely to result in vastly improved services for the people who use them, even though difficulties may be experienced in applying the theory in practice.

To summarize this section, there are certain groups within society which are devalued: treated as unimportant or less than human. Such groups include people with learning difficulties and people with a mental illness; these groups are typically regarded as clowns, evil or menaces and may experience a life characterized by segregation, isolation and lack of choice. Advocates of normalization argue that these groups experience devaluation not only in society generally but also in services designed to cater for their needs. Services reflect the attitudes and values of society and though set up to help they often hinder the development of the service users. Proponents of normalization contend that services need to change, become conscious of what they are doing and set about accomplishing positive outcomes with and for their customers.

THE VICIOUS CIRCLE

A deviancy career is a vicious circle in which a person comes into contact with widely held stereotypes and comes to incorporate them into his value system. The process is shown in the form of a diagram in Figure 3.2. The vicious circle may start with negative beliefs about the worth of a group of people being attributed to an individual who has one or more of the stereotyping conditions characteristic of the group. The individual accepts the negative value placed on him so he plays the role expected of him and because he plays the role he reinforces the stereotype. Thus, the circle is maintained.

The existence of the vicious circles in services is particularly damaging. Not only does it further damage the individual in the service but it also transmits very strong messages to people outside the service about the people who use it. After all, if professional people employed to improve a person's quality of life hold negative stereotypes of their clients and demonstrate low expectations of them they set an extremely harmful example to the general public. Rather

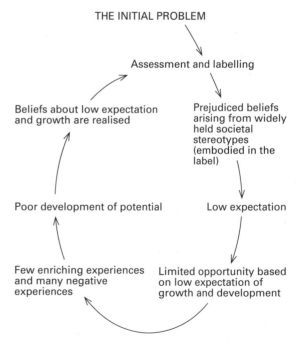

Figure 3.2   Incorporating stereotypes into a value system.

than focusing on the processes involved in the maintenance of the vicious circle, and breaking it, services may simply deal with the individual problems as they arise.

THE APPLICATION OF THE PRINCIPLES OF NORMALIZATION

In this section normalization theory is viewed from two perspectives:

- the individual in the service
- the service as it seeks to support the individuals who use it.

Service is in turn examined under three main headings, namely work, social life and accommodation. Each of the perspectives is considered under the following headings:

- Community presence
- Making choices and advocacy
- Developing and maintaining skills
- Gaining respect
- Positive relationships
- Being treated as an individual
- Having one's rights supported
- Continuity
- Dignity of risk.

The individual in the service

Community presence

People should not be segregated from other citizens in residential, day and leisure facilities but have the right to live, work and socialize within the wider community.

Making choices and advocacy

Individuals should be assisted to develop and maintain a wide range of choices, from small everyday decisions to major life decisions. This requires that people are given information, are listened to and priority given to ensuring people assert their rights and preferences.

Developing and maintaining skills

In order to live in their local community, indi-

viduals may need help to acquire and maintain practical and social skills at all levels.

Gaining respect

It is important that efforts are made to enable individuals to fill valued roles in the community that give them dignity and respect. Recognition should be made of the adult status of those people using adult services and everything should be done to prevent people being seen as second-class citizens.

Positive relationships

It should be a priority that people are given the help and encouragement they need to meet and mix with other valued citizens. In practice, this means that opportunities must be made available to help people form a wide range of relationships from acquaintance to intimate friend.

Being treated as an individual

It is necessary to recognize that people have varied needs and wants which can be provided for only by an approach which is flexible and tailored to the individual. Services should be fitted to the individual rather than the person to the service.

Having one's rights supported

People should have claim to all the rights enjoyed by other citizens, irrespective of the level of support they require. This includes people having access to information regarding their rights, support to assert those rights and safeguards to ensure them.

Continuity

The social networks which people have already developed should be supported and encouraged. The role of the service should be to build on established networks within the local area and culture which support the individual, rather than attempting to replace them.

Dignity of risk

In order to grow and gain competence across the fullest range of activities individuals need to be supported to engage in activities which may contain an element of risk. Services should ensure that all reasonable precautions are taken to safeguard the individual but should not exclude individuals from activities which would be stimulating and challenging through the overzealous application of rules which are limiting and overprotective.

The service as it seeks to support those who use it

Work

Community presence

People with learning difficulties should, wherever possible, have the right to be engaged in a job of work in an integrated setting. This means a job which provides realistic pay for the work done in a workplace populated by other valued citizens. The role of the service should be to provide such support as may be necessary to enable individuals to secure meaningful employment and retain it.

Making choices and advocacy

Services should earnestly attempt to discover each person's interests and aptitudes and provide support in actively pursuing these preferences. This should not be confined to a limited range of jobs seen as suitable for 'disabled' people, but take in the entire range of employment and employment practices, i.e. flexible hours, job sharing and co-working.

Developing and maintaining skills

The role of services is to provide and create access on behalf of service users to acquire skills which are tailored to the individual's wishes and in demand in the workplace. Initially, this may require the provision of sheltered work placements for certain individuals. Placements on such schemes should not however be seen as a permanent option but rather as a means to an end, the end being work with reward. Where an individual has limited experience of the world of work, services should support individuals to explore different kinds of work through work experience before attempting to ascertain the individual's preferred employment. The underlying assumption should be that everyone can learn and, provided the right level of support is available, the vast majority can hold down a job.

Gaining respect

People should be encouraged to seek valued employment and efforts made to help people develop their career structure. It is important that the work done is widely held to be of worth and that the wage paid for the job adequately reflects that worth and is, at the very least, the same as any other citizen doing the same work would receive.

Positive relationships

Employment can provide opportunities for relationships with other citizens which are based on an ability to do a job of worth and shared experience as a colleague, rather than on disability. Working relationships should be encouraged and supported both in and outside the workplace.

Being treated as an individual

Support should be tailored to each individual's need and will change according to the individual's circumstances. Some people require little support while others may need a great deal over a long period of time.

Having one's rights supported

Services should ensure that people have access to information about their employment rights – about trade union membership, staff organizations and employment contracts, and assistance to understand their relevance where necessary. Services should also work actively to ensure these employment rights are properly safeguarded.

Continuity

It is important that people are properly equipped both to begin a working life and to retire at the appropriate time. This requires services to engage in purposeful discussion of employment opportunities with young adults, career development and retirement. Discussion about employment should be in line with locally based opportunities and expectations.

Dignity of risk

Services should not exclude from the range of possible employment any occupations which are considered to carry an element of risk. The role of the service is to support, enable and equip the individual with due regard to access on behalf of the individual's health and safety in the workplace. In recognizing the need to support individuals, services must not neglect their responsibility nor should they be restrictive through a tendency to overprotection.

A social life

Community presence

The social life of individuals with learning difficulties should be centred in the community with all that this entails in respect of local opportunities for leisure, recreation and health. Services should facilitate, support and encourage people to pursue their leisure interests in nonsegregated settings, i.e. clubs, hotels and community centres and similarly receive other services available to ordinary citizens in the community, i.e. health care in health centres. There should not be a requirement for people with learning difficulties to form segregated clubs for entertainment due to a lack of other opportunities.

Making choices and advocacy

The support services provided in respect of exercising choice and advocacy should be available in two ways. Firstly, people should be helped to discover the social opportunities available in local areas and to make choices about participa-

tion. Secondly, services should actively help people engage in their interests.

Developing and maintaining skills

It is through the experience of social situations that people develop skills of social interaction, e.g. conversation and social 'etiquette'. The belief that people leading restricted social lives improve their social skills in segregated settings before entering the mainstream of social activities is very questionable. While there is a place for providing sheltered environments for some people with learning difficulties there is an associated danger of the protective environment becoming restrictive. The challenge to services is to facilitate integrative social contact through which people with learning difficulties may be exposed to real social contact while supporting them in learning from this experience.

Gaining respect

Services should promote opportunities for people not only to pursue their interests but also to take responsibility for them and play a major role in managing them. Roles which may be developed as a result of people taking greater ownership of their social lives include that of host or guest which convey status on the individual and command respect.

Positive relationships

Traditional models have assumed that people with disabilities only relate well to other people with disabilities. Services should find opportunities for people to meet and develop relationships with other people which are founded on mutual interest, outlook and hobbies and not on common disability.

Being treated as an individual

Services must not be based on a professional's opinion regarding what people might enjoy. Patterns of leisure provision should be determined by the individual's interests and wishes.

Having one's rights supported

Some people with learning difficulties may find it difficult to assert their rights. The challenge to services is to develop systems of communication which are 'user-friendly' and to listen and support individuals who express a wish to pursue their interests. Advocacy may be appropriate when individuals experience difficulty in asserting their rights. Some people may require further assistance through the offices of a citizen advocate – someone not engaged by services who may speak on the individual's behalf.

Continuity

In most instances, services should support people in maintaining and developing their social networks. The severing of local ties and friendships upon a change of residence could be avoided by facilitating and encouraging contact by letters, phone calls and visits.

Dignity of risk

People with learning difficulties are at risk from suffering loss of dignity in many ways. They may be ridiculed for behaving inappropriately or saying the wrong thing in the wrong place, or they may be trivialised through other people holding low expectations of success and minimizing their achievements. Services can minimalize these risks through preparation prior to social engagement. However, services are limited in what they can do to protect individuals in helping them to develop strategies for coping with embarrassing and challenging situations. Though there is an element of risk involved in mixing with nonmentally handicapped people, services can support individuals by helping them to deal with situations as they arise so that these experiences can be learned from.

Accommodation

Community presence

People with learning difficulties should, as a matter of priority, be assisted to remain in their own homes with their families for as long as they wish to. However, support to remain at home should not preclude the right to leave and establish more independent living, either in single tenancies or shared residencies, with a level of support appropriate to individual requirements. In the event of a move from home being advocated, the new accommodation should, where possible, be situated in the area with which the individual is familiar and has a sense of belonging. People leaving home to live elsewhere should be encouraged to maintain family bonds and personal relationships.

Making choices and advocacy

Adults with learning difficulties should have a choice of accommodation which is wide ranging and based on individual preferences and needs. Where shared tenancies are desirable the choice as to who may share with whom should be on the basis of personal compatibility (decided upon by the sharing tenants), rather than by common degree of disability. In the event of prospective tenants being unable to express a point of view someone who knows the individual very well may assume an advocatory role. Such a step should only be taken when an individual *cannot* express a view him- or herself. The role of advocate should be adopted as an aid to decision-making only as a second option; great care should be taken to elicit a choice from the individual before recourse to consultation with others. Adults within their own home (home being the place where the individual spends most of his time, i.e. the base where his personal belongings are stored and where the individual sleeps – this may be a ward in an institution) should be able to take a large part in decision-making regarding their living arrangements on a day-to-day and long-term basis.

Developing and maintaining skills

The support made available to people either in their own homes or in supported accommodation is to assist him or her to create and/or maintain a home and a home life. Each individual should receive a level of support that is neither underestimated nor overestimated, both of which are likely to diminish opportunities to learn and consolidate new skills. Each person should have a plan of action, which is both challenging and achievable and which reflects the ambition and desire of the individual to become more competent in the administration of his or her own home. This requires that support workers possess a wide range of skills (either as individuals or as part of a wider support team) from simple assistance with budgeting to counselling and resolution of challenging behaviours.

Gaining respect

In all but the most exceptional of circumstances it should not be necessary to build houses specially for people with learning difficulties. Where a requirement to build is paramount the accommodation should be situated in the area of origin of the prospective occupants, be in keeping both in terms of style and size for the immediate neighbourhood and should not, through its design or appointments, draw attention as being anything other than a home for the people who live there. Designs which draw the attention of the public as being for 'different people' should be avoided. However, from time to time alterations such as ramps or lifts may be essential for individual residents. Where the provision of special adaptations or design is essential, care should be exercised to ensure its visual impact is kept to a minimum. The role of professional staff engaged in the support of individuals in their own homes, be it in institutional or community settings, should be on an equal adult-to-adult basis with the service user.

Positive relationships

For those who choose to live in a shared situation the choice of who they live with should rest primarily with the service user. Large groups of people with disabilities should be avoided lest 'service ghettos' develop. Accommodation which is situated close to non-disabled citizens is more likely to facilitate the formation of positive relationships with neighbours than if it was removed from other accommodation. Sharing situations should reflect individual preferences and intensity of relationships, from acquaintances sharing accommodation to couples living together.

Being treated as an individual

The requirement for a flexible, skilled pool of support workers is essential in order that help may be provided to meet the needs of the individual. It should not be a requirement that service users move through a range of accommodation of different support levels as the individual develops – rather the intensity and content of support should revolve around the individual in his or her own home. Each person should have adequate space to store, display and use items of personal property which reflect the individual's preferences, without fear of disapproval or theft. Residents should be encouraged to acquire and assume responsibility for personal possessions.

Having one's rights supported

Each person with learning difficulties should have access to the full range of rights enjoyed by other citizens, whether or not the individual is in his or her own home. The role of support workers is to ensure these rights are not infringed or abused and to guide, counsel and support people with learning difficulties in exercising these rights.

Continuity

Changes in service provision such as accommodation and support should be provided in ways which minimally disrupt the life of the individual. This requires that services pay high regard to existing relationships between the person and his or her friends and families and with his or her support workers. Use of a key worker will avoid the trauma of a large number of disparate professions descending on the individual.

Dignity of risk

When designing or altering prospective accommodation for people with learning disabilities every effort should be made to arrive at a 'barrier free' home. Barrier free housing is that which has the necessary aids and adaptations for the user to perform the activities of daily living with the minimum of assistance from others. Many activities in the home have the potential of being dangerous or risky. A careful balance must be struck between protecting the individual resident from unnecessary risk and overprotection through excluding the resident from any potentially dangerous task because of some disability, i.e. epilepsy.

IMAGE AND COMPETENCY – A DILEMMA

In normalization theory, two main strands of thinking (image and competency) affect each of the core themes when put into practice. For example, the image projected by the use of an aid such as a walking stick is one of differentness, illness or disability; yet without the aid the person becomes a prisoner of his or her own home, denied the opportunity to use the resources of the community and reliant upon his or her friends to visit for social contact. In such circumstances, the strict application of normalization theory (if given the same weighting) may result in failure to meet at least one of the goals of the core themes. Professional judgement involves weighing the pros and cons of image and competency enhancement to consider the relative gains (or losses) of each before helping the person decide on his or her course of action, e.g. whether or not to use a walking stick.

Damage to the image of the individual by using the aid may be considered less important than the effect on the person's social and personal skills of not using the aid. The decision-making does not however end there! Normalization principles challenge us to examine the problem again to seek the best possible aid for the individual not only in terms of doing the job, but also in terms of impression management.

The importance attached to impression management may be seen in the complaint regarding disabled TV presenters by a dissatisfied viewer. The viewer complained that high-profile disabled TV presenters who were in possession of chrome wheelchairs could wear a wide variety of colour coordinated clothing while she was stuck with an airforce blue wheelchair which was unattractive and limited her choice of wardrobe! The impact of this apparently small detail regarding the colour of her aid to mobility, while appearing to be of little significance to you or me, was of great significance to the viewer.

The issues of image and competence are relevant to all aspects of the core themes and are often in tension one with the other. In PASS and PASSING, aspects of image and competence are examined thoroughly both in terms of service design, structure and organization, and in terms of the effectiveness of the service in achieving desirable outcomes for the people who use the service. Each of the nine headings we have considered contain elements which require careful consideration, in terms of the image projected by an action when applying the principles in practice and likewise with competency.

MISUNDERSTANDINGS ABOUT NORMALIZATION

- *Normalization means making people 'normal'.*
  Normalization does mean that people can often acquire more appropriate behaviour and appearances through positive expectations and supportive environments and techniques. However, the principle does not claim to eliminate differences nor to 'cure' handicaps. It is therefore applicable to all people, regardless of the severity or permanence of their conditions.
- *'Normalization means treating people as if they were not handicapped.'*
  Normalization does not mean moving people into mainstream society without making available specialized forms of help. It does, however, constantly challenge us to find ways to provide the assistance at times, in settings and with procedures which cater for their needs without the help itself being stigmatizing.

- *'Normalization denies people the right to be different or individualistic' or (just the opposite) 'Normalization means that any behaviour, appearance, or activity is acceptable because free choice and individual differences are 'normal'.'*

  Normalization requires that service programmes and personal interactions enable and actively encourage people to demonstrate behaviours, characteristics and experiences which are normative, i.e. familiar or valued in our society. However, normalization does not deny a person the right to choose a nonnormative option, provided the alternatives and consequences are real and clearly recognized by the person.

- *'Normalization means making things 'nice' for handicapped people' and 'Segregated services are acceptable if they are like similar services for nondisabled people.'*

  The primary focus of normalization is on creating social change – on increasing the physical presence and valued participation of handicapped people within the community. Well-meaning attempts to *simulate* the real world – even its most positive aspects – are inconsistent with the spirit of the principle.

- *'Normalization is impractical, too ideal.'*

  It is impossible to make progress towards a goal without clearly and sytematically defining that goal and the means to reach it. Undoubtedly, normalization as an ideal at times will be in tension with 'reality', but it is important that any compromises which must be made be clearly recognized as such.

- *'Normalization is common sense, nothing new' and 'Normalization is the same as deinstitutionalization, community services, mainstreaming . . . we're already doing it.'*

  Any serious study of the implications of normalization would reveal that our society and our helping services have much to accomplish in order to carry out normalization. Concepts such as 'deinstitutionalization', 'community services' and 'mainstreaming' focus on one service type, location, or technique without specifying the desired quality of life which is the goal. As a result, these concepts are often implemented in ways which are inconsistent with normalization.

Normalization and social role valorization – what is the difference?

The simple answer is that there is no difference – they are one and the same theory and principle. The term normalization has been considered to be confusing and has led to common misunderstandings, some of which are stated above. 'Normalization' is not about making people 'normal'. Social role valorization is considered a more accurate phrase that reflects the theory and principles described.

A major criticism of the social role valorization perspective is that it expects too much of the people being supported, and the community at large, and is therefore unrealistic. People with a mental handicap are seen as being better off in segregated settings where they can be with their peers and avoid the prejudices that exist in integrated community settings. For example, some religious organizations have built their services on principles of specialist nonintegration rather than integration though sharing many of the other values central to the normalization and social role valorization philosophy.

QUALITY ASSURANCE – OTHER SYSTEMS AND MEASURES

The impetus to look at quality assurance in nursing care springs from three important documents published in the 70s and 80s. The first, *Towards a Theory of Nursing Care* (Inman 1975), postulated a systematic approach toward the design and application of nursing practice. The second, *Standards of Nursing Care* (Committee on Standards of Nursing Care 1979), examines the delivery of nursing practice in terms of standards of good practice which are achievable and realistic. The third, *Report of the NHS Management Enquiry* (The Griffiths Report, DHSS 1983), advocated greater service accountability and put the customer or patient at the centre of the quality assurance drive by focusing on the recipient of care as being a legitimate judge of quality.

What does 'quality' mean?

Quality is not an absolute. One person's view of quality in a service (or a product) will not necessarily be the same as that of another. Quality is about that which is perceived to be good or bad and is essentially subjective and value based. The development of quality services (and quality measures) is elusive, difficult to define in any lasting sense and subject to the vagaries of professional fashion, consumer expectation and political direction.

The dimensions of quality

Quality has many dimensions, the relevance and importance of each varying from situation to situation. The dimensions include:

- speed of delivery
- reliability of provision
- accuracy of information
- capacity for choice
- ease of access
- freedom from mistakes
- effective use of technology
- helpfulness in contact
- courtesy and respect
- redress
- competence in performance
- understanding of the needs and problems
- knowledge
- credibility
- security.

The question 'Who determines the quality of the service?' is central to the establishment of quality assurance systems. The answer may appear obvious, that is the service user, e.g. client, patient or resident. However, expectations of other groups may also be relevant. These include care staff managers, professional and voluntary agencies, politicians and watchdog bodies, such as the Mental Welfare Commission and Scottish Hospitals Advisory Service, or the National Development Team in England and Wales.

Quality may be judged to be good or bad on behalf of the users of the service (customer) by those others who have the interests of the client at heart, though judged from different perspectives and perhaps using different criteria, for example, the criteria used by a manager may differ from that used by a care worker. One way of standardizing criteria is to examine the primary function of the service and the values on which it is based.

The goal of services, expressed in the corporate statement of intent, may be broken down to statements of specific objectives to be attained within a specific timescale. A corporate statement is the basis of the operation of every part of the organization. Success of an organization in meeting its objectives depends on the degree to which each part meets its own specific objectives derived from the corporate statement. As nursing constitutes by far the biggest part of most health care systems, success of the system depends largely on how successful nurses are in meeting their objectives in providing a high quality of service. The corporate statement of intent is based upon a set of values pertinent to service users, their carers and families. These values require a commitment from service personnel and should be adhered to as the basis for service provision.

Frameworks for quality assurance in nursing

Two broad frameworks for quality assurance have been developed for application in the health care field as it relates to mental handicap. The frameworks for quality assurance can be categorized as:

- structure, process, outcome (Donabedian 1966, developed by Kitson 1986)
- problem solving (Collard 1981).

Probably the most frequently used approach to quality assurance is that described by Donabedian (1968) based on the industrial model of quality assurance of input, throughput and output. In applying this model to nursing, input becomes resources (or structure), throughput becomes actions (or process) and output the results (or outcomes). Care should be taken when considering the relative merits of each of these dimensions though many nurses consider that process is especially relevant to nursing in ensuring quality of service (Fig. 3.3).

Structure

Structure is defined as the resources necessary to successfully engage in and complete a task. These include:

HEALTH BOARD QUALITY ASSURANCE INITIATIVE		

STANDARD OF CARE/SERVICE INDEX NO. _____ TI/CS/003(S)

RATIFIED BY _____ DATE _____ 14 March 1992

SOURCE OF PRODUCTION _____ STANDARD SETTING WORKSHOP

STANDARD TOPIC _____ SAFETY

NAMED COORDINATOR OF SST _____

SUB TOPIC _____ LIFTING AND HANDLING OF PATIENTS

DATE FOR FULL IMPLEMENTATION OF STANDARD _____ 1 May 1992

CARE GROUP _____ PATIENTS IN THE COMMUNITY

DATE FOR REVIEW OF STANDARD _____ 30 April 1993

STANDARD STATEMENT

STRUCTURE <----------------------------------> PROCESS <----------------------------------> OUTCOME

STRUCTURE	PROCESS	OUTCOME
1. UKCC Code of Professional Conduct Nos. 1, 2 and 10. 2. Staff are trained in the principles of kinetic movement. 3. Mechanical lifting aids are available when required. 4. Staff receive instructions in the use of mechanical lifting aids.	1. The District Nursing Sister will assess the patient's condition, identify the individual's needs and degree of help required. 2. The District Nursing Sister will prescribe in the patient's care plans the resources required. 3. The District Nursing Sister will demonstrate the appropriate techniques to the patient and carers. 4. The District Nursing Sister will review the plan of care in consultation with colleagues, patient and carers. 5. When a mechanical aid is required the District Nursing Sister will liaise with other agencies regarding the installation. 6. The District Nursing Sister will ensure that the maintenance of mechanical aids is carried out as per supplier's instructions.	1. Patient is lifted in a safe manner. 2. Patient feels secure and confident during the procedure

MEASURING AND MONITORING

1. All accidents occurring to patients while being lifted or handled by staff should be recorded and reported to the nurse manager.
2. By nurse manager randomly visiting with their staff observing technique and informally interviewing the patient and carer(s).

Figure 3.3 Example of a structure/process/outcome form.

- buildings
- equipment
- support services
- domestic services
- policies and procedures
- rules and regulations
- staff – numbers, training and expertise
- organizational framework.

Process

Process encompasses the actions undertaken by staff toward a stated level of achievement or outcome. These include:

- assessment techniques and procedures
- intervention strategies
- method of documentation:
  — description of and specific action to be taken
  — method of communication or information exchange
  — evaluation of compliance with procedures and policies.

Outcome

Outcome is concerned with the desired result of intervention and education (on the action taken) in terms of specific objectives. These include:

- increased level of knowledge
- increased level of specific skills, e.g. social interaction
- expressed level of satisfaction by service user
- increase in desirable behaviour
- decrease in undesirable behaviour.

Standards

A standard is an agreed level of performance appropriate to the target service group and should be understandable, specific, concise, achievable, clinically sound and measurable. The standard setting and application cycle can be represented diagrammatically as shown in Figure 3.4.

Problem-solving

The problem-solving approach differs from the

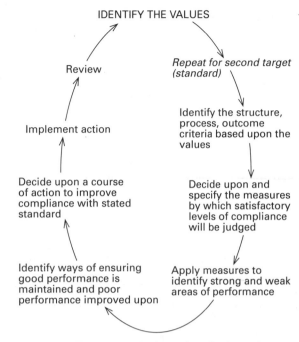

Figure 3.4 The standard setting and application cycle.

structure, process, outcome approach in that, instead of setting a standard and clearly mapping the pathway to that standard, the service staff are required to seek and overcome the blockages to achieving the higher standard. The first step is to identify a standard then to examine the existing structure or system to ascertain what changes must be made to achieve the standard. To enable the service personnel to undertake the task a number of problem-solving techniques are taught or the personnel are led through the process by someone familiar with the process who acts as facilitator.

Cause and effect analysis

The first step in identifying the most salient problems is the compilation of a table indicating the problems and the possible causes. This exercise is carried out by a group representing those involved in service provision. The major causes are written under general headings, i.e. manpower, equipment, materials, methods. As a rule it is best to keep the main headings to a minimum. Under each major heading the minor headings are added. An example of a problem identified by a group which may serve to illustrate the analysis is IPP (Individual Programme Plans planning) (Fig. 3.5).

From the diagram a number (or all) of the problems are chosen and further investigated to establish which are considered the most serious. One method is to administer a questionnaire following each IPP meeting, detailing problems and asking people to assign a level to the problem they felt contributed to the failure of each meeting. The results may then be tabulated in the form shown in Figure 3.6, which indicates that the most serious problem identified is the presentation of assessment results. After identifying this and other major problems strategies are agreed upon to resolve them.

Finally, to test the effectiveness of the process and to identify and correct any unforeseen consequences of the solution, solution effect analysis is employed. This is the same as the cause effect analysis but round the other way – instead of working through the causes *to* the effect, we examine the solution's impact *on* the effect (Fig 3.7).

Quality assurance audits

Quality assurance audits are the application of

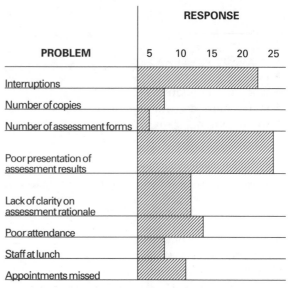

Figure 3.6 Weighting of significance of problems identified.

standardized measures over a range of similar services to determine the services, compliance with a stated level of quality and performance in relation to each other. Complex though many audits are, the audit only tells you what the situation is – not how to tackle problems identified. Furthermore, if the audit is based on a set of values not shared by the organization which is subject to the audit, then the usefulness of the tool is flawed from the outset.

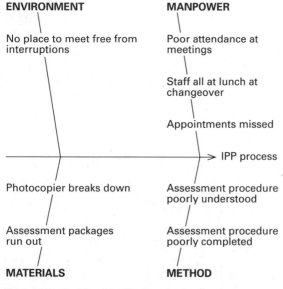

Figure 3.5 Problem identification.

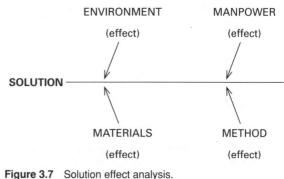

Figure 3.7 Solution effect analysis.

TOTAL QUALITY MANAGEMENT (Fig 3.8)

1. Total quality management (TQM) is a corporate management approach which

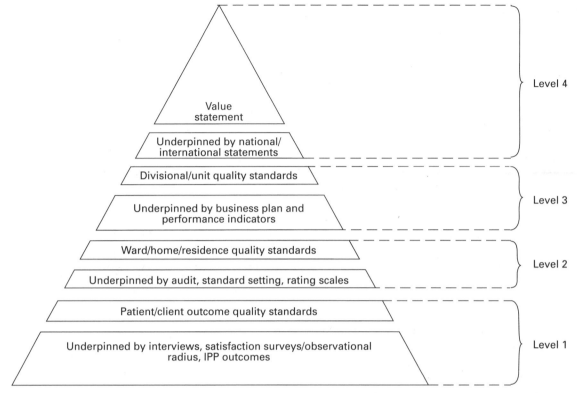

Figure 3.8 A TQM framework.

recognizes that customer needs and business goals are inseparable.

2. Puts in place processes and systems which will promote excellence, prevent errors and ensure that every aspect of the business is aligned to the *needs of its external* (patients) and *internal* (nurse, social worker, doctor) customer and the advancement of the organization's goals *without* duplication, waste or errors.

3. TQM originates at the chief executive level and is promoted in *all* activities. Quality is thus achieved by personal involvement and accountability applied to a continuous improvement process with measurable levels of performance by all concerned.

4. It involves every department, function and process in an organization and the active commitment of everyone to meeting customer needs.

The major objective of TQM is to improve quality within the resources available. This may be done by:

- decreasing unit costs and improving efficiency, thus releasing resources for other activities
- attracting business
- fostering a work force that is proud of its organization.

TQM is management led.

Meeting the customer's true requirements, whether internal or external, involves:

- a management-led commitment to excellence
  The first steps to TQM are awareness and understanding of the aims of the service that are clearly signalled in a quality policy document or mission statement.
- a participative environment
  Development of the team approach with active participation and ownership is advocated; this approach leads to:
  — greater motivation
  — breakdown of professional barriers
  — pooling of knowledge, skills and expertise.

- A good quality system
  A vital key to TQM is recognizing and understanding the supplier/customer interfaces and managing the organization in such a way that the customer, internal and external, is consistently satisfied.

REFERENCES

Bandura A 1977 Social learning theory. Prentice-Hall, Englewood Cliffs, NJ

Christie H, O'Reilly M 1984 Quality circles. Nursing Mirror February 16–19

Collard R 1981 The quality circle in context. Personnel Management, 9

Collard R 1989 Total quality; success through people. IPM, London

Committee on Standards of Nursing Care 1981 Towards standards: a discussion document. RCN, London

DHSS 1983 Report of the NHS management enquiry. DHSS, London

Donabedian A 1966 Evaluating quality of medical care. Millbank Memorial Fund Quarterly 5: 39–50

Donabedian A 1968 Promoting quality through evaluating the process of patient care

Donabedian A 1984 Quality assessment and monitoring: evaluation and the healthcare professions 6: 363–375

Inman V 1975 Towards a theory of nursing care. RCN, London

Kitson A L 1986 Framework for quality. Nursing Standard 5

RCN Committee on Standards of Nursing Care 1979 Standards of nursing care. RCN, London

Wolfensberger W, Glenn L 1987 Program analysis of service systems (PASS): a method for the quantitative evaluation of human services. York University, Ontario

Wolfensberger W 1972 The principle of normalization in human services: York University, Ontario.

Wolfensberger W, Thomas S 1983 Program analysis of service systems implementation of normalization goals. York University, Ontario

---

FURTHER READING

Brost M M, Johnson T Z 1982 Getting to know you: one approach to service assessment and planning for individuals with disabilities. WCAZ, Madison

Donabedian A 1980 The definition of quality and approaches to its assessment: explorations in quality assessment and monitoring, vol 1. Ann Arbor Science, Oxford

Independent Development Council for People with Mental Handicap 1987 Kings Fund, London.

MSC 1986 The development of quality circles programmes. MSC, London

Peters T, Waterman R H 1986 In search of excellence. Appleton-Century-Crofts, New York.

Raynes N V 1988 Annotated directory of measures of environmental quality. University of Manchester

Tyne A 1981 The principle of normalization: a foundation for effective services. CMHERA, Reading

Promotion of skills

SECTION CONTENTS

4. Physical causes and conditions   61

5. Social causes   83

6. Associated conditions   93

7. Helping with learning difficulties   119

8. Helping with sensory impairments   135

9. Helping with behavioural problems   149

10. Helping with social issues   211

11. Helping with multiple handicap   229

12. Helping with communication through movement   269

Section 2 is the main section of the book and is concerned with ways in which the carer can help the person with learning disabilities maintain or improve the quality of his or her life. It is based on the principle of providing holistic care by regarding the individual as a single entity embedded in his or her social context. Each chapter focuses on a specific issue while retaining the principle of holistic care. The central aim of the section is to develop in the individual the knowledge and skills to improve his or her quality of life.

CHAPTER CONTENTS

Introduction 61

Chromosomes and genes 62

Chromosomes 62
Types of autosomal abnormalities 63
    Numerical 64
    Structural 64
Types of sex chromosome abnormalities 64
Conditions caused by autosomal abnormalities 64
    Down syndrome 64
    Cri-du-chat 66
    Wolf syndrome 67
Conditions caused by sex chromosome abnormalities 67
    Klinefelter syndrome 67
    Turner syndrome 67
    Triple X syndrome 67

Genes 67
Autosomal dominant inheritance 67
Autosomal recessive inheritance 68
Sex-linked recessive inheritance 68
Polygenetic inheritance 69
Conditions caused by autosomal dominant genes 69
    Tuberous sclerosis (epiloia) 69
    Neurofibromatosis 69
Conditions caused by autosomal recessive genes 69
    Phenylketonuria 71
    Galactosaemia 72
    Hurler syndrome 72
    Cerebromacular degeneration 72
    Hepatolenticular degeneration (Wilson's disease) 72
Conditions caused by sex-linked recessive genes 73
    X (sex)-linked hydrocephalus 73
    Hunter syndrome 73
    Fragile X syndrome 73
Conditions caused by polygenetic inheritance 73
    Sturge-Webber syndrome 73
    Cornelia de Lange syndrome 73
    Hydrocephalus 74
    Hypothyroidism (cretinism) 74

Acquired conditions 74
Prenatal problems which can lead to brain damage 74
Infections 74
    Bacterial 75
    Viral 75
    Protozoal 76
Maternal nutrition 76
Maternal-fetal incompatibility 76
Toxic agents 76
Physical factors 77
Postnatal and developmental factors 78
    Infection 78
    Gastroenteritis 78
    Meningitis 78
    Encephalitis 78
    Trauma 78
    Toxic agents 78

Conclusion 79

Summary 79

Glossary 80

4

Physical causes and conditions

G. Petrie

Key points
- For the vast majority of people with learning disabilities there is no discernible or easily identifiable biological cause for their disability
- Chromosomal abnormalities are normally caused by mistakes in the creation of sex cells, ova or sperm, during meiosis and to a lesser degree during mitosis (conception)
- The process of changes within genes is difficult to identify though the effects on the individual are frequently all too clear
- Many pre-(non-genetic), neo- and postnatal causes have been identified and health promotion approaches including the recommendation of changes in life styles have been employed
- Care of people with learning disabilities, particularly those who are severely mentally handicapped, is likely to be enhanced by a greater understanding of the cause and process of the underlying condition

INTRODUCTION

An understanding of the causes of mental handicap is important for all groups involved in caring for people with learning disabilities even though only a small percentage have a condition with an identifiable cause or can be classified within a particular grouping or syndrome. The more severely handicapped individuals are found within these more clearly identifiable syndromes. Nurses trained in caring for those with learning disabilities are likely to have the greatest degree of contact with this group of people. Other less severe forms of mental handicap are considered to have been the result of a combination of multiple factors–constitutional, environmental and interactional. Many individuals affected require little or no specialist professional help and nurses will have less contact with them. Nevertheless, a background knowledge of all possible causes of mental handicap can enable workers in hospital and community settings to provide the most appropriate care, play a full role in detection and prevention of mental handicap at a primary and a secondary level, help and support families of people with a mental handicap and give meaningful advice and counselling. A wider role in health education is also possible through an understanding of the principles of inheritance, and the dangers from infection, toxic agents and trauma in the causation of mental handicap.

An appreciation of the possible clinical features associated with a particular condition can be a useful guide to planning all aspects of care, as in Down syndrome, where many physical and mental characteristics are common in those with the syndrome. However, caution must be exercised to prevent any 'label' given to a person with learning disability becoming an additional handicap. Care for each person with a mental handicap must be based on the needs revealed by and appropriate to individual assessment. Assumptions about physical and intellectual deficits must never be made on the basis of subjective visual assessment, causation factor or any other label imposed on a person.

The overview of causes and conditions shown in Figure 4.1 will be examined in the chapter to provide a framework for examining the causation factors that can lead to mental handicap. Such a framework can also provide a context for understanding, detection and prevention. The overview has limitation, as with any system of classification of mental handicap, and will contain overlaps.

CHROMOSOMES AND GENES

Hereditary characteristics can be considered as either chromosomal or genetic. Each chromosome

---

Box 4.1 A MODEL FOR CARE
Classification based on clinical features can narrow the view taken of the individual. Statistics about incidence and prevalence, information about screening techniques for detection and lists of features of a condition can lead to a medical view of the person affected. A medical model of care is inappropriate in dealing with a person with a mental handicap. The three-dimensional model shown in Figure 4.2 is offered as a reference point to enable the carer to avoid the restriction of any one approach to care. The model also illustrates the uniqueness required when responding to each individual client, whatever the reason for carer involvement.

is made up of thousands of genes. Characteristics which are referred to as 'chromosomal' result from specific chromosomal configurations, e.g. sex is determined by the presence of an extra 'leg' in the 23rd chromosome in women and the absence of this 'leg' in men. A huge number of hereditary characteristics arranged along the chromosomes, such as eye colour, result from the effect of one or more genes and so are referred to as 'genetic'.

CHROMOSOMES

Contained within the nucleus of all human cells is a supply of genetic material, organized as strands, known as chromosomes. Humans have 46 chromosomes grouped in pairs: 22 pairs are referred to as autosomes and 1 pair as sex chromosomes. The autosomes are matched. In the female the sex chromosomes are matched and referred to as XX. In the male they are unmatched and referred to as XY.

By convention, chromosomes are numbered from 1 to 23 according to the Denver system. The largest pair is number 1 and they are arranged by size to the smallest, number 22. In an alternative system of classification several pairs of chromosomes are grouped by size under a letter, alphabetically from A to G. This facilitates the description of normal and abnormal karyotypes, or chromosome pictures. The larger the chromosome affected the greater the severity of the potential handicap or the more life threatening the outcome.

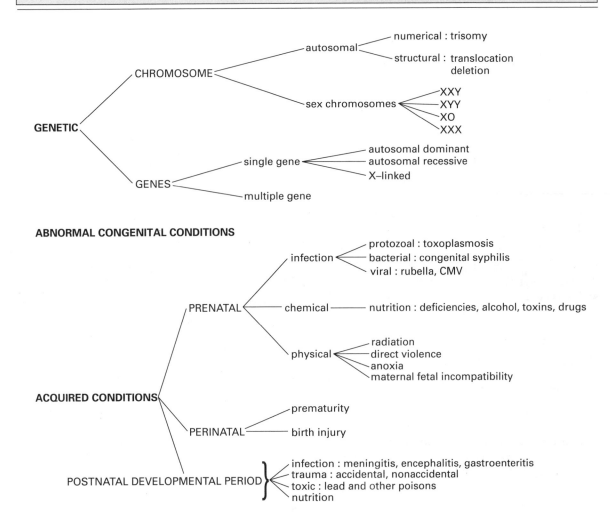

Figure 4.1 Framework of causation factors.

The only cells in the human body that do not contain 23 paired chromosomes are the sex cells (the ovum and the sperm) which have 23 unpaired chromosomes. The fusion of the ovum and the sperm at conception forms the zygote which has 46 chromosomes. Each parent contributes 1 chromosome to each pair found in the offspring. As many as 50 chromosome abnormalities have been identified although most are very rare.

Types of autosomal abnormalities

When abnormalities occur in the autosomes both male and female clinical sufferers will be

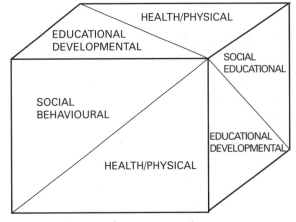

Figure 4.2 A model for care.

found. There are two main types of autosomal abnormality: numerical and structural.

Numerical

A numerical abnormality is where there is the loss or gain of one or more chromosomes. The main abnormality of this type is the presence of an extra chromosome, called trisomy. This is usually the result of nondisjunction which is a failure of two members of a chromosome pair to separate during cell division in the formation of gametes. This process of cell division is known as meiosis. Examples of autosomal trisomies are:

- Down syndrome – trisomy in pair 21
- Edward syndrome – trisomy in pair 18
- Patau syndrome – trisomy in pair 13.

Structural

Translocation. The transfer of all or part of a chromosome during meiosis to a chromosome of another pair is a translocation. A balanced translocation carrier is generally physically and mentally normal. Such carriers are, however, at a high risk of producing a clinical sufferer who will have 46 complete chromosomes plus an extra segment. The monosomic form, where one chromosome only of the pair is present, is non-viable, i.e. the developing individual does not survive. A balanced carrier, male or female, has in theory a 1-in-3 chance of producing a normal noncarrier child, a 1-in-3 chance of producing a balanced carrier who would be clinically normal and a 1-in-3 chance of producing a child with a clinical abnormality. The actual risk of producing a child with an abnormality is less than the theory suggests, although remaining high. Unidentified factors may intervene to reduce the probability. A female carrier is at greater risk than a male carrier of passing on the abnormality (1:6 risk for a female carrier, 1:20 risk for a male carrier). An example of translocation is:

- Down syndrome – the extra chromosome segment may be attached to a member of one of the following pairs : 13, 15, 21 or 22.

Deletion. This abnormality occurs when part of a chromosome is missing. Examples of deletion are:

- Cri-du-chat syndrome – deletion of the short arm of a number 5 chromosome.
- Wolf syndrome – deletion of the short arm of a number 4 chromosome.

Mosaicism. In some individuals a percentage of cells have an abnormal chromosome count while the other cells have a normal chromosome count. The nondisjunction responsible for mosaicism occurs after fertilization during mitosis, unlike the numerical abnormalities mentioned above which occur during meiosis. Mosaicism occurring in autosomes and sex chromosomes have been noted. Examples of mosaicism are:

- Down syndrome – between 2% and 4% of people with Down syndrome are mosaic
- Klinefelter syndrome – a sex chromosome abnormality.

Types of sex chromosome abnormalities

Nondisjunction of the sex chromosomes leads to a number of abnormalities. Basically two female and two male sex chromosome abnormalities are found:

Phenotype female
- Turner syndrome—karyotype:XO (only 1 member of the pair present)
- Triple X syndrome—karyotype:XXX.

Phenotype male
- Klinefelter syndrome—karyotype:XXY
- XYY syndrome—karyotype:XYY.

Cases have been noted where more than one extra sex chromosome has been present, e.g. XXXX, XXXY.

Conditions caused by autosomal abnormalities

Down syndrome

Down syndrome is the best known condition which results in mental handicap. It was referred to as Mongolism in the past but this is an unacceptable title which is derogatory, inaccurate and racist. The condition was first described by Dr John Langdon Down in 1866, but it was not recognized as a chromosomal abnormality until 1959. There has been a decrease in the incidence of Down syndrome and a change in parental age group of those with a Down child since the change in the Abortion Law in 1967 and the improvement in antenatal techniques and genetic counselling.

The prevalence of Down syndrome has not shown a corresponding decrease as the life expectancy of sufferers has improved, i.e. although there are fewer children with Down syndrome being born these individuals are more likely to live longer than previously.

Incidence. The overall incidence of Down syndrome in populations of European origin is approximately 1:700 (Smith & Berg 1976). Incidence is similar in other racial groups. Prevalence is not related to any specific geographic area, although there are claims that clusters of people affected can be found around nuclear installations.

The incidence of the trisomy 21 type of Down syndrome increases with maternal age. For a mother around 20 years of age the risk is approximately 1:2300 and at 45 years of age 1:40 (Siggers 1978). As indicated above there is a change in the pattern of births and it is now more likely that the mother of a person with Down syndrome will be in the earlier childbearing years at the birth of her child (Pueschel 1988). Age is not significant with the translocation type of Down syndrome; either parent can be the carrier, but the risk of translocation Down syndrome is greater if the mother is the balanced carrier.

Characteristics. A large number of common features are exhibited by those with Down syndrome. This results in a degree of similarity in appearance and makes it possible to identify

Table 4.1 Types of Down syndrome (Richards 1974)

Cause	% of sufferers
Trisomy 21	90+
Translocation	4–5
Mosaicism	2–4

most people who have Down syndrome, though the similarity to each other may be less than family likeness. Not all features will be seen in every individual and when features of the condition are present they may vary in degree and impact in each individual. Care must be taken when assessing the needs of those with Down syndrome to take account of the wide range of physical and intellectual variation possible. All those involved in the care of a person with Down syndrome may find a knowledge of the features of the syndrome a helpful guide to care needs. Individual assessment is essential to ensure the best possible care and to avoid generalizations about the person affected which could limit his or her potential.

Head and brain. The head is usually small (brachycephalic) and round with a reduced cranial capacity. The brain is 'simple' in structure and underweight. Intellectual deterioration frequently occurs from middle age. Coordination is often poor, libido is reduced. Epilepsy and cerebral palsy are rare, unlike other conditions producing learning disabilities. During infancy and childhood those with Down syndrome tend to be slow for the expected milestones of development and tend to lag further behind as they grow older. Early intervention, from the first days of life, is vital to enable maximum potential to be realized. In infancy the Down child is often described by parents as being a 'good' baby who is undemanding. This can have its dangers as the infant is not interacting with the environment thus limiting developmental progress.

Hair tends to be dry, sparse and fine. The scalp and skin can become dry and flaky. The face is 'flat' as is the occiput. Ears are small with poorly developed lobes.

Eyes. The eyes are usually upward and outward slanting. Strabismus, nystagmus and cataract are common, as is an epicanthic fold on the inner aspect of the upper eyelid. The iris is often poorly developed and Brushfield's spots are to be found flecked through the iris. Chronic conjunctivitis and blepharitis are common due to lack of lysozyme, an enzyme in tears which acts as an antiseptic. Poor sight is also a common problem.

Nose.   The bridge of the nose is poorly developed and mouth breathing is common. The risk of respiratory tract infection is, therefore, high. Before the advent of antibiotics severe and repeated respiratory tract infections meant that few people with Down syndrome survived beyond early adulthood.

Mouth.   The mouth is often small with a high narrow palate, whereas the tongue is large with horizontal fissures. As a result, the mouth tends to be open with the tongue protruding. Teeth are late, abnormal in size, shape and alignment. Mouth breathing, a protruding tongue and increased likelihood of dental decay make infection a problem.

In the past, respiratory infection and heart defects resulted in up to 50% of Down syndrome sufferers dying by 5 years of age. This is no longer the case but poor circulation for those with heart defects can be present and can add to the problems of skin care and infection already mentioned. The presence of a heart defect should not lead to overprotection as this could lead to understimulation of the cardiovascular system.

Body.   The adult with Down syndrome is usually small and broad in stature, rarely being more than 1.5 m (5 feet) in height. There is a tendency to hypotonia, with joints having an abnormal range of movement. The abdomen tends to be protuberant with umbilical hernia being common. The hypotonia can lead to the adopting of abnormal postures.

Hands and feet.   Hands and feet are characteristic. The hands have a square palm with a palmar crease and a wide gap between the thumb and second digit. Fingers are short and stumpy. A gap between the great toe and the second toe is common.

Genitalia.   In the male, genitalia are underdeveloped. On the basis of testicular histology Down males cannot be considered sterile (Pueschel 1988). On the rare occasions when a female with Down syndrome conceives the risk of a Down child is almost 50% (Smith 1982).

Those with Down syndrome are mentally handicapped to some degree. Almost 10% fall in the profound and moderate range with the majority in the IQ range 25–49. There are many individual exceptions but females have been found to have higher mean IQ scores than males (Lane & Stratford 1985). Many people with Down syndrome can learn to read and write and acquire adaptive behaviour skills that improve the chances of independence in adulthood.

The wide range of intellectual ability, and the variety and degree of physical manifestation of the syndrome, require individual assessment and subsequent planning of care and education on an individual basis. Intellectual stimulation will be dependent on the person leading as normal and full a life as possible without unnecessary constraints. The negative impact and the generalizations of the label Down syndrome, especially those related to intellectual impairment, must be put aside by parents, other carers and school teachers. An optimistic approach is essential and justified. Early intervention, from the first weeks of life, with programmes of intellectual stimulation and physical care, will enable the individual with Down syndrome to reach his or her maximum potential and optimum physical status.

Care should extend beyond the individual with Down syndrome to include the family. Almost all younger people with Down syndrome live at home with their families and on reaching late adolescence and young adulthood are, in the majority of cases, able to leave home and begin a life of their own in independent or sheltered accommodation.

Cri-du-chat

Cri-du-chat, or 'cry-of-the-cat', syndrome is an autosomal abnormality. There is a deletion of the short arm of one of the number 5 chromosomes. The condition is rare, with an incidence of 1:50 000 (Wiedemann 1985).

The cry is distinctive, a high-pitched wailing like a cat, and in infancy is diagnostic. Microcephaly is common. The eyes slant downward, the chin is small and the ears are low set. Characteristically, sufferers are small in stature. Birth weight is low, in the early months there is a failure to thrive and there is a poor sucking reflex. Life expectancy is variable but can be into adulthood. Intellectual impairment is normally severe and the development of speech is limited.

Wolf syndrome

Wolf syndrome is caused by the deletion of the short arm of one of the number 4 chromosomes.

Conditions caused by sex chromosome abnormalities

Only a proportion of people with sex chromosome abnormalities are intellectually impaired. XYY syndrome is not associated with mental handicap. A number of years ago XYY syndrome was linked with psychopathic and criminal behaviours but this link has been questioned (Kingston 1989).

Klinefelter syndrome

In this condition the individual presents as male with the sex chromosomes XXY. Such an individual is described as chromatin positive male. The incidence of the syndrome is approximately 1 in 500 male births (Wiedemann 1985). Many people with Klinefelter syndrome are of normal intelligence and of those with an intellectual impairment the majority are found in the mild and borderline groups. Just over 1% of mentally handicapped males suffer from Klinefelter syndrome.

Development until puberty appears normal, but at puberty it becomes evident that secondary sex characteristics are failing to develop. Testes are small or undescended, body hair is sparse and the body shape appears feminine due to the distribution of body fat. There is tendency to breast development; sufferers are infertile and psychotic and personality problems are common (Wiedemann 1985).

Secondary sex characteristics are promoted by giving male hormone, such as testosterone. Support and care are especially important during adolescence.

Turner syndrome

Diminished secondary sex characteristics are features of Turner syndrome. The individual presents as female but lacks ovarian tissue and sex hormones, is sterile and shows primary amenorrhoea. Other physical features include dwarfism, webbing of the neck and a low hairline at the back of the neck. The incidence of Turner syndrome is 0.4 per 1000 in live female infants (Kingston 1989) with only 20% being intellectually impaired. Those who are mentally handicapped are often of very low intellect. Oestrogen replacement therapy can help minimize the physical impact of the condition. As in all conditions care needs and subsequent treatment must be determined on the basis of individual assessment.

Triple X syndrome

Triple X syndrome is fallaciously called 'superwoman'. There are no specific physical characteristics which typify this group of women. They are found through the whole range of intellectual impairment and can be of normal intelligence. Skeletal and neurological problems are common and psychotic disorders are more frequent among women with triple X than in the normal population. Incidence is thought to be about 0.65 per 1000 female births (Kingston 1989). There are reports of triple X women bearing normal children.

GENES

Genetically determined conditions can be considered under four headings:

- Autosomal dominant inheritance
- Autosomal recessive inheritance
- Sex-linked (X-linked) recessive inheritance
- Polygenetic inheritance.

Autosomal dominant inheritance (Fig. 4.3)

1. There is a degree of manifestation, i.e. the condition is present to a greater or lesser extent in all cases.

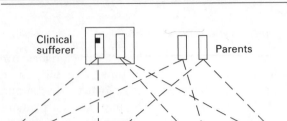

Figure 4.3 Autosomal dominant inheritance.

2. There is variation in degree of manifestation over time.
3. A constant risk of 1 in 2 exists that the condition will be passed on.
4. Clinical sufferers can be of either sex.
5. Spontaneous mutations occur. The more serious the clinical impact of the condition, the higher will be the mutation rate as those who survive with the condition, but with severe handicaps, will be very unlikely to reproduce.

Examples of autosomal dominant conditions are tuberous sclerosis (epiloia), neurofibromatosis (Von Recklinghausen's disease), and Huntington's chorea.

Autosomal recessive inheritance (Fig 4.4)

1. Both parents must carry the gene, but they do not suffer clinically.

2. Clinical sufferers can be of either sex.
3. A constant risk of 1 in 4 exists that carrier parents will have offspring with the recessive condition.
4. A constant risk of 1 in 2 exists that carrier parents will have a carrier child, who will be clinically normal.
5. A child with a rare recessive condition is more likely to be born if parents are related because related individuals have a high percentage of genes in common, including rare recessive genes.

Examples of autosomal recessive conditions include phenylketonuria (PKU), galactosaemia and Tay-Sachs disease. There is a large number of autosomal recessive conditions most of which are very rare.

Sex-linked (X-linked) recessive inheritance (Fig. 4.5)

1. Males are affected when they inherit the recessive gene on their X chromosome. There is a constant risk of 1 in 2 for the male child of a carrier mother suffering from the condition.
2. Females carry the condition, with a constant 1-in-2 risk of a carrier female child being born to a carrier mother.
3. All female children of male sufferers will be carriers of the condition.
4. Male children of male sufferers will be neither sufferers nor carriers.

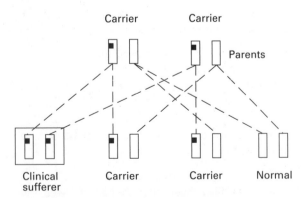

Figure 4.4 Autosomal recessive inheritance.

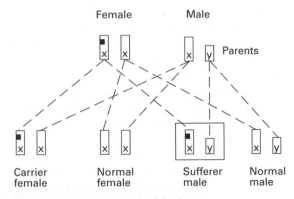

Figure 4.5 X-linked recessive inheritance.

Examples of sex-linked recessive inheritance are Hunter syndrome (a form of 'gargoylism'), fragile X syndrome, Lesch-Nyham syndrome, Duchance muscular dystrophy and a rare form of hydrocephaly.

Polygenetic inheritance

A number of congenital conditions are thought to be caused by a number of genes acting together. The risk of inheritance is much less than in single gene inheritance; the risk is not constant. Indications for increased risk will depend on the condition. In some conditions such as Hirschsprung's disease the size of lesion will indicate the risk factor for siblings or offspring. In other conditions an increased number of first degree relatives with the condition would indicate an increased risk.

Conditions caused by autosomal dominant genes

Tuberous sclerosis (epiloia)

Tuberous sclerosis, also called epiloia, is a rare condition caused by a dominant gene of poor penetrance, i.e. the condition varies in manifestation, physical and intellectual. The condition was thought to be very rare, but tuberous sclerosis is sometimes inherited from an unsuspecting parent who has the dominant gene but does not have fits or intellectual impairment, there being a poor penetrance of the dominant gene. The condition only rarely presents in its severest form and it has been difficult to estimate the numbers affected as physical and intellectual manifestations do not always present as obvious conditions.

Incidence is thought to be about 1 in 10 000 (Osbourne 1990). Approximately 60% of those with the gene will present varying degrees of mental handicap. When epilepsy and the facial rash are also present this gives the three cardinal signs of the condition.

The facial rash, adenoma sebaceum, which appears over the cheeks and the bridge of the nose, is found in a butterfly distribution. The rash is caused by an overgrowth of the sebaceous glands. Argon laser treatment can reduce the impact of the facial rash and is of benefit to the individual and his or her family as the rash is often the cause of considerable distress.

'Shagreen patches', which are raised areas of skin, are sometimes present in the lumbrosacral region. Tumours are frequently found in the muscle wall of the heart, kidneys, lungs and brain which often become calcified.

The child who is eventually diagnosed as having tuberous sclerosis would typically be slow in reaching milestones, with the adenoma sebaceum becoming evident by 4 or 5 years of age. Initially, the facial rash appears like grains of rice under the skin, but in later life the rash can become red and pronounced. Mental and physical deterioration may occur resulting in deterioration of skills. Life expectancy in severe cases will be reduced.

Neurofibromatosis

Von Recklinghausen's disease is the other name given to this autosomal, dominantly inherited condition in which about one third of sufferers are mentally handicapped. Mental handicap is more likely when lesions are found in the brain. Skin tumours are common and café-au-lait patches are found on the surface of the body. The skin tumours are painless, and can be present in vast numbers in some people, although the number of skin tags is unrelated to intellectual impairment. Complications include epilepsy, cerebral palsy, deafness and blindness. Periodic deterioration tends to occur in sufferers resulting in or adding to physical and/or mental handicaps.

Conditions caused by autosomal recessive genes

There are a large number of autosomal recessive disorders, many of which are associated with mental handicap:

- phenylketonuria
- maple syrup disease

- galactosaemia
- Tay-Sachs disease
- Hurler syndrome (a form of gargoylism)
- hepatolenticular disease (Wilson's)

- Laurence-Moon-Biedl syndrome
- some cases of microcephaly, 'true microcephaly'
- Niemann-Pick disease
- some cases of hypothyroidism

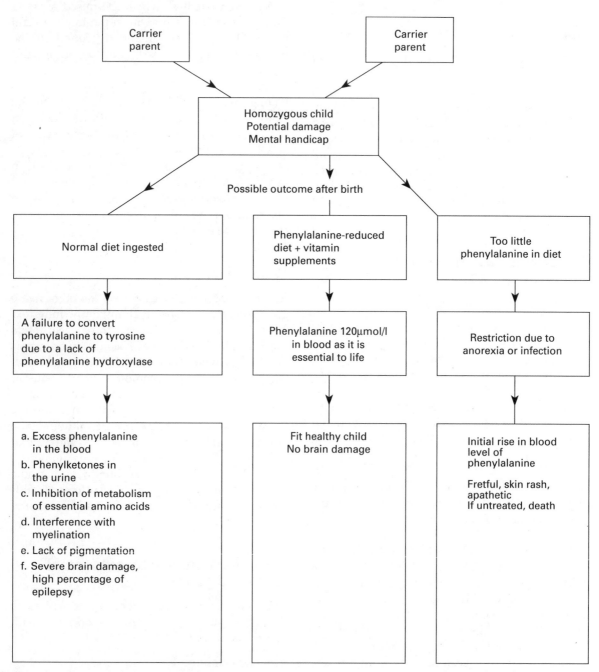

Figure 4.6 Phenylketonuria's genetic progress.

Many of these recessive disorders are metabolic.

Phenylketonuria

Phenylketonuria is one of the best-known genetic conditions which, if untreated, can result in mental handicap and a number of associated conditions. The overall incidence is about 1 in 12 000 (Nichols 1988) with variations in different geographic areas. The condition is found most frequently in areas of Britain with a high immigrant Irish/Celtic population, such as Liverpool and the industrial west of Scotland.

Phenylketonuria is a disorder of protein metabolism which can be detected by a blood test. The Guthrie test is carried out routinely on all babies around the 5th or 6th day of life, provided that milk has been ingested. If it is established that a baby is phenylketonuric, a phenylalanine-reduced diet must be commenced at once. It is necessary to include some phenylalanine in the diet to meet nutritional requirements for normal physical and mental development.

When there is dietary restriction, caused by food fads or anorexia in infection, there is a breakdown of body protein (catabolism). Blood levels of phenylalanine will show an initial rise and urine testing will be positive for phenylketones. There will be no lasting effect if corrected quickly, but if the situation becomes chronic the child will become fretful, fail to thrive, become apathetic and could die (Fig. 4.6).

Blood levels of phenylalanine rise and phenylketones appear in the urine. Phenylalanine is not converted to tyrosine due to lack of the enzyme phenylalanine hydroxylase (Fig. 4.7). Vomiting and irritability in a child slow to reach milestones is characteristic. By the second half of the first year of life the child becomes hyperactive and brain damage becomes apparent. Tyrosine is a precursor for melanin and most sufferers show lack of pigmentation of eyes, hair and skin. Eczema is common as are autistic features. There is resistance to cuddling and a tendency to self-mutilation. Many damaged sufferers are epileptic. The degree of intellectual impairment in the completely untreated cases is severe.

A blood level of phenylalanine maintained between 0.125–0.250 µmol will result in a fit healthy child. The phenylalanine-reduced diet is possible by giving protein substitutes and must be accompanied by vitamin supplements and tyrosine. Food products suitable for those on a phenylalanine-reduced diet include Albumaid, Cymogran, Minafen and Lofenalac. The effectiveness of the diet is monitored by regular urine tests for phenylketones and blood tests to ensure correct levels of phenylalanine.

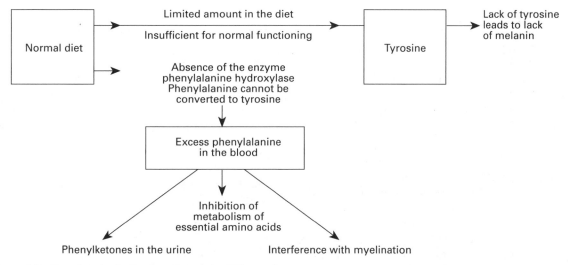

Figure 4.7 Phenylalanine in the phenylketonuric child.

There is considerable debate about when the diet can be stopped without negative repercussions. It is thought best to continue dietary treatment after 8 years of age although a measure of relaxation can probably be tolerated by that age (Simpson 1989). It is advisable for carrier women – and this includes successfully treated sufferers – to be on a phenylalanine-reduced diet prior to conception and during pregnancy (Simpson 1989).

Galactosaemia

Galactosaemia is an autosomal recessive disorder of carbohydrate metabolism. It is a rare condition with an incidence of approximately 1-in-20 000 live births. Brain damage can be prevented with a milk-free diet. Prenatal diagnosis is possible. In galactosaemia there is a failure by the liver to convert galactose into glucose with the result that galactose builds up in the blood. The untreated infant presents as lethargic, with liver enlargement and jaundice in the first few weeks of life. There is a failure to thrive together with progressive mental deterioration. If it is untreated the condition may be fatal. Treatment must be started as early as possible with the removal of dietary galactose. Galactomin and Nulramigen are food products which are given to provide the appropriate milk-free diet.

Hurler syndrome

Abnormal storage of mucopolysaccharides in connective tissue is a feature of a number of degenerative conditions, many of which are autosomal recessive. The incidence of all forms of the mucopolysaccharidosis is 1:25 000 (Nichols 1988). Gargoylism is a name given to sufferers from the condition because of their physical appearance which is said to resemble the figures which project from Gothic buildings. Hurler syndrome is an example of an autosomal recessive form of the condition.

Although prenatal diagnosis is possible, the condition is not apparent at birth but becomes evident during the first year of life. The facial features are distinctive: the head is large with frontal bossing, the supra-orbital ridges are prominent and the bridge of the nose is depressed. Eyebrows are coarse and hairy. Ears are low set and there is corneal clouding in the majority of cases. (In the X-linked form of this syndrome, which only affects males, there is no corneal clouding.) The teeth are irregular and are late in appearing. The neck is short and thick. Kyphosis, due to abnormal vertebral deposits, develops. The individual is short in stature as the limbs are relatively short. There is limited extension of the joints. Mental and physical deterioration usually lead to death in adolescence.

Cerebromacular degeneration

Tay-Sachs disease is an example of an autosomal recessive disorder of lipid metabolism. Incidence in the general population is 1:500 000 but in Ashkenazi Jews is 1:5600 (Scheerenberger 1987).

There are a number of lipid metabolism disorders under the general title of cerebromacular degeneration, known in the past as amaurotic family idiocy. Age of onset differentiates between the various manifestations of the disease. The condition can be detected in the prenatal period by amniocentesis. Tay-Sachs disease develops early in life, usually in the first year. There is progressive mental deterioration for which no treatment is available. As the condition develops in the early months mental deterioration is accompanied by spastic paralysis, blindness and convulsions. A 'cherry red' spot is found in the macula of the retina. Death occurs in the 3rd or 4th year of life (Paritzky 1985).

When the onset of the disease is delayed until the 6th or 7th year of life, death is likely to occur in mid teens, the disease having followed a similar course to the early onset type. The late onset type is called Batten's disease.

Hepatolenticular degeneration (Wilson's disease)

Wilson's disease is a rare disorder of copper metabolism with excessive absorption of copper from the diet and a deficiency of copper-carrying protein in the blood called caeruloplasm.

A failure to thrive and jaundice are followed, usually in adolescence or young adulthood, by mental deterioration. This is accompanied by involuntary choreiform movements and progressive difficulty in articulation and swallowing. There is also a tremor present. Contractions and muscle wastage are found with rigidity in the muscles of the trunk, limbs and face. These are associated with copper deposits in the lenticular nuclei of the brain.

Copper is excreted in the urine and deposits are found in the outer margin of the cornea forming what are known as Kayser-Fleischer rings. Liver and kidney functions are affected. A reduction of dietary copper and the use of chelating agents such as D-penicillamine can help reduce physical and mental deterioration. Liver transplant can lead to clinical improvement (Nichols 1988).

Conditions caused by X-linked (sex-linked) recessive genes

A number of genetically determined conditions associated with mental handicap are inherited in an X (sex)-linked manner. Males are affected, while females may be carriers of the condition.

X (sex)-linked hydrocephalus

In those affected by this rare form of hydrocephalus the aqueduct of Sylvius fails to develop fully and without surgical intervention cerebrospinal fluid accumulates in the ventricles and brain damage may occur.

Hunter syndrome

This is a form of mucopolysaccharidosis (gargoylism) which affects males. The condition is similar to Hurler syndrome but with a much slower rate of physical and mental deterioration and sufferers usually survive into adulthood. There is no corneal clouding.

Fragile X syndrome

A non specific X-linked mental retardation with an incidence of 1.8 per 1000 males has become apparent in recent years. This group of mentally handicapped males helps to explain the larger number of males as compared with females in the mentally handicapped population. Fragile X syndrome is second to Down syndrome as a specific cause of mental handicap (Scheerenberger 1987). There is a fragile site on the X chromosome detectable in the laboratory. Clinical manifestations of the condition include a large forehead, ears and jaw, and following the onset of puberty macro-orchidism (enlarged testicles). Behavioural characteristics, reported in those with the condition, are hyperactivity, autism and self-mutilating behaviour. Intellectual impairment can be profound with most cases being said to be moderate.

Conditions caused by polygenetic inheritance

A large number of conditions, most of them very rare, with a suspected polygenetic origin, or with no known cause but with readily identifiable features, are associated with mental handicap.

Sturge-Webber syndrome

This syndrome, also known as naevoid amentia, is rare and the cause is unknown. The condition is typified by a facial naevus. Part or all of the trigeminal nerve is affected on one side of the face. The facial marking is referred to as a 'port wine stain'. A meningeal angioma is found on the same side as the naevus. In some cases there may be calcification in the meningeal angioma and the cerebral cortex. Epilepsy is common, as is spasticity. Hemiplegia occurs on the opposite side of the body to the facial marking. The degree of intellectual impairment can be severe.

Argon laser treatment for the port wine stain is now possible, the clotted blood capillaries being replaced by colourless, fibrous tissue so reducing the colour of the mark. There is little evidence of scarring.

Cornelia de Lange syndrome

In 1933 a Dutch paediatrician, Cornelia de Lange,

described this syndrome, which has become known as Amsterdam dwarfism. The incidence of de Lange syndrome is approximately 1 in 40 000. The cause is unknown. Microcephaly, facial hair, confluent eyebrows, downward slanting eyes, small palate and irregular teeth typify the syndrome. The person is dwarfed with limb abnormalities and small hands and feet. Genitals are underdeveloped. In infancy feeding problems are common due to sucking difficulties. All sufferers are intellectually impaired and this is often severe.

Hydrocephalus

Hydrocephalus is due to an increase of cerebral spinal fluid (CSF) within the skull, in the ventricles or in the sub-arachnoid space. A whole range of different processes can end in hydrocephalus. These include:

- congenital malformation, which can cause a blockage to the pathways through which the CSF flows (the aqueduct of Sylvius is a common site for such blockage)
- brain tumours
- infections, such as meningitis and encephalitis
- overproduction of CSF
- failure of absorption of CSF into the venous circulation.

A considerable increase in head size can occur without evidence of significant brain damage. However, when the damage to brain substance reaches a critical point with dilation of the ventricles the degree of intellectual impairment can be severe. Surgical intervention is necessary in many cases. Excess fluid can be drained by the insertion of a ventriculo-atrial shunt; drainage into the peritoneal cavity is also possible.

With early detection and advances in surgical treatment few cases of grossly distended skulls and accompanying severe mental handicap should occur. The main visual features of the untreated condition are a grossly distended head, with a thin skull and dilated veins. Blindness and deafness are common, as is paralysis, and convulsion can occur. In the past early death was common in a considerable number of cases.

Spina bifida and hydrocephalus frequently occur together.

Hypothyroidism (cretinism)

Hypothyroidism is the name given to a group of conditions casued by a deficiency of thyroxine, which is secreted by the thyroid gland. Hypothyroidism can be caused by a number of different metabolic errors, all of which result in a similar clinical picture. Several of the errors are thought to be caused by autosomal recessive genes. Incidence of the condition is around 1 in 4–6000 (Craft et al 1985). Girls are more frequently affected in a 70:30 ratio (Wiedemann 1985).

The problem is treatable with thyroxine, usually given orally, and treatment should be commenced as early as possible, within the first few months of life. Screening, by making use of dried blood, is possible but is not routine in the United Kingdom.

The untreated person frequently presents as a child with retarded growth who is apathetic, poor at feeding and sucking and a noisy breather due to an enlarged tongue which protrudes. The condition is characterized by a small stature, severe mental impairment and delayed acquisition of speech, till 7 or 8 years of age. Skin is yellowish, loose and wrinkled with thickening of eyelids, nostrils, lips, hands and feet. Hair is usually scant. Puberty is late and external genitals fail to develop.

ACQUIRED CONDITIONS

Prenatal problems which can lead to brain damage

A number of causes of mental handicap operate during pregnancy. The causation factors are not as clear as in genetic cases and statistical risk is not so easily identified. A knowledge of the causation factors is particularly important in the prevention of mental handicap.

Infections

Examples of maternal infection which have

Box 4.2   Genetic counselling

Genetic counselling is a service to parents and potential parents. Risk of genetically inherited conditions can be given and such risk put into perspective. Knowledge of the possible birth of a child with a treatable genetic condition, e.g. PKU, can make early, effective treatment possible and so avoid or minimize damage. A secondary purpose of genetic counselling is the reduction of the birth frequency of genetically determined conditions.

Genetic counselling is appropriate in a number of instances:

1. When a person suffering from a genetically inherited condition wishes to have a family.
2. In families with a member who has a recognized genetically inherited disease, or parents who already have a child with a genetically inherited condition.
3. Women who are pregnant, or planning a family, and who are over 35 years of age.
4. Women who have had multiple miscarriages.

A careful diagnosis of the condition which brings a person for genetic counselling must be made. This can be achieved with the help of cytogeneticists, biochemists, neuropathologists and, if the condition involves mental handicap, a team with a high level of expertise in the clinial aspects of mental handicap. A computerized data base of the large body of relevant literature will be very important.

Increasing numbers of genetically inherited and congenital conditions can be diagnosed in utero, giving the mother information on which to consider the possibility of termination. An accurate family tree, in some cases, can enable the mode of inheritance to be determined and risk established according to statistical probability. An explanation of the facts of the disease is given, with the inheritance pattern. The person's ability to understand the facts presented should be taken into account. It must also be remembered that a person's attitudes, beliefs and hopes will influence the way they interpret the facts they receive and the action they wish to take. Rapport between parent and counsellor is also important, with an acknowledgement of the likelihood of the person experiencing psychological and emotional turmoil. Counselling should be nondirective, but care must be taken to ensure that decisions made reflect realistically the alternatives available. Genetic counselling can lead to a number of alternatives for people who wish to have a family or parents who wish to increase their family. It may be that assurance of minimal risk can be given. The choice will be influenced by the disease, the degree of risk of inheritance and the views and feelings of the person being counselled. Where prenatal diagnosis is possible, therapeutic abortion can be offered if tests indicate the fetus has inherited a genetic condition or is damaged in some detectable way. Sterilization, contraception and adoption are alternatives which can be considered. In some countries, these options may not be so readily available to people, particularly abortion. However, more liberal laws are likely to be passed and attitudes towards issues such as abortion are changing slowly.

---

been implicated as a cause of mental handicap can be considered under three main headings:

- bacterial
- viral
- protozoal.

Bacterial

Congenital syphilis, resulting from maternal infection, is less common than in the past as a cause of mental handicap. In the early 1980s there was evidence of an increase in the incidence of syphilis. Improved antenatal care and the use of antibiotics have reduced the number of mentally handicapped people damaged by the bacteria.

In untreated children physical and mental development can be affected. Jaundice at birth is common. There is a failure to thrive and growth is stunted. The typical facial appearance includes a saddle back nose, opacities of the cornea, stra-bismus and nystagmus. Teeth are peg-shaped, especially the upper incisors. The effect on the central nervous system is variable as is the possible degree of mental handicap. Epilepsy may also be present.

Viral

Rubella, also known as German measles, is the best-known maternal infection which can be a cause of mental handicap. A number of other viruses have also been implicated in causing damage to the developing fetus, including mumps and poliomyelitis virus, and infections such as chicken pox.

With rubella the danger time is during the first trimester. The earlier the infection strikes during pregnancy, the more severe will be the damage in affected cases and the more extreme the degree of intellectual impairment. Subclinical infection can cause damage and so rubella in the expectant mother can go undetected. The overall risk to the developing fetus from rubella virus in the first 16 weeks of pregnancy is about 21%. Approximately 70% of infants whose mothers have rubella in the first 10 weeks of pregnancy will have some degree of handicap (Peckham 1988).

Affected children show a wide range of defects. Problems include congenital heart lesions, deafness, blindness and microcephaly. Where mental impairment is a feature of the damage the degree varies from mild to profound.

Other viral infections implicated in the causation of mental handicap, but much rarer, would include:

- cytomegalovirus disease
- chicken pox
- influenza.

Protozoal

In Britain 36% of the population in rural areas and 22% in urban districts are infected by protozoa by adulthood. It presents a danger if the infection occurs in a woman between the 2nd and 6th months of pregnancy. Spontaneous abortion or stillbirth occurs for about 10% of cases where there has been an infection during pregnancy with approximately one third of babies born to mothers who have had the infection also being infected.

Only a small proportion of those born with the infection have severe manifestations which, when it is severe, would include mental handicap, blindness and neurodevelopmental abnormalities.

Maternal nutrition

The unborn child is totally dependent on the mother. If there is an interruption to the supply of nutrients, including oxygen, over the placental barrier the developing fetus will be affected. Abnormal development of the placenta can result in placental insufficiency. Cardiovascular disease in the mother can limit blood supply to the placenta and severe diabetes mellitus in the mother puts the fetus at risk. There can be underdevelopment of the fetus in multiple pregnancy.

Box 4.3 Conditions in which microcephaly is, or may, be found

- 'True microcephaly' (autosomal recessive inheritance)
- Cornelia de Lange syndrome (Amsterdam dwarfism)
- Bird headed dwarfism
- Cri-du-chat syndrome
- Phenylketonuria
- Damage caused by maternal infection, e.g. rubella
- Damage caused by radiation, usually early in a pregnancy

Maternal–fetal incompatibility (kernicterus)

Rhesus factor incompatibility can also result in brain damage, including athetosis, in the newborn. Incompatibility occurs when a woman does not have the Rh factor in her blood. She is described as Rhesus negative. If the child has inherited the Rhesus factor from the father there is a high risk of Rh positive blood from the child entering the mother's bloodstream and antibodies will develop against the Rh factor. A first child is usually unaffected as antibody level only increases sufficiently during subsequent pregnancies to pass through the placental barrier and destroy the Rh positive blood in the fetus. At birth such a child will be jaundiced and brain damage will occur if untreated. Formation of the dangerous antibodies can be prevented by injecting the Rh negative woman within 48 hours of delivery of a first child with anti-D gammaglobulin. Exchange transfusion can be carried out in utero or immediately after birth if blood is being destroyed.

Toxic agents

A number of toxic agents can injure the developing fetus. In some instances the agents are ingested, as with alcohol, smoking and drugs. Environmental pollutants have been implicated as a causation factor in certain cases of mental handicap, mercurial poisoning being a notable example. The intake of alcohol during pregnancy may have detrimental consequences. It is impossible to give the precise amount of alcohol which has to be consumed to damage the fetus but there is a consensus view (Plant 1987) that alcohol should not be consumed during pregnancy. Major damage occurs between the 24th and 40th days of gestation. 'Binge drinking' in a pregnant woman puts the developing fetus at particular risk.

Damage to the fetus by alcohol can lead to fetal alcohol syndrome. In one study (Brooke et al 1989) women consuming 100g of alcohol or more a week before the 14th week of gestation showed a significant trend toward lower birth weight. In such children, microcephaly has been noted and also a failure to thrive. Motor performance has been found to be less developed. There may be as many as 75 000 women of childbearing age in Britain who have an alcohol problem (Shaw 1980) and present a risk to their fetus. A relationship has been established between smoking and reduced birth weight. One study (Brooke et al 1989) showed an average 241g decrease in birth weight in women who smoked more than 15 cigarettes per day and 140g average decrease in those smoking 1–14 cigarettes per day.

Smoking in pregnancy has also been linked with an increased risk of abortion. It is thought that vasoconstriction in the placenta and increased CO_2 in the blood reduce oxygen-carrying capacity. Smoking can cause deficiency of vitamins A, B_6 and C (Margeotta 1984).

Smoking does not in itself cause mental handicap but may lead to underdeveloped babies who are more likely to have a low birth weight. A link between drugs ingested during pregnancy and fetal damage has been positively established in a number of instances, the most publicized case concerning thalidomide. Only drugs prescribed should be taken during pregnancy. Addiction to hard drugs, such as heroin, puts the fetus at considerable risk of physical and intellectual damage.

Physical factors

The effect of radiation from excessive use of X-rays during pregnancy has been found to cause damage to the fetus, especially if the exposure is early in the pregnancy. Microcephaly in the children of women who were pregnant and were contaminated in the atomic bomb blasts in Japan was noted, as have been subsequent chromosomal abnormalities and mutant genes. Ultrasound screening techniques are used for diagnostic purposes during pregnancy.

A recognition of the effects of external influences on the developing fetus is essential. The provision of good antenatal care and increased awareness through health education can help reduce the impact of these influences and so reduce the risk of damage to the developing fetus.

Direct violence may lead to stillbirth or abortion. Physical violence to the developing fetus can lead to brain damage. The stage of gestation and the nature and severity of the violence will all be important factors in determining the extent of the damage caused.

If the brain is deprived of oxygen for 4–5 minutes irreversible changes occur in the brain. There are a number of causes of oxygen deprivation in the perinatal period, including:

- eclamptic fit
- prolonged second stage of labour
- coiling of the umbilical cord round the neck of the child during delivery
- reduction in respiration due to excessive maternal sedation
- severe respiratory infection in the immediate period after birth.

Parts of the brain most affected by oxygen deprivation are:

- cerebral cortex
- cerebellum
- hippocampus
- basal ganglia.

Administration of an atmosphere too rich in oxygen can be dangerous and can result in blindness (retrolental fibroplasia).

Other possible causes of birth injury include:

- excessive moulding of the head
- instrument delivery
- breech presentation.

In the immediate period after birth untreated

hypocalcaemia, hypernatraemia and hypogly-caemia in the infant can result in brain damage (Soothill et al 1987). Cerebral palsy and epilepsy as well as mental handicap can occur during the perinatal period. The extent of the damage and the part or parts of the brain affected will determine the nature and the extent of the resulting brain damage.

Monitoring the fetus is essential during labour. This can be done with the aid of ultra-sound and other electronic monitoring equip-ment, enabling early signs of fetal distress and potential danger to the fetus to be detected.

This, together with knowledge of fetal size and presentation and placental size and site, can reduce the risks of damage to the fetus.

Postnatal and developmental factors

During development, before birth and after birth the brain can be damaged and mental handicap and a number of associated conditions can result. In the period after birth a number of factors can result in brain damage.

Infection

Various infections in childhood carry the risk of brain damage as a complication and so mental handicap and associated handicaps may be manifested in some instances.

Gastroenteritis

This is especially dangerous in the very young. Dehydration can occur very quickly with this infection, leading to brain haemorrhage which can result in permanent brain damage. The subsequent intellectual impairment can range from mild to profound.

Meningitis

Acute pyogenic and chronic glandular meningi-tis can lead to damage to the brain and to mental impairment. Improved health care can reduce the incidence of such infections and the compli-cations associated with them.

Encephalitis

Following viral infections, such as rubella, chicken pox and mumps, the brain substance can become infected resulting in encephalitis. Post-vaccination encephalitis is rare but has been noted following whooping cough and other vaccinations. While the incidence of encephalitis is rare the degree of damage to the brain can be severe.

Trauma

Severe assault to the head in an accident can cause brain damage, e.g. a child being thrown through the windscreen of a car. Any accident where oxygen deprivation to the brain occurs, be it due to a blow to the head or to prolonged submersion in water, can result in irreversible brain damage if the deprivation lasts more than several minutes.

Battered baby syndrome is the term used when the damage to the child is nonaccidental. The injuries in such cases are usually caused by a parent or guardian. The extent of the brain damage and the degree of physical and mental handicap will be dependent on the extent and site of the injuries. Close monitoring of children at risk of such injury is essential and will involve the cooperation of social workers, health visitors, GPs and families.

Toxic agents

As in the prenatal period toxic substances can damage the developing brain. Lead intoxication was fairly common in the past when water supply pipes were lead and when the base for paint contained lead. These sources of lead have been recognized as potentially damaging and have been reduced or eliminated in many areas, though they may still exist in old buildings in such places as inner city dwellings. The danger of lead in motor vehicle exhaust fumes is increas-ingly recognized as contributing to a degree of brain damage (Yule et al 1981), especially in urban areas. There has been an increase, encour-aged by price differential, in the use of unleaded petrol in the UK.

Other materials, from industrial sources in particular, which are increasingly polluting the environment are being linked with brain damage. Substances seen as detrimental in the developmental period would include mercury (a community in Japan was badly affected when mercury entered the food chain, the humans being damaged by ingested mercury in fish), copper, manganese and strontium.

Nutrition factors can have an effect on the mental development of a child. Severe malnourishment in infancy has been shown to lead to poorer performance in school. A lack of protein during periods of rapid central nervous system development is especially serious. Those infants who are malnourished, either through inappropriate diet or through the relative poverty of their parents, will also be in a group where little value is placed on educational attainment.

CONCLUSION

Classification of mental handicap can be organized in various ways, none of which is wholly satisfactory. In all systems of classification there are anomalies and overlaps.

Whatever system is used classification should never be the most important or overriding factor for carers, whether parents or professionals. Knowledge about causation and specific features should be used as a means of improving care and quality of life.

MacKay (1982), in his report on the severely mentally handicapped population (those in most need of care and support) in England, states that in over 80% of people with learning disabilities causation of their condition was detectable. Of the detectable cases 55% were prenatal, 20% perinatal and 10% occurred during the developmental period. A similar study aimed at the identification of a specific cause or grouping by recognizable characteristics was not possible for people who were mildly mentally handicapped.

SUMMARY

Hereditary characteristics which have resulted in mental handicap are the result of abnormality

---

Box 4.4 Detection and prevention (Fig. 4.8)

AMNIOCENTESIS
Amniocentesis is the most common method of obtaining fetal cells for analysis. The test can only be done after the 14th week of pregnancy. 10–20 ml of amniotic fluid is withdrawn through the mother's abdominal wall. Ultrasound is used to ensure that there is no injury to the fetus by showing the location of the placenta and the position of the fetus.

CHORIONIC VILLUS SAMPLING
Chorionic villus cells located in finger-like projections of the membrane surrounding the embryo early in pregnancy carry the same genetic information as the developing fetus. The test can be done between the 9th and 11th week of pregnancy. The sample is obtained with the aid of ultrasound by inserting a catheter through the vagina and cervix and into the uterus, or by a needle inserted through the abdominal wall. Results can be obtained earlier and more quickly by this method than by amniocentesis.
    Risk of miscarriage following CVS is significantly higher than in amniocentesis.

NEW ANALYTIC TECHNIQUES
Recombinant DNA technology in the analysis of fetal cells looks directly at the structure of the human genome, making it possible to determine if the fetus has a specific abnormal gene. This is especially useful in the diagnosis of PKU. The abnormal enzyme is produced by liver cells and such cells cannot be collected by other prenatal sampling methods, but with recombinant DNA methods a fetus with the abnormal gene can be identified.

ULTRASOUND
Ultrasound is a valuable aid when obtaining amniotic fluid or in CVS. Advances in this technology have enabled highly skilled clinicians to detect a variety of skeletal and connective tissue disorders. Central nervous system defects such as anencephaly and hydrocephaly can be detected as can kidney abnormalities and urinary tract obstructions.

MATERNAL SERUM ALPHA-FETOPROTEIN SCREENING
Alpha-fetoprotein found in the serum of all pregnant women has been found to be useful as a tool in prenatal diagnosis. Raised AFP levels are found in women carrying fetuses with spina bifida and other related defects of the central nervous system.
    Lower than expected levels of AFP have been found in women carrying a fetus which has Down syndrome.

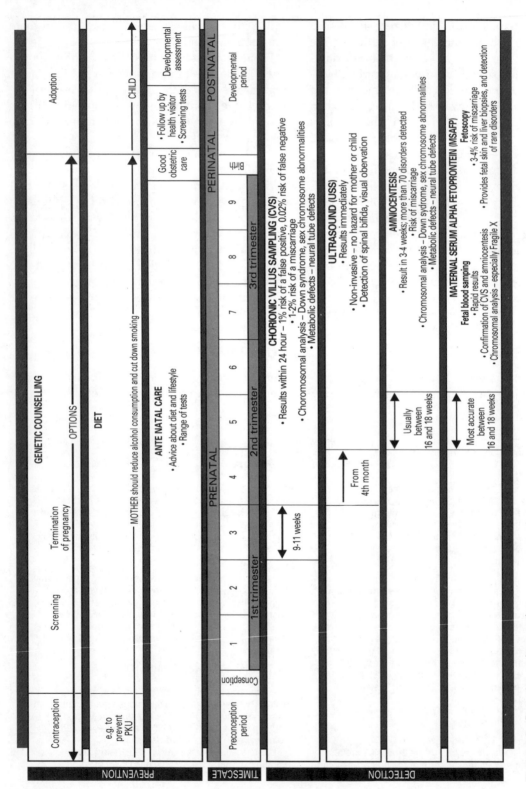

Figure 4.8 Detection and prevention.

occurring in the genetic make-up of the body in the autosomes, sex chromosomes or specific genes. Clinical features and prognosis of a particular condition should be used as an aid to planning care and should never impose rigid care planning which is unresponsive to individual need.

Not all features of each syndrome or abnormality will be exhibited in every case so individual assessment must take account of the wide range of variation. With advances in technology and scientific investigation prenatal diagnosis of many genetic conditions is now possible. A wider range of options for treatment and prevention through genetic engineering will be possible as knowledge and techniques advance.

Nongenetic causes of mental handicap stem from infection, nutritional and chemical factors, and assault from toxic agents, such as alcohol and drugs. Damage can occur at any time during pregnancy, at the time of birth and through the developmental period after birth. In some instances damage may be unavoidable, but provision of health education, good quality antenatal and obstetrics care, regular screening and high quality health care during the developmental period can reduce the chance of damage that could lead to mental handicap.

Once it is established that a person is mentally handicapped, parents and care staff must ensure that secondary handicaps, physical and mental, do not occur. This can be prevented by ensuring from the outset that each person is given their right to individualized holistic care, objective assessment and care delivery that is responsive to individual need.

GLOSSARY

Autosome	A chromosome, other than a sex chromosome
Chromosome	Rod-shaped bodies in the cell nucleus, which contain the hereditary units, the genes.
Congenital	Any abnormality which is present at birth.
Deletion	Where part of a chromosome is missing.
Gamete	A reproductive cell; the male is the sperm, the female the ovum. The gamete contains half the chromosomes and so half the genes of the parent.
Gene	The biological unit of genetic information which occupies a specific site on a chromosome.
Karyotype	The chromosomal make-up of an individual; 46 XX for a normal female, 46 XY for a normal male.
Meiosis	The process of gamete formation.
Mitosis	The process of cell division and multiplication.
Mutation	An abrupt change in phenotype due to a change within a gene or a chromosome.
Nondisjunction	The failure of two members of a chromosome pair to separate during cell division. Both chromosomes will thus pass to the same daughter cell.
Phenotype	The outward visible expression of genetic material.
Sex chromosomes	The X and Y chromosomes that are involved in sex determination.
Sex linked	This refers to genes which are carried on the sex chromosome.
Translocation	The transfer of all or part of a chromosome to a site on another chromosome.
Trisomy	The presence of three chromosomes instead of a pair.
Zygote	The fertilized ovum.

REFERENCES

Brooke O G, Anderson H R, Bland J M, Peacock J L 1989 Effects on birth weight of smoking, alcohol, caffeine, socioeconomic factors and psychosocial stress. British Medical Journal 298: 795–801

Craft M, Bicknell J, Hollins S 1985 Mental handicap: a multidisciplinary approach. Ballière Tindall, London

Kingston H M 1989 Chromosomal disorders 11. British Medical Journal 298: 813–816

Lane D, Stratford B 1985 Current approaches to Down's syndrome. Holt, Rinehart and Winston, London

MacKay R 1982 The causes of severe mental handicap. Developmental Medicine and Child Neurology 24: 386–393

Margeotta P 1984 The importance of preconceptual nutrition. Nursing Times: Health Visitor Supplement 11–12

Nichols E 1988 Human gene therapy. Harvard University Press, Harvard

Osbourne J, Fryer A E 1990 Tuberous sclerosis. Tuberous Sclerosis Association of Great Britain, Worthing

Paritzky J 1985 Tay Sachs: the dreaded inheritance. The American Journal of Nursing, March 260–264

Peckham C S 1988 Infection and the fetus. Medicine International 51: 2107–2110

Plant M 1987 Women, drinking and pregnancy. Tavistock, London

Pueschel S 1988 The young person with Down's syndrome from adolescence to adulthood. Paul Brooke, London

Richards B W 1974 Investigation of 142 mosaic mongols; cytogenic analysis and maternal age at birth. Journal of Mental Deficiency Research 18: 199

Scheerenberger R 1987 A history of mental retardation. Paul Brooke, London

Siggers D C 1978 Prenatal diagnosis of genetic disease. Blackwell Scientific, Oxford

Shaw S 1980 Women and alcohol. In: Camberwell Council on Alcoholism. Tavistock, London

Simpson D 1989 Phenylketonuria. Midwives Chronicles and Nursing Notes 102 (1213): 37–41

Smith D W 1982 Recognisable patterns of human malformation. W B Saunders, London

Smith G F, Berg J M 1976 Down's anomaly. Churchill Livingstone, Edinburgh

Soothill P 1987 Prenatal asphyxia. British Medical Journal 294: 1051–1053

Wiedemann H R 1985 An atlas of human characteristic syndromes. W B Saunders, London

Yule W, Lansdown R, Miller I B, Urbanowicz M-A 1981 The relationship between lead concentrations, intelligence and attainment in a school population. Medicine and Child Neurology 23: 567–576

FURTHER READING

Bromham D R 1988 Prenatal diagnosis. Update: 193–201

Crawfurd M da 1988 Prenatal diagnosis. Update 297: 502–506

Donnai D 1988 Screening for Down's syndrome. British Medical Journal 297: 876

Gibson D 1978 Down's syndrome. Cambridge University Press, Cambridge

Jakab I 1982 Mental retardation. Karger, London

Kingston H M 1986 Patterns of inheritance. Maternal and Child Health January 9–13

Kingston H M 1989 Mendelian inheritance. British Medical Journal 298: 375–378

Kingston H M 1989 Detection of carriers. British Medical Journal 298: 508–511

Kingston H M 1989 Estimation of risk. British Medical Journal 298: 449–451

Kingston H M 1989 Chromosomal disorders 1. British Medical Journal 298: 663–665

Kingston H M 1989 Prenatal diagnosis. British Medical Journal 298: 1368–1371

Kingston H M 1989 Genetic disorders. British Medical Journal 298: 1499–1501

MacKenzie I Z 1988 Chorion villus sampling and antenatal diagnosis. Update 1 January 1394–1399

Pembrey M 1988 Recent advances in clinical genetics. The Practitioner 232: 1152–1155

Plant M 1990 Advising on alcohol. Nursing Times 86: 64–65

Slack J 1986 Prenatal screening. The Practitioner 230: 711–716

Wald N J 1988 Maternal serum screening. British Medical Journal 297: 883–887.

Young I D 1986 Identifying families at risk of inherited disease. The Practitioner 230: 705–708

CHAPTER CONTENTS

Introduction   83

Social classes   84
Genetic perspective   85
Social environment perspective   86

Identification of cultural differences   87
Patterns of child/parent interaction   87
Locus of control   87
Sociolinguistics   88
Self-fulfilling prophecy   88

Conclusion   89

Summary   90

5

Social causes

G. Petrie

Key points
- Mild mental handicap most prevalent in social classes 4 and 5
- Class differential due to genetic factors or result of social environment!
- Existing bias toward middle class culture in the education system and IQ tests
- Working class culture reinforces negative influences
- Social environment causes can be remedied
- Genetic engineering offers opportunities and risks

INTRODUCTION

There is a danger that professionals and volunteer workers dealing with people with learning disabilities have a distorted view of the prevalence of mental handicap. They often fail to appreciate that they are dealing with a very small percentage of those people in society who are thus labelled. This is particularly the case when contact is with those in the moderate, severe and profound categories, or when there are additional handicaps including disruptive behaviours or debilitating physical handicaps.

The largest number of people with cognitive disabilities are in the mild category. Of the 2–3% of the population who are considered to be mentally handicapped between 80 and 90% fall in the mild category with less than 4% in the severe and profound range (Table 5.1 and Table 5.2). The majority of people who are in the mild range of mental handicap live relatively independent

Table 5.1 Percentage of the mentally handicapped population

	%
Mild	86.7
Moderate	10.0
Severe and profound	3.3

lives with little contact with care providers and support services.

The majority of people with learning disabilities in the mild category, unlike those in the moderate, severe and profound range, come from classes 4 and 5 in the Registrar General's classification scheme (Table 5.3). These classes, also referred to as the 'working class', contribute a disproportionate percentage of people who are designated as mildly mentally handicapped. In his revision of the Stanford-Binet scale McNemar (1942) estimated that the IQ score of children in class 1 (professional) was 116 while in class 5 (unskilled) the average score was 96. This contrasts the situation in the more severe range of mental handicap where the whole range of classes is proportionately represented.

SOCIAL CLASSES

The category of classes 4 and 5 is part of a system of socioeconomic classification using such criteria as education, occupation and income. These criteria seem to correlate with such ill-defined factors as spending patterns, attitudes and IQ scores. Housing, transport, nutritional status and opportunities for access to leisure and recreational facilities are likely to be less good for those in class 4 and 5, as compared to opportunities open to classes 1 to 3, the 'middle class'.

The Registrar General in the UK has used this system to identify 'people whose social, cul-

Table 5.2 Classification of mental handicap (World Health Organization, 1968)

Classification	IQ
Mild	50–75
Moderate	35–50
Severe	20–35
Profound	0–20

Table 5.3 Registrar General's classification scheme

Class	Occupation
1	Professional (doctors, lawyers, engineers)
2	Retail (retailers, farmers, nurses, teachers)
3(i)	White collar workers (office workers)
3(ii)	Skilled manual (tradesmen)
4	Semi-skilled
5	Unskilled (labourers)

tural and recreational standards and behaviour are similar'. There is frequent overlapping of characteristics between classes and a degree of movement between the groupings. Despite this, social class has become an accepted and convenient way of classifying groups in our society. In the Registrar General's classification scheme the following divisions emerged using occupation as the main criterion (Table 5.2):

- Professional
- Retail
- White collar
- Skilled manual
- Semi-skilled.

The term 'working class' refers approximately to classes 4 and 5, i.e. semi-skilled and unskilled workers, while 'middle class' refers to the remainder.

An important issue when considering the social causes of mental handicap (an issue of great interest to sociologists, psychologists and educationalists) is why there is a significant difference in school performance and IQ scores between those in classes 1 and 2 and classes 4 and 5. There are two main theories that attempt to account for this difference – the genetic theory and the sociological theory.

The genetic theorists take the view that over a period of generations individuals with low intelligence tend to gravitate or drift into semi-skilled occupations because they cannot cope with more intellectually demanding work. It would also be suggested by the genetic theorists that they tend to socialize with and marry people of similar background thus building up a poor genetic pool. The theory would suggest that the converse would be true of highly intelligent people. Sociological theorists, in contrast, would see the social environment of the working class as being responsible for the poor performance in IQ tests and at school.

Genetic perspective

There are two main sources of evidence cited when considering the inheritance of intelligence:

1. Studies correlating IQ scores between people of various degrees of genetic relationship.

Studies involving identical twins reared together and reared apart have been important in this area of research. Those identical twins reared apart share the same genetic material but not the same environment.

Closeness of genetic relationships to similarities in IQ score is measured in terms of a correlation scale. The scale runs from +1 through to –1. The closer to +1 the correlation score lies, the higher the relationship between two events. For example, if a mother and child are tested, a positive correlation would suggest a close relationship and a similar test score; a correlation of 0 would indicate a negative relationship; and a correlation near to –1 would indicate a negative relationship and dissimilar test scores.

Erlenmeyer-Kimling & Jarvik (1963) concluded that the closer the genetic relationship the more similar are the IQ scores. Average correlation between the IQs of various relationships is shown in Table 5.4. These studies point to a high degree of influence of genetic factors.

2. Studies of IQ differences between racial groupings have been used to support genetic theories.

Methodology used in studies in this area and the analysis of data have been put under considerable scrutiny and the conclusions supporting

genetic theorists from this source must be considered with great care. IQ scores in some studies in the USA have shown scores 10–15 lower for blacks than whites. In Britain and the USA the majority of blacks do comparatively poorly at school, end up in unskilled occupations and have low incomes.

In Social Trends 21 (1991) it is stated that unemployment rates in Britain are lower among the white population than for other ethnic groups. Quoting employment statistics for the years 1987–89 Social Trends 21 points to Pakistani and Bangladeshi ethnic groups as having the highest unemployment rates and that when figures for those with no qualifications are examined the Pakistani and Bangladeshi group are more than twice as likely to be unemployed than their white counterparts. Unemployment rates for the ethnic minorities remain higher than for the white population, but the gap is narrowing and the overall rate for ethnic minorities fell by over a quarter between 1985 and 1989.

A major proponent of the genetic theory, Jensen (1969), concluded that differences in IQ scores reflected real differences between blacks and whites. His claims have been supported by a psychologist working in England, Eysenck (1971). The proponents contend that these differences indicate a difference in intellectual ability. The view that blacks have lower intelligence than whites has led to intense political and emotional debate. The main argument against the genetic theory concentrates on the inference that IQ scores reflect levels of intelligence of individuals from different cultures. However, the tests on which IQ scores are based are not totally culture free. Nor is it possible to eliminate the influence of environmental, social, educational and other variants relating to the conditions under which blacks and whites are raised:

As long as systematic differences remain in the conditions under which blacks and whites are raised (and as long as the effects of these differences cannot be reliably estimated) no valid conclusions can be drawn concerning innate differences in intelligence between races. (Hilgard et al 1975)

Layzer (1974) concentrates his criticism on

Table 5.4 Correlation between genetic relationship and IQ scores (Erlenmeyer-Kimling & Jarvik 1963)

Genetic relationship	Correlation
Parents and their natural children	0.50
Parents and their adopted children	0.25
Fraternal twins	0.55
Identical twins reared apart	0.75
Identical twins reared together	0.90

the methodology used by Jensen in making the comparison between blacks and whites. He concluded that:

Published analysis of IQ data provides no support whatever for Jensen's theory that inequalities in cognitive performance are due largely to genetic differences.

In this nature versus nurture debate, as in so many situations where apparently contradictory views are expressed, there seems a good case for the middle ground, i.e. that both genetic and social factors play a part. The argument should not be an 'either-or' debate but a consideration of the importance of the factors in determining intellectual development.

In reviewing studies, Scarr-Salapatek (1971) concluded that genetic factors account for between 60 and 80% of the variance in IQ scores while Jencks et al (1972) postulated that 45% of the variance is accounted for by genetic factors, 35% by environment factors and the remaining 20% by the correlation between genes and the environment. There is little that can be done at present to change the effect of genes on intellectual development and any future developments in genetics, which could make such changes possible, will cause a great deal of controversy and debate. Improvement in IQ scores by tackling environmental causes of intellectual impairment is more likely. A scrutiny of environmental influences on intellectual development may indicate areas where social engineering may occur.

Social environment perspective

The heading 'social environment' is used in preference to the terms 'cultural deprivation' or 'subcultural' handicap, used by Forrest et al (1973), as both these terms have unacceptable connotations. While they are useful in emphasizing the different cultural influences of the social environment both imply that the group of people described are inferior, i.e. that they are a subordinate culture or that they have been deprived of culture. The notion of a subordinate or deprived culture disregards the richness of working class culture and reflects a dominant bias by a 'superordinate' culture, i.e. by those doing the classifying (usually members of the middle class). In order to overcome these possible objections the more general and less judgmental heading of 'social environment' is used.

Studies that blame the social environment for low IQ scores and poor school performance have concentrated on children whose social conditions have altered and who subsequently exhibited marked changes in IQ score.

Skeel & Dyke (1939) cited a case where 13 children who had been moved from an orphanage with few staff to an institution where residents who were classified as having a mild mental handicap acted as mothers. Following this change the children had made gains in IQ score ranging from 7 to 58 points. A control group of 12 children who remained in the orphanage actually showed a decline in IQ scores. As adults those who remained in the orphanage ended up in wards of institutions, mental hospitals and mental handicap hospitals. The children who had moved from the orphanage became independent as adults and compared well with other noninstitutionalized people, i.e. the general population.

Davis (1947) described a case where a child spent the first 6 years of her life in an attic, in an environment with little stimulation or social interaction. On discovery, her IQ was assessed at 25; three years later her IQ score was found to be within the normal range.

Kugel & Parsons (1967) in a 2-year investigation studied IQ changes that coincided with social environmental changes in children between 3 years and 6 years of age. The children studied had no apparent organic brain damage and had been diagnosed as moderately or mildly mentally handicapped. A special educational programme was implemented that involved changes in the children's home life and at their school. At the end of 2 years there were increases in IQ scores of up to 51 points.

Garber (1975), in recording aspects of the Milwaukee experiment, reported major changes in IQ scores as a result of special programmes.

One group of black children were given experiences aimed at developing their cognitive powers while another similar group of black children from the same background were not given any special programme (the control group). At the age of 7 years (the experiment had been running from shortly after birth) the average IQ of the former group was 106 and the score of the control group was 85.

One consistent finding in these and other studies into low IQ scores is the relationship between social class and IQ score. There are two main interpretations of this finding:

1. Actual deficiencies in cognitive functioning may result from the social environment of classes 4 and 5. These deficiencies are measured by IQ scores and are reflected in poor school performance.

2. Poor scores on IQ tests and poor school performance do not reflect deficiencies in cognitive functioning. Cole & Bruner (1971), Ginsburg (1972) and Baratz (1979), argue that poor performance may reflect nothing more than the existence of sets of values, language codes and motivation that are different from those of the measuring middle class culture. Socializing someone to the norms, values and attitudes of the dominant culture may merely improve their score at an IQ test and equip them to deal with the 'hidden curriculum' at school. This view does not imply that cognitive disabilities do not exist. Instead it emphasizes the fact that bias in assessment of intellect exists against certain classes, resulting in a greater likelihood that membership of such classes can result in being considered mentally handicapped.

Care providers and other professionals themselves must avoid imposing their norms, values and attitudes on people with cognitive disabilities so disadvantaging them further. Providers of services should be sensitive to the client group and not impose inappropriate provision as had occurred when the Education Act of 1944 designated large numbers of youngsters with learning difficulties as ineducable, hence depriving them of the very provision they required to help them reach their potential.

IDENTIFICATION OF CULTURAL DIFFERENCES

Patterns of child/parent interaction

One of the earliest studies on the differences between working class child/parent interaction and that of the middle class was carried out by Hess & Shipman (1965). They concluded that middle class mothers tended to use a reasoning and person-oriented means of control. Unlike working class parents they did not depend on the power of authority and did not rely on their own position or role to exercise control. This difference in child/parent interaction was emphasized by Bernstein (Trudgill 1974) who described two possible types of family structures:

1. The positional family
In this type of structure, mainly working class, the influence on decisions made depended on the formal status of each member of the family, i.e. it is not so important what is said but who it is that says it.

2. The person-orientated family
In this type of structure, mainly middle class, greater credence is given to the individual and there is much less adherence to the person's position in the family hierarchy. As a result, according to Hess & Shipman (1965), the middle class child learns to depend on reason both in interpreting disciplining by others and in giving justification for his own behaviour, while the working class child learns to be passive and unquestioning.

White & Watt (1973) compared the behaviour of mothers and found that middle class mothers tended to spend much more time interacting with their children, particularly in naming things and explaining about them. They also encouraged up to three times more activity than they discouraged. Working class mothers tended to be much more controlling and discouraged activity more than they encouraged.

Locus of control

Working class people are socialized to being accepting and passive, seeing no possibility of changing their circumstances (Battle & Rotter 1963). They live in relative poverty with limited financial resources, experience high levels of unemployment, lack job security, have poor housing and feel they have no control over their lives. This contrasts with the outlook of many middle class children who learn that they can change things in their life through their own initiative and have an awareness of the opportunities of doing so. In other words, middle class people feel that the power to change things resides within themselves (internal locus of control) while working class people feel that events outside their influence control their lives (external locus of control).

Research into the effect on school performance of different loci of control showed that locus of control was a good predictor of later school success (Coleman 1966). If a person feels that his own efforts have little influence on how well he gets on, then he is liable to put little effort into trying which in turn is liable to result in low achievement.

Sociolinguistics

According to the Whorfian theory, language determines the way we think (Whorf 1956). In other words people with different language think differently. While Whorf's theory has been subjected to severe criticism it has become more accepted that language, while not determining the way we think, at least influences our thinking.

Bernstein (1967) examined the different types of language used by the working class and the middle class and postulated that the type of language used may account for the differences in performance in school. He identified two different codes of speech:

- Elaborated code – used by the middle class
- Restricted code – used by both working and middle class.

Restricted code involves simple sentence structure with a limited repertoire of structures and vocabulary. The subject matter of conversation is more concrete and less abstract than that of those who use elaborated code. The speaker is less explicit, depending on shared assumptions with the listener in the same way as between intimate friends where a single exclamation will instantly convey a wealth of meaning without further elaboration being necessary.

The implications for education of Bernstein's theory are that elaborated code may be seen as an important requirement for learning and those who only use restricted code cannot think as effectively as those with elaborated code and, consequently, are at considerable disadvantage at school. The solution would seem to be that working class children should be taught elaborated code in order to improve their thinking capacity and hence their school performance.

Teaching programmes such as Operation Headstart implemented in the USA proved to be unsuccessful in attempting to improve the school performance of black children, despite the many millions of dollars poured into it. The emphasis here was to teach these children to use Standard English (as distinct from Non-Standard or Black English).

Another view of Bernstein's theory is that elaborated code is merely a social convention and in education it is demanded as the appropriate style of communication. Working class children are not necessarily any less intelligent: the only difference between middle class and working class children is that the working class way of communicating is not accepted by members of the dominant culture. Those students who use elaborated code tend to be more successful in our educational system and their arrival in positions of authority perpetuates the use of elaborated code in education. The solution to this problem may be to change attitudes toward working class speech and to develop a greater understanding of working class culture and ways of communicating.

Self-fulfilling prophecy

Rist (1970) described how the teacher's expectations influence her behaviour in class. In an all-black kindergarten the teacher assigned each child to one of three groups: fast learners, average learners and slow learners on the basis of having taught them for 8 days. Rist felt that this period of time was too short for an accurate assessment to be made. He observed that children designated fast learners were generally neat and clean while slow learners were untidy and often smelled of urine. Slow learners were more likely to have parents on state benefit. The teacher's behaviour toward the children varied according to the grouping she had made. For example, the teacher stood closer to the fast learners (the slow learners were furthest from the front) and addressed her remarks to them rather than to the whole class. She involved the fast learners in classroom activities much more frequently than the slow learners, in such things as projects and in demonstrations to the class. After a year, the teacher commented that the slow learners did not have an idea about what was going on in the class and 'were off in a world all by themselves'. She felt that her teaching was not responsible for the poor performance of the slow learners but was due to their being 'low achievers'. In other words she felt that teaching the low achievers was of little use and responsibility for poor performance resided within the child and not within her. This attitude had been reflected in her classroom behaviour.

Rosenthal & Jacobson (1968) clearly demonstrated the effect of the teacher's expectation on the child's performance. They gave a class of children an IQ test to complete and informed the teachers that certain children were going to show marked improvement over the coming year. In actual fact the children named were selected at random and not on the basis of the IQ scores. A year later the IQ test was repeated. The children described as liable to show marked improvement actually did show significant improvement; the other children showed no change in IQ score.

CONCLUSION

Genetic factors seem to play an important part in determining the level of intellectual functioning of the individual. The main debate now centres on the relative influence these factors exert.

A useful way of viewing this issue is to see genetic factors as representing the individual's potential which is affected by the huge number of influences in the social environment in which he or she lives. Two examples of the influence of social environment are:

1. The person with a genetic potential for a high level of intellectual functioning may experience adverse social conditions, as described in the studies of children in institutions, and so fail to reach that potential and end up functioning at the level of mild mental handicap.
2. A person with low genetic potential who experiences favourable social conditions is likely to get close to maximum intellectual potential.

The culture (working class or middle class) into which a person is born represents an important part of their social environment. It has been shown to influence IQ score and school performance. The view that working class culture is responsible for deficiencies in intellectual functioning is not clear cut. The low IQ scores gained by members of the working class may be due to factors other than the person's level of intelligence and may include:

- different values
- different language codes
- different motivational factors
- the bias of IQ tests toward the middle class
- the bias of the educational system toward the middle class.

From a purely practical point of view there is little that can be done to alleviate the genetic factors responsible for low intelligence. However technological advances are occurring in the field of genetic engineering. As such advances are made many moral and ethical considerations will have to be addressed.

Sociological factors would appear to be more amenable to manipulation, but there are no simple answers to what is a multifaceted issue. The areas for manipulation can be controversial and lead to wide-ranging social and political debate.

The way ahead for exponents of the 'no deficiency theory' would be to alter the educational system to have a less middle class bias and to devise IQ tests that are culture free or, as in California, use different tests for different ethnic groups.

Those who believe there is a deficiency in cognition would argue that further identification with and possible emulation of the socialization patterns of the middle class for children of working class background may offer the best solution.

SUMMARY

Most people with learning disabilities fall into the category of 'mild' mental handicap. According to a socioeconomic classification based on occupation, education and income the prevalence of mild mental handicap is concentrated in social classes 4 and 5; severe and profound handicap is spread over all 5 social classes.

This class differential has been explained by:

- genetic theory – the inheritance of intelligence
- social theory – the effect of environment.

Studies support the view that class culture is responsible for school failure and low IQ scores and that a bias exists towards middle class culture. Additionally, working class culture exerts a negative influence through less effective child / parent interaction, lack of focus of control, restricted use of language and the impact of self-fulfilling prophecy.

Where deficiency in cognition is caused by genetic factors no improvement is possible. However, if the deficiency is caused by the social environment, then attention should be turned to improving individual components of that environment, e.g. the educational system, to alter any bias.

REFERENCES

Baratz S S, Baratz J C 1979 Early childhood intervention: the social science base of institutional racism. Harvard Educational Review 40: 29–50

Battle E S, Rotter J B 1963 Children's feelings of personal control as related to social class and ethnic group. Journal of Personality 31: 482–490

Bernstein B 1967 Social structure, language and learning. In: Dececco JP (ed) The psychology of language thought and instruction. Holt, Rinehart & Winston, New York

Central Statistical Trend 1991 Social Trends 21 1991 Edition, pg 78, Government Statistical Service

Cole M, Bruner J S 1971 Cultural differences and inferences about psychological processes. American Psychologist 26: 867–876

Coleman J S 1966 Equality of educational opportunity. US Dept of Health and Welfare

Davis K 1947 Final note on a case of extreme isolation. American Journal of Sociology 57: 432–457

Erlenmeyer-Kimling L, Jarvik L F 1963 Genetics and intelligence. A review science 142: 1477–1478

Eysenck H 1971 Race, intelligence and education. Temple Smith, London

Forrest A, Ritson B, Zealey A 1973 New perspectives in mental handicap. Churchill Livingstone, Edinburgh

Garber H L 1975 Intervention in infancy: a development approach. In: Begeb M J, Richardson S A (eds) The mentally retarded and society: a social science perspective. University Press, Baltimore

Ginsburg H 1972 The myth of the deprived child. Prentice Hall, Englewood Cliffs, New Jersey

Hess R D, Shipman V 1965 Early experience and socialization of cognitive modes in children. Child Development 36: 869

Hilgard E D, Atkinson R C 1975 Introduction to psychology. Harcourt Brace, New York, p 419

Jencks C et al 1972 Inequality: a reassessment of the effect of the family and schooling in America. Basic Books, New York

Jensen A R 1969 How much can we boost IQ and scholastic achievement? Harvard Educational Review 39: 1–123

Kugel R B, Parsons M H 1967 Children of deprivation. Washington: Children's Bureau Pub. No.440 Welfare Administration DHEW

Layzer D 1974 Heritability analysis of IQ scores: science or numerology? Science 183: 1259–1266

McNemar Q 1942 The revision of the Stanford-Binet scale. Houghton Mifflin, Boston

Rist R C 1970 Students' social class and teacher's expectations: the self-fulfilling prophecy in ghetto education. Harvard Education Review 40: 411–451

Rosenthal R, Jacobson L 1968 Pygmalion in the classroom. Holt, Rinehart & Winston, New York

Scarr-Salapatek S 1971 Race, social class and IQ. Science 174: 1285–1295

Skeel H M, Dyke H B 1939 A study of the effects of differential stimulation on mentally retarded children. Proceedings and addresses of the AAMD 44: 114–136

Trudgill P 1974 Sociolinguistics: an introduction. Penguin, Harmondsworth, p 51–56
White B L, Watt J C 1973 Experience and environment: major influences on the development of the young child.
Prentice Hall, Englewood Cliffs, New Jersey
Whorf B L 1956 Language thought and reality. Wiley, M.I.T, New York

FURTHER READING

Cole M, Bruner J S 1971 Cultural differences and inferences about psychological processes. American Psychologist 26: 867–876
Cocking I, Surinder A 1990 A special case for special treatment. Social Work Today 8 Feb: 12–13
Cratt M, Bicknell J, Hollins S 1985 Mental handicap. Baillière Tindall, London
Ingalls R P 1978 Mental retardation. Wiley, New York

Richardson S A 1975 Reaction to mental subnormality. In: Begeb M J, Richardson S A (eds) The mentally retarded and society: a social science perspective. University Press, Baltimore
Smith D J 1977 Racial disadvantage in Britain (The PEP report). Penguin, Harmondsworth, p 51–56
Tomlinson S 1989 Asian pupils and special issues. British Journal of Special Education 16 (3): 119–122

CHAPTER CONTENTS

Epilepsy 93
Control of epilepsy 94
'The epileptic personality' 94

Cerebral palsy 95
Causation 95
Classification 95
  Spasticity 95
  Athetosis 95
  Ataxia 95
  Mixed types 96
Care of the individual with cerebral palsy 96
  Eating 96
  Pathological tongue thrust 96
  Communication 97
  Music, rhythm and melody 97
  Physiotherapy 97
  Paralytic dislocation of the hip 98
  Surgery 98
  Drugs 98
  Coping behaviour of families 98

Stereotyped behaviour 98
Theories 98
Behavioural approaches 99

Hyperkinetic syndrome 99
Hyperactivity 99
Distractibility 99
Short attention span 100
Impulsiveness 100
Temper tantrums 100
Destructiveness 100
Aggressiveness 100
Treatment 100
Diet 101

Autism 101

Mental illness 102
Affective psychoses 103
  Depression 103
  Mania 105
Schizophrenia 106

Organic reactions 108
Delirium 108
Dementia 109

Neurotic disorders 112

Conduct disorders 112

Forensic psychiatry 112

Acquired immune deficiency syndrome 113

Summary 115

6

Associated conditions

F. Quinn   A. Mathieson

Key points

- People with epilepsy have not only its physical aspects to deal with but also the social consequences
- Cerebral palsy can cause extreme difficulties for people performing basic activities of living if unaided. Help may involve a plethora of specialists the coordination of whom may itself cause problems
- Hyperkinetic behaviour can be debilitating for the carers as well as the person affected
- Considerable sensitivity is required in identifying a person with severe learning disabilities who is experiencing mental illness
- Because of the move to the community this vulnerable group may be at risk from HIV infection

EPILEPSY

The purpose of this section is to focus on the effects that epilepsy can have on the life of the affected person and to explore some of the attitudinal prejudices people with epilepsy face.

For some members of the general public, epilepsy is a condition which raises enormous fears and anxieties (Hopkins 1981). Beliefs that it denoted possession by evil spirits persisted well into the 19th century and may still exist today in some cultures. In Western culture, the fears tend to be based upon the perceived unpredictability of events. The sufferer is liable to 'drop' in a fit at any moment, he may or may not come out of it, indeed, he may or may not survive it, and if he does his behaviour might be bizarre, even violent, and what if he has a fit in the bath, or next to an open fire, or while cooking . . .? The list of nightmare scenarios is considerable. When allied to mental handicap, a concept which raises similar anxieties about unpredictable and bizarre behaviour, it is understandable how the person with a mental handicap and associated epilepsy can become a figure not only to be shunned and ostracized but also feared.

All those who work alongside people with mental handicap have a responsibility to engage the larger community in education aimed at demystifying these ideas and correcting misconceptions. Perhaps the two greatest misconceptions which exist are, firstly, that epilepsy is uncontrollable and, secondly, that such an entity as the 'epileptic personality' exists.

Control of epilepsy

The advent of drugs such as sodium valproate have made management much safer and more successful. It has been estimated that 50–90% of sufferers achieve successful medical control of their seizures (Shorvan 1987), although the figure may be lower for people with profound mental handicap. The efficacy of treatment allows people with epilepsy to indulge in activities which might hitherto have been prohibited to them, such as swimming, horse riding, and cooking.

People with epilepsy have the same right to make decisions and take risks as other groups in society, yet it is also appreciated that those with learning disabilities and epilepsy often require care staff to offer supervision and advice (Brechin & Swain 1987).

The tendency in the past when dealing with people with mental handicap has been for supervision to be more akin to custodianship, and advice more like orders, usually the prohibitive kind. Restrictive and prohibitive cossetting is even more likely if the individual also suffers from epilepsy. A balance must be struck between freedom and supervision.

Careful assessment and identification of the pattern of epileptic seizures, likely predisposing

factors and the types of behaviour which can be expected to initiate a fit allow identification of risks associated with the person indulging in certain behaviours to be made. The affected individual can then be helped to make informed decisions on activities and lifestyle commensurate with the risks involved. While there will always be some element of unpredictability associated with epilepsy, the more we know of how individuals are affected the better prepared we are to help them discriminate between high and low risk activities.

A survey carried out for the British Epilepsy Association (BEA) showed that 72.3% of a sample of almost 2000 epilepsy sufferers claimed to have experienced problems in finding employment, and over half of them described their problem as 'serious' (BEA 1990). Again, the figures are likely to be higher for those who are also mentally handicapped. These figures indicate that despite the educational work of organizations like BEA those with epilepsy are at a disadvantage when competing for jobs.

'The epileptic personality'

The characteristics of the 'epileptic personality' have been described as devious, manipulative, egocentric, selfish, argumentative and a variety of other similarly pejorative traits. The evidence to support this perception is extremely scant (Laidlaw & Laidlaw 1984). Admittedly, some people with epilepsy may have personality problems but these are neither indicative of, nor peculiar to, that condition. The factors which govern the personality of a person with epilepsy are likely to be the same as those which govern others; there is probably a genetic link and the effects of environment, stimuli, stressors, education, balance of approval against disapproval, encouragement, opportunity and sense of personal value are all considered important contributing factors.

Nurses working with these clients can do nothing about the genetic factor but they can influence some of the environmental factors. The person with epilepsy who lives in a caring, stimulating, educational and approving environment has a greater chance of realizing his potential and achieving a sense of self-worth.

A particularly influential factor relates to the level of stress felt by clients. All of us require a certain level of stress in order to function positively, but each individual has 'critical levels': below these levels, lack of stress leads to indolence and frustration; above it, too much stress leads to worry, anxiety and a sense of failure (Bond 1986). It is suggested that people suffering from epilepsy are more prone to epileptic fits when in the latter state (Laidlaw & Laidlaw 1984). A sensitive nurse who can identify the signs of under- and overstimulation in a client, and who intervenes appropriately, is setting the right kind of atmosphere in which people can grow emotionally and intellectually.

CEREBRAL PALSY

The term 'cerebral palsy' is used to describe varying disorders of posture and movements, which result from a defect occurring in the motor areas of the developing brain. The clinical picture varies considerably as the disorders present varying levels of muscle tone, involuntary movements and ataxia. Many people with cerebral palsy, in addition to having to cope with the primary defects of motor control, may experience secondary handicaps, such as intellectual impairment, epilepsy, defects of hearing and vision, speech and emotional disruptions.

Causation

The condition may be inherited or arise from factors occurring before, during or after birth. Woods (1969) reported that it is estimated that 5–10% of cerebral palsy is inherited. In other cases, brain cells may be damaged by anoxia, caused by infectious diseases or birth damage. Rubella can cause cerebral palsy in association with blindness, deafness and microcephaly. Chickenpox, cytomegalovirus infection and toxoplasmosis may affect the fetus and account for cerebral palsy in some people. Blood group incompatibility may cause athetosis but this is rare nowadays due to advances in this field.

Postnatal factors include meningitis, encephalitis and direct violence.

Classification

Spasticity

Damage to the cerebral motor cortex causes the most common type of cerebral palsy, namely rigidity of the limbs and an inability to relax the muscle. Damage to other areas of the brain may result in athetosis or ataxia. Hitchcock (1978) reported that it is estimated that 70% of those with cerebral palsy show spasticity. The extent and part of the body involved varies:

- hemiplegia – the arm and leg of one side of the body are affected
- monoplegia – only one arm or leg is affected
- paraplegia – both legs are affected
- quadriplegia – all four limbs are affected
- diplegia – involvement of four limbs with the legs more affected than the arms
- triplegia – involvement of three limbs.

Athetosis

Damage to the basal ganglia causes frequent involuntary movements which interfere markedly with normal movements of the body. These movements may be slow or fast, writhing, jerky from swiping or rotatory patterns, or they may be unpatterned. The involuntary motion is increased by excitement, insecurity and the effort to make a voluntary movement. Factors which decrease athetosis are fatigue, drowsiness, fever, prone lying or the individual's attention being deeply held (Levitt 1983). Hitchcock (1978) reported that approximately 10% of cerebral palsied people show athetosis.

Ataxia

Damage to the cerebellum results in poor body balance, unsteady gait and hand/eye coordination difficulties. According to Hitchcock (1978) approximately 10% of people suffering from cerebral palsy show ataxia.

8) reported that approximately
i͞   ͞ral palsied people present mixed
forms c͞ ͞e above three types. Others may
show different types of muscular tension, such
as dystonia, hypotonia and hypertonia.

Care of the individual with cerebral palsy

Adequate and appropriate treatment depends
on detailed assessment of motor function,
hearing, vision and communication testing,
and psychological testing.

Assessment dictates the approach of care
staff in care and management. The abilities of the
individual are compared with the developmental norm expected of his age group. Failure to
assess and implement a systematic programme
will result in the acquisition of abnormal postures which prevent people with cerebral palsy
from acquiring certain skilled movements. The
orderly development of motor patterns as in
noncerebral palsied individuals fails to take
place. The physical handling of the person with
cerebral palsy, e.g. when helping to eat, dress,
bath and the social interaction, e.g. the way the
person is spoken to and interacted with, should
be seen as part of a systematic programme.

Cerebral palsy is a multifaceted problem and
involves the work of many disciplines, e.g. care
staff, physiotherapists, speech therapists and
parents. Therapy generally aims at improving
coordination of posture and movement and
building up all the basic movement patterns of
head control, turning, sitting, kneeling, standing
and balance. Changes of position both night and
day inhibit the development of pressure sores. A
daily bath is important for skin care and presents
an opportunity for carrying out passive exercise.

Eating

One of the most important basic skills we learn is
the ability to feed ourselves. We need to eat to
live, but we must also, in our society, eat tidily
and presentably if we are to be socially accept-

able. Appropriate eating patterns are important
for the person with cerebral palsy. He must learn
to use tools, e.g. he should at least be able to
manage a spoon, as finger feeding is not socially
acceptable as he gets older. Very often people
with cerebral palsy need specific help to overcome feeding difficulties. The ability to bring
the hand to the mouth, as well as being essential
in feeding oneself, also plays an important part
in developing hand/eye coordination, so vital in
later life for more complex motor skills. In addition, an inability to develop feeding patterns may
cause difficulties with the development of speech.

Helping a person to eat in the reclining
position excludes him from his peer group at
mealtimes and makes him less socially accessible. It also reinforces the extended position. All
individuals with cerebral palsy can be placed in
an upright position for feeding. The extension
spasm is prevented by fully flexing the hips
and bringing the shoulders and arms forward.
If the individual is too large to be held he can
be placed in a special chair that allows full
support for his thighs with his feet on the foot-
rest. The aim is to sit the individual in a position
as near normal as possible with minimum support. A harness and groin straps aid positioning
initially. Various aids are available to prevent
the plate from slipping on the table. The care
staff can sometimes assist the less handicapped
person to learn to feed himself by sitting on his
dominant side and guiding him by supporting
his elbow and correcting the angle as his hand
nears his mouth. If the individual is unable to
feed himself, the staff should allow him time
to look and see the food he is eating; inform
him when food is placed in his mouth so he can
concentrate on it, thus preventing choking and
startle reactions.

Food may be given in small amounts to prevent gag reflex. A wooden spoon is used if the
'bite reflex' is severe. This reflex is stimulated by
touching around the mouth and gums but can be
reduced by stroking those areas during the day.

Pathological tongue thrust

Pathological tongue thrust, or reverse swallowing, is associated with cerebral palsy. Thompson et al (1979) reported that observable tongue thrust in a 10-year-old mentally handicapped male was modified during mealtime using operant conditioning techniques. Their findings suggest that operant conditioning is a desirable alternative to surgical or mechanical procedures in dealing with this problem.

Communication

The person with a mental handicap and associated cerebral palsy often has great difficulty in communicating. He may be unable to control his limbs or communicate his needs in an effective manner to other people. He may have additional handicaps of a sensory nature affecting his perception. These difficulties may give rise to behavioural problems, e.g. aggressive outbursts (Oswin 1967) and learning difficulties. A considerable number of perceptual deficits may occur in children with cerebral palsy. These will have further implications for the person's daily activities and educational performance.

The speech therapist aims to help the individual control the muscles of the lips, tongue and throat in order to learn correct movement. All opportunities to link speech with objects and activities aid development and all spontaneous attempts at verbal imitation are immediately rewarded by praise. Speech therapy is essential to develop and improve communication skills and facilitate interpersonal relations. For the person with a mental handicap who has failed to develop spoken language the use of nonverbal communication techniques as an alternative or supplementary form of communication, is important. Makaton is commonly used in the United Kingdom. This system can be used to facilitate language, can help to develop understanding of lexical and expressive abilities, and is a medium of communication for those with restricted communication potential. A major requirement for its success is that those in contact with the handicapped person, e.g. nurses, must use it if effective communication is to be achieved.

Music, rhythm and melody

This can be an integral part of the person's learning programme. The power of music to soothe, energize and bring people together is universal. The elements of melody, harmony and rhythm contained in musical experience have an appeal for most human beings.

All aspects of human experience and feeling can find expression in music. It is a nonverbal medium which allows the person to respond and channel inner feelings of joy, sadness, aggression and tranquillity. For people who experience communication problems, music can become a real, active and living expression of self and a release from the restrictions that encompass their lives (Nordoff & Robbins 1988). Musical activity and expression encourage the person to use his or her limbs and voice and so they become a means of communication and a way of developing relationships. Attempts at rhythmically moving to musical sound also aid physical coordination.

Physiotherapy

Following assessment, physiotherapy is concerned with improving balance and head/neck control, maintaining joint mobility, preventing contracture and deformities, the use of reflex-inhibiting posture and concentrating on the person's antigravity muscles. The care staff and physiotherapist work very closely in relieving 'spasm'. This can be done at bath time, as warm water relieves spasm, or through the use of a pool which provides relaxation and greater freedom of movement. Another technique to relieve spasm is that of 'shaking' the limbs.

After relieving spasm, both active and passive exercises may be carried out. Various aids, e.g. 'standing frame' and 'walkiepen' are useful in aiming for independence. Balance is taught by reducing support, using the 'tailor sitting' position and using a mirror which allows the person to see himself off-balance.

Temple Fay, a neurosurgeon in Philadelphia, recommends that cerebral palsied children be taught movement according to their development in evolution. Lower animals carried out basic movements of progression; similarly, they can be carried out by humans with cerebral cortex damage. Temple Fay patterning counteracts the asymmetrical tonic reflex posture and can be used to unlock clenched fists and to correct ankles.

Paralytic dislocation of the hip

Hip and spinal deformities may occur in combination. Those most likely to develop hip dislocation are people with severe quadriplegia (Howard et al 1985). Scoliosis may or may not be associated with hip dislocation. Hip dislocation without scoliosis tends to occur between the ages of 3 and 11 years (Cooke et al 1989). Scoliosis with hip dislocation may occur up to 18 years of age. The later the dislocation the more likely it is to be associated with athetosis (Cooke et al 1989). Samilson et al (1972) reviewed 1013 institutionalized patients, most of whom were unable to walk, and found hip dislocation or subluxations in 28%. This condition can be prevented by surgery but Moreau et al (1979) found that surgical treatment for already dislocated hips is reserved in many cases for the neurologically mature and athetoid patient.

Surgery

Orthopaedic surgery may be used to assist walking by lengthening the Achilles tendon, and stabilization of joints may be achieved by arthrodesis. Neurosurgery, e.g. hemispherectomy, may alleviate associated epilepsy. Hitchcock (1978) reported that stereotactic surgery, which involves destruction of parts of the basal ganglia, may achieve a reduction in involuntary movement and alleviate articulation problems.

Drugs

Muscle relaxants, e.g. diazepam, may be used but large doses cause side effects, such as drowsiness. Excess salivation may be reduced by drugs such as benzhexol. Associated epilepsy is controlled by anticonvulsants.

Coping behaviour of families

Investigations have shown how families cope with the varying difficulties that handicap can present (Schilling et al 1985). The importance of social support for families has been highlighted (Brandt 1984). The positive effects of parent support groups composed mainly of mothers with disabled children have been studied by Haggerty (1980) and Mardiros (1982).

Byrne & Cunningham (1985) indicate that mothers in families with a handicapped child carry the major burden. Areas documented in a long term follow-up study of cerebral palsy children and coping behaviour of parents by Hirose & Ueda (1990) include the feelings, thoughts and actions of parents at the time their children were diagnosed as having cerebral palsy; the crisis periods in raising the children; the important persons who supported the parents during the acceptance phase and the role of mothers and fathers in raising the children.

STEREOTYPED BEHAVIOUR

This type of repetitious behaviour is characteristic of individuals with a severe mental handicap (Ingalls 1978). It is ritualistic and has no apparent adaptive purpose. Common examples of stereotyped behaviour include innocuous rocking, rolling of the head, jumping up and down, twirling of the fingers in front of the eyes, flapping of the arms and picking at oneself. Extreme forms include slapping of the face, banging of the head, biting of fingers or hands and poking of the eyes.

Theories

Various theories have been suggested to explain this type of behaviour. It may be related to boredom or sensory deprivation. People with severe mental handicap living in institutions lack adequate stimulation in their environment and resort to stereotyped behaviour (Ingalls 1978) Berkson & Mason (1964) give evidence of stereotyped behaviour in chimpanzees who were deprived of the opportunity to interact with other chimpanzees. Forehand & Baumeister (1970) showed that with increased stimulation the frequency of the stereotyped behaviour decreased. Other theories include explanations that stereotyped behaviour increases if the individual is frustrated (Hollis 1971) or deprived of the opportunity for adequate exercise (Levy 1944).

Behavioural approaches

The use of behavioural approaches in the modification of stereotyped behaviour is a useful contribution to the management of people with severe mental handicap displaying such behaviour. Young & Clements (1979) have indicated the importance of the behavioural approach in stereotyped behaviour. However, in extreme forms of stereotyped behaviour, it is very important to check that there is not in fact some clear reason related, for example, to skin irritation or general irritation, in the area that is being injured. The choice of a particular approach is dependent upon the individual and his situation. The reason why a child does what he does must be considered when choosing a means of management if a successful outcome is to be achieved (Cullen et al 1977).

Various behavioural techniques are used in an attempt to modify stereotyped behaviour, for example:

- withdrawing of social rewards
- rewarding alternatives to the problem behaviour
- over-correction
- aversion – which must be administered under certain controlled conditions
- time-out – which must be carefully monitored.

HYPERKINETIC SYNDROME

Hyperkinesis, overactivity, hyperactive behaviour are descriptive terms indicating patterns of abnormal behaviour in childhood. This condition of motor unrest can be a symptom of great disruption within the family, giving rise to pressure, stress and disarray in the home. The child, in his pursuit of constant lively attention can, in some cases, cause the breakup of the family unit.

In our everyday existence it can be argued that restlessness is a symptom of boredom and detailed concentration can result from challenge and interest. The pathological implications of overactivity can be seen in the field of psychiatry. Overactivity, associated with mood elevation, is a distressing and upsetting feature of mania; restless, violent, impulsive and unpredictable behaviour is a result of catatonic excitement in schizophrenia; restlessness and irrational behaviour often present themselves in delirium as a result of acute organic disorders.

Corbett (1975) reported that hyperkinesis may overlap epilepsy and is common in mentally handicapped people. In association with behaviour problems, perceptual and conceptual difficulties are likely to be encountered. The syndrome is characterised by several types of behaviours:

- hyperactivity
- distractibility
- short attention span
- impulsiveness
- temper tantrums
- destructiveness
- aggressiveness.

Hyperactivity

The hyperactive child wanders about in an apparently purposeless manner and appears to be unable to control the degree of reaction to a given situation. Care staff aim to channel this behaviour into socially acceptable pursuits. Recreational and leisure pursuits, such as music, mime, drama and sporting activities, can be constructed as positive responses to frantic, aimless, noisy and destructive behaviour.

Distractibility

One interpretation of hyperkinetic behaviour sees the child as being unable to filter important and unimportant details in his environment. He is bombarded by the constant activity emerging from the surroundings and trivial background details emerge to compete for his attention. He perceives only parts of the whole situation and is sidetracked and distracted in an attempt to try to deal with all stimuli in his environment. Individual attention in small family units is considered desirable in setting realistic goals that avoid frustration. Care staff need to manipulate the environment to effect learning.

Short attention span

A short attention span causes difficulty in concentration and interferes with learning programmes. From adequate assessment, a clear understanding of what the child can do can assist the care staff in identifying potential and allowing for limitations. A quiet room is desirable and distractions must be minimized, as excessive stimuli tend to make the child over excited and impulsive. A planned sequence is used in a teaching programme, as structured and concrete planning reduce the need for excess control. Toys, clothing and furniture should be strong and durable, as fragility may invite destruction.

Impulsiveness

As people develop and mature, they progress to controlled behaviour from emotional functioning. As they progress they develop a checking mechanism that allows inhibition of impulses. The person with hyperkinetic behaviour is often unable to do this and, consequently, overreacts emotionally sometimes in a panic-type reaction.

Temper tantrums

Difficulty in perceiving the environment and paying attention can cause frustration in the child and he may react in an explosive outburst, such as a temper tantrum. Ignoring the incident may work; he learns that such behaviour does not produce what he wants. If it occurs in situations where ignoring it is not possible, such as crowds of people, removal to a quiet situation may be appropriate. It is important to remain calm and in control of emotions if such an incident arises.

Destructiveness

The child is often attracted by stimuli and is prone to touch many objects, overexplore, mishandle or cause breakages. A patient and consistent approach is important in handling him. Attitudes towards him must be firm and supportive.

Aggressiveness

This child may be aggressive to siblings, parents and care staff without provocation. He needs help in constructing his behavioural boundaries. Care staff need to teach him what is, and what is not, acceptable. Rules regarding acceptable and nonacceptable behaviour give him security, and allow attainable behavioural goals to be set for him.

Treatment

Improvement in the behaviour of some severely disturbed children by the administration of amphetamine drugs has been widely described, particularly in the United States of America, but the long-term beneficial effects are questionable (Shaffer 1977). In addition, considerable objections have been raised about the use of amphetamines in view of the problem of drug dependency. Winsberg et al (1972) reported that imipramine, a tricyclic antidepressant, had received favourable mention in reducing overactivity.

Major tranquillizers, e.g. thioridazine, from the phenothiazine group, and haloperidol, from the butyrophenone group, are sometimes used in controlling the syndrome. Lithium carbonate is used by some doctors, especially if associated with mood disturbance, as in mania (Cantwell 1977). As in epilepsy, the use of drugs for hyperkinesis is not to treat a specific illness but to control symptoms. There has been extensive and optimistic literature on the use of operant conditioning techniques in the treatment of children with hyperkinesis. Christensen (1975) has advocated a token reinforcement programme as a viable alternative to the use of stimulant drugs in mentally handicapped people. Perhaps the best approach is to view each of the methods of treatment as options that can be used either singly or in combination to deal with the problems of each individual.

Diet

Dietary factors have been examined as potential causes or contributing factors especially sugar, food additives and preservatives, caffeine and chocolate.

In 1977, the West German government became alarmed at the effects of food additives on its youth. Many cases were reported, indicating that unruly and hyperkinetic behaviour were preceded by ingestion of food additives (Dieter 1978). There were also indications that these same additives produced learning difficulties.

In some children diet, toxic metals, food additives and food allergies were shown to contribute to hyperkinetic behaviour (Schauss 1980).

AUTISM

This disorder was first described by Kanner in 1943. He described the outstanding features as a lack of response to other people, a delay in the acquisition of speech and an insistence on the preservation of sameness in the environment. Population based studies (Lotter 1966, Wing & Gould 1979, Gillberg 1980, 1984, Bohman et al 1983, Steffenburgh & Gillberg 1986) indicate figures of 4.0–6.7 per 10 000 children. There appears to be no major difference in frequency between urban and rural areas. Boys outweigh girls at a ratio of 1.4:4.8 (Lotter 1966, Brask 1970, Steinhausen & Brienlinger 1986).

Omenn (1973) argues that high boy/girl ratio in a given medical condition favours a biological cause, presumably genetic or partially genetic.

Studies indicate that the great majority of autistic children are also mentally handicapped (Clark & Rutter 1979).

Between half and two-thirds of all autistic children are severely mentally handicapped with IQs below 50 (Carr 1976). A majority of those with autism have an 'islet' of special ability which does not signal underlying superior talent but is rather the only intact area of mental functioning in the otherwise highly deviant child (Shah & Frith 1983).

Associations between epilepsy and autism have been reviewed by Coleman & Gillberg (1987) and they conclude that an association does exist but that there have been insufficient scientific studies as to the nature of the relationship.

Autism is a feature of certain disorders affecting half of those with tuberous sclerosis and around 10% of those with fragile X syndrome. Creak (1961) classified the behavioural characteristics of autism into a 9-point scale and Clancy et al (1969) extended the scale, listing 14 behavioural symptoms indicative of the condition. He indicated that if seven or more of these were present, autism should be considered:

- stand-offish manner, communicates very little with other people; treats them as objects rather than people
- great difficulty in mixing and playing with other children
- strong resistance to any learning of new behaviour or skills
- resists change in routine
- acts as if deaf
- no eye contact
- repetitive and sustained odd play
- not cuddly as a baby
- unusual attachment to particular objects
- marked physical overactivity
- spins objects, especially round ones
- prefers to indicate needs by gesture
- lack of fear about realistic dangers
- laughs and giggles for no apparent reason.

Rutter (1970) formulated his four essential points:

1. delayed and deviant language development which has certain defined features and is out of keeping with the child's intellectual level
2. impaired social development which has a

number of special characteristics and is out of keeping with the child's intellectual level
3. insistence on sameness, as shown by stereotyped play patterns, abnormal preoccupations, or resistance to change
4. onset before the age of 30 months.

The autistic child, behaviourally, is characterized by extreme withdrawal and little interest in people. It is likely to be a lifelong handicap with profound effects on the person's ability to relate. He shows an inability to concentrate on anybody or anything. He cannot tolerate emotional demands and is unable to offer an emotional response. In order to help him, care staff aim to communicate with him to build a relationship with him. Contact is the foundation of a relationship and all use is made of any means available to do this. Withdrawn children may enjoy playing with or in water. They enjoy the texture and sound of sand trickling through their fingers; such activities create the opportunity to join in and play with the child. Rhythmical movements may offer the autistic child a satisfying outlet; rocking and swinging offer the communicator a chance to break through to his inner world. Music may elicit a response and offer the chance of singing a tune or playing a musical instrument. These simple approaches allow the formation of a channel of communication. The child will avoid any situation that makes demands of him so making use of his ritualistic mannerisms allows an opportunity to experience and share. We must create an environment that is undemanding for him and offers a warm and accepting climate. His eccentricities must be accepted and his concepts of normality and reality not reinforced. Close observation of his obsessional and bizarre behaviour will often indicate that he is telling us more by his actions than he could ever consciously communicate in words.

Other people, including care staff, are themselves the most important aid to communication for the autistic child. They communicate by word, gesture, eye contact and expression. Patience, understanding and good humour are essential assets in doing so. They may be the child's only link with reality: the bond between his fantasy worlds and the real world. They create the situations in the environment which allow the child to become more aware of himself and other people. His emergence into the real world, if at all, is slow. He can quickly withdraw into his private world but the aim is to extend his level of participation. Much ingenuity is required to make use of the child's own motivational systems and the ability to rely on normal praise and social reward as communication is established is very important. Ferster and De Meyer (1961, 1962) demonstrated the efficiency of the operant conditioning of nonverbal responses with autistic children. Nelson and Evans (1968) showed that the amalgamation of speech therapy techniques and operant conditioning principles can have some success.

MENTAL ILLNESS

Estimates of the incidence of mental illness in people with a mental handicap have varied widely over the last 20 years. Heaton-Ward (1977) produced a figure of 10% among patients in mental handicap hospitals, while other surveys suggest a figure of up to 60% (Jancar 1988). The Office of Population Censuses and Surveys (1976) stated that 25% of adults and 5% of children in hospital had behavioural problems serious enough to be regarded as such by professionals, and identified anxiety states, manic depressive disorders, obsessional neuroses and organic confusional states amongst the most common presenting conditions, while Day's (1985) work with long-stay hospital residents over the age of 40 years revealed that 30% exhibited signs of significant psychiatric disorder. Today, these figures are likely to be a gross underestimation, with only those individuals who have the most disabling conditions being retained in hospitals.

What seems clear from such figures is that it is difficult to compile statistics on the prevalence of mental illness in people with a mental handicap because diagnosis is problematic due to communication difficulties (Russell 1987). The mental handicapping condition may result in distorted images of self, crises of confidence and negative public attitudes, leading to rejection, segregation and isolation. These experiences may predispose to the development of mental illness. But it is also important to recognize that the strains and stressors of complex societal demands which affect millions of people may adversely affect people with mental handicap to a greater extent; appreciation of this fact will enable nurses to consider the mental health of their clients as integrally linked to individual and general environmental and emotional factors.

Goldberg et al (1970) established a method using the standardized psychiatric interview for use in community studies. Ballinger et al (1975) showed that the modified version of Goldberg's standardized interview for use with the mentally handicapped was valid, reliable and applicable.

Affective psychoses

These are disorders where the primary disturbance is that of affect or mood. The term 'mood' refers to the existing emotional make-up which affects the person's total experience and outlook. The disorders consist of depression and mania. Both are usually classed together as manic depressive disease of pathological origin or bipolar affective disorder. Any sequence of depression and mania can occur, but depression is more common than mania. Many residents have depression only and, even in people who have both, depressive episodes are the more frequent. It may be that some unipolar cases represent an entity distinct from bipolar cases. Unipolar affective disorders are disorders where the person has either mania or depression (one pole). Bipolar is where the person's mood is likely to swing from one extreme (mania) to the other extreme, depression, sometimes within a few months.

Manic depressive psychoses associated with mental handicap have been studied for many years. Kraepelin (1896) indicated that 'imbecility may form the basis for the development of other psychoses, such as manic depressive insanity'. Rohan (1936), in his description of 36 mentally handicapped people, some suffering from affective psychoses, indicated that accompanying delusions tended to be grandiose and expansive.

Penrose (1938), Hayman (1939), Herskovitz & Plesset (1941) indicated that the more severely mental handicapped showed fewer typical features of psychoses. Prevalence rates for inpatient populations range from 6% found by Penrose in 1938, 1.2% by Reid in 1982 and 1.2% quoted by Heaton-Ward in 1977. This compares with 3-4 per 1000 of the general population (Hamilton 1980). In mental handicapped outpatient populations, Neustadt (1928) found 8% and Craft (1958) quoted 6%. Corbett in 1979 carried out a detailed study of all mentally handicapped individuals over 15 years of age in Camberwell attending mental handicap services. He indicated a prevalence rate of 1.5% for bipolar affective psychoses and 2% for depressive illness.

Sovner & Hurley (1983) concluded that people with mental handicaps can experience the full range of disorders which are seen in people without such handicaps.

Depression

There are few people who have not experienced some state of depression. In some, the symptoms are trivial and disappear quickly; in others the symptoms persist and are so severe that they affect the person's ability to cope.

Psychological features. The resident looks sad, preoccupied, self-concerned and tired. He is fatigued and suffers loss of energy. His facial expression may be distressed, tormented or may show little or no emotion. Dysphoria is a feature. He loses interest and withdraws: everything looks gloomy and hopeless. Psychomotor activity is inhibited—movement is slow and dragging; speech is slow and monotonous; there is poverty of thought and lack of concentration. Diurnal variation, suicidal tendencies and delusions of guilt about his moral worth may be experienced; also hypochondriacal delusions regarding his bodily health, delusions of poverty pertaining to financial worries, and paranoid delusions in relation to interpersonal relationships and social status. Hallucinations are rare but may be limited to reproaching voices; agitation and stupor when they occur cause added difficulties.

Physical features

- insomnia – variations of sleep disorder occur. It may be marked at the beginning, middle or latter part of the night
- change in weight, usually anorexia and loss of weight, though weight gain sometimes occurs
- constipation is common and may be linked to hypochondriasis
- palpitations and tight feelings in the chest
- amenorrhoea in women
- progressive retardation of thought processes and activity may lead to a depressive stupor, with no response to stimuli.

A number of factors may cause difficulties in identifying depression in people with mental handicaps:

- difficulties in communication
- distinguishing the effects of the underlying brain damage from the symptoms of depression.

Many mentally handicapped people have communication difficulties and may lack the ability to describe a mood of depression; lack of verbal skills can lead to difficulties in diagnosis (Pawlarcyzk & Beckwith 1987). Depressive symptoms may be masked behind a statement, such as 'I'm very fed up', or acted out in aggressive or agitated states of behaviour. Kielholz (1973) indicated that the more handicapped the person, the more likely is his depressive illness to be 'masked'.

Reid (1982) indicated that disturbance of sleep, appetite, bowel habits, headaches, abdominal pain, hysterical fits, bizarre gaits and persistent attention-seeking hypochondria may indicate depression without having to rely on the subjective reporting of depressed mood. Underlying brain damage in people with a mental handicap can modify the effects of otherwise characteristic symptoms of mental illness (Menolascino 1974).

A major caring problem in dealing with a person who is depressed is suicide. When a person is feeling hopeless and helpless he may consider this option. Reid (1982) reported that suicide and attempted suicide are not unknown among people who are mentally handicapped.

Often the suicide attempt is ineffective and may contain an element of plea, though all attempts should be treated very seriously.

Care and management. Early identification of the condition is an important feature in caring for the person with learning difficulties; the nurse may have to depend solely on observation of physical appearance and behaviour changes. Facial representations of mood states, such as immobility or frequent crying, combined with behaviours, such as difficulty in getting to sleep or waking up early in the morning, may constitute signs of a depressed mood.

A very depressed person needs close observation and the care and management of a skilled, tolerant, sympathetic and understanding staff.

Establishing a therapeutic relationship may involve indicating to the patient that you appreciate his difficulties, understand his problems, are interested in what happens to him and that he can trust you. The act of remaining with the person gives him emotional support though outwardly he may not show this by his apparent lack of interest and uncommunicativeness.

A balance should be struck between offering the person a secure and safe environment and allowing the person the freedom of movement and privacy that other nondepressed people experience. An environment should be created by care staff that allows for close observation (bearing in mind suicidal tendencies) and permits moderately stimulating surroundings. Basic observation must include knowing the level of depression, where he is and what he is doing without necessarily being constantly at the person's side.

Drugs. People with depression may be prescribed antidepressant drugs which return the abnormally depressed mood towards its usual state. It is the nurse's duty to administer these drugs in the correct dose, to the correct patient, at the correct time. There are two main groups of antidepressants:

- *Tricyclic* group, e.g. imipramine or amitriptyline
- *Mono-amine oxidase inhibitors* (MAOI), e.g. phenelzine.

Tricyclic group. The tricyclic group appears to be safer, i.e. it causes less severe side effects and is more widely used. Their pharmacological action is to increase the concentration of nor-adrenaline at receptor sites, inhibiting the reuptake of released noradrenaline. They start producing an effect after 7–14 days. They also have some sedative effect, thus easing the agitation experienced in some depressions.

Side effects include those due to:

- its effect on noradrenaline. It is potentiated by, or potentiates, other drugs which increase the concentration of amines, hence there is a risk of hypertensive crisis, excitability and excess body temperature if they are combined with:
  - mono-amine oxidase inhibitors
  - amphetamines.
- its anticholinergic or atropine-like properties, e.g. dry mouth, constipation, blurred vision, urinary retention, tachycardia and difficulty in micturition.

Care must be taken with elderly people who have benign prostatic hypertrophy and patients suffering from glaucoma, as these drugs can cause a further increase in intraocular pressure.

Usually, these drugs are well tolerated and Reid (1982) indicates that a dosage level of 100–200 mg per day of amitriptyline or imipramine, in divided doses, is in an acceptable range.

Mono-amine oxidase inhibitors. The mono-amine oxidase inhibitors are probably less frequently used because of the danger of more problematical side effects. Their pharmacological action is to inhibit the enzyme mono-amine oxidase which aids the breakdown of noradrenaline, causing an increase in the noradrenaline concentration at the nerve endings. These drugs produce an antidepressant effect which takes 2–4 weeks to have optimal effect.

Side effects can arise as a result of an increase in amine concentration, e.g. the risk of hypertensive crisis with a risk of subarachnoid haemorrhage. The patient complains of a severe throbbing headache and vomiting. This is especially likely where:

- the person takes substances, e.g. amphetamines,

adrenaline, isoprenaline, ephedrine or procaine, which liberate noradrenaline at the sympathetic nerve endings
- the person takes foodstuffs rich in certain amines, e.g. cheese, wines, beer, yeast, bovril and marmite. They contain tyramine which is normally broken down by MAO in the liver but in the absence of MAO it is absorbed into the bloodstream. It is essential to issue the patient with a card containing a list of foods to be omitted on it and to notify those involved in the preparation of their food
- the person takes MAOI, in combination with tricyclic antidepressants.

If the depression is severe, electroconvulsive therapy (ECT) may be prescribed as antidepressant drugs may take a considerable time to act or are ineffective. Drugs may then be used to prevent a relapse. Reid (1982) indicates caution in using ECT in mentally handicapped people because of the high prevalence rate of structural brain abnormality, unless the indications are imperative.

Mania

Clinical features. Mania is the pathological elevation of mood with euphoric excitement which makes a person especially cheerful and optimistic. Behaviour is in a manner compatible with feelings. The person is overactive and very restless; all inhibitions disappear. He may be domineering, arrogant and reject control. Irritability with a quick temper and anger may suddenly manifest itself. Lability of affect with interchange of cheerfulness, suspicion and irritability occurs. He can be aggressive, destructive, tactless and extravagant. He is often easily distracted and has a short concentration span. There is pressure of speech and flight of ideas. Delusions of grandeur and an attitude of superiority are often in evidence. There is lack of insight with impaired judgement and foresight.

Reid (1982) indicates that elevation of mood and overactivity may be poorly sustained in mentally handicapped people and some lability is common; restlessness may be severe. Components of the following may be in evidence:

- irritability
- excitability
- impulsiveness leading to assaultive behaviour
- delusions and hallucinations appropriate to the mood, but often naive, grandiose and wish-fulfilling
- hysterical symptoms
- sexual disinhibition.

Care and management.   The emphasis here is on the creation of a quiet, controlled and un-stimulating environment. The care staff need a blend of patience, kindness, firmness, good humour, tolerance and tact in caring for this person. Close observation is needed to protect him from exhaustion and from injury, both to himself and others. Supervision of personal hygiene and encouragement of adequate amounts of food and fluid intake, and channelling the person's activities into nondestructive behaviour, are all important aspects of care.

Drugs.   Major tranquillizers of the phenothiazine group, e.g. chlorpromazine, or of the butyrophenone group, e.g. haloperidol, are used in the treatment of mania. They are readily absorbed and have a rapid onset of action; this allows a quick control of manic overactivity. Craft & Schiff (1980) indicate that they are well tolerated in mentally handicapped people, but side effects may be more obvious because of the existing brain damage. The care staff must observe carefully for any side effects. Dosage is measured against response and side effects. Reid (1982) advises 100–400 mg of chlorpromazine per day in divided doses and haloperidol 5–15 mg per day in divided doses. Larger doses may be required in acute manic states but as mania subsides the tolerance disappears.

Lithium carbonate is used in the treatment of mania but it takes 10 days before acting. It is often combined with haloperidol or chlorpromazine in the early stages. Blood serum levels are checked every 5 days to ensure that the optimal therapeutic level of 0.6–1 mmol/l is not surpassed. The dose is varied according to the need of the individual, but the average daily divided dose of lithium is between 1000–1200 mg. Side effects can be very serious and include nausea, vomiting, diarrhoea, tremor of the hands, polyuria, polydipsia, weight gain, oedema, sleepiness, vertigo, dysarthria and occasionally hypothyroid goitre.

Schizophrenia

Schizophrenia is a disabling and misunderstood mental disorder. The term 'schizophrenia' was introduced in 1911 by a Swiss psychiatrist, Eugen Bleuler, to describe what he considered to be a group of severe mental illnesses with related characteristics. Schizophrenia replaced the earlier term, 'dementia praecox', which was first used in 1899 by a German psychiatrist Emil Kraepelin to distinguish the illness from manic depressive psychosis.

Schizophrenia describes a variety of psychotic disorders affecting thought, perception, emotion and behaviour.

Prevalence.   Among residents in a mental handicap hospital, Penrose (1938) reported 3%, Craft (1958) 4% and Heaton-Ward (1977) 3.4%, suffering from schizophrenia. In the Camberwell survey of adults with a mental handicap in hospital and in the community Corbett (1979) reported a prevalence rate of 3.5%. Other surveys of inpatient populations of mental handicap hospitals in the UK have come up with prevalence rates of around 3.5% (Reid 1985).

Clinical features.   These include:

1. Thought disorder – thought blocking where the train of thought suddenly stops and a completely new one begins. Speech ranges from vague woolliness to incoherence with neologisms. Echolalia – repetition of the spoken word – occurs. Flight of ideas may be in evidence.
2. A delusion is a false or irrational belief that is firmly held despite obvious or objective evidence to the contrary. Delusions may be of a religious, paranoid, sexual or hypochondriacal nature.
3. Hallucinations, false sensory perceptions (especially auditory) that are experienced

without an external stimulus but are 'real' to the person concerned, can occur. However, any type of hallucination, i.e. visual and, less commonly, tactile, olfactory, bodily, gustatory, may occur. Voices may be hostile, abusive, critical, directive, or reassuring. Noises and sounds that are associated with machines may be heard.

4. Abnormalities of affect; flattening of affect, emotional blunting with coldness and loss of finer feelings. Incongruity of affect is when the emotional response is not appropriate to the situation, e.g. laughing during a funeral.
5. Disturbance of volition; lack of drive and initiative; negativism.
6. Disturbance of movement with strange mannerisms, grimacing, posturing – called catatonia.
7. Disorders of behaviour—tics, disturbed, unpredictable, destructive, impulsive and aggressive behaviour may manifest itself.

Types

Simple. The simple type begins insidiously in late adolescence or early adult life. There is a gradual deterioration, with indifference, shallowness of emotional response and loss of drive. Thought disorder is prominent; social deterioration occurs. Earl (1961) and Shapiro (1979) maintain that this type of schizophrenia is particularly common. Reid (1982) and Heaton-Ward (1977) state that it is often difficult to identify such an ill-defined illness in people with a severe mental handicap.

Hebephrenic. The onset of this type is between 15–25 years, with a less insidious onset and more florid characteristics. Thought disorder, incongruity of affect, volitional disorder and disorganization of the whole personality occurs.

Catatonic. The onset of this type is between 15–40 years, with sudden onset. Features may include catatonic stupor, in which the person becomes completely withdrawn from outside stimulation and adopts strange postures, and catatonic excitement, where he is very restless, impulsive, unpredictable and often violent. Echolalia, echopraxia, and rituals may occur.

Paranoid. The paranoid type tends to occur later in life, after the age of 30 years, but it can occur earlier. Persecutory delusions and auditory hallucinations are prominent. Disturbance of thinking, feeling and volition, and mannerisms may occur though in some much of their already established personality is relatively unaffected.

Care and management. Care and management may be based on a systematic nursing approach using the stages of assessment, planning, action and evaluation. Although there is a wide variety of problems experienced by people who have schizophrenia there are common responses nurses can make aimed at helping the person deal with them. Building up consistent and constructive interpersonal relationships with the person with schizophrenia involves the acceptance that the person's interpretation of the external world may be different from others who are not affected by schizophrenia.

Care staff must not attempt to dissuade him in his beliefs but acknowledge that they simply do not share them. The staff must accept his behaviour, however antisocial, disturbed or degraded, as representing his sense of reality. Disruptive or dangerous behaviour, however, must be checked, though without conveying any sense of rejection to the person. Care must be geared to increasing the person's personal identity and degree of responsibility, to maintaining a stimulating environment, and to creating an individual programme of care using a systematic nursing approach.

A major goal of the care programme may be to increase the person's previous level of interaction with his environment. Recreational and occupational activities are important aspects of this programme. He should spend part of each day in gainful employment or at recreational and occupational tasks that are rewarding and fulfilling to him.

Another goal of the care programme may be to lessen the feelings of paranoia. The delusional and hallucinatory world may convey to the person that he is being poisoned. This can result in refusal of food. The carers need to find out what the person's motive is for refusing food. He may reject food from some members of staff and accept it from others. If offered a selection of food, he may select some items. He may eat if the carers also eat the food. It may be necessary to allow him to prepare his own food, or to provide him with items which cannot be tampered with, such as tinned foods. The person may only accept fluids so frequent drinks of milk, Complan or other such foods will help to ensure adequate nourishment.

The person may be urged by auditory hallucinations to act aggressively. An aggressive outburst is disturbing not only for the carers but also for the person, as he is often afraid of his own aggression. The creation of a relaxed, friendly atmosphere where the person feels secure and accepted is important. A satisfactory relationship allows anticipation of an aggressive outburst as each person has his own way of showing tension. Mutual trust and respect are prerequisites to effective communication which is essential when dealing with situations that anger the person or that he perceives as hostile.

Drugs. The phenothiazine group of tranquillizing drugs has been a major advance in controlling schizophrenic behaviour. Chlorpromazine and thioridazine are commonly used. The longer-acting, injectable preparations, e.g. fluphenazine deconate and flupenthixol, have a useful role to play. Reid (1982) reported that butyrophenones have also been used in the treatment of schizophrenia with varying success.

The use of tranquillizer drugs in the treatment of schizophrenia can also cause unpleasant side effects. These include skin photosensitivity, blood dyscrasias, liver disorders, dystonic reactions, parkinsonism, rigidity, akathisia and oculogyric crises. Tardive dyskinesia, a syndrome of repetitive involuntary movements affecting the mouth, lips, tongue, trunk or extremities, develops in up to 25% of people receiving long-term treatment with antipsychotic drugs, and there is at present no effective treatment for this complication.

If the person refuses his medication, gentle persuasion may succeed in encouraging him to take the drug. It should be explained that the medication is to help his symptoms. Care must be taken to ensure that the person has, in fact, swallowed the tablets. If he refuses to take tablets, he may take an elixir of the drug. If not, the drug may need to be administered by injection.

Criminal behaviour. The criminal behaviour of individuals with schizophrenia in Sweden was investigated using data from the Central Police Register (Lindqvist & Allebeck 1990). People treated for schizophrenia who were discharged from hospital in Stockholm in 1971 were followed for 15 years. The authors found that the crime rate among men was almost the same as that in the general male population, whereas for women it was twice that of the general female population. The rate of violent offences was four times higher than the general population.

In a less sophisticated study based on a case-note review, Buckley et al (1990) found that of 698 schizophrenic patients studied over a 5 year period, only 19% had performed a serious physical assault since the onset of their illness. The majority of these patients were psychotic at the time of these violent episodes, with delusions and command hallucinations being of clear relevance in 30% of cases.

ORGANIC REACTIONS

Organic reactions are found in those conditions characterized by some abnormality of structure or function of the brain. Structural brain pathology is common among mentally handicapped people (Reid 1982). These reactions are conventionally divided into two groups, the acute form, called delirium, and the chronic type, called dementia. In the acute form the symptoms are reversible if the underlying condition can be corrected. In the chronic group the conditions tend to be irreversible so that paramount damage to the central nervous system may result.

Delirium

This is usually a short-lived, reversible disorder of cerebral function; as the cause is treated so the confusion tends to disappear. It is characterized by clouding of consciousness and impairment of perception of the environment, with disorientation. The person's memory of recent events is impaired; illusions and hallucinations may occur, with impulsive and disturbed behaviour. It is difficult to engage his attention; his concentration is impaired; he is apprehensive and restless. Physical symptoms, such as perspiration, dehydration, tachycardia, and chest and renal complications, may be in evidence and fits can occur. There is nothing distinctive about delirious reactions in people with learning difficulties. Many such people suffer from structural brain abnormality and it may be that, as a result, delirium is particularly readily provoked in them (Reid 1982). The treatment of delirium is the removal of the underlying cause. The restlessness may be treated by drugs such as chlorpromazine or chlormethiazole.

Care is aimed at preventing confusion in a familiar environment with familiar staff; orientation of the person to his environment helps to reduce disorientation. Adequate diet with sufficient fluids and relief of constipation and urinary retention is essential. Nutritional and fluid balance need to be carefully observed and accurately recorded.

Dementia

Dementia is a disease which is becoming more common: it has been suggested that the incidence of dementia between the years 1975 and 2000 could increase by 54% in the developed regions of the world, and by 123% in the less developed regions (Kraemer 1980).

While dementia can present in a number of forms and a variety of age groups (Table 6.1), the only uniquely distinctive feature about dementia in relation to people with mental handicap is the great increase in the incidence of Alzheimer's disease found in people with Down syndrome. Thase (1982) found 45% of Down syndrome subjects had signs of Alzheimer's disease after the age of 45, while it has also been suggested that virtually all affected individuals who die after the age of 40 years show neuropathological changes indicative of Alzheimer's disease (Malamud 1972).

Alzheimer's disease is a progressive, degenerative illness characterized histologically by the presence of plaques (neuritic plaques containing a core of amyloid protein) and tangles (neurofibrillary tangles) found in the neocortex and hippocampus of the brain (Yates 1986). Typically, the sufferer demonstrates a gradual deterioration in intellectual and physical function; his abilities to problem-solve, to understand environmental stimuli and to remember (initially) events from the recent past and ultimately events from throughout life gradually diminish. Change in personality has been reported, with previously compliant individuals becoming stubborn and argumentative, and vice versa (Jacques 1988).

The disease is usually accompanied by a

Table 6.1 Examples of types of dementia

Disease	Type of damage	Treatment	Prognosis
Alzheimer's disease	Senile plaques, neurofibrillary tangles	Symptomatic	Gradual deterioration (1–10 years)
Multi-infarct	Brain infarcts	Symptomatic	Episodic deterioration
Tay-Sach's	Genetic	Symptomatic	Rapid deterioration (0–4 years)
Normal pressure hydrocephalus	Physical	Insertion of ventricular shunt	Improvement after treatment
Wilson's disease	Toxic damage	Chelating agent (penicillamine)	Improvement after treatment
Alchohol-related	Toxic damage	Abstinence	Moderate–good improvement after abstinence
Multiple sclerosis	Damage to white matter	Symptomatic	Gradual–rapid deterioration
General paralysis of the insane	Syphilis infection	Penicillin	Treatment has potential benefits even in advanced cases
AIDS dementia	Cortical atrophy, ventricular enlargement	Symptomatic	Gradual–rapid deterioration

parallel diminution in physical capabilities, reduced concentration span and restless wandering. A reduction in food intake, with subsequent weight loss and general health problems, is also characteristic. The course can be slow and gradual but more commonly there is a fairly rapid deterioration towards death; Bergman et al (1978) noted a 30% mortality rate within one year of initial diagnosis, with 70% requiring institutional care within the same time span.

Diagnosis is not straightforward; research suggests that doctors overdiagnose the condition (Homer 1988), with other forms of dementia, acute confusional states, pseudodementia (a form of depression found predominately in the elderly) and AIDS being mistaken for Alzheimer's disease. Tests are carried out to exclude infections, mental illness, cancers, constipation, anaemias, fluid and electrolyte imbalances, diabetes and other conditions which can mimic its presentation (Rabins 1985).

The link with Down syndrome has been the source of much research over the years. The mode of development of Alzheimer's disease is still unclear; postulation ranges from inheritance (Matsuyana et al 1985) through heavy metal poisoning (Bartus 1986) to viral infection (Greutzner 1988) and, indeed, all three may well be active to greater or lesser degrees. The evidence for the link with Down syndrome is predominately histological, with examination of brain tissue of Down syndrome people even from the age of 30 showing neuritic plaques and neurofibrillary tangles (Matsuyana et al 1985). Controversy exists, however, over whether these histological changes actually produce the emotional, intellectual and behavioural disturbances typical of Alzheimer's disease. Arie (1985) asserts that 'almost all' individuals with Down syndrome who live beyond the age of 35 develop the clinical, as well as the neuropathological, features of Alzheimer's disease, and demonstrated that six out of seven of the subjects over 50 years he investigated had changes in behaviour and intellectual functioning indicative of dementia. But Ropper and Williams (1980) suggest that neuropathological changes at postmortem are not necessarily consistent with clinical features in life; it seems possible that a 'critical number' of plaques and tangles must be present before clinical signs become manifest. Such controversies, allied to the difficulties presented by diagnosis, suggest that debate and speculation about the link between Down syndrome and Alzheimer's disease will persist for some time.

Care and management. There is as yet no drug therapy which will arrest or inhibit the progress of Alzheimer's disease, so management is geared towards helping the individual and his family cope with the devastating effects of the illness.

Understanding of the abilities of a person with Down syndrome before the onset of Alzheimer's disease is important in acting as a baseline from which subsequent deterioration can be measured (Barr 1991). There are a variety of behavioural (Pattie & Gilliard 1979), psychological and activities-of-living (Mathieson 1988) assessment tools available which can assist in understanding the progress of the disease, but these are of little use unless they actually contribute to the plan of care which is formulated.

The general principle of management is that it should be based on a thorough assessment of individual need; this will help to ensure that set goals are reasonable and are within the person's capabilities. More broadly, care should be governed by an understanding that the person's capacity to store and retrieve new information is limited and will, in all probability, continue to deteriorate. It is reasonable, therefore, to attempt to achieve stability in the person's physical, social and recreational environments.

The notions of strict routines and rigidly enforced timetables which leave little room for improvisation and initiative are now largely discredited and are not advocated here as providing the basis of a suitably therapeutic environment in which to care for people with Alzheimer's disease. There may be advantages, however, in increasing a sense of security by ensuring that changes in the person's environment are introduced very gradually (whenever possible) in order to allow the person with compromised cognition to comprehend the relevant implications.

Complementing the principle of stability is the introduction of a primary nursing system of care (Manthey 1980), where an identified registered nurse assumes responsibility for the patient's overall care and seeks to develop a therapeutic relationship with him. The method, which shares many similarities with the key worker concept in social care (Sines 1988), would seem well suited to meeting the needs of Alzheimer's disease sufferers, and Armitage (1990) has reported that its introduction to two long-term psychiatric wards resulted in an increase in the resident's self-sufficiency and independence. Primary nursing has supporters who claim it is successful in various branches of nursing (Manley 1989, Wright 1990) although there is as yet insufficient empirical evidence to give unequivocal support to this.

Even if primary nursing can be successfully utilized in the care of dementia sufferers, a multi-disciplinary approach to the management of the individual problems presented by each person is most likely to achieve positive results (Jacques 1988). The skills of psychologists, occupational therapists, physiotherapists, speech therapists and dieticians, help in managing the various emotional, cognitive and physical disabilities which are present. The patient's family can also be considered as part of the team and, with support from professionals, can assist the individual to maximize his existing abilities.

More formal methods of management include reality orientation (RO), reminiscence and validation therapy (VT). RO is a technique which attempts to give the dementia sufferer a secure understanding of his environment by persistent reminders about time, place and identity of appropriate individuals (Holden & Woods 1988). The therapy can be carried out informally at each interaction with the person or in formal group sessions. It has proved successful with elderly nonmentally handicapped persons who are in the very early stages of Alzheimer's disease, and whose biggest problem is failing memory. There is no conclusive evidence that it helps mentally handicapped people, but Hong (1989) reports that after six months of working in RO groups, mentally handicapped people had increased levels of concentration and, just as important, were enjoying the experience.

The theory of reminiscence is that it allows people to review life experiences in the hope that they gain new wisdom and insights which promote a positive self image (Brooking 1986). Again, it can be facilitated in individual or group sessions and utilizes a variety of props, such as old photographs, newspapers and clothing, which aim to stimulate the person to converse about the significance of objects and events in his life. It may be of some value in providing stimuli to a person with mental handicap who has Alzheimer's disease.

VT is a therapy developed in the United States (Feil 1989) which is designed to increase communication and understanding with individuals with moderate to severe dementia. The technique hinges on a belief that elderly people with dementia are unable to articulate the many 'unresolved conflicts' of their lifetimes, and instead compensate by giving vent to varying degrees of emotional disinhibition. The therapist, instead of concentrating on the verbal content of the disorientated person's conversation, focuses on the emotional feeling behind the message and attempts to help the patient express what the real problem is. Success is claimed for the therapy in the United States and Canada (Mattice 1990); work in this country is still in its infancy (Bleathman 1988), and has concentrated on elderly people, but it is not inconceivable that nurses working with people with learning difficulties will wish to explore its potential.

Witnessing the deterioration of the intellectual and physical capacities of a family member, and having to adjust to his or her 'new' personality, may be a painful and difficult experience for others in the family. Feelings of frustration and helplessness can surface, and be compounded by social withdrawal and isolation if the individual's personal habits and other behaviours deteriorate to a socially unacceptable level. Education about the disease, its progress and management, and details of help available to the family from professionals, fellow carers, state agencies and voluntary bodies can enhance the provision of care to the person affected (Scottish Health Education Group 1988).

Nurses may find it useful to develop an awareness of the services offered by organizations and be prepared to advise carers accordingly.

NEUROTIC DISORDERS

This term is used to describe emotional disorders in which a sense of reality is preserved. It includes states of disproportionate anxiety, panic and fear, phobias, hypochondriasis, unhappiness, depression, sensitivity, shyness and relationship problems, e.g. sibling jealousy (Reid 1982). People with a mental handicap are, like others, exposed to stress, strain, anxiety and apprehension throughout their lives. Feelings of guilt, embarrassment and inadequacy felt by the family may be projected on to the handicapped member. This can result in rejection or overprotection. Difficulty in learning and coping with educational demands may give rise to a sense of failure as well as being stigmatized and the subject of jokes and unfair comparisons with nonhandicapped siblings and other children. Failure to grasp the rules of social interaction can result in a person with learning difficulties misjudging social situations.

The symptoms of anxiety are physical, psychological and behavioural. Anxiety, especially if experienced as a panic attack, can give rise to a definite set of physical symptoms, such as palpitations, difficulty in breathing, dry mouth, sweating, dizziness, trembling and tightness in the throat. Psychological reactions include difficulty in concentration, irritability and extreme restlessness.

The behavioural reaction is one of avoidance – to run from the feared situation or object.

Rutter (1970) commented that intellectual retardation in children is associated with an increase in neurotic and conduct disorders. Reid (1980) notes that neurotic disorders could be diagnosed in children with learning difficulties. A team approach is indicated to try to isolate the significance of the symptoms and modify the situation for the person affected. Care should be taken to consider the patient's limitations and potential to avoid excess pressure in trying to achieve certain goals. The assistance of the psychologist is useful in defining behavioural treatment approaches, which include various deconditioning procedures such as systematic desensitization.

Phobic disorders may be treated by the use of behavioural therapy, psychotherapy and antianxiety drugs. The uses of behaviourally orientated psychotherapy involving gradually increased exposure to phobic situations is very useful in enabling the person to 'unlearn' his patterns of fear and avoidance.

Symptoms may be relieved by drugs such as the butyrophenone group, e.g. haloperidol or the benzodiazepine group, e.g. diazepam. Depressive features may respond to antidepressant drugs, e.g. phenelzine.

CONDUCT DISORDERS

Socially unacceptable behaviour, such as aggression, destruction and sexual misdemeanours or eating disorders, e.g. anorexia nervosa, may be shown by some people with a mental handicap. Disorders with a physical manifestation may also occur such as stereotyped movements. Inability and inconsistency in handling such conduct may create additional problems of antisocial behaviour, particularly in those with a mild degree of mental handicap. Identifying and curtailing the factors which are reinforcing the conduct and substituting an alternative behavioural pattern is one approach in dealing with conduct disorders.

FORENSIC PSYCHIATRY

The relationship between mental handicap and criminality is the subject of much debate and research (Woodward 1955, Bluglass 1966, Walker & McCabe 1973). The subject has aroused interest in recent years with the growth in awareness of the rights of people with learning disabilities and the moves towards community living.

Many people with a mental handicap are trusting and may be easily manipulated. Because of this they may be easily led into petty crime and exploited. They may lack the ability to conceal any involvement in the criminal activity and be liable to police apprehension. The police may decide not to prosecute and discharge the individual home or direct to a hospital or care centre. On the other hand, the police may charge the individual. People with a mental handicap may have limited social skills and suffer from possible victimization as members of a minority group that does not have the resources to put its case (Hewitt 1985).

Very little information is available regarding the more common mentally abnormal offenders who commit petty offences (Bowden 1977). The Butler Report (Home Office & DHSS 1975) scarcely addressed the issue and described these offenders as 'inadequates'. These offenders are described as limited or damaged personalities because of chronic schizophrenia, personality problems or mental handicap. The report suggested more facilities for support but little has resulted from the recommendation.

It has been suggested that crimes committed by the mentally handicapped relate mainly to the category of minor socially undesirable acts (Crompton 1986).

It is questionable whether mentally abnormal offenders have been adequately dealt with. Scarce resources tend to be directed to the small number of dangerous offenders while the majority who commit minor offences are sent to whichever establishment or agency is prepared to accept them.

Reid (1982) reported that it would seem there is no link between defectiveness of intelligence and crime beyond sexual offences and arson. Perhaps this results from the fact that the mentally handicapped male may have great difficulty securing a suitable partner and have little awareness of the significance of socially appropriate sexual behaviour.

Publications regarding the management of mentally handicapped offenders are available and include consideration of how they are dealt with by the police and the courts (Anonymous 1985, Gibbons et al 1981, Marsh et al 1975) and in institutions (Kugel et al 1968, Menolascino 1974, French 1983, Reinke-Scorzelli & Scorzelli 1976, Rockoff 1973).

The Police and Criminal Evidence Act 1984 (PACE) came into effect in January 1986. It contains a number of sections concerning the treatment of people in police custody, including safeguards for people who are mentally ill or mentally handicapped. Safeguards are crucial to prevent people with mental disorders being sent to prison inappropriately (Thomas 1986).

Various factors may improve our understanding of criminality and the person with learning disabilities in the future. The introduction of tape recording at all police interviews will undoubtedly improve the quality of interviews and the techniques used in them but failure to mention the implications for mentally handicapped people in the new code of practice (Home Office 1988) is most disappointing to many.

As the emphasis nowadays is for community care for people with a mental handicap, a strong network of social support may help avoid the problems of antisocial behaviour which can lead to criminality.

ACQUIRED IMMUNE DEFICIENCY SYNDROME

Acquired immune deficiency syndrome (AIDS) is a terminal illness which is caused by infection but, unlike many other infections, it is not responsive to immunization or treatment by chemicals or antibiotics. The unique biological mechanisms of the responsible virus, the human immuno-deficiency virus (HIV), of which more than one strain is active, ensure this; the virus is able to invade and then destroy human cells (commonly T-lymphocytes, which are involved in the body's immune system), but is also able to replicate itself within the cell. Once released, these new viruses can go on to invade and destroy more cells (Pratt 1988).

Remarkably, given the devastating impact the virus has had on the population of the world over the last 10 years, it is a fragile virus which is not very infective and can survive in only a few particular media. Outside the body, modest heat and household bleach can destroy it in seconds. Once inside the body it is, as yet, indestructible.

The initial response of identifying individuals or groups who were considered to be at high risk has now been succeeded by an understanding that all human beings are potential carriers of the virus (Hart 1991). There remain, however, clearly identifiable high-risk activities, involving exposure to blood and other body fluids which may harbour HIV. These activities include having sexual intercourse with more than one partner (hetero- or homosexually) and communal use of intravenous injection equipment. This section will concentrate on the relationship of people with a mental handicap to the former activity.

Given that medical science cannot offer protection in the form of immunization or cure, the only way people can protect themselves from this fatal illness is by modifying personal, behavioural and social habits; the implications of this in terms of emotional, motivational and ethical considerations can be enormous, and offers humankind its greatest health challenge.

The immense complexity of this issue is magnified when applied to the question of how to protect people with a mental handicap from becoming infected. Trying to influence the behaviour of people capable of reasonably assessing the risks involved is problematic; how much more difficult it is to affect the behaviour of people who may not have the ability to conduct their own intellectual assessments. This leads nurses and carers into an ethical minefield, where consideration of responsibilities to protect are weighed against the absolute necessity to allow people with a mental handicap to enjoy the same liberties as everyone else.

The trend towards normalization in the care of people with a mental handicap (Nirje 1980) has led to an increasing awareness of the right of such individuals to learn about and express their own sexuality. The need to receive and express love, and to acknowledge and appropriately express sexual desires, are undeniable rights for every individual.

Some people with a mental handicap are sexually active. For years this activity has been carried out amidst ignorance and subterfuge (Wolfensberger 1972). Large institutions discouraged mixing of the sexes unless under extremely controlled conditions; the inevitable corollary was the development of close sexual relationships with members of the same sex, which in turn was implicated in high rates of hepatitis B infection among male institution populations (Kay 1990).

The watchword of care for people with a mental handicap has for too long been 'control' (Kay 1990). This control touched every aspect of the institutionalized patient's life (Ryan & Thomas 1980), governing when he got up in the morning, what he ate, where he sat, who he saw, when he bathed and when he went to bed again. The legacy of this kind of custodial environment, of control and lack of opportunity for decision-making, is that there are now generations of people with a mental handicap who have difficulty in making decisions and exercising choice. The dilemma which this now presents for nurses who employ normalization techniques, and who encourage independence of thought and action in their clients, is that those clients may still be insufficiently skilled and practised in making decisions. In the field of human relationships since the advent of AIDS, one wrong decision might mean becoming infected and in turn infecting others. The crucial questions for nurses relate to balance: how to balance the need to protect individuals from exploitation and harm against individuals' right to express themselves as they see fit; how to balance the urge to be prescriptive and prohibitive in an attempt to protect clients from contracting a deadly disease against people's right to arrive at their own decisions; how to have constructive relationships simultaneously with a mother who wants her mentally handicapped daughter protected at all costs, and a daughter who wants the freedom to enjoy relationships.

It is in the nature of dilemmas not to promote easy, or even any, solutions (Benjamin & Curtis 1981). There are no stock answers for nurses who grapple with this problem every day. There are some activities and attitudes, however, which nurses may find constructive.

Firstly, nurses must be aware when their own moral sense is entering into the debate; this is not to say that the nurse's ethical beliefs should be ignored, quite the contrary, but the nurse should be aware that they may be interfering with her ability to remain objective and are obstructing meaningful discourse. Inevitably, questions about human relationships will raise issues which individuals strongly disapprove of, or even find repugnant; the nurse who has a secure sense of her own values and a sound understanding of her professional role will be able to adopt a mature, facilitative and constructive role which will help individual clients and leave her emotionally unscarred.

Secondly, the only weapon we have against this disease is education and we must use it (Jones 1987). Teaching people with a mental handicap about 'safe' or 'safer' sex is not offering a licence to promiscuity; rather, the nurse might find it much more constructive to include the subject in discussions about relationships, about love and commitment, ensuring that the topic is not presented in isolation (Royal College of Nursing Society of Mental Handicap Nursing 1991).

Lastly, the nurse can work to dispel inaccurate and misleading notions about transmission; accurate information will not encourage complacency, but will allow people with a mental handicap to focus on the real high risk activities and subsequently help them to understand and adopt safe practices.

SUMMARY

Mental handicap is often found in association with other impairments. Factors which affect the development of the brain may interfere with bodily development. The conditions outlined produce profound physical, intellectual and emotional effects on the individual concerned and create anxiety, fear and apprehension which can create problems for individual families and for the general public.

Epilepsy may be controlled by anticonvulsant drugs but the psychological implications of the condition must be carefully considered.

It is vital to ensure that people with a mental handicap who also suffer from cerebral palsy achieve their maximum potential and that every assistance to the process of communication is delivered.

Abnormal behaviour may pose problems and require modification by drug treatment or operant conditioning techniques. When stereotyped behaviour occurs in institutionalized people with a mental handicap it is often self-destructive. Hyperkinesis is characterized by excessive motor activity, distractibility, poor concentration, impulsiveness, temper tantrums and possible aggression towards others. Autism is evident in early childhood: autistic children are handicapped in language development and display no response to other people.

Mental illness may be superimposed on mental handicap. Psychosis, in which a drastic change in a person's personality occurs, can present itself in the form of affective disorders and schizophrenia. Delirium and dementia are the two types of organic states, delirium presents in a dramatic and urgent way while dementia is a slow, insidious process. Neurotic disorders describe emotional disorders in people of any age, in which reality is preserved.

The link between criminality and mental handicap is the subject of much debate and research. Continued research is vital and safeguards must be developed to prevent people with mental disorders being sent to prison needlessly. The immense complexity of AIDS is magnified when applied to the question of how to protect people with a mental handicap from contracting the disease. It creates innumerable ethical and moral dilemmas for carers in an era when the rights of mentally handicapped people to learn about and express their own sexuality are highlighted.

REFERENCES

Anonymous 1985 Mentally disabled offenders. Mental and Physical Disability Law Reporter 9: 20–21

Arie T (ed) 1985 Recent advances in psychogeriatrics. Churchill Livingstone, Edinburgh

Armitage P 1990 Changing care: an evaluation of primary nursing in psychiatric long term care. (Unpublished.) School of Nursing Studies, University of Wales, Cardiff

Ballinger B R, Armstrong J, Presly A S et al 1975 Use of a standardised psychiatric interview in mentally handicapped patients. British Journal of Psychiatry 127: 540–544

Barr O 1991 Down's syndrome and Alzheimer's disease – what's the link? Professional Nurse, June 465–468

Bartus R T (ed) 1986 Controversial topics on Alzheimer's disease: intersecting crossroads. Neurobiology Ageing, 7, 6

Benjamin M, Curtis J 1981 Ethics in nursing. Oxford University Press, New York

Bergman K et al 1978 Management of the demented elderly patient in the community. British Journal of Psychiatry 132: 441–449

Berkson G, Mason W 1964 Stereotyped behaviour of chimpanzees: relation to general arousal and alternative activities. Perceptual and Motor Skills 19: 635–652

Bleathman C 1988 Validation therapy with the demented elderly. Journal of Advanced Nursing, July 551

Bluglass R S 1966 A psychiatric study of Scottish convicted prisoners. MD thesis, University of St Andrews

Bohman M, Bohman I L, Bjorck P O, Sjoholm E 1983 Childhood psychosis in a northern Swedish county: some preliminary findings from an epidemiological survey. In: Smidt M H, Remsmidt H (eds) Epidemiological approaches in child psychiatry vol 2. Georg Thieme, Stuttgart

Bond M 1986 Stress and self awareness: a guide for nurses. Heinemann London

Bowden P 1977 The current management of the mentally disordered offender. Proceedings of the Royal Society of Medicine 70: 881–884

Brandt P A 1984 Social support and negative life events of mothers with developmentally delayed children. Birth Defects 20(5): 205–244

Brask B H 1970 A prevalence investigation of childhood psychosis. Paper given at the 16th Scandinavian Congress of Psychiatry

Brechin J & Swain A 1987 Changing relationships. Harper & Row, London

British Epilepsy Association 1990 Towards a new understanding. British Epilepsy Association, Leeds

Brooking J I 1986 Dementia and confusion in the elderly. In: Redfern S J (ed) Nursing elderly people. Churchill Livingstone, Edinburgh

Buckley P, Walshe D, Colohan H A et al 1990 Cluain Mhuire Family Centre Dublin, Ireland : Violence and schizophrenia—a study of the occurrence and clinical correlates of violence among schizophrenic patients. Irish Journal of Psychological Medicine 7: 102–8

Byrne E A, Cunningham C C 1985 The effects of mentally handicapped children on families – conceptual review. Journal of Child Psychology and Psychiatry 26(6): 847–864

Cantwell D P 1977 Hyperkinetic syndrome. In: Rutter M, Herson L(eds) Child psychiatry – modern approaches. Blackwell Scientific, Oxford

Carr J 1976 The severely retarded autistic child. In: Wing L (ed) Early childhood autism, 2nd edn. Pergamon Press, Oxford

Christensen D E 1975 Effects of combining methylphenidate and a classroom token system in modifying hyperactive behaviour. American Journal of Mental Deficiency 3: 226–276

Clancy H, Dugdale A, Rendle-Short J 1969 The diagnosis of infantile autism. Developmental Medicine and Child Neurology 11: 432–442

Clark P, Rutter M 1979 Task difficulty and task performance in autistic children. Journal of Child Psychology and Psychiatry 20: 271–285

Coleman M, Gillberg C 1987 The biology of the autistic syndromes, 2nd edn. Praeger, New York

Cooke P W, Cole W C, Carey R P L 1989 Dislocation of the hip in cerebral palsy. Journal of Bone and Joint Surgery (Br) 71B (3): 441–446

Corbett J A 1975 Aversion for the treatment of self-injurious behaviour. Journal of Mental Deficiency Research 19: 79–95

Corbett J A 1979 Psychiatric morbidity and mental retardation. In: James F E, Snaith R P (eds) Psychiatric illness and mental handicap. Gaskell Press, London

Craft M J 1958 Mental disorders in the defective. Royal Institution, Starcross, Devon

Craft M J, Schiff A A 1980 Psychiatric disturbance in mentally handicapped patients. British Journal of Psychiatry 137: 250–255

Creak M 1961 Schizophrenia syndrome in childhood. British Medical Journal 2: 889–890

Crompton S 1986 Criminal treatment? Disability Now February 5–7

Cullen C N, Hattersley J, Tennant L 1977 Behaviour modification: some implications of a radical behaviourist view. Bulletin of the British Psychological Society 30: 65–69

Day K A 1985 Psychiatric disorder in the middle age and elderly mentally handicapped. British Journal of Psychiatry 147: 660–667

Dieter H 1978 Das heimliche gift, Stern 40: 31–38

Earl C J C 1961 Subnormal personalities. Baillière Tindall, London

Feil N 1989 Validation: the Feil method. Edward Feil, Cleveland, Ohio

Ferster C B, De Meyer M K 1961 The development and performances in autistic children in an automatically controlled environment. Journal of Chronic Disabilities 13: 312–345

Ferster C B, De Meyer M K 1962 A method for the experimental analysis of the behaviour of autistic children. American Journal of Orthopsychiatry 32: 89–98

Forehand R, Baumeister A A 1970 The effects of auditory and visual stimulation on stereotyped rocking behaviour and general activity of severe retardates. Journal of Clinical Psychology 26: 426–429

French L A 1983 The mentally retarded and pseudoretarded offender: a clinical/legal dilemma. Federal Probation 46: 55–61

Gibbons F X , Gibbons B N, Kassin S M 1981 Reactions to the criminal behaviour of mentally retarded and non-retarded offenders. American Journal of Mental Deficiency 86: 235–242

Gillberg C 1980 Maternal age and infantile autism. Journal of Autism and Development Disorders 10: 293–297

Gillberg C 1984 Infantile autism and other childhood psychoses in Swedish urban regions: epidemiological aspects. Journal of Child Psychology and Psychiatry 25: 35–43.

Goldberg D P, Cooper B, Eastwood M R et al 1970 A standardised psychiatric interview for use in community surveys. British Journal of Preventive and Social Medicine 24: 18–23

Greutzner H 1988 Alzheimer's: a care givers' guide and sourcebook. John Wiley, New York

Haggerty R J 1980 Life stress illness and social support. Developmental Medicine and Child Neurology 22: 391–400

Hamilton M (ed) 1980 Fish's outline of psychiatry. Wright, Bristol

Hart S 1991 Blood and body fluid precautions. Nursing Standard, 5(25) 25–27

Hayman M 1939 The interrelations of mental defect and mental disorder. Journal of Mental Sciences 85: 1183–1193

Heaton-Ward A 1977 Psychosis in mental handicap. British Journal of Psychiatry 130: 525–533

Herskovitz H H, Plesset M R 1941 Psychoses in adult mental defectives. Psychiatric Quarterly 15: 574–588

Hewitt S E K 1985 Interviewing people at risk: following police codes of practice. Mental Handicap 13: 150–151

Hitchcock E F 1978 Stereotactic surgery for cerebral palsy. Nursing Times 74 (50) : 2064–2065

Hirose T, Ueda R 1990 Long-term follow-up study of cerebral palsy children and coping behaviour of parents. Journal of Advanced Nursing 15: 762–770

Holden U P, Woods R T 1988 Reality orientation, 2nd edn. Churchill Livingstone, Edinburgh

Hollis J H 1971 Body rocking: effects of sounds and reinforcement. American Journal of Mental Deficiency 75: 642–644

Home Office and Department of Health & Social Security 1975 Report of the committee on mentally abnormal offenders. (Chairman Lord Butler) Cmnd 6244 HMSO, London

Home Office (1985a) Police and Criminal Evidence Act 1984 (s.66) Codes of Practice. HMSO, London

Home Office 1988 Police and Criminal Evidence Act 1984 (s.60(1) (a)) Code of Practice (E) on Tape Recording. HMSO, London

Homer A 1988 Diagnosing dementia: do we get it right? British Medical Journal 297: 894–896

Hong C 1989 Doubly disadvantaged. Nursing Times 85 (32) 69–70

Hopkins A 1981 Epilepsy: the facts. Oxford University Press, Oxford

Howard C B, McKibbon B, Williams L A, Mackie I 1985 Factors affecting the incidence of hip dislocation in cerebral palsy. Journal of Bone and Joint Surgery (Br) 67B: 530–532

Ingalls R P 1978 Mental retardation – the changing outlook. John Wiley, New York

Jacques A 1988 Understanding dementia. Churchill Livingstone, Edinburgh

Jancar J 1988 Consequences of longer life for the mentally handicapped. Geriatric Medicine 18(5): 81–87

Jones C 1987 AIDS and people with mental handicaps. Mental Handicap, 15, 4

Kanner L 1943 Autistic disturbances of affective contact. Nervous Child 2: 217-250

Kay B 1990 Mental Handicap and AIDS: the issue. Nursing Standard 4(23) 30–34

Kielholz P (ed) 1973 Masked depression. Hans Huber, Bern

Kraepelin E 1896 Psychiatrie. Translated in: Clinical Psychiatry 1902 by Deferndorf A R, New York

Kraemer L 1980 The rising pandemic of mental disorders and associated chronic disease and disabilities. In: Stromgren E et al (eds) ACTA, Psychiatrica-Scandinavica, Supplement 285

Kugel R B, Trembath J, Sagar S 1968 Some characteristics of patients legally admitted to a state institution for the mentally retarded. Mental Retardation 6, 2–8

Laidlaw M V, Laidlaw J 1984 People with epilepsy: how they can be helped. Churchill Livingstone, Edinburgh

Levitt S 1983 Treatment of cerebral palsy and motor delay. Blackwell Scientific, Oxford

Levy D M 1944 On the problem of movement restraint. American Journal of Orthopsychiatry 14: 644–671

Lindqvist P, Allebeck P 1990 Schizophrenia and crime: longitudinal follow-up of 644 schizophrenics in Stockholm. British Journal of Psychiatry 157: 345–350

Lotter V 1966 Epidemiology of autistic conditions in young children, I–prevalence. Social Psychiatry 1: 124–137

Malamud N 1972 Neuropathology of organic brain syndromes associated with ageing. In: Gaitz CM (ed) Ageing and the brain. Plenum Press, New York

Manley K 1989 Primary nursing in intensive care. Scutari Press, Harrow

Manthey M 1980 The practice of primary nursing. London, Blackwell

Mardiros M 1982 Mothers of disabled children: study of parental stress. Nursing Papers 14(3), 47–56

Marsh R L, Friel C M, Eissler V 1975 The adult MR in the criminal justice system. Mental Retardation 13: 21–25

Mathieson A 1988 Rating needs. Nursing Times 84 (35) 38–41

Matsuyana S S, Jarvik L F, Kumar V 1985 Dementia: genetics. In: Arie T (ed) Recent advances in psychogeriatrics. Churchill Livingstone, Edinburgh

Mattice M 1990 Caring for confused elders (reality orientation/validation therapy). Canadian Nurse, December 16

Menolascino F J 1974 The mentally retarded offender. Mental Retardation 12: 7–11

Moreau M, Drummond D S, Rogala E, Ashworth A, Porter T 1979 Natural history of the dislocated hip in spastic cerebral palsy. Development Medicine and Child Neurology 21: 749–753

Nelson R O, Evans I M 1968 The combination of learning principles and special training techniques in the treatment of non-communicating children. Journal of Child Psychology and Psychiatry 9: 111–124

Neustadt R 1928 Psychoses of defectives. Karger, Berlin

Nirje R 1980 The normalization principle. In: Flynn R J, Nitsh K E (eds) Normalization, social integration and community services. University Park Press, Baltimore

Nordoff P, Robbins C 1985 Therapy in music for handicapped children. Victor Gollancz, London

Office of Population Censuses and Surveys 1976. HMSO, London

Omenn G 1973 Genetic issues in the syndrome of minimal brain dysfunction. In: Waltxer S, Wolff P (eds) Minimal cerebral dysfunction in children. Grune & Stratton, New York.

Oswin M 1967 Behaviour problems amongst children with cerebral palsy. John Wright, Bristol

Pattie A H Gilliard C J 1979 Manual of the Clifton assessment procedures for the elderly. Hodder & Stoughton, Sevenoaks

Pawlarcyzk D, Beckwith B E 1987 Depressive symptoms displayed by persons with mental retardation: a review. Mental Retardation 25: 6, 325–330

Penrose L S 1938 A clinical and genetic study of 1280 cases of mental defect. Special Report Series of Medical Research Council No 229. HMSO, London

Pratt J 1988 AIDS: a strategy for nursing care. Edward Arnold, London

Rabins P V 1985 The reversible dementias. In: Arie T (ed) Recent advances in psychogeriatrics. Churchill Livingstone, Edinburgh

Reid A J 1980 Psychiatric disorders in mentally handicapped children: clinical and follow up study. Journal of Mental Deficiency Research 24: 287–298

Reid A H 1982 The psychiatry of mental handicap. Blackwell Scientific, Oxford

Reid A H 1985 Psychiatry and mental handicap. In: Craft M, Bicknell J, Mollins S Mental Handicap: a multidisciplinary approach. Baillière Tindall, London

Reinke-Scorzell M, Scorzelli J F 1976 An area of neglect: the mentally retarded offender. American Archives of Rehabilitation Therapy 24: 37–39

Report of the committee of enquiry into mental handicap nursing and care 1979 HMSO, London

Rockoff E S 1973 The mentally retarded offender in Iowa correctional institutions. Dissertation abstracts 34: 3–94

Rohan J C 1936 Mental disorder in the adult defective. Journal of Mental Science 82: 551–563

Ropper A H, Williams R S 1980 Relationship between plaques, tangles and dementia in Down's syndrome. Neurology 30: 639–644

Royal College of Nursing Society of Mental handicap Nursing 1991 AIDS – a proactive approach to mental handicap. Scutari Press, Harrow

Russell 1987 Presentation of psychiatric illness in mentally handicapped people. Medicine 2 (44): 1826–1829

Rutter M 1970 Autistic children: infancy to adulthood. Seminars in Psychiatry 2: 435–450

Ryan J, Thomas F 1980 The politics of mental handicap. Harmondsworth, Penguin

Samilson R L, Tsou P, Aamouth G, Green W M 1972 Dislocation and subluxation of the hip in cerebral palsy. Journal of Bone and Joint Surgery 54A: 863–872

Schauss A 1980 Diet, crime and delinquency. Parker House, California Ch IV, p50–60

Schilling R F, Schinke S P, Kirkham M A 1985 Coping with a handicapped child: differences between mothers and fathers. Social Science and Medicine 21(8)

Scottish Health Education Group 1988 Coping with dementia, 2nd edn. Scottish Health Education Group, Edinburgh

Shaffer D 1977 Drug treatment in child psychiatry. In: Rutter M, Herson L (eds) Child psychiatry. Blackwell Scientific, Oxford

Shah A, Frith V 1983 An islet of ability in autistic children: a research note. Journal of Child Psychology and Psychiatry 24: 613–620

Shapiro A 1979 Psychiatric illness in the mentally handicapped: an historical survey. In: James F E, Snaith R P (eds) Psychiatric illness and mental handicap. Gaskell Press, London.

Shorvan S 1987 The treatment of epilepsy by drugs. In: Hopkins A (ed) Epilepsy. Chapman and Hall, London

Sines D 1988 Maintaining an ordinary life. In: Sines D (ed) Towards integration: comprehensive services for people with mental handicaps. Harper & Row, London

Sovner R, Hurley A H 1983 Do the mentally retarded suffer from affective illness? Archives of General Psychiatry 40: 61–67

Steffenburgh, S, Gillberg C 1986 Autism and autistic-like conditions in Swedish rural and urban areas: a population study. British Journal of Psychiatry 149: 81–87

Steinhausen H C, Brienlinger M 1986 A community survey of infantile autism. Journal of the American Academy of Child Psychiatry 25: 186–189

Thase M E 1982 Reversible dementia in Down's syndrome. Journal of Mental Deficiency Research 26: 111–113

Thomas T 1986 The police and social workers. Gower with Community Care, Aldersholt 1986

Thompson Jr G A, Iwata A, Poynter H 1979 Operant control of pathological tongue thrust in spastic cerebral palsy. Journal of Applied Behaviour Analysis 12(3): 325–333

Walker N, McCabe S 1973 Crime and insanity in England. New solutions and new problems. Edinburgh University Press, Edinburgh, vol II

Wing L, Gould J 1979 Severe impairments of social interaction and associated abnormalities in children: epidemiology and classification. Journal of Autism and Developmental Disorders 9: 11–29

Winsberg B, Bialer I, Kupietz S et al 1972 Effects of imipramine and dextroamphetamine on behaviour of neuropsychiatrically impaired children. American Journal of Psychiatry 128: 1425–1431

Wolfensberger W 1972 The principle of normalization in human services. National Institute of Mental Retardation, Toronto

Woods G E 1969 The causes. In: Blencowe SM (ed) Cerebral palsy and the young child. E & S Livingstone, Edinburgh

Woodward M 1955 The role of low intelligence in delinquency. British Journal of Delinquency 5: 281–303

Wright S 1990 My patient – my nurse. Scutari Press, Harrow

Yates C M et al 1986 Monoamines and peptides in ageing. Alzheimer's type dementia and Down's syndrome. In: Bebbington P E, Jacoby R (eds) Psychiatric disorder in the elderly. London Mental Health Foundation

Young R Clements J 1979 The functional significance of complex hand movement stereotypes in the severely retarded. British Journal of Mental Subnormality 25: 79–87

CHAPTER CONTENTS

Introduction 119

Background 119
Early classifications of children with learning
   difficulties 120
Extending the system to all children with learning
   difficulties 120
The Warnock Report and after 121

The development of thought and learning 122
The sensorimotor stage 122
The preoperational stage 124
The stages of concrete operations and formal
   operations 125

Effective teaching and learning 126
Applied learning theory 127
   Developmentally appropriate reinforcement 127
   Respecting personal preferences 127
   Sensible reinforcement 128
   Teaching useful skills 128
   Diagnostic teaching 128
   Beyond teaching 128
Adult/child interaction 128
Curriculum 129
   Communication 129
   Problem-solving 129
   Environmental studies 130
   Expressive arts 131
Administrative procedures 131

Educational integration 132

Questions 133

7

Helping with learning difficulties

G. MacKay

Key points
- Educational provision for children with learning difficulties has been developing for 100 years
- Understanding children's level of development gives guidance when selecting the educational tasks they can tackle
- Learning and teaching can be made more effective by attention to various principles of learning and curriculum theory, and by consultation between school and home
- Educational integration is a desirable aim but is not an easy option

INTRODUCTION

The modern era of education in the United Kingdom began with the passing of Education Acts in the 1870s which entitled children between the ages of 5 and 13 years to schooling. Soon after the passing of these Acts, it was recognized that children with learning difficulties offered a challenge to which the general system of schooling was not making a satisfactory response. In consequence, special educational provision for these children began to be provided. This chapter begins by outlining the history of the development of that provision. This will set the context for a consideration of various practical issues concerned with providing the best possible service from the education system for children with learning difficulties.

BACKGROUND

What are the educational implications of having

a learning difficulty? It may mean having unusual difficulty in solving practical and abstract problems, in detecting patterns and other conceptual structures, and in communicating. In addition, many people with learning difficulties acquire knowledge and skills more slowly than others. Children who have problems handling complexity and speed of learning are likely to have educational difficulties. The new education systems of the 1870s were for all pupils, recognizing only those who were blind as having any special needs. However, the case for special assistance for pupils with learning difficulties was sufficiently clear by the end of the 19th century so special schools and classes were established for them too.

Early classifications of children with learning difficulties

Who were these children whose need for special education was recognized by this legislation? The Scottish legislation of the period labelled them 'mentally defective' and defined them as being 'not merely dull and backward' but 'not imbecile', and as 'incapable of receiving proper benefit from the instruction in the ordinary schools'. In the legislation, mental defect was a more troublesome condition than being 'merely dull and backward', but less troublesome than being 'imbecile'. 'Merely dull and backward' children attended the mainstream schools. 'Mentally defective' children attended the new special schools and classes, where these were provided. But 'imbecile' children had such serious difficulties that the educational provision for 'defective' children did not extend to them. Even less consideration was given to the children who were known as 'idiots' at that time; they had more severe difficulties than those of the 'imbeciles', and were not mentioned in the Acts at all.

'Imbeciles' and 'idiots' were still specifically excluded from the provisions of the main, mid-century Education Acts 40 years later. Indeed, it was not until 1970, in England and Wales, and 1974, in Scotland, that their right to education was guaranteed. Thus, a clear conceptual structure for the education of pupils with learning

difficulties took more than 100 years to emerge.

Extending the system to all children with learning difficulties

Although special schools for children with the most severe degrees of learning difficulty were slow to appear, some forms of provision were made for them quite early. Residential institutions for children with severe and complex learning difficulties had been established during the 19th century. Day provision for them also began to appear soon after the turn of the century in the form of 'occupation centres' (England and Wales) or 'occupational centres' (Scotland). Under the Mental Deficiency Acts of 1913, which covered the whole of the United Kingdom, children with severe and profound learning difficulties became the responsibility of their parish councils which were the antecedents of the present local authorities and health boards. However, it was nearly a quarter of a century before provision by education authorities became statutory with the group of Education Acts which appeared around the end of World War II. For instance, the Education (Scotland) Act 1945 required Scottish education authorities to make provision for 'ineducable but trainable mental defectives' in 'occupational centres'. Three details of this Act are particularly worth noting.

First, the word 'trainable' appears, making a distinction between 'training', which was provided by instructors in the occupational centres, and 'education' which was provided by teachers in the ordinary schools and in the special schools which were established at the start of the century. No attempt is made to tease out an essential difference between training and education, though one official publication suggests that the difference lay in the content of education and training. The content of training was a set of skills which would 'render (pupils) as self-reliant, adjusted and acceptable to normal society as (their) potentialities allow' (Working Party 1961). Presumably, the content of education was that which occurred in the ordinary schools.

Second, no educational provision was made

for the most severely disabled children, that is, those who were 'ineducable and untrainable', but they were not forgotten. Official policy was that they would not benefit from attendance at occupational centres and that they should be referred to the local health authority for placement in a 'day centre'.

Third, the new legislation required education authorities to have a concern for children from the age of only 2 years, thus signalling a concern with early intervention which still exercises legislators and the providers of services.

The major milestones in the 45 years between the 1945–6 Acts and today are clustered between 1970 and 1981. An intense increase in interest in the abilities of people with severe and profound learning difficulties occurred in the 1960s when it became clear that they could learn many skills if they were taught systematically, using the principles of operant learning which will be discussed later.

One critical feature of this period was an increasing faith in the educability of children with severe and profound learning difficulties. This affirmation was given substance in England and Wales in 1970 by the Education (Handicapped Children) Act, which entitled all children to education irrespective of the severity of any disabilities they might have. This Act had near contemporaries in other countries: Scotland in 1974, the USA in 1975 and Norway in 1976. The American Act, Public Law 94–142, has had an influence well beyond its national boundaries on account of its powerful declaration of the educational rights of children with disabilities.

The United Kingdom Acts led to the renaming of all occupational and care centres as 'schools'. This change was a jolt to the system. The labels had changed but the children had not. The most profoundly handicapped pupils might be functioning at the developmental level of children in the first few days of life; the most able still had much more difficulty than their age peers in solving problems, learning new facts and processes, and in communicating in a wide range of situations in everyday life. Whatever their degree of learning difficulties, many of the children would also be affected by sensory and physical disabilities. Yet they all had to be educated.

The Warnock Report and after

Probably the most significant publication on special education since World War II has been the Warnock Report, *Special Educational Needs* (HMSO 1978). In November 1973, Mrs Margaret Thatcher, then Secretary of State for Education and Science in England and Wales, announced the formation of a Committee of Enquiry in to the Education of Handicapped Children and Young People, including those with learning difficulties. This committee, chaired by Mrs Mary Warnock, was to review special educational provision in England, Wales and Scotland, and make recommendations about its future development. Its report stated that preschool provision, postschool education and teacher education were three areas of first priority for development, but it also included proposals on identifying pupils 'with special needs', on providing appropriate education, on the involvement of parents, on the provision of services which would offset the effects of disabilities, and on many other matters. The report has also stimulated considerable debate on the issue of the educational integration of pupils with special educational needs.

Overall, the Warnock Report effected a major change of attitude from concern with pupils' handicaps to a focus on meeting their needs so that they might, as far as possible:

enlarge (their) knowledge, experience and imaginative understanding and thus (their) awareness of moral values and capacities for enjoyment; and to enable (them) to enter the world after formal education is over as . . . active participant(s) in society and . . . responsible contributor(s) to it, capable of achieving as much independence as possible (Committee of Enquiry 1978, para. 1.4).

The Education Acts of 1981 were the legislative response to the Warnock Report. They had three major effects:

● the abolition of the statutory categories of handicap which had existed since the mid-1950s

- the appointment of Named Persons (a parents' guide with no real power or role)
- establishment of Records of Needs (Scotland) or Statements of Needs (England and Wales) to note children's educational needs and how they should be met.

The 1981 Acts have disappointed many people because they required little more than what was standard practice in many education authorities: identification of children with difficulties, consultation with parents, and assessment by teams of specialists. A more fundamental problem with the Act is that it is grounded on an understanding of the concept 'needs', which seems quite superficial. 'Respond to needs, not handicaps' is a good slogan, but these are needs for the prescription of support or special provision more often than not.

This introduction has been a brief overview of the development of special educational provision for children with learning difficulties. The remainder of the chapter will examine learning difficulties themselves from an educational point of view. In practical terms, helping people to overcome learning difficulty depends on an understanding of the complexity of what they are expected to learn, and an understanding of what is involved in effective teaching and learning. The complexity of tasks is probably best understood by looking at them in terms of the development of thought and learning. The understanding of effective learning involves a consideration of the factors which influence good teaching.

THE DEVELOPMENT OF THOUGHT AND LEARNING

There is no single correct way to describe the development of thought and learning, but the principles which the Swiss psychologist, Jean Piaget, began describing in the 1920s still have many useful applications. For Piaget, understanding (or 'intelligence', or 'thinking') developed through a series of stages, ranging from the virtually reflex acts of newborn babies through to the abstract reasoning of adult intelligence.

Progress through the stages results from our experience of having to respond to tasks of everyday living which become progressively more complex as a result of our success in rising to the challenge of earlier ones. The ability to function at any of the higher stages seems to be impossible unless a person has become proficient at the lower stages. Piaget's system is useful in the context of people with learning difficulties because it illustrates the learning difficulty of not being able to handle such degrees of complexity as most people of one's own age and background.

The sensorimotor stage

At the earliest stage, the sensorimotor, the origins of purposeful behaviour appear in reflex responses to stimulation of the senses of vision, hearing, touch, movement and so on. This may well be the highest level at which some people with the most profound degrees of learning difficulty are functioning, and therefore an appropriate education for them is going to be far removed from the conventional curriculum of primary and secondary schools. Nevertheless, it is possible to arrange a full timetable for them around stimulation of the senses. Table 7.1 gives examples of these in the settings of classroom, home and outdoors.

Fortunately, there are few people whose level of functioning is so restricted that sensory stimulation is the major part of their education. In fact, the sensorimotor stage, which is often described as lasting from birth to the appearance of speech, is characterized by activity of considerable complexity. Most children at this stage are growing rapidly in their power of thinking as a result of their responses to stimulation from their surroundings. Piaget considered that there were six types of sensorimotor behaviour which could be detected, and these may be summarized as:

- *object permanence*: recognizing that out of sight does not mean out of mind
- recognizing simple *cause-effect* relationships
- *deliberate actions* to achieve a purpose

Table 7.1 Examples of activities for sensory stimulation (based on MacKay and Dunn, 1989, pp. 27–76)

Sensory area	Classroom	Outdoors	Home
Vision	Displays of computer graphics	Visits to parks, shops and fields	Watching fish in tank
Sound	Playing percussion and other instruments to the children	As for vision	Try to discover musical likes and dislikes
Taste	Stimulate taste receptors for saltiness, bitterness, sweetness	Visits to cafés	Try to discover likes and dislikes
Smell	Scent dispenser, collection of scents and other smells in bottles	Visits to cafés, shops, farms, zoo and the seaside	Spend time in all rooms in house, and let child see what occurs in them
Touch	Surfaces of different texture to lie on	Horseriding	Bathtime: washing and drying
Movement	Activities on soft-play equipment	Swimming pool	Home-based physiotherapy (consult child's therapist, and Finnie, 1974)

- understanding the *importance of the position* of objects in relation to each other
- *imitation*, both vocal and gestural
- *manipulating* objects in increasingly complex ways.

The importance of knowing about these actions is that they can give teachers and parents useful guidance on types of activity which may be carried out with children long before they are able to understand speech. There are also many adults with severe learning difficulties who can understand little or no speech, and knowledge of these six types of action may be helpful in finding appropriate activities for such adults in training centres or at home. Knowledge of the six types of action can also be a useful guide to observation of one's pupils, students and clients, for assessing their intellectual ability. Table 7.2 gives examples of an early and of a more advanced activity for each of these types of sensorimotor action.

An enjoyable way of charting children's progress through the later phases of the sensorimotor stage, and into the preoperational stage beyond, is to watch their development of imagi-native play. At its earliest levels, play consists of acts which are overlooked easily, such as holding objects or gazing at them. Later, children will play by exploring the properties of objects in ways such as knocking spoons against different surfaces, splashing their hands under a running tap, and hiding toys under their pillows. Later still, they will play complicated games with dolls and soft toys, bathing them, feeding them and putting them to bed.

Play seems to be essential for the development of emotional and intellectual functioning in later life, and it is a process in which adults can assist. Firstly, they should give children opportunities to play by ensuring that they have the essential resources of time, space and objects. Also, they should make themselves available to be with the children and join in their play. They can do this by bringing objects to the children's attention if they seem to be ignoring them, by showing the children how a new toy works or how surfaces such as food containers and metal trays produce different sounds when struck with a stick or a spoon. And, of course, they can join in some of the longer episodes of imaginative play, making sure that all the soft toys are fed

Table 7.2 Examples of early and later actions in Piaget's six types of children's activity at the sensorimotor stage (based on MacKay & Dunn, 1989, pp. 77–165)

Type of action	Early level	More advanced level
Object permanence	Watching a toy drawn through the visual field	Searching for objects concealed in adults' hands or under boxes
Connecting cause and effect	Child is agitated when adult stops performing an amusing activity	Switches on TV, makes mechanical toy work
Deliberate actions	Reaching for a desired object	Going to cupboard for food
Position and gravity	Knocking objects off table onto floor	Building with blocks and other constructive toys
Imitation	Makes any vocalization after adult vocalizes	Imitates animal noises; imitates words of own accord
Manipulating objects	Holds object in hand and looks at it	Makes good imitation of adult activities such as sweeping or washing

in a tea party, or that a doll is tucked into bed properly.

The clearest message to adults working with children at the sensorimotor stage is that they should be given every opportunity to find life interesting, by exploring their own immediate surroundings and by visiting a range of other surroundings beyond home and school. Parents and care givers should feel a sense of success if they see children emerging from the sensorimotor stage with a lively interest in what is going on around them, with the ability to play in ever more imaginative ways, and with a desire to do things for themselves.

The preoperational stage

The developmental stage beyond sensorimotor is the preoperational. There is not a distinct break between one stage and the next, yet there are important differences. Probably the most noticeable difference between children at this stage and those still at the sensorimotor is that they are able to speak and understand language (unless they are disabled by hearing loss or physical disorder). However, it is not language ability which characterizes functioning at this level, but the way in which the children use their powers of reasoning. Preoperational reasoning exists when the child is able to use a set of rules for

organizing experiences into categories or into a simple pattern. For instance, children at the preoperational stage will show increasing proficiency with jigsaws, and eventually will be able to put into the sequence of tallest to shortest a series of cut-out figures, (e.g. animals, cars or people) which differ only in size. However, children at this stage are not adept at concentrating on two (or more) sets of rules simultaneously.

Piaget's classic examples of this showed the difficulty preoperational children have in understanding that the volume of water in a tall, slim container can be identical to that in a short, broad one. Doubt has been cast on the validity of Piaget's conclusions about children's thinking at this stage, on the grounds that he did not take sufficient account of the children's understanding of language and of the fluency of their language, and that he was not sufficiently attentive to the detail with which he arranged his experiments. Yet, his detractors have not really produced any improvement which is as useful as the development of stages for expressing the different qualities which children's thinking shows as they grow up.

For that reason alone, it is unwise to to ignore him, but there are also practical applications of his psychology which are relevant to work with people with learning difficulties who are functioning at the preoperational stage. Difficulties in working with two or more sets of rules at once are not a problem but a natural stage of development through which adults can help children to pass more easily. This is an area in which situations of 'structured play' between adults and children can be set up so that the children have to solve problems in practical play activities in the sand tray, in building with blocks and other apparatus, in water play and so on. There are also opportunities in everyday activities for developing more complex levels of thinking. These include setting out the correct number of plates and cutlery for meals, in making sure that everyone's coat has a peg, and in learning the sequence of the main events of the day such as mealtimes, time for going out and time for going to bed. Structure in play should not make it inhibiting, of course, for it is vital that children acquire habits of taking responsibility for their own development. Therefore, they need their own space and time to explore, to play with objects and materials which interest them, and to learn how to form warm and appropriate relationships with other people. They should also not be prevented from letting their imagination express itself in personal fantasy in life or in art, for the preoperational stage is when mystery, magic and reality are naturally bound together in the thinking of young children. Balancing the demands of as much freedom as possible with the setting up of opportunities in which individual children may grow is one of the key skills of teachers working at the nursery and early primary stages of the schools.

Communication by language is a critical faculty which makes its appearance at the start of the preoperational stage; first words are usually heard from normal infants of 12–18 months approximately, though factors such as hearing loss or a domineering sibling may cause delayed onset of speech in children with no other learning difficulty. A great deal has been written on how to encourage the development of language in children who are late in starting to speak, e.g. Gillham 1979, McConkey & Price 1986, MacKay & Dunn 1989. From an educational point of view, the appearance of speech at the preoperational stage, and its development

in the stages beyond, develops hand-in-hand with powers of thinking such as reasoning, problem-solving, recognizing and understanding the world. The relationship of language to thinking was stated powerfully by the Soviet psychologists Luria (1961) and Vygotsky (1962), and their views have filtered through to the standard teaching practices in nursery and primary schools, such as:

- teachers making sure that they use words as well as actions to describe visual and motor experiences such as construction activities, painting and the formation of letters in handwriting
- children being encouraged to use language in the course of their classroom activities
- teachers making sure that the children are using their language to perform a variety of *functions* such as describing, asking, imagining and solving problems.

The development of communication, the exchange of ideas, has the highest priority in modern primary, nursery and special education. In the case of literacy, which is discussed later in the chapter, confidence and competence in communication are more important than any phonic drills or exercises in visual perception. Teaching children to understand mathematics, the environment and social relationships is often based on the principle that the skills will be learned more effectively and efficiently if they are put into words right from the start. The reason for drawing attention to the importance of communication here is that many people with severe learning difficulties may show preoperational thinking throughout life because of the extent of their disability. However, the skills which they do possess may grow if their ability to communicate lets them use these skills regularly and purposefully in an exchange of ideas with other people.

The stages of concrete operations and formal operations

Children who have attained the stage of concrete

operations are able to use several sets of rules simultaneously, and work out actions in their head without having to perform them physically. For example, they will be able to give good reasons for safety procedures such as looking left and right before crossing the road. They will also be able to tell why outwardly different objects have underlying similarities: a pear and a peach are alike because you can eat them, and a car and a bus are alike because they take you to school. Many children are showing clear signs of being able to think at this level around the age of 7 years, yet it is a level of thinking which is quite adequate for a great number of important everyday tasks, and one which we use all the time in adult life, irrespective of our degree of intelligence.

Concrete operational thinking is attained by many people with quite marked learning difficulties. This is why so many have shown that they can live valued and independent lives as adults. Straightforward, concrete rules are learned by many people with learning difficulties, and by the rest of us, for attending to tasks at home such as cooking, cleaning, hygiene, personal appearance and the elementary maintenance of buildings and equipment. Outside the home, obeying equally simple rules will let us travel independently, use resources in the community, such as shops and public offices, and carry out a surprising amount of unskilled (and sometimes semi-skilled) employment. People with learning difficulties may have problems handling money, coping with the wide range of interpersonal relationships in which we are assumed to be competent, and in underlying employment skills, such as good timekeeping and sustained effort. However, poor attainment in these skills is not an inevitable consequence of having difficulty with learning. It may be the result of lack of opportunity for people to acquire the skills, of underestimation of their potential, and of the reluctance of teachers, parents and care givers to make normal demands on them. These causes of secondary disability are avoidable; avoidance begins with recognition of them and continues with deliberate attempts to promote skills which are genuinely useful for increasing self-sufficiency and for promoting healthy, appropriate relationships with other people. The matter of which skills are 'genuinely useful' is not easy to resolve, and is dealt with later in the chapter.

The stage of formal operations is usually thought to begin at the upper end of the primary school years, around the age of 11. The characteristic type of thinking at this stage is the ability to recognize the principles which underlie problems of ethics and concepts, rather than just the functional attributes of these problems which begin to be understood at the stage of concrete operations. In the case of the earlier examples, children who can use formal operational thinking will state that pears and peaches are alike because they are fruit, and that cars and buses are alike because they are forms of transport. In school, reasoning like this lies behind successful performance in the abstract problems which are set in mathematics, in the interpretation of English literature and in speculating about the circumstances which have led to certain events (in science and social subjects). Such children will also be able to give 'adult' reasons for ethical matters by saying, for example, that we should not tell lies because this will lose us the trust of other people.

People who use formal operational thinking do not have the global difficulty with learning which characterizes mental handicap, and therefore it does not require further discussion here. It is sufficient to emphasize that formal operational thinking is unnecessary for possibly the great majority of tasks in everyday living and that, especially for people who can use concrete operational thinking, what matters most from an educational point of view is that they should have the chance to broaden and strengthen their skills in as wide a range of practical situations as possible.

EFFECTIVE TEACHING AND LEARNING

Effective teaching and learning depend on a number of factors. A few of the most important will be considered here. First, account must be taken of applied learning theory which has influenced practice in education, health and social work for approximately 40 years. Next, there is a note on the dynamics of adult/child interaction with children who are young developmentally. The value of good teacher/pupil relationships is not questioned in the school years, but it is equally important in the preschool years, and in working with people who have profound difficulties. The quality of the curriculum, the experiences provided by schools, should also be considered as it has been in a period of rapid development since the Warnock Report (HMSO 1978). The guiding principle now is that the curriculum must be relevant to pupils' lives at and beyond the school years. Special mention will be made of literacy in the curriculum section. Finally, all those who work with children who have learning difficulties should know about the formal and informal administrative procedures for keeping pupils' progress under review, to ensure that their special educational needs are being met.

Applied learning theory

It is usual to date the scientific study of learning from the conditioning of natural reflexes carried out by Pavlov and other Russian psychologists in the 19th century. However, the theory which implicitly or explicitly underlies a great deal of current educational practice is 'operant learning', which began to make a significant impact on psychology, education and health care practice in the 1950s, and which is discussed elsewhere in this manual under headings such as 'behaviour modification'. The principal figure in the formation of operant learning theory was B. F. Skinner, late Professor of Psychology at Harvard University. For Skinner, successful teaching and learning were achieved by appropriate 'reinforcement', which he defined as 'events which strengthen behaviour'.

In formal education and in health care, the behaviours to be strengthened are usually chosen for the learner so deciding how best to reinforce them can often be a delicate art. Matching the learner to the desired goal and the reinforcement may be difficult, as may the gradual withdrawal of reinforcement so that the behaviour is under the learner's control entirely. Moreover, in real life, reinforcement may come from no more than noticing that we have completed an action, or from satisfaction with what we have accomplished: we provide our own motivation to act and to learn. As far as possible this should be the aim of education too: to enable learners to gain sufficient satisfaction (or reinforcement) from what they are doing that they have to rely on reinforcement provided by others as little as possible. The specifics of applied learning theory are dealt with in greater detail elsewhere in the manual, but it is worth noting the following aspects of it which have particular relevance to the education of children.

Developmentally appropriate reinforcement

In education, reinforcement often means 'letting the learner know that a desired behaviour has occurred'. How the learner is told this must depend in part on the person's developmental level. Those who can talk can be told verbally what they have done and that they have done it well. Those who do not understand speech may be reinforced in nonverbal ways, such as smiles, physical contacts or small amounts of favourite food or drink. Children with the most profound learning difficulties require a different type of reinforcement, particularly if their behaviour consists mainly of reflex actions. In such cases, appropriate reinforcements are the stimuli which evoke the reflex acts, such as stroking of the child's limbs, face and neck to produce movement, or bringing bright objects into the visual field to produce eye fixation.

Respecting personal preferences

Each child is an individual and reinforcement which works for one may not work for another. Some children like being told that they are doing well, some do not; some will work hard for special play activities, others will work badly to avoid them. Some will stop undesired behaviour when ignored on one occasion but will get worse if it is ignored next time.

Sensible reinforcement

In the past, pieces of breakfast cereal or chocolate have been given in reinforcement in lavatory training. Perhaps they have strengthened a desired behaviour, but the association of lavatory and food seems to be an odd one to build up. There are also many people who are not keen on using sweets as reinforcers at any time for reasons of dental hygiene.

Teaching useful skills

Applied learning theory is an effective way of getting other people to do what we want. Leaving aside the civil rights issue in this, it is also worth questioning the educational value of what is taught. At one end of the developmental scale, much time is spent teaching children with severe and profound learning difficulties to give prolonged eye contact to adults, without any evidence that this is normal behaviour, or even behaviour which promotes effective learning. At the other end of the scale, postadolescent males may be taught how to use a safety razor, when disposable razors and electric shavers are the cultural norm.

Diagnostic teaching

It may be necessary to reconsider the analysis of a task if the teaching is not bringing results. Was the child assessed correctly in the first place? Is the appropriate reinforcement being used? Is the child afraid to try, or failing to pay attention? Does the child have a physical disability which should be compensated for by a different position of sitting or lying? Should the single stage being worked at be broken down into smaller steps? Is the task too difficult, too easy, boring or irrelevant?

Beyond teaching

Aim to make children enjoy learning for its own sake. Does the child with profound difficulties watch fish in an aquarium after the adult has gone away? Does the preverbal child play happily alone at the sand tray? Does the teenager who can read a little look at the television section of the newspaper voluntarily? If 'yes' is the answer to questions like these, they are being helped to become independent learners.

Adult/child interaction

For a number of years it has been known that babies come into the world all ready to take an active part in forming relationships with other people, particularly their mothers (see, for example, Trevarthen 1988). They are a long way from being passive organisms just waiting for stimulation. In fact, they seem to be programmed to take part in very complex interactions soon after birth. They do not need to wait for their mothers to begin the interaction: often it is the baby who will set in motion these early turn-taking games of smiling, vocalizing and imitating. Children with severe developmental difficulties may have sensory, cognitive or motor disorders which prevent them initiating activity with their mothers, or which prevent their mothers being aware that they are trying to initiate activity. In addition, the babies may show little or no clear responsiveness to activities which their mothers initiate. The babies' lack of responsiveness discourages mothers from reacting as consistently, spontaneously and immediately as they might, thus creating a secondary source of difficulties beyond those created by the pathology which has given them difficulties with learning.

Fortunately, it is possible to avoid at least some of the disadvantages of faulty reactions by adults. For example, children with conditions such as Rett syndrome, which cause profound degrees of learning difficulty, may be helped by techniques such as movement therapy and music therapy. The aim in both therapies is to use vocalization, movement and bodily contact to establish a relationship between the child and the therapist which is very like the interplay in the mother-and-infant games described by Trevarthen. This contact is likely to be much more than mere stimulation, for it requires the therapist to be attentive to reactions from the child, and to respect these as active attempts to make contact with the therapist.

Similar principles apply to work with individuals whose difficulty with learning is not so severe. For example, Arkell (1986) has suggested that mothers have a natural facility for teaching their children to communicate by reacting to their children's vocalizations and behaviour as if they were meaningful. It does not matter too much that the mother interprets the vocalization incorrectly: that reaction may encourage the child to be more accurate next time. What does matter is that she has shown respect for an attempt to communicate and this seems to be a powerful method of encouraging the child to persevere with purposeful communicative behaviour. The importance of purpose should be underlined because there is still a popular belief that children should be taught to imitate words. Adequate ability to imitate is probably useful for the development of intelligible pronunciation but it is less important than having a need to communicate.

Also, Cheseldine & McConkey (1979) have shown ways in which mothers can be more successful at encouraging their children with learning difficulties to understand and use speech. They should not try to drag words from them by artificial techniques, such as holding up objects or pointing to pictures and asking the children to name them. Playing at teachers is best left to children! Instead, they can draw children's attention to important words by using them as often as possible (in a natural way) in the routines of daily living, by using speech sparingly so that 'target' words are not lost in a fog of other words, and by encouraging children to play imaginatively and explore so that they will have a need to communicate arising from the events which they are experiencing.

Curriculum

Education is concerned with enabling pupils to live fulfilling lives, with enlarging their knowledge, experience, imagination and understanding, and with preparing them for life after school. These aims are no different for pupils who have learning difficulties, though the curriculum through which they are realized will often be different from that for pupils with average or above-average ability in mainstream schools. Different priorities make this necessary. In general, the greater the pupils' degree of learning difficulty, the greater will be the emphasis put on helping them to communicate (verbally or by a sign-system) and on helping them to acquire practical skills which will enable them to look after themselves as much as possible.

Currently, the curriculum in mainstream primary schools and special schools is often divided into four broad areas as sources of activities for meeting these aims:

- communication
- problem-solving
- environmental studies
- expressive arts.

Each of these areas will now be considered individually with reference to pupils who have learning difficulties.

Communication

Communication includes literacy (reading and writing), speaking and listening. Although literacy is a special case, speaking, listening, and their nonverbal equivalents for those who will not be able to understand speech, or not be able to use it, are essential skills to develop in order to reduce the barriers between people with learning difficulties and the broader world. Some years ago, there was a strong emphasis on teaching people with learning difficulties to imitate adult words and adult forms of language. Nowadays, more importance is placed on the functions of communication which were referred to in the discussion of the preoperational stage. It is important to give pupils with learning difficulties plenty of opportunities to meet other people so that they can practise their own communicative skills in a variety of settings, and become accustomed to the imperfections of the communication of others.

Problem-solving

Problem-solving includes arithmetic and other

aspects of mathematics, and the premathematical activities which are used in nursery schools to enable children to understand size, shape, quantity and volume. Some pupils with learning difficulties are quite proficient at arithmetical processes like addition and subtraction, although their understanding of the practical application of what they are doing may not be great. This is one area of schooling in which computer programmes can be very useful for teaching basic number facts, and also important skills such as using money, estimating quantities and applying number facts to real problems. As in so many other things, people with learning difficulties may have acquired a real knowledge of number without anyone realizing it, as the following example shows.

The staff of an adult training centre (ATC) had decided that it would be good idea to have a clients' committee. Early videotapes of the group in action showed very little happening. There was no real discussion, and most of the proceedings were dominated by a man with Down syndrome talking about nothing in particular. The members of the committee were fulfilling one of the common stereotypes of people with learning difficulties, the inability to reason verbally and make generalizations. Then one day the videotapes were transformed. The man with Down syndrome was sidelined and his dominant role within the group was taken by a woman who hitherto had never spoken. She led discussions which involved most members of the group and which produced outcomes. The reason for this dramatic change was that the staff had given the committee £20 to spend. At a stroke, there was a real reason for having a committee meeting, and the members were able to respond with common sense, and an understanding of group processes and arithmetic which surprised and pleased everyone.

Environmental studies

Environmental studies include science, knowledge of the community, practical skills, health and similar topics. In many primary schools, environmental studies bring together many differ-

ent subjects in a topic study. For example, the topic 'babies' might consider the young of different species, reproduction and development. Older pupils might put together a map of the public resources in their neighbourhood, with information on how to travel to them and how to use them. Neighbourhood themes are often considered in special schools as a means of showing pupils the attractive things which exist beyond school hours and school days, and as a means of motivating them to make use of them.

Sex education is a difficult topic which is often tackled as a branch of environmental studies. Current practice approaches the subject within the framework of 'relationships', and the following intriguing approach, 'circles', has been found useful for promoting discussion with pupils who have learning difficulties. In this approach, the individual is at the centre of a group of concentric circles. People with the right of greater or lesser access to the privacy of the person at the centre are in the outer circles. In the circle closest to the individual are people, such as parents, siblings and a few special friends, who can be allowed to be very close to the individual, physically and emotionally. In the outmost circle are complete strangers. In between, the individual has to locate members of the extended family who are less intimate than those in the circle closest to the centre, and professionals such as teachers, nurses, doctors and social workers who have good reason to be physically or emotionally close to the individual at certain times.

Locating people within circles is not a once-and-for-all task because the nature of relationships changes; displays of physical intimacy which are considered acceptable between adults and young children are likely to be unacceptable between adults and those in the teenage years and beyond. Neither is the location of people within circles a simple or a painless task; people with learning difficulties may have had little encouragement to believe that they are entitled to a private, inner circle of their own, from which they have a right to exclude other people, including those in the nearest circle of relatives and friends. At a very serious level, lack of awareness of this right may leave them open to physical abuse but, more insidiously, it may take the form of an emotional smothering which inhibits the development of self-esteem and maturity.

Expressive arts

Expressive arts include art, music, drama and movement (physical and outdoor education). Sometimes religious education is included within the expressive arts, sometimes it is seen as an area on its own. The aim is to let pupils express themselves in a wide variety of ways, as this is considered to be valuable for the development of the individual personality, for finding and knowing oneself. It is in this area of the curriculum that parents and care givers can most easily complement, and probably improve on, the opportunities provided by the school. There may be more time and relaxation at home to devote to these matters, and the adults at home may attend (as spectators or participants) a range of social, cultural and sporting activities which interest the child more than what happens at school. In addition, many children with learning difficulties enjoy attending youth organizations and clubs in their spare time.

Administrative procedures

The aim of this section is to give readers some information about administrative procedures concerning special education as they may, on occasion, find that parents of children with learning difficulties ask for advice about matters of procedure, or because they themselves may have to act on a child's behalf in dealings with the local authority.

Despite regional and national variations, certain common principles and practices exist. There are formal procedures for noting that a child has pronounced learning difficulties. There are also formal procedures for appealing against decisions of the local authority concerning special educational provision. For example, parents may wish to challenge the authority's decision to place their child in a special school (when they, the parents, believe that a mainstream school would

be more appropriate), or the decision to place the child in a mainstream school or class (when they believe that special provision would be more appropriate). The decision of the local authority is not final if parents are unhappy about the outcome. Disputes about the substance of education and about evaluation of children's needs may ultimately be taken to the Minister of Education; disputes about school placement may be settled in the sheriff or county courts.

One of the glaring anomalies of the 1981 Education Acts was the apparent lack of responsibility of education authorities to provide special services which children with disabilities might require. However, a number of parents have now challenged their local authorities successfully on the matter of the lack of special provision, referring to local authorities' duties under the 1980 Education Acts to provide adequate and efficient education for all children.

Parents should also expect that any of their children who are receiving special education will have that provision, and that their children's response to it will be reviewed regularly. For example, the headteachers of many special schools organize annual reviews of all their pupils, and invite to the review meetings the children's parents and all professionals who work with the children and their families. Attending these meetings can be a stressful procedure for parents, especially for those attending for the first time, or for those who normally make few informal contacts with the school and other agencies on their children's behalf. Yet, parents and professionals should see each other as members of a team, all with valued information, questions, challenges, support and opinions, though all should also take account of the parents' unique monitoring role as consumers of the services which are being provided.

Finally, the 1981 Acts require education authorities in Scotland, England and Wales to have a formal meeting to consider the future needs of older teenagers who have Records (Scotland) or Statements (England and Wales) of special educational needs. These meetings ought to be valuable for taking stock of pupils' careers at schools, and for building contacts with the further education and social work services which these young people are likely to use in the years after school. The attendance of parents or carers at these meetings, and if possible the young people themselves, is of considerable value.

EDUCATIONAL INTEGRATION

The chapter would not be complete without reference to the educational integration of pupils with learning difficulties, a subject about which there has been considerable debate over the last 20 years. In part, this is because the right to equality of educational opportunity is often equated with identical educational provision for all pupils, and this is difficult to envisage in practice. Yet it is also recognized that segregated special education may be too sheltered an experience, too limited in its level of interest and challenge, and inadequate in preparing pupils for as full a life as possible in the community. Therefore, it is worth considering what forms integration takes and what the implications are for good practice in the schools.

The Warnock Committee classified three types of integration: locational, social and functional. Loosely speaking, locational integration has the least degree of integration, social integration is in the middle, and functional integration has the greatest. In practice, locational integration would mean that pupils with and without learning difficulties made use of the same educational locations and equipment, though there may be little or no contact between the two groups of pupils. Examples of locational integration include pupils from a special school visiting a mainstream school to make use of its gymnasium or home economics room, but with no real contact with the mainstream pupils. Social integration would involve providing opportunities for pupils with learning difficulties and those with none to meet in activities like games, concerts and other social gatherings. Examples of this include pupils from a special class or school joining pupils from a mainstream school for 'non-academic subjects' such as games and outdoor pursuits. Functional integration combines

social integration and locational integration, and adds the requirement that all pupils should be educated together, irrespective of the severity of any learning difficulties which they may have.

Locational and social integration are often easy to accomplish when there is goodwill and good communication among staff in the mainstream and special sectors. Functional integration is different, both because of the practical difficulties which it raises and because of areas of educational philosophy which have to be confronted. These issues can be illustrated by reference to examples from two extremes of the range of learning difficulty: a child with profound difficulty learning whose difficulties are complex because of sensory loss and motor disorder, and a child with moderate difficulty learning. Let us assume that both are in classes where the average age of the pupils is 10 years.

The child with profound learning difficulties is unlikely to be able to take part in any lessons taken by the other children so it would seem that integration is working at locational and social levels only. However, it can be argued that this social integration is providing the pupil with valuable experience of interaction with other children, and is valuable for developing the social awareness of the rest of the class to the existence and the needs of people with disabilities. Provision of an extra teacher would also allow the pupil with profound difficulties to have individual work in the class or to be withdrawn to a room for individual programmes of teaching.

Unfortunately, that solution is too simple. The financial and logistic investment required to provide adequate human and material support for such a pupil is considerable. There is also the educational argument that much of the pupil's time in the company of the other pupils might be better spent attempting to meet cognitive and skills objectives which are as important as the social objectives which may (or may not) be met by passing the day sitting or lying in a mainstream class. The case for practical, functional integration of pupils with profound learning difficulties has yet to be made convincingly.

The example of the child with moderate difficulty learning is different. He or she is likely to be able to take part in all classroom lessons, but will probably have difficulty understanding abstract problems in mathematics and in understanding written and spoken English at the same complexity as that which can be tackled by most of the class. However, the case for providing segregated education for the majority of pupils in this loose category becomes ever more difficult to sustain, even though they are still the largest single group of pupils receiving special education in the United Kingdom. It has been recognized for many years that it is very difficult to identify moderate learning difficulty.

Sometimes the reason for transfer has not been very good: the children have been failing at school; their behaviour may have disrupted teachers and pupils in mainstream classes; or they may have had difficulties with learning which were the results of social disadvantage or a poor curriculum rather than congenital disabilities (Galloway & Goodwin 1987). But at the same time, this disparate group of pupils includes children whose difficulties result from clinical syndromes, genetic abnormalities or problems of the central nervous system. It

is important that consultation procedures such as the Statement and Record of Needs should be used to do proper credit to the complex reasons for pupils having moderate difficulty learning so that the decision about where a child should be educated is not based on assumptions that the current structure of special and mainstream education will remain unchanged, nor on slogans about integration which masquerade as ideals.

It is worth remembering that integration is just one of the three main cornerstones of Wolfensberger's 'social role valorization' (Wolfensberger 1983), which is discussed in Chapter 3. In that philosophy, integration is not so much an end in itself but a means of ensuring that people receive services which enable them to live valued lives. Regarding school placement, then, the aim is not necessarily integrated education but, always, appropriate education. Of course, 'appropriate', like 'needs', is a value-laden term which depends for its implementation on personal, educational and sociological forces, but it seems more worthwhile to make the effort to find out what it means in practice than to put too much faith in narrow practical and theoretical interpretations of educational integration.

REFERENCES

Arkell J E H 1986 The language teaching device. Childcare, Health and Development 12(3): 151–166

Cheseldine S, McConkey R 1979 Parental speech to young Down's syndrome children: an intervention study. American Journal of Mental Deficiency 83(6): 612–620

Committee of Enquiry 1978 Special educational needs (the Warnock report). HMSO, London

Finnie N R 1974 Handling the young cerebral palsied child at home. Heinemann, London

Galloway D, Goodwin C 1987 The education of disturbing children. Longman, Harlow

Gillham B 1979 The first words language programme. George Allen & Unwin, London

Gillham W E C 1978 Reconstructing educational psychology. Croom Helm, London

Luria A R 1961 The role of speech in the regulation of normal and abnormal behaviour. Pergamon, Oxford

McConkey R, Price P 1986 Let's talk. Souvenir, London

MacKay G F, Dunn W R 1989 Early communicative skills. Routledge, London

Shakespeare R 1970 Severely subnormal children. In: Mittler P (ed) The psychological assessment of mental and physical handicaps. Methuen, London p 519–541

Terman L M, Merrill M M 1960 Stanford Binet intelligence scale: manual for 3rd revision. Harrap, London

Trevarthen C 1988 Infants trying to talk. In: Söderbergh R (ed) Children's creative communication. University of Lund Press, Lund p 9–31

Vygotsky L 1962 Thought and language. MIT Press, Cambridge, Massachusetts

Wolfensberger W 1983 Social rôle valorization: a proposed new term for the principle of normalization. Mental Retardation 21(6): 234–239

Working Party on Standards of Assessment for Special School Children 1961 Degrees of handicap. HMSO, Edinburgh

QUESTIONS

1. What special educational provision exists in the area in which you work? What range of pupils and students does it serve?
2. What channels of communication exist between your local special educational provision and the families of the children served by it?
3. At which stage of Piaget's scheme are the children you know thinking and acting? What are your reasons for that assessment?
4. To what extent do any children with learning difficulties known to you enjoy an integrated life in the community beyond school?
5. What useful 'environmental text' exists in your local community, in the shops, transport and other services? How could it be used to make children aware of purposeful reading?
6. How would you set about teaching the message 'Don't go with strangers' to children with poor powers of verbal communication?

CHAPTER CONTENTS

Introduction 135

Hearing impairments 136
Characteristics of hearing impairments 137
   Time of onset 137
   Degrees of deafness 137
   Types of deafness 137
Hearing aids 138
Communication 138

Visual impairments 138

Sensory multiple impairments 141
Deaf-blind 142
   Congenital visual impairment with an acquired
      hearing impairment 142
   Congenital hearing impairment with an acquired
      visual loss 143
   Acquired visual and hearing impairments 143
   Congenital or early-onset deaf-blindness 143
Sensory and multiple impairments 143
   Visual and multiple impairments 143
   Hearing and multiple impairments 144

Assessment 144

Bringing meaning to the world 145

The total approach 146

Conclusion 147

8

Helping with sensory impairments

G. Morbey

Key points

- Blindness and deafness are not 'all or nothing' phenomena rather they present degrees of severity
- Alternative means of communication can supplement impaired hearing or vision
- Those with visual, hearing and learning difficulties require a multiplicity of techniques to help them communicate basic needs
- There is a danger of the whole person getting lost in the plethora of services catering for specific needs of the person

INTRODUCTION

The term 'sensory impairment' covers a wide range of special needs and levels of ability. This chapter attempts to identify some of the different aspects of sensory impairment while also looking at some practical issues. We are therefore concerned here with vision and hearing.

Even looking at hearing alone, for example, there is a wide range of damage and therefore variation in levels of ability. The term 'deaf' is a misleading one; 'hearing impairment' is more suitable. 'Deaf' implies a total hearing loss when in fact a person may have partial or residual hearing. Equally, it makes a difference *when* hearing loss occurs.

A person born deaf, congenitally or prelingually deaf, will be faced with particular difficulties in acquiring language. However, those who become deaf in later life, perhaps through the ageing process, have a different set of difficulties and, consequently, different needs.

There are also wide variations in visual impairment, ranging from partial sight through to blindness. There are different types of visual conditions, for example, tunnel vision, light sensitivity and retinal damage, all resulting in disparate sets of needs. As with hearing impairment, the time of onset of visual impairment also affects a person's view of the world. A congenitally blind person will not have gained a visual perception of his or her environment whereas someone who becomes blind later in life will have stored up visual memories.

The terms 'deaf' and 'blind' are therefore simplistic and do not begin to address the issues involved in sensory impairment. Nolan (1984) states that the term 'deaf' is an 'inappropriate description because it conveys to the lay person an impression of someone who hears no sound whatsoever.' The area can be further confused if both distance senses are damaged – visual and hearing impairments occurring together. Equally, there are people who have severe learning difficulties who also have a sensory impairment.

The number of people affected by damage to one or both distance senses is a significant part of the population of a mental handicap hospital. A study undertaken by the Royal National Institute for the Blind (RNIB) (1987) estimated that there were 4300 mentally handicapped visually impaired people aged between 16 and 64 residing in mental handicap hospitals.

There are difficulties in acquiring accurate statistics partly because of the difficulties in identification and assessment. Sebba (1987) notes 'The prevalence of additional impairments such as hearing or visual problems among people who have a mental handicap is far greater than in the general population.' Furthermore, the occurrence of these problems becomes more likely with increasing severity of mental handicap. Studies in hospitals and in the community have indicated that many people with learning disabilities suspected of having hearing or visual problems have not received specialized assessment and have therefore not been provided with glasses or hearing aids mainly because of the difficulties they present in terms of testing.

Sensory impairment in the area of mental handicap has been recognized for some time. Wolf & Anderson (1973) described visual limitations in over 50% of children with cerebral palsy. Lawson et al (1977) found that as many as 70% of a sample of mentally handicapped children had visual defects. Cunningham & McArthur (1981) noted a high prevalence of hearing impairments in Down syndrome children, and audiologists Tucker & Nolan (1984, 1986) recommended that all people with a mental handicap should receive audiological assessments.

What does all this mean in terms of nursing or working with someone who has sensory impairment? In fact, it means a great deal. If we are working with a person who perhaps has profound learning difficulties, a very small amount of residual vision can be important. For example, understanding that someone possibly has a small amount of peripheral vision will mean that we will not get eye-to-eye contact. The person may have developed strategies to maximize visual information and may therefore turn their head to the side. In understanding the situation, we can then appreciate that he or she is not ignoring us, not turning his or her head away to avoid us, but rather to pay attention.

It is useful to consider in more detail the definitions and variations within sensory impairment, starting with hearing impairments.

HEARING IMPAIRMENTS

It is important to know about the physiology of the ear so we understand that when the nerve cells are damaged in the cochlea, the levels of deafness which occur are dependent on the number and types of cells damaged. Severe, profound and partial loss can occur and these may be high, low or a mix of frequency loss. As noted in the introduction, time of onset is also an important factor.

Deafness does not mean that a person will hear nothing or hear everything at a lower level. It does not help to shout! Moreover, the old description 'deaf and dumb' is offensive and untrue.

A classic study by Schlesinger & Meadow (1972) documented the acquisition of signing (manual communication) by two deaf children of deaf parents and the signed words compared more than favourably with hearing children. Meadow (1980) further stated that vocabulary growth, grammar and syntax were all equally comparable to hearing peers.

Our main concern is usually with sensorineural deafness. Although some people may have conductive deafness, perhaps resulting from chronic middle ear infections, many conductive losses can be treated and cured either through antibiotics or, in the case of malformation, surgery may be used. Conductive loss is fairly common. Some 10% of children may suffer from short term losses. It is therefore important to be aware of ear infections so that early treatment can be offered.

Sensorineural deafness, on the other hand, is permanent, often severe and for the best part cannot be treated medically, although work with cochlear implants is increasing.

Characteristics of hearing impairments

There are a number of factors involved when considering hearing impairment: *time of onset*, *degree* and *type* of hearing impairment being three main factors.

Time of onset

It is likely that a person who acquires deafness later in life will have speech whereas a congenitally deaf person may not. However, this rather sweeping statement is dependent equally on the degree and type of hearing loss. Other factors that may affect this are associated with the person's ability to lip read, interpret environmental cues and understand body language. Speech therapy has a huge contribution to make to a person acquiring deafness later in life. The conservation of speech is a crucial area.

Degrees of deafness

This refers to the measurement of volume. One important measure of sound is the loudness of volume. This is measured on a decibel scale. To give you a better idea of sound, the following list indicates at what decibel level various sounds can be heard.

- 140dB – pain threshold
- 120dB – aeroplane taking off
- 80dB – shouting in a loud voice
- 60dB – ordinary conversation
- 20dB – quiet whisper
- 0dB – threshold of hearing

Thus, if a person is noted as having a 60dB loss, this refers to his or her threshold of hearing. However, with the use of hearing aids, a 60dB loss can be greatly helped and the person may be able to hear ordinary conversation. A 25dB loss would be considered a mild hearing impairment and, again, amplification through hearing aids may be useful. The degree of loss can vary right through to a profound 95dB hearing loss, although audiologically it is very rare for someone to hear nothing at all.

Types of deafness

Sound travels in waves: the more frequent the waves, the higher pitched the sound. You can get an idea of the transmission of sound by using tin cans linked by knotted string stretched tight, one tin acting as the speaker and the other as the receiver. Messages can be transmitted in this way. Sound waves travel from their source at a speed of 760 miles per hour. The number of waves arriving at the ear in one second is the frequency of sound.

A high frequency loss may cause great difficulty in understanding speech even though the person is aware of talk going on around them. Speech sounds can be put into two categories: consonants and vowels. Vowel sounds are generally lower in frequency than consonants. It is the consonants that make speech intelligible. Take, for example the phrase 'School starts at nine o'clock'. Omitting either consonants or vowels results in:

- vowels only :   ---oo- --a--- a- -i-e o'--o--
- consonants only :   sch--l st-rts -t n-n- -'cl-ck

A range of test stimuli across frequencies is therefore used to assess hearing. Nolan (1984) states that it is vitally important for clinicians to ensure, when applying a hearing test, that a person's ability to hear both vowel and consonant information is assessed.

Hearing aids

People often forget that using a hearing aid involves practice and training if it is to be used properly. Hearing aids simply amplify *all* sound therefore the sound of cutlery will be at the same level as conversation. People are often frightened by the resulting perplexity of noise and reject hearing aids. It is important to understand this and help a person to make better use of a hearing aid. Dr Jan van Dijk refers to the 'hazardous experience' of fitting hearing aids to children but equally notes the importance of keeping the 'auditory pathways' open. Van Dijk (1982) suggests singing, music and other forms of auditory stimuli.

Sometimes, a step-by-step introduction to the hearing aid will help, perhaps starting with 1 hour a day and gradually building it up. There are various types of hearing aid. However, the three basic types are postaural (behind the ear), body worn and radio aids. Postaural aids tend to be the most common and are often preferred because the wearer will receive sound more naturally at ear level. Body worn aids, where the microphone rests on the chest, will mean that sound will be received at chest level and then transmitted through two wires to ear level. The radio aid allows for the microphone to be separated from the amplifier, e.g. the parent wears the microphone and the child wears the amplifier. These are particularly useful for classroom situations as they allow the teacher's voice to be transmitted directly to the listener while cutting out background noise.

Communication

Communication for people with hearing impairments varies depending on all the aspects we have touched on earlier. It is a complex area and a simple division between manual communication and speech does not give the complete picture – environmental cues, motivation, understanding of body language and speech therapy all play a part.

Those deaf people who use sign can choose from a number of systems. British Sign Language (BSL) is a language in its own right and is often used by deaf adults. It uses sign and finger-spelling in a particular grammatical order. Signed English uses BSL signs with fingerspelling in English word order, and Paget-Gorman sign system is an artificial sign language which exactly represents the structure of English. There are over 3000 signs within this system.

The Royal National Institute for the Deaf, the National Deaf Children's Society and the British Deaf Association are useful sources for further information on signing. There are other forms of communication for deaf people who have also got severe learning difficulties, such as Makaton, 'Hands on', symbols, objects or the deaf-blind manual. Makaton is based on BSL signs and has a total of 237 signs divided into eight stages with a ninth containing additional vocabulary. The deaf-blind manual is a touch alphabet system. The use of objects and symbols is discussed later in this chapter when a total communication approach is considered.

VISUAL IMPAIRMENTS

There are many types of visual impairment, each with different outcomes. The visual acuity and type of ocular disease which causes the eye defect have varying effects. For instance, a person with tunnel vision (retinitis pigmentosa) may focus on a door handle without seeing the door. Others may see at the side of their eyes, having peripheral vision only, while other situations may create a patchy vision and partial view of the world.

As in the situation of training a person to use a hearing aid, people often need help and support to use residual vision. Clearly, a person has to be interested to use vision. In an obscure environment a person's vision may not be stimulated enough. Van Dijk (1982), when considering deaf-blind children, notes the importance of the fitting of glasses and further states the importance of an interesting visual environment, such as a child's favourite colour or the use of a moving toy to encourage 'tracking'. In the same way as total deafness is rare equally the majority of people with significant visual deficiencies retain some functional vision though their limited experiential and cognitive abilities may lead to a tendency for their residual vision to remain largely unused.

The main aspects of testing vision concern the distance at which an object can be seen, the visual clarity and the size of the object. The environmental conditions will also play an important part, particularly the level of lighting.

When considering lighting levels, just as it is not helpful to shout at a deaf person, it is not helpful simply to expose a visually impaired person to strong sources of light. This can often be a hindrance, creating glare, and rather than enhancing residual vision will limit it. Levels of lighting should avoid glare and create contrasts. Lighting should be directed from behind the person with the major area of light falling on the object or table you wish the person to see.

Remember, a blind person will depend on you for most, if not all, of the information around them. He or she will not know who you are, the size or colour of a room, who is in the room or what is on their dinner plate, unless you tell them. If you stop reading for a moment and try to place yourself in the position of a visually impaired person, then you may begin to appreciate some of the difficulties they face. Even better, try blindfolding yourself and do some simple tasks like trying to make coffee or dusting.

Best (1987) outlines further:

Different perceptions
Imagine a person who is blind exploring an orange. What aspects of it are likely to be most important to him? Its shape? Its temperature? Its smell? Its sponginess? Its rough texture? These aspects are not the ones that you would probably find most interesting and important when looking at the same orange. For you, the most striking qualities are likely to be its shiny skin and bright colour.

What does the word 'horse' convey to a blind person? Probably the sound of hooves, snorting, and neighing; its smell, its smooth or rough coat. These impressions are quite different from the picture of a well-proportioned beast cantering smoothly across a field that the word might convey to you or me.

Speed of observation
Look at a chair. How long does it take you to notice all the main features? 1 second? At the most, 2 or 3 seconds. Now imagine someone who is blind exploring the same chair. How long would it take him? He has to explore each part separately and then try to imagine all the parts fitted together into a whole object. Would this take 10 seconds? 20 seconds? Longer? If he is mentally handicapped as well as blind, he may have great difficulty in puzzling out the way the parts fit together and may take a very long time to decide it is a chair he has found; or he may not succeed at all.

The cartoons reproduced in Figure 8.1 highlight other aspects of visual impairment which can cause difficulties.

Many services are available to people with visual impairments, either through local social work or related departments, or through societies for the blind. These services range from low visual aids (magnifiers and torches) to assist in reading, to talking watches. There is also a range of talking books (taped stories and news) and materials available in Braille and Moon.

Visually impaired people can read through tactile systems. Braille is the best known and is considered to be universal and flexible. It is multilingual and capable of representing short-hand, mathematics and musical notation. Nevertheless, braille is often difficult for an older, newly blind person to read. Dr William Moon developed the alternative Moon system which is confined to English. The raised shapes of the letters are based on the Roman alphabet. Braille is based on raised dots so is a more intricate system requiring tactile awareness. In Moon, however, the symbols are larger and easier to read through fingertips. Furthermore, the Moon-writer has greatly increased the effectiveness of writing as well as reading.

Braille, Moon and large print are all used by visually impaired people, depending on their abilities. People who read Braille tend to have an excellent knowledge of language; Moon, on the other hand, is regarded as slightly easier to

Guiding is an important aspect of assisting a person with visual impairment

Figure 8.1 'It's not funny being blind.' (Reproduced by kind permission of Strathclyde Regional Council Social Work Department.)

learn and is often introduced to elderly visually impaired people.

SENSORY MULTIPLE IMPAIRMENTS

The first part of this chapter dealt with people who have either a visual impairment or a hearing impairment. Most people with a single impairment will be in the community. The next part of the chapter considers sensory impairment combined with other impairments and is therefore likely to be more relevant to a person caring for an individual with learning disabilities. However, the brief overview of visual and hearing impairments is also important to the knowledge and understanding of a person with additional difficulties.

When considering visual impairment earlier in this chapter we highlighted some aspects associated with maximizing the function of residual vision, such as lighting, contrast and an interesting environment. This process is not so straightforward with people who have a combination of disabilities. Ouvry (1987) states that children with profound handicaps, including sensory deficits, may be unable to acquire a satisfactory level of stimulation from their surroundings, or they may be confused and overwhelmed by the impressions they receive and their inability to filter and organize the information. We must therefore consider not only how to maximize residual vision and hearing but also how damage to these senses interferes with the whole person.

The rest of the chapter considers people who have complex difficulties, such as those who are born deaf-blind, multihandicapped visually impaired, or multihandicapped hearing impaired. While it is acknowledged that every person's needs are individual, and each person is to be respected and understood within that context, it is necessary to generalize to some extent.

The reader may be asking why is it so important to consider the sensory impairment when a person has severe and complex learning difficulties? The answer literally is that unless we consider all aspects of a person, all abilities and disabilities within a 'whole' person view, we are unlikely to fully understand an individual or provide adequate resources or support.

Often, difficulties arise because of the complexities of need and various practitioners' well-founded commitment to do the very best for a given client. This frequently, unfortunately, results in the client being referred to one service or another so that the appropriate 'bits' of him or her can be considered. Thus he or she goes to one expert for vision, another for hearing and another for specialist aids and welfare. The picture becomes even more confusing when the information a person is receiving through these services is scrutinized in any detail. It is not only confusing but also, on occasions, conflicting as well. What can the client make of these resources? Typically, a 30-year-old man can be found residing in a hospital for the mentally handicapped and labelled 'aggressive'. He does not wear hearing aids and his vision has not been tested for 10 years. In fact, his so-called 'aggression' is due to his lack of communication skills, and he has found that the only way to receive attention is to create a 'scene'. Instead of considering such people as 'multiply' handicapped, and being overwhelmed by the complexity of need, it is vital to consider and be constantly aware of the sensory deficits they experience and, therefore, the distorted information they receive. In a variety of ways, deaf-blind people may have fallen between services.

Diversity of needs cuts across a multitude of services which must be delivered in a coordinated fashion. It is only by recognizing the specific disability of deaf-blindness that related services will, on the one hand, have a resource to turn to and, on the other hand, be aware of the need to do so.

Communication must be entered into in a number of ways. Having some skill in using the deaf-blind manual alphabet is not enough and may not even be appropriate. Rather, total communication philosophies may be more useful; various combinations of tactile, smell, and movement can be utilized, combined with hands-on techniques for communication.

Furthermore, particularly if we are working with people who have severe and profound impairments, we are likely to be overwhelmed by the complexity of problems. In all aspects of our lives we require feedback and reinforcement for what we do. A person who only rocks or appears aggressive whenever we approach may not be regarded very sympathetically by us and therefore receive less attention. It is important to be honest in considering our own feelings here. Working with people who have complex needs is a two-way process, and we are half of that interaction.

If we are overwhelmed by a person's difficulties, it is very useful to stand back and consider all aspects of his or her abilities and impairments. There is no reason why a multihandicapped hearing impaired person should not be seen by practitioners in hearing impaired services; equally, there is no reason why that person should not be considered for a hearing aid. Sadly, because of the difficulties in assessment, and perhaps our own perceptions, we can underestimate our clients, reaching negative conclusions as to their needs.

The following sections look broadly at some of the categories in the area of sensory multiple impairments. The first section considers the deaf-blind population. The second section looks at the population with sensory and some other impairments.

Deaf-blind

A useful social definition of people who are considered deaf-blind is that they have a severe degree of combined visual and auditory impairment resulting in problems of communication, information and mobility. Best (1982) states:

The deaf-blind child has one of the least understood of all handicaps; he is not just a blind child who cannot hear or a deaf child who cannot see. Rather he is a multiply sensory deprived child who has been denied the effective use of both senses.

Deaf-blindness is therefore a complex area. Aitken & Morbey (1987) note that it is only within the past ten years that deaf-blindness has come to be recognized as a specific handicap. Several factors combine to warrant consideration

of those who are deaf-blind as having a specific disability.

Congenital visual impairment with an acquired hearing impairment

This group of people may lose hearing through trauma, age and a variety of other conditions. Generally, these people have relied greatly on their hearing because of the lack of information they receive through sight, and therefore any loss can have a major disabling effect. When age has been the cause of hearing loss, this group very typically becomes isolated. They are often unable to learn new communication skills and therefore conversation is often reduced to shouting, resulting in stress for all participants.

If the person is able to learn new communication skills, the Deaf-Blind Helpers' League and Sense can provide further information. For example:

- Where new communication skills are learned, the deaf-blind manual is used to communicate with the person. Occasionally, 'hands on' signing is utilized.
- The person will then speak back.
- Depending on amount of residual vision, Braille or large print are used.
- Great use is made of technology, such as the Hasicom telephone system.

This group of the deaf-blind population are very able and can, with appropriate aids, live almost entirely independently.

Congenital hearing impairment with an acquired visual loss

This group tends to have more difficulty with communication, largely because their hearing impairment is congenital. Loss of their second distance sense can have a massive disabling effect because of the reliance placed on vision. Very often the condition is caused by Usher syndrome. Woodford's study (1989) describes the isolation and communication difficulties such people may experience. These communication difficulties include the following:

- Either 'hands on' or the deaf-blind manual is used to communicate with them. Problems can arise if signing has been their main mode of communication because as vision decreases signing becomes more difficult.
- In return, the manual and/or signing will be their form of expressive communication, and a very skilled communicator is required.
- Mobility becomes increasingly difficult – unlike the person with speech, they cannot use voice with the general public to explain their distress. In this area, Forfar Guide Dogs for the Blind has pioneered work into the use of guide dogs for deaf-blind people. This is now proving to be extremely successful and can offer them some independence.
- New technology can be extremely helpful to this group.

Acquired visual and hearing impairments

This group can have very similar communication patterns to those congenitally visually impaired who later acquire hearing loss. Trauma, illness, (e.g. meningitis) and old age can all be causal factors. The extent of their independence and their needs will vary greatly with the age of onset. Because of the later loss, this group will usually have competent knowledge of language and may use speech.

Congenital or early-onset deaf-blindness

There is no formal definition of deaf-blindness recognised in the United Kingdom, and Sense has previously utilized the Nordic Council definition. The definition given at the beginning of this section is directed to proposing a framework based on a more functional approach.

Sensory and multiple impairments

The second functional category we referred to is the person with sensory and multiple impairments. Typically, he or she has needs which are similar to those who are early or congenitally deaf-blind. This group of people, along with those who are congenitally deaf-blind, present very complex difficulties to service providers.

Visual and multiple impairments

There are difficulties with those people who are visually impaired with additional problems and who also have a functional difficulty with hearing. Again, they are considered multiply handicapped and the practical outcome is that they are not seen by teachers for the visually impaired. Their needs do not match the way services are delivered. Aitken & Morbey (1987) noted that 'The more services a person requires can often result in them receiving less'.

Hearing and multiple impairments

People with hearing and multiple impairments may not be afforded any mode of communication because of their complexity of need. It is not uncommon to find that they have no hearing aids and are not seen by teachers or specialists in the field of hearing impairment.

Increasingly, organizations for the deaf and the blind have become more aware of the complex needs of this population. This has been emphasized further by the increased integration of visually and hearing impaired people and is very clearly seen in special schools, where the population of children who have 'only' hearing or sight losses is being replaced by those with more complex disabilities.

Any service to deaf or blind people should attempt to offer resources to both these groups. Mobility training, for example, may be required in a specialist form. When there are hearing and functional communication difficulties, a mobility officer must also have specialized communication skills.

ASSESSMENT

Assessment is often the key to what services are offered and how to relate to a person. It is crucial that many elements of expertise are considered, for example, physiotherapy and psychology. Equally, it is crucial that such assessments are not seen as isolated components. The physiotherapist cannot simply consider limb movement unless the whole person is considered. Assessment must follow an integrated approach and be part of a meaningful life plan for a person.

Moreover, assessment should be dynamic, imaginative and ongoing. The needs of an individual will change and regular assessments should, therefore, be undertaken. (Deaf-Blind Services Liaison Group 1988).

If the reader works in a hospital, the assessment is likely to be based on a medical model, that is to say, clinical and more rigorous testing will be emphasized. We do not wish to diminish the importance of the medical model but rather raise some questions about it and alternatives to its use.

Ouvry (1987) identified the problems children with complex learning difficulties have in filtering and organizing information. She stated that without a consistent pattern of response to sensory stimuli in any given channel neither perception nor the lack of perception can be assumed. She added that it may be necessary to teach a response before introducing a range of stimuli in any modality in order to help to establish a response threshold in any one sensory area.

If the assessment is carried out in an unfamiliar, badly lit environment the person may be stressed and not respond to the stimulus presented. Equally, if the test materials we use are not motivating or interesting to the individual we may well end up with a visual assessment that concludes that the person is totally blind. Furthermore, the person testing the individual may be unfamiliar with him or her and not have an in-depth knowledge of the whole person. Consequently, the remarks on the case notes may state that the person is blind. Once the diagnosis is formalized subsequent observations are likely to be coloured by it. For example, in a ward situation the multihandicapped visually impaired person can see his or her hamburger on a white plate and attempts to pick it up. The nurse may discount her perception, assume she is mistaken and continue to treat the person as dependent on her.

We acknowledge assessment of ability is difficult, particularly the level of sensory impairment. However, the recognition that many factors exert influence on the accuracy of assessment, e.g. motivation or lighting, may temper the weight given to such measures. A mixed model approach where both physiological and psychological elements are considered offers a holistic approach to assessment. In addition, an awareness of the skills and weaknesses professionals bring to the assessment process is also important. In recognizing all these factors we may be able to approach assessment in an imaginative and positive fashion.

BRINGING MEANING TO THE WORLD

Under this heading we will try to explore motivation, mobility and communication. We are purposely considering these large areas together because we are attempting to follow a holistic approach. Communication is central to all aspects of working with people with sensory impairments; the links between language, thought and cognitive ability have been discussed and debated for centuries, from Descartes to Piaget and from Vigotsky to Chomsky.

Let us consider a deaf-blind person who is also mentally handicapped sitting in his chair in the ward. John Grant does very little all day, except perhaps rocking and engaging in some self-injurious behaviour. He is also incontinent and cannot feed himself.

The nurse comes to take John for his bath. He resists – like the visually impaired person in the cartoon on page 140. John is likely simply to be showing fear. He has had no warning of the nurse coming and perhaps demonstrated a startle response when the nurse touched him. Even his sense of touch, a sense that could be so crucial to him, is one that only warns John of things to come. John's sense of touch has been damaged; it is not being used to explore or calm or give him any sense of enjoyment.

How much better it would be both for John and the nurse if the activity was undertaken in the way described in Box 8.1.

Communication can be developed further for

Box. 8.1   Giving meaning to John's world

John always sits in the same seat – this is made known to him by a piece of felt tied round one of the arms, and John is encouraged to feel this every time he sits down.

The nurse makes John aware of her approach by stamping her feet and wearing some scent, then she touches the arm of John's chair.

She can further identify herself by placing John's hand on a personal reference, e.g. this nurse always wears a watch, or a special ring – it is unique to her. Natural objects are best, but if you run out of ideas you may have to contrive ones – a cotton reel, or a small bell tied round the wrist. Each member of staff has their own 'identifier' that they put on when they come on duty.

Having introduced herself, the nurse now has to try to tell John what is happening next. She does this by giving John a sponge. She then takes his hands and does a washing action with them. She uses her hands on top of John's, using a sign close to the activity in a 'hands on' motion.

John's chair is next to the wall and near the bathroom door. By using 'hands on' technique again, the nurse raises John's hand to indicate that he is to leave his seat. John is given the sponge again and then the nurse guides him to the wall. On the wall is a mobility route, which could be a rope with bells and shiny paper or a natural line in the wall – it all depends on how much reinforcement and help John needs.

John's hand is guided to the rope and he is encouraged to follow the route to the bath. The nurse, on finally arriving in the bathroom, will reinforce the whole activity by encouraging John to touch the sponge again, use the sign and explore the bathroom. Thus mobility and communication have been considered in one activity.

John. He may learn to use signs but may, on the other hand, require real objects – the sponge, a cup or swimming trunks – for some time. He could perhaps have a soft bag hanging from his chair with some of these articles in it. Therefore, if John himself wished to communicate that he wanted a bath or a drink, he could take out the object. In developing this it is important to remember that the activities and objects chosen should be interesting and rewarding to John.

Similarly, if John is incontinent, we must consider if he has ever been 'shown' the toilet. The same methods used in the example of the bath can be adapted for the toilet.

We also noted that John does not feed himself. Again, by using 'hands on' techniques we should guide John's hands round his plate. He is not being messy by touching his food; indeed, at this stage, it is important that he does so. He should be encouraged to explore what is on his plate and consider textures. John can be encouraged to hold the spoon and his hand guided to his mouth. If John throws his spoon away it is important that the nurse does not pick it up for him. John has no way of knowing what happens when he throws the spoon – he can't see where it goes and he can't hear it land. If the nurse picks it up perhaps John will think that the spoon can fly! Rather, John's hand should be guided to where the spoon fell.

Of course, John may resist all of this, and whatever kind of programme is carried out, it is likely to be a slow process.

THE TOTAL APPROACH

If John is resistant to touch it may be necessary to do some work in this area first. The term is 'tactile sensitive' or 'defensive'. If you can imagine being blindfolded then someone placing your hands in a bowl of jelly, the likely outcome is that you would resist and withdraw your hands. Life is a bit like this for John – he is confused and frightened.

Touch is a very important sense for John yet it is one that he may be frightened to use. Touch may only be known to him as a means of conveying instructions, i.e. John is pulled when it is time to leave his chair. We noted the startle response earlier when the nurse tried to take John to the bathroom – one of John's most important senses is denied him.

In considering touch in more detail there are a number of areas that may affect John's understanding and knowledge of the 'touch world'. Ouvry (1987) concluded that tactile sensations can be differentiated by general properties such as duration, intensity and location, and also by characteristics which are specific to the source of stimulation. It is difficult for us to fully appreciate these aspects of touch as tactile awareness is a secondary sense: we literally take it for granted.

Certain techniques can be employed to help John be less defensive, for example, a gradual introduction to different textures, using creams and scented lotions, dough and lentils. John should be encouraged not only to use his hands but also his feet. Again, this will all be gradual and John may start by tolerating only a few seconds. Ouvry (1987) gives an idea of the opportunities that may be available to us in using touch. Passive experience involves direct contact, such as massage, stroking and the use of different textures and scents. Nondirect contact considers the use of different textures and vibration. Vibration is used in a variety of ways, not least music therapy. Wet, dry, hot and cold are all aspects of touch. Ouvry then outlines more active forms of tactile work where weight, shape and solidity are important. Equally, touch is an important tool to find out about more permanent objects. If a person is always shown the minibus door, door may become associated with movement rather than the whole bus. It is rather like the Rudyard Kipling poem where three blind men were introduced to an elephant, all felt different bits of the elephant and all left with completely different ideas about how an elephant looks!

Van Dijk (1982) notes an even more fundamental starting point when studying tactile techniques, considering direct contact within a theory called 'appetite versus aversion'. When discussing his work with deaf-blind children Van Dijk explained that he tried to determine, by carefully touching the child at different places on his body, the types of contact stimuli that the child pays more attention to than others.

Smell and taste are other senses we may underestimate yet they can be important sources of information for John. We often see the negative side of this, for instance, it is not uncommon to find that severely sensory impaired people are fussy about their food, not tolerating new tastes or textures well. We can encourage the use of smell by training someone to be aware of it in the first place; use of different strong smells can simply draw John's attention to this sense. We can then use it to reinforce a message – the sponge for bath has the same scent on it, John's

swimming trunks use another scent and so on. Furthermore, aromatherapy is being used as a relaxation aid and again this could be developed for John.

To do any of these things John will need to trust the people he is with. The importance of building relationships, respect and understanding cannot be overemphasized. We can never view the world from John's point of view but we can try, and in doing so we may bring meaning to his world.

CONCLUSION

In this chapter we have taken a very brief view of a wide range of sensory impairments. Physical and mental handicaps have been recognized for some time, but sensory handicap has only recently been regarded as a specific area of disability. Given that our distance senses of sight and hearing contribute most of our information about the world around us, it is not surprising that damage done to one or both creates learning difficulties. If this is further compounded by, for example, mental handicap, the person is likely to have a distorted and often confused view of the world.

We have considered the effects of a visual or a hearing impairment alone and then gone on to consider people with sensory multiple impairments. It was noted that a wide range of abilities and needs is covered by the term 'sensory impairment' and we further discussed a wide range of aspects affecting these abilities. Broadly, we discussed the time of onset, the degree of impairment and the type of disability. We looked at how damage to both distance senses can have a profoundly disabling effect and how this would alter and distort the person's view of the world. In order to gain an insight into these complexities we considered assessment in some depth. Assessment is the key to most services and often affects our approaches to a client. Finally, we considered all this together through a case study and looked in more detail at a total approach, maximizing all possible routes of residual vision and hearing, touch, smell, taste and environmental cues. Building in routine is an important aspect of bringing order to the day. Through routine we can help John to anticipate what comes next and, as discussed, we can increase touch, smell and object information when taking John to the bathroom.

The complexities of John's needs challenge us personally and professionally and much of the onus of responsibility rests with us to meet John's challenge. A useful starting point, as in all impairments, is, firstly, to examine our own attitudes and views and, secondly, to try and understand John's view of the world. If we are aware of visual and hearing impairments in more than a physiological way but actually examine the implications of that disability for John – what it means for *him* – we can go some way towards meeting John's needs. John hopes that you can rise to his challenge.

REFERENCES

Aitken S, Morbey G 1987 Look I'm here. Sense in Scotland, Glasgow

Best C 1982 The new deaf-blind. University of Birmingham, Birmingham

Best A B 1987 Steps to independence. BIMH, Worcester

Beveridge M, Jeffree D, Nolan M, Warner J 1987 In: McCartney E (ed) 1987 Helping adult training centre students to communicate. BIMH, Worcester

• Cunningham & McArthur 1981 In: Hogg J, Raynes V (eds) 1987 Assessment in mental handicap. Croom Helm, London

Dale P S 1976 Language development, structure and function. Holt Rinehart & Winston, London

Deaf-Blind Liaison Group 1988 Breaking through developing services for deaf-blind people. Deaf-Blind Services Liaison Group, Glasgow

Foster R B 1991 It's not funny being blind. Strathclyde Regional Council Social Work Department, Glasgow

Hewson S, Jeffree D, McConky M 1977 Teaching the handicapped child. Souvenir Press, London

Hogg J, Sebba J 1987 Profound retardation and multiple impairment vol 1: development and learning, Croom Helm, London

International Association for the Education of the Deaf-Blind 1989 Sensory impairment with multihandicap current philosophies and new approaches. Proceeding of Warwick Conference. IAEDB/Sense, London

Lawson et al 1977 In: Hogg J, Raynes V (eds) 1987 Assessment in mental handicap. Croom Helm, London

McAnespie H 1985 The education of hearing impaired children with additional handicaps. Paper 9: Screening for hearing loss in children with serious handicaps. University of Glasgow, Glasgow

Meadow 1980 In: Van Dijk J (ed) 1982 Rubella handicapped children, 2nd edn. Swets & Zeitlinger B V, Netherlands

Nolan M 1984 In: McCartney E (ed) 1987 Helping adult training centre students to communicate. BIMH, Worcester

Ouvry C 1987 Educating children with profound handicaps. BIMH, Worcester

RNIB 1987 Out of isolation: a plan for the growth of services to multihandicapped visually impaired people. RNIB, London

Schlesinger & Meadow 1982 In: Van Dijk J (ed) 1982 Rubella handicapped children, 2nd edn. Swets & Zeitlinger B V, Netherlands

Sebba J 1987 Assessment of physical development hearing and vision that can be used by education and care staff. In: Hogg J, Raynes N V (eds) 1987 Assessment in mental handicap. Croom Helm, London

Tucker & Nolan 1987 In: McCartney E (ed) 1987 Helping adult training centre students to communicate. BIMH, Worcester

Van Dijk J (ed) 1982 Rubella handicapped children, 2nd edn. Swets & Zeitlinger B V, Netherlands

Wolf & Anderson 1973 In: Hogg J, Raynes V (eds) Assessment in mental handicap. Croom Helm, London

Woodford D 1989 Out of touch. Sense in Scotland, Glasgow

CHAPTER CONTENTS

Introduction 149

Challenging behaviours 150
Prevalence of behaviour problems 150
Causative factors 150

The behavioural approach 151
Defining a problem 152
Organizational issues 152

The nursing process 154

Assessment 155

Functional analysis 155
Antecedents 156
Behaviour 156
Consequences 156
Performing a functional analysis 157

Measuring, recording and analysing 161
The baseline measurement 161
Special equipment 165
Presentation of data 166
Reliability 169
Skills assessment 170
The process of assessment – a summary 172

The way forward 172
Setting treatment goals 173
Planning the treatment programme 174
Deciding on appropriate treatment methods 175

Increasing appropriate behaviours 176
The manipulation of antecedents and consequences 176
The use of reinforcement 176
Skills teaching methods 180

Decreasing inappropriate behaviours 188
The reflective approach 189
Adjusting antecedents 189
Adjusting consequences 189
Medication 193
Programme design 194

Evaluation: measuring treatment success 195
If satisfied with treatment results 195
If not satisfied with treatment results 196

Gentle teaching 197

The ethics of the behavioural approach 197
Consent 198
Rationale 198
Using the least intrusive methods 200
The use of reinforcement 200
Applying specialist knowledge 201

Conclusion 201

9

Helping with behavioural problems

M. McCue

Key points
- Behaviour must be identified, defined and looked at in relation to the environmental setting
- Positive reinforcement is always a part of therapy
- Unwanted behaviour should be reduced by differential reinforcement before resorting to more invasive approaches
- The key to success lies in the recording systems
- Therapy is the business of the whole team, otherwise it will be less effective

INTRODUCTION

In recent times, as government and mental health policies have become increasingly orientated towards the relocation of people with a mental handicap to smaller, community-based facilities, the implications of behavioural difficulties presenting within this client group have become crucially significant to the success of community placement. Research studies have consistently shown the presentation of behavioural problems to be not only a major obstacle to effective community adjustment but also a reliable predictor of initial admission, or readmission, of people with a mental handicap to hospital-based facilities.

If the basic tenets behind the philosophy of normalization (also known as social role valorization) are to be respected then surely it is essential to address any and all issues which may impinge upon, or even preclude, people with a mental handicap from achieving their rights and their entitlement to valued social roles. Since behavioural difficulties may not only interfere with the development and well-being of an individual as well as that of his family and friends, the requirement to provide skills and services to remedy these problems is paramount.

Throughout this chapter reference is made to the individual as client, subject or person. This is dependent on the context and is not done to confuse. Similarly, reference is made exclusively to the male gender. This is done for ease of explanation and consistency and is not meant to have any other implications.

Behaviour therapy, or modification, has proven to be both a desirable and effective treatment method in the amelioration of behavioural difficulties presented or experienced by people who have a mental handicap. There is no intention to provide a historical account of behaviour therapy but rather an account of those methods most often used to treat people with a mental handicap who have behavioural problems. It is also the intention to provide an outline of the main components of a behavioural approach. Suggested further reading should afford the reader the opportunity to become more familiar with the historical development of behaviourism and the behavioural approach.

CHALLENGING BEHAVIOURS

Behavioural problems or difficulties are sometimes referred to as 'challenging behaviours'. This more contemporary descriptor is used to accentuate the challenge which such behaviours present to care providers and services. The nature of those challenging behaviours which may act to deter or obstruct the social and/or educational development of a person is almost beyond quantification. Each presents a unique testament to the individuality of the person and his circumstances. Despite being somewhat of an oversimplification, it is helpful to view behavioural difficulties as being manifest in a manner which allows categorization into two main groups:

- *behavioural excesses* – behaviours which we may seek to reduce

- *behavioural deficits* – behaviours which we may seek to increase.

The judgmental inferences of such a dichotomy may frequently rest uneasily. After all, who is to decide whether a particular behaviour, or group of behaviours, is in excess or deficit? For that matter, who is to decide whether a behaviour presents a problem? Some guidelines and suggested criteria are provided later. This will hopefully allow the reader to develop answers to such pivotal, yet rarely simple, dilemmas.

Prevalence of behaviour problems

There have been relatively few studies conducted to establish the prevalence of behavioural problems in people with a mental handicap. Of those known to this author most estimate prevalence to be about 40% of total populations surveyed and, for example, Kiernan & Moss (1990) found that over 40% of the population of a large mental handicap hospital exhibited either moderately or severely disordered behaviour. Generally speaking, findings are that behavioural problems are present to only a slightly lesser degree in community settings, perhaps reinforcing the essential requirement for services within the community to be responsive to the needs of people with a mental handicap who present with challenging behaviour.

Causative factors

There are a number of factors which may influence the likelihood of a person presenting with behavioural problems. The following list is not exhaustive but represents the most commonly found causes.

Physiological factors

Throughout our day-to-day lives we may experience peaks and troughs of physical well-being which may have a very subtle, or very obvious, effect on the way in which we behave. This is no less true of a person who has a mental handicap. Pain or discomfort from, for example, a toothache or headache may lead to a lower tolerance threshold and increased sensitivity. In turn, our behaviour may change. For example, we may become socially withdrawn and less communicative. We might even become short-tempered and react to normally unprovocative stimuli in a hostile or aggressive manner. Therefore, behavioural change may sometimes present as a manifestation of a transient physiological illness.

More chronic physiological difficulties may have similar significance in the presentation of behavioural problems. Examples of such are organic brain disease and epilepsy. The former may give rise to problems of functional impairment due to disorientation and confusion, while in the latter it would appear that, in some instances, seizure frequency and type have influenced self-injurious and aggressive responding.

Conditions associated with mental handicap

Challenging behaviours may also be more likely to present in conditions associated with mental handicap: for example, in fragile X, Lesch-Nyhan and Tourette syndromes. In each of these conditions, behavioural problems have been observed as being fairly common. In people with rubella damage or autism some form of behavioural difficulty may be a feature. It must be stated clearly, however, that none of these conditions are predictive of the development of challenging behaviours.

Psychiatric disorders

Research has indicated that people with a mental handicap are at a greater than average risk of developing psychiatric disorders (Borthwick-Duffy & Eyman 1990). The presence of psychiatric illness in people with a mental handicap has given rise to a classification of 'dual diagnosis', a term emanating from the United States of America.

There may be an association between the presence of a mental illness and behavioural difficulties, for example, due to a prevailing emotional or personality disorder.

Sensory impairments

Impairment in, or absence of, hearing or vision may predispose to behavioural problems. Similarly, physical handicap and/or communication difficulties may give rise to frustration and anger – emotions which may be the precursor to challenging behaviours.

Social factors

An individual with a mental handicap who has been the subject of an impoverished quality of care, or who has suffered rejection by society, may experience feelings of inadequacy or worthlessness. He may have extreme difficulty in establishing relationships which are both valued and gratifying. These factors may make the emergence of behavioural problems more likely.

Environmental factors

There appear to be numerous environmental factors which can contribute to the presentation of challenging behaviours. Some of the more common of these are: increased noise level, lack of personal space, limited social interaction, lack of recreational opportunity and conflict in interpersonal relationships. Any permutation of these may influence behavioural problems.

Emotional factors

As a consequence of any or all of the causes described, a person with a mental handicap may harbour feelings of tension, stress, anxiety, hopelessness and anonymity. He may, due to difficulty in resolving or coping with these feelings, subsequently experience and present behavioural problems.

THE BEHAVIOURAL APPROACH

As stated in the introduction to the chapter, the utilization of behaviour therapy techniques can effectively ameliorate behavioural problems. Therapy is provided via the behavioural approach: an approach which is based on a systematic and scientific analysis of behaviour, working towards specific goals of treatment by a methodology firmly rooted in tested and proven techniques. Behavioural theory and practice are based on learning processes, that is, the ways in which behaviour patterns are learned and, therefore, by which different patterns of behaviour may be taught and learned. Historically, the behavioural model has dealt with that which can be observed, measured and evaluated. In doing so it has, to an extent, excluded the influence of thoughts, feelings and desires on behaviour, not because these were viewed as being insignificant but rather because their extent and influence on behaviour could not be readily and accurately measured.

In recent times, however, behavioural analysis and therapy have been more attentive and responsive to the effects which emotional and cognitive factors may have on behavioural responding. As a result of treatment methods being based on a more accurate and detailed assessment of the cause and function of challenging behaviours there have been more successes. Through a scientific analysis of the individual and his interaction with the environment, the behavioural approach affords an individualized treatment plan which is in many ways 'custom-built' to resolve the unique difficulties being experienced or presented by an individual.

It cannot be overstated that behaviour therapy is not a 'ready-to-use' package of techniques which can be conveniently prescribed to resolve particular behavioural problems; it is neither finite nor fixed. A major element of the behavioural approach is its empiricism, and this is the driving force behind its continual development and reformation. This ensures that the methodology for analysis and therapy is responsive to the individuality of each person and his problem or difficulty.

Defining a problem

How do we establish if a problem exists? Who defines the parameters of acceptable or unacceptable behaviour? These are difficult but crucial considerations. To attempt to define the presence or nature of challenging behaviour subjectively or in isolation is therefore inadvisable. An alternative, and more desirable approach may be to ensure a confluence of opinions and involvement of significant others, for example, the client, his family, his friends and his care providers.

There are a number of dimensions within which behaviour should be measured in order to define the existence and extent of a problem:

- Consideration of personal, social and culturally normative values is important. What is acceptable or alluring to one individual, his society or culture may be seen as unacceptable or even aberrant to another.
- Consideration from a temporal perspective may reveal that yesterday's taboo is tomorrow's custom.
- Perhaps the most important criterion we can use to identify whether or not a problem exists is the extent to which a circumstance intrudes on the physical, mental or emotional well-being of an individual or others. Reference was made in the introduction to the right of the person with a mental handicap to equal value, opportunity and services within society. The presence of a behavioural problem, for example, physical aggression, may seriously obstruct or even preclude that person's access to that right. Such challenging behaviour may also impinge on the rights of others to enjoy the same sense of well-being and having their needs and wishes respected.

In a similar fashion, behavioural difficulties such as self-injury or stereotypy may intrude on the acquisition of new skills by preventing access to educational opportunity. This situation has an obvious inference if the individual's abilities are to be maximized.

In essence, if it is decided that an individual's behaviour constitutes a problem either for himself, for others, or both then we may seek to find ways of overcoming that problem. In doing so, however, we may find ourselves confronted with a new set of dilemmas:

- What exactly requires to change?
- How is that change to be effected?
- Who is to be involved in the process of change?
- Where will therapy take place?

The assessment process begins here, therefore, as we endeavour to quantify the existence, nature and extent of an individual's behavioural difficulty and also to determine the requirement for therapeutic intervention, the nature of any proposed treatment plan and the resolution of specific organizational issues.

Organizational issues

A detailed and accurate assessment of the problem behaviour, its possible causes and the resources required to implement therapeutic change is the key to resolving organizational issues surrounding treatment. There will be elaboration of the mechanics of the assessment process later. Reference is made here to assessment in broad terms.

Any number of organizational issues may require to be settled prior to the implementation of any therapeutic programme. Some of the most common issues found are:

- setting priorities
- the use of resources
- location.

Setting priorities

Once it has been established exactly which behaviour or behaviours appear to constitute a problem, we may wish to target a particular behaviour or combination of behaviours for treatment. Therapy may be aimed at increasing or decreasing target behaviour, depending on whether it is a goal of therapy to encourage or discourage this behaviour. We may then select specific treatment goals for each behaviour we wish to change. Since establishing priorities is seldom a simple or fleeting affair, it is not only expedient but also necessary to involve other relevant parties as an integral part of this decision-making process. Wherever possible, the individual being helped should have the opportunity to provide the maximum contribution towards decision-making. Where an individual's capacity to make such a contribution is limited, or even precluded, his wishes should be expressed through his parents, guardian or responsible advocate. Informed consent is a major ethical prerequisite for the use of any behavioural assessment or treatment.

Since each individual's problem and situation will present uniquely there can be no entirely prescriptive criteria for the establishment of priorities. However, common considerations are:

- Which behaviour, or aspect of behaviour, presents the greatest danger or difficulty to the individual or others?
- Which behaviour appears to lend itself most readily to change?
- Which behaviours serve to prevent change in other behaviours?
- Which behaviour, if encouraged or taught, may serve to inhibit performance of 'problem' behaviour?
- Which behaviours, if encouraged or taught, would best meet the needs of the individual?

The use of resources

Resource implications are a vital consideration in the planning and subsequent implementation of any behavioural treatment plan. The availability of sufficient time, manpower, materials and expertise may be instrumental to the success of therapy. Therefore, a thorough evaluation of resources, both existing and required, is indicated prior to the organization of therapy. There may be a reciprocal influence between resource availability and the design of a treatment plan. At times, resource limitations may direct certain aspects or components of treatment, while in other instances the proposed therapy may dictate the requirement of further resources.

It is important to state, however, that one should never passively accept insufficient resources, especially where this may compromise the effectiveness of therapy; neither should resource deficiency preclude that therapy. The aim is to help the individual via an approach which appears to be not only the least restrictive alternative in terms of its effect on the individual but also is the most desirable and proven in its therapeutic efficacy. If achieving this aim involves increasing resources then attempts must be made to effect this as much as is realistically possible.

Again, it is testament to the individuality of the person and his situation that the chosen treatment approach should be responsive to the resource requirements of that person.

A major resource requirement may be that of specialist knowledge and skills appropriate to therapy. To ensure effective organization and intervention it is important that all treatment approaches be adequately monitored and evaluated. Those involved in the care of people with a mental handicap will inevitably differ in the extent of their knowledge and experience of the use of behavioural approaches. In consequence, some may be more confident and competent in their use of these than others. Most people, however, will usually seek the involvement of a professional person with specific training and expertise in the use of behavioural change techniques, whether that involvement is in an advisory capacity or at a practical level, or both. Where other specialist involvement is required, contact may be made with the relevant professionals such as nurses, physiotherapists, occupational therapists and speech therapists. A multidisciplinary approach ensures the availability of specialist supervision and support wherever required. The identity of those persons directly involved in the organization, implementation and evaluation of therapy is largely dependent on the location of the therapy.

Location

Resource availability or deficiency may also at times influence the location of therapy. A therapeutic environment should both accommodate and promote effective treatment. This may involve the provision of living conditions which provide the fundamental entitlements of the person, such as adequate personal space, opportunity for privacy and recreation and attractive and comfortable furnishings. It may similarly involve the introduction of resources more specific to therapy, such as specialist support, increased staffing and the provision of particular equipment or appliances designed to help the person with his behavioural difficulty.

Many behavioural problems appear to be environmentally specific: that is, the behaviour seems to be caused and/or maintained by certain aspects of the environment in which it takes place. Similarly, many behaviours may be inhibited by environmental factors. Research has shown that it may be more desirable to attempt to change behaviour within the environment in which it occurs. Therefore the provision of specialist support and services within that environment may best serve the needs of the individual.

Where, however, a person's behaviour presents a danger to either himself or others, and resources cannot be provided to sufficiently minimize that danger, while also facilitating appropriate treatment within the existing environment, then intervention outwith that environment may have to be considered. Despite the continuing development of initiatives across the country to provide specialist support and services for people with challenging behaviours, problems continue to present in both the management and treatment of these individuals, not only in community settings but also in hospital and residential settings. The creation of a specialist behavioural unit to resolve these difficulties has been a popular response, though debate about the relative merits and inadequacies of these units has been somewhat scarce. Favourable points raised include the provision of a safer environment and a staffing complement with specialist knowledge and skills.

A major criticism, however, is the apparent failure of most units to address the issues of maintenance and generalization of improvement in behaviour outwith the units concerned. If it was seen as a specific aim of specialist units to address these issues then the therapeutic value of the units would increase immeasurably. Irrespective of the location of therapy, its organization may remain largely the same.

The nursing process

The behavioural approach and the nursing process share a common address to therapy involving four main stages:

- assessment
- planning

- implementation
- evaluation.

Throughout these stages those involved in therapy may require support, education and supervision about whether a programme is to be run at home, in hospital, in a hostel, in a training centre or in a combination of these settings.

Consistency in the application of a treatment programme is crucial to the likelihood of its success. Therefore, all those responsible for implementation, from the client himself to care providers (possibly across a variety of different settings), should be fully aware of their role in therapy. In order to facilitate this and ensure a regular and thorough evaluation of treatment effects, there should be effective communication maintained between all relevant parties and a healthy exchange of information regarding significant changes in behaviour and/or circumstances.

ASSESSMENT

When dealing with issues related to assessment, reference will be made to the behaviour being assessed as the 'target' behaviour. In issues related to the stages of planning, implementation and evaluation, the term 'target' behaviour is used to denote that behaviour which is to be increased or decreased.

Similarly, with regard to assessment, the term 'subject' is frequently used to refer to the person who is the focus of the assessment. In the planning, implementation and evaluation stages, the term 'subject' is used in reference to the person requiring help with their behavioural difficulties.

Advances in the methodology for observation, recording and analysis of behaviour have contributed substantially to the development of innovative and effective behaviourally based treatment methods. A detailed and accurate assessment and analysis of the problem behaviour, and those factors which may be encouraging or discouraging to its performance, are critical to the likely success of any subsequent therapy. Groden (1989) puts some perspective on the importance of the assessment process:

To attempt to alter a problem behaviour by consequence manipulation, without careful scrutiny of the possible maintaining variables, and also of those antecedent variables which might be responsible for the onset of the behaviour, is both potentially inefficient and unethical.

An essential prerequisite in the assessment and analysis of a particular behaviour is to define the behaviour under study in terms which are clearly understandable and allow the behaviour to be accurately observed and recorded. For example, a person may be described as exhibiting 'aggressive', 'disruptive' or 'destructive' behaviour. However, each of these terms is too vague if a behaviour is to be measured accurately. In order to achieve this a clear and objective definition of the behaviour is required. An example of 'aggressive' behaviour may be 'kicking others on the legs'; disruptive behaviour may be 'throwing food onto the floor while at the dining table', and an example of destructive behaviour might be 'tears up items of clothing'. Of course, the behaviour we are seeking to assess or analyse may not always be an undesirable behaviour. We may wish to measure desirable behaviour, in which case, we would still require a clear definition of that behaviour or skill, such as 'John uses the toilet', 'Sally uses her knife and fork' or 'Ian puts on his own clothes'.

For assessment purposes, these types of definition allow each behaviour to be measured in terms of when, where, in what situation and how often each occurs. They may also be expanded to include a set of criteria in relation to specific conditions and the degree of success under which the behaviour should be performed. For example:

- 'John uses the toilet without assistance when given a verbal prompt by a member of staff.'
- 'Sally uses a knife and fork without help and without spilling any food at every mealtime.'
- 'Ian puts on his own clothes correctly every morning, with mum's supervision only.'

These extended definitions may be used as behavioural objectives as part of a goal planning system (which will be dealt with in detail later).

There are a number of different methods

and devices which may be used to observe and analyse behaviour. In behaviour therapy, the most important of these methods is the behavioural or functional analysis.

FUNCTIONAL ANALYSIS

Functional analysis involves the analysis of behaviour and the environment in which it takes place. Typically, a scrutiny of situations and events surrounding the performance, or nonperformance, of the behaviour is conducted. Circumstances before and after the behaviour are investigated to establish if any aspect of these could be contributing to the performance or nonperformance of behaviour. This approach towards the study of behaviour is sometimes referred to as an 'ABC analysis' since it involves an analysis of:

- Antecedents: factors prevailing prior to a behaviour which may be influential in the performance of the behaviour.
- Behaviour: the *exact* behaviour which takes place and is under analysis.
- Consequences: factors which prevail following a behaviour which may have an influence on the performance of the behaviour.

In Figure 9.1, possible relationships between the antecedents to, and the consequences of, behaviour are demonstrated.

Antecedents

The example in Figure 9.1 illustrates John's situation and activity (or in this case lack of activity) prior to performance of the problem behaviour. We can observe that John was alone and unoccupied. We may hypothesize, therefore, that his inactivity and the lack of attention given to him may have triggered the problem behaviour. We

cannot be certain, however, since other antecedent factors may have been influential. For example, physiological discomfort due to headache or stomach upset may have been a predisposing factor. Similarly, being asked to do something which he does not enjoy doing may be an antecedent event which promotes performance of problem behaviour. Medical investigation may eliminate or confirm physiological factors. Further observation of episodes of problem behaviour in the absence of prior demands or requests may similarly confirm or discount these as precursors to problem incidents. However, if further episodes took place when John was left alone or inactive, our initial hypothesis would be strengthened. Any number of physiological or other 'setting' events may require investigation as potential antecedent factors.

Behaviour

Recording the exact details of the nature of John's behaviour is of crucial importance. In doing this it is possible to examine both the nature of the behaviour and the events surrounding it.

Consequences

Investigation of potentially significant consequences is as important as analysis of antecedent events. In the example given, it could be initially hypothesized that problem behaviour may be rewarded by the delivery of a picture book. However, other consequential factors may be relevant. For example, John may enjoy the noise he is making or the disruptive effect on other persons or the environment. He may also find staff attention, verbal reprimand included, to be a rewarding consequence. If John's behaviour settled down following delivery of the picture

Antecedent	Behaviour	Consequence
John was seated alone at a table in the sitting-room; he appeared to be sleeping. I asked him to go and wash his hands before lunch.	John started to scream and shout, and then he began to bang the table with his hands.	Judy told John to stop making such a noise. She gave him a picture book to look at and he calmed down.

Figure 9.1 Functional analysis of John's behaviour.

book as a single consequence, then this would strengthen the hypothesis that problem behaviour may be maintained by the presentation of stimulating material as a consequence of that behaviour. If, however, delivery of the picture book does not reduce or remove the performance of problem behaviour, then other potentially influential factors would require investigation to establish their significance.

Since manipulation of antecedent and consequential influences can have a dramatic effect on behaviour, it is vital that these are analysed in detail in order that only the relevant factors are isolated and used in therapy, if the aim is to increase the likelihood of such behaviour being performed and repeated in the future. Similarly, in dealing with behaviour we wish to decrease, we can use antecedents and consequences which may lessen the likelihood of behaviour being performed and repeated in the future. In behavioural terms, a consequence which renders a behaviour *more likely* to be repeated is often referred to as a reinforcer, or a reinforcing consequence. A consequence which renders a behaviour *less likely* to repetition is sometimes referred to as a punisher, or a reducing consequence.

Performing a functional analysis

The most common methods of obtaining a functional analysis of behaviour are by means of:

- interviewing methods
- recording methods
- methods of direct observation.

Interviewing methods

Information regarding a person's behaviour can be obtained by interviewing a number of relevant persons, especially the subject of the study. The ability of the subject to respond to questioning will naturally depend on his having full understanding of the questions posed and the communication skills necessary to answer appropriately. If the latter is an obstacle, it may be possible to use some form of mediator during the interview process, such as an individual who has the ability to communicate effectively with the subject or the use of a signing system, to obtain the desired information. Where it is not possible or practicable to conduct an interview with the subject, it may be necessary to interview someone who knows the subject very well, such as a parent or primary care provider. It is important that a reliable source of information is used in order that as comprehensive and accurate a collection of data as possible is obtained.

Some interviews may be less structured than others, but most will attempt to extract similar kinds of information. It is useful to use a set format for interview and there are some ready made schedules available for use, such as the Behavioural Interview and Analysis Schedule or BIAS (Barker 1982) and the Basic ID (Lazarus 1976). Some of the more relevant questions to be asked are as follows:

Behavioural definition. What exactly is it that the person does or does not do which presents as a problem? It should be remembered that here we are looking for as quantitative a description of the behaviour as possible. As mentioned previously, vague or general terms such as 'aggressive' or 'uncooperative' behaviour are insufficient descriptors.

Behavioural dimensions. Here we are looking for information that is as exact as possible with regard to the frequency, intensity and duration of the behaviour. For example, does the behaviour take place daily, every hour, or a number of times in each hour? Is the behaviour improving or becoming worse? How long does it last? For a set period of time? Does the length vary? How long at the extreme? How short at its best and worst?

Behavioural specifics. It is helpful to establish any patterns regarding the behaviour in respect to locations, persons or situations. For example, does the behaviour occur or fail to occur in certain places or under certain conditions? Does it happen when particular people are present or absent? Does it happen during particular activities or at a set time of the day?

Behavioural history. By examining the history of the subject's behavioural difficulty we may be able to determine those factors which are relevant to the onset of the problem. For example, significant life events, changes in medication or environment, or onset of physiological discomfort. One would also be interested in any previous therapy aimed at helping the subject and the outcome of such therapy in terms of success or failure. Any proposals for treatment would take cognisance of past results.

Analysis of antecedents. Antecedents may be relevant either as proximal antecedents, i.e. those events occurring immediately prior to the behaviour under study, or distal antecedents, those events which took place some time prior to the behaviour.

Distal antecedents influential on behaviour may have taken place minutes, hours, days or even weeks before that behaviour is exhibited. This makes significant distal antecedents somewhat more difficult to isolate in comparison to proximal ones.

Antecedents may also be distal in a physical as well as a temporal sense. For example, the presence of a particular individual in the same room or building as the subject may be sufficient to elicit a particular behaviour.

In analysing proximal antecedents, the following information may be of use:

- Location – where was the subject when the behaviour occurred?
- Activity – what was the subject doing before the behaviour occurred? Was he talking to someone? Whom? What was said?
- Social – what was taking place around the subject?
- Covert behaviour – it is frequently difficult, and sometimes impossible, to establish what the subject was thinking or imagining prior to the onset of behaviour. Certain thoughts and thought patterns may be instrumental in determining behaviour so it is important to attempt to obtain this information as far as is possible.
- Physiological state – there may be some physiological change which the subject experiences prior to the onset of the behaviour. If so, the subject may be able to tell us about them or we may observe such changes. Examples of observable changes may

be changes in facial expression, excess sweating or flushed appearance.

Analysis of consequences. Consequences of behaviour may be analysed using the same format as for antecedents. Relevant questions would include:

- Where was the person following the performance of behaviour?
- In what ways, if any, did others react to the behaviour?
- Did the subject do or say anything following the behaviour? If so, what?
- How did the subject feel afterwards? What did he think about afterwards?

As with antecedents it may be important to attempt to identify any distal consequences which may be relevant to the performance of the behaviour.

The process of obtaining a detailed functional analysis is seldom easy, especially when retrospectively examining the details surrounding past episodes of the target behaviour. In examining previous notes and records of an individual's behaviour it is frequently difficult to isolate potentially significant antecedent or consequential factors. It is common to see phrases such as 'for no apparent reason', 'unprovoked' or 'due to no observable cause'. By widening the range of analysis to include distal antecedents and consequences, and by interviewing significant other persons, it, may be possible to achieve a more comprehensive and informative assessment of the behaviour under analysis than would otherwise be the case.

The motivational assessment. It is also necessary to gain insight into factors which may have influenced the performance or nonperformance of a behaviour. In simple terms we may say that a person is motivated by likes and dislikes, and these may fall into a range of categories, such as activities, consumables, materials and persons. Naturally, individual likes and dislikes will be influential on the behaviour, making it more likely to recur in response to the same or similar situations.

What one tries to establish is a fairly exhaustive list of the more specific likes and dislikes of the subject which will be unique to that individual. For example:

Person A	**Likes**	**Dislikes**
• Activities	Going to the cinema	Taking a bath
• Materials	Books, records	Soft toys
• Places	Theatres, parks	Buses, busy shops
• Consumables	Spicy foods, milk	Fizzy drinks, eggs
• Persons	Brother, Cliff Richard	Uncle Tommy

When it is established what factors are most pleasurable or displeasing to the subject, these may then be used as components of therapy, if required. An individual may also be motivated by the praise and approval of others, by achieving success or by gaining greater independence. The support and encouragement of friends and family may also be a motivating factor.

The most effective way of establishing what motivates a person is to ask him. However, this is not always possible. It may then be necessary to rely on an informant who knows the subject and his likes and dislikes well.

Recording methods

Obtaining information about behaviour using a specifically designed recording format is both useful and cost-effective. One example of an in-depth recording format is the *Detailed Behavioural Analysis Guide* (Groden 1989). This format seeks to obtain the majority of information which may be gathered via interview methods.

A more concise format for recording behaviour is presented in Figure 9.2. This 'incident record' provides the opportunity to obtain a number of potentially relevant details regarding a specific behaviour or number of behaviours. To avoid subjective interpretation of the behaviour being recorded a specific definition of the behaviour is given at the top of the form. In this example the behaviour is recorded as 'John kicking another trainee on his legs'.

Following the chart from left to right, it also provides information about:

- the date and time of the incident (this may establish whether the behaviour occurs at particular times of the day or days of the week)
- where the subject was immediately prior to the incident (this may establish if the behaviour is specific to a location)
- what the subject was doing immediately prior to the incident
- what exactly happened (an exact description is required to determine whether the behaviour is in response to a particular event or situation)
- who else was involved (this may give evidence of the presence or absence of a

DATE AND TIME	5/7/92 @ 2.45pm
WHERE WAS HE/SHE?	John was in the woodwork room.
WHAT WAS HE/SHE DOING?	He was sanding down the legs of a table he was making.
WHAT EXACTLY HAPPENED?	Tony approached John. John turned round – told Tony to leave him alone – and then kicked Tony on the left shin with his right foot.
WHO ELSE WAS INVOLVED?	Only Tony and John! 7 other trainees were in the woodwork room with myself. We were all choosing a wood-stain colour for a rocking chair. We were about 15 feet away from Tony and John when the incident took place.
WHAT HAPPENED AFTERWARDS?	Tony withdrew from John as quickly as he could. John was shouting. He accused Tony of always telling him what to do. I asked John to apologize to Tony – which he did, about 5 minutes later.
SIGNATURE	M.MsC.

Figure 9.2   Record of John's behaviour.

person or persons who are influential)
- what happened afterwards (giving clues to contributory events or situations which have a consequential effect on the behaviour)
- signature (the person witnessing the event should complete the form – this allows subsequent questioning to be conducted to elicit further details).

The design of the form tends to provide more detail of proximal than distal antecedents and consequences, therefore a follow-up interview may be necessary to elicit more distal factors. Data should be recorded as soon as possible after the event to ensure that memory lapse does not occur.

Touchette et al (1985) describe the use of a 'scatter plot'. This allows the collection of data about frequency of a particular behaviour as performed during specified time intervals throughout the day. The scatter plot allows a visual presentation of the data which may highlight patterns and thus lead to the identification of influencing factors.

Specific formats to record behaviour are useful and different formats may be designed to obtain whatever kinds of information are required. It is crucial that the person completing the form is aware of the methodology and its importance.

Recordings may be complex and time consuming, depending on the amount and depth of information required. There are many types of forms available. The form presented in Figure 9.2 is, however, a good example of how a substantial amount of objective and potentially relevant information can be recorded quickly and effectively.

Direct observation methods

Using observational methods as a means of obtaining a functional analysis is generally more time consuming than completing recordings following the occurrence of a behaviour. Information obtained by interview or the use of specific recordings may highlight particular times of day or particular circumstances which predict the onset of a behaviour. In such a case, direct observation can be employed around those times or situations. Thus it may be possible to determine more precisely significant antecedent or consequential factors which could have a bearing on the behaviour.

Observational methods are not however without their own problems. It is considered unethical to purely observe behaviour which is a danger to the subject or others, such as aggression or self-injury. It may also be difficult to obtain a clear line of sight in a situation, thus making observation more difficult. The subject may be aware of the observer and respond differently than would be 'normal'. This is described as an 'observational effect'.

The use of special equipment may help to resolve observational difficulties. Mace & Knight (1986), for example, used a mirror to observe a subject to avoid making eye contact with him. Also, furniture may be moved to provide a clear view during the observation period. It is important not to change the setting too much as this could have an effect on the subject and thus alter the behaviour displayed. The key to an observation session is to gather as much information as possible while remaining as discreet as possible.

Where no obvious antecedent or consequent factors can be isolated through interviewing and recording methods it may be possible to conduct a series of direct observations at a variety of times in different locations or settings in an attempt to identify factors influencing behaviour. Some studies, referred to as 'analogue studies' (Iwata et al 1982, Sturmey et al 1988) have been conducted where different conditions were deliberately created for the subjects in order to test behavioural responses to each condition. Information thus gained would then be used as a basis for subsequent treatment methods. The use of such methods is, however, restricted to extremely difficult behaviours, and carried out under strict clinical control with specific ethical guidelines, therefore it would not be considered lightly or entered into arbitrarily.

To enumerate all possible factors which may influence the performance or nonperformance of behaviour would be an impossible task. Some of the more common factors are:

Factors contributing to the performance of problem behaviour:

- *Antecedent factors*
  — physiological discomfort, e.g. due to pain from toothache
  — lack of stimulation
  — lack of sufficient recreational opportunity
  — noisy environment
  — provocation from others
  — fear, stress, anxiety
  — being asked to perform a difficult or disliked activity
  — copying another person's behaviour.
- *Consequence factors*
  — attention provided by others, approval or disapproval (some people seem to enjoy being told off or corrected)
  — the achievement of sensory stimulation, e.g. from compulsive body rocking or hand waving
  — deriving enjoyment from causing disruption or upset
  — the removal of the request to perform a difficult or disliked task.

Factors influencing inhibition or non-performance of behaviour:

- *Antecedent factors*
  — where there is no, or little, opportunity for the behaviour to take place
  — where there is no, or little, assistance for the behaviour to take place
  — where there is no, or little, encouragement given to the performance of the behaviour.
- *Consequence factors*
  — where performance of behaviour is given no, or insufficient, encouragement for repetition
  — where performance of behaviour is given no, or insufficient, attention or praise.

MEASURING, RECORDING AND ANALYSING

The baseline measurement

The baseline is a measure of a person's behav-

iour under 'normal' conditions prior to any therapy being instituted. Information is obtained regarding the nature and extent of a person's behaviour which may assist in determining whether or not therapy is indicated, which behaviour, or behaviours will be a target for therapy and by retrospective comparison the effects of therapy. Since a range of statistics usually emerge from baseline study, results are commonly presented as averages, such as 'averaging 3 times per hour', or '4–7 times per week', or 'averaging 10.5 seconds' duration each minute', or 'averaging 3.2 hours per day'.

Baseline measurement is a prerequisite to effective evaluation of therapy. Following treatment, a measurement of behaviour would be taken under baseline conditions and the results presented in the same form as the original baseline in order that effectiveness can be determined.

Where an individual exhibits a behaviour which may be potentially harmful to himself or others it is not ethically sound to perform a conventional baseline assessment. In such instances a retrospective baseline would be taken and would be sufficient for the purpose. Typically this involves the scrutiny of past recording, notes and records in order to find information relating to past episodes of the behaviour under study. Sometimes these accounts may be vague or incomplete. However, an adequate base for evaluation of therapy may still be obtained.

There are a number of methods by which behaviour may be measured. The most commonly used techniques are:

- frequency or event recording
- duration recording
- latency recording
- interval recording
- time sampling recording
- measurement by permanent product
- checklists: logbooks, record charts and rating scales.

Frequency or event recording

This involves the measurement of the number of times that a target behaviour occurs within a set period of time. The total number of observed behaviours can then be divided by the time of observation to provide an average frequency of occurrence. Figure 9.3 shows that a total of 29 incidences of behaviour were observed within a 10-minute observation period, (Session 1). Dividing frequency by time gives an average frequency of 2.9 behavioural responses per minute. If a series of 10-minute observation periods was performed one could divide the total number of responses observed in all sessions (182) by the number of sessions (10) to give an average number of responses (18.2) per session (Fig. 9.3).

Not all behaviours are best measured by frequency recording. For example, those which do not appear to have a clear start and/or finish and which last for a considerable amount of time. Behaviours suitable for such recording may include throwing food, breaking crockery or lifting a spoon. Unsuitable behaviours may include watching television or reading a book.

Duration recording

In some instances behaviour may occur relatively infrequently but may be performed for lengthy periods of time. In such circumstances it may be more appropriate to measure the amount of time spent engaged in the behaviour. As with all behavioural recording, a clear definition of the behaviour to be observed is essential to ensure consistency and accuracy in measurement. Behaviours such as getting dressed, playing sports or prolonged screaming may be suitable for duration recording.

Latency recording

This is similar to duration recording, but is concerned with how long it takes a person to start or finish performing a particular behaviour. It may be desirable, for example, to quantify how long it takes a person to walk to work or to have a bath. In conducting this form of recording it is necessary to clarify what exactly constitutes the start or finish of the behaviour. For example, should measurement begin when the person is prompted to leave for work or when he actually leaves? Similarly, should recording cease when the person steps out of the bath or when he leaves the bathroom fully dressed?

Interval recording

This method involves dividing an observation session into equal time intervals. For example, a total observation period of 30 minutes may be divided into 30 1-minute intervals or 60 30-second intervals. The observer then records whether the target behaviour occurs during each interval. Since only performance or nonperformance of the behaviour is recorded for each interval the length of each interval should be sufficiently short to accommodate only one single occurrence of the behaviour being measured, otherwise potentially valuable information may be lost. Figure 9.4 illustrates a typical interval recording form. At the end of each observation period the number of intervals during which the target behaviour occurred can be expressed as a fraction or percentage of the total.

Interval recording is best suited to behaviours which are of variable duration and can stop and start very quickly. For example, speaking, chewing food or rocking back and forth.

SESSION NO.	LENGTH OF SESSION	NUMBER OF INCIDENCES OF BEHAVIOUR OBSERVED
1.	10 minutes	29
2.	as above	17
3.	as above	31
4.	as above	14
5.	as above	9
6.	as above	27
7.	as above	16
8.	as above	20
9.	as above	8
10.	as above	11

Figure 9.3 Frequency record.

Subject's name: ....

Location ....

Date: ....**Length of session:** ....

Session commenced: ....**Length of intervals:** ....

Session completed: ....**No. of observers** ....

Target behaviour ....

Please record incidents of target behaviour by using a tick (√). Leave blank if no target behaviour is observed. Use a cross (x) if subject is absent or if observer's vision is obscured.

1	2	3	4	5	6	7	8	9	10

11	12	13	14	15	16	17	18	19	20

51	52	53	54	55	56	57	58	59	60

Total no. of intervals with target behaviour [ ]   % of intervals with target behaviour [ ]   Observer ....

Figure 9.4 Interval recording form

Technically, interval recording procedures appear to afford some measure of both frequency and duration. Results can, however, be misleading because a recording of a single performance is made irrespective of how many discrete performances of the target behaviour occur during that particular interval. Similarly, if intervals are set at, e.g. 15 seconds in length, then no account is given of whether the behaviour lasted for only a few seconds or for all 15 seconds of that interval. To overcome these problems 'whole interval' recording may be used if the target behaviour takes place throughout the entire interval and 'partial interval' recording if the behaviour only takes place during part of the interval.

Frequency may be more accurately recorded by using a 'frequency within interval' recording. This involves taking a measure of every occurrence of the target behaviour within the interval.

The interval recording system may be designed to allow the observer to record and observe simultaneously, or have consistent breaks in observation during which the observer records the results.

Some formats may be more complex, involving the collection of data in relation to a number of behaviours. Generally speaking, the more complex the format, the more skilled the observer needs to be in both observation and recording techniques to ensure accuracy of data and to avoid losing potentially valuable information. A major disadvantage of interval recording is the considerable demand made on the surveillance and concentration skills of the observer.

Time sampling recording

This is a method which may be used to measure the amount of time a person engages in a particular behaviour without requiring continuous observation. It involves the observer in recording the performance or nonperformance of behaviour at the end of a set period of time. Figure 9.5 shows a fairly typical time sampling recording form. Using this format the observer would visit the location of observation at hourly intervals. If, at that precise time, the subject was performing the target behaviour, this would be recorded with a tick. Nonperformance would be recorded with a cross. If no observation was possible, for

example, because the subject was absent, this would be recorded by using a single slash mark against the entry time. If a number of behaviours were to be recorded then these could be coded with a letter or number. As with interval recording, the instance of behaviour may be reported as a percentage of the total number of samples taken. In Figure 9.5, for example, 50% of the samples taken revealed performance of the target behaviour.

A major advantage of time sampling is that it is not intensely time consuming. It allows for a number of subjects and behaviours to be studied simultaneously. A major disadvantage is the danger that potentially valuable information may be lost as the observer is unable to witness every episode of the target behaviour. This can be countered to a large extent by introducing random time sampling which has no

---

Subject's name: .... Date: ....

Location: .... Sample frequency ....

Target behaviour ....

Please record observed target behaviour with a tick (√). Leave blank if no target behaviour is observed. Use a single slash mark (\) if no observation was possible at sample time.

1.	√		13.			25.	
2.			14.			26.	
3.	√		15.			27.	
4.	√		16.			28.	
5.			17.			29.	
6.	√		18.			30.	

10.	√		22.			34.	
11.			23.			35.	
12.	√		24.			36.	

Total no. of samples	12	No. of samples with observed target behaviour	6	% of samples with observed target behaviour	50

Figure 9.5 Time sampling record.

fixed pattern to the observation times. Instead, the observation times are predetermined on a randomized schedule. This can give a more accurate picture of the target behaviour as episodes which would have been missed on a fixed time sample are more likely to be observed in a random schedule.

Measurement by permanent product

This is a relatively simple and non-time consuming method by which to record behaviour. Only behaviours which produce a measurable outcome can be recorded using this method. For example, it is possible to assess how well a person has dressed himself by rating his appearance, i.e. how many items of clothing have been correctly put on. Similarly, it is possible to measure a person's destructive behaviour by recording the number of items broken or damaged. In order for recordings to be accurate and valid it has to be ascertained that the measured product was due to the behaviour of the subject and not attributable to the influence or actions of others.

Checklists: logbooks, record charts and rating scales

Using a checklist is a quick and straightforward method to record performance or nonperformance of the behaviour under study. A logbook format is an example of one type of checklist which may be highly motivating for a person and can encourage self-recording and self-management of behaviour. Figure 9.6 shows a daily segment of one form of behavioural logbook recording system. Specific behaviours are recorded by ticking whether or not each is performed. More sophisticated designing of logbooks can afford the inclusion of prompting levels, ratings of performance and other relevant comments. Happy or sad 'faces' may be used to represent appropriate or inappropriate behaviour where the subject has a greater degree of learning difficulty. Use of brightly coloured materials can enhance the attractiveness of the logbook. Modifications can

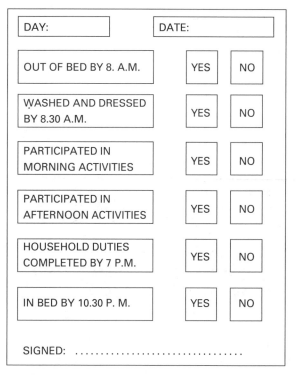

Figure 9.6 Daily segment of behavioural log.

be made to accommodate people with sensory loss. For example, the use of braille type or punch holes can be used for people with visual impairment.

Record charts can be used to log details of behaviour such as self-care skills. As with other recording systems, one or several behaviours can be incorporated into the form. People with learning difficulties may have problems with daily living skills or social skills. Specifically designed behavioural rating scales may be used to assess an individual's ability in the behaviours which are a part of these skills, such as eating, dressing, using appropriate gestures, and making eye contact. Figure 9.7 shows a rating scale designed to assess performance of social skills.

There are numerous recording systems and formats which can be used to quantify behaviour. The prime consideration is that the format chosen should be suited to the individual needs of the subject and the nature of his behavioural difficulties.

Subject's name: ....

Location: ....

CRITERIA FOR RATING

1	2	3	4	5
VERY POOR	POOR	AVERAGE	GOOD	VERY GOOD

BEHAVIOUR	SESSION NUMBER (WITH DATE UNDERNEATH)					
	1	2	3	4	5	6
	RATING	RATING	RATING	RATING	RATING	RATING
1. USES APPROPRIATE FACIAL EXPRESSIONS						
2. MAKES APPROPRIATE EYE CONTACT						
3. USES APPROPRIATE BODY POSTURE						
4. USES APPROPRIATE TONE OF SPEECH						
5. USES APPROPRIATE SPEED OF SPEECH						
6. LISTENS ATTENTIVELY TO OTHERS						

Figure 9.7 Sample from social skills rating form.

Special equipment

There are a number of devices which may be used to enhance the speed and accuracy of recordings. Some of these are relatively easy to use and are readily available. Others are more complex, expensive and difficult to obtain. It may be helpful to suggest a few inexpensive and accessible items of equipment which could prove to be useful. Apart from the variety of recording systems and forms previously outlined the following may be of use:

Timers and stopwatches

These devices are invaluable for duration, latency, time sample or interval recording techniques.

Event recorders or tally counters

These are particularly useful for recording be-haviours which occur at low duration and high frequency. Different types of event recorder are available, most of which can be easily concealed and are unobtrusive to use.

Tape recorders

Audio recording equipment can be used to record interviews or an observer's verbal account of behaviours or events which may be extremely detailed and complex and which would make written recording of data difficult. The use of very small recorders and accessories such as ear-pieces, can afford discreet and reliable recording of data.

Video equipment

Although more expensive and cumbersome than other devices, the video camera and recorder remain popular and effective tools for the observation and recording of behaviour. The therapeutic value of the use of video equipment has been demonstrated in a number of treatment programmes. Video taped behaviour also allows a variety of different analyses to be conducted on a single period of observation. It is also extremely valuable as an evaluative tool, comparing subject behaviour pre- and post-treatment, as well as allowing ample opportunity for measuring the reliability of observations.

Computers

Despite a high cost the use of computer systems can be very helpful in eradicating a number of errors and faults associated with more conventional recording equipment and techniques. They also afford a considerable saving in time and effort. Research studies have demonstrated the usefulness of computer systems in the collection and analysis of observational data (Repp & Felce 1990).

Presentation of data

It is important that, once relevant and accurate data have been obtained, they are presented in a form that is both appropriate and comprehensible. Graphs and charts are popular methods by which pertinent information may be presented in a visual form.

Graphs

The graph is one of the simplest and most effective ways of displaying data. It is usually designed to illustrate change in behaviour over periods of time. The vertical axis may be used to represent frequency or duration of behaviour and the horizontal axis is usually used to represent units of time, or the number of observational or treatment sessions carried out. Figure 9.8 shows a typical graph illustrating the frequency of a particular behaviour over a number of days. The average or mean (in this case the average number of behaviours performed daily) is represented by the broken horizontal line travelling through the graph. In situations where the number of recordings along the horizontal axis becomes extensive, these can be grouped into larger time periods (e.g. days into weeks, weeks into months). In these cases mean or average

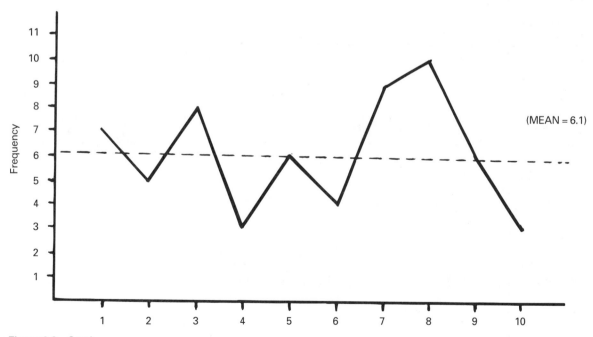

Figure 9.8 Graph.

frequencies of scores can be plotted in a graph to show change over time.

Changes in different types of behaviour may be represented on the same graph to contrast and compare trends. However, plotting too much data may result in the graph becoming visually confusing. In situations where several sets of data are to be presented it may be better to use a bar chart.

Bar charts

Bar charts are a useful method of displaying data about several behaviours over a number of variables, such as different locations, days of the week and months of the year. They use a number of columns, usually of a uniform width, placed alongside each other for easy comparison. Figure 9.9 shows a bar chart illustrating the daily frequency of four different types of behaviour. Each behaviour may be represented by a different form of shading (different colours may also be used) to improve presentation. A legend may also be provided to allow each behaviour to be readily identified. A number of behaviours may be represented using a single column with respective frequencies highlighted by the amount of shading or colour used to represent each behaviour.

Pie charts

These are useful charts with which to illustrate behavioural performance relative to a whole entity, for example, total behaviour, one observational session or an entire day. In Figure 9.10 the circle is used to represent the entire period of one observation session. Each segment represents the percentage of the whole period which was taken up by performance of a particular behaviour. Since the entire circle is expressed in degrees the whole period is expressed as 360°. Each segment is then calculated as a percentage of 360°. In order to do this, the total amount of time spent performing each behaviour is calculated as a fraction of the total observational period. This fraction is then multiplied by 360 in order to obtain the angle by which a segment should reflect the behaviour it represents.

Figure 9.11 illustrates the same information contained in the pie chart but presented as a bar chart, with each behaviour being shown as a percentage of the total period. Each segment

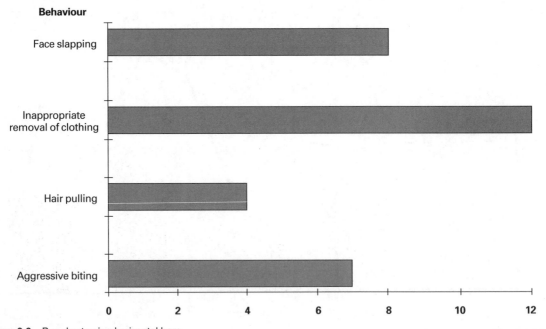

Figure 9.9   Bar chart using horizontal bars.

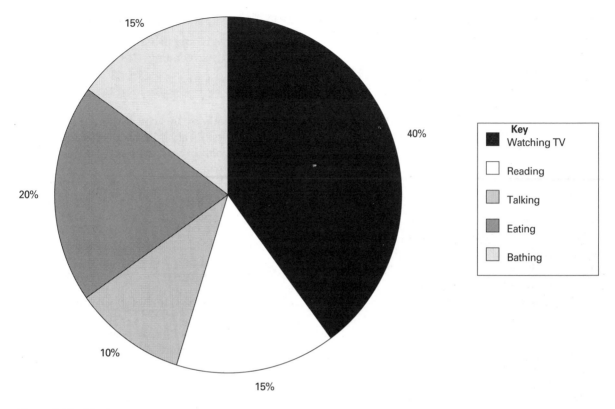

Figure 9.10   Pie chart.

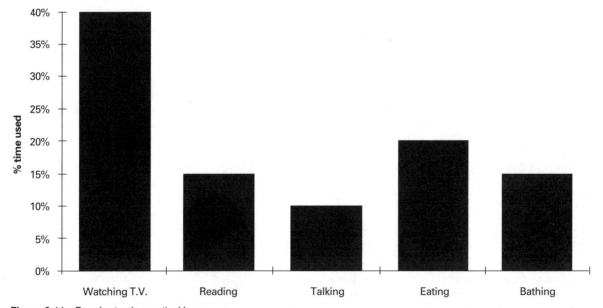

Figure 9.11   Bar chart using vertical bars.

of a pie chart may be shaded or coloured in the same way as a bar chart. Again, a legend is essential for easy identification of data.

Selecting the most effective method of presentation of data is not prescriptive. What is to be used will depend on the nature and amount of the data to be presented and which particular aspects or dimensions of the information require to be highlighted.

Reliability

Throughout the process of observation and measurement of behaviour, effort has to be made to ensure that only significant and accurate information is being obtained. By calculating the reliability of data, it is possible to achieve a gauge of the accuracy of that data. Reliability measurement is used to assess the extent of observer agreement, which in turn may be indicative of consistency in both the definition and scoring of target behaviour.

Different procedures may be used to test reliability depending on the observational methods used. All procedures require to have at least two observers. One of these is usually referred to as the primary observer, i.e. someone who observes and records target behaviour. During all observation sessions the second observer, who may vary between sessions, independently observes and records the same target behaviour. This person may be referred to as the reliability observer. A frequently used measure of reliability is that of inter-rater reliability, i.e. the extent to which both observers obtain the same results. This can be expressed numerically. The formula for calculating inter-rater reliability is:

$$\frac{\text{Number of observer agreements}}{\text{Number of observer agreements} + \text{number of observer disagreements}} \times 100$$

For example, if the total number of observation intervals used equalled 50, and the total of agreements between observers was 40, with the number of disagreements being 10, then the calculated percentage agreement by observers or inter-rater reliability would be:

$$\frac{\text{Number of agreements (40)}}{\text{Number of agreements (40)} + \text{number of disagreements (10)}} \times 100$$

$$\frac{40}{50} \times \frac{100}{1} = \frac{4000}{50} = 80\%$$

Different methods of calculation allow other measurements of reliability of observation using inter-rater reliability. A measure of 90% or above is generally considered to be reflective of satisfactory data, although a reliability of 80% or above may be accepted if the behaviour under study is complex and extremely difficult to define.

Skills assessment

Thus far, consideration has been given to the assessment and analysis of behaviour irrespective of whether that behaviour requires to be increased or decreased, encouraged or discouraged. A skills assessment affords the opportunity to highlight those aspects of a person's behavioural repertoire which require to be encouraged or strengthened. This type of assessment also makes it possible to focus on one skill or a group of skills in particular. Where a person exhibits a behaviour which is considered inappropriate, one may wish to examine skills the person already has, or may be taught to have, which may replace performance of the problem behaviour. One can look at skills which are, or would be incompatible with, performance of the problem behaviour, i.e. those which preclude or interfere with the performance of the problem behaviour. Examples of these two approaches would be:

1. A person may perform an inappropriate behaviour in an attempt to gain attention. If attention is consistently paid to appropriate behaviour or skills, then emphasis may be removed from the inappropriate behaviour and placed on the performance of appropriate behaviour. Since the latter now serves the same function as the former, i.e. gaining attention, it is possible to succeed in encouraging appropriate behaviour.
2. Similarly, a person may engage in stereotypic

hand-waving behaviour. If this person is encouraged to engage in an appropriate behaviour which involves the use of his hands, such as modelling clay or building a construction kit, performance of hand-waving behaviour will be difficult since the appropriate and inappropriate behaviours described are mutually exclusive, i.e. performance of one does not allow the simultaneous performance of the other.

Interest has to be expressed, therefore, in the skills and abilities which a person may have or can be taught. In assessing those skills the following may be considered:

- Does the person have, or has he ever had, the skill being assessed?
- If so, does he use it when necessary?
- Does he perform the skill independently?
- Does he perform the skill if assisted?
- How much, if any, assistance is required and does this vary?
- Is the skill always performed satisfactorily and in the appropriate situation?
- Is the skill only performed sometimes and only in certain situations?

Skills can be assessed using the following methods:

- direct interview
- assessment schedules
- observation
- testing.

Direct interview

By interviewing the person himself, or someone who knows him well, it is possible to obtain the desired information. The accuracy of this information is dependent on both the honesty of the informant and his ability to provide the information. If interviewing someone other than the subject, it is important that the informant has observed performance or non-performance of the skill being assessed, rather than providing information based on what has been heard from others or in anticipation of what the subject may or may not be able to do.

Assessment schedules

There are a variety of skills assessment schedules available for use. Some of these may have been designed specifically for use within certain environments and with a particular clientele in mind. Hogg & Raynes (1987) provide an outline of the more commonly used and readily available formats. Generally speaking, most assessment schedules have a similar basic design. Skills are usually categorized into a number of broad areas, such as personal hygiene, socialization and communication. Each area may then contain a number of more specific skills pertinent to its heading. Individual skills may then be scored or rated according to the person's proficiency in performance of that skill. Some assessment schedules may have prescribed criteria for scoring and may also take account of factors relating to performance, such as availability of opportunity and physical ability. Some may investigate the presence of challenging behaviours such as damage to property, aggression and self-injury.

Presentation of findings using a visual profile is a useful feature of many assessment schedules. It is frequently a task in itself to find a format which is sensitive to the needs and abilities of the subject. However the majority of assessment schedules are relatively easy to use and can save a substantial amount of time, making any search required well worthwhile.

Observation

Where there is uncertainty about a person's ability in a certain skill or group of skills, observation provides the opportunity to carry out a quantitative and potentially most informative assessment of that skill. However, direct observation in the person's natural environment can be time consuming, especially if a number of skills require to be assessed in this manner. It is also advisable, and may often prove essential, to carry out several observations of the skill being demonstrated in order to obtain an accurate assessment.

There may be factors which influence the person's performance or nonperformance of the skill. For example, he may feel unwell, or he may not be motivated due to the presence or absence of particular people, or because of the time of day. Despite these disadvantages – and particularly if several observations are carried out – direct observation affords a precise and detailed measurement of a person's skills and is therefore a popular and well-used method of assessment.

Testing

Where there may be difficulty in assessing a particular skill due to limited opportunity for the subject to perform the skill, or if performance occurs only rarely, it is possible to assess by creating a situation that is as natural as possible. For example, if there was a need to assess a person's ability to 'buy single items across a shop counter' and the person is not due to go into town until the following week, or the assessor cannot accompany him on his next trip, precluding a timeous assessment, then performance can be tested in a created situation outwith 'real life' but in as natural circumstances as is possible. It should be emphasized that there is often a significant variance in a person's ability to perform skills under different environmental conditions, therefore assessment in 'natural' conditions is preferable to 'test' conditions. The latter nonetheless can provide information which may be useful for short-term assessment and which may help determine suitable approaches to care planning and implementation.

The process of assessment – a summary

Selecting suitable methods of obtaining information may be influenced by a number of factors. In most instances, consideration will be given to the nature and extent of the behaviour under study, the conditions under which it does or does not take place, which persons are to observe, interview or be interviewed and what resources are available in terms of time, expertise, manpower and materials. Whatever methods are used to measure behaviour prior to treatment should be reapplied for evaluation. The baseline affords not only a foundation for the design of therapy but also an opportunity for continuous and careful evaluation. This may typically involve observation of behaviour under exactly the same circumstances and using the same observers, otherwise different variables (such as observation times) may influence results, thus clouding the effects of therapy.

The use of some assessment techniques may subsequently indicate the use of others. For example, interview or incident recording may reveal that a behaviour occurs at certain times of the day, in which case direct observation sessions may be conducted around those times. The results of these direct observations may in turn reveal which behaviour, or aspect of a behaviour, appears to be most frequent or intense thus indicating which form of measurement of that behaviour will be most useful.

The most important reason for the assessment and analysis of behaviour is its relevance in the planning and implementation of effective therapy. A thorough and accurate assessment may mean the difference between success and failure in any treatment plan based on that assessment.

THE WAY FORWARD

The assessment process should produce a wealth of relevant information on which to develop an appropriate treatment plan. This plan may be aimed at increasing appropriate behaviours and may also be directed to decreasing inappropriate behaviours. Consideration is therefore given to those factors about the individual and his environment which may be used to achieve the desired therapeutic change. One way to isolate these factors is to separate them into two main categories: strengths and needs.

- *Strengths*
  These should include the person's character and abilities, personal relationships and environmental factors, including:
  — the person's skills – both actual and potential
  — people whom he appears to like and responds well to

— the situations or activities which appear to discourage the performance of inappropriate behaviour

— significant antecedent or consequential factors which appear to initiate or encourage appropriate behaviour

— resources and materials which may be usefully employed to encourage appropriate behaviour.

● *Needs*

These should be factors which require to be provided or resolved in order to encourage appropriate behaviour or discourage inappropriate behaviour. Needs should be expressed positively and not simply represent a list of the person's faults or vulnerabilities, or indeed be a catalogue of resource or service deficiencies. For example, someone's need may be positively expressed as, '. . . needs to learn to sit quietly and peacefully at the dining table' as opposed to the more negative expression, '. . . needs to stop shouting and fidgeting at meal times'. The positive statement of a need is more purposeful and may be clearly directive of the objectives of a therapeutic management plan.

When compiling a list of needs the following may be considered:

● Those skills which a person has which may be strengthened, or those skills which may be taught in order to bring about a reduction in inappropriate behaviour.

● Relationships which may be built upon and utilized to effect therapeutic change.

● Environmental factors, resources and materials which may be of use in the facilitation of desired results.

● Significant antecedent or consequential factors which may be manipulated to promote and strengthen appropriate behaviour or discourage inappropriate behaviour.

Figure 9.12 shows an example of a strengths and needs list.

Setting treatment goals

Once it has been decided which behaviours re-
quire attention a statement may be made of the exact changes which treatment is designed to achieve. This may begin with the presentation of the statement as the ultimate or long-term goal of therapy. Some examples of long-term goals would be to:

● completely dress himself without difficulty every morning

● shop unsupervised in town for selected items of food

● sit quietly, without banging cutlery or shouting, every mealtime

● converse with others each time they initiate conversation.

When a goal is expressed in this clear manner, the extent to which a person is achieving the goal can be more readily evaluated. If goals are expressed in a broad and ambiguous manner then evaluation is more difficult since it is not clear as to how exactly the goal is to be achieved. Examples of broad and indistinct goals for the above behaviour might be:

● improve self-help skills
● buy food
● decrease disruptive behaviour
● increase social interaction.

Generally speaking, it is unrealistic to expect a person to achieve a long-term goal in a short period of time. It is usually necessary therefore to subdivide and break down each goal into smaller and more readily achievable goals or subgoals. These would become gradually more difficult as they approach the nature of the long-term goal itself. The person would progress gradually but systematically towards the final goal by successively mastering each of the subgoals. Figure 9.13 shows how a goal may be logically broken down into smaller, progressive subgoals or stages.

Systems for goal planning are commercially available and the reader is referred to these to obtain a more detailed account of the processes of writing goals, setting objectives and breaking down more complex skills into achievable steps.

If an individual does not demonstrate a particular skill, this does not necessarily mean that

SKILL HEADING		STRENGTHS	NEEDS
PERSONAL HYGIENE			
S U B - T O P I C	WASHING	Can wash hands and face properly when prompted	To self-initiate hand and face washing when appropriate
	DRESSING	Can put clothes on independently	To learn how to fasten shirt buttons and trouser zip fasteners
	GROOMING		
COMMUNICATION			
	GESTURES	Can indicate by pointing and miming actions	To learn more formal ways of signing e.g. makaton
	LANGUAGE	Can make word sounds sporadically	To have help with forming and sounding of words
	COMPREHENSION	Will follow simple instructions from time to time	To be able to express the lack of understanding
SOCIALIZATION			
	PARTICIPATION	Will participate in activities if prompted and guided	To gain pleasure from engaging in activities
	GROUP ACTIVITY	Will sit as part of a group in organized events	To actively participate in group-orientated events

Figure 9.12 Strengths and needs lists.

the ability to perform the skill is deficient. It may be the case, rather, that he is simply not motivated to perform the skill. A skill may also be absent or incomplete due to an associated problem, such as sensory impairment, organic disorder, illness or physical incapacity. Consideration of the nature and cause of the difficulty is pivotal in the setting of realistic therapeutic goals. Availability of resources may also influence these goals.

The setting of goals which are realistically achievable is paramount to the cultivation and preservation of morale and motivation both for the person and for those involved in implementing the treatment plan.

Planning the treatment programme

When the goals of therapy have been set and prioritized, the process of intervention planning may commence. Issues relating to the organiza-

tion of therapy have been discussed earlier in this chapter; however, it is worth highlighting some of the more common problems which may be encountered in the planning stage:

- inadequate resources available for the treatment plan to be implemented as desired
- persons involved in implementation may be suspicious of, or feel threatened by, the programme
- consent for treatment being withheld due to particular components of therapy
- too many or too few people being involved in the implementation of the treatment plan, resulting in uncertainty and inconsistency in approach.

These represent only a few examples of the difficulties which may be encountered and which can obstruct effective programme planning. Solutions corresponding with the above problems might be:

LONG-TERM GOAL:	SUBJECT WILL INDEPENDENTLY COMPLETE THE PROCESS OF DRESSING

SUBGOALS

1. Subject will select items of clothing with assistance

2. Subject will select items of clothing independently

3. Subject will select items of clothing independently and dress with assistance

4. Subject will select items of clothing and dress independently (with assistance in fastening/securing buttons, clips, zippers etc.)

5. Subject will select items of clothing and dress independently (without assistance in fastening/securing buttons, clips, zippers, etc.)

LONG-TERM GOAL	SUBJECT WILL INDEPENDENTLY COMPLETE THE PROCESS OF DRESSING

Figure 9.13   Breakdown of a long-term goal into subgoals.

- To design or modify the treatment plan so that it can safely operate within available resources. Compromise is often necessary but should only be made for sound and therapeutic reasons.
- Identify those who may be involved in programme implementation from the early stages of planning in order that they can feel part of the entire process of therapy.
- Provide a detailed cost-benefit analysis of therapy to substantiate treatment methods. Ensure that treatment plans are negotiated carefully with the client or advocate and that therapy is in line with ethical guidelines for practice (a topic covered later in the chapter).
- Involve only those people who require to be involved in treatment. Emphasize to all concerned that their individual role, no matter how small it might seem to be, is crucial to the success of therapy.

Anticipating and resolving difficulties is a crucial part of treatment planning. Generally, the more detailed the process of planning is, the greater are the chances of circumventing organizational difficulties and subsequently achieving success. Within the clinical setting, the similarities between the nursing process and the behavioural approach facilitate both effective record keeping and a systematic and scientific approach to therapy, both philosophies sharing a staged approach to treatment through assessment, planning, implementation and evaluation. Irrespective of the location of therapy, however, there are a number of planning and progress recording systems available for use. The Bereweeke Skills Teaching System (Jenkins et al 1983) is an excellent example of such a system which facilitates the planning, implementation and evaluation of programmes of care.

Deciding on appropriate treatment methods

There are a number of considerations which may contribute to the decision about which techniques are to be used in therapy. Many of these may have already influenced the formulation of specific treatment goals, e.g. the nature of the problem, location of therapy, and availability of resources. These will continue to be important factors influencing the use of particular methods of treatment. Some other considerations are:

- The likelihood of particular treatment methods being effective for this client.
- The efficacy of the chosen techniques and whether this has been demonstrated and satisfactorily evaluated by research.
- Does the therapy, and chosen methods of same, conform to ethical guidelines for practice? For example, has informed consent been given by the subject or appointed advocate? Does treatment involve using non-aversive – and the least restrictive – approaches? Is there some sound justification for using an alternative approach?

Whatever methods of treatment are chosen, they should reflect the needs and wishes of the person undergoing therapy so he should be involved as much as possible throughout the entire process, from assessment to evaluation.

Although the outline of treatment methods was separated above into those aimed at increasing behaviour and those aimed at decreasing behaviour, it was not the intention to divorce one from the other. Methods used to increase appropriate behaviour are the more therapeutically desirable and should always be considered over techniques designed solely to reduce inappropriate behaviour. The use of methods to decrease inappropriate behaviour may be considered when more positive approaches have been properly used and have proven to be unsuccessful. Even then, however, reduction methods should be used in conjunction with those designed to increase appropriate behaviour and should never be used in isolation. The approach which is characterized by the building up of patterns of appropriate behaviour in order to replace undesirable behaviour is known as the constructional approach (Goldiamond 1974, 1975). This approach has proven to be ethically preferable and practically effective. Consideration will now be given to examples of this approach and some of the more commonly used methods.

INCREASING APPROPRIATE BEHAVIOURS

The manipulation of antecedents and consequences

Antecedent control

Certain antecedent and/or consequential factors may influence the performance of behaviour and these may be used to effect the desired change. To increase appropriate behaviour those antecedents which make the desired behaviour more likely can be presented. For example, the decision may be made to encourage a person in the construction of a jigsaw puzzle. In order to make this behaviour more likely to occur, he may be systematically provided with encouragement and verbal prompting to engage in the behaviour. Similarly, antecedent factors which make the desired behaviour less likely to occur are either removed or minimized. For example,

assessment results may indicate that the subject appears to be easily distracted by noise and the presence of others. In order to encourage the performance of the desired behaviour the person may be removed to a quieter and less populated area in which he may engage in jigsaw construction.

Consequence control

There may also be consequential factors which impede or preclude the performance of desirable behaviour. It may be desirable to remove or modify these to increase the likelihood of appropriate behaviour occurring. For example, if the existing consequences of a person's ability to demonstrate domestic skills are that the performance of these skills goes largely unnoticed, and the person is asked to perform more chores of that nature then, assuming both consequences are undesired by the subject, he may reduce or cease the performance of these skills.

In order to make it more likely that the behaviour will occur by consequence alteration, attempts would be made to ensure that more desirable consequences are provided to display of the behaviour, such as praise and attention when domestic skills are performed and the removal of unwanted extra chores.

The use of reinforcement

The principle of reinforcement provides the foundation on which a considerable number of treatment methods used to promote desirable behaviour are based. Reinforcement is best described as any event following a behaviour which increases the likelihood of future repetition of the behaviour. The inherent value of reinforcement is not in its potential appeal to the individual but rather in its ability to strengthen behaviour. The concept of reinforcement as being something which is pleasing or desirable can be misleading. The pivotal concern is that of individual preference. What is pleasing or desirable to some people may not necessarily harbour the same qualities for others. The experience of pain or humiliation would not be regarded by the majority of people as pleasurable, yet some people would appear to derive satisfaction from these. In addition, an event consequent to a behaviour may be pleasurable or desirable to an individual but not to the extent that it is sufficient to increase the frequency of a particular behaviour. It is only by serving that purpose that a consequence may be described as reinforcing. Where a consequence is presented following a behaviour and that behaviour is thereby strengthened then positive reinforcement is said to have occurred. A frequently confusing concept is that of negative reinforcement. As the term reinforcement implies, this is also concerned with the strengthening of behaviour. However, in negative reinforcement this process is brought about not by the presentation of a pleasing event but by the removal of an unpleasant event. The same behaviour may be strengthened by the use of positive and negative reinforcement. The crucial difference lies in the *presentation* of a pleasing stimulus in positive reinforcement as opposed to the *removal* of an unpleasant stimulus in negative reinforcement.

Negative reinforcement involves the performance of a behaviour in order to escape from or avoid an unpleasant experience. People with learning difficulties may perform undesirable behaviours, such as body rocking or hand-biting, in order to escape from or avoid unpleasant situations or experiences. Such situations might be the request of their participation in a particular task or activity, or an overcrowded and noisy atmosphere. If performance of undesirable behaviour removes or prevents these unpleasant experiences then this process serves to negatively reinforce inappropriate behaviour. It is necessary, therefore, to understand the learning process involved in negative reinforcement. The use of negative reinforcement as a part of treatment is relatively rare, particularly with people who have learning difficulties. There is little need therefore to deliberate further on this concept.

Types of reinforcement

Reinforcement can be provided in many different forms. Four main categories have been suggested (Hemsley & Carr 1987). These are:

- primary
- secondary
- social
- stimulating.

Primary reinforcers are those which are natural and prerequisite to life, such as food, drink and warmth. Secondary reinforcers are those which have developed reinforcing characteristics through their ability to access other reinforcers. The most obvious secondary reinforcer is money – of no value in itself but readily exchangeable for other things. Anything which can be used to access other important items (often referred to as 'back-up' reinforcers) could be usefully employed as secondary reinforcers. Tokens, stickers or points earned may be later exchanged for back-up reinforcers like consumables or materials. The value of secondary reinforcement is learned through this process rather than being intrinsic.

Social reinforcement, such as smiles, praise and touch may be readily provided as a consequence of desirable behaviour. Social reinforcers are often paired with the delivery of primary or secondary reinforcers, particularly in the early stages of programme implementation. The desired result of the pairing process is that the potency and value of social reinforcement is thereby enhanced, facilitating the phasing out of primary or secondary reinforcement in favour of social at a later stage in therapy.

Stimulating reinforcement provides the fourth category. Examples are: sensory stimulants (e.g. flashing lights or different sounds), toys, preferred activities and leisure pursuits. The extent to which these will appeal to the individual and be enjoyed may be demonstrated by that person's attention and involvement with such items and events. Where desired, stimulating reinforcers may be provided in exchange for secondary reinforcement, i.e. used as back-up reinforcers.

In the process of development and maintenance of appropriate behaviour, reinforcement can provide a crucial and potent motivator. In everyday life, most of us perform under the control of reinforcement. We may work harder or dress smartly to earn the praise, approval and respect of our family, friends, peers or bosses, thereby learning patterns of behaviour in response to the delivery of social reinforcement. Some degree of social and environmental control may therefore influence our motivation to behave in a particular way. Sometimes, where an individual has a learning difficulty, it may be necessary to use reinforcement in order to strengthen that person's motivation to engage in desirable behaviour.

Reinforcement selection

Potential reinforcers may already have been highlighted during the assessment process. If possible, the subject may be asked directly which preferences he or she has. This may be done by using a specially designed questionnaire or inventory. Where the subject is unable to provide this information directly then an individual who is familiar with him may be consulted.

It can often be difficult to isolate reinforcers, particularly where effective communication proves difficult. In consideration of this several studies have involved the sytematic assessment of preferences by direct observation of the subject's response to different stimuli (Green et al 1988, Pace et al 1985, Wacker et al 1985). These studies proved to be effective in determining reinforcement preferences which could then be used in training programmes.

When individual reinforcers have been identified then decisions may be made about which reinforcers to use, when to use them, for how long and how frequently. Choosing a reinforcer may depend on how easily it can be obtained and delivered, which behaviour is to be strengthened and how suitable it is for the subject concerned. For example, should we wish to encourage someone to engage in conversation, we may use social reinforcement, such as smiling and eye contact, as a result of the person's initiating conversation.

This is a good example of natural reinforcement, as part of the process of conversing with another generally involves making eye contact and perhaps smiling from time to time. Wherever possible the natural consequence of a behaviour should be given first consideration. However, returning to the example, the subject may not be motivated by smiling and eye contact. It may therefore be necessary to choose an alternative reinforcer which is more appealing. A token or a tick in a behavioural log book, which could later be exchanged for a preferred item, would not only allow speech to continue but also provide a topic of future conversation. Similarly, if the desired behaviour is weight loss, for example, it would be quite inappropriate to use food as a reinforcer. It is crucial that the chosen reinforcement will not interfere with the behaviour being strengthened or the health of the person having treatment.

Contingency

A contingency is the relationship between a response or behaviour and its consequence. When delivering reinforcement there should always be a distinct relationship between the desired behaviour and the consequence of that behaviour. It is frequently advised that reinforcement should immediately follow the desired behaviour. The purpose of this is to avoid strengthening another non-target behaviour which may occur at some point between performance of the desired behaviour and the delivery of reinforcement. The pivotal consideration in determining how quickly reinforcement should follow the desired behaviour is the person's level of understanding, i.e. their ability to associate the delivery of reinforcement with performance of the desired behaviour, even if that reinforcement does not follow immediately. If a person's ability to make such a clear association is in doubt, then it may be expedient to clarify the contingency by immediate delivery of reinforcements. In this case, therefore, we must be careful also to select a reinforcer which can be readily (and perhaps frequently) delivered in order that little time is used in obtaining same. If, on the other hand, a person is capable of making a clear association between performance of a desired behaviour, and delivery of reinforcement, reinforcement may be delayed. The use of secondary or conditioned reinforcers, such as tokens, ticks or stars in a logbook or diary can be effective in bridging the gap between performance of the desired behaviour and the delivery of back-up reinforcers. Social reinforcement may be used in a similar way, since these are more natural responses to desired behaviour. Social reinforcement should be given warmly and enthusiastically, if the person receiving it is to make a clear association between his delivery and his performance of desired behaviour. Consistency is a crucial issue in the building and strengthening of behaviour. Everyone involved in the delivery of reinforcement should be clearly aware of exactly which behaviour is to be reinforced, the nature of reinforcement, and how and when reinforcement is to be given.

Reinforcement scheduling

When reinforcement is delivered as a consequence of a desired behaviour every time that behaviour takes place, this is referred to as continuous reinforcement. This method of reinforcement scheduling appears to be the most effective in strengthening behaviour. Another advantage of a continuous reinforcement schedule is that it is usually uncomplicated to use and therefore consistency may be relatively more easy to achieve. A major disadvantage, however, is that when the reinforcement is suddenly withdrawn, the target behaviour stops very quickly. The process of sudden withdrawal of reinforcement is called extinction. This may be avoided by the systematic and gradual phasing out of reinforcement. This can be achieved by using alternative schedules of reinforcement. The crucial dimensions of these schedules are frequency and time. A ratio schedule of reinforcement is determined by the frequency of behaviour, and an interval schedule of reinforcement by performance of behaviour, following a set period of time. In addition, ratio or interval schedules may be either fixed or variable. When using a fixed ratio, or FR schedule, reinforcement may be delivered following a certain number of performances of a behaviour. For example, if a child is being rewarded for every 3rd marble he places in a jar, this schedule of reinforcement would be on a fixed ratio of 3, i.e. FR3; delivering reinforcement for every 4th marble placed in the jar would be FR4, and so on. Using a variable ratio schedule involves delivery of reinforcement following a variable frequency of responses whose average is the number determined by the ratio. Returning to our example, if the variable ratio schedule of 5 (or VR5) is set, the child may be reinforced for the 4th, 10th, 16th and 20th time he puts a marble in the jar. Reinforcement is thereby being given, on average, every 5th time the child performs the desired behaviour.

Interval schedules are useful for reinforcing behaviours which tend to last for a significant period of time, e.g. reading or drawing. Using an interval schedule involves reinforcing the target behaviour when it is first performed following a specified period of time. For example, if the desired behaviour is reading, and the selected time interval is 15 minutes, a fixed interval schedule would require reinforcement to be delivered following the first performance of reading behaviour after the 15 minute interval had expired. By using a variable schedule, where intervals last, on average, for 15 minutes (VI 15 minutes) it is possible to avoid the potential difficulty of the person being able to calculate the time of reinforcement delivery under a fixed schedule. The use of variable schedules of reinforcement renders the desired behaviour more resistant to extinction. However, variable schedules tend to be more difficult to apply efficiently than fixed schedules. In the process of phasing-out of reinforcement, and substituting more natural consequences to appropriate behaviour for consumable and material items, effective scheduling is a major contributor to success.

Satiation

When reinforcement is delivered frequently and without change, it may lose its appeal to the person and therefore its ability to maintain performance of desired behaviour. This process is called satiation, and may be surmountable by using an assortment of preferred reinforcers which may be offered to the person as a choice, delivered in a random sequence, or used to substitute the old reinforcer. Satiation may also be avoided by ensuring that the reinforcers being used are not readily available to the person in situations which do not require performance of the desired behaviour. Some reinforcers may be particularly resistant to satiation, especially tokens or money, since these can normally be exchanged for a number of different items or events, or may be kept for use when they are most needed by the person. Sometimes, the value of reinforcement may become associated with the person responsible for its delivery. In a similar fashion, the appeal of the person providing reinforcement may diminish if he is the only person who delivers it. Generally speaking, it is advisable to use a number of persons who can provide variety in the provision of reinforcement. This may not only avoid a satiation process but will assist in the generalization of performance of desirable behaviour. The issue of generalization will be discussed in more detail later in the chapter.

The Premack principle

This is a reinforcement technique named after its founder, David Premack (Premack 1959). The principle states that any high probability behaviour (HPB), which is made a consequence of performance of a low probability behaviour (LPB), will reinforce the low rate behaviour. An example of the use of this technique might be a person who loves to watch sport on television (HPB) but who detests having to take a shower (LPB). If it is arranged and agreed that the person can only engage in watching television if he has taken a shower, then the HPB (watching sport on TV) would strengthen the performance of the LPB (taking a shower).

As with other methods of reinforcement, this technique may only be effective if the person is able to make a clear association between performance of the desired behaviour and the reinforcing consequence.

Contingency contracting

This is a behavioural change method in which the subject and significant others, e.g. parents, carers or therapists, agree to a contract which outlines the consequences of the subject's performance or nonperformance of desired or undesired behaviour. This typically involves a written agreement which contains details of the positive and negative results of specific behaviours, e.g. 'If subject brushes his teeth mum will take him shopping, ' or 'If subject becomes aggressive he will be required to stay alone in his room for one hour'. Both parties agree on the details of the contract and sign it as an expression of this agreement. The four main ingredients of the contract are:

1. *The desired behaviour*
   What exactly is required of the subject? This should be stated explicitly.
2. *Positive consequences*
   Clearly specify privileges for desired performance.
3. *Negative consequences*
   Penalties for nonperformance, or other violation of the agreement, should be negotiated and outlined in detail.
4. *Bonuses*
   This may involve extra privileges as an incentive for extra special or consistently satisfactory performance.

The contract agreement may circumvent the problem of the subject manipulating the programme or forgetting verbal negotiations.

Skills teaching methods

There are many techniques which may be used to build and strengthen appropriate behaviour. Many of the skills teaching methods outlined in this section may be used in a variety of permutations and combinations, in order to train people who have a learning difficulty to overcome problems of living. To attempt to provide even a single example of a treatment approach relative to each individual difficulty encountered is a far more protracted exercise than is worthwhile, if not an impossible task. Therefore, as with social skills training, the attention of the reader is directed towards the appropriate literature for more detailed information.

In this section, the following methods will be considered:

- prompting
- fading
- shaping
- chaining
- modelling
- role play
- social skills training
- relaxation training
- self-management skills.

Prompting

Prompting is a method which is used to encourage a person to perform the desired behaviour whenever the appropriate situation arises. The most commonly used types of prompts are physical, gestural and verbal. Each of these is characterized by the extent to which help is provided to ensure performance of the behaviour. Generally speaking, physical prompting involves the most intensive instruction, followed by gestural prompting, with verbal prompt usually being the least intensive. Each form of prompting itself may involve using different intensities of instruction, e.g. from full or maximum physical prompting to partial or minimal physical prompting. It is important to provide an exact behavioural definition of the level of prompting to be used within the treatment programme, e.g. minimal physical prompting may be defined as 'physically guiding the subject's hand throughout the sequence of behaviour using the instructor's hand to lightly hold his wrist'. This procedure would be classed as physical prompting since some degree of physical guidance or assistance was provided in order for the person to perform the target behaviour. A gestural prompt involves demonstrating the target behaviour to the subject by the use of gestural signals, e.g. beckoning or pointing. A verbal prompt involves the use of words to instruct and guide the person towards performance of the target behaviour.

Assessment of the person's ability to perform the desired behaviour may indicate the level of prompting which appears to be required. It is considered best to use the minimum amount of prompting necessary for the target behaviour

to be performed. However, if verbal prompts alone prove unsuccessful then gestural prompts may be used. If these also fail, then it may be necessary to use physical prompting also. The timing of prompts may be very important in teaching skills which should eventually be demonstrated in response to the natural stimulus for same, e.g. if someone is being taught to clear the table following mealtimes prompting should be provided at these times. By doing this, the person may ultimately learn to perform the desired behaviour in response to the situational cue, i.e. once the meal is finished, rather than continue to rely on prompting.

Fading

Fading is the process by which prompts are reduced and eventually removed. This is usually done on a very gradual basis since the quick removal of prompts can result in the person losing the skill he is being taught or encouraged to perform, due to discontinued assistance and support. It is important, therefore, to ensure that prompts are systematically faded in response to simultaneous improvement in or satisfactory maintenance of performance. Fading usually reverses the process of the building up of prompts. Just as we may move from giving verbal prompts to using gestural then physical as a necessary progression towards the teaching of a desired skill, we may gradually fade or reduce the level of prompting from physical to gestural to verbal before eventually removing prompts altogether as the behaviour occurs in response to a natural situational or environmental cue.

Shaping

Shaping is a technique which involves the gradual construction of a desired behaviour by the strengthening of progressive approximations of that behaviour. Many behaviours are made up of intricate sequences of behaviour as opposed to a solitary act. Shaping allows the reinforcement of a behaviour which can be used to facilitate the learning of the desired response. Sometimes this may involve the strengthening of responses which appear to be, in some way, related to the target behaviour. On other occasions, the initial behaviour being reinforced may appear to have little in common with the target behaviour. However, the reinforcement of successive responses shaped to resemble the final target behaviour may systematically lead to actual performance of that behaviour. As with fading, it is advisable to ensure that each sequence or stage of behaviour has been satisfactorily learned before moving on. It may also be desirable to end the training session on a successful note. Shaping can be a tiring and stressful procedure for trainee and instructor alike. If a sequence of behaviour appears to be too demanding to be mastered during the session, the previous (albeit lower) stage could be repeated, performed correctly and heavily reinforced. This would allow the session to end in a positive fashion, preserving motivation and morale. Shaping is often used in conjunction with prompting in order to teach and elicit target behaviours.

Chaining

As with shaping procedures, chaining is used when the target behaviour is capable of being dissected into smaller component steps involving a number of different behavioural responses. A method which can be effectively employed to afford this dissection is a detailed analysis of each of the steps which together make up the whole behaviour. This is sometimes referred to as a 'task analysis'. Box 9.1 illustrates a possible task analysis for putting on and buttoning a shirt. Chaining involves teaching the individual components or steps, one at a time. When these are linked together, i.e. performed in sequence, the chain of behaviour gradually extends until the final target behaviour is achieved. When the initial step in the behaviour is taught first, this process is referred to as forward chaining. Conversely, when the process involves teaching the last sequence of behaviour first, this is known as reverse chaining or backward chaining.

In the example in Box 9.1 the first step to be taught via backward chaining would be the final step, i.e. fastening the collar button. Steps

Box 9.1 Task Analysis: Putting On a Shirt
Given that the subject is right handed; can tell right from left; has full manual dexterity and can follow verbal instructions.

Step no.
1. Select shirt from wardrobe.
2. Check that all buttons are on shirt but are undone.
3. Hold shirt by collar using left hand.
4. Turn shirt until front is facing you.
5. Insert right hand in sleeve which hangs on the left hand side as shirt faces you.
6. Use left hand to pull shirt sleeve over entire right arm until right hand reaches out of sleeve cuff.
7. Pull shirt over left shoulder using right hand.
8. Hold shirt with right hand while putting left hand in vacant sleeve.
9. Push left arm through sleeve until left hand reaches out of sleeve cuff.
10. Pull collar round neck.
11. Pull shirt sides round to meet in front.
12. Use right hand to fasten left cuff button.
13. Use left hand to fasten right cuff button.
14. Fasten shirt from bottom button to top button, leaving collar open if desired.
15. Fasten collar button if desired.

would continue to be taught in reverse sequence once each previous skill was mastered. A lot of prompting and reinforcement may be used to facilitate the person's learning of each step. Through forward chaining, steps would be taught in a logical progression from first to last. Again, prompts and reinforcement may be used as required. Prompts may be faded depending on the level required for the individual to perform the desired behaviour. Delivery of reinforcement following successful performance of each sequence of behaviour may be necessary to preserve the motivation of the trainee. Once each step has been learned, it may be sufficient to reward that step with social reinforcement, whereas each new step may require back-up reinforcement when being taught initially.

It is generally considered that, of the two methods, backward chaining is the more effective technique for skills teaching. The rationale is that, in backward chaining, the last step is taught first thereby immediately completing the chain and achieving success. This performance is heavily reinforced, therefore completion of the final step assumes the properties of secondary reinforcement due to its pairing with that reward. Where difficulty in linking steps in the chain of behaviour is experienced, this may be due to the progression being too much for the person to cope with, or because he is not being sufficiently motivated to perform the desired behaviour. The addition of smaller, easier steps to link the behaviour sequence, and the use of more potent reinforcement to boost motivation may surmount these obstacles to progress.

Modelling

Modelling is a very effective method of teaching behaviour, and is based on social learning theory. The principal research on social learning was carried out by Albert Bandura (Bandura 1977). Social learning theory differs from the other behavioural learning theories in one major respect: that it is not totally reliant on direct experience. In very simple terms, social learning theory purports that learning takes place not only by direct experience but also by indirect experience, i.e. by the observation and imitation of others. Obviously, this process can be the mediator in the acquisition of inappropriate, as well as appropriate, patterns of behaviour. A good example of the potency of social learning is the way in which some fears and anxieties are acquired. Many people are afraid of snakes or lizards yet may never have a personal experience of them. They develop a fear, often based on reading about or listening to the bad experiences or the fears of others.

Modelling as a technique to teach behaviour involves a process of observational learning and imitation. The procedure typically involves presenting a demonstration of the desired behaviour. This may be done either in a live or imagined situation, or through the use of video, presentation of pictures or visual cues. The emphasis is on a visual demonstration of the desired response, with the intention that the viewer will learn how to perform that response from the model. The demonstration attempts to present the appropriate situational cues and reinforcing consequences to the performance of the target behaviour, in order that these features will also be learned.

There are a number of considerations which may add to the efficacy of the modelling procedure:

- The model should be regarded highly by the observer.
- The model should be of the same sex and of similar age to the observer.
- The model should demonstrate the desired behaviour clearly and precisely.
- The observer should be able to attend to the model without any distraction or interruption.
- The observer should have the physical and mental capacity to both retain and subsequently initiate the desired response.
- Sufficient opportunity should be available outwith the training session for the observer to reproduce the desired behaviour. For example, there should be ample provision of appropriate situational cues and delivery of preferred reinforcement when the desired response is performed.

Modelling may be used in conjunction with other skills teaching methods to successfully increase appropriate behaviour. Its efficacy has been well demonstrated in the training of social and independent living skills, relaxation techniques and the self-control of anger and anxiety.

Role play

This is a widely used technique in the teaching of social and behavioural self-management skills. Role play typically involves the performance of desired behaviour in an artificially created situation, rather like acting. The behaviour being taught is exactly that which it is expected will be performed in the natural environment, despite the simulated situation. Usually the therapist will act out a particular scenario in a manner designed to both elicit and respond to the desired behaviour from the subject receiving training.

Social skills training

Social skills training incorporates a number of techniques and is used to increase the person's proficiency in, and range of, skills related to social functioning. Training may commence following a thorough assessment of the individual's abilities with regard to expression, interaction and perception. As with any analysis of desired behaviour, the question of a skill versus a motivational deficit requires to be satisfactorily answered, i.e. can the person perform the desired behaviour? If so, is he choosing not to do so? Why? What do we need to do to encourage performance? Most social skills training studies have been based on a skills deficit. Using this criterion, the treatment approach may involve a combination of verbal instruction, modelling, role play and social reinforcement. Training sessions, either in an individual or group format, are usually conducted two or three times per week and typically last for about 1 hour. The content of each session may be based on social skills problems identified from the assessment process. Usually, the least difficult problem is dealt with first and progression takes place systematically, working through those problems causing most difficulty. Therapist-assisted practice enables the therapist to supervise the performance of learned responses by accompanying the subject or subjects within the natural environment. The reader is referred to the appropriate references in the Further Reading list for more specific information regarding the assessment and teaching of a variety of social skills.

Relaxation training

In recent years there has been an increase in research evidence supporting the use of relaxation techniques with people who have a learning difficulty and behavioural problems. Relaxation methods with such people appear to be the modification of these techniques in response to their special needs and level of understanding. Two of the more commonly used forms of relaxation training for people with learning difficulties are behavioural relaxation training (BRT) and abbreviated progressive relaxation (APR). Behavioural relaxation training involves the demonstration of unrelaxed and then relaxed states in 10 different body areas. The person has

to first watch and then imitate the relaxed state. The therapist provides prompting and feedback according to performance. A few examples of the relaxed versus unrelaxed states are:

- overall unrelaxed posture – then relaxed posture
- quick breathing – then slow breathing
- eyes tightly closed – then eyes lightly closed or open and still
- feet moving – then feet still.

Abbreviated relaxation training is similar and involves the therapist demonstrating:

- sitting in a relaxed posture
- tension release cycles in the hands and face
- breathing slowly and deeply.

The subject is then asked to copy each of these responses and instructed to use the tension-release cycles in different parts of the body, e.g. arms, face and legs.

Alternative methods of relaxation include deep breathing exercises and listening to soothing music. Evaluation of the effects of relaxation training may be carried out by the measurement of the subject's pulse rate before and after each session. Relaxation rating scales may also be used to assess results. If possible, the subject may give a self-report on the presence of a relaxed or tensed state, e.g. by verbal or gestural indication. Training sessions typically last for around 1 hour and may take place daily or three or four times per week. Once the person has mastered the techniques, it is hoped that he will use them in response to anger or anxiety provoking situations in order to become relaxed and calm. Audio-taped instructions or soothing music may facilitate self-initiated relaxation.

People who have a learning difficulty may experience a number of fears and anxieties in everyday life. The process of relocation from a hospital to a community setting, for example, may render the manifestation of these problems more likely. In some instances, the presence of behavioural difficulties such as phobia or aggression may hinder or preclude the relocation process itself. Relaxation training may be a potentially efficacious component of any treatment plan aimed towards the amelioration of these difficulties.

Self-management skills

The use of self-control and self-management techniques to ameliorate behavioural difficulties experienced by individuals or people who have a mental handicap is a development of major significance. Although the available literature regarding the teaching and use of these skills with people who have a learning difficulty remains far from extensive (in this country, at least), research findings to date indicate favourable evaluation and highlight the potential usefulness of these behavioural change methods. In broad terms, self-management involves the subject's independent use of specific procedures in order to regulate his own behaviour. To successfully attain this goal, the person receives education regarding the behavioural principles inherent in these techniques, as well as the instruction needed to apply it appropriately and effectively. Typically, self-management training will involve the use of four main procedures:

- self-monitoring
- self-instruction
- self-evaluation
- self-consequation.

Self-monitoring. This entails the person being responsible for examining the nature and extent of his own behaviour. Usually, a detailed and systematic recording of behaviour and surrounding events and circumstances is made by the individual. The act of self-monitoring alone may result in a change in the characteristics of the behaviour being monitored. This reactive effect may be particularly pronounced if the person is highly motivated towards changing his behaviour. Thus, the technique of self-monitoring may not only provide an accurate record of an individual's behaviour but also influence that behaviour.

Self-instruction. By using a self-instruction procedure, the individual may manipulate the events or situations which cue the target behaviour. In order to effect the desired response, self-instruction can be used to provide a series of positive self-statements which will help to promote appropriate behaviour. For example:

I know what I have to do . . . I've done it before . . . let's go, then . . . wait just a minute . . . that's right . . . I'm doing well . . .

Similarly, these positive self-statements may be used to replace any negative thoughts or statements which may cue or fuel feelings of anger, anxiety or frustration, which in turn might lead to inappropriate or undesirable behaviour. Initially, coping statements may be used to reduce feelings of anger, anxiety or frustration. For example:

Be calm . . . that's it . . . stay cool . . . let's think this over . . .

Further self-statements may then be introduced in order to cue and promote appropriate behaviour. For example:

That's better . . . what was all that fuss about . . . I'm fine now . . . I can deal with this . . .

Self-instruction such as this operates at a cognitive level, that is, it requires the person to employ certain thinking patterns and strategies in order to avoid, cope or deal appropriately with potentially problematic situations. On a more overt or observable level the individual may modify his actions or environment in order to promote or discourage performance of certain behaviours, for example, a freshly cleaned and ironed suit left hanging outside his wardrobe may serve as a reminder that he should dress smartly the following day. Similarly, a person may choose to leave a room in which others are arguing, rather than stay and risk getting involved himself.

Self-evaluation. By a process of self-evaluation, the person may determine if his behaviour has been satisfactory or unsatisfactory. This self-assessing procedure may be performed in line with predetermined criteria regarding whether his behaviour is considered 'good' or 'bad'. Honest and accurate self-evaluation is a pivotal component of self-management, since it may not only determine the nature of self-consequation, but also provide an opportunity for determining the efficacy and desirability of self-instructive techniques. In turn, this may produce direction for progress in the entire self-management process and stimulate motivation to achieve the desired results.

Self-consequation. Depending on the outcome of the self-evaluation process, the individual may deliver to himself a rewarding consequence (self-reinforcement) or an unpleasant consequence (self-punishment). Specific reinforcing or punitive consequences may be self-selected or negotiated with others, and may be written as part of a contract agreement between the subject and 'himself' (through self-contract) or between the subject and significant others, e.g. parent or carer. Self-reinforcement or punishment may be covertly delivered or overtly delivered, as in the following examples:

Covert delivery
● Self-reinforcement – by creating thoughts or images which provide and stimulate rewarding and pleasant feelings. For example:

I've done really well . . . I've proved I can do it . . . Everyone is pleased with me . . . I've made a good impression . . . I feel good having done that and done it well . . .

● Self-punishment – by creating thoughts or images which provide and elicit unpleasant or undesirable feelings. For example:

I've let everyone down . . . I don't feel good about myself . . . I feel guilty . . . I've disappointed myself and others . . .

Overt delivery
● Self-reinforcement – by self-administration or access to desired regards, e.g. consumables, activities, tokens.
● Self-punishment – by self-denial of desired rewards, e.g. not engaging in preferred activities, 'fining' oneself tokens, giving consumables intended for regard to another person.

Using self-management skills

When using self-consequation with people who have a learning difficulty, it may be inadvisable to use covert self-punishment as this could fuel negative feelings of inadequacy and frustration, perhaps resulting in further problems. The use of encouraging self-statements to maintain motivation and promote future improvement may prove more desirable and beneficial to the individual. Examples of these are:

That's OK . . . don't worry . . . I'll do better next time . . . I didn't do so well that time . . . I'll work harder to improve things . . .

Self-management involves the use of a number of skills and techniques in order to achieve behavioural change. In order to effectively control desired change in his behaviour the individual may require help and training in:

● identification of those situations and events which promote or discourage certain behaviour
● identification and selection of appropriate and effective solutions to deal with behavioural difficulties
● the performance of appropriate responding
● evaluation of his performance
● the application of appropriate consequences to success and failure in self-management.

More intensive cognitively orientated self-management techniques will often require a higher level of intellectual functioning if they are to be most effective. However, appropriate modifications to self-management training may be made in order to render it relevant to individual abilities. The majority of research studies on self-management procedures appear to be conducted with people who have mild or moderate learning difficulties; although favourable results have been reported with people who have a more severe learning difficulty.

Other behavioural change methods and the use of specially designed materials can be utilized in order to enhance the effectiveness of self-management. Modelling, role play, prompting, feedback and reinforcement are some of the more common external behavioural change methods used in conjunction with self-management approaches. Wrist counters, special cue cards, behaviour recording charts and behavioural logbook recording systems are examples of special materials which may be used to complement self-management skills. The aforementioned are particularly useful where the individual has difficulty in comprehension and/or communication. In theory, self-management and self-control techniques appear to have the capacity to promote the process of generalization, since the skills involved can potentially mediate behavioural change across time, location and situation.

Although questions remain regarding the generalization and maintenance of acquired self-management skills, studies have demonstrated satisfactory outcomes with regard to these issues. The use of self-management skills offers a number of advantages over those behavioural change strategies implemented exclusively under external influences. At a fundamental level, the individual is heavily involved in contributing to the nature and design of the treatment approach. Self-management also falls in line with ethical guidelines to employ the least restrictive and intrusive treatment option in respect of individual rights. Self-management skills are consistent with the underlying philosophy of normalization, in that they promote independence via self-control and can assist in access to valued social roles for the individual. External behavioural change methods tend to impose substantial demands on the time and effort of others, which can interfere with the independence of the individual and may lead to problems in the generalization of appropriate behaviour and skills. Despite the fact that the use of external influences to promote the desired behavioural change may be incorporated into a self-management approach, the emphasis on behavioural self-control enables the individual to become more responsible for his or her actions and thus more independent of external factors for behavioural change.

A major difficulty with self-management may lie with self-consequation. For example, a person may self-reinforce without performing the desired behaviour or in spite of performance of undesirable behaviour. There is, therefore, a strong reliance on the honesty and motivation of the individual to utilize self-management skills appropriately.

Self-management methods have been used, both independently and in conjunction with other behavioural change methods to ameliorate a variety of behavioural difficulties. For example, in skills teaching they have covered social skills (Matson and Andrasik 1982), vocational skills (McNally, Kampik and Sherman 1984) and self-help skills (Alberto et al 1986). They have been used with various undesirable behaviours, including agitated-disruptive behaviours (Reese, Sherman and Sheldon 1984), socially undesirable behaviours (Rosine and Martin 1983), high-rate disruptive behaviours (Cole, Gardner and Karan 1985) and verbal and physical aggression (Bradley and McCue 1988).

Generalization and discrimination

Once new skills have been learned, it is crucial that the individual can perform these satisfactorily within the natural setting. The performance of a behaviour in the presence of similar stimuli, across a variety of situations, is known as generalization. The treatment process is incomplete unless generalization takes place. Some skills may require to be performed across a diversity of location, time of day and persons. For example, when we teach an individual to use a cooker as part of a formal training session, it is envisaged that eventually he or she will be able to use a cooker in a number of different locations – in a friend or relative's house, or in a holiday apartment. If a person learns to initiate a conversation within a small group, it is hoped that he or she will ultimately be able to converse with a number of different people, at any time of day, and in a variety of situations and locations. Someone who learns how to behave appropriately at the dining table should be encouraged to show the same behaviour whenever and wherever he or she is seated for a meal.

Unless a person is specifically trained to generalize an acquired skill, he or she may fail to demonstrate that skill in new situations. Generalization training requires the desired behaviour to be reinforced by natural consequences within the new situation. Therefore, it is important that any artificial reinforcers are systematically and successfully phased out while being replaced by the naturally reinforcing events which will be present within the new environment. Social skills, for example, are necessary and valued within everyday living situations. These are generally reinforced and maintained by people exchanging smiles, eye contact and conversation, thus increasing the likelihood of a wider use of these skills. In order to facilitate generalization of skills, it is best to teach them in the environment in which they require to be performed. Where this is not possible, the training situation could be altered to resemble the natural environment as much as possible. In doing this, the important stimuli which exist in the natural situation could be provided within an artificial situation. These stimuli would be used to cue the performance of the desired skill, as would be done naturally, thereby facilitating the generalization process.

Discrimination is an important element of skills acquisition and performance. Discrimination refers to the ability to respond differently to certain cues or stimuli. A person must have the ability to detect changes in environmental conditions if discrimination is to take place. Certain behaviours are only appropriate in response to certain stimulus or environmental conditions. For example, a young boy has just learned to use the toilet seat appropriately and independently within his own home. Whilst visiting a large DIY store with his parents, the young chap then undoes his clothing and 'performs' in the toilet seat which is part of a bathroom suite display. In this instance, the boy has failed to discriminate, by performing a learned skill in response to an inappropriate stimulus condition. Although we may wish him to generalize the learned skill, e.g. by using a friend or relative's toilet, we also want him to discriminate toilet usage by visiting the Gents, rather than the Ladies toilet. Discrimination and generalization are closely related. Some inappropriate behaviours arise from a failure to discriminate, e.g. having an intimate conversation with a total stranger or overdressing on an exceptionally hot day. Discrimination therefore involves recognition of the very often subtle differences in similar stimulus conditions. Discrimination training involves the reinforcement of a desired response to an appropriate stimulus and the nonreinforcement (or extinction) of a response to an inappropriate stimulus. If this procedure is carried out consistently, the desired response will occur only in the presence of appropriate stimulus conditions. Ultimately, it is required that the desired behaviour will occur in response to the appropriate stimulus conditions within the natural environment.

DECREASING INAPPROPRIATE BEHAVIOURS

In the previous section, reference was made to the fact that preference should be given to techniques which promote an increase in appropriate behaviours. The constructional approach offers a methodology for behavioural change based on such techniques. The use of this, and alternative nonaversion approaches towards the reduction of undesirable and inappropriate behaviours, should always be employed first to produce the desired behavioural change. However, the presence of some behaviours, for example, self-injury or aggression, may render the teaching and building up of appropriate skills and behaviour an extremely challenging and protracted process. Severely challenging behaviour may also present immediate danger to the well-being of the individual and/or other persons. In such instances, the use of alternative decelerative techniques may be considered for use in conjunction with – rather than in preference to – nonaversive and constructional approaches. In this section, therefore, attention will be given to some of the nonaversive and decelerative techniques which may be contemplated.

In comparison to the section dealing with skills teaching, methods and techniques used to increase behaviour, this section is considerably less extensive in its outline of decelerative treatment approaches. This is done quite deliberately, not only to emphasize the preference for positive and nonaversive methods, but also to alert the reader to the ethical considerations in the use of certain strategies to decrease problem behaviour. Firstly, the chosen method of treatment should be the least restrictive to the rights and freedom of the individual. Secondly, and as previously stated, decelerative techniques should be used in conjunction with constructional and nonaversive approaches. Thirdly, the chosen treatment should conform to ethical guidelines. Fourthly, the entire process of therapy, from assessment to evaluation, should involve the application of specialist knowledge relevant to treatment. These key considerations are appropriate to the implementation of any behavioural treatment approach but are greatly amplified with respect to decelerative techniques.

In this section, reference is made to problem, difficult or challenging behaviour as that which is viewed to be inappropriate or undesirable.

The reflective approach

This is a particularly useful exercise by which we may consider the function or purpose of challenging behaviours and possible measures to deal with them. Through this approach we can reflect on those relevant factors which predispose our own emotional or behavioural difficulties and identify their consequences. We may then consider appropriate measures which can be taken in order to reduce or remedy these difficulties. This reflective process may help us to understand the behavioural problems of others through our own personal experiences. In turn, this insight can point us towards strategies which may be effective in achieving the desired behavioural change with other people. People who have a mental handicap are frequently exposed to intensely more devaluing and frustrating life experiences than ourselves. If we can reflect clearly on our own concerns, desires and frustrations this may help us to identify, understand and address the difficulties being both experienced and presented by others.

Adjusting antecedents

Behavioural analysis may reveal the occurrence of a particular problem to be related to existing antecedent factors. For example, a young man is reported to have frequent outbursts of verbal aggression when at home or within hostel-type accommodation. No such outbursts have ever been reported as occurring within his day centre or at work. Where it appears that this aggressive behaviour is related to factors prevailing at home or within the hostel – for example, lack of structured activity or adequate stimulation – the environmental conditions within the home or hostel may be adjusted so that the desired antecedent factors (opportunities for activities preferred by the individual) are created. By achieving this we may reduce or eliminate verbally aggressive episodes.

It has been explained previously how internal antecedents to problem behaviour, such as dysfunctional or negative thought processes, may be modified via self-instructional techniques. Similarly, specific antecedent events which precipitate undesirable behaviour may be altered or removed in order to reduce such a difficulty. For example, a young girl has been observed to self-injure at mealtimes by fiercely biting her hands. Such behaviour has never been observed at other times. The girl is unable to communicate but it has been reported that she appears to be sensitive to noise and becomes upset in particularly noisy situations. The other people who sit with her at mealtimes have recently begun to exhibit rowdy behaviour. A change in seating arrangements may eliminate the problem, with the difficulties being shown by the others to be addressed separately, if indicated.

Adjusting consequences

A wide variety of consequence-related procedures can be used to reduce behavioural problems. As with the selection of any behavioural change method, the chosen approach should be responsive to the needs of the individual and his or her problem, therefore the assessment process and outcomes will be pivotal in the identification and implementation of treatment. Specific techniques using a consequence orientated approach differ greatly with regard to complexity, restrictiveness and desirability. However, those chosen here fall under four headings:

- Presentation of reinforcing consequences
- Prevention of reinforcing consequences

- Removal of reinforcing consequences
- Presentation of punitive consequences.

As mentioned previously, most of these descriptions are given briefly. However, once again, the reader is directed to the reference list for more detailed information.

Presentation of reinforcing consequences

The reader may be perplexed by the apparent reiteration of a set of procedures outlined earlier in this chapter. However, any confusion may be readily attributed to the decision to include differential reinforcement techniques in this section rather than that dealing with increasing appropriate behaviour. The rationale for this preference is that, although differential reinforcement methods are used to strengthen more appropriate forms of behaviour, this is usually done with the intention of eliminating problem behaviour. Further description of the individual techniques involved will clarify this point.

The two most common methods of differential reinforcement are differential reinforcement of other behaviour (DRO) and differential reinforcement of incompatible behaviour (DRI). DRO involves the delivery of reinforcement at the end of a specified time interval during which no instances of the problem behaviour occurred. The duration of the time interval being used is determined by the nature and frequency of the problem behaviour. For example, if the behaviour occurred, on average, every 5 minutes, the first interval may be set at 4 minutes, in order to allow an opportunity for reinforcement of nonperformance of problem behaviour to take place. Subsequent time intervals may be increased as periods of nonperformance of problem behaviour become longer. It is crucial to plan the reinforcement schedule so that periods of appropriate behaviour are being strengthened via a clear association of reward for same and for nonperformance of problem behaviour. Care must be taken not to unintentionally reinforce other forms of inappropriate or undesirable behaviour which may occur during the specified time interval. It may therefore be necessary to provide reinforcement contingent on nonperformance of a number of predetermined and defined problem behaviours.

DRO has a number of significant advantages, including its proven effectiveness in the treatment of a variety of behaviour problems, its compatibility with other behavioural reduction methods and, most importantly, its nonaversive properties in comparison to other decelerative techniques. Disadvantages appear to be slight; for example, difficulty in using DRO in situations where the therapist is working with a number of individuals. Also, in instances where reinforcement intervals are necessarily of short duration, the DRO procedure can demand a considerable use of time and manpower.

DRI is a response-specific strategy which involves the reinforcement of those behaviours which are directly incompatible with performance of the identified problem behaviour, i.e. behaviours which cannot be performed simultaneously. For example, a person who self-injures by scratching his forehead may be reinforced for appropriate use of his hands.

Prevention of reinforcing consequences

These procedures involve the removal of the reinforcing consequences of problem behaviour.

Interruption. This is a method used to prevent a problem behaviour from being reinforced by stopping its completion. A person may appear to be gaining sensory reinforcement from performance of a particular problem behaviour, for example, hand waving/flapping. A behavioural interruption procedure to treat this problem may, for example, involve actively preventing the subject from continuing with the problem behaviour immediately it is observed. The person may then be directed towards alternative, more appropriate behaviour, preferably that which is incompatible with the problem behaviour. A DRI procedure may also be used in conjuction with the interruption procedure in order to achieve the desired outcome.

Extinction. This procedure involves the elimination of the reinforcing consequences of a behaviour. For example, if a problem behaviour is being reinforced by attention removal of that attention following performance of the problem behaviour should lead to a reduction in, and eventual elimination of, that problem. Extinction is potentially a very powerful method of decreasing undesirable behaviour. However, it must be used consistently in order to achieve the desired results.

Application of an extinction procedure frequently results in an extinction burst, which involves the person displaying an initial increase in the frequency of problem behaviour in an attempt to elicit the desired consequence. A subsequent decline in the frequency of problem responses usually follows if this extinction burst fails to produce the reinforcing consequence. Due to the high probability of an extinction burst taking place, an extinction procedure should not be used in the treatment of behavioural problems which present actual or potential danger to the individual or others, for example, physical aggression or self-injury.

Sensory extinction. This extinction technique utilizes the removal of sensory effects, which as consequences of the performance of problem behaviour, reinforce and strengthen that behaviour. One example of this might be an individual who frequently bangs their arms and hands on the wooden arm supports of a chair in order to produce noisy sounds. By padding the arms of the chair we can muffle the resultant sounds considerably, thereby leading to a reduction, if not the elimination, of the problem behaviour. Once again, consistency is crucial. If the individual had ready access to other chairs which had no padded arm supports, he or she may continue to display the problem behaviour while sitting in them.

Removal of reinforcing consequences

The procedures described here involve the removal of the opportunity to enjoy the reinforcing consequences of appropriate behaviour, as a result of performance of problem behaviour.

Time out. Time out (often referred to as time out from positive reinforcement) is a procedure which involves the removal of reinforcement as a consequence of the performance of problem behaviour. An essential prerequisite for the use of time out is that positive reinforcement is being made readily available for the individual.

A time out procedure may be used in different ways. For example, the removal of social interaction or attention with an individual may be used as a consequence of inappropriate behaviour. It is desirable that the duration of time out be kept as short as is necessary. Using our example, therefore, social interaction or attention would be resumed following, say, 2 minutes, providing the undesirable behaviour was not being demonstrated. In this instance, it would be crucial not to resume interaction or attention with the individual while problem behaviour was being performed, as this may unintentionally reinforce that behaviour.

An alternative form of time out could be the removal of reinforcement by taking reinforcing materials from the person for a short time following performance of undesirable behaviour. These could then be reintroduced when the undesirable behaviour had ceased. A practical example of this form of time out could be the removal from and reintroduction of sensory stimulating materials to a person, as a consequence of the performance and nonperformance of problem behaviour respectively. A further example of the use of time out might be the withdrawal of the opportunity to earn reinforcement for a certain period of time. This form of time out would be used where a formal reward system was established, for example, by the allocation of points or tokens which can be exchanged for reinforcing consequences. As the result of performance of problem behaviour, the person may be denied the chance to earn points or tokens leading to rewards for a certain amount of time.

The least desirable form of time out involves the removal of the person himself from the reinforcing situation as a consequence of problem behaviour. A major consideration here is that the person is removed to a situation which is nonreinforcing. Release from time out, and the subsequent return of the individual to the reinforcing situation, would be made following as short a duration of time as required. Return to the reinforcing situation would be made when appropriate behaviour was being shown by the individual. There are a number of crucial issues to be considered regarding the use of this form of time out and these should be thoroughly reflected upon and resolved prior to any consideration being given to its use.

Response cost. This procedure, similar to fining, involves the permanent removal of positive reinforcement as a result of the performance of problem behaviour. Response cost should always be used in conjunction with an existing reward schedule and should never infringe upon the everyday entitlements of the individual. In a response cost procedure a person might lose points, tokens or the opportunity to take part in certain 'treat' activities as part of a formally organized reward system, due to performance of problem behaviour.

Presentation of punitive consequences

The following procedures involve the application of unpleasant or punitive consequences as a result of problem behaviour being performed. These procedures may require to be carried out by the individual or by another person.

Overcorrection. Overcorrection refers to two types of procedure which may be used either independently of one another or together to correct the consequences of problem behaviour and to create more appropriate forms of behaviour.

Positive practice overcorrection requires the person to repeatedly perform an appropriate behaviour which is similar in form to, and often incompatible with, the problem behaviour itself. For example, a young girl was required to brush her hair for 2 minutes following each observed episode of the problem behaviour, which was pulling her own hair (Barrett & Shapiro 1980). The appropriate behaviour used in positive practice should be an unpleasing alternative for the individual if the procedure is to be effective.

Restitution is a form of overcorrection which requires the person to rectify the consequences of his or her undesirable behaviour. Typically, this involves the restoration of the environment,

him or herself, or others to a state which is at least the same as, but preferably improved upon, its existing condition prior to performance of the problem behaviour. Thus, after having overturned a chair and broken it during an episode of destructive behaviour, a person may be required to help mend the chair, polish it and return it upright to its original location. Similarly, someone who has deliberately torn items of clothing might be expected to help mend, wash and iron these. Since the desired response in overcorrective procedures is the active participation of the subject, the use of graduated prompting may be required in order to achieve this. Overcorrection may not be suitable for use with individuals who are particularly volatile or aggressive as it may only serve to antagonize. Generally speaking, however, overcorrection appears to be an effective technique for the deceleration of some problem behaviours. However, as with all punitive procedures, a great deal of consideration must be given to its level of restrictiveness of individual freedom and social acceptability.

Social disapproval and verbal reprimand. This involves an expression of disapproval and/or verbal reprimand immediately following an episode of problem behaviour. A stern look and tone of displeasure may accompany the expression in order to maximize the effect. Similarly, gestures can accompany the reprimand, wherever necessary, to improve communication and promote understanding. It is crucial that the individual clearly associates the expression of disapproval with the behaviour we are trying to reduce. It should be remembered that verbal reprimands may act as reinforcing consequences for some individuals. Careful evaluation of the frequency of the problem behaviour should indicate whether or not the use of social disapproval or reprimand is having the desired effect.

Social disapproval and verbal reprimands should always be used in conjunction with other decelerative techniques, where these have been found to be necessary. This allows the systematic fading of these procedures while, the more acceptable consequence of reprimand and disapproval retains a decelerative effect through stimulus association. It should also be remembered that it is insufficient to suppress behaviour, by merely saying, 'No ... don't do that' or 'That's wrong!'. Every time a problem occurs, the individual should also be told which behaviours are more acceptable, and clearly directed and encouraged towards more desirable responses.

Negative practice.   This aims to reduce problem behaviour by requiring the subject to deliberately and repeatedly perform that behaviour. The rationale for this is that the problem behaviour will eventually assume unpleasant properties for the individual due to the requirement for repeated practice, i.e. the problem behaviour will become a reducing consequence for itself. An example of this might be to request a person who screams inappropriately to practise screaming repeatedly for, say, 5 minutes following the initial screaming behaviour. This procedure should not be considered for use with behaviours which may have an effect on the wellbeing of the individual or others. Indeed, the desirability and applicability of this technique may be extremely limited.

There are a number of other decelerative techniques which involve the application of unpleasant experiences as a consequence of problem behaviour. Only some have been listed and the reader is directed to other sources for further information on the use of punitive techniques. In doing this, it is to be hoped that the reader will become aware of the use of aversive techniques as a last resort, and that they will subsequently redirect their reading and research towards more constructional approaches and alternatives to punishment. The search for the most appropriate treatment approach is described well in a statement by Morgan (1989), who says:

The most critical and challenging issue seems to be that of identifying behavioural procedures that are most effective, most acceptable and least restrictive in producing desired outcomes, while preserving the individual's right to remain free from harm.

Other punitive techniques include:

- facial screening (Barmann & Vitali 1982)
- water mist spray (Dorsey et al 1982)
- restraint procedures (Altmeyer, Williams & Sams 1985)
- the application of unpleasant tastes, smells or noises (Marholin et al 1980)
- electric shock (Fox et al 1986).

Medication

There can be a number of major disadvantages in using medication to reduce difficult behaviour, including unwanted side effects and over sedation, resulting in interference with the person's learning capacity. However, the potential benefits of using medication, either in conjunction with or separate from behavioural management strategies, should not be disregarded. Studies illustrating a combination of behavioural and pharmacological interventions for self-injury have demonstrated these to be very effective (Durand 1982, Luiselli 1986, 1991). Evidence has been shown that lithium therapy has proven effective in dealing with screaming, stripping, aggressive, depressed and self-injurious behaviour (Craft & Mathews 1984). Barrett et al (1989) found very favourable results when the drug naltrexone hydrochloride was used to treat the self-injurious responding of a 12-year-old girl with a mental handicap. However, an earlier study by Szymanski et al (1987) revealed that naltrexone hydrochloride had no measurable effects on self-injurious behaviour. Presland (1989), mentions studies which 'show that suppression of problem behaviour by medication can sometimes make it easier to use behavioural approaches to develop appropriate behaviours'. Gedye (1989a, 1989b) has suggested that aggressive and self-injurious behaviours can sometimes be attributed to the presence of frontal lobe seizures. Perhaps medication may have a part to play in the suppression of these seizures?

The reader is strongly directed towards the appropriate reading materials wherever the use of medication is being considered. As part of the intervention process, the use of medication will require extensive discussion, research and control. Effective monitoring by appropriately qualified personnel is also paramount. The administration of any form of medication cannot be taken lightly.

Programme design

Prior to behavioural intervention, details regarding programme implementation should be formally written. It may be helpful to review some of the major considerations prior to discussing formal programme design. These may include:

- Definition of the target behaviours – are definitions clear and precise?
- Specific goals of treatment – are these in the best interest of the client? Are they realistic and achievable?
- Have relevant others been identified and approached regarding therapy? How best can they help? How can they assist in the generalization and maintenance of the desired behavioural change?
- How motivated is the client towards behavioural change? How can we best encourage and maintain that motivation?
- Does the programme involve the client as much as possible? Has he or she the mechanism option to cease therapy if so desired?
- Does therapy fall in line with ethical considerations?
- Do the projected benefits of therapy significantly outweigh the projected costs?
- Is there an appropriate educational and support service for those involved in therapy?

The next stage is to formally design the treatment plan. This involves the writing of a detailed, step-by-step behavioural management programme, which those involved in therapy can easily understand and implement. Any anomalies or misunderstandings should be identified and resolved prior to formulation of the final draft of the treatment plan. The chosen treatment approach may be written up as part of the subject's overall care plan records or similar individual treatment recording system. The programme can also be an entirely separate document. The important factor is that everyone involved in implementation of the chosen treatment ap-

proach should have complete understanding of its content, and ready access to a written copy of same. The following guidelines may help in the formal preparation of a behavioural treatment programme:

1. Ensure that the target behaviours and treatment goals have been clearly defined.
2. Provide comprehensive, step-by-step instructions for those who are to be involved in programme implementation.
   Consider any procedural variances which may be determined by a difference in location, persons, situation and time of day.
3. Specify any antecedent factors which the programme aims to use to advantage, in order to promote the desired behavioural change.
4. State clearly the planned consequences to behavioural responses.
5. Stress the importance of those components of the treatment plan aimed towards promotion, generalization and maintenance of the desired behavioural change, for example:
   — programming of familiar stimulus conditions
   — planning treatment to extend within natural environments
   — encourage self-management skills wherever possible.
6. Detail specific procedures which may require to be used in conjunction with the overall treatment plan, for example:
   — prompting
   — relaxation training
   — role play exercises.
7. Emphasize the nonaversive and constructional components of the treatment plan.
8. Emphasize the importance of consistency in approach, and the timeous and accurate recording of relevant data.
9. Accentuate the need for continuous and effective communication between the client (where able) and those involved in treatment.
   Set times and dates for regular review of therapy.

10. Stress the importance of natural reinforcing consequences to strengthen appropriate behaviour and facilitate systematic fading of tangible or conditioned reinforcement.

EVALUATION: MEASURING TREATMENT SUCCESS

Evaluation is a process which should begin with the implementation of the chosen treatment plan and be continuous throughout therapy. At different times and stages of treatment, specific measurement will require to be taken in order to monitor therapeutic effect. Sometimes this may prove difficult to quantify. However, there are a number of criteria which may assist in the accurate evaluation of treatment. Those considered to be most helpful are:

1. The comparison of data between the treatment phase and baseline conditions – are the desired results being achieved regarding the frequency, intensity and duration of the target behaviours? If a comparison with baseline conditions is being made ensure that the target behaviour is being evaluated under the same conditions as during baseline recordings, i.e.:
   — in the same circumstances
   — in the same location
   — at the same time of day
   — using the same measurement recording tools, formats and observers.
   If these factors are not held as constant as possible it will prove difficult to definitively attribute any behavioural change to the treatment plan itself, since any number of potentially influencing variables might be involved. Remember also the extinction burst effect if extinction-based techniques are being used.
2. Treatment results may be evaluated against identified therapeutic goals, i.e. are results better or worse than expected at a particular stage of treatment?
3. Treatment results may also be compared with results achieved with others using the same treatment methods. Measurement can be taken against previous treatment approaches

or research studies. Once again, however, accurate evaluation may only be possible if these were the same, or markedly similar, approaches in terms of the individual subject, his or her difficulty, situation, method of treatment and system of recording.
4. A measurement of treatment success may be obtained by the self-reporting of the client or consultation with significant others, for example, those involved in therapy, carers, relatives and friends. Self-evaluation is a crucial part of self-management, as previously described. However, it may be used to measure the subject's perception of behavioural change in response to other treatment approaches. Feedback from the client or relevant others may be quite informal, for example, by expression of opinion at any stage of therapy. More formal and detailed measurement may be taken by requiring the client and others to complete a set rating scale, questionnaire, or behavioural report. By using these methods, evaluation of satisfaction with individual components of treatment, how these are being applied and achieved results might be carried out in light of findings. The treatment plan might be adjusted, for example, if greater opportunity and encouragement towards the desired behavioural change need to be provided.

Although treatment results may vary substantially within the parameters of success and failure, they fall broadly into two categories – results which are satisfactory and results which are not. The following guidelines will assist direction in the light of both conclusions.

If satisfied with treatment results

- Do not withdraw treatment immediately.
- Involve the client as much as possible in any changes to the treatment plan.
- Use procedures to phase out treatment systematically.
- Use natural antecedents and consequences to replace artificial ones, with full prompting to change verbal cues to stimulus cues within a natural situation. Replace tangible

reinforcement with natural consequences, e.g. social praise.

- Adjust schedule in order to gradually withdraw tangible reinforcement.
- Encourage the client to use self-management approaches, e.g. self-monitoring and self-consequation.
- Use methods to promote generalization and maintenance in the desired behavioural change, e.g. continue to provide social praise and attention for appropriate behaviour.
- Continue to provide opportunity and encouragement for performance of a desired skill or behaviour.
- Give special treats sporadically to encourage progress.
- Systematically record all changes to the treatment plan.
- Redesign it, if it has changed significantly.
- Inform all relevant others of planned changes in order to ensure consistency in approach.
- Reinforce their efforts to maintain motivation.
- Continue careful evaluation of treatment results until formal intervention is phased out in line with same.

If not satisfied with treatment results

- If undesirable behaviour worsens significantly in the absence of extinction-based techniques being used discontinue the chosen treatment approach until a cause can be identified and resolved, otherwise allow a realistic amount of time for the treatment plan to have a desired effect. Generally, 3 or 4 weeks is enough time to observe at least some significant behavioural change.
- If the desired behaviour change is only slight look to make minor alterations to the treatment plan in order to produce better results. Allow more time for results to improve.
- If changes are practically non-existent consider which aspects of the programme or the evaluation process may be at fault, for example:
  — Is the reinforcement scheduling not tight enough?

— Has the available reinforcement lost its potency?
— Are there insufficient cues for appropriate behaviour?
— Are the treatment procedures being wrongly applied?
— Are expectations of progress set too high?
— Is the client sufficiently motivated to change?
— Are the therapists sufficiently motivated to help him or her to change?
— Are the chosen techniques not working?
— Are evaluative tools insufficiently sensitive to detect the desired changes?
— Are evaluative recordings being completed accurately?
— What variables have changed since baseline recordings, or programme design and implementation?

If any, or a combination of the above are causing problems, take the appropriate action to rectify them, for example:

— Adjust the reinforcement scheduling accordingly.
— Use different reinforcers.
— Provide the necessary opportunities and encouragement for appropriate behaviour.
— Reeducate regarding application of treatment procedures.
— Redefine and reset treatment goals, or set subgoals.
— Encourage client motivation by outlining and emphasizing potential benefits of treatment.
— Reinforce the importance of treatment success for the client and others. Provide sufficient feedback, encouragement and praise for therapists.
— Review treatment methods. Consider addition of facilitative procedures, e.g. prompting, modelling and role play.
— Review evaluative methods and modify accordingly or use alternative measurements of behavioural change.
— Stress the importance of timeous and accurate recordings; if necessary, reeducate regarding their completion.

— Attempt to identify significant variables and take account of these if alteration is to be made to the treatment plan.

— Where necessary discontinue the existing treatment plan and redesign in light of failure.

GENTLE TEACHING

Gentle teaching claims to be a nonaversive intervention strategy which has been used in the care of people with a mental handicap who exhibit challenging, and often severe, behavioural difficulties, such as aggression and self-injury. The approach was developed by John McGee and colleagues at the University of Nebraska in the USA. McGee (1987) writes that:

Gentle teaching is based on a posture that centres itself on the mutual liberation and humanization of all persons, a posture that strives for human solidarity and one that leads care givers to teach bonding to those who attempt to distance themselves from meaningful human interactions.

'Bonding' appears to be the key component of gentle teaching; it is a process which is achieved by the teaching of value in human relationships. In turn, bonding promotes a mutual closeness and warmth between care giver and client, and leads to the recognition of human interdependence. Brandon (1989) states that in gentle teaching we use ourselves rather than simple techniques. He goes on to describe gentleness as 'a process of melting rather than breaking down defences'. Claims for gentle teaching as an innovative approach have not gone unchallenged. Turnbull (1990) states that gentle teaching is a collection of well-tested behaviour modification procedures that are all nonaversive in themselves. It has also been suggested that gentle teaching could be 'behaviourism at its best?' (Jones 1990).

McGee (1990a) points out that, although many of the supportive techniques used within the intervention model of gentle teaching are well-tested behavioural ones, they differ from typical behavioural approaches with regard to primary goals. He describes the primary goals of typical behavioural approaches as being control and compliance, rather than 'establishing a mutual relationship based on feelings of safety and security, participation and valuing' (McGee 1990a). Gentle teaching, he states 'assumes that frequent and unconditional value giving is central to interactional change'.

The 'unconditional value giving' to which McGee refers involves the delivery of 'encouraging words, gazes, pats on the back and smiles', whether or not current behaviours are adaptive or maladaptive. McGee claims that 'everyone has an inherent longing for affection and warmth' which will eventually respond to unconditional valuing. He advocates further that there should be a process of mutual change in both care giver and client, with the carer's actions towards the client shifting from dominating to value-centred.

The therapeutic value of gentle teaching has been reported on, for example, Moore (1989) and McGee et al (1987). However, two studies (Jordan et al 1989, Jones et al 1991) have demonstrated the apparent superiority of visual screening over gentle teaching with regard to its effectiveness in controlling the behavioural difficulties of stereotypy and self-injury respectively. Visual screening is a behavioural procedure where the subject's vision is very briefly blocked as a consequence of undesirable behaviour. In addition to superior effect, both studies report having brought about the same amount of bonding with both the visual screening and the gentle teaching procedure. Emerson (1992) has further suggested that the gentle teaching approach may be highly distressing for individuals who find social interaction to be aversive, for example, people who have autistic characteristics.

The reader is strongly urged to consult the available literature on gentle teaching in order to satisfy his or her knowledge with regard to its relative advantages and disadvantages.

THE ETHICS OF THE BEHAVIOURAL APPROACH

Both Yule and Carr (1987) and Presland (1989) contain comprehensive and thought-provoking chapters which deal with ethical issues in the care of people with a mental handicap who have behavioural difficulties. In light of these recommended sources of further reading, it is the intention within this section to discuss those ethical concerns which are considered to be most important and most commonly encountered.

The Mental Health Act (1983) and professional codes of conduct tend to provide broad parameters of ethical conduct, whereas the Zangwill Report (1980) contains recommendations specific to the ethical practice of behaviour therapy. The latter report arose from a government-sponsored working party whose membership included representation from the Royal College of Psychiatrists, the Royal College of Nursing and the British Psychological Society. International Codes of Practice are addressed, to some extent, in the 1971 United Nations Declaration on the Rights of Mentally Retarded Persons. In the domestic sphere, the King's Fund Report (1987) and the BIMH Document, *Service Responses* advocate access to an ordinary life and everyday rights for people with a learning difficulty and challenging behaviour.

Although ethical concerns are by no means unique to the application of behavioural techniques there are, nonetheless, particular issues which may become amplified in relation to them. Behavioural change methods can be extremely powerful and effective, therefore there is a need for detailed guidelines to ensure that misuse is precluded and that the techniques involved are applied to therapeutic and ethical satisfaction.

Consent

Before assessment of the nature of a person's behavioural difficulties begins, it is essential that consent to do so is obtained. This approval of intention and process of assessment should extend throughout treatment and into the evaluative stage. The crucial property of consent is that it should be informed. Informed consent implies that, as far as is possible, the subject of assessment and any subsequent treatment is fully aware and understanding of the implications of these procedures. There is, therefore, a responsibility to ensure that a detailed explanation of the rationale and methodology of assessment and treatment is given to the client or responsible advocate. A negotiative process is the most desirable, with the client having sufficient latitude to have his or her wishes fully expressed and taken account of, and with the therapists' and carers' views and perspective delivered in the best interests of the client, and not distorted in sympathy with personal value and belief systems.

Obviously, the ability of the client to give informed consent and make informed decisions is a major consideration which in itself may pose an ethical dilemma. A similar difficulty may arise in deciding who should act as a suitable advocate for the client in the event of his or her being unable to make informed decisions. A multidisciplinary forum can be a very effective platform for consultation and discussion to produce outcomes which will best reflect the needs and wishes of the client. Self-advocacy skills may be taught and encouraged, in order to assist clients towards making informed choices in their own interest. Historically, people with a mental handicap have been farthest removed from the decision-making process affecting their own lives. As carers, we must be fully committed to our efforts to ensure that this injustice is redressed.

Rationale

- Who decides whether or not a person's behaviour is acceptable?
- Who decides what is a priority concern and what is not?
- Why use a behavioural approach?

These are merely a few of the ethical considerations which must be resolved in order to justify the use of a behavioural approach to treatment. In examining the nature of acceptability, it can be considered a useful (but not infallible) rule of thumb that a person's behaviour may be considered to be unacceptable if it compromises the well-being of that person or others. This is a rather broad, and perhaps somewhat ambiguous, criterion which will frequently require further and deeper analysis according to individual circumstance. The pivotal justification for behavioural change is that change is sought in the best interests of the client and not merely to serve the interest of those effecting change, although improving the quality of life for carers and significant others may frequently be a desirable, if essentially secondary, goal of treatment. For example, carers may decide that a client needs to stop screaming during mealtimes. The desired behavioural change may be justified if the rationale is to better that client's relationship with his or her peers and broaden his or her experience of eating out in fast food diners and restaurants. However, the use of behavioural change methods to reduce screaming solely because carers find this to be an aversive experience, would not be a satisfactory justification for intervention.

Frequently, the presence of challenging behaviours limits educational and social experiences and opportunities for people with a mental handicap. Clearly, if this client group is to be afforded the same rights and life experiences as others, we may be justified in attempting to reduce these challenging behaviours in an effort to improve quality of life. Setting priorities for treatment can, and should, be negotiated between client and carers wherever possible. Once again, multidisciplinary involvement may facilitate the identification of priorities for treatment, using a decision-making process which reflects the client's best interests. A cost-benefit analysis could be conducted in order to identify the most desirable targets for intervention. This should be done for each identified behavioural difficulty. Anticipated costs, i.e. undesirable outcomes, should be enumerated and compared alongside perceived benefits, i.e. desirable outcomes. Where expected benefits significantly outweigh costs, this may help to indicate favourable priorities for treatment.

Sometimes a behaviour may be identified as a priority because it directly interferes with the treatment of another behavioural difficulty. For example, we may decide to attempt a reduction in cutlery throwing behaviour before we teach feeding skills to a particular client. Alternatively,

we may decide, using this example, that it may be possible to effect a reduction in the former behaviour by focusing on the direct teaching of the latter. Obviously, the building and strengthening of adaptive patterns of behaviour should be used, wherever possible, to influence reduction in maladaptive behaviours. There are, however, situations which may require the initial focus of therapy to necessarily fall upon the reduction of problem behaviour which is more severe, and perhaps even life-threatening, for example, self-injury.

Any intervention strategy should be firmly based on a thorough and detailed functional analysis of the behavioural difficulty which it seeks to resolve; for example, it would be unethical to use a reinforcement based treatment plan aimed towards encouraging and strengthening a behaviour which was not being demonstrated due to a skill, rather than a motivational deficit. It is essential, therefore, to differentiate between a skill and motivational deficit when the aim of therapy is to encourage a particular behaviour. As an illustration of this, we would establish that a client had the necessary skill or knowledge in order to deal appropriately with anger-provoking situations before negotiating a treatment package with him or her which involved delivery of rewarding consequences for periods of nonaggressive responding. If we are entirely satisfied that the person possesses the necessary knowledge and skills to behave appropriately, then we are using a reinforcement package based on the ethically sound intention of increasing motivation to behave nonaggressively. If, however, we are uncertain, or consider that the prerequisite skills are lacking or incomplete, then we would firstly attempt to teach these skills before using the suggested treatment approach. We would not be ethically justified in offering reward as a consequence of a skill which our client cannot demonstrate. Similarly, it would not be equitable to expect a person to effectively control a behaviour which was being performed due to physiological discomfort or an epileptiform disturbance. It is crucial, therefore, that assessment takes into consideration possible causes of the client's difficulty, and that the chosen treatment approach both reflects and is responsive to this.

Using the least intrusive methods

We have a responsibility to ensure that our clients have access to the most effective and least intrusive methods of behavioural change. Regular updating of research findings will indicate which tried and tested techniques encapsulate the desired properties of therapeutic effect, social acceptability and minimal interference in the liberty and rights of the client. Many studies present valuable comparisons of available treatment methodologies. There may be a number of important considerations in choosing the desired approach; for example, speed of effect, generalization properties or resource implications. However, the most crucial quality of any behavioural intervention plan should be its ability to produce the desired results with the least restrictiveness on the client. Constructional approaches based on desired therapeutic goals should be employed initially. Environmental control may be preferred to addressing change within the client. All decelerative treatment plans should incorporate constructional approaches in order to build and maintain positive behavioural repertoires. There should be formal and systematic recording and review throughout treatment to ensure that both desirable and undesirable outcomes are closely evaluated and that identified safeguards are taken. Treatment approaches should also take cognisance of, and be responsive to, the rights and well-being of significant others – minimum restrictiveness applies to them also. Self-management strategies should be used wherever appropriate. The client or appointed advocate should be kept regularly informed of significant developments in treatment and should have the ability to withdraw from therapy whenever desired.

The use of reinforcement

A number of ethical concerns have been voiced regarding the use of reinforcement procedures as part of treatment. In some instances reinforce-ment may have been viewed as merely an insincere lure to induce client compliance. The influence of reinforcement, however, can serve a far more subtle and therapeutic purpose. All of us in every day life conform to socially acceptable codes of behaviour which operate under the principles of reinforcement. Many behaviours produce intrinsic reinforcement via the natural pleasure we gain from performing them. Feelings of satisfaction, achievement and self-esteem are typical examples of intrinsic reinforcement which we experience from day to day. Subsequently, these reinforcers serve to strengthen our motivation to perform those behaviours which produce them, on a more frequent or regular basis. Similarly, reinforcement of a more extrinsic nature, such as a social reward (praise, encouragement or smiles) tends to achieve the same outcome. People who have a mental handicap, however, are frequently denied the opportunities to experience and appreciate the value of social and intrinsic reinforcement. Consequently, motivation to perform those behaviours which may access such reinforcement is extremely limited, or nonexistent. In an effort to afford these persons the opportunities to enjoy and benefit from social and intrinsic reinforcement, therefore, it may be necessary to employ more tangible motivators via extrinsic reinforcement, such as preferred consumables, materials and activities. This should, however, be done on a temporary basis, with a systematic reduction in the frequency of these types of reward in favour of gradual substitution by social and intrinsic reinforcers. This process is very much one of teaching the value of more naturally reinforcing events.

Ethical concerns may also arise from the nature and delivery of reinforcement. For example, would we be justified in using the reward of preferred foods for a client who was significantly overweight, or whose physical well-being was affected by the ingestion of certain additives contained in these foods? Reinforcers should be negotiated with the client or responsible advocate in order that they are a valued incentive and safe to deliver. In addition, reinforcement should never compromise the everyday rights and entitlements of the client. To this end, selected reinforcers should be superfluous to routine access. Not only would this preclude any interference with the client's entitlement, but it would also facilitate the preservation of reinforcement potency.

Applying specialist knowledge

Applying behavioural change methods without sufficient competence in the appropriate skills is an obvious ethical concern. Therefore, opportunity for the necessary instruction of carers is essential if they are to act in the best interest of their clients. Access to suitable courses regarding the management of challenging behaviours and the application of advocacy skills will no doubt vary according to geographical location and resource availability. As mentioned earlier, training clients in the use of self-advocacy skills and self-management skills may enable them to make more informed decisions and act in ways which will best reflect their personal needs and wishes. Access to specialist support and supervision by a suitably qualified person would be invaluable, especially where carers do not have any related experience or training.

Ignorance of the rationale and methodology of any behavioural treatment plan can breed fear, mistrust, concern or suspicion. Education is the effective remedy for ignorance. Discussion with, and thorough instruction of, relevant persons involved in treatment will minimize anxiety and misunderstanding regarding the nature and process of therapy. Preparation and circulation of clear and concise guidelines will also facilitate comprehension of, and consistency in, the application of the treatment plan.

Widening parameters towards education of the public regarding the theory and practice of behaviour therapy would help to reduce misconceptions and resolve uncertainties surrounding the desirability and therapeutic value of behavioural techniques. Deliberation over ethical concerns is not a process which should be rejected but rather one which should be welcomed and valued, since it provides a framework through which the best interests of the client and significant others

may be both identified and acted upon. Multiagency, and multidisciplinary involvement in the decision-making process may avoid treatment outcomes arising from the bias of subjectivity or isolated deliberation. Working groups should be formed in order to devise and review ethical codes of practice, sound operational and risk taking policies, and qualitative standards of care.

In an American study, Morgan et al (1992) reviewed a number of State Department Standards with regard to the regulation of behavioural procedures for individuals. This author is not aware of any comparative study which reviews current domestic standards or practices, but such an undertaking would prove useful.

Decision-making processes should embrace a philosophy respecting the rights of people with a mental handicap to be treated as equals. Individuals should have access to so called 'normal' life experiences and opportunities in order to maximize personal development and well-being. Consequently, the outcomes of that process will serve the best interests of the client and satisfy ethical requirements.

CONCLUSION

There has been a significant theoretical bias in the content of this chapter although reference has been made to practical issues wherever this was relevant. The highly specific (and often unique) circumstances surrounding each individual treatment precludes an exhaustive analysis of practical considerations. Box 9.2 highlights some of the more common practical difficulties encountered during the stages of therapy. There are, however, two particular practical points which require further consideration. These are the provision of training and of resources.

Carers require the reassurance and support which can be provided by the experience of appropriate training. This not only serves to clarify and advance their knowledge but can also provide the necessary opportunity for carers to both develop and practise specialist skills which they can then confidently and effectively employ to the advantage of their clients. There is therefore

Box 9.2 Potential pitfalls and problems in the organization, implementation and evaluation of behavioural care plans

Problems in behavioural assessment
- Choosing inappropriate and/or insubstantial assessment methods
- Differences in opinion and normative values
- Using unreliable or limited sources of information
- Identification of significant behavioural antecedents or consequences
- Using, and relying on, a limited width of analysis
- Difficulty in or impossibility of, analysis of covert behaviour
- Isolating potent reinforcers
- Using persons unfamiliar width the implications and mechanics of behavioural assessment methods
- Ambiguity in nature and description of behaviour being assessed

Problems with programme design
- Poor identification, or lack of identification, of treatment goals
- Lack of a suitable timescale
- Choice of inappropriate change techniques
- Failure to consider ethical implications
- Presenting a programme which is unrealistic in terms of resources available
- Designing a programme based on nontherapeutic, or unrealistic, expectations
- Under- or overinvolvement of co-therapists, or client
- Use of unsuitable reinforcement components
- Use of inappropriate reinforcement scheduling
- Insubstantial attention paid to relevant research papers
- Lack of feedback component for care staff involved

Problems in programme implementation
- Inconsistency in approach by those involved in programme running
- Limitations in resources, e.g. staffing levels, time spent on running programme
- Internal politics at ward, departmental or managerial levels
- Insufficient educational input to those involved in programme implementation

- Failure of consistency in approach and programme management across care setting
- Deliberate or unintentional sabotage; alteration or manipulation of the components of the programme by care staff or client
- Inadequate supervision and evaluation of programme by therapist
- Difficulties with reinforcement potency, contingency or scheduling
- Failure or therapist to recognize the need for programme modification or to admit defeat

Problems in programme evaluation
- Identifying which components of the programme are in fact working and which are not
- Determining accuracy of recordings
- Establishing if the programme is being implemented correctly and consistently
- Identifying changes in environmental or stimulus conditions
- What needs to change? Programme? Attitudes? Environment?
- Determining how best to modify and adapt the programme given improvement or deterioration regarding the target behaviours
- Ensuring that visual or verbal feedback is continuous for those involved in programme running.

This is not intended to represent a comprehensive list of problems involved with behavioural intervention: difficulties will often require to be dealt with spontaneously. If, however, we can prepare ourselves to avoid, deal or cope with as many problems as we can realistically envisage, we will go a long way towards helping our intervention to be successful.

Always consider the *main* characteristics of the behavioural approach:
1. systematic assessment
2. explicit treatment goals
3. well-defined techniques
4. careful evaluation.

a need for a strong commitment to training opportunities from employers and training agencies. The provision of specialist input at basic and postbasic levels within professional education would be invaluable. Similar input would of course also be useful to parents and informal carers at a more individual level.

Specialist training courses and packages are available (for example, Foxen & McBrien 1981, McBrien & Felce 1992, Clements & Zarkowska 1992). These provide the opportunity for learners to acquire knowledge of behavioural treatment methods through structured programmes delivered by presenters with experience in the field.

Also of fundamental importance is the provision of adequate resources before effective planning and implementation of treatment can be undertaken. Sufficient human and material resources need to be available in order to respond to individual needs. This requires a clear understanding of the behavioural approach and a shared view as to the value of such an approach by both practitioners and those controlling resources. In the absence of such shared understanding and commitment it becomes very difficult, if not impossible, to provide truly therapeutic environments which are conducive to behavioural change.

There is a danger that the use of behavioural change methods is perceived as cold and mechanistic. By presenting the behavioural approach as scientific in its base, formal in its planning, and systematic in its application this chapter may have run the risk of reinforcing (no pun intended) such a view despite the contrary views of this author. There is a possibility that some of the terminology used in behaviour therapy may in fact obscure the therapeutic purpose and value of the approach. Behaviour therapy is changing in the light of both changing ideology and research findings. This is a highly desirable process. What is not desirable, however, is that the preoccupation by practitioners and researchers to sustain this momentum may cause behaviour therapy to stumble on its own wordiness.

The most important point to emphasize in behaviour therapy is the fundamental desire to do something *with* people rather than to do things *for* them or, worse still, *to* them. Barker (1982) comments that behaviourism and humanism may be seen as 'strange bedfellows'. This may be due to the historical dichotomy between a model of control and one of autonomy. Behavioural interventions should be based on a therapeutic relationship of mutual caring and respect with treatment being negotiated in the light of the individual needs and wishes of the client. Lovett (1985) states that 'the one attitude that disturbs me most though is the idea that we must choose between being 'nice' and being 'therapeutic'. Rather than being mutually exclusive, I think that they are mutually inclusive.'

The cold, mechanistic application of behavioural techniques is therefore not the desired method by which to achieve therapeutic change. Rather, interventions based on a relationship which reflects mutual caring, dignity and respect appear to hold the key to behavioural change. Thus, the interpersonal skills of the therapist become emphasized and also become as important (if not more important) than the methods employed in achieving success.

It is to be hoped that behavioural intervention strategies are becoming more sensitive of and responsive to the environmental and social contexts of behavioural difficulties. Thus, environmental and social change may be viewed as desirable, if not essential, accompaniments to individual change. One of the most productive forms of behavioural analysis is that of introspection – the examination of those environmental, social and individual characteristics which influence personal behaviour. Heightened awareness of the influence of these on the behaviour of the therapist contributes to a greater understanding of these factors in the difficulties experienced by clients. In many instances, clients are, or have been, exposed to relatively impoverished environmental and social circumstances. Awareness of this may prompt an urgency to redress the situation by creating opportunities for clients to have access to valued experiences and social roles. The purpose of therapists should be to promote therapeutic strategies which attract rather than repel clients and which seek to befriend rather than estrange. Environmental, social and individual factors can serve a preventative as well as ameliorative function. Therefore, the opportunity to acquire and practise socially appropriate behaviours and skills needs to be provided. Indeed the preventative and ameliorative use of behaviour therapy has expanded throughout health education and into other professional arenas, such as commerce and sport.

Flexibility and adaptability are major assets of the behavioural approach. These attributes when used functionally add to the therapeutic value. For example, behaviour therapy may form part of a treatment package involving other treatment components, such as speech therapy, music therapy and physiotherapy. Similarly, its versatility is demonstrated in the adaptation to other approaches, such as the use of self-monitoring and anger management. The field of applied behavioural analysis continues to stimulate and direct innovative and effective practice (for example, Iwata et al 1982, 1990).

Behaviour therapy will continue to develop and expand into new approaches, and be influenced by new ideas and findings. If it is to have any relevance in the future, however, it must maintain contact with and be responsive to the dignity and quality of life of the client group it serves.

REFERENCES

Alberto P A, Sharpton W R, Briggs A, Stright M H 1986 Facilitating task acquisition through the use of a self-operated auditory prompting system. Journal of the Association for Persons with Severe Handicaps 11: 85–91

Bandura A 1977 Social learning theory. Prentice Hall, Englewood Cliffs, New Jersey

Barker P 1982 Behaviour therapy nursing. Croom Helm, London

Barmann B C, Vitali D L 1982 Facial screening to eliminate trichotillomania in developmentally disabled persons. Behaviour Therapy 13: 735–742

Barrett R P, Feinstein C, Hole W T 1989 Effects of naloxone and naltrexone on self-injury: a double-blind, placebo-controlled analysis. American Journal on Mental Retardation 93, 6: 664–651

Barrett R P, Shapiro E S 1980 Treatment of stereotyped hair-pulling with overcorrection: a case study with long term follow-up. Journal of Behavioural & Experimental Psychiatry 11: 317–320

Borthwick-Duffy S A, Eyman R K 1990 Who are the dually diagnosed? American Journal on Mental Retardation 94, 6: 586–595

Bradley P, McCue M 1988 Self-management of verbally and physically aggressive behaviour. Unpublished material

Brandon D 1989 How gentle teaching can liberate us all. Community Living 2, 4: 9–10

Clements J, Zarkowska E 1992 Advanced level training in the behavioural approach. BIMH, Kidderminster

Cole C L, Gardner W I, Karan O C 1985 Self-management training of mentally retarded adults presenting severe conduct difficulties. Applied Research in Mental Retardation 6: 337–347

Craft M, Mathews J 1984 Lithium in mental handicap: a review. Mental Handicap 12: 117–118

Durand V M 1982 A behavioral/pharmacological intervention for the treatment of severe self-injurious behavior. Journal of Autism and Developmental Disorders 12, 3: 243–251

Emerson E 1992 Self-injurious behaviour: an overview of recent trends in epidemiological and behavioural research. Mental Handicap Research 5, 1: 49–81

Foxen T, McBrien J 1981 Training staff in behavioural methods: the EDY in-service training course for mental handicap practitioners. Trainee workbook. Manchester University Press, Manchester

Foxx et al 1986 The successful treatment of a dually diagnosed deaf man's aggression with a program that included contingent electric shock. Behavior Therapy 7: 170–186

Gedye A 1989a Episodic rage and aggression attributed to frontal lobe seizures. Journal of Mental Deficiency Research 33: 369–379

Gedye A 1989b Extreme self-injury attributed to frontal lobe seizures. American Journal on Mental Retardation 94, 1: 20–26

Goldiamond I 1974 Towards a constructional approach to social problems. Behaviourism 2: 1–84

Goldiamond I 1975 The constructional approach to self-control. In: Schwartz A, Goldiamond I (eds) Social casework: a behavioral approach: 67–138. Columbia University Press, New York

Green C W et al 1988 Identifying reinforcers for persons with profound handicaps: staff opinion versus systematic assessment of preferences. Journal of Applied Behavioral Analysis 21, 1: 31–43

Groden G 1989 A guide for conducting a comprehensive behavioral analysis of a target behavior. Journal of Behavioral Therapy & Experimental Psychiatry 20, 2: 163–169

Hemsley R, Carr J 1987 Ways of increasing behaviour: reinforcement. In: Yule W, Carr J (eds) Behaviour modification for people with mental handicaps. Chapman Hall, London

Hogg J Raynes N V 1987 Assessment in mental handicap: a guide to assessment practices and checklists. Croom Helm, London

Iwata B A et al 1982 Toward a functional analysis of self-injury. Analysis and Intervention in Developmental Disabilities 2: 3–20

Iwata B A et al 1990 Experimental analysis and extinction of escape behavior. Journal of Applied Behaviour Analysis 23: 11–27

Jenkins J et al 1983 The Bereweeke skills teaching system. NFER Nelson, Windsor

Jones L J, Singh N N, Kendall K A 1991 Comparative effects of gentle teaching and visual screening on self-injurious behaviour. Journal of Mental Deficiency Research 35, 1: 37–47

Jones RSP 1990 Gentle teaching: behaviourism at its best. Community Living 3: 9–10

Jordan J, Singh N, Repp A 1989 An evaluation of gentle teaching and visual screening in the reduction of stereotypy. Journal of Applied Behavior Analysis 22: 1, 9–22

Kiernan C, Moss S 1990 Behaviour disorders and other characteristics of the population of a mental handicap hospital. Mental Handicap Research 3, 1: 3–20

Lazarus A A 1976 Multimodal behavior therapy. Springer, New York

Lovett H 1985 Cognitive counselling and persons with special needs. Praeger, New York

Luiselli J K 1986 Behavior analysis of pharmacological and contingency management interventions for self-injury. Journal of Behavioral Therapy & Experimental Psychiatry 17, 4: 275–284

Luiselli J K 1991 A non-aversive behavioral-pharmacological intervention for severe self-injury in an adult with dual sensory impairment. Journal of Behavioral Therapy & Experimental Psychiatry 22, 3: 233–238

Mace F C, Knight D 1986 Functional analysis and treatment of severe pica. Journal of Applied Behavior Analysis 19: 411–416

Marholin D II et al 1980 Response contingent taste-aversion in treating chronic ruminative vomiting of institutionalised profoundly retarded children. Journal of Mental Deficiency Research

Matson J L, Andrasik F 1982 Training leisure time social interaction skills to mentally retarded adults. American Journal of Mental Deficiency 86, 5: 533–542

McBrien J, Felce D 1992 Challenging behaviour and severe

learning difficulties: a practical workshop package. First Draft Publications, Kidderminster

McGee J J et al 1987 Gentle teaching: a non-aversive approach to helping persons with mental retardation. Human Sciences Press, New York

McGee J J 1990a Gentle teaching: the basic tenet. Nursing Times 86, 32: 68–72

McGee J J 1990b Self-injury. Current Opinion in Psychiatry 3: 613–615

McNally R J, Kampik J J, Sherman G 1984 Increasing the productivity of mentally retarded workers through self-management. Analysis and Intervention in Developmental disabilities 4: 129–135

Moore S 1989 Thinking positive. Entourage 4, 4: 5–8

Morgan R L 1989 Judgements of restrictiveness, social acceptability and usage: review of research on procedures to decrease behavior. American Journal on Mental Retardation 94, 2: 121–133

Morgan R L et al 1992 Regulating behavioural procedures for individuals with handicaps: review of state department standards. Research in Developmental Difficulties 12, 1: 63–85

Pace C M et al 1985 Assessment of stimulus preference and reinforcer value with profoundly retarded individuals. Journal of Applied Behaviour Analysis 18, 3: 249–255

Parrish J M et al 1985 Behavior analysis, program development, and transfer control in the treatment of self injury. Journal of Behavioral Therapy & Experimental Psychiatry 16, 2: 159–168

Premack D 1959 Towards empirical behavior laws: 1–positive reinforcement. Psychological Review 66: 219–233

Presland J L 1989 Overcoming difficult behaviour. BIMH Publications, Worcester

Reese R M, Sherman J A, Sheldon J 1984 Reducing agitated-disruptive behavior of mentally retarded residents of community group homes: the role of self-recording and peer-prompted self-recording. Analysis and Intervention in Developmental Disabilities, 4: 91–107

Repp A C, Felce D 1990 A microcomputer system used for evaluative and experimental behavioural research in mental handicap. Mental Handicap Research 3, 1: 21–32

Rosine LPC, Martin G L 1983 Self-management training to decrease undesirable behavior of mentally handicapped adults. Rehabilitation Psychology 28, 4: 195–205

Sturmey P, Carlsen A, Crisp A G, Newton J T 1988 A functional analysis of multiple aberrant responses: a refinement and extension of Iwata et al's (1982) methodology. Journal of Mental Deficiency Research 32: 31–46

Szymanski L, Kedesdy J, Sulkes S, Cutler A, Stevens-Our P 1987 Naltrexone in treatment of self-injurious behavior: a clinical study. Research in Developmental Disabilities 8: 179–190

Touchette P E, MacDonald R F, Langer S N 1985 A scatter plot for identifying stimulus control of problem behavior. Journal of Applied Behavior Analysis 18: 343–351

Turnbull J 1990 The emperor's new clothes? Nursing Times 86, 32: 64–66

Wacker D P et al 1985 Evaluation of reinforced preferences for profoundly handicapped students. Journal of Applied Behavior Analysis 18, 2: 173–178

Yule W, Carr J (eds)1987 Behaviour modification for people with mental handicaps, 2nd edn. Chapman Hall, London

Zangwill O L (Chairman) 1980 Behaviour modification: report of a joint working party to formulate ethical guidelines for the conduct of programmes of behaviour modification in the NHS: a consultation document with suggested guidelines. HMSO, London

Zarkowska E, Clements J 1988 Problem behaviour in people with severe learning disabilities: a practical guide to a constructional approach. Croom Helm, London

FURTHER READING

Abraham C 1989 Supporting people with a mental handicap in the community: a social psychological perspective. Disability, Handicap & Society 4, 2: 121–129

Ager A, Reading J C 1992 Teaching skills through the enhancement of natural antecedents. Journal of Intellectual Disability Research 36: 157–168

Allen E A 1989 Behavioural treatment of anxiety and related disorders in adults with mental handicaps. Mental Handicap Research 2, 1: 47–60

Altman K, Krupsaw R 1983 Suppressing aggressive-destructive behavior by delayed overcorrection. Journal of Behavioral Therapy & Experimental Psychiatry 14, 4: 359–362

Altmeyer B K, Williams D E, Sams V 1985 Treatment of severe self-injurious and aggressive biting. Journal of Behavioral Therapy & Experimental Psychiatry 16, 2: 159–167

Axelrod S 1987 Functional and structural analyses of behavior: approaches leading to reduced uses of punishment procedures? Research in Developmental Disabilities 8: 165–178

Bailey S, Pokrzywinski J, Bryant L E 1983 Using water mist to reduce self-injurious and stereotypic behavior. Applied Research in Mental Retardation 4: 229–241

Baker B L, Heifetz L J, Murphy D M 1980 Behavioral training for parents of mentally retarded children: one year follow up. American Journal of Mental Deficiency 85, 1: 31–38

Barker P, Fraser D (eds) 1985 The nurse as therapist: a behavioural model. Croom Helm, London

Barron A, Earls F 1984 The relation of temperament and social factors to behavior problems in three-year old children. Journal of Child Psychology & Psychiatry 25, 1: 23–33

Bellack A S, Hersen M (eds) 1985 Dictionary of behaviour therapy techniques. Pergamon Press, Oxford

Bellack A S, Hersen M (eds) 1988 Behavioural assessment: a practical handbook, 3rd edn. Pergamon Press, Oxford

Benson B A 1986 Anger management training. Psychiatric Aspects of Mental Retardation News 5, 10: 51–55

Benson B A, Rice C J, Miranti S V 1986 Effects of anger management training with mentally retarded adults in group treatment. Journal of Consulting and Clinical Psychology 54, 5: 728–729

Benson B A, Ivins J 1992 Anger, depression and self-concept in adults with mental retardation. Journal of Intellectual Disability Research 36: 169–175

Berkowitz B P, Graziano A M 1972 Training parents as behaviour therapists: a review. Behaviour Research & Therapy 10: 297–317

Bird F, Dores P A, Moniz D, Robinson J 1989 Reducing severe aggressive behaviors with functional communication training. American Journal on Mental Retardation 94, 1: 37–48

Blair A 1992 Working with people with learning difficulties who self-injure: a review of the literature. Behavioural Psychotherapy 20, 1: 1–23

Blunden R, Allen D 1987 Facing the challenge: an ordinary life for people with learning difficulties and challenging behaviour. King's Fund, London

Bouras N, Drummond C 1992 Behaviour and psychiatric disorders of people with mental handicaps living in the community. Journal of Intellectual Disability Research 36, No.4

Brandon D 1990 Gentle teaching. Nursing Times, January 10, 86, 2: 62–63

Bridgen P, Todd M 1990 Challenging behaviour. Mental Handicap 18: 99–104

Carr E G, Newsom C D, Binkoff J A 1980 Escape as a factor in the aggressive behaviour of two retarded children. Journal of Applied Behavior Analysis 13, 1: 101–117

Carr E G, Durand V M 1985 Reducing behavior problems through functional communication training. Journal of Applied Behavior Analysis 18, 2: 111–126

Carr E G, Newsom C D 1985 Demand-related tantrums. Behavior Modification 9, 4: 403–427

Carr J 1988 Continuous reinforcement to facilitate extinction of counter exhaustion. Behavioural Psychotherapy 16, 1: 64–68

Carr J 1991 Recent advances in work with people with learning difficulties. Behaviour Psychotherapy 19, 1: 109–120

Castellani P J, Downey N A, Tausig M B, Bird W A 1986 Availability and accessibility of family support services. Mental Retardation 24, 2: 71–79

Causby V D, York R O 1991 Predictors of success in community placement of persons with mental retardation. British Journal of Mental Subnormality 37, 1, 2: 25–34

Cummings R et al 1989 Challenging behaviour and community services: establishing services. Mental Handicap 17: 13–17

Davies R R, Rogers E S 1985 Social skills training with persons who are mentally retarded. Mental Retardation 23, 4: 186–196

Day H M, Horner R H 1986 Response variation and the generalization of a dressing skill: comparison of single instance and general case instruction. Applied Research in Mental Retardation 7: 189–202

Day H M 1987 Comparison of two prompting procedures to facilitate skill acquisition among severely retarded adolescents. American Journal of Mental Deficiency 91, 4: 366–372

Deitz S M, Repp A C, Deitz D E D 1976 Reducing inappropriate classroom behavior of retarded students through three procedures of differential reinforcement. Journal of Mental Deficiency Research 20: 155–170

Delprato D J 1981 The consrtuctional approach to behavioral modification. Journal of Behavioral Therapy & Experimental Psychiatry 12, 1: 49–55

Delprato D J, Pappalardo P A, Holmes P A 1984 The role of response-reinforcer relationship in discrimination learning of mentally retarded persons. American Journal of Mental Deficiency 89, 3: 267–274

Demchack M A, Halle J W 1985 Motivational assessment: a potential means of enhancing treatment success of self-injurious individuals. Education and Training of the Mentally Retarded: 25–37

Donkersley M, Thorpe M 1989 Video assisted learning for adults with mental handicaps. Mental Handicap 17, 2: 70–73

Dorsey M, Iwata B A Ong P, McSween T E 1980 Treatment of self-injurious behavior using a water mist: initial response suppression and generalization. Journal of Applied Behavior Analysis 13, 2: 343–353

Dorsey M. J, Iwata B A, Reid D H, Davis P A 1982 Protective equipment: continuous and contingent application in the treatment of self-injurious behavior. Journal of Applied Behavior Analysis 15, 2: 217–230

Duker P C, van Dreunen C, Jol K, Oud H 1986 Determinants of maladaptive behavior of institutionalized mentally retarded individuals. American Journal of Mental Deficiency 91, 1: 51–56

Emerson E, Emerson C, 1987 Barriers to the effective implementation of habilitative behavioral programs in an institutional setting. Mental Retardation 25, 2: 101–106

Emerson E et al 1987 Challenging behaviour and community settings: introduction and overview. Mental Handicap 15: 166–169

Emerson E et al 1988 Challenging behaviour and community settings: who are the people who challenge services? Mental Handicap 16: 16–19

Emerson E et al 1989 Challenging behaviour and community services: evaluation and overview. Mental Handicap 17: 104–107

Emerson E, McGill P 1989 Normalization and applied behaviour analysis: rapprochement or intellectual imperialism? Behavioural Psychotherapy 14, 4: 316–322

Emerson E 1990 Self-injurious behaviour: some of the challenges it presents. Mental Handicap 18: 92–98

Evison R 1986 Self-help in preventing stress build-up. The Professional Nurse, March: 157–159

Eyman R K, Call T 1977 Maladaptive behavior and community placement of mentally retarded persons. American Journal of Mental Deficiency 82, 2: 137–144

Eyman R K, Borthwick S A, Miller C 1981 Trends in maladaptive behavior of mentally retarded persons placed in community and institutional settings. American Journal of Mental Deficiency 85, 5: 473–477

Favell J E et al 1981 Physical restraint as positive reinforcement. American Journal of Mental Deficiency 85, 4: 425–432

Favell J E, McGimsey J F, Schell R M 1982 Treatment of self-injury by providing alternate sensory activities. Analysis and Intervention in Developmental Disabilities 2: 83–104

Felce D et al 1987 To what behaviors do attending adults respond? A replication. American Journal of Mental Deficiency 91, 5: 496–504

Fidura J G, Lindsey E R, Walker G R 1987 A special behavior unit for treatment of behavior problems of persons who are mentally retarded. Mental Retardation 25, 2: 107–111

Firestone P 1976 The effects and side effects of timeout on an aggressive nursery school child. Journal of Behavioral Therapy & Experimental Psychiatry 6: 79–81

Fleming I 1984 The constructional approach to 'problem behaviour' in an institutional setting. Behavioural Psychotherapy 12: 349–355

Fleming I, Tosh M 1984 Self-control procedures. Mental Handicap 12: 110–111

Fletcher R 1984 Group therapy with mentally retarded persons with emotional disorders. Psychiatric Aspects of Mental Retardation Reviews 3, no. 6

Flynn M 1986 Adults who are mentally handicapped as consumers: issues and guidelines for interviewing. Journal of Mental Deficiency Res 30: 369–377

Fovel J T, Lash P S, Barron D A Jnr, Roberts M S 1989 A survey of self-restraint, self-injury and other maladaptive behaviors in an institutionalized retarded population. Research in Developmental Disabilities 10: 377–382

Friedrich W N, Greenberg M T, Crnic K 1983 A short form of the questionnaire on resources and stress. American Journal of Mental Deficiency 88, 1: 41–48

Gardner W I, Clees T J, Cole C L 1983 Self-management of disruptive verbal ruminations by a mentally retarded adult. Applied Research in Mental Retardation 4: 41–58

Gardner W I, Cole C L, Davidson D P, Karan O C 1986 Reducing aggression in individuals with developmental disabilities: an expanded stimulus control, assessment, and intervention model. Education and Training of the Mentally Retarded, March: 3–12

Gardner W I, Cole C L, Berry D L Nowinski J M 1983 Reduction of disruptive behaviors in mentally retarded adults. Behavior Modification 7, 1: 76–96

Goldfried M R, DeCanteceo E T, Weinberger L 1974 Systematic rational restructuring as a self-control technique. Behavior Therapy 5: 247–254

Green C 1987 The importance of behaviour modification for the nursing process in mental handicap. Nurse Education Today 7: 59–62

Griffin J C et al 1986 Self-injurious behavior: a state-wide prevalence survey of the extent and circumstances. Applied Research in Mental Retardation 7: 105–116

Halpern L F, Andrasik F 1986 The immediate and long-term effectiveness of overcorrection in treating self-injurious behavior in a mentally retarded adult. Applied Research in Mental Retardation 7: 59–65

Harchik A E, Sherman J A, Sheldon J B 1992 The use of self-management procedures by people with developmental difficulties: a brief review. Research in Developmental Disabilities 13: 211–227

Harris J (ed) 1991 Service responses to people with learning difficulties and challenging behaviour. Seminar Papers No. 1, British Institute of Mental Handicap, Kidderminster

Harrop A, Daniels S M, Foulkes C 1990 The use of momentary time sampling and partial interval recording in behavioural research. Behavioral Psychotherapy 18, 2: 121–127

Hemming H 1986 Follow-up of adults with mental retardation transferred from large institutions to new small units. Mental Retardation 24, 4: 229–235

Henry G K 1987 Symbolic modelling and parent behavioral training: effects of non-compliance of hyperactive children. Journal of Behavioral Therapy & Experimental

Psychiatry 18, 2: 105–113

Hill B K, Bruininks R H 1984 Maladaptive behavior of mentally retarded individuals in residential facilities. American Journal of Mental Deficiency 88, 4: 380–387

Hobbis V, Williams T 1986 Uses of mechanical vibration in the education of multiply handicapped blind children. Journal of Visual Impairment & Blindness, Dec: 1003–1004

Hobbs S A, Forehand R 1977 Important parameters in the use of timeout with children: a re-examination. Journal of Behavioral Therapy & Experimental Psychiatry 8: 365–370

Hoefkens A, Allen D 1990 Evaluation of a special behaviour unit for people with mental handicaps and challenging behaviours. Journal of Mental Deficiency Research 34: 213–228

Howard A et al 1989 Psychotherapy in mental handicap with potentially violent people. Mental Handicap 17: 54–56

Hurley A D 1989 Individual psychotherapy with mentally retarded individuals: a review and call for research. Research in Developmental Disabilities 10: 261–275

Intagliata J, Rinck C, Calkins C 1986 Staff response to maladaptive behavior in public and community residential facilities. Mental Retardation 24, 2: 93–98

Iverson J C, Fox R 1989 Prevalence of psychopathology among mentally retarded adults. Research in Developmental Disabilities 10: 77–83

Jackson H J, Boag P G 1981 The efficacy of self-control procedures as motivational strategies with mentally retarded persons: a review of the literature and guidelines for future research. Australian Journal of Developmental Disabilities 7, 2: 65–79

Johnson W L, Baumeister A A 1978 Self-injurious behavior. Behavior Modification 2, 4: 465–487

Johnson W L, Baumeister A A, Penland M J, Inwald C 1982 Experimental analysis of self-injurious, stereotypic and collateral behavior of retarded persons: effects of overcorrection and reinforcement of alternative responding. Analysis and Intervention in Developmental Disabilities 2: 41–66

Jones J L, Singh N N, Repp A C 1989 An evaluation of gentle teaching and visual screening in the reduction of stereotypy. Journal of Applied Behaviour Analysis 22: 9–22

Jones RSP, Baker LJV 1990 Differential reinforcement and challenging behavior: a critical review of the DRI schedule. Behavioural Psychotherapy 18, 1: 35–47

Kleinberg Y, Galligan B 1983 Effects of deinstitutionalization on adaptive behavior of mentally retarded adults. American Journal of Mental Deficiency 88, 1: 21–27

Kornblatt E S, Heinrich J 1985 Needs and coping abilities in families of children with developmental disabilities. Mental Retardation 23, 1: 13–19

Krishnamurti D 1990 Evaluation of a special behaviour unit for people with mental handicaps and challenging behaviour: a riposte. Journal of Mental Deficiency Research 34: 229–231

Lakin K C et al 1983 New admissions and readmissions to a national sample of public residential facilities. American Journal of Mental Deficiency 88, 1: 13–20

Lambert M E 1987 A computer simulation for behavior therapy training. Journal of Behavioral Therapy & Experimental Psychiatry 18, 3: 245–248

Lancioni G E, Hoogeven F R Non-aversive and mildly aversive procedures for reducing problem behaviours in people with developmental disorders. Mental Handicap Research 3, 2: 137–160

Lattal K A, Freeman T J, Critchfield T S 1989 Response-reinforcer dependency location interval schedules of reinforcement. Journal of the Experimental Analysis of Behavior 51, 1: 101–117

Lennox D B, Miltenberger R G, Spengler P, Erfanian N 1988 Decelerative treatment practices with persons who have mental retardation: a review of five years of the literature. American Journal of Mental Retardation 92, 6: 492–501

Levine H E 1985 Situational anxiety and everyday life experiences of mildly mentally retarded adults. American Journal of Mental Deficiency 90, 1: 27–33

Lindsay W R et al 1988 Dog-phobia in people with mental handicaps: anxiety management training and exposure treatments. Mental Handicap Research 1, 1: 39–48

Lindsay W R, Baty F J 1989 Group relaxation training with adults who are mentally handicapped. Behaviour Psychotherapy 17, 1: 43–51

Lindsay W, Kasprowicz M 1987 Challenging negative cognitions. Mental Handicap 15: 159–162

Lindsay W, Richardson I, Michie A M 1989 Short-term generalised effects of relaxation training on adults with moderate and severe mental handicaps. Mental Handicap Research 2, 2: 197–206

Luce S C, Delquardi J, Hall R V 1980 Contingent exercise: a mild but powerful procedure for suppressing inappropriate verbal and aggressive behavior. Journal of Applied Behavior Analysis 13, 4: 583–594

Luiselli J K 1984 Treatment of an assaultive, sensory-impaired adolescent through a multicomponent behavioral program. Journal of Behavioral Therapy & Psychiatry 15, 1: 71–78

Luiselli J K, Gleason D J 1987 Combining sensory reinforcement and texture fading procedures to overcome chronic food refusal. Journal of Behavioral Therapy & Experimental Psychiatry 18, 2: 149–155

Luiselli J K, Greenidge A 1982 Behavioral treatment of high-rate aggression in a rubella child. Journal of Behavioral Therapy & Experimental Psychiatry 13, 2: 152–157

Luiselli J K, Slocumb P R 1983 Management of multiple aggressive behaviors by differential reinforcement. Journal of Behavioral Therapy & Experimental Psychiatry 14, 4: 343–347

Lund J 1989 Measuring behaviour disorder in mental handicap. British Journal of Psychiatry 155: 379–383

MacDonald L, Barton L E 1986 Measuring severity of behavior: a revision of part II of the adaptive behavior scale. American Journal of Mental Deficiency 90, 4: 418–424

Mace F C, Knight 1986 The role of reinforcement in reactive self-monitoring. Applied Research in Mental Retardation 7: 315–327

Mace F C, Browder D M, Lin Y 1987 Analysis of demand conditions associated with stereotypy. Applied Research in Mental Retardation 18, 1: 25–31

Mace F C, Kratochwill T R, Fiello R A 1983 Positive treatment of aggressive behavior in a mentally retarded adult: a case study. Behavior Therapy 14: 689–696

Mace F C, Lalli J S, Lalli E P 1991 Functional analysis and treatment of aberrant behaviour. Research in Developmental Difficulties 12, 2: 155–180

Mace F C, Page T J, Ivancic M T, O'Brien S 1986 Analysis of environmental determinants of aggression and disruption in mentally retarded children. Applied Research in Mental Retardation 7: 203–221

Mank D M, Horner R H 1987 Self-recruited feedback: a cost-effective procedure for maintaining behavior. Research in Developmental Disabilities 8: 91–112

Martin G, Pear J 1988 Behavior modification: what it is and how to do it, 3rd edn. Prentice-Hall, New Jersey

Masters J C, Burish T G, Hollon S D, Rimm D C 1987 Behaviour therapy: techniques and empirical findings, 3rd edn. Harcourt Brace Jovanovitch, London

Matson J L 1986 Self-injury and its relationship to diagnostic schemes in psychopathology. Applied Research in Mental Retardation 7: 223–227

Matson J L, Gorman-Smith D 1986 A review of treatment research for aggressive and disruptive behavior in the mentally retarded. Applied Research in Mental Retardation 7: 95–103

Matson J L, Keyes J B 1990 A comparison of DRO to movement suppression time-out and DRO with two self-injurious and aggressive mentally retarded adults. Research in Developmental Disabilities 11: 111–120

Matson J L, Stephens R M, Smith C 1978 Treatment of self-injurious behaviour with overcorrection. Journal of Mental Deficiency Research 22: 175–178

Matson J L, Taras M E 1989 A 20-year review of punishment and alternative methods to treat problem behaviors in developmentally delayed persons. Research in Developmental Disabilities 10: 85–104

McBrien J 1987 The Haytor unit: specialised day care for adults with severe mental handicaps and behaviour problems. Mental Handicap 15: 77–80

McBrien J A 1985 Behavioural training for nurses in mental handicap: an application of the EDY course. Journal of Advanced Nursing 10: 337–343

McCaughey R E, Jones R S P The effectiveness of gentle teaching. Mental Handicap 20, 1: 7–14

McCool C et al 1989 Challenging behaviour and community services: structuring staff and client activity. Mental Handicap 17: 60–63

McCrea C, Summerfield A B 1988 A pilot study of the therapeutic usefulness of videofeedback for weight loss and improvement of body image in the treatment of obesity. Behavioural Psychotherapy 16, 4: 263–284

McDevitt S C, Rosen M 1977 Adaptive behavior scale, part II: a cautionary note and suggestions for revision. American Journal of Mental Deficiency 82, 2: 210–212

McGee J J, Menolascino F J 1991 Beyond gentle teaching: a non-aversive approach to helping those in need. Plenum, New York

McKeegan G F, Estill K, Campbell B 1984 Brief report, use of nonexclusionary timeout for the elimination of a stereotyped behavior. Journal of Behavioral Therapy & Experimental Psychiatry 15, 3: 261–264

McKeegan G F, Estill K, Campbell B 1987 Elimination of rumination by controlled eating and differential reinforcement. Journal of Behavioral Therapy & Experimental Psychiatry 18, 2: 143–148

Measel C J, Alfieri P A 1976 Treatment of self-injurious behavior by a combination of reinforcement of incompatible behavior and overcorrection. American Journal of Mental Deficiency 81, 2: 147–153

Meichenbaum D H 1977 Cognitive behavior modification. Plenum Press, New York

Murphy G et al 1991 MIETS: a service option for people with mild mental handicaps and challenging behaviour or psychiatric problems 1. Philosophy, service and service users. Mental Handicap Research 4, 1: 41–66

Murphy G et al 1991 MIETS: a service option for people with mild mental handicaps and challenging behaviour or psychiatric problems 2. Assessment, treatment and outcome for service users and service effectiveness. Mental Handicap Research 4, 2: 180–206

Naglieri J A 1985 Assessment of mentally retarded children with the Kaufman assessment battery for children. American Journal of Mental Deficiency 89, 4: 367–371

Newman I, Emerson E 1991 Specialised treatment units for people with challenging behaviours. Mental Handicap 19, 3: 113–119

Nihira L, Nihira K 1975 Jeopardy in community placement. American Journal of Mental Deficiency 79, 5: 538–544

O'Connor N 1987 Cognitive psychology and mental handicap. Journal of Mental Deficiency Research 31: 329–336

Partridge K, Chisholm N, Levy B 1985 Generalisation and maintenance of ward programmes: some thoughts on organisational arrangements. Mental Handicap 13: 26–29

Pichot P 1989 The historical roots of behavior therapy. Journal of Behavioral Therapy & Experimental Psychiatry 20, 2: 107–114

Qureshi H, Alborz A 1992 Epidemiology of challenging behaviour. Mental Handicap Research 5, 2: 130–145

Rapoff M A, Altman K, Christopherson E R 1980 Suppression of self-injurious behaviour: determining the least restrictive alternative. Journal of Mental Deficiency Research 24: 37–46

Reid A H 1984 Gilles de la Tourette syndrome in mental handicap. Journal of Mental Deficiency Research 28: 81–83

Reid A H 1989 Psychiatry and mental handicap: a historical perspective. Journal of Mental Deficiency Research 33: 363–368

Repp A C, Singh N N, Olinger E, Olson D R 1990 The use of functional analyses to test causes of self-injurious behaviour: rationale, current status and future direction. Journal of Mental Deficiency Research 34: 95–105

Riley G 1990 Prompting strategies for those with a severe mental handicap. Behavioural Psychotherapy 18, 3: 193–206

Rix K 1988 Teaching a mother to attend differentially to her mentally handicapped child's behaviour. Behavioural Psychotherapy 16, 2: 122–132

Roberts P, Iwata B A, McSween T E, Desmond E F Jnr 1979 An analysis of overcorrection movements. American Journal of Mental Deficiency 83, 6: 588–594

Robertson I, Richardson A M, Youngson S C 1984 Social skills training with mentally handicapped people: a review. British Journal of Clinical Psychology 23: 241–264

Rogers R C, Simenson R J 1987 Fragile X syndrome: a common etiology of mental retardation. American Journal of Mental Deficiency 91, 5: 445–449

Romer D, Heller T 1983 Social adaptation of mentally retarded adults in community settings: a social-ecological approach. Applied Research in Mental Retardation 4: 303–314

Sachs D A 1973 The efficacy of time-out procedures in a variety of behavior problems. Journal of Behavioral Therapy & Experimental Psychiatry 4: 237–242

Sajwaj T, Libet J, Agras S 1974 Lemon juice therapy: the control of life-threatening rumination in a six-month-old infant. Journal of Applied Behavior Analysis 7, 4: 557–563

Salend S, Ehrlich E 1983 Involving students in behavior modification programs. Mental Retardation 21, 3: 95–100

Samson D M, McDonnell A A. 1990 Functional analysis and challenging behaviours. Behavioural Psychotherapy 18, 4: 259–271

Schmid T L 1986 Reducing inappropriate behavior of mentally retarded children through interpolated reinforcement. American Journal of Mental Deficiency 91, 3: 286–293

Schramski T G 1984 Role playing as a therapeutic approach with the mentally retarded. Psychiatric Aspects of Mental Retardation Newsletter 3, 7–8

Senatore V, Matson J L, Kazdin A E 1982 A comparison of behavioral methods to train social skills to mentally retarded adults. Behavior Therapy 13: 313–324

Shapiro E S 1979 Restitution and positive practice overcorrection in reducing aggressive-disruptive behavior: a long-term follow-up. Journal of Behavioral Therapy & Experimental Psychiatry 10: 131–134

Singh N N, Dawson M J, Manning P J 1981 The effects of physical restraint on self-injurious behaviour. Journal of Mental Deficiency Research 25: 207–216

Sisson L A, Dixon M J 1986 A behavioral approach to the training and assessment of feeding skills in multihandicapped children. Applied Research in Mental Retardation 7: 149–163

Skinner B F 1988 The operant side of behavior therapy. Journal of Behavioral Therapy & Experimental Psychiatry 19, 3: 171–179

Smith M D 1986 Use of similar sensory stimuli in the community-based treatment of self-stimulatory behavior in an adult disabled by autism. Journal of Behavioral Therapy & Experimental Psychiatry 17, 2: 121–125

Spreat S, Lipinski D, Hill J, Halpin M E 1986 Safety indices associated with the use of contingent restraint procedures. Applied Research in Mental Retardation 7: 475–481

Steen P L, Zuriff G E 1977 The use of relaxation in the treatment of self-injurious behavior. Journal of Behavioral Therapy & Experimental Psychiatry 8: 447–448

Sturmey P 1992 Goal planning for adults with a mental handicap: outcome research, staff training and management. Mental Handicap Research 5, 1: 92–108

Switzky H N, Haywood H C 1991 Self-reinforcement in mildly mentally retarded adults: effects of motivational orientation and instructional demand. Journal of Mental Deficiency Research 35: 221–230

Tarnowski K J, Rasnake L K, Mulick J A, Kelly P A 1989 Acceptability of behavioral interventions for self-injurious behavior. American Journal on Mental Retardation 93, 5: 575–580

Tarrier N, Main C J 1986 Applied relaxation training for generalised anxiety and panic attacks. British Journal of Psychiatry 149: 330–336

Thorpe G L, Amatu H I, Blakey R S, Burns L E 1976 Contributions of overt instructional rehearsal and 'specific insight' to the effectiveness of self-instructional training: a preliminary study. Behavior Therapy 7: 504–511

Thorpe G L, Olson S L 1990 Behavior therapy: concepts, procedures and applications. Allyn & Bacon, Boston

Tierney K J, Smith H V 1988 The effect of different combinations of continuous and partial reinforcement schedules on response persistence in mentally handicapped children. Behavioural Psychotherapy 16, 1: 23–37

Tomporowski P D 1983 Training an autistic client: the effect of brief restraint on disruptive behavior. Journal of Behavioral Therapy & Experimental Psychiatry 14, 2: 169–173

Toogood A et al 1988 Challenging behaviour and community settings: planning individualised services. Mental Handicap 16: 70–74

Van Hasselt V B, Sisson L A, Aach S R 1987 Parent training to increase compliance in a young multihandicapped child. Journal of Behavioral Therapy & Experimental Psychiatry 18, 3: 275–283

Van Houten R, Rolider A 1988 Recreating the scene: an effective way to provide delayed punishment for inappropriate motor behavior. Journal of Applied Behavior Analysis 21: 187–192

Walker G R, McLaren K P, Bonaventura S 1985 Changing places: a look at some realities of institutional behavior management. Mental Retardation 23, 2: 79–81

Watson J, Singh N N, Winton A 1986. Suppressive effects of visual facial screening on self-injurious finger-sucking. American Journal of Mental Deficiency 90, 5: 526–534

Whitaker S 1985 Can all parents teach their own children? Mental Handicap 13: 49–50

Whitman T L 1987 Self-instruction, individual differences and mental retardation. American Journal of Mental Deficiency 92, 2: 213–223

Wieseler N A, Hanson R H, Chamberlain T P, Thompson T 1985 Functional taxonomy of stereotypic self-injurious behavior. Mental Retardation 23, 5: 230–234

Winton A S, Singh N N, Dawson M J 1984 Effects of facial screening and blindfold on self-injurious behavior. Applied Research in Mental Retardation 5: 29–42

Wolfensberger W 1983 Social role valorization: a proposed new term for the principle of normalization. Mental Retardation 21, 6: 234–259

Wolfensberger W 1984 A reconceptualization of normalization as social role valorization. Mental Retardation 34, 2: 21–27

Wolpe J 1989 The derailment of behavior therapy: a tale of conceptual misdirection. Journal of Behavioral Therapy & Experimental Psychiatry 20, 1: 3–15

Wurtele S K, King A C, Drabman R S 1984 Treatment package to reduce SIB in a Lesch-Nyhan patient. Journal of Mental Deficiency Research 28, 4: 227–234

Yapa P, Roy A 1990 Depressive illness and mental handicap. Mental Handicap 18: 19–21

Zegiob L, Klukas N, Junginger J 1978 Reactivity of self-monitoring procedures with retarded adolescents. American Journal of Mental Deficiency 83, 2: 156–163

CHAPTER CONTENTS

Introduction 211
Mental handicap 212
Social well-being 212

The social well-being of people who have a mental handicap 214

Service users' perspectives 217

A residential carer's perspective 218

A community nurse's perspective 220

A social worker's perspective 221

A parent's perspective 222

Policies which can facilitate the promotion of social well-being 223

10

Helping with social issues

A. Kay

Key points
- Using the term 'mental handicap' draws attention to the social disadvantages accrued from being so labelled
- The awareness by the carer of the person's understanding of himself or herself and his or her situation is central to the promotion of social well-being
- The quality of services may depend on the extent to which care staff are empowered to make decisions about the use of resources
- The trend towards separating services to deal with the individual's health needs and his or her social needs may run counter to the philosophy of holistic care
- The nature of interpersonal relationships determines the person's social identity and well-being

INTRODUCTION

The World Health Organization's definition of health as a state of complete physical, mental and social well-being, and not merely the absence of disease and infirmity, provides an all-encompassing view of health which is not apparent when looking at the way in which our own society plans, manages and delivers services for individuals and groups of citizens. There is a sharp administrative divide between health care services and social care services; the former being largely the responsibility of central government and the latter falling within the sphere of local authority control. This separation may well serve a useful purpose in relation to certain types of problems experienced by people within society, but for those with complex and continuing care requirements it has often meant that services have been piecemeal, and slow to respond to changing needs. Recognition of the unsuitability of institutional models of service provision for people with a mental handicap has not automatically led to rapid and fundamental change in the planning, management and delivery of a more acceptable range of services. The highly critical Audit Commission Report *Making a reality of community care* (1986), highlighted some of the underlying problems impeding the development of comprehensive community care services, and pointed to 'organizational fragmentation and confusion' (p. 49). Having been asked by the government to advise on options for action to improve this situation, Sir Roy Griffiths (1988) commented:

Community care has been talked of for 30 years and in few areas can the gap between political rhetoric and policy on the one hand, or between policy and reality in the field on the other hand, have been so great. (p. iv)

Subsequent changes in policy, and changes in the way that services are structured, have been received with varying degrees of enthusiasm and cynicism. The National Health Service and Community Care Act (1990) has adjusted the boundaries of responsibility between central and local government agencies but whether or not it will be able to create partnerships in the delivery of care, which was Sir Roy Griffiths' vision, remains to be seen. What is clear, however, is that there remains a need for individual concern and personal commitment both to develop and to deliver a range of services which are sensitive to the wishes of users and responsive to their requirements.

It would be impossible to list comprehensively the ways in which the well-being of someone with a mental handicap can be enhanced; every person is a unique individual with idiosyncratic strengths, preferences, needs and problems. Rather, it is my intention in this chapter to suggest ways of thinking about relationships between service users and service providers which

can lead to effective actions to promote social well-being. Before going on to look at some of the issues which are central to its achievement it may be useful if I explain my understanding of the terms 'mental handicap' and 'social well-being'.

Mental handicap

The term 'mental handicap' is neither particularly descriptive nor, in my experience, particularly well liked by people to whom it is applied. Heron & Myres (1983) have pointed out that the terms 'intellectual impairment' and 'intellectual disability' are probably more accurate descriptions. It needs to be remembered, however, that these terms, as well as 'learning difficulties' and 'learning disabilities', may be just as unacceptable as 'mental handicap' when applied to a person who views his or her main problem as a lack of employment opportunities or as being treated in a condescending manner. The World Health Organization (1980) differentiates between the terms 'impairment', 'disability' and 'handicap' in its definitions:

Handicap is a disadvantage for an individual, resulting from an impairment or a disability, that limits or prevents the fulfilment of a role that is normal (depending on age, sex, and social and cultural factors) for that individual. (p. 32)

There is no general agreement on the usefulness of this definition but it certainly helps to clarify that 'handicap' is not a necessary consequence of impairment; the 'disadvantage' that 'limits' may well be imposed on an individual by means of discrimination or victimization. I use the term 'mental handicap' in this chapter because it is in general use but would hope that it also serves to draw attention to the social disadvantages which accrue when people are so labelled. Changing the label will not remove the factors which lead to disadvantage. That will require a much more fundamental shift in the way that people are viewed and treated within society.

Social well-being

Social perspectives attempt to describe and understand human behaviour and experience within the context of the society in which the individual lives. The starting point is the identification and recognition of influences which are external to the individual and include, as relevant subject matter, the structure and functions of groups, individual roles, personal expectations and understandings of others, and systems of interaction.

The relative importance of biological and environmental factors in determining human nature, and the extent to which an individual is able to exercise control over his or her own destiny, are issues which arouse considerable controversy. Similarly, attempts to establish a conceptual framework which will take account of the inter-relatedness of external and internal influences has proved problematic. The work of George Herbert Mead (1934), an American social psychologist, served to highlight the extent of the complexity but has also provided a perspective on social action which has continued to have considerable influence:

Mind can never find expression, and could never have come into existence at all, except in terms of a social environment; that an organized set or pattern of social relations and interactions (especially those of communication by means of gestures functioning as significant and thus creating a universe of discourse) is necessarily presupposed by it and involved in its nature. (p. 204)

Mead's contention that the development and existence of 'mind', 'self' and 'society' are inextricably interconnected has had considerable impact on the development of thinking within the social sciences. His emphasis on the role of personal meaning in social actions was continued and developed within the framework of 'symbolic interactionism' (Meltzner et al 1975), has been a major source of ideas within social psychology (Farr 1980) and has contributed to the development of humanistic sociology (Mechlin 1986). Additionally, as Doise (1986) has pointed out, Mead's work can help to throw light on the study of human cognitive development.

Mead was closely associated with the development of a philosophical viewpoint described as pragmatism, which was based on the notion that human thought has a functional basis and is sig-

nificant only in as much as it has consequences for actions. Pragmatism offered new ways of considering fundamental questions about the nature of human beings and, as Nakhnikian (1963) has pointed out, it rendered the notion of 'dualism' unproblematic:

The human mind could now be conceived as an emergent capacity in principle understandable in purely naturalistic terms. Knowledge, as product, was warranted belief; warranted belief was the product of inquiry; to inquire was to act in certain ways in certain situations and to believe was to be disposed to act in certain ways in certain situations. There were no mysterious inner goings on to be a basis for contrasting mentality with the lack of it. There was no dualism of mind and matter; no dualism of nature and supernature; and no dualism of method. (p. 159/160)

For Mead it was important to recognize, and act on, an understanding of the interconnectedness of the individual and society. This required the development of methods of inquiry which could illuminate personal meanings associated with social acts, each person being socialized into an existing social world of concepts and actions. As he pointed out, people are not merely passive recipients of ideas which are received from others in society; their every act changes and reconstructs society:

In our reflective conduct we are always reconstructing the immediate society to which we belong. We are taking certain definite attitudes which involve relationships with others. Insofar as those relationships are changed, society itself is changed. We are continually reconstructing. (p. 386)

This theme of the reconstruction of society on the basis of interaction and discourse has been developed within the framework of symbolic interactionism. This approach emphasizes the importance of establishing both personal and shared meanings which are involved in relationships. It is based on a recognition that people have a concept of *self* and that through experiences of interacting with self and others the symbolic meaning of behaviour, interaction and events will be established. This has implications for how we view the world but particularly it suggests that it is essential to try to understand an individual's perspective from his or her own viewpoint rather than by attributing reasons for behaviour and action on the basis of our own predetermined understandings. Similarly, it suggests that a process of *reflection* is possible in that we are able to consider our own behaviour and actions in light of both personal symbolic meaning and in relation to the shared meanings which emerge through communication with others.

The ideas of Mead have contributed to the development of approaches to understanding and explaining complex social interactions through the use of qualitative data. The 'social' in social well-being means that the focus is on the way that people interact, rather than on the individual as a separate biological organism or as a separately defined 'self', but what of 'well-being'?

It has been pointed out by Benner and Wrubel (1989) that the World Health Organization's definition of health is unrealistic, being based on the achievement of an 'ideal state'. As an alternative they suggest an interpretation of the term well-being which 'reflects the lived experience of health'.

Their approach represents a phenomenological perspective (that is, the subject matter of study is individual experience and personal meaning rather than objectively observed behaviours or externally analysed motives and intentions). Within this context they define well-being as: 'congruence between one's possibilities and one's actual practices and lived meanings and is based on caring and feeling cared for'. (p. 160) From this viewpoint well-being is to do with personal history, current meanings and future experiences of the social world which each person inhabits. It is the bringing together of an individual's 'situated possibilities' with the experienced reality of his or her life and is underpinned by the central importance to human well-being of the establishment of caring relationships.

By combining these meanings of social and well-being I would suggest promotion of someone's social well-being to be 'actions which can bring about a situation in which an individual's interaction with others is experienced as positive, valued and caring'. I hope that it is clear from this definition that promotion of the social well-being of someone with a mental handicap can take many forms; it can involve all sorts of different types of activity by one individual who interacts with that person, and will be influenced by the actions of many different people who have contact with the person. It means that the ways in which a single relationship is experienced need to be considered as well as the cumulative meaning for an individual of the totality of his or her social relationships.

THE SOCIAL WELL-BEING OF PEOPLE WHO HAVE A MENTAL HANDICAP

People with a mental handicap sometimes require special services in the form of assistance which can enable them to achieve a satisfactory quality of life, but they can only be given this assistance if the people with whom they come in contact have the will to bring about necessary changes. The well-being of someone with a mental handicap is entirely dependent on the goodwill, personal concern and level of commitment shown by others who are significant in that person's life. Individual actions can, and do, make a difference at both interpersonal and organizational levels. Outmoded institutional models of care *are* being replaced by services which seek to enhance lifestyles and promote choice rather than emphasizing the need for containment and control. As the Audit Commission (1986) noted:

There are many good community care schemes developing – in spite of the system rather than because of it. Many people are working hard to thread a way through the organizational maze and to overcome the financial obstacles because they believe that community care is the best way forward for their clients. (p. 65)

Development may be slow but looked at from an historical perspective there has been significant incremental progress. Alaszewski (1988) has pointed out that attitudes towards people with a mental handicap, as characterized by social welfare policies, have changed during the course of this century; having been treated as 'villains' people with a mental handicap are now more commonly viewed as 'victims of past attitudes and inappropriate services' (p. 12).

Whether social welfare policies have been responsible for determining how people with a mental handicap are treated by others in society or whether they simply reflect the beliefs, values and wishes of members of society is open to question. Decisions to place large numbers of people in institutions have tended to be accompanied by the widespread belief that they must deserve to be there. Similarly, an increased incidence of homelessness in Britain can be tolerated and justified by the belief that all those who are homeless must have brought this state about by their own actions.

The alternative to adjusting one's beliefs to fit in with current reality is to take the view that change is possible; that health and social welfare policies and practices *can* be developed which will enable people to attain a state of physical, mental and social well-being. Within this context, Ackoff (1974) has provided an interesting overview on the way in which changes in the approach to thinking and problem-solving of people who are living in modern industrial societies can affect social structures. According to Ackoff we are in the process of moving from the 'machine age' to the 'systems age'; from a general preoccupation with reductionism, analysis and mechanistic modes of explanation towards expansionism, synthesis and the idea of the indivisible whole. For Ackoff this change heralds hope that solutions can be found to seemingly intractable organizational and social 'messes':

Although we give a great deal of attention to changes in the state and behaviour of man, we tend to neglect changes in the way he views and thinks about these changes. Changes of our point of view and way of thinking not only give rise to new interpretations of what is happening but also to new ideas as to what can be done about it. (p. 7)

Most people with direct experience would agree that the way in which people with a mental handicap and their carers have been treated represents an organizational and social 'mess'. Moreover, it would appear to be the case that many of the ideas and concepts which currently underpin the process and direction of change emphasize the importance of looking at the 'whole person' and of considering the individual's place within society: the person as part of a 'social whole'.

These days, the problems faced by someone who has a mental handicap are very rarely described simply in terms of medical aetiology and/or physiological or mental impairment. It is now more common for emphasis to be placed on the ways in which factors which contribute to handicap can be removed or ameliorated. Since the 1970s the concepts of normalization and social role valorization (Wolfensberger 1983) have undoubtedly provided professionals with direction and impetus for changing the way in which services are planned and provided. A number of distinctly different interpretations of normalization have emerged and, as well as highlighting some of the ways in which they feel the term has been 'misapplied', Perrin and Nirje (1990) have pointed out that as originally conceived it was intended to mean 'making available to all mentally retarded people patterns of life and conditions of everyday living which are as close as possible to the regular circumstances and ways of life of society'. (p. 220)

The concept of normalization has been useful because it highlights ways in which people with a mental handicap are treated differently from other people within society and provides a direction for change. It is also clear, however, that many of the problems which are experienced by people with a mental handicap and their carers are similar to those which affect other socially disadvantaged groups. The term which is perhaps most widely used to describe the notion of imbalance and disadvantage in social relationships is 'oppression' and the term which is often used to describe the restructuring of relationships in a way which will overcome oppression and promote social well-being is 'empowerment'. However, as Gibson (1991) has pointed out:

Empowerment is a difficult concept to define and is easier understood by its absence: powerlessness, helplessness, hopelessness, alienation, victimization, subordination, oppression, paternalism, loss of a sense of control over one's life and dependency. (p. 355)

Bayley (1991) has suggested that normalization is a useful tool but more fundamentally there is a need to base policy 'unambiguously on unconditioned valuing of people with a mental handicap as they are' (p. 99). This theme has been central in the development of 'gentle teaching' as an alternative to behaviour modification in preventing the continuation of an individual's self-injurious and life threatening actions. As McGee et al (1987) point out:

Gentle teaching is based on a posture that centers itself on the mutual liberation and humanization of all persons, a posture that strives for human solidarity. (p. 11)

If the main thrust of normalization is to promote social integration the main difficulty must be how to create the conditions whereby people can establish relationships based on mutual unconditional valuing. An increase in the willingness to accept, and to provide the means to bring about, the complete integration within mainstream society of people with a mental handicap certainly requires more than a change in the way that *professionals* plan and deliver services. It will entail a radical shift in the way that *people*, generally, relate to each other – perhaps what Havel (1978) has described as an 'existential revolution'. As Brechin (1988) points out:

The creation of a society in which people value each other for what they are, without seeking first and foremost 'to interfere, to control, to change, to improve' would bring rewards for us all. Not only those with learning difficulties would gain from a greater sense of humanity. (p. 122)

The notion that it is desirable to allow, and encourage, people with a mental handicap to have more control over their own lives, and to provide service users with opportunities to influence the ways in which resources are allocated, has becoming increasingly important; one of the stated intentions of the 1989 White Paper *Caring for People* was to 'give people a greater individual say in how they live their lives and the services they need to do so'. (p. 4)

To be able to enhance an individual's social well-being requires, firstly, a willingness to understand the viewpoint of another person. If well-being is a personally defined state of balance between possibility and actuality it is impossible to act in ways which will increase congruence without establishing personal meanings. Secondly, it will require that interaction be based on recognition of that individual's personal value and worth. The way in which people view themselves and others is of crucial importance in determining how people interact. It is likely that someone who thinks of a person with a mental handicap as a 'villain' will act very differently towards that person than will someone who views him or her as a 'victim'. Equally, if someone sees 'level of intellectual functioning' as the sole determinant of human worth it is likely that he or she will treat a person with a mental handicap as being less than human. Each person has a different way of understanding the world and as Lalljee & Abelson (1983) have pointed out:

The tendency to seek explanations for physical events, social processes, and human behaviour seems as pervasive a human tendency as any other. An explanation serves to demystify an event, to impose a particular sort of stability and predictability upon the world, and to enable the individual to act toward it in a systematic manner. (p. 239/240)

The starting point for considering aspects of the relationship between service users and service providers must be a willingness to listen to the explanations which people give for their actions and the actions of others. The following are extracts of conversations which I have had with five people who are directly involved in receiving or providing services for people with a mental handicap and their families. They are intended to act as a starting point for considering and understanding ways in which the social well-being of others can be promoted. As Denzin (1989) points out, however, understanding inevitably involves personal interpretation:

Understandings rest on an interpretive process that leads one to enter into the emotional life of another. *Interpretation*, the act of interpreting and making sense out of something, creates the conditions for *understanding*, which involves being able to grasp the meanings of an interpreted experience for another individual. (p. 28)

I have interpreted the comments made to me during these conversations, have edited them, and have placed them within a framework of my own beliefs and values. Each of us develops understandings based on the expressed views and related experiences of others. Our actions are based on the conceptual understandings which we form and in recording these comments I have carried out a process of selection and interpretation which is intended to make explicit a process that is implicit within all social interactions.

SERVICE USERS' PERSPECTIVES

Pat and Davy had known each other earlier in their lives, but when they met again in 1987 they found that they enjoyed each other's company to such an extent that they married in April 1989. They are now living in a small district council flat. There is nothing particularly unusual in their story except that both were 'in care' from an early age and both have spent a considerable part of their adult lives in mental handicap hospitals.

Davy has been trying hard to find out about his childhood and early family life. He remembers the children's home he was admitted to when he was 7 years old and recalls being transferred to a mental handicap hospital when he was 17. His memories of his stay in hospital are not all bad and he views positively opportunities he had to work in the gardens and to assist the hospital painters. Individual acts of kindness and respect also made a lasting impression. He 'took to the hills' on one occasion and experienced life in a variety of hostels for homeless people. A conviction for shoplifting eventually led to his return to hospital and he recalls that the reaction from staff was not as bad as he had been expecting:

I was in the kitchen and the Charge Nurse said, 'Have you got a smoke?'. I said, 'No, I've no smokes' and he said, 'Well there's 20 Woodbine and a box of matches'. Then a nurse came in and said, 'Right, you've to come for a bath'. I wouldn't go with her and she said, 'I'll go and get the Charge Nurse' so I said, 'You go and get him and I'll tell him I'm not a low grade patient'. The Charge Nurse came up and said, 'For crying out loud, you're not a low grade patient' and he told the nurse 'He can bath himself'. He also said I could wear my own clothes.

Having become an 'informal patient' Davy discharged himself in 1979 (he's still got the letter which the Charge Nurse asked him to sign to say that he was leaving against the advice of staff) and went to live with another ex-hospital patient. He didn't find it easy to adjust:

When I came out of hospital into society – I call hospital 'another society' – at first it didn't work. I moved from digs to digs and ended up in the (homeless unit) again.

Eventually his social worker felt that Davy would have a better chance of receiving support within the framework of mental handicap services and arranged for a short period of assessment in a social work department hostel. His name was then put forward for a place in a supported housing development for people with a mental handicap and he moved into a self-contained flat. Davy found it difficult to live on his own and, despite the efforts of staff to provide support and assistance, he feels that it is likely that he would have returned to being homeless if it had not been for his relationship with Pat.

Pat thinks that she was taken into care when she was 18 months old and, like Davy, can remember when she was first admitted to a mental handicap hospital:

Someone said to me, 'You're going to a nice home' – a nice home with a scrubbing brush! It was a 'nice' surprise, a 'nice' shock. You'd to get up and scrub the dormitory before breakfast and you had the whole place to clean before you went out to your work in the morning.

Pat has both pleasant and unpleasant memories of people she knew and incidents which occurred during her time in hospital. When leaving hospital she remembers spending the night outside in the cold before going to see a member of staff and asking for help to find somewhere else to live:

I said I've nowhere to go and she said, 'I'll try and get you somewhere'. Then she said she'd take me to a hostel. I didn't mind sleeping with other people in the room – I liked the residents there and as long as I had a bed that was the main thing.

Having been admitted to a social work hostel for people with a mental handicap Pat was keen to move on to a place of her own. She experienced a few setbacks before finally achieving her goal of setting up home and, in retrospect, feels that it would have been very difficult for her if she had been on her own. The development of a close relationship with Davy, however, meant that she was able to plan ahead on the basis of sharing a flat and sharing her life. As Pat says:

It's made a wonderful difference – we have each other and we've got a home. Davy needs a decent life, someone to care for him.

Davy also recognizes the difference to him that his relationship with Pat has made:

Since I've met Pat my life's got better. We've had our ups and downs but if I've got any troubles I can go to Pat or if she's got any troubles she can come to me. I feel settled now. I wasn't brought up to care for people but I've got a wife now, someone to care for. I've got responsibility now. I haven't had that in the past.

Pat and Davy both view the relationship which they have established with each other as the crucial ingredient which has transformed their lives. Both feel that an essential part of that relationship is being concerned about each other's well-being. Both have had experiences which make them shudder and which rekindle anger about the ways they have been treated while living in institutions and settings which span the full range of residential care provision for people with a mental handicap. In many ways their life experiences epitomize the rationale behind the development of the concept of community care – firstly, as a reaction against long-term hospitalization and the inherently institutionalizing patterns of interaction between 'them and us' which is associated with hospital care, and, secondly, as a reaction against the notion that smaller institutions called 'hostels' rather than 'hospitals' would be able to resolve this problem. They focus on the way that people have interacted with them as being the important factor in their experience of residential settings and their comments also highlight the value to both of them of being able to *care for* someone else rather than simply *being cared for*.

Their comments would also suggest that what is important to Pat and Davy is not how they were treated in the past but how they are treated now. Both have been 'handicapped' by being de-nied opportunities to adopt normal roles within society as a consequence of having been labelled 'mentally handicapped'. The label did not in itself produce this outcome but the attitudes towards the label because they involved seeing people with a mental handicap as members of a group, who should be treated in certain ways. This primarily involves removing choice and exerting control.

Everyone has had experience of being treated in a manner which they feel is unjust and inappropriate, and it would be unusual for someone to be able to journey through life without, at some point, being made to feel stupid, worthless or downright malicious. For some of us this occurs as a temporary inconvenience which can be shrugged off, a minor obstacle which needs to be overcome to allow us to attain personal goals and objectives. For others it clouds our view of humanity long after the irritant has been removed; experiences of this sort affect the most well-balanced of people. For Pat and Davy, being treated as inferior and unimportant has been part of their experience of everyday life during both childhood and adulthood; not only in terms of the way in which many of the people who have played central roles in their lives have interacted with them but also in the way that they have been treated by society as a whole. Within this context it is perhaps surprising that they are not more aggrieved about the ways in which their lives have been restricted in the past, but it also suggests that the effects of oppression are not irreversible.

A RESIDENTIAL CARER'S PERSPECTIVE

As a member of the management team working within a local authority hostel Patricia sees her role as creating conditions which will allow staff to work effectively with residents. To try to maximize the effectiveness of staff in working with individual residents a key worker system is used, though as Patricia points out:

The system works well for some staff and not so well for others. It works well for people who are prepared to take on responsibility. Other people who have been given the same opportunities don't seem to want, or are not able, to take on the full responsibility that is possible with the key worker role.

Patricia feels that there are a number of explanations which can help to account for the reluctance which some staff show towards the acceptance of responsibility for the coordination of care for an individual resident:

Some staff don't see their job as encouraging residents to be involved in activities outside the home. They see their job as being in the home and 'looking after' residents; to see that people are fed, washed and changed. That is what some people think is the role of the residential worker.

Another problem which Patricia identifies is the reluctance of staff to accept risk or to allow and encourage residents to take risks. She feels that this can lead to the unnecessary limiting of residents' lifestyles and a reduction in the choices which are open to people. According to Patricia, the question of risk is often a central one for residential care staff and she highlighted the complexities of the issues involving risk for a resident who has diabetes. This young woman requires a daily injection of insulin which is administered by a district nurse.

Initially her meals were cooked in the central kitchen and she was not involved in the preparation. This meant that her intake of food was largely controlled and she didn't have the same access to food as she has now. However, she's capable of doing a lot for herself and doesn't need hotel-like services. She's now in a semi-independent unit and as such has got more access to food.

Staff within the hostel have worked closely with medical and nursing staff to ensure that the young woman's blood glucose levels are monitored, and that an effective carbohydrate exchange system has been worked out. They feel confident that everything has been done to control the condition; however, as Patricia points out:

She knows the principle of the carbohydrate exchange system and she knows when she's 'cheating'. She's also got a limited understanding of the risks she takes when she doesn't stick to her diet.

Staff have been trying to encourage this resident to take on responsibility for her own well-

being rather than have staff 'watching over' her. Having attended an adult training centre for some time she fairly recently started on an employment training scheme. Patricia notes that there was some concern over this arrangement, but it seems to be working out:

It has meant that she has had to make up a packed lunch every night. She does this herself, counting out her carbohydrate exchanges. Staff usually check what she has prepared but 9 times out of 10 there is no problem.

Patricia feels that it is important that the medical problems associated with diabetes do not prevent this resident from having opportunities to lead a full and varied life and that the requirement for staff to safeguard and protect the individual is balanced against the desirability of personal freedom and responsibility. She points out that there appears to be a tendency for residential care staff to be preoccupied with residents' physical care requirements and, though this is important, it is only part of the picture.

Patricia's comments highlight the complexity of factors which influence the types of interaction which take place between staff and residents within a residential setting. An individual's personal understanding of his or her role in caring will have considerable impact on the way that individual and group interactions take place and perceptions among staff and between staff and residents can be very different. Efforts to devise and implement systems such as the utilization of a key worker for each resident represent an attempt to establish the relationships which will counteract the tendency for institutional patterns of behaviour which are associated with group treatment. As Patricia points out, however, it can be difficult to establish a shared understanding of the purpose and value of this approach within a setting which has been designed with other priorities in mind.

The Independent Review of Residential Care chaired by Wagner (1988) reviewed the role of residential care services in relation to people with a mental handicap and commented:

Supporting people with mental handicap in ordinary houses on a large scale within the community is uncharted territory. Finding and training workers who can live alongside without dominating, and who enable rather than direct, is a crucial challenge for service providers. The extent to which agencies succeed in meeting the demands will closely affect the spread and quality of community provision. (p. 105)

From this perspective the development of a more appropriate range of residential settings is not simply about smaller groups of people living in smaller houses, it is also about the construction, from scratch, of caring services which enable rather than dominate or direct. It would appear to me, however, that Patricia's description and explanation of the work going on with a particular resident in a particular hostel suggest that the framework already exists for the creation of a more appropriate and sensitive range of services. Perhaps the problem does not lie in having an existing workforce which has been badly selected or wrongly trained as the Wagner Report implied. In the same way that it is possible for staff to apply their interactional skills *either* to meet institutional requirements for control and containment *or* to facilitate personal growth and development it may well be that the quality of residential services is dependent on the extent to which staff are empowered. Situations in which carers are given opportunities to acquire suitable facilities, have access to sufficient resources, are provided with educational and training opportunities, and are offered an organizational framework which encourages the establishment of user-led service development are still being seen as 'experiments' in community care. As Alaszewski & Hayes (1990) point out:

It is important managers not only believe in the philosophy and principles [of normalization] but demonstrate this belief. In addition they must be willing to take the necessary risks which are essential to its success. (p. 280)

A COMMUNITY NURSE'S PERSPECTIVE

Having trained and worked within a hospital for people with a mental handicap Ann-Marie now works within a community mental handicap nursing team. She has a caseload of around 30 clients:

My role is to look after the health care needs of the person with a mental handicap. This involves providing support, advice and guidance to people, including families and other professionals.

Ann-Marie feels that it is not always easy to differentiate between 'health problems' and 'social problems' and points out that because someone has a mental handicap it does not necessarily follow that person will have health problems or health care needs. She cites the example of a recent referral where she felt that community nursing involvement would not be appropriate:

People assumed that because he has Down syndrome he automatically required health care services, but he doesn't have health deficits which require a nurse to deal with them. He needs social involvement and social contact. He needs educational support and training. He needs somewhere to live. These are the primary problems, but I was being asked to become involved because he has Down syndrome.

Ann-Marie thinks that many of the people whom she sees have problems which arise out of the lack of available resources to meet the emotional and social needs of individuals and families:

If there were sufficient resources a lot of referrals for health care services would not be necessary. People need to get help and advice to recognize the ways their needs can be met, but often the resources required are those which social workers are expected to provide.

The clients with whom she works most intensively tend to have a complex combination of problems. She cites the example of one young man who was referred by a consultant:

The initial problem was to do with a combination of problems with epilepsy and aggressive outbursts. I've been involved in looking at family dynamics, personal relationships, personal development, family support, liaison with other agencies. I'm carrying out a life plan assessment to help him identify what his needs are, to try to help him to focus on the fact that he's a young man who shouldn't be afraid to have an opinion.

For Ann-Marie this client's neurophysiological problems cannot be considered in isolation from his social environment. She feels that there is still an expectation amongst other professionals that a nurse will only be involved in aspects of physical care and that not everyone recognizes that medical problems and health needs are different. She works closely with social workers and points out that the role of the community nurse and the role of the social worker are not always clearly differentiated:

Sometimes it doesn't matter whether it is a social worker or a nurse that is involved as long as that person is able to provide a service which enables the individual to maintain balance in their health and social well-being.

Community mental handicap nurses are a relatively recent phenomenon in the provision of services for people with a mental handicap, but it is widely recognized that they are able to make a valuable contribution within the framework of community health care services. As Ann-Marie points out, the community nurse's role involves focusing on the health care needs of the individual and acting in ways which will lead to the creation of a situation in which the person is able to function at an optimum level. For Ann-Marie it is impossible to consider the individual's health and well-being in isolation from his or her social environment and much of her work entails interacting with others who are important in that person's life. Within this context social well-being is a manifestation of health.

Ann-Marie points out that someone who has a mental handicap will not necessarily require the involvement of a community nurse and though she recognizes the problems faced by the person who was referred to her 'because he has Down syndrome' she feels that other services would be more appropriate for their resolution. This highlights one of the problems which is inherent within a fragmented health and social care system – the possibility that individual health and social care services may fail to respond to the needs of an individual whose problems are not defined in terms which are compatible with the remit of existing services. By that I do not mean to imply that Ann-Marie should have accepted the referral, but rather to suggest that the divide between health care and social care services for people with a mental handicap is administratively imposed and is arbitrary.

There has been much debate about how best to provide a coherent and comprehensive service for people with a mental handicap and their families. The provision of joint National Health Service and local authority community mental handicap teams has been seen to be one way of ensuring that service provision is coordinated to provide a 'one door' approach for people who are assessed as requiring specialist services. The very fact, however, that there is need for specialist services suggests that the organizational framework of both general health and generic social care services has failed to address the issues associated with mental handicap. Brown (1990) has pointed out that despite some problems community mental handicap teams have played an important role in highlighting the needs of people with a mental handicap by 'listening to the voice of the powerless' (p. 19).

A SOCIAL WORKER'S PERSPECTIVE

Jennifer is a generic social worker within an area team. She trained as a social worker after having worked for a voluntary agency involved with people with mental health problems and has a mixed caseload of around 25 clients. She is involved with a small number of families who are caring for a child or adult with a mental handicap and also receives referrals when acting as duty officer within the area office. For example:

One woman who had been living alone since her mother died was referred by her family in view of concerns over her general coping abilities; it was to do with bills, finances, accounts and things like that.

Although the client was assessed as having a mild mental handicap Jennifer felt that this client's main difficulty arose from her hearing impairment:

She enjoyed her life and she didn't necessarily live the way that her family wanted her to live. It was very difficult in that she saw me as siding with the family.

In view of medical concerns this client was admitted to a mental handicap hospital for a period of assessment and it was decided that when she left hospital a home help should provide support and the possibility of day care within a local centre for elderly people should be considered:

It was felt that she would benefit from having a home help and she does. She needs that level of support and to know that there's a reliable person around. Someone who she can trust who is independent from her family. We looked at the possibility of day centre attendance and suggested it from the point of view of her assisting others, not necessarily as a recipient of the service. Unfortunately, she saw it as her being used as a 'skivvy'.

This client's lifestyle has been enhanced by the establishment of the relationship with her home help and, as Jennifer points out:

She still spends her money the way she chooses and knows what's expected of her in terms of 'if you don't pay your electricity you'll get cut off so what do you want to do?'. The options are pointed out and she realizes she needs to pay her bills. Whatever's left she does with as she wants. I really think that she's quite happy now. She's fairly friendly with her family again and I think that they've grown to respect that she does know her own mind. There are things that she does need a bit of help and support with, but it's help rather than control.

The people with a mental handicap whom Jennifer is involved with are usually more highly dependent. She sees her role as working with the family and the individual client, but points out that these two roles do come into conflict at times:

Without the parents' cooperation very little can be achieved. There are legal actions which social workers can take, but there are also different styles and approaches.

Jennifer feels that it is important that she is able to work with people who have different types of problems, with the common thread for social work involvement being to help people during periods of transition.

When introduced, generic social work departments were seen to be a major step forward in providing continuity of service provision for individuals, families and groups who could face a multiplicity of problems requiring the involvement of previously separate social care agencies. The extent to which informal neighbourhood care can provide support will vary (Department of Health 1989) and, as Jennifer's comments

highlight, a generic social worker can evaluate existing support and assess additional service requirements. The problems faced by the woman who was referred to Jennifer were managed in a sensitive manner with the person's right to have choice and to maintain personal responsibility being enhanced. In this instance there was no need to involve specialist services as the client's needs could be met by the involvement of a home help.

Jennifer describes her role in terms of 'helping during periods of transition' and many of the individuals and families with whom she is involved have extreme difficulties and are facing acute crises. Within this context the role of the social worker has often come to be associated with reaction to a crisis rather than the proactive promotion of social well-being. It is perhaps within this context that service development issues have tended to be taken on board by specialist practitioners rather than by generic workers. Within the context of the All-Wales Strategy for people with a mental handicap (AWS) McGrath & Grant (1990) note:

The AWS presented social services departments with a massive challenge in terms of reappraising accepted values and philosophical aims, as well as establishing a new culture where contributions to planning and delivery of services were to be expected of both consumers and front-line staff. (p. 25)

Jennifer highlighted an issue which is not easy to resolve when professionals and parents or other carers have different perceptions of what is in the best interests of someone with a mental handicap.

A PARENT'S PERSPECTIVE

Margaret's son, Derek, suffered brain damage when he was young. He is now 21 and lives at home with his parents and his brother. Looking back she feels that there are a number of things that she would do differently:

I was overpossessive with Derek and I was too critical of him. It's good for kids to have a chance to talk for themselves and to mix with others – they can learn how to socialize which is more important than anything.

She is also highly critical of many of the services which have been provided for Derek:

I feel that I've not always had a fair hearing – it's maybe natural that professionals will stick together. I think that it would be a good idea to give parents a say in the running of places. Even if the parents were involved in employing people they would know if a person has a good attitude. After all the parents know better than anyone.

She feels that there is better financial help now for families but that people have to go out of their way to find out about what is available:

There's money that people can get, but only if you're getting full attendance allowance. I've given other people advice.

Margaret thinks that Derek's main difficulties just now are his lack of confidence and his inability to communicate and express himself. She also feels that the way that Derek is viewed by others is unfair:

It's important for him to get confidence and usually you get confidence with maturity, particularly if you're given the right guidance. Everyone is shy when they're young and you need to be encouraged and learn confidence. Derek can be very annoying at times, but he's also got his good points. If you're a bit handicapped, or seen to be handicapped, you're not allowed to have normal reactions. As a kid if you hit somebody back, even when they're annoying you, you're not seen to be 'hitting' somebody, you're 'attacking' somebody. You're actually expected to be more controlled than an 'ordinary' person.

In terms of Derek's future Margaret thinks that it would be better for him to remain at home with his parents, but she is unsure of the long-term possibilities:

There might be miracles that can happen later on in life, but the way that he is just now he doesn't have confidence. If he moved in somewhere it would be horrible to think of someone taking advantage of him, taking money off him. If he did want to move somewhere it would be nice if he had his own flat in something like a sheltered flat with a warden. I think that it must be very lonely though for someone who's not very clever. I'd really like to think that same day he would be able to have a little job. I just don't know what's in front of Derek – he might even get married. I don't know just how much potential he does have.

The concerns which Margaret expresses about Derek's future will be shared by many people who have a family member who has a mental handicap. Similarly, she will not be alone in feeling that professionals tend to play down the significance of the knowledge which a parent has about the difficulties that are faced by a son or daughter. The ideal of creating a partnership between parents and professionals which combines the best of both worlds to ameliorate the problems associated with mental handicap is well established, but personal experiences of family members suggest that this is not often their reality. Mothers tend to be the predominant carers for people with a mental handicap living at home and as Grant (1988) has pointed out in relation to the long-term care of adult family members with a mental handicap:

For some mothers, and other informal carers, their commitment shades into stoicism, a reluctance to share responsibilities, and a refusal to transfer those responsibilities to others in the face of personal adversity. There is an urgent need to extend to those families, from an early point in the life-cycle, counselling services and more accessible and tailored forms of domiciliary, relief and residential care to prevent them from feeling that sharing or transferring care means an abdication of personal responsibility. (p. 91)

The fact that these services have often not been available is not the fault of parents. If a partnership is to be created the onus must surely be on the professional to show that he or she is willing to find out about the difficulties which family carers experience and then act in ways which will help to solve their problems. To do this, however, there must be a mechanism by which tailored forms of services can be developed to meet the particular requirements of individuals and families.

POLICIES WHICH CAN FACILITATE THE PROMOTION OF SOCIAL WELL-BEING

Blumer (1969) has suggested that two main methods of inquiry can be useful in helping to understand social phenomena – exploration and inspection. The former allows the development of a clearer understanding of what is going on and the identification of useful explanatory or 'sensitising' concepts, and the latter facilitates examination of these concepts in the light of evidence. Within this context the personal views of service users and service providers which I have included provide a means of exploring issues and concerns which have a bearing on the promotion of social well-being. I have commented on a number of the issues which were raised during the conversations from the point of view of my own understandings but would point out that other interpretations may be equally valid.

The extracts of conversations also serve to highlight different ways in which people with a mental handicap are viewed. The recollections of Pat and Davy illustrate that people with a mental handicap have tended to be treated in ways which create social inferiority and foster marginalization. Swain (1990) has argued that 'learned helplessness' is the 'psychological price of powerlessness in which oppression becomes internalized' (p. 116). That people with a mental handicap should be treated with dignity, and deserve to be afforded basic human rights, is widely acknowledged, but the question of how best to bring this about appears to be more problematic. The comments of Patricia, Anne-Marie and Jennifer indicate an approach which emphasizes the encouragement of independence, choice and personal freedom, with the professional providing a client-centred service and acting as advocate. The extent to which professionals can combine loyalty to the organization which they represent with actions which are in their clients' best interests may well be dependent on individual determination and the maturity of service managers. With regard to the ability of professionals to act as advocates Gostin (1984) has pointed out:

Staff who are dedicated to the treatment and care of mentally ill or mentally handicapped people feel they are the advocates, and probably always have been. Some social workers refer to their work in terms of 'casework advocacy' or 'child advocacy'. It is important that staff continue to assume this role, but the cornerstone of advocacy is the independence of statutory authorities if conflicts of interest and loyalties are to be avoided. (p. 7)

Margaret's comments would suggest that a

situation of 'them and us' is not unprecedented in relationships between professionals and parents. Fish (1991) has suggested that there are currently two divergent models of professionalism. On one hand, there is the 'technical rational model' which 'strives for objectivity . . .' and 'seeks to remove, as far as possible, human fallibility' (p. 28). On the other hand, there is the 'professional artistry model' which 'sees professional activity in terms of structure, patterns, principles, and it values creativity and the room to be wrong' (p. 30). To provide a service which is relevant and effective each professional will require to find out about the views and expectations of carers. Equally, however, service providers must be willing to indicate clearly the scope and limitations of the services which they are able to provide.

The comments of Pat and Davy provide evidence that people with a mental handicap can benefit from self-advocacy. Sutcliffe (1990) has outlined various ways in which people with a mental handicap can be encouraged to 'speak up for themselves' and Grant (1990) has pointed out that there has been considerable growth in the involvement of consumers in the planning of services for people with a mental handicap in Wales:

Beyond self-advocacy there are signs that many of the new community based services, by virtue of their adopted organizational culture and ideology, are involving people with a mental handicap in the planning and organization of day-to-day activity while at the same time enabling them to encounter and to be embraced by surrounding communities of interest. A particularly positive sign in this connection is that it is becoming increasingly difficult to distinguish consumers from coworkers or service providers. It would be invidious to single out particular projects to provide examples as there are now so many that could claim these signal achievements. Because of the way they have been designed many of the new services are at an advantage over existing services in these respects. It is important however that individuals in long-stay hospitals or who use other services which group and segregate them from the community are not neglected in the search for effective methods of promoting consumer involvement. (p. 32)

Within the context of promoting social well-being one of the main issues which must be ad- dressed is how best to ensure that opportunities exist for the establishment of a range of interper- sonal contacts which can contribute to an indi- vidual's sense of belonging to a community. For most of us this is an intrinsic and important part of our understanding of *self*. Dowson (1989) has pointed out that the term 'community' is often used to refer to a geographical neighbourhood but that a sense of belonging is more often expe- rienced by an individual in relation to a unique community consisting of a network of relation- ships and acquaintances.

It may consist of family members, some of the neighbours, and perhaps the local shopkeeper or the regulars at the pub or club; but it may also stretch far beyond the neighbourhood, to the workplace and to old friends many miles away. It also includes mainstream services such as the family doctor, college or adult education centre. (p. 4)

Different meanings of 'community' and of 'community care' have been utilized to describe services which can provide alternatives to hospi- tal or institutional models. It has been pointed out (Kay 1990) that one of the consequences of the White Paper *Caring for People* (1989), was implicit clarification of the meaning of the term commu- nity care as 'the creation of political, social and economic systems and mechanisms which foster a network of interpersonal contacts to enable each person to lead as full and meaningful a life as possible' (p. 6).

This definition indicates the link between so- cial well-being and community care for people with a mental handicap. Community care is to do with the organizational framework constructed by government to fulfil the aims of its social wel- fare policies. Community care cannot be achieved without the transfer of resources within society; it requires the provision of formal services to supplement the care being provided by indi- vidual citizens. The alternative to community care is community neglect.

Creating conditions which will encourage pro- motion of the social well-being of people with a mental handicap is a necessary part of commu- nity care but individual actions are dependent on personal initiative rather than on the alloca- tion of resources. The desire to enhance the life- style and life-chances of people who are vulner- able underpins the caring actions of individual citizens and service providers and, though this may well entail actions which encourage the formation and implementation of social welfare policies which foster rather than hinder the es- tablishment of enabling relationships, it also in- volves thinking about how best to enable – how to empower rather than oppress. Promoting the social well-being of another person is part of being human, constructing community care is about creating a civilized society.

The National Health Service and Community Care Act (1990) reiterated that responsibility for social care lies with local authorities and indi- cated that consultation should take place with other agencies to ensure that an appropriate and cost effective mix of services is provided. Wright (1990) has pointed out that policy changes are intended to create a demand-led or user-led system of social care provision to replace the current supply-led or provider-led approach which involves centrally planned service devel- opment. Within this context local authorities will be expected to ensure that an assessment of needs is carried out and to adopt an enabling role rather than acting primarily as the providers of services. It is suggested that the main mecha- nism by which this can be achieved is through the role of the care manager who will be respon- sible for putting together a package of care. Early studies of care management systems (Challis & Davies 1986) would suggest that there are considerable advantages in a resource alloca- tion system that is more closely tuned into the requirements and wishes of service users. It cer- tainly appears to offer a useful alternative to the process whereby large numbers of professionals meet together to decide fairly trivial matters but are unable to take more important decisions because they do not have the necessary author- ity. However, as Beardshaw & Towell (1990) point out there are a range of models which have very different implications. It is clear that deci- sions have to be taken about how best current services can be deployed and, as Ann-Marie points out, health and social work services have different budgetary responsibilities. If progress is to be made, an effective mechanism for change and development in the range of available services is required.

To achieve this goal demand-led, needs-led and user-led approaches to service development have been suggested. The idea of demand-led service provision is associated with free market economics. In theory, customers will buy goods and services which they desire and can afford and suppliers will make available what will sell. Decisions about what is produced within the economy will depend, therefore, on the overall effect of decisions taken by individual consumers. The alternative, a supply-led approach, involves decisions being taken by a planning group. What is to be produced within the economy is determined centrally. A demand-led system depends on consumers having money to spend on the basis of 'wants' but in relation to services for people with a mental handicap the idea of 'wants' is often replaced by the notion of 'needs'. In their Policy Guidance booklet (1991) the Department of Health have outlined ways in which community care policies should be implemented to foster a 'needs-led approach' (p. 25). This document defines key terms and within the glossary 'assessment' is defined as:

The process of objectively defining needs and determining eligibility for assistance against stated policy criteria. It is a participative process involving the applicant, their carers and other relevant agencies. (Appendix B/1)

There are a number of issues which cannot be clarified until systems are fully implemented on a widespread scale, but it is likely that the notion of 'objectively defining needs' will prove problematic. It is impossible to consider 'needs' without taking into account subjective experience and it is inevitable that in any particular situation there will be differences of opinion about the nature of an individual's needs. It could be argued, for instance, that Pat and Davy's needs were being met by institutionalization.

Brandon & Towe (1989) have pointed out that an inordinate amount of power lies with service providers and have suggested that 'service brokerage' incorporates elements which are neces-sary to alter the balance of control away from planners and professionals and towards service users. Service brokerage represents a user-led approach with resources being allocated to individuals who can then determine, with assistance, the services which will best meet their requirements.

Ann-Marie indicates that her work with a particular client has included a 'life plan assessment'. This illustrates one way in which professionals can ensure that an individual's social well-being is taken into account and that a user-led approach is encouraged. Berger et al (1974) suggested the notion of an individual's life plan as 'the totalization of all the relevant timetables, their grand sum and their integrative meaning' (p. 69). Their idea was not that people necessarily plan out every aspect of their lives in advance, but rather that individuals tend to think about both their own situation and the situation of others within society by reference to progressional pathways. Within this context people will have various 'careers' or 'timetables' that are to do with, for instance, their involvement in occupational activities, educational development, family relationships, their financial state or the development of hobbies and leisure interests. In discussing Derek's prospects for the future Margaret refers to employment, housing arrangements and marriage and suggests that he will face a greater degree of uncertainty than most people. For people with a mental handicap there are considerable obstacles which need to be overcome if they are to have options for development in *any* of these areas. A life plan assessment may help to establish the idea that someone with a mental handicap has the right to develop and can assist in formulating a plan of action which takes into account the sorts of progressional pathways through life which other people take for granted.

Promotion of the social well-being of people with a mental handicap requires acceptance of full personal responsibility for ensuring that the many examples of good practices which are now around are perpetuated and extended and that examples of bad practices are eliminated and replaced. Listening to, and reflecting on, the views of people who are directly involved in providing services will generate ample evidence of the current situation and the views and everyday experiences of people who are service users will highlight ways in which services can be changed for the better.

It is maybe encouraging to note that when Vaclav Havel wrote in 1978 about the need for an 'existential revolution' he was under house ar-

rest as a dissident in communist Czechoslovakia and 12 years later he was elected President of the country. As he pointed out in his essay *The power of the powerless:*

The real question is whether the 'brighter future' is really always so distant. What if, on the contrary, it has been here for a long time already, and only our blindness and weakness has prevented us from seeing it around us and within us, and kept us from developing it? (p. 122)

REFERENCES

A Report to the Secretary of State for Social Services by Sir Roy Griffiths, 1988 Community care: agenda for action. HMSO, London

Ackoff R L 1974 Redesigning the future: a systems approach to societal problems. John Wiley & Sons, Chichester

Alaszewski A 1988 From villains to victims. In: Leighton A (ed) Mental handicap in the community. Woodhead-Faulkner, London

Alaszewski A, Hayes S 1990 Lessons from the Croxteth Park project. In: Alaszewski A and Ong B N (eds), Normalization in practice: residential care for children with a profound mental handicap. Routledge, London

Audit Commission for Local Authorities in England and Wales 1986 Making a reality of community care. HMSO, London

Bayley M 1991 Normalization or 'social role valorization': an adequate philosophy? In: Baldwin S and Hattersley J, Mental handicap: social science perspectives. Routledge, London

Beardshaw V, Towell D 1990 Assessment and case management, briefing paper No. 10. King's Fund, London

Benner P, Wrubel J 1989 The primacy of caring: stress and coping in health and illness. Addison-Wesley, California

Berger P L, Berger B, Kellner H 1974 The homeless mind. Pelican Books, Middlesex

Blumer H 1969 Symbolic interactionism. Prentice-Hall, Englewood Cliffs, NJ

Brandon D, Towe N 1989 Free to choose: an introduction to service brokerage. Good Impressions Publishing, London

Brechin A 1988 Personal relationships and personal fulfilment. In: Leighton A (ed) Mental handicap in the community. Woodhead-Faulkner, London

Brown S 1990 Community mental handicap teams practice papers series: No 4 Managing care. Centre for Research in Social Policy, Nottingham

Challis D, Davies B 1986 Case management in community care: an evaluated experiment in the home care of the elderly. Gower, Aldershot

Denzin N Z 1989 Interpretive biography. Qualitative Research Methods vol 17. Sage Publications, London

Department of Health 1989 Neighbourhood care and social policy. HMSO, London

Department of Health 1989 Caring for people: community care in the next decade and beyond. HMSO, London

Department of Health 1991 Community care in the next decade and beyond: policy guidance. HMSO, London

Doise W 1986 Levels of explanation in social psychology. Cambridge University Press, Cambridge

Dowson S 1989 Going beyond Griffiths: a reassessment of community care. CMH, London

Farr R M 1980 Homo socio-psychologicus. In: Chapman A J and Jones D M (eds) Models of man. The British Psychological Society, Leicester

Fish D 1991 But can you prove it? Assessment and evaluation in higher education 16: 1 pp 22–36

Gibson C H 1991 A concept analysis of empowerment. Journal of Advanced Nursing, 1991, 16, 354–361

Gostin L 1984 Foreword. In: Sang B and O'Brien J Advocacy: The UK and American experiences. King Edward's Hospital Fund, London

Grant G 1988 Stability and change in the care networks of mentally handicapped adults living at home: first report. Centre for Social Policy Research and Development, University College of North Wales, Bangor

Grant G 1990 Consumer involvement and the all Wales strategy: a research note for all Wales advisory panel subgroup on consumer involvement. Centre for Social Policy Research and Development, University College of North Wales, Bangor

Havel V 1978 The power of the powerless. In: Vladislav J (ed) Vaclav Havel: living in truth. Faber & Faber, London

Heron A, Myres M 1983 Intellectual impairment: the battle against handicap. Academic Press, London

Kay A 1990 Clarifying community care. Senior Nurse 10(4): pp. 6–8

Lalljee M, Abelson R P 1983 The organization of explanations. In: Hewstone M (ed) Attribution theory: social and functional extensions. Blackwell, Oxford

McGee J J et al 1987 Gentle teaching: a nonaversive approach to helping persons with mental retardation. Human Sciences Press, New York

McGrath M, Grant G 1990 Supporting 'needs-led' services: implications for planning and management systems. Centre for Social Policy Research and Development, University College of North Wales, Bangor

Mead G H 1934 Mind, self and society. University of Chicago Press, Chicago

Mechlin J 1986 The Jamesian Berger. In: Hunter J D and Ainlay S C (eds) Making sense of modern times: Peter L Berger and the vision of interpretive sociology. Routledge & Kegan Paul, London

Meltzner B N, Petras J W, Reynolds L T 1975 Symbolic

interactionism: genesis, varieties and criticism. Routledge & Kegan Paul, London

Nakhnikian G 1963 John Dewey 1895–1952. In: Alston W P, Nakhnikian G (eds) Readings in twentieth century philosophy. Crowell-Collier Publishing, New York

Perrin B, Nirje B 1990 Setting the record straight: a critique of some frequent misconceptions of the normalization principle. In: Brechin A, Walmsley J (eds) Making connections: reflecting on the lives and experiences of people with learning difficulties. Hodder & Stoughton, London

Report of the Independent Review of Residential Care (Chaired by Wagner G) 1988 Residential care: a positive choice. National Institute for Social Work. HMSO, London

Secretaries of State for Health for the United Kingdom 1990 The National Health Service and Community Care Act. HMSO, London

Sutcliffe J 1990 Adults with learning difficulties: education for choice and empowerment. National Institute of Adult Continuing Education, Leicester

Swain J 1990 Learned helplessness theory and people with learning difficulties: the psychological price of powerlessness. In: Brechin A and Walmsley J (eds) Making connections: reflecting on the lives and experiences of people with learning difficulties. Hodder & Stoughton, London

Wolfensberger W 1983 Social role valorization: a proposed new term for the principle of normalization. Mental Retardation vol 12, No. 6, 234–239

World Health Organization, 1980 International classification of impairments, disabilities and handicaps. World Health Organization, Geneva

Wright K 1990 Creating a market in social care: the problems for community care. University York Centre for Health Economics, York

CHAPTER CONTENTS

Introduction   229

The nature of profound multiple handicap   230

The effects of profound multiple handicap   232
Sensory handicaps   232
    Hearing   232
    Vision   233
    Speech   233
Physical handicaps   234
    Physical deformities   235
    Patterns of physical disability   236
    Primitive reflexes   236
    Other physical phenomena   238
Behavioural disorders   239
Mental handicap   240
    A new group of people with profound multiple
    handicap   241

Management   241
Preventing further deterioration   241
    Positioning and handling   241
    Correcting asymmetries   244
    Managing physical problems   247
Developing functional self-help skills   249
    Feeding   249
    Dressing   256
    Toileting   257
    Personal hygiene skills   259
Developing a system of communication   260
    Helping the person communicate   260
    Pain and distress   261
    Augmentative and alternative communication
    techniques   261

Beyond basic care   262
Attaining mobility   262
Promoting rest   262
Recreation and play   264
Safety   264

Alternative treatment methods   265
Snoezelan   265
Conductive education   265
Progressive patterning   266

11

Helping with multiple handicap

P. Bradley   P. Darbyshire

Key points

- The person with profound multiple handicap has a complex set of needs unique to him
- Providing effective care requires a holistic and systematic approach
- Effective total care requires close cooperation between a large range of carers and professionals
- Helping with activities of daily living provides a basis for the development of the individual's abilities
- Eclecticism is a legitimate strategy in care

INTRODUCTION

The treatment and care of a person with a profound multiple handicap involve addressing and managing a wide range of associated conditions and complex problems. To this end, the role and function of professional carers are vital. The expertise of therapists from all areas of the caring world must be incorporated into a coordinated client-centred approach to care. So diverse are the potential problems presented by individuals with profound multiple handicaps that a single profession unilateral approach to management may only deal with a fraction of the problems which that person has. It would be fair to say that no professional programme of education intends to, or can, prepare practitioners to fully

Note: This chapter has been revised for this edition by
Patrick Bradley, based on the original version
prepared by Philip Darbyshire for the first edition.

meet the comprehensive needs of a person with profound multiple handicap.

In order to secure an approach to care which has the optimum chance of meeting the varied needs of individuals with profound multiple handicap an interdisciplinary approach to care is advocated. In advocating multiprofessional practice in caring this text cannot limit itself to addressing the needs of any one group of workers. Indeed the reality is that many facilities composed of different professional disciplines, will be asked, at least in the midterm, to facilitate the needs of individuals with profound multiple handicap. For this reason, this text describes the functions and offers principles of care which professionals from all disciplines can utilize.

Professionals, when charged with the responsibility to meet the needs of individuals under their care, must be prepared to share their specialist skills, knowledge and experience within the care team. They must also be willing to approach, work with and learn from the competent practice of other skilled professionals. In short, the interdisciplinary approach to meeting the care requirements of the profoundly multiply handicapped should encourage carers to share their skills and learn new skills from others, to the benefit of individuals with profound multiple handicap.

In the past, authors documenting specifics of care have been served well by the practice of using the condition of cerebral palsy as a vehicle for exploring the nature and effect of profound multiple handicap on individuals. There are, without doubt, similarities in the disabilities which can be found in the two conditions. However, the inclusion of cerebral palsy within Chapter 6 of this book provides a more than adequate résumé of that specific condition and allows this chapter to view profound multiple handicap from as broad a perspective as is possible. Much of the following, therefore, remains as valid in caring for individuals with cerebral palsy, and a degree of mental handicap, as it is in caring for individuals who have profound multiple handicap. Readers are therefore encouraged to approach both chapters as being complementary in nature.

THE NATURE OF PROFOUND MULTIPLE HANDICAP

There has been much discussion recently within the care sector concerning the definitive features of both profound mental handicap and profound multiple handicap (Kiernan & Moss 1990, Hogg & Sebba 1986a, Browning et al 1983). This discussion has enabled clinicians to use similar terms almost interchangeably, and also led to a subsequently increased degree of unnecessary confusion among professionals as to the extent and prevalence of the problem.

Profound mental handicap, as a descriptive term, has been in common usage in the educational provision of the Strathclyde area during the period of the Browning survey (1983). When asked to elucidate on the meaning of that term, headteachers from within that area's specialist provision identified individuals with profound mental handicap as displaying:

- multiple handicaps
- little or no language; difficulties in communication
- stereotyped behaviours; often withdrawn
- limited self-help skills
- needing constant and careful supervision.

The expectations of experienced professionals in the field of mental handicap care were clearly that individuals diagnosed as profoundly mentally handicapped would present difficulties which were many but which were not exclusive to the presence of a mental handicap. 'Multiple handicap' appeared to be a more apt descriptor.

Such findings were not peculiar to Scotland. Pressland (1982) describes 'special care children' as displaying a typical portfolio of disabilities. Such people were seen to have no language, were barely ambulant, displayed difficulty in manipulating objects, were unable to feed, dress, or toilet themselves, displayed severe behaviour problems and were thought of as having a profound degree of mental handicap.

The results of these studies allow justifiable inferences to be drawn. Within the teaching profession in the United Kingdom there appeared to be some anxiety over the relevance, and descriptive suitability, of the definition of profound mental handicap. Within this one area of care the nature of profound multiple handicap is seen to be imprecise.

In practical terms, the use of a multitude of divergent terminologies to describe and define an almost typical group of similar problems presented by individuals who have multiple handicaps may serve only to fragment and polarize the expertise of all caring professions and cause confusion amongst carers.

This confusion over the formulation of precise terminology which carers and clinicians might use to describe the effects of profound multiple handicap is by no means confined to the teaching profession alone. One need only read through the reference material dedicated to describing profoundly handicapped individuals to appreciate the scale of the problem which surrounds appropriate definition.

Almost every care-providing profession perceives such individuals differently, while utilizing varying descriptive terms for what is ostensibly the same client group. Indeed, as the Browning study indicates in a clear manner, within care sectors different terms are in use to describe the same symptoms and disabilities.

The origins of this dilemma can be traced back to the practice of equating an individual's mental ability (or lack of it) with an intellectual performance, established by the subjective process of intelligence testing. Common practice within this framework has customarily accepted that profound mental handicap is characterized by Intelligence Quotient (IQ) scores of less than 24 (Grossman 1983). The reliability and usefulness of determining the presence and severity of mental handicap exclusively by this procedure has led writers to question the validity of this practice.

Critics of this system insist that the tools used in the measurement of IQs rarely relate to exact measurements of vision, hearing or physical impairments, all of which contribute to cognitive ability and are affected by the presence of profound multiple handicap. Individuals with such handicaps are disadvantaged by an inherent failure within the process, in whole or part, to recognize the detrimental effects of those learning handicaps on that person's capacity for scoring in intelligence testing. Subsequently, intelligence, when quantified in such a fashion, can only be a small part of any meaningful definition of profound multiple handicap.

Indicative of that school of thought the findings of studies (Kiernan & Moss 1990, Hogg & Sebba 1986a, Browning et al 1983) provide sufficient evidence to suggest, with some degree of authority, that in people who have a profound level of mental handicap a high prevalence of additional impairments to that individual's learning capacity will also be found. Those additional impairments correlate directly with the handicaps identified within the Browning et al and Pressland studies.

Such disabilities can best be examined by using the broad categories of:

- sensory handicaps (including auditory, visual, and oral disabilities)
- physical handicaps (represented in a degree of impairment to full mobility)
- behavioural disorders (involving self or others)
- mental handicap or learning difficulty (some degree will usually result, if only as a consequence of the effects of the related impairments) (Fig. 11.1).

What is more difficult to determine is the degree of mental handicap and the relationship between that learning impairment and the additional handicaps which might be present.

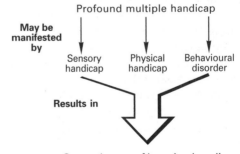

Figure 11.1 The relationship between profound multiple handicap and mental handicap.

THE EFFECTS OF PROFOUND MULTIPLE HANDICAP

In the past, due to the difficulties associated with accurate diagnosis, little comprehensive empirical data existed which detailed the handicaps of individuals with profound multiple handicap. What was true of the past cannot be held to be the case today. Recent shifts in health care trends and cumulative social policy review have encouraged clinicians and researchers alike to look more closely at the effects of profound multiple handicap and address the implications of providing a good quality of care to this group.

The results of this work, much of which is embryonic in nature, offers indicative rather than definitive insight as to the effects of profound multiple handicap and should be viewed as such by readers.

Sensory handicaps

(This section should be read in conjunction with Chapter 8, *Helping with Sensory Impairments.*)

Problems associated with hearing, vision and speech are difficult to quantify and qualify. In the same way as indications of cognitive function are dependent upon replies which can only be represented in motor function, quantitative assessments of specific sensory capacity, or defect, employ procedures which rely on the respondents related ability in motor, cognitive and social functioning. Sensory abilities too often demand cognitive and motor elements which cannot be assumed to be present in people with profound multiple handicap (Jones 1991).

Sensory impairment as a term, whether generic or relating to a specific sensory function, is intended to cover a broad range of sensory loss from partial to total incapacity. As such, the true prevalence of sensory deficit may never be fully established within groups or individuals.

Hearing

The profoundly multiply handicapped person may suffer from many specific problems in this area. Ball (1991) suggests that hearing impairment can be divided into two important areas: conductive loss and sensorineural loss.

Conductive hearing loss is caused by anything which impedes the transmission of sound entering the ear while on its journey to the nerve endings in the cochlea. Effects can vary from a relatively mild form of high or low tone deafness to complete, and far more serious, loss of hearing. The most common condition leading to a conductive hearing impairment is 'glue ear' caused by a build-up of fluid behind the ear drum itself, which may manifest as painful or painless. Milder forms of this condition are transient in nature. However, a prolonged episode of glue ear will lead to infection which interferes with the conductive mechanism of sound, causing hearing impairment.

Sensory neural hearing impairment is caused by malformation or significant damage to the auditory nerve, or the cochlea, which transmits sound signals from the inner ear to the sound centres of the brain. Damage to the auditory cortex of the brain itself would also cause sensory neural hearing loss.

In general terms, conductive types of hearing impairment are curable and can be alleviated by treatment of causal factors. Otitis media, an infection of the structures of the middle ear which is responsible for much of the incidence of partial hearing loss, can be treated, with expectation of complete recovery, by short-term antibiotic therapy. An obstructive build-up of cerumen (wax) within the external ear can also cause hearing difficulties which can be easily and speedily treated.

More profound types of hearing loss are normally sensory neural in origin, associated with organic problems of the inner ear mechanisms which conduct sound waves. Some of these hearing defects are treatable by medical and surgical intervention while others are not.

A person with sensory neural loss might well hear some sounds, leading carers to assume that the person has a selective ability to hear. The effect of such pathological disability only serves to exemplify the difficulties which are associated with objectively assessing hearing in the profoundly multiply handicapped.

Kropka (1983) indicates that 10.6% of the total hospital population under study suffered from a degree of hearing loss. This study goes on to suggest that as the degree of severity in an individual's mental handicap progresses so too does the severity of hearing impairment increase. Furthermore, Hogg & Sebba (1986a) draw attention to these, and other, results as representative of an underestimate of the extent of the problem. Precise audiometric testing is not a typical feature of the care traditionally afforded to individuals with profound multiple handicap.

Kropka's figures appear valid, however, when compared to Browning et al (1983) whose study of profoundly multiply handicapped children returned a comparative figure of 8% demonstrating hearing problems. Kiernan & Moss (1990), in one of the most recent surveys (of a Greater Manchester hospital population) return similar statistics of 6.9% of all tested showing hearing impairment.

In summary, it appears to be the case that at least 1 in every 10 individuals with profound multiple handicap will have a decreased hearing capacity.

Vision

A wide range of visual impairments can be found in individuals with profound multiple handicap. Defects, affecting one or both eyes, can range from fairly minor abnormalities such as strabismus (or squint) and nystagmus (an involuntary rapid movement of the eyeball) to, more seriously, a total or partial loss of function resulting in blindness.

It has been estimated that in hospital wards providing care for individuals with profound multiple handicaps the incidence of complete blindness may be as high as 11% (Warburg 1977). Browning (1983) suggests that 21% of the Strathclyde study showed visual defect (9% blind; 12% having partial sight loss). Kiernan & Moss (1990) found a rate of 7.1% in their study cohort.

Jones (1991) goes some way to explaining away the disparity when he details the difficulties associated with determining the visual acuity of developmentally immature individuals with multiple handicaps. The practice he advocates to achieve a truer representation of visual functioning in this group is a more functional method of assessing the near vision of individuals. This assessment method (using graded sizes of food items in this single case study) shows early promise in producing more reliable results, leading to more effective treatment of visual defects.

Difficulty in assessment method may account for the figures presented by Black (1980) who found visual abnormalities in 78% of cerebral palsied children who also had a profound degree of multiple handicap, or it may represent a true summary of the extent of this problem which carers must address in formulating care plans. What does appear to be clear from reviewing available studies is that the more profoundly handicapped individuals are, the more difficulties are associated with the assessment of their vision (Hogg & Sebba 1986a).

Speech

There are two main contributory factors which will determine the extent of a speech problem in a person who has a profound multiple handicap. Organic causes of speech impairment, found typically in individuals with cerebral palsy, result in difficulties which can present as articulation defects or in complete lack of speech. Secondary factors can then delay vocal abilities. An organic, initial delay can be further enhanced by that person's subsequent exposure to a limited language range. This diminished expectation on the part of carers has been seen to result in the increased use of immature vocabulary (Wehman 1979, Hogg & Sebba 1986a).

Pathological defects, such as paralysis of the muscles which control and regulate movement in the lips, tongue, larynx and pharynx might well render individuals completely without language or, at very least, limit attempts at communication to unintelligible sounds. In individuals who have physical handicaps the loss of ability to emphasize spoken words with gesture and movements compounds an inability to speak. Dental problems, commonly encountered in profoundly handicapped individuals, will complicate speech attainment too. The effects of poor oral hygiene and inadequate dental maintenance will debilitate people with profound multiple handicaps as it would do others. Paralysis of the muscles in the region of the mouth indicates a possible problem in the process of oral clearance. The prolonged existence of food debris in the mouth increases the chances of decay to teeth and gums, with resultant increase in extractions, fillings and toothache.

Quite apart from the effects on the structure, and thereby the function, of such a person's mouth, motivation to speak in an accepted and recognizable style may be diminished.

Studies which detail the incidence of speech difficulties which might be expected within the group of people who have a profound multiple handicap are thin on the ground. Most commentators discuss the relationship between auditory, visual and vocal development and conclude that exact or approximate details are best expressed in terms of communication. While falling short of providing exact incidence of communication difficulties, Hogg & Sebba (1986a) provide a framework by which the vocal deficits of individuals with profound multiple handicap may be recognized within the complex problem of communication.

Effective communication is made of two component parts:

- the general cognitive, developmental and sensory mechanisms which underlie the ability to express semantics of speech
- knowledge of specific meanings which are to be conveyed.

By acknowledging the importance of the sensory components in communication (Ellis 1986, Kropka & Williams 1986), and the knock-on effects that impaired vision and hearing have on the development of language, the reader might be brought to an understanding of the verbal difficulties which a person with a profound multiple handicap can face. Studies offer only conflicting insight into the deficiencies of a specific individual's verbal ability. For this reason carers must be aware of the complex way in which speech is developed

and be prepared to establish the prerequisite ability an individual has in communication (by means of sound assessment techniques), if they are to be effective in developing a form of language for and with that person.

Physical handicaps

Amongst those who suffer the effects of profound multiple handicap, individuals who have cerebral palsy seem most at risk of developing physical deformities. Such deformities can be either unfixed or fixed. An unfixed deformity (occurring in a joint or joints) can, as the term suggests, be manipulated back into an anatomically correct position by physical intervention. This intervention can be actively achieved with the person's assistance or passively carried out by the carer.

A fixed deformity, however, cannot be fully corrected by physical therapy alone. Passive exercise may be utilized to achieve a minimum degree of reduced mobility at the affected joint for that individual but more usually surgical treatment is indicated.

Physical malformation is not the only physical handicap which people with profound multiple handicap may expect to develop. Many individuals will suffer from physical illnesses caused by infections (to the respiratory, urinary and digestive tracts) or due to the side effects of commonly encountered chronic disorders (epilepsy, incontinence and pressure sores). Other physical problems relate directly to the presence of pathological conditions. The prolonged existence of primitive reflexes in cerebral palsy, for example, leads to reduced mobility in many individuals. Immobility causes muscles to atrophy and shorten. Tendons and ligaments lose their elasticity and fixed contractures can result.

If muscle tone is impaired, as in hypotonicity (where the muscle tone is reduced) or in hypertonicity (where the tone is greatly increased), bones can be pulled out of alignment by the abnormal pull of the surrounding muscles and deformities can result.

Asymmetries can arise through muscle imbalance or as a result of the person maintaining a constant preferred position which almost always involves one side of the body only. If an asymmetry is allowed to persist it may lead to an uncorrectable physical deformity. Deformities such as these can often present during periods of growth spurt, such as adolescence.

Physical deformities

Contractures.   If a person's limbs are kept in the same position for a prolonged period of time, for example, sitting in a wheelchair or lying in bed, then the muscle fibres surrounding immobilized joints begin to atrophy and soon (due to inadequate oxygenation) shorten in size. This shortening of muscle fibres results in reduced mobility at the joint with resultant reduced function in the movement of the joint and associated limbs. As the joint becomes increasingly immobile more muscle fibres contract in size until eventually the joint becomes fixed in one abnormal position, causing little or no movement to be possible in the affected limbs.

If contractures are allowed to form, the effect on that individual is progressively debilitating. Contractures occurring in, for example, the muscle groups located in the hand can (given time and lack of intervention) progress along the chain of interconnected muscles until the entire arm is pulled from the normal anatomical position and develops abnormally. Resulting from this misplaced arm position, the muscles of the chest can become contracted and mal-

formed with subsequent knock-on effects presenting within the person's internal organs (such as lungs, liver and spleen).

Smith (1986) details the extent to which such progressive malformation can affect one person and notes the occurrence of chronic indigestion, or heartburn, as a particularly debilitating condition which requires constant intervention on a multiprofessional level.

Windswept hips (Fig. 11.2).   This deformity involves difficulties in movements of the hips. Adduction, flexion and medial rotation are all movements which may be hard to achieve. When lying on his back the person will be unable to move his legs to the midline, instead he will be forced to lie to the side. This position can often lead to dislocation of the hip on the side of the adducted leg.

Spinal deformities (Fig. 11.3).   Malformations in the development of the spine can also occur in individuals with profound multiple handicaps. The most common problems include:

- scoliosis – a sideways curvature of the spine
- kyphosis – a flexion deformity of the spine, where the person's spine will protrude at some point on his back
- lordosis – an extension deformity of the spine (located usually in the person's lumbar region) where the spine curves towards the front
- kypho-scoliosis – as the name suggests this condition is a combination of kyphosis and scoliosis.

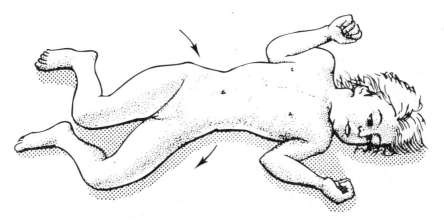

Figure 11.2   Windswept hips.

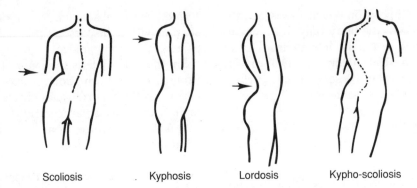

Scoliosis   Kyphosis   Lordosis   Kypho-scoliosis

Figure 11.3 Spinal deformities.

Patterns of physical disability

Unfortunately, all too commonly carers working with groups of individuals with profound multiple handicap will discover typical specific problems in the pattern of immobility each person has. The descriptive classification below may provide a clear and useful framework for carers to discuss and share knowledge of specific treatment interventions which they can then incorporate in their practice:

- monoplegia – only one limb is affected by paralysis
- paraplegia – the lower limbs of the body are affected, normally resulting in flaccid paralysis, attributable to a specific lesion on the spinal column
- diplegia – both lower limbs are usually affected by spastic paralysis
- hemiplegia – both limbs on the same side of the body are affected by paralysis
- quadriplegia – all four limbs are affected.

Golding & Goldsmith (1986) offer a good if rudimentary commentary on the mechanisms which commonly lead to disabled patterns of movement. The danger in using such a classification system is that the individual is typically viewed, and subsequently provided for, in terms of the limbs which are affected by mobility loss. This negative practice serves merely to accentuate perceived difficulties by focusing on the weaknesses of the person and ignoring his strengths. Thus, a person suffering paralysis of one limb only is described as having monoplegia.

The fact that three limbs can function perfectly well is overlooked by this label and concentrates on the negative deficiencies of that person. Carers, if aware of this potential, are best placed to overcome the possible difficulties of a negative approach to profound multiple handicap.

Primitive reflexes

A newborn baby, if observed over a period of time, would be seen to possess a number of behaviours which exist purely due to the innate abilities of humans. No learning could have taken place to explain the existence of these reflex behaviours. They appear to be instinctive and are displayed automatically. Numbered among such behaviours are the ability to suck, grasp, the protective Moro response and the cardinal points reflex (for a fuller discussion see Illingworth 1991 and Inge 1987). These reflex actions are common to all children.

In normal development these reflexive behaviours are refined to become functional. Many reflexive behaviours are built upon to become essential to the performance of larger sophisticated skills in later life. A developmentally healthy child can assimilate the response into his range of skilled behaviour. For example, grasping and sucking is incorporated into the complex behaviour of eating. Alternatively, the reflexive action can be outgrown and the child cease to display it, as with, for example, the cardinal points reflex and the Moro response.

Some children with profound multiple handicap are diagnosed by the existence of reflexive responses well into the time that healthy children have left them behind. For this reason, carers must be aware of the effects of the primitive reflex patterns of movement.

There are many examples of the incidence and persistence of primitive reflex movements. These are defined by reference to abnormal movements. The main categories of movements are described by the following variations:

The asymmetrical tonic neck reflex (ATNR) (Fig. 11.4). A child with this abnormal response will typically respond to the turning of his head to one side by the limbs of that side of the body extending while the limbs of the other side contract. This movement occurs spontaneously and involuntarily as a response to the initial head movement. Therefore, a person in ATNR responds when one arm is flexed by extending the other one with the head turning towards the extended arm also. This response will make face-to-face feeding, for example, very difficult and also prevent the person from being able to bring his hands to his mouth.

The symmetrical tonic neck reflex (STNR) (Fig. 11.5). The effects of this response on the person are similar to the ATNR, with an important distinction. The differing responses of contraction and extension of limbs across the

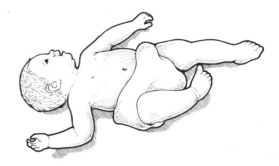

Figure 11.4 Asymmetrical tonic neck reflex activated by child's head postion.

vertical midline of the individual is seen, in the STNR, across the horizontal of the body. A child lying flat, when the chin is raised, will respond by extending the upper body. The head is pushed back and the upper limbs, the arms, stretch out. At the same time the lower body contracts so that the legs are pulled up to the buttocks.

Tonic labyrinthine reflex (TLR). This response is unlike the previous two in that this is not a reflex typically seen in normal development. An increased extensor tone will persist if the child is placed upon his back in a flat position. As a consequence, he will be unable to raise his head and will not be able to sit or bring his arms together at the body's midline. If the child is placed flat

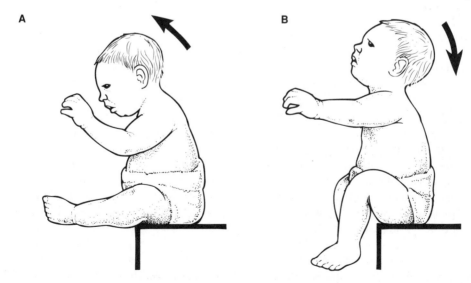

Figure 11.5 Symmetrical tonic neck reflex activated by child's head moving forwards (A) and backwards (B).

on his stomach then the response is a persistent flexor tone. This prevents him from lifting his head, propping upon his forearms, or moving towards an upright or sitting position.

In all of the physical deformities described, carers should expect to find enhanced difficulties when the handicap is found in adults. A combination of factors make this likely:

- prolonged periods of immobility
- the progressive natures of both physical malformation and contracture development
- inadequate physical therapy
- the reduced expectations of carers with resultant reductions in care goals being set (Hogg & Sebba 1986a)
- the effects of the ageing process.

All these factors will further debilitate an individual who has a physical handicap. It is most important then that effective treatment of specific problems be secured and systematic management principles of care be implemented at an early stage of that person's life.

Other physical phenomena

Respiratory tract difficulties. Many individuals with a multiple handicap will encounter specific problems in maintaining efficient respiratory function with consequent inadequacy in the exchange of oxygen and carbon dioxide. This may be due to paralysis of the muscles of respiration or to an associated physical deformity affecting the thoracic cavity (such as kyphosis, lordosis or asymmetrical chest moulding). Prolonged immobility may also result in impaired respiratory function and complicate normal anatomical development.

It is still, unfortunately, the case that some people with profound and multiple handicaps may spend the majority of the day being cared for while lying on their backs, either on bed rest or dressed but placed on the floor upon mats or bean bags. This practice increases the likelihood of the person developing acute episodes of respiratory infection, or hypostatic pneumonia, with subsequent infection due to the secretions of the respiratory tract or, more dramatically, to the inhalation of saliva, regurgitated foodstuffs or vomit. Chaney et al (1979) identify the effects of respiratory disorders as the most common cause of death among profoundly handicapped people.

The main factors which conspire to impair the process of oxygenation in a person with a profound multiple handicap are:

- a reduction in blood volume and red cell mass which alters the carrying capacity of the blood
- venous stasis which decreases cardiac output thus reducing the oxygen transport process to the body's tissues
- restricted chest and lung expansion due to paralysis or other damage occurring in the nervous conducting pathways, resulting in the person's adopting very shallow breathing patterns which limit the movement of respiratory secretions.

Normally, mucus within the tract is swept outward to excretion by ciliary action within the organs of respiration. When a person becomes upright and moves normally the mucus lines the bronchioles evenly, draining by force of gravity. However, when a person is immobilized and in the supine position the mucus in the bronchioles will tend to arrange in pools in the lower extremities of the lungs, with the upper areas becoming dry. This mucus may eventually form into a plug which can then block the structure of the bronchioles, causing a hypostatic pneumonia. Static pools of secretion provide an environment which encourages the growth of bacteria and promotes the development of chest infection. The diameter of the bronchioles also tends to decrease in size when a person is continually placed in the supine position.

Chest infections are usually treated by medical intervention and the prescription of antibiotic therapy. Initially, this may be a broad spectrum antibiotic but could be changed to a drug with a more specific action when the causative organism of the infection has been identified. Administration of drug therapy, observation for side effects, analysis of prognosis, as well as management of the effects of the condition, should all be incorporated into the overall individualized care plan.

The easiest method for the person to take medicines is often in the form of a liquid preparation. Although these preparations, typically suspensions, may appear to be pleasantly flavoured we need only recall our childhood experiences to appreciate the difficulties involved in administering them! Carers may find that the person will need to be encouraged to take the drug or drugs prescribed for him. A pleasantly flavoured drink taken after the medicines helps to remove any natural inhibitions.

There is also a link between recurrent chesty congestive conditions and conductive types of hearing loss (Ball 1991).

Incontinence. Charlett (1990) states that a high proportion of people with a profound handicap will be incontinent. An exact estimate of this high proportion is difficult to gauge, but indicative figures are available for incidence of incontinence among a group of people with cerebral palsy whom Hogg et al (1990) suggest are in one of the three main categories associated with multiple handicap. Urinary incontinence has been reported to be as high as 67% in total population studies (Shaw 1990). In the same study carers (in this case all were families) had only attempted to train half of all of the cerebral palsied children. Shaw (1990) presents a small study which suggests that 97% of individuals with cerebral palsy achieved reliable levels of continence in a 5-week period.

Far from accepting that a necessarily high proportion of all people with multiple handicaps must suffer the effects of incontinence, carers' scarce resources may be better employed in the pursuit of continence rather than in coping with the effects of incontinence. Some individuals, due to the severity of their neurological impairment and the extent of their additional handicaps, could prove to be resistant to benefiting from a toilet training programme. Others, potentially a large majority, may derive significant advantage from this type of intervention, but if carers do not attempt continence planning then the true outcome may never be known.

Epilepsy. The occurrence of epilepsy in people with a profound multiple handicap is common. The MENCAP survey *Profound retarda-tion and multiple impairment* (Hogg et al 1990) states that some 64.3% of all people with a multiple handicap will exhibit some degree of epileptic activity. That the prevalence and severity of epilepsy is seen to increase commensurately with the degree of learning difficulty is being readily accepted by most commentators (Clarke 1990).

A more detailed summary of this condition and the carer's role in managing the effects of epilepsy is given in Chapter 6.

Behavioural disorders

The use of behavioural strategies in the care of individuals with a degree of learning difficulty is often focused on techniques which can be utilized in an attempt to decrease the behavioural excesses of individuals. Thus, the practice of behaviourism is often equated with eradicating those maladaptive, unacceptable, and unpalatable behaviours from presenting in individuals with profound multiple handicap, often at the insistence and discretion of carers who have difficulty managing such manifestations. Zarakowska & Clements (1988) suggest that as many as 50–60% of people with learning difficulties are likely also to present with a significant behavioural disorder.

In relation to behavioural excesses it would appear that there is substantial evidence which suggests that poor communication skills, language problems and physical problems are associated with people who self-injure (Emberson & Walker 1990). It also seems to be agreed that self-injury is more common among the most profoundly handicapped (Murphy & Wilson 1985) and therefore may typically be the type of behavioural problem seen by carers of people with profound multiple handicaps. Face slapping, scratching, head banging, hand biting, skin picking, hair pulling and gouging have all been documented as frequent self-injurious behaviours in people with profound multiple handicap (Oliver et al 1987, Emberson & Walker 1990, Kiernan & Moss 1990).

Presland (1991) provides a fuller description of the range of behavioural excesses with which people with profound multiple handicaps might present. Stereotypies such as engaging in apparently purposeless, repetitive rocking or hand flapping have been reported. Violent episodes, rumination, regurgitation and pica (the eating of unsuitable substances) are also reported.

Hogg & Lambe (1988) report that when asked about the time families spend in caring for their children with multiple handicaps on average in excess of 7 hours per day was spent in a variety of activities which were directly linked to the children's inability to perform certain behaviours. Among this group of behaviours were listed such activities as washing, feeding, dressing and toileting. Barker (1982) called such inabilities 'behaviour problems caused by behavioural deficiency'.

This lack of functional behaviours is clearly as problematic to carers as the range of excess behaviours catalogued above. This inability to perform skills is tackled later in this chapter and also more fully related in Chapter 9 which addresses the role of the carer in managing behavioural interventions. Many individuals with profound multiple handicap will present carers with problems composed of both excesses and deficits in their behavioural repertoire (Barker 1982).

Mental handicap

As was discussed in relation to abilities such as hearing and seeing the assessment of ability is a difficult exercise. Diagnosis of those inabilities may well become fraught with the problem of subjectivity. In much the same way, the accurate diagnosis of a person's mental capacity or ability is a difficult concept to quantify scientifically.

The studies quoted above either explicitly assume the presence of a degree of mental handicap or infer, because of the nature and designated function of the facilities used in collecting the data, that mental handicap is part of the cocktail of disabilities found in people who have a profound multiple handicap. There are implications in such an acceptance.

When the range of documented handicaps related to people who are classed as having a pro-

found multiple handicap is considered (visual, communicative, physical and medical) the main debilitating effect that each individual handicap brings to a person is in restricting the opportunity for that person to learn. Therefore, it could be contended that it is very likely that each individual is in some way learning disadvantaged.

The degree of learning difficulty is the unspecified area in this equation but that may be the variable which carers can exert some influence on. In reviewing the relevance of learning theory to profoundly handicapped people Remington & Evans (1988) are explicit in asserting that there is sufficient evidence on empirical grounds to claim that people with even the most profound mental handicap are capable of at least some degree of learning under certain conditions. It follows, therefore, that the opportunity to learn should be considered. In a person with a profound multiple handicap this may be very difficult indeed, but such opportunities do occur although they may appear very slight.

The person may learn to turn his head towards a stimulus when lying over a foam wedge, try to push his arm into his sleeve when dressing or smile and show pleasure when being handled in a particular way. These improvements may only come after many months of effort from carers, yet they are improvements which indicate that the person has learned.

Purely physical care activities will take up a large part of the person's day and these activities can be viewed as potential learning experiences. Otherwise, physical care may become almost a passive routine whereby the care giver performs care tasks *to* rather than *with* the person. Activities can be used as opportunities to build a relationship. This rapport cannot be established overnight. The person has to become accustomed to his care givers, trust their handling, recognize their voices and sense their affection. It is perhaps unreasonable to expect the person to show signs of progress if these relationships have not been made.

Consistency in approach is an important element in the successful pursuit of learning. In presenting the same activity in the same way the person is afforded the opportunity to become familiar with the activity and possibly to anticipate a response or action. He may become confused if his care is carried out by many people in many different ways.

A new group of people with profound multiple handicap

Jacobson, Sutton & Janicki (1985) suggest that the traditional view of people with a profound multiple handicap being a minority proportion of individuals within the mental handicap care sector is under review. While looking at the percentage ratio of individuals with learning difficulty who were further classed as being profoundly handicapped, Jacobson et al found that 50% of the people in the study were over 40 years of age. Indeed, 40% of the whole sample were over 60 years old, with 20% of individuals with profound handicaps being over 80 years old. Of all the people Jacobson et al studied, 1-in-4 were over 80 years of age. They concluded that the life span of people with mental handicap, as a group, has increased, with individuals living longer than in the past. The effects of this occurrence have not, they concede, been as marked in individuals classed as having a profound degree of mental handicap, but what does seem to be apparent from this work is the principle that, in general terms, as the age of the person with mental handicap increases then the corresponding abilities in function, intellect and sensory capacity diminish.

Enough evidence exists to allow for the suggestion to be made that in future carers may well be faced with an increasingly elderly and more dependent group of people to care for.

MANAGEMENT

A systematic approach to care has been consistently and authoritatively advocated for ensuring that an optimal quality of care is delivered to individuals with profound and multiple handicaps across care settings (Darbyshire 1986, Sines & Bicknell 1985, Green 1985). Indeed, the cumulative weight of government policy as expressed in the National Health Service and Community Care Act (1990) necessitates that care be arranged around the component steps of a systematic approach.

Given the range of problems which will challenge the carers' skillbase in caring for people with profound multiple handicaps, the question is, 'How can the management which is necessary for effective care be best arranged?'. One framework carers could usefully employ is that of achieving three broad but attainable aims. Carers might strive to:

1. Prevent any further deterioration in the abilities of individuals with profound multiple handicaps.
2. Encourage the development of functional self-help skills.
3. Develop some means of communication.

Preventing further deterioration

Positioning and handling

As the majority of people with a profound handicap have physical handicaps resulting in varying degrees of immobility, a large part of the daily care of such a person involves helping him to adopt a posture and positions which benefit the daily activities of living. A programme aimed at good functional positioning actively prevents secondary physical deformities from developing.

It is important that the team involved in care includes a qualified physiotherapist who can organize programmes of movements, exercises, positions and strategies for prevention of deformities. Physiotherapy staff can advise and inform the day-to-day work of carers and ensure the ongoing provision of integrated physical therapy to the person.

Sitting. The importance of being able to sit upright is often overlooked by carers who can perform this function routinely and almost subconsciously. The person who is left for long periods of time in the lying position is deprived of the benefits of sitting upright. The environmental interaction for such a person is often restricted to that of a passive view of one particular area of the ceiling as information has to come from above. Achievement of a more upright posture results in the presentation of a more dynamic environment which can provide opportunity for spontaneous stimulation (Fig. 11.6). The sitting position also provides the opportunity for the person to begin to be more actively involved in activities such as feeding and playing.

Difficulty in attainment of adequate independent trunk and head control makes it impossible for the person to achieve such postures alone. It can, however, be achieved by provision of appropriate support. A specially constructed wheelchair, for example, can provide both support and increased comfort. There is a danger, however, in using the wheelchair to exclusively achieve that necessary support for an individual in all circumstances. The person can become dependent on the chair and be confined to it for long periods of time.

The attainment of good postural positioning can also be achieved by use of a body brace which will provide improved support to the spine and prevent deformities from occurring or progressing. Such braces are normally made from materials which mould to the exact contours of the person's body, providing support where it is needed. As the person grows such supportive braces need to be modified, and perhaps recast, if the brace is to perform its function adequately.

There are management problems when using aids, however. For example, the chafing effect

Figure 11.6 Sitting properly.

of a poorly fitting or ill-used support brace can have damaging effects on the person's skin.

Nonambulatory people who have good postural control can often benefit from having their own wheelchair. In such circumstances these chairs are required to provide good postural support which contributes to sitting balance. Modifications, such as chair footrests which prevent the person's feet from dragging on the floor, also offer a sound anchor base for the maintenance of a sitting posture which enables functional movement. Adaptations to the chair may also include side supports which prevent the person toppling over. For individuals who tend to slide forward when sitting a groin strap harness can be fitted to correct this problem. As well as securing a comfortable position for the person the harness will help prevent further postural damage to the spine. Chairs can be fitted with a table so that the person has the opportunity to handle objects more easily.

The principles of sitting which relate to wheelchairs can also be applied to any ordinary chairs which the person might have occasion to use.

Finally, in relation to the sitting position, in recent years the use of beanbags has become fashionable. These objects, while useful for individuals with little physical handicap, appear to offer little support to the seated but immobile person and therefore should be used advisedly. When placed on a beanbag a person with multiple handicaps derives little spinal support and often ends up in an uncomfortable curled position with flexed arms, scissored legs, and his head tipped backwards away from the presentation of stimuli.

Standing. In addition to securing a beneficial sitting position the carer might also attempt to secure for the person a variety of other therapeutic positions. By widening the range of positions in which he can be placed an important goal is achieved in his development. Positioning variety can aid the development of the neuromuscular system, maintain the integrity of the skin and accommodate the experience of new stimuli.

The person with a severe physical handicap can be helped to experience the standing position for short periods during the day by the use of standing frames. These boards usually incline at an angle of approximately 45°. The person is placed against the board and support straps are fixed to the legs and trunk. The board has a table at about shoulder height so that the person can engage in some activity with his hands (Fig. 11.7). There are also special tables which have cut-out sections where the person can stand supported by straps and a back piece. In this position the person can enjoy play and practise functional skills on the table top.

Lying. There are times during the day when the person may lie down for a nap or simply lie as another variety of position. However, persistently lying on his back will encourage deformities, such as scoliosis and windswept hips and increases the risk that he might also inhale secretions or vomit (Fig. 11.8). Many alternative postures can be chosen; for example, in the side lying position the person is laid on a floor mat with a pillow or sandbag at his back to prevent him from rolling over. In order to absorb any secretions which drain from the mouth a pad or tissue can be placed under his face. Another pillow or wedge can be placed between the hips to keep them in abduction (Fig. 11.9).

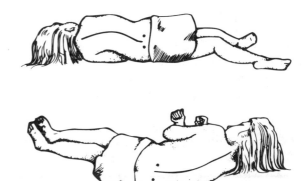

Figure 11.8 Uncorrected side-lying positions encourage deformities.

Both hands can then be brought forward and in children some toys can be placed within their reach to encourage spontaneous movement. If a prone lying position is chosen, then the person can be placed lying over a foam wedge. This has an advantage over flat lying in that the person will find it much easier to use whatever head control he has, and also to reach out for toys or objects which are placed within his reach. This position is especially good as it encourages the adoption of a symmetrical body position.

Hand function. Many people with profound multiple handicaps have difficulty in using their hands due to the very limited range of movements associated with this condition. This means that they will not be able to bring their hands to the midline as readily as nonhandicapped individuals where hands can then be looked at and played with. This can also happen if the person is poorly positioned.

Even if a good range of shoulder and arm movements is present the person with cerebral palsy in particular, but multiply handicapped

Figure 11.7 Prone standing board in use.

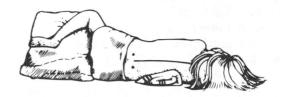

Figure 11.9 Wedge placed between hips to keep them in abduction.

people in general, often have no ability to grasp. The thumbs are flexed across the palm of the hand and the fingers clench tightly over it. The wrist is often also bent to a degree which renders its function useless.

Care staff can help the person to become more aware of his hands during their daily activities with him. Positioning is again very important in enabling the person to have his hands in front of him where he can more easily see and play with them. Not only is it dangerous to allow his hands to dangle over the sides of his wheelchair but also this offers him little therapeutic benefit.

Care staff can stimulate awareness of hands when carrying out activities such as bathing. Gently open the clenched hand by first straightening and turning out the arm. The hands can then be soaped and rubbed. Special 'feelie mats' and surfaces of different textures offer a variety of tactile sensations. Some jam or syrup placed on a finger may encourage a child to bring a hand to his mouth. Noisy toys, such as rattles, fixed in position to the hands may also stimulate movements.

Correcting asymmetries

One of the aims of good positioning and handling of the handicapped person is to try to counteract the detrimental effects of asymmetries of the body and to attain symmetrical postures and movements. It is important to be particularly aware of the person who sits with his head turned to one side, or the person who uses the same arm and hand continually, or the person who is able to 'bottom-shuffle' along the floor but always using the same side of the body. These patterns can be discouraged by stimulating the use of the other side of the body, e.g. by talking to the person from the other side or presenting material to the person's least-used hand.

Handling. Care staff who are inexperienced in working with severely handicapped people often show a degree of reluctance and uncertainty when handling the handicapped person. This is very understandable, for a very frail multiply handicapped child often looks as though he might break were he to be lifted too roughly. However, this reluctance to handle can often lead to the person being restricted and deprived in his level of movement, range of experiences and opportunities for learning. Also, he will be deprived of much-needed physical contact through touch and careful handling. Careful handling by all care staff is important if the person is to have a wide range of movement experiences and helps to ensure his comfort during carrying and positioning; it can also help to prevent the development of secondary physical deformities.

Specific handling techniques may be decided upon after discussion with the physiotherapist; however some general guidelines should be followed.

Handling should always be done gently and carefully. Tell the person what you are about to do. Never snatch or grab him suddenly, as unexpected movements can frighten the person and increase spasticity or trigger off abnormal reflex patterns. It is also important to maintain symmetry when working with the person.

When helping the person to move from one position to another, perform the movement slowly in order that he is given the chance to participate actively where possible.

When lifting the person who has very little postural control of his head, trunk and limbs, do not pull him up by the hands, leaving his head to hang backwards. Instead, raise him gently by holding each shoulder.

Avoid carrying the severely handicapped person as if he were a baby, with one arm under the shoulders and another behind the knees. This encourages spinal curvatures, allows the person no chance to move actively and greatly reduces the visual field (Fig. 11.10). It is better to carry the person, if possible, astride your hip or abdomen with his legs well parted. This encourages outward movement of the hips and bending of the knees. While one hand supports the person's bottom the other can support his back which will be much straighter. The person's head is now in a better position for looking around and engaging in conversation (Fig. 11.11).

When handling the person always encourage

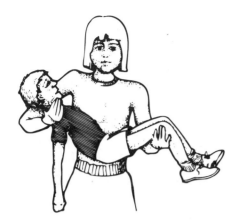

Figure 11.10   Unsupported carrying position (incorrect).

Figure 11.11   Supported carrying position (correct).

any purposeful movements which the person initiates, for example, helping to push an arm into a jumper sleeve.

There is little merit to be had in handling people with profound multiple handicaps using sound therapeutic techniques if those techniques are detrimental to the carer. Both the care giver and the person must have confidence in the handling. If the person feels insecure this can cause him to go into abnormal reflex or spasm patterns.

If the carer is injured during lifting procedures then the danger of dropping the handicapped person is increased. Also, the carer's ability to perform effectively is compromised and his or her health and employment state diminished.

For more detailed advice, and illustrations

showing how to handle the physically handicapped person correctly, readers are referred to Nancie Finnie's widely recommended book *Handling the Young Cerebral Palsied Child at Home* (1990). Although primarily intended for parents who are caring for their handicapped child at home it contains information and clear illustrations which would be invaluable for care staff working with the person with a profound multiple handicap.

Physical deformities.   The person with a severe physical handicap is prone to the development of secondary physical deformities. As well as creating problems for him, these deformities pose problems for care staff. It is difficult to dress a person with an incontinence pad whose hips are so tightly drawn together and legs so scissored that they cannot be separated. Similarly, trying to put a pair of trousers on to someone whose legs are severely contracted in the bent position is problematic.

There are, as previously stated, many factors which may contribute towards the development of physical deformities. A knowledge of these factors is the first step towards preventative care.

Prevention of deformities.   Frequent changes of position should be planned throughout the day for the person with profound multiple handicap. He should be encouraged to experience regular varied movements which follow as normal a pattern as possible. Both passive and, where possible, active movements have a part to play. Passive movements, however, while preferable to no movement at all, are to be viewed as merely a substitute for movements initiated and performed by the person himself. The use of passive movements alone in mobilizing people is not an entirely acceptable goal for carers. The danger of a regime built entirely on passive exercise is in the possible interpretation by care staff of such task orientation as simply picking up limbs and putting them through a limited range of movements (Seivwright 1982) while failing to use this contact as an opportunity for therapeutic interaction with the handicapped individual. At the same time, a unilateral regime of passive movements may also neglect important areas such as the hips and spine. Of far greater benefit to the person is a planned programme of functional movements and positions which can be used as part of all of the person's daily activities (Finnie 1990, Levitt 1983).

Attempting to force or stretch spastic muscles will only increase the level of spasticity. Instead, the limb will benefit from very gentle and smooth movements. Massaging the muscles may help to decrease the level of spasticity within the muscle. Music and movement classes can also be helpful in providing the person with a scheme of exercises and beneficial movements. To be effective these sessions should be held on a regular basis and, where possible, with the guidance of the physiotherapist. The exercises may be entirely passive to begin with; the person will eventually develop a conditioned reflex whereby he will recognize a particular tune and move appropriately.

As group exercises these sessions provide an invaluable communal activity, something that is often missing in the lives of severely physically handicapped people. Individual exercise sessions also have a part to play as they can be adapted, depending on the nature of the person's handicaps (Fig. 11.12).

Pool activities can provide many benefits for the person with profound multiple handicaps; they:

- provide a change of environment
- encourage relaxation
- improve circulation
- encourage autonomous active movements
- promote leisure and play activities.

This is an area where the direct care staff and the physiotherapist can work very closely together.

Some general points regarding the management of the profoundly handicapped person who has superimposed physical handicaps can be made:

1. Techniques of moving, positioning and handling are not the exclusive province of the physiotherapist but should be part of the skills of all carers involved with people who have profound multiple handicaps.
2. It is impossible to divorce the techniques and principles of good positioning and handling from the person's activities of daily life, such as feeding, sleeping, sitting and moving. It is counterproductive to divide the person into 'areas' for each therapist, such as mouth for the speech therapist or limbs for the physiotherapist. All disciplines must cooperate and work effectively to provide total care for the handicapped person.
3. Programmes of positioning and exercises must be repeated regularly and frequently to

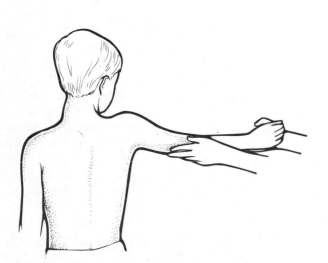
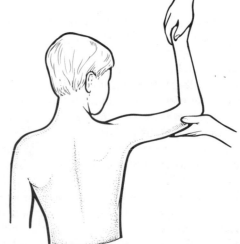

Figure 11.12 Passive movement to straighten the arm.

be effective. Instant results are neither looked for nor expected.

4. The needs of each person will be different due to the wide variety of manifestations handicaps may take. The nature of each individual person's handicaps has to be considered and his care planned accordingly.

Managing physical problems

Despite being given a high level of care the person with profound multiple handicap might still develop infection. Commonly this infection will occur within the respiratory tract and present as a chest infection. For this reason, and in order to commence appropriate treatment as early as possible, carers must be familiar with the range of symptoms which suggest the presence of infection:

- difficulty in breathing (dyspnoea)
- prolonged rise in body temperature (pyrexia)
- persistent cough, which may produce expectorated mucus and pain when breathing
- noisy, bubbly respirations which can be heard as the person breathes
- loss or reduction in the appetite
- general listlessness
- pallor, which in extreme cases of dyspnoea may give way to a bluish colour (cyanosis), indicating serious respiratory distress.

Skin care. The person with profound handicaps, due in large part to restricted mobility, is in constant danger of developing sores or decubitus ulcers. Such sores can be difficult to heal, especially in the debilitated person. For this reason, and also because of the pain and discomfort that they cause, the prevention of pressure sores is a constant concern and is a key aim for carers. Factors which predispose to the development of pressure sores are:

- immobility
- thinness and debilitation
- damage to the central nervous system, including sensory loss
- having unusual bony prominences due to physical deformities

- incontinence, with possible consequential skin breakdown
- iatrogenic factors (factors resulting from care practices), such as the person being pulled up into a sitting position rather than being lifted, or being left in one position, such as lying in bed or sitting in a wheelchair for several hours
- vascular factors, such as peripheral vascular disturbance resulting in poor circulation.

Prevention of pressure sores. The prevention of pressure sores is not an isolated treatment carried out once or twice a day but an awareness of the problem which informs the actions of all carers as they work with the handicapped person. Basically, pressure sores are caused by unrelieved pressure. The person, therefore, requires to be moved frequently throughout the day. Pressure sores can develop just as easily while he is sitting in a wheelchair as they can lying in bed. Changes of position are seen as part of the person's total care as this is also an integral part of maintaining good postures and positions, and in preventing secondary physical deformities.

Regular and frequent checks are necessary to ensure that the person with incontinence is not left in a wet or soiled condition, as this can lead to skin breakdown. The integrity of the person's skin can be checked when undressing, changing and bathing, particularly for any areas of redness.

There are several areas of the body where pressure sores are most likely to develop and these areas should be examined especially carefully. The sacrum, heels and ankles, hips, shoulders, occiput (back) of the head (especially in hydrocephalus) and the buttocks must all receive particular attention.

If an area of redness is noted it is vital that all pressure is kept off this area. The practice of vigorously rubbing a person's skin in order to stimulate the circulation has been shown to increase the likelihood of pressure sores developing (Dyson 1978). This practice should be abandoned in favour of brief gentle rubbing when washing the skin.

Clinicians (Rithalia 1992, Fletcher 1992) are now suggesting that preventive care is best served by addressing such causative variables as dietary factors. Diet is clearly an important aspect in the prevention of pressure sores (Bader 1990, Fletcher 1992). The aim is to help the person to achieve the best possible nutritional status for his height, build and physical condition. A diet high in calories and protein may be appropriate for the person who is susceptible to developing pressure sores.

The clear message is that prevention is patently a better strategy than relying on curative measures. A more detailed overview of the pathogenesis, prophylaxis and treatment of pressure sores can be found in Bader (1990).

Other skin problems. In common with most young people the handicapped person going through adolescence may suffer from acne. Skin cleanliness helps prevent pores becoming blocked and a proprietary deep cleansing lotion may be useful after routine face washes. If the acne is very severe an antibiotic, such as tetracycline, may be prescribed. If the person tends to rub or scratch the affected areas his nails should be kept clean and short in order to prevent further skin abrasion and infection.

People who have to wear any kind of orthopaedic brace or appliance may suffer from skin abrasions, redness or sores. This is especially common if the appliance is new, has not been put on properly, has been outgrown by the person and is now too small or where the person has to wear plaster of Paris casts following orthopaedic surgery.

Dental care and oral hygiene. Healthy teeth and gums are important because they allow proper biting and chewing, help in proper speech development and give an attractive appearance. In addition to the range of problems which can affect the nonhandicapped person, such as dental caries, gum disease and toothache, the person with a handicap may be faced with the following dental problems:

- *Malocclusion* is commonly found in people with cerebral palsy. The teeth are irregularly arranged in the jaws which results in the accumulation of food debris with a consequent rise in the level of decay and gum disease. Malocclusion also adversely affects the person's appearance.

- *Bruxism*, or tooth grinding, is more common in severely handicapped people and can result in increased and irregular wear on the teeth.
- *Poor oral clearance* can occur because many profoundly handicapped people lack the ability to use their tongue and lips effectively. This can result in an excessive build-up of plaque on the teeth and an increase in decay and gum disease. Some profoundly handicapped people who also suffer from epilepsy may experience difficulty in clearing food from their teeth and gums, due to hypertrophy or overgrowth of their gums caused by the use of certain anticonvulsant drugs.

Other dental problems can be created for the person if he is receiving a diet which consists of sugary foods. Programmes involving the use of sweets to reward good behaviour can also unintentionally increase the chances of tooth decay occurring.

Should the person with severe communication problems develop oral pain or toothache he may be unable to communicate this effectively to his care givers, resulting in periods spent in pain and discomfort. If a profoundly handicapped person were to lose his teeth through decay it is less likely that he would be able to cooperate in the wearing of dentures.

Toothbrushing. There are many practical difficulties involved in efficiently cleaning the mouth of a severely handicapped person. He may dislike the procedure and offer resistance to it by constantly moving his head and biting on the toothbrush.

The object of toothbrushing is to remove plaque from the teeth, to remove food debris from spaces between the teeth and to massage gums. Even people without teeth benefit from brushing. An additional aim is to leave the person's mouth feeling clean and fresh. In normal practice it is best to use a fluoride toothpaste but in special circumstances, where the person has a particular problem, such as dental plaque or inflammation of the gums (gingivitis), a chlorhexidine gel may be used (Gibbons 1983).

A good position for toothbrushing is to stand behind the person while supporting his head and opening his mouth with the free hand.

When using this method it is important to let the person know that you are going to clean his teeth, in order that he is not suddenly frightened. Another position, suitable for adults, is for the person to sit on the floor below the care giver who can sit on a chair and hold the person's shoulders with his legs. This leaves both hands free for toothbrushing.

The wide range of toothbrushes available makes choosing the correct type difficult; however, a small-headed brush allows better access to corners of the mouth. A dentist or dental hygienist may help in the selection of the proper toothbrush for each person. It is best to replace toothbrushes approximately every 2 months.

Oral hygiene. Profoundly multiply handicapped people often breathe through their mouths. This can cause the mouth, tongue and lips to become dry and cracked. If left unattended this condition can lead to an increased risk of tooth decay and unpleasant halitosis. To prevent this the person can be given regular small drinks to help to keep his mouth moist. Lips can be treated with petroleum jelly smeared around the mouth: this prevents chafing and cracking. The mouth itself can be cleaned occasionally with a solution of sodium bicarbonate in tepid water or a chlorhexidine preparation, both of which prevent the formation of harmful plaque and gingivitis.

The process of washing the mouth can be achieved by means of a clean gauze swab wrapped around the person's or carer's finger; alternatively, a proprietary brand of foam-topped spatula can be used.

Dental hygienist. One of the most effective improvements in dental services for people with a mental handicap has been the increasing use of the dental hygienist. The hygienist has an important role to play in the prevention of dental and oral problems through regular dental inspections and treatments, and can offer direct care staff much in the way of advice and information. The hygienist, therefore, has an important role to play in teaching good dental care practices not only to the person with the handicap but also to his carers.

The person should receive a dental examination at approximately 6-monthly intervals. Most people are usually apprehensive at the thought of a visit to the dentist and the profoundly multiply handicapped person may also find this a frightening experience. An experienced care giver who has a good rapport with the person is best-placed to accompany a multiply handicapped person to the surgery. This carer should make sure that all the information the dentist may require is available (such as records, the care plan and prescription sheets which list any medication that the person is receiving). The carer is then available to stay with the person and assist the dentist and hygienist, by helping with communication, for example, but more importantly by providing comfort and support to the person having treatment.

Developing functional self-help skills

There are a host of skills within the domain of self-help which offer advantages both to the carer and the individual with a handicap. This chapter concentrates on four main areas of skill:

- feeding
- dressing
- toileting
- personal hygiene.

These have been chosen because, as common problems, they offer scope to discuss generic principles which can be applied to, and utilized in, teaching more specific skills to individuals with profound multiple handicaps.

Feeding

Common feeding problems. Factors which directly affect the external organs of digestion can further complicate the process of feeding in a person who has profound multiple handicap. Bulbar palsy, causing paralysis of the muscles which regulate movement of the lips, tongue, larynx and pharynx can lead to pronounced problems in coughing and swallowing functions. This makes coordination of these structures, which is so essential for effective chewing and swallowing, almost impossible to achieve.

Serious problems in feeding will, if not overcome, increase the dependency of the individual on others, thereby increasing the handicap. In addition to the obvious outcome of diminished nutritional state, feeding difficulties can lead to more serious problems. Regurgitation, rumination and choking all serve to differentiate between, and devalue further, the social status of individuals with multiple handicaps. They also constitute a potential life-threatening episode for the person with the handicap. Inhalation of foodstuffs following digestive irregularities can commonly lead to inhalation pneumonia.

Occasionally, the care provider encounters a person who has increased salivation. This will increase the difficulties which that person may have in swallowing and as a result the person may drool continually. This hypersecretion may be attributable to problems in the swallowing reflex mechanism or to the side effects of particular drugs.

If the person is very floppy (hypotonic) and has little or no postural control, most noticeably in the area of head control or in cases of severe spasticity, he may adopt a characteristic position of hyperextension where the whole body is stretched out in extension. In this position it is almost impossible to feed the person properly.

The existence of involuntary reflex responses may also complicate a skill which most of us take for granted. The person may have such severe neurological damage that he possesses only infantile sucking and swallowing reflexes and will be unable to progress to biting and chewing. If, on the other hand, he exhibits a strong sucking pattern, then tongue thrust may be a problem, i.e. the tongue tends to push food out of the mouth rather than gathering it and taking it backwards into the mouth.This can lead to much of the person's meal being lost.

A bite reflex is another serious feeding problem which affects many people with profound handicaps. When the person's lips or gums are touched (especially with a metal spoon) he clamps his mouth closed tightly. This means that either food cannot be put into the mouth or that he will bite hard onto the spoon until the spasm ends. This can be a very painful and unpleasant experience for the handicapped person. Try

biting on a large ball of silver paper to get some idea of how this might feel!

The handicapped person may also have physical abnormalities affecting his oral region, such as an abnormally high palate, unusually large tongue or dental malocclusion. A cleft lip or palate may also be present in very young children who have not yet had these abnormalities surgically repaired. If the person is not given any opportunities to try more solid foods, then he never learns to bite or chew and infantile sucking patterns, with associated tongue thrust and spillage, persist. There are other problems associated with the persistence of a soft diet, such as a resultant weakness of muscles of feeding and speech. These can result in poor lip closure and consequent persistent dribbling of saliva. The presence of specific enzymes in the saliva can cause skin breakdown around the person's mouth, chin and neck and persistent drooling can also necessitate frequent changing and washing of clothing. The nature of drooling is such that it can lead to the person being shown less consideration and reinforcement and may also lead to his experiencing rejection (Purdy 1987). Positive results in reducing drooling in particular circumstances have been reported, however. For an expansive discussion of treatment techniques see Lancioni et al (1989).

Facilitating patterns of feeding. One of the most basic skills we all learn is how to feed ourselves. This is an obvious nutritional necessity, but the ability to feed in an efficient and tidy manner is demanded by society if we are to be socially acceptable. This area, however, is one where the profoundly multiply handicapped person is almost certainly going to experience a great deal of difficulty (Ayer & Alaszewski 1984). Indeed, many people are unable to feed themselves and are completely dependent upon carers to ensure that their nutritional needs are met.

Positioning. Positioning and the maintenance of correct posture in the person with a profound multiple handicap are important factors in encouraging functional feeding patterns. As a general rule, the supine or flat position should be avoided. Laying the person flat on his back while feeding him can lead to a fatality – should the person choke, regurgitate food or vomit when in this position the foodstuff might be inhaled. The upright position seems best suited to feeding procedures as any secretions or foreign bodies will be prevented from passing into the respiratory tract (Fig. 11.13).

In certain circumstances, where the person's physical condition precludes an upright posture, a side lying position can be substituted. The use of a pillow or similar support, placed behind the back, will prevent the possibility of his accidently rolling into the supine position.

Developing normal feeding patterns

Sucking. Sucking is a reflex mechanism which is present at birth or shortly afterwards. It is an important survival mechanism. Sucking is achieved by closing the lips around the nipple or teat to prevent the intake of air instead of liquid. To suck efficiently there must be a negative pressure inside the mouth in order to draw in the liquid. This is achieved by tight closure of the lips around the teat or nipple and by the back of the tongue raising to the soft palate to prevent air entering the mouth from the nose.

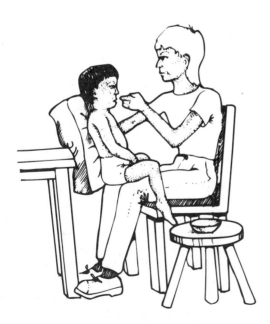

Figure 11.13 Using the upright position for feeding.

Swallowing. This is another reflex mechanism, which is stimulated by the bolus of food touching the back of the throat. Although swallowing is automatic the ability to chew and form the food into a bolus and pass it to the back of the throat is not.

Biting and chewing. These abilities develop with the introduction of more solid food into the child's diet and with the emergence and growth of the first teeth. Unlike sucking and swallowing, biting and chewing are skills which the child must learn.

Head control. The head is the first part of the body which the child learns to control. This is an essential part of the development of feeding and many other functional skills. Achievement of good hand–eye coordination, for example, is dependent upon the attainment of head control. This ability will enable the child to bring food to his mouth using his hands. In general terms, the nonhandicapped child is able to eat using a spoon and with fairly little spillage by about 2 years of age.

Drinking. Initially, a newborn baby sucks from the breast or bottle instinctively. By around 9 months he can drink from a feeding cup with a mouthpiece. At around 15 months he can drink from an ordinary cup, even if rather messily. By 18 months–2 years of age a child is usually capable of drinking from an ordinary cup with little spillage as his lip closure has improved greatly.

Management of feeding problems

Positioning. As previously suggested, probably the most important aspect of developing good feeding technique is the person's position. Inexperienced carers often attempt to feed a handicapped person by tilting his head backwards or by laying him on his back. They may explain that this will help him swallow his food more easily and cause less mess due to food spilling from his mouth. In fact, this practice is potentially dangerous and should be discouraged (Fig. 11.14). Any attempt to feed the person who is in a flat lying position severely limits the field of vision and sensory experience. It also accentuates the outstretched extensor position which

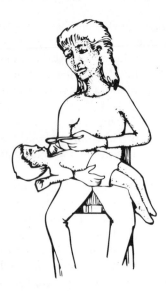

Figure 11.14 Dangerous practice – feeding child tilted backwards.

must be counteracted for success to occur. The most urgent consideration, however, is that of safety. The person is very likely to gag or to choke while feeding if he is fed in a reclining position. This is a common cause of inhalation pneumonia and, subsequently, death among profoundly multiply handicapped people, many of whom have impaired cough and swallow reflexes. To appreciate just how difficult it is to feed in this position the reader is encouraged to lie on his or her back and try to drink from a cup with a spout or a bottle.

The basis of a good position for feeding is that the person is sitting upright. This is something which can be achieved even with the most severely physically handicapped person. He should be seated in a comfortable and properly fitting chair. This means that his hips should be flexed and his bottom should be well to the back of the chair. A groin strap can be used to help prevent him going into the extensor position and perhaps sliding off the chair. A good upright position can also be achieved when the person is sitting in a wheelchair. For the young child an excellent feeding position is for him to sit on the carer's lap, facing the carer, with his hips flexed and legs astride those of the carer. The child's back and shoulders can

be supported by a pillow laid against the edge of a table.

Whichever position is chosen it is important that the carer sits in front of the person to feed him. This face-to-face feeding is especially important with the sighted person who may learn actions such as opening his mouth by watching and copying the actions of the feeder.

Preparation of food. A well-balanced diet includes adequate fats, carbohydrates, protein vitamins, minerals, water and roughage. Several important aspects of nutrition should be considered when planning the diet of the profoundly multiply handicapped person. If, for example, he is confined to a wheelchair and is either totally immobile or has very reduced mobility then his energy requirements will consequently be reduced. A poorly balanced diet coupled with reduced levels of physical exertion can result in his becoming obese, which will make his physical management more difficult.

A much more common problem is the person who is underweight for height. This is especially common in people with severe cerebral palsy and those who have very pronounced feeding problems. Experienced carers will recognize the characteristic features which accompany this state of undernutrition, such as diminished growth, poor skin lustre, tendency towards constipation, listlessness and reduced spontaneous activity. This undernourished state can be extremely difficult to correct once established, even with intensive effort from the entire care team. The person's diet may have to be radically altered to consist of several small snacks per day rather than two or three main meals. Foods high in calories and protein can be chosen with the help of a dietitian or nutritionist. These may be everyday foods, such as carbohydrates and starches, or special preparations such as 'Hycal' drinks. Vitamin and iron preparations may have to be included as a dietary supplement for the profoundly multiply handicapped person. These can be given in an easily taken liquid drops form, such as Abidec multivitamins.

When ordering food or planning meals it is important to ensure the provision of a good dietary pattern which will meet the person's requirements for all nutrients. This can sometimes be difficult when carers have to rely on a large hospital kitchen which by its very nature is involved in mass catering. A more individualized and improved standard of food can often be achieved for residents by involving the catering manager or dietitian in discussions and the planning of the management of the person's feeding problems and special nutritional needs.

Variety in diet. The actual manner in which the food is prepared will depend on the feeding capabilities of the handicapped person. The most severely impaired people may require to have all meals liquidized and puréed. They may be able at a later stage to progress to more solid foods. Carers tend to underestimate the ability of the person to progress to eating more solid foods. It is undesirable for the handicapped person to be kept on a liquidized diet and not be given the chance to learn to bite and chew more solid foods. This progression is best made gradually, from liquidized to mashed or minced food and then to solid food, but may not be possible for all profoundly multiply handicapped people. It is hard to tell who is capable unless foodstuffs are varied in a planned and systematic way.

Another important aspect of food preparation is that the person's likes and dislikes are respected. It occasionally surprises some carers that a person who is thought to be incapable of almost any mental functioning can indicate a like or dislike of a particular food. Carers who are familiar with particular individuals will have a knowledge of their preferred foods. For those not yet in this position a trial and error system of tasting can be embarked upon but not before friends, relatives or prior carers are used as a source of this information. It would be petty and harsh for carers to attempt to force this person to eat food which he shows that he dislikes or to deprive him of a particular favourite food on the grounds that it is 'pandering to his food fads'.

The amount of food which is served is also important. The profoundly multiply handicapped person may require less food because of his lower level of physical activity. As a general rule, it is better to serve frequent small meals rather than one or two large three-course servings. When offered too much food at one sitting the person is more likely to vomit or regurgitate the meal. Frequent small meals also offer more opportunities to practise developing good feeding patterns.

Overcoming specific feeding difficulties. Problems such as tongue thrust and bite reflex are very difficult to overcome, especially in older people if they have become firmly established.

Bite reflex. Bite reflex is stimulated by touching the sensitive area around the mouth and gums; it is increased by the use of metal spoons which can be avoided. The use of metal spoons can also cause traumatic damage to the person's teeth and gums. An unbreakable plastic or polythene spoon is preferable when feeding a handicapped person with a strong bite reflex. Occasionally stroking the person's mouth and gums prior to mealtimes can help to desensitize this area.

Tongue thrust. Tongue thrust may be overcome by placing a small spoonful of food on the front of the person's tongue as it is being put into his mouth. His lips can then be helped to close over the spoon. The most widely used method of overcoming tongue thrust is for the feeder to place alternate spoonfuls of food into the rear side of the person's mouth between his back teeth. In this way the tongue is less able to push the food out.

Poor lip closure. Poor lip closure is a common cause of food spillage from the person's mouth. When placing the spoonful of food into the mouth, the food is not scraped off the spoon by the person's top teeth. This happens when the person is usually fed from above and is not given the chance to try to use his lips. The feeder can gently push the person's top lip down onto the spoon to pull off the food. The feeder can also encircle the person's head with her arm and use the first two fingers of one hand to help hold the person's lips closed.

Finnie (1990) provides a description of this and other helpful techniques which carers can utilize in an effort to increase independence in feeding for the profoundly multiply handicapped.

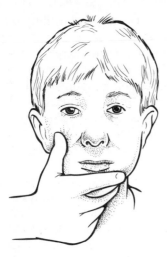

Figure 11.15 Three-fingered jaw control.

The three-fingered lip control method has proved to be particularly effective. This procedure achieves an element of control in the mechanical aspects of chewing thereby allowing the handicapped person to participate in the successful eating process. The carer can secure the person's jaw by placing the thumb on the jaw joint, the index finger between the chin and lower lip and the middle finger under and behind the chin. By applying constant firm pressure the mouth is insulated from involuntary movements and the movements used in chewing can be simulated and regulated (Fig. 11.15).

Choking and gagging. Choking and gagging are also common difficulties. Often, the cause of choking is simply that the feeder is trying to feed the person too quickly. When feeding another person it is necessary to feed at the person's own rate. Speeding this process up will result in a great deal of spilled and dribbled food plus an increased chance that the person will choke or vomit. The person may occasionally choke or gag if there are lumps in his food to which he is unaccustomed. For this reason, new and more solid foods should be introduced gradually. Another very common cause of choking and gagging is that the feeder has tilted the person's head too far backwards while feeding him. This practice is dangerous.

Care staff are encouraged to learn an effective way of helping the person who is clearly choking during a meal. The most favoured method is the Heimlich manoeuvre (Richards 1977). When using this technique the care giver stands behind the choking person, puts both hands firmly under his diaphragm and pushes upwards. This forces air from the lungs upwards thus dislodging any food or foreign bodies trapped in the person's glottis. If there is any object or particle of food visible in the person's mouth this can be hooked out with a finger.

The person may have difficulty in chewing and swallowing, especially if he suffers from a bulbar paralysis. Chewing can be encouraged by offering the person pieces of toast, biscuit or apple to chew on. This will be extremely difficult for the person and instant success should not be expected. The feeder can help him to chew by gently manipulating the jaw in chewing motions.

Occasionally the person may have difficulty in swallowing. He may retain a mouthful of food for an extremely long time without swallowing or may have a very uncoordinated swallowing mechanism. The feeder can help to stimulate the person's swallow reflex by gently stroking under the person's chin. The head must remain forward, however, as a reclining head position makes swallowing very difficult.

Drinking. Drinking efficiently can pose extreme problems. It is important to maintain the person in an upright position as drinking is even more difficult and dangerous for the person if he is tipped backwards or lying down. Feeding cups with spouts are often used to give drinks to multiply handicapped people but are rarely used properly. They are not intended for pouring fluid into the open mouth of the person from a height of several inches. This will not improve his ability to drink from a cup.

A good position is to stand behind the person while supporting his chin and lower lip with your hand. Place the rim of the cup between the person's lips and tip the cup until he is able to take fluid into his mouth. Avoid tipping his head backwards and close his lips to help him to retain and swallow the fluid. If the person has great difficulty in swallowing fluids without choking and gagging then a slightly thicker fluid can be tried, or drinks can be thickened with a proprietary brand of thickener.

Hydration. Dehydration is a potential hazard as the person may be unable to ask for a drink or even to indicate thirst by gesture. Neurological damage may even have impaired his sensation of thirst. The carer who is having a busy day may think that drinks are too messy or time consuming and may leave them 'until later', which can result in the person having a very poor fluid intake. Common signs of dehydration to watch out for are dry tongue, wrinkled skin and decreased urinary output, with an associated increase in the urine's concentration bringing with it a distinctive smell. If this dehydration becomes more severe then the person may suffer from constipation, weight loss, anorexia, lethargy and confusion.

Special equipment. There are a great many aids and pieces of special equipment which may be of use to some profoundly multiply handicapped people. Cutlery can be specially manufactured or ordinary cutlery adapted by adding built-up handles; plates and bowls are better if they have a wide base because they are then less easily tipped over; a high-sided bowl or plate helps with scooping out food; non-slip mats help stabilize bowls and plates and two-handled mugs promote bimanual activity and are more stable. For most people mealtimes are social occasions. Their purpose is not simply to ingest food and drink but to enjoy the food and conversation. For the profoundly multiply handicapped person living in institutional care, however, these events are rarely enjoyed. Indeed, Oswin (1978) described mealtimes in wards for profoundly multiply handicapped children as being 'the crisis of feeding'. Mealtimes were viewed by care staff as occasions when the ward routine could easily be hindered. Food would often arrive late or in an unsatisfactory condition from the kitchen and might have to be returned. The meals could be delayed and 'run in' to staff meal breaks. Perhaps one or two care staff were left to organize and feed 20 or more people with very severe feeding problems. They often had to cope with shortages in essential equipment such as bibs, plastic spoons and other aids. If mealtimes were not completed within a certain time care staff also risked being criticized by other therapists for not having the children ready for school or therapy in time.

Clearly, this overall atmosphere of mealtimes being a chore which must be accomplished as quickly as possible is against everyone's best interests. It creates tension among care staff who worry about getting people ready in time.

Carers were also seen to worry about their own abilities to feed those people with serious feeding problems but for inappropriate reasons. Often, they were not concerned about feeding the person correctly and paying careful attention to his specific problems and nutritional needs but were worrying about whether they could get the food inside the person as quickly as other staff could. Failure to do this can lead to the carer being viewed as less than capable of feeding 'difficult' people. This rush to complete mealtimes does not benefit the handicapped person and reduces mealtimes to the level of mere refuelling stops.

Thoughtful, basic care can make all the difference to feeding technique. Try not to put spoonfuls of food into the mouth of an unsuspecting person who has had no prior warning of its arrival. He may well be trying to cope with food already in his mouth or be about to swallow or cough or sneeze when, unannounced, the next heaped spoonful is inserted. Nonhandicapped people do not eat meals at breakneck speed and in a stony silence. We ought not to expect the profoundly multiply handicapped person to do this for the sake of keeping ahead of the routine.

Establishing good feeding patterns is important for the multiply handicapped person. It is not only important from a purely nutritional point of view but also because good feeding patterns are important for the possible future development of speech and also in the development of good sitting postures and coordination. Mealtimes are also potentially very valuable sessions between the care giver and the handicapped person where communication can be established.

The management of feeding problems is a good example of an area where multidisciplinary cooperation is essential if progress is to be made. The advice of a physiotherapist would be helpful regarding the most suitable feeding positions for people with various degrees of physical handicap. The physiotherapist can also advise on positions and techniques which will help to counteract undesirable reflexes, such as extensor and asymmetrical tonic neck reflex. The advice of a speech therapist should be sought regarding actual feeding techniques which will help overcome problems such as tongue thrust and bite reflex and help to establish proper patterns of eating and drinking. If it is thought that the handicapped person will be able to make some progress with self-feeding, then an occupational therapist could provide specialist advice on the most suitable feeding aids for that individual such as special cutlery, plates and mugs and, where necessary, demonstrate their proper use.

Dressing

Selection of appropriate clothing. When we choose clothes to wear we do not think only of protecting ourselves from the weather but of many aspects of clothing. We may wish to cover parts of our bodies to preserve our modesty or we may wish to show off parts of our bodies. We also reveal a great deal about our beliefs, attitudes and position in society by the way in which we dress. Sadly, the same amount of thought is often not shown when clothing is selected for the profoundly handicapped person, especially in living environments which have institutionalized practices.

The clothes which some people in residential care wear immediately proclaim to the world that they are different. For this reason, perhaps it is wise to attempt to ensure that carers who are aiding or advising on the purchase of clothes are of approximately the same age as the intended wearer. Dressing people in colours and styles which are incongruous with their ages and lifestyles results in their looking every bit as institutionalized as the grey shadowy figures who have walked the corridors of some of our large institutions in the past. Carers who appreciate the important role which clothing plays in the life of the handicapped person will realize that clothing and grooming can have a marked effect on the attitudes and behaviours of those who come into contact with the handicapped person.

There are special considerations which carers make when selecting clothing for the profoundly multiply handicapped person. Wherever possible the handicapped person should be given the opportunity to participate in selecting his own clothing. This may not be possible for the most profoundly handicapped person, but even the very severely handicapped person may be able to indicate a preference for a particular colour or garment by a subtle gesture, such as a nod or a smile.

If the person is not present when clothes are being bought for him it is important that carers have an accurate list of his current measurements; guesses should never be made as the person may be small for his age and may have physical deformities. The clothes may require to be loose fitting as tight clothing can cause skin irritation and discomfort. Tight clothing can also inhibit movement, make any physical deformities more obvious and can be very difficult for the person to put on and take off, especially if he has only a limited range of movements.

The profoundly handicapped person may require several changes of clothing in any one day, as a result of incontinence or feeding difficulties but with the enormous range of choice of attractive, and relatively cheap, clothes available in shops and stores today there is no justification for the handicapped person being stigmatized as a result of his dress.

Dressing and undressing. It is likely that most profoundly handicapped people will only be able to offer minimal assistance and will require to be helped in the process of dressing by their carer. It is important that all of the person's clothes are assembled and ready before beginning to help him to dress. This saves the carer from making repeated trips to the wardrobe and disrupting the dressing exercise. Dressing affords the carer the chance to show the person a good position, to help make him more aware of his body, to perform a limited range of passive movements and to communicate with him through talking and careful handling.

Depending on the nature of his physical handicaps the person will be dressed while in either the sitting or lying position. It is a good idea to vary the position used for dressing in order to provide some variety of movement experience for the person. Lying on the back on every occasion is not particularly beneficial. If the person has a more affected side this is dressed first. Try to straighten gently any stiffly flexed limbs and put the limb into the sleeve or trouser leg rather than pulling the clothes over the flexed limb and missing an opportunity to exercise it.

It is essential to talk to the person as you dress him. Explain what you are doing, name the different parts of his body as you dress them and talk about the colours of the clothes. Sighted people may enjoy being dressed sitting in front of a mirror where they can follow their movements as they get dressed. Carers should observe closely for any sign of active cooperation from the person such as pushing an arm into a sleeve, and encourage such developments.

People enjoy being told how nice they look or how pretty their clothes are. An ultimate, if not immediately achievable, aim for the profoundly multiply handicapped person will be the progression towards some degree of independence in dressing.

Toileting

The processes of eliminating waste products from the body are essential to health; however, the whole area of helping the person with elimination may not be afforded the priority it deserves. The successful elimination of waste products from the body is not likely to feature highly in any list of topics of conversation. It is, however, an elementary function which must be maintained in caring for profoundly multiply handicapped individuals. In order to attain optimal levels of health for such individuals the process of eliminating body waste

products must be addressed. Yet, despite the fundamental importance of this task, and bearing in mind the implications of failing to manage successful excretion, the daily management of elimination is often left to the most junior or untrained care staff.

The aims of carers in the management of elimination should include the following:

1. Attempt where at all possible to attain continence for the person.
2. If merely ensuring that the effects of incontinence are minimized then:
   — ensure that the person is kept as clean and dry as possible
   — prevent secondary problems due to elimination difficulties, such as constipation, urinary tract infection, faecal impaction or skin breakdown.
3. Carry out toileting procedures with due regard for the person's right to privacy and physical comfort.
4. Keep the handicapped person's environment as pleasant and odour free as possible.

When attempting to achieve a degree of continence for the person with profound multiple handicap, carers must be aware of the latency period between achieving total continence and any level of deficit in function. Subsequently, an integral part of continence training must be the management of bouts of incontinence.

Urinary incontinence. It is very important that the incontinent person is checked at frequent intervals throughout the day to ascertain whether he is dry or wet. If he has been incontinent of urine he should obviously be changed immediately on discovery. The normal pH of urine is between 5.5 and 7 which is acidic. If urine is left for a length of time it will react with bacteria on the body and become alkaline. This is the cause of the characteristic 'ammonia' smell of a wet incontinence pad which has not been changed for a long time. In either its acidic or alkaline state urine can rapidly cause skin irritation and breakdown, even to the extent of causing a urine 'burn' which is similar in appearance to any burn caused by corrosive chemicals such as acids or alkalis.

It is important, therefore, when changing the person that the skin around his perineal area be carefully cleaned with soap and water and dried afterwards, with special care being taken to dry the skin folds around the groin. A barrier cream such as zinc and castor oil can be used to protect the skin. A wide range of incontinence aids is available. Advice can be obtained from incontinence advisers as to what might best suit a particular individual.

Certain routine observations can be made when changing the person. His skin should be checked for any signs of redness or rashes which may be the first indication of an impending pressure sore or other skin breakdown. The carer may also use such an opportunity to smell the urine for an unusually strong smell, the presence of which may indicate that a urinary tract infection is present or that the person is dehydrated and his urine is overconcentrated. If the care giver suspects either of these causes it is advisable to check the person's temperature. An increase in temperature (pyrexia) may be an indication of systemic infection. The person's intake of fluids should also be increased and it would be wise to record exactly how much fluid he receives daily. A clean specimen of urine may be required for bacteriology tests to identify definitely whether or not an infection is present.

Faecal incontinence. The goals of management in urinary incontinence in multiply handicapped individuals are also applicable to the person who is incontinent of faeces. The same frequency of checking and even more scrupulous washing and drying during changes is required.

Observations of the person's skin condition can also be made while changing. Any abnormalities of the faeces should be noted; for instance, if they are unduly loose and foul smelling this may indicate a gastrointestinal infection. Stools which are very hard may again indicate dehydration. Other abnormalities can be detected by observation of faeces, such as blood and intestinal parasites like tapeworm.

Preventing complications. One of the most important aspects of the management of elimination is the prevention of complications arising from the person's disordered patterns of elimination. The range of potential problems faced by the individual is great and as such requires a multidisciplinary approach to management. In this way, a comprehensive approach to the benefit of the individual will be secured.

Many people with profound multiple handicaps are prone to recurrent episodes of severe constipation. Several factors are responsible for this:

1. The level of immobility causes weakening of the abdominal and perineal muscles.
2. Gastric motility is reduced.
3. The person's diet may contain insufficient roughage and dietary fibre.
4. The person may be receiving insufficient fluids. If he is kept in the lying position for long periods of time normal stimulation of the urge to defaecate is reduced.
5. There may also be specific neurological damage affecting the nerve supply to the gastrointestinal tract.

As severe constipation is a painful and distressing condition it is important that carers are aware of the various measures which can be taken to minimize the possibility of its occurrence. Frequent exercise plays an important part in the prevention of constipation. The provision of suitable exercise for the profoundly handicapped person is closely interrelated with programmes of physiotherapy and positioning for daily activities. Dietary measures also play an important part and the diet should contain a high percentage of fibre or roughage which can be found in foods like wholemeal bread, green vegetables, fresh fruit, bran cereals and baked beans. The person also requires an adequate fluid intake.

Despite careful attention to exercise and diet some profoundly impaired people will require regular help from laxatives or enemata. This should be administered under the guidance of a doctor. In residential care settings there should be a clearly recognized policy for the administration of these medications. Oral laxatives are preferable to suppositories or enemata as they do not involve invasion of body privacy and are much less uncomfortable for the handicapped person.

Where oral laxatives are found to be ineffective a laxative suppository or an evacuant enema may be prescribed. An important principle to remember before administering any laxative or evacuant enema is that the carers must be sure that the stools which are to be passed will be soft and formed. If this precaution is not taken then the profoundly handicapped person may have to strain in severe tenesmic pain and distress trying to pass a large bulk of very hard stools. Anyone who has experienced such pain will vouch for its severity.

If the person has not had a bowel movement for several days then a rectal examination may be indicated in order to ensure that the stools are sufficiently soft not to cause pain and discomfort when they are passed. Should it be discovered during examination that the stools are unduly hard, then a stool softening preparation such as dioctyl medyl syrup or perhaps an olive oil enema can be given prior to attempting evacuation of the faeces.

One of the most serious consequences of disordered bowel function is that the handicapped person may not have a bowel movement for such a long period that he develops faecal impaction where a large mass of hard faeces occludes the bowel and is very difficult to remove. Faecal impaction may make the person appear irritable and distressed. If the carer were to palpate the person's abdomen he or she may be able to feel the mass within the bowel. This diagnosis can be confirmed by means of a rectal examination, if necessary. If the mass is low down in the descending colon it will be easily felt. Carers should be alert to the possibility of faecal impaction in the person prone to constipation. This condition has often been misdiagnosed and the person sent to the local general hospital suffering from an 'acute abdomen' or 'query appendicitis'.

The signs of faecal impaction are sometimes deceptive in that small amounts of faeces often leak around the site of the impaction giving the false impression of regular or even loose bowel movements. For this reason, many experienced carers hold as a truism that a diagnostic sign of constipation is diarrhoea. If faecal impaction is suspected or discovered the person may have his level of fluid intake increased. Providing the site of the impaction is low down the carer can often remove it by very gently removing small pieces of the impacted mass at a time using a well lubricated glove. If the mass is higher up in the bowel then further medical advice should be sought. Manual evacuation of faeces is a very unpleasant and distressing event for the person, particularly if he does not understand the necessity for it. The procedure should always be carried out with the greatest care and with due regard to the privacy of the person.

The other most common problem associated with disordered bowel function is diarrhoea. This is often caused by simple dietary indiscretion but occasionally it may have an infective cause, as in gastroenteritis or dysentery. In a unit caring for larger numbers of people with profound multiple handicaps these and similar infectious disorders tend to spread at a rapid rate. Physical isolation of the infected person or persons, and the instigation of a barrier regime with scrupulous hygiene measures, may prevent the spread of these and similar infections.

In a residence where a large number of residents are incontinent it is the responsibility of the carers to ensure that the environment remains as pleasant and odour free as possible. Smells of urine and faeces which are present long after toileting procedures have been carried out make working and living conditions very unpleasant for all concerned. Unpleasant odours will be reduced if the incontinent person is washed and changed immediately, and soiled or wet linen is put directly into the appropriate receptacles, which should always be covered by a lid (if bags are used, they should be tied at the neck). Receptacles are kept in one prespecified area where the door can be closed. The unit must be well ventilated and windows opened where weather and climate permit. Proprietary air fresheners can be used in areas prone to unpleasant odours.

Personal hygiene skills

The maintenance of a high level of personal

hygiene is very important for the multiply handicapped person as any neglect can result in physical problems, such as skin disorders, and perhaps a reduced level of social interaction. Extra care is required if the person is incontinent or prone to excessive perspiration, due perhaps to his wearing special aids or appliances, or to his sitting in a plastic or vinyl-covered wheelchair for long periods.

The person will benefit from a daily bath or shower, preferably in the morning prior to the day's activities. A daily bath is essential, not only to ensure skin cleanliness and freshness but also to perform several other important functions. Bathtime gives the carer the opportunity to examine the person's skin closely for any signs of redness or rashes which may indicate an incipient pressure sore. Any urine or sweat rashes or other skin irritations can be noticed also. Bathtimes also provide an ideal opportunity for play, fun and stimulation between the person and his carer.

Privacy is an important fundamental right of the individual during bathing and carers must take steps to ensure that this principle translates well in to practice.

When bathing the severely physically handicapped person it is important to wash carefully those 'awkward' areas such as skin folds, the inguinal areas and in between clenched hands. Any crusts which have formed in the nose or eyes should be removed by gently cleaning with a moistened cotton-tipped bud. Careful drying after the bath is important as areas which are left wet can cause chafing and soreness of the skin. Before dressing, talcum powder or deodorant may be applied to the skin at the discretion of the individual. Zinc and castor oil cream can be smoothed over the perineal region prior to putting on the person's incontinence pad if they require this layer of dressing. Carers should avoid the excessive use of toiletries. It may be uncomfortable for the person if talc and cream are allowed to cake into lumps on his skin, thus negating their purpose.

Hair should be shampooed frequently with a shampoo suited to the person's hair type. People with persistent dandruff will benefit from a shampoo with anti-dandruff properties many of which are easily available in commercial form. If practical, and desired by the individual, wet hair can be dried by use of a hairdryer. This will not only achieve the desired end of drying hair but will allow for personal interaction and provide extra stimulation for the profoundly handicapped person.

Developing a system of communication

Helping the person communicate

Although communication is discussed in more detail in other parts of this book, several aspects are very closely related to the care of the profoundly multiply handicapped.

The handicapped person may have many problems which will make communication between him and his carers difficult, such as the inability to speak or indicate his needs by gestures; there may also be sensory problems which further augment communication difficulties. When so much of a person's day may be involved in purely routine aspects of care, communication between the person and his carer must become an integral part of these care procedures. When carrying out any care procedure with the handicapped person communication and rapport with the person can be established by using every available channel of communication – verbal and nonverbal – including play, touch and handling.

It is often difficult for carers to see the importance of talking to the handicapped person who seems not to understand or respond. This seeming lack of response often leads to the carer giving up attempts at verbal communication. However, the development of responses and building of rapport take some time and carers should not become discouraged if immediate responses are not forthcoming.

The carer can try to vary her voice to make it as understandable and interesting as possible in order to evoke a response from the person. A funny voice or a whisper in the ear can sometimes produce a smile. Nonverbal forms of communication, such as the use of facial expression by the care giver, can give greater emphasis to what is being communicated. Touch is a very important system of nonverbal communication in all care settings and can be incorporated with ease into care practice. Feelings of affection, security and fun can all be conveyed by touch and handling. For example, the way in which a person is lifted from his bed or carried to the bath can be done in such a way as to let him experience warmth, security and enjoyment.

Fun and enjoyment can also be conveyed by tickling, and through games such as 'round and round the garden' and 'hickory dickory dock'. Seemingly unresponsive children will often smile and show pleasure during such simple physical contact exercises. Many strategies can be employed to stimulate the sensory impaired child. Tactile signs can be used as a substitute for other forms of communication. For example, the presence of a particular carer might be announced to a person with profound multiple handicap by blowing gently on their face. In much the same way sensory cues can be used to represent the arrival of dinnertime or bedtime (see Ch. 8). A wealth of advice on the provision of a multisensory environment can be found in the NDBRA's interesting and readable *Stimulating the Sensory-impaired Child* (1989).

Pain and distress

One of the vital areas of communication with the profoundly multiply handicapped person is that of detecting any signs of pain, distress or discomfort which the person may be showing. Nonhandicapped people can indicate pain or distress relatively easily. They can complain of pain and describe and locate it. They can use gestures to point to painful areas or to relieve the pain by, for example, holding a sore head or stomach. They call also cry, groan and moan very expressively. There are, however, many people with profound multiple handicaps, susceptible to painful and uncomfortable conditions, who are unable to make known their pain and discomfort by any of these means.

Attempts to indicate pain and distress may be very subtle and detection of such signs calls for acute powers of observation on the part of the care staff. The signs include:

- crying – which may not be loud, overt crying and is often unaccompanied by tears
- vocalizations – grunts, groans and moans
- facial expressions – grimaces or 'pained looks'
- nonverbal body communication – holding the jaw when there is toothache or drawing up the knees when there is abdominal pain
- undirected aggression – self-injurious behaviour
- movement disorders – any movement pattern which is abnormal for the person, e.g. restlessness, fidgeting and fussing behaviours or, alternatively, a reluctance to move
- eating disorder – loss of appetite is a common feature of pain and distress.

The signs and signals may be such a subtle change in the person's behaviour pattern that they may only be noticed by the observant carer who is experienced in working with the particular individual. For this reason, in residential care settings, information about how the person indicates discomfort or pain can be gathered from parents, friends or carers and written in the care plan or case notes where this information can be easily accessed by new care staff or other therapists.

Carers should not underestimate the importance of this aspect of communication. If the carer has limited knowledge in this area, or has poor observational skills, then the person can be left to suffer pain and distress. This is incompatible with achieving the best possible quality of care for the handicapped person.

Augmentative and alternative communication techniques

The use of augmentative forms of communication is an increasingly frequent practice (Snell 1987, Arthur 1989). Augmentative communication refers to the use of aids or techniques which supplement the existing vocal or verbal communication skills which the person has. Alternative systems of communication can be used by individuals without the ability to express themselves vocally (Mustonen et al 1991). A person with a communication difficulty, regardless of his level of physical and cognitive development, possesses at least a rudimentary means of expression and as such has potential to acquire additional skills which can indicate needs and desires.

There are many forms of speech enhancing communication systems which can help such development (Reichle et al 1991). The choice of a particular system will be determined by the extent of language deficit the person presents with and the ease by which this new language can be used and understood by both sides in the communicative process. It would be misleading to criticize the wealth of augmentative and alternative communication techniques which have been seen to effectively aid the abilities of communication-impaired people without reference to the specific abilities and needs of the individual.

As the potential point on the spectrum of communication ability and need is best known by the individual and his carers, it is inappropriate to be discursive here. However, we can direct carers to further, more detailed reading and stress the development of relationship and common meaning as the prime elementary requirement for building an effective communication system with and for people with profound multiple handicap. The final decision on choosing a system of communication is not the care giver's but the care receiver's and as such there is no requirement for formal systems to be used; many good communication systems are developed on a daily basis between carers and those they care for.

BEYOND BASIC CARE

If the basic aims of care can be incorporated into the daily life of the person with a profound multiple handicap then carers can begin to address other important facets of care which will increase the quality of that person's life. Indeed, if a systematic, comprehensive assessment of an individual's abilities and needs is used to determine priorities of care which do not require the intervention detailed then carers may substitute different aims of care which, are more relevant to the person's well-being then that of the above. Some of these aims may be drawn from the following passages which detail additional care objectives.

Attaining mobility

As discussed earlier in this text, the use of handling and the achievement of good postural positioning can greatly aid the work of carers in their daily interactions with people who have profound multiple handicaps. The principles detailed in the section concerning positioning and handling (pp. 241–247) achieve much prophylactic benefit for individuals while enabling small purposeful movements to occur, such as participation in bathing and feeding. These techniques can also be applied to achieving independent and spontaneous movement from one area to another. If, however, the person's physical handicap severely limits the prospect of independent ambulation, carers could examine methods where minimal movement can be transferred into maximum ambulation. The development of technological aided propulsion has moved apace since the introduction of the manually powered wheelchair. Electronic and electrical movement can be achieved easily for a person with even minimal lip movement when coupled with computer know-how. Carers can consult with wheelchair clinics (most health boards provide access to this resource) and physiotherapists to discover the best way to maximize the movements of individuals with profound and multiple handicaps. As with all positioning and supportive prosthesis the importance of accurate assessment and appropriate use is essential if benefit is sought from use.

Promoting rest

Many people with profound handicaps display erratic or unusual sleep patterns. It is thought that the ability to sleep deeply develops along with maturation of the central nervous system.

An area deep within the brain called the hypothalamus is thought to have a prominent part to play in arousal and sleep.

There has been a tendency to underestimate the importance of sound sleep and many people think of it as a very negative state where nothing is really happening. However, it is now widely recognized that a disturbed sleep pattern can seriously affect a person's emotional and physical well-being. Ask a mother with a young baby who cries inconsolably night after night how she feels during the day as she tries to cope with all of her activities and relate to her family, having had little or no sleep.

In addition to central nervous system damage there may be other factors which prevent the profoundly handicapped person from having a sound night's sleep. His level of activity during the day is an important consideration. If left to lie in bed or to sit in a wheelchair for an entire day, a person is unlikely to sleep well during the night. Here a pattern of sleep reversal may occur whereby the person may sleep during the day and be alert during the night. Sleep can also be disturbed by pain, discomfort, drug effects, hunger or thirst, or strong emotional and environmental factors.

There are several ways in which carers can help promote a sound night's sleep. It should be beneficial if the person's day has been filled with interesting activities. Changes of position, play and games, exercises, music and movement, going for walks or playing outdoors can all be used to provide a variety of activities. It is very difficult to fall asleep if you are hungry or thirsty. Carers can alter mealtimes for individuals to reduce this cause of sleeplessness. The effects of incontinence will create discomfort and cause difficulty in getting to sleep so night attire should be checked and changed if necessary.

There is often a quiet period in the evening just before bedtime when carers can spend time in settling the handicapped person. This would also be a good time to talk to the person and try to evoke a response. Oswin (1978) found, through observation in several units for multiply handicapped children, that children were receiving an average of 5 minutes of mothering attention (cuddling, play and talking to) in a 10-hour period. Surely carers can find more time to spend in meaningful human interaction however busy their day is.

During the night, carers may have to perform certain tasks, such as changing the person's position, washing and changing the person who is wet or soiled and perhaps administering medication. As far as possible, such activities should be carried out together in order to minimize the disturbance to the handicapped person and those around him.

Night-time positioning is an integral part of the positioning programme which is aimed at reducing or preventing the development of secondary physical deformities. If the severely physically handicapped person were to be placed in bed in the supine position, he would tend to adopt a preferred position from which he could not move for the entire night. The position of lying on his back is, as we can now appreciate, a poor sleeping position. It promotes many of the causal factors of deformity mentioned earlier. The principles of positioning set out earlier in this chapter can and should be applied to sleep postures. Support can be offered by means of padding or foam blocks which are often used in the side-lying position to try to counteract any curvature of the spine. For instance, if the person has a spinal curvature to his right side:

- when lying on his right side a pad would be placed under his ribs
- when lying on his left side a pad or block would be placed under his hips.

There is now good evidence that a muscle needs to be continually stretched for normal growth to occur (Tardieu et al 1988, Stern 1990). Night splints may be used to help prevent the onset of contractures and achieve this end. Carers should, if engaged in this practice, attempt to ensure the optimal level of comfort and be prepared to act if sleep is being disrupted over long periods. If the person has been used to lying in a preferred position he may indicate discomfort and attempt to resist these new positions, but it is important that this programme of good positioning be continued throughout the night if the efforts during the day are not to be negated.

If a side-lying position is contraindicated for any reason – such as an acute chest infection – the person may be sat up in as symmetrical a position as possible. His head should be supported and not allowed to extend backwards. Arms and hands are brought forward in the midline and hips and knees are bent in a sitting position. A sandbag at his bottom can prevent him from slipping down the bed, and counteract the effects of involuntary reflex movements.

As with so many things, carers must be aware of subjectively judging others by their own norms and standards. A sleep pattern which differs from that normally enjoyed by the carer is not necessarily a sleep problem for the individual with profound multiple handicap. A problem can only be judged to exist when that person's sleep habits begin to differ from his normal pattern.

Drugs have a limited role in helping the multiply handicapped person achieve a good night's sleep. Hypnotic drugs should only be requested when all other measures previously outlined have been conscientiously tried but have been insufficient on their own to help the person sleep. Among the most commonly used of these hypnotic drugs are nitrazepam (Mogadon) and chloral hydrate. It should not be assumed that giving the person an increased dose will help him to sleep more soundly.

Recreation and play

The provision of suitable recreational and play experiences forms an important part of giving physical care. Routine tasks such as dressing and bathing can often be made into games to provide learning opportunities. The carer should try to think of ways in which this extra dimension can be incorporated into the daily care of the multiply handicapped person. Spontaneous play, if not present in individuals, can be encouraged if this is desired. Murphy et al (1985) stipulate that play skills can be taught to indi-

viduals by the use of potent reinforcement of play behaviours, by structured training programmes or by a combination of these two methods. What the carer then has to decide upon is the appropriateness of the type and age of play to the person being cared for.

Safety

Even when he or she is aiming for constructive therapeutic practices the carer's first duty is to ensure that no harm comes to the person with profound multiple handicap. In an environment potentially fraught with danger it is difficult to list every accident which can happen and prescribe preventive action for each one. Many people, however, feel that the profoundly multiply handicapped person is very unlikely to have accidents due to the fact that he may lead a life of limited mobility and therefore incur little risk, unlike the more lively and mobile handicapped person who will run around and explore while showing little regard for any dangers. This is, unfortunately, a belief which leads to complacency. Constant vigilance is required from carers if the person's environment is to be kept safe.

Accidental burns can be caused by serving food which is far too hot. Filling baths with hot water before adding cold is also a potentially dangerous practice as the handicapped person may put a limb into the water before the cold water has been added. The commonplace radiator can also cause severe burns if the person is left sitting too close and is unable to communicate his feelings of pain and discomfort to care staff.

Aids and appliances can often be involved in accidents. If people in wheelchairs are not given tables to place their hands and arms on, their arms can hang at the sides of the chair where fingers may be caught in the spokes. People should never be pushed in a chair with their arms hanging over the sides. Painful injuries can easily result if the carer tries to push the person's chair through a narrow doorway.

There are potential dangers even in bed. If

the person is a restless sleeper cot sides may be kept in position to prevent him from falling out of bed. Occasionally, padded cot sides may be necessary to protect the person who repeatedly injures himself against the cot sides or bed rails, perhaps as the result of particularly severe seizures. Such a practice when indicated, however, cuts down the person's view of his surroundings and causes an unnecessary degree of sensory deprivation.

Carers are reminded Florence Nightingale said that a prime function of a hospital is that it should do the sick no harm. This is equally true for any place of residential care.

ALTERNATIVE TREATMENT METHODS

Snoezelen

Snoezelen, rather than provide a framework for intervention, attempts to secure the provision of leisure resources for profoundly multiply handicapped people. This approach, already well established in its Dutch homeland, is being integrated into mainstream care services across the country at a breathtaking pace.

The Snoezelen concept is based on a recognition of the therapeutic value of leisure activities. These leisure activities, because of the nature of profound handicap, utilize a multisensory media in an attempt to fully stimulate the sensations and emotions of participants as they interact with the environment. Most centres which offer Snoezelen activities provide:

- adventure facilities – where robust play can be safely facilitated
- water areas – which stimulate movement and relaxation
- sitting room – where people can rest, wait or recharge their batteries
- sound and light room – state of the art lighting and sound simulators at the direct control of the individual user provide auditory, tactile and visual stimulation
- white room – where the serene environment encourages deep relaxation

- tactile areas – where individuals may explore the environment through touch.

The essence of Snoezelen is to create a feeling of safety, novelty and stimulation which is under the user's control (Haggar & Hutchison 1991). Readers wishing to explore further the world of Snoezelen are directed to Hulsegge & Verheul (1987) who write very fully on the subject.

Conductive education

Conductive education is the name given to an educational system originally intended to prepare motor-impaired children for the mobility and learning demands of mainstream education. McKinlay (1990) contends that conductive education is also being used as a preventative tool because it is now aiming to achieve intervention from a very early age.

The philosophy, based on the work of Andras Peto in The State Institute for the Motor Disabled in Budapest, utilizes the work of both learning theorists and neurological researchers. The main thrust of the practice of conductive education centres on three principles:

1. The use of conductors.
2. The practice of rhythmical intention.
3. The need for structured events within the groups of pupils being taught.

When brought together in the practice of conductive education these principles attempt to deliver a curriculum which assures for individuals a sequential progression through normal developmental stages using task series.

Central to the success of this work is how the care is arranged by the conductors. Indeed, some influential practitioners would claim that understanding conductive education depends on understanding the role of the conductor (Hari & Akos 1988). Rhythmical intention, based on the proposition that motor behaviours can best be regulated and controlled through the verbalization of that activity, has two main elements (Hogg & Sebba 1986b, Hari & Akos 1988). The importance of rhythm is the first factor. To achieve this rhythm in practice the conductor defines a goal in speech, expressing verbal intention and the group then carry out that command to the accompaniment of a spoken count. In such a way the second element of rhythmical intention, that of making activity voluntary, is achieved. The work of the conductor in the provision of a structured learning day appears to have much to offer to carers of people with profound multiple handicaps as its delivery characterizes a necessarily well coordinated team approach.

Further detail about the philosophy and practice of conductive education can be found in Hari & Akos (1988). If the theories which underpin conductive education cannot be readily accepted by carers it appears that the actual practice of care delivery offers much from which to learn.

Progressive patterning

Representative of the neurological approach to physical incapacity, the Doman-Delacato 'progressive patterning' exercises have evolved from study of the stages of typical movement development. The movement patterns are divided into six stages, ranging from prone, lying with head and trunk rotation from side to side, through to a walking pattern. The theory behind these treatments is that 'silent neurological pathways' can be opened by the constant repetition of the movements performed during the patterning. However, the treatment has been the subject of much controversy. The very labour intensive nature of the patterning exercises may benefit the person with profound multiple handicap in that he will be receiving the individual attention and stimulus of approximately five people. Viewed simply as exercises, this form of therapy can help greatly in the prevention of secondary physical deformities.

For a detailed account of how to perform these patterning exercises, see Levitt (1982).

Most commentators agree that there is merit in every school of thought currently used in the treatment of individuals with profound multiple handicap. For this reason, and due to the individual effects of this type of handicap, an eclectic approach to care which selects relevant ideas and methods from each philosophy is popular amongst carers.

A review of the nature of eclecticism is provided in Hogg & Sebba (1986a) who suggest common concerns central to all approaches.

REFERENCES

Arthur M 1989 Augmentative communication systems for learners with severe disabilities: towards effective assessment and practice placements. Australian and New Zealand Journal of Developmental Disabilities, 15, 2, 119–125

Ayer S, Alaszewski A 1984 Community care and the mentally handicapped – services for mothers and their mentally handicapped children. Croom Helm, London

Bader D L 1990 Pressure sores – clinical practice and scientific approaches. Macmillan, London

Ball B 1991 Hearing and the multihandicapped child. Talking Sense, Spring 18–19

Barker P J 1982 Behaviour therapy nursing. Croom Helm, London

Bernsen A H 1981 Severe mental retardation among children in a Danish urban area. In: Mittler P Frontiers of knowledge in mental retardation. University Park Press, Baltimore, vol 2

Black P D 1980 Ocular defects in children with cerebral palsy. British Medical Journal 281, 487–8

Browning M M, Bailey I J, Clark O 1983 Schools and units for profoundly mentally handicapped children in the Strathclyde region of Scotland. Jordanhill College of Education, Glasgow

Chaney R H, Eyman R K, Miller C R 1979 Comparison of respiratory mortality in the profoundly retarded and the less retarded. Journal of Mental Deficiency Research 23, 1–7

Charlett J A 1990 Hygiene. In: Hogg J et al Profound retardation and multiple impairment. Chapman & Hall, London, vol 3 ch 10

Clarke M 1990 Epilepsy: identification and management. In: Hogg J et al Profound retardation and multiple impairment. Chapman & Hall, London, vol 3 ch 9

Darbyshire D 1986 Physical aspects of care of the profoundly mentally handicapped. In: Shanley E (ed) Mental handicap: a handbook of care. Churchill Livingstone, Edinburgh

Dyson R 1978 Bed sores – the injuries hospital staff inflict on patients. Nursing Mirror 146, 30– 32

Ellis D 1986 Sensory impairments in mentally handicapped people. Croom Helm, London

Emberson J, Walker E 1990 Self-injurious behaviour in people with a mental handicap. Nursing Times 86, 23, 43–46

Finnie N 1990 Handling the young cerebral palsied child at home. Heinemann, London

Fletcher A 1992 Pressure sores. Wound Management 2, 1, 12–13

Gibbons S E 1983 Mouth care procedures. Nursing Times 79, 30

Golding R, Goldsmith L 1986 The caring person's guide to handling the severely multiply handicapped. Macmillan, London

Green C 1985 Nursing process: what is it? Adapted for Mental Handicap Nursing: after Heath J, Law G M. Learning Resources Unit, Sheffield

Grossman H J 1983 Classification in mental retardation. American Association for Mental Deficiency, Washington

Haggar L E, Hutchinson R B 1991 Snoezelen: an approach to the provision of leisure resource for people with profound and multiple handicaps. Mental Handicap 19, 51–55

Hari M, Akos K 1988 Conductive education. Tavistock-Routledge, London

Harris S R, Purdy A H 1987 Drooling and its management in cerebral palsy. Developmental Medicine & Child Neurology 29, 807–811

HMSO 1989 Caring for people: community care in the next decade and beyond. HMSO, London

Hogg J, Lambe L J 1988 Sons and daughters with profound retardation and multiple handicaps attending schools and social education centres. Profound Retardation and Multiple Handicap Project Paper 6. Mencap, London

Hogg J, Sebba J 1986a Profound retardation and multiple impairment, vol 1: development and learning. Croom Helm, London

Hogg J, Sebba J 1986b Profound retardation and multiple impairment, vol 2: education and therapy. Croom Helm, London

Hogg J, Sebba J, Lambe L 1990 Profound retardation and multiple impairment: medical and physical care and management. Chapman & Hall, London, vol 3

Hulsegge J, Verheul A 1987 Snoezelen: another world. Rompa UK, Chesterfield

Illingworth R S 1991 The normal child – some problems of the early years and their treatment. Churchill Livingstone, Edinburgh

Inge K J 1987 Atypical motor development and cerebral palsy. In: Orelove F P & Sobsey D Educating young children with multiple disabilities. Paul Brookes, Baltimore

Jacobson J W, Sutton M S, Janicki M P 1985 Demography and characteristics of ageing and aged mentally retarded persons. In: Janicki P M, Wisniewski H M Ageing and developmental disabilities. Paul Brookes, Baltimore

Jones P R 1991 Functional assessment of near vision in children with profound and multiple handicaps. Mental Handicap 19, 14–17

Kiernan C, Moss S 1990 Behaviour disorders and other characteristics of the population of a mental handicap hospital. Mental Handicap Research 3: 1, 3–20

Kropka B 1983 A summary of the results of the questionnaire into hearing impairment and the mentally handicapped in NHS hospitals and hostels in England and Wales. Unpublished report, British Institute of Mental Handicap, South West Division, Exeter

Kropka B, Williams I 1986 The epidemiology of hearing impairment in people with a mental handicap. In: Ellis D Sensory impairments in mentally handicapped people. Croom Helm, London

Lancioni G E et al 1989 Use of automatic cueing to reduce drooling in two multihandicapped students. Journal of Multihandicapped Person 2, 3, 201–210

Levitt S 1982 Treatment of cerebral palsy and motor delay. Blackwell, London

McKinlay M 1990 Conductive education in Hungary and Britain. Health Visitor 63, 9, 298–300

Murphy G, Wilson B 1985 Self-injurious behaviour. BIMH Publications, Kidderminster

Murphy G, Callias M, Carr J 1985 Increasing simple toy play in profoundly mentally handicapped children: 1. Training to play. Journal of Autism and Developmental Disorders 15, 4, 375–385

Mustonen T, Locke P, Reichle J Solbrack M, Lindgren A 1991 An overview of augmentative and alternative communication systems. In: Reichle et al Implementing augmentative and alternative communication. Paul Brookes, Baltimore

National deaf blind & rubella association 1989 Stimulating the sensory impaired child. Talking Sense 35, 6–7

Oliver C, Murphy G H, Corbett J A 1987 Self-injurious behaviour in people with a mental handicap: a total population study. Journal of Mental Deficiency Research 31, 147–162

Oswin M 1978 Children living in long-stay hospitals. Heinemann, London

Presland J L 1991 Problem behaviours and people with profound and multiple handicaps. Mental Handicap 19, 66–71

Presland J L 1982 Paths to mobility in special care. British Institute of Mental Handicap, Kidderminster

Reichle J, York J, Sigafoos J 1991 Implementing augmentative and alternative communication. Paul Brookes, Baltimore

Remington B, Evans J 1988 Basic learning processes in people with profound mental handicaps: review and relevance. Mental Handicap Research 1, 1, 4–23

Richards N C G 1977 Treatment of choking. Nursing Times 73, 856–857

Rithalia S V S 1992 Pressure sores and leg ulcers. Wound Management 2, 1, 14

Seivwright J 1982 An unconventional approach to therapy. Remedial Therapist 4, 21

Shaw J 1990 Continence in cerebral palsy. Health Visitor 63, 9, 301–302

Sines D, Bicknell J 1985 Caring for the mentally handicapped in the community. Harper & Row, London

Smith P 1986 Comfort for a child with multiple handicap. Nursing Times 17, 49–51

Snell M E 1987 Systematic instruction of persons with severe handicaps. Charles E Merrill, Columbus

Stern L M 1990 The management of cerebral palsy. Journal of Paediatric Child Health 26, 184–187

Tardieu C, Lespargot A, Tabray C, Bret M D 1988 For how long must the soleus muscle be stretched each day to prevent contracture? Developmental Medicine & Child Neurology 30, 3–10

Warburg S 1977 Blindness among 7600 mentally retarded children in Denmark. University of Nottingham, Nottingham

Wehman P 1979 Curriculum design for the severely and profoundly handicapped. Human Sciences Press, New York

Zarakowska E, Clements J 1988 Problem behaviour in people with severe learning disabilities. Croom Helm, London

USEFUL ADDRESS

Specialist advice on equipment and aids and appliances can be obtained from:

Cerebral palsy helpline
Tel: 0800–626 216

This line is provided by the Spastics Society and is manned 7 days a week between the hours of 1 p.m. and 10 p.m.

CHAPTER CONTENTS

Introduction   269

Role of nonverbal communication   270
Channels and codes   271
    Limited range of channels   271
Nonverbal features   272
    Proxemics   272
    Physical contact   273
    Looking   274
    Gesture   274
    Posture   275
    Nonverbal leakage   275
    Regulatory function   276

Movement   276
Observing and interpreting movement   277
Movement provides a common link   278

Communication and expression   279

Early communication   279

Interactional synchrony   281

Communication through movement – general
points   282
Appropriate stimulation   284
Adaptable approach   284
Microscopic details   285

Summary   287

12

Helping with communication through movement

B. Burford

Key points

- Verbal skills are not essential for communication
- Communication is a two-way process
- Cultural, social and environmental factors influence nonverbal expression and communication
- The context in which body movement occurs gives it meaning and purpose
- Poor interactional synchrony can cause difficulties in communicating and forming relationships
- Communicating effectively through movement requires that caregivers monitor their own actions and are sensitive to the cues, reactions and moods of the person with learning disabilities

INTRODUCTION

Communication is a fundamental part of human life yet generally we pay it scant attention when it is working to our satisfaction. Words such as 'interaction', 'expression' and 'interpersonal communication' are seen by many people as vague areas with no real substance or meaning: each one is just 'something' that 'happens'. We often take our ability to communicate and form relationships for granted. When everything is running smoothly we give little thought to the underlying mechanisms which enable us to communicate and relate to each other. It is when we do encounter difficulties in our attempts to communicate, e.g. with someone with profound multiple learning disabilities, that we may begin to realize that these vague areas are of importance in everyday life. The ways a person uses to communicate depend on his or her needs, intentions and abilities. The most successful and appropriate form of communication for people with profound multiple learning disabilities is nonverbal, since they are unlikely to be able to communicate through speech and have little understanding of language. Physical handicaps may further restrict a person's range of nonverbal communication and expression. However, the capacities he or she does have available can be used effectively if caregivers adapt the means of communication to suit the person, rather than trying to fit the person into a predetermined framework.

This form of communication is concerned with developing social relationships rather than exchanging factual information. It is a partnership in which each person influences the other through looks, facial expressions and body movements. This way of communicating gives caregivers the opportunity to help the person with profound multiple learning disabilities to become part of the social world. Little by little, the person can become aware that he or she can have some influence on others, e.g. realizing that a certain movement will prompt a caregiver to repeat an action song. In this way people with profound multiple learning disabilities are given an opportunity to learn that they can have some degree of control over their world. In fact, nonverbal communication has a central place in all human communication and is important for everyone, whether they have learning disabilities or not.

When we begin studying nonverbal communication, its research and literature, we enter a world which isolates tiny elements of human communication and then examines them in even greater detail. High significance is given to apparent fragments from the vast range of nonverbal communication. Yet these details *are* significant and can play a crucial role in everyday communication.

ROLE OF NONVERBAL COMMUNICATION

Body communication plays an important part in our lives from infancy. Its usefulness, although more apparent during the preverbal phase of development, does not diminish with the onset of speech. Nonverbal communication has a multipurpose role and its functions and structures are the subject of much theorizing and research. Let us take a brief look at three viewpoints concerning the role of nonverbal communication.

Farb (1977) believes that speech determines the gestural system, as he calls it, and that it is the spoken language that determines exactly which movements will be used. He says that when someone learns a language he also unconsciously learns an accompanying gestural system.

Birdwhistell (1968) believes that there is a language of movement which is comparable to spoken language. He views communication as a multichannel system in which all the channels are equally necessary to the whole system. Though no single channel is in constant use, there are always one or more channels in operation (Birdwhistell 1971). According to Birdwhistell, the fact that language is characteristic of humans does not mean that it is the central or most important communication channel: interaction does not stop when the people involved stop talking.

Argyle (1972) views nonverbal communication as part of an overall system with complex rules of structure and sequence. He says it must be accepted that most human social behaviour involves speech. Much speech is accompanied by nonverbal communication which may depend on structures similar to speech or which may even have been learnt as part of the skill of verbal communication.

Whatever the views that may be held about the nature and function of nonverbal communication, its general purpose is an interactive one. We wave in greeting to a friend, look at others when talking to them or use gestures to help give directions to a stranger. Importantly, it is a rich and effective medium for expressing and sharing our feelings; it allows us to express and convey emotional communication (Buck 1984).

Body movements and nonverbal expressions are useful and powerful aids to language, and the rhythm and intensity of speech can be matched by similar rhythm and intensity in movement. Our speech is accompanied by nonverbal signs and cues which can complement, enhance or contradict what we are saying. Sometimes we may deliberately use certain nonverbal features to emphasize what we wish to convey, e.g. facial expression to emphasize displeasure, or a certain stance of the body to convey an outward appearance that belies how we are really feeling inside. However, for a large part of the time we are unaware of our constant use of facial expressions, gestures, eye contact and postures, and indeed we may have nonverbal habits of which we are completely unaware. We pay a lot of attention to other people's nonverbal behaviour, observing and interpreting their moods and attitudes towards us and this influences how we respond to people and the opinions we form about them.

Channels and codes

Communication requires channels to send messages and codes to carry the message. The two main channels, verbal and nonverbal, can be subdivided into a multiplicity of channels, e.g. people can communicate nonverbally through gestures, touch, facial expressions, or with their eyes. The meaning of the message depends on the context in which it occurs. For example, a look can be used to express warmth or hostility. Meaning can also be affected by conflicting messages being sent at the same time. For example, one person can agree with another in words and, at the same time, express his misgivings nonverbally.

Limited range of channels

The person with profound multiple learning disabilities often has a limited range of channels for communication, all of which are nonverbal. Where physical handicaps limit the range even more, we have to look at the communication channels he or she is still able to use. If someone is blind, has very limited movement and does not use or understand language, then touch, tone

of voice and vocalizing become important as a means of communicating to the person. However, communication from the person need not be restricted to these same channels, e.g. facial expression or body movements might be used. Repeated observations will show how the responses are expressed. Even if a response is a spontaneous expression of pleasure rather than a deliberate attempt to communicate, it can still provide some indication that the caregiver is having an effect. Familiarity through regular contact with the person will show how he or she communicates. Through time it may be possible to develop this into two-way communication in which the person is a more equal partner.

Two-way communication with the person with profound multiple learning disabilities does not develop easily. The person may readily respond in some way to communication from other people, yet still show no attempt to make the first move. Thus, the interchangeability and adaptation which are features of two-way communication are missing. Picture a child with learning disabilities who is unable to speak, who smiles at others, laughs appropriately, looks at another, vocalizes in a communicative way and seeks and reaches out to others – she already possesses interactive skills and initiates as well as responds to communicative contact . She is an *active participant* in communication. Now picture a child, also unable to speak, who never smiles or laughs, does not look at people, makes only random sounds and does not seek and reach out to others – she does not have interactive skills. She gives no feedback to those who attempt to communicate with her and so communication is one-sided. She is not a participant in interaction and the first task is to find a way of gaining entry into the child's world, which will enable us to develop some way of communicating with her.

Picture a third child with no speech development. He smiles when approached, laughs when amused, cuddles in when picked up, looks at others and vocalizes when someone talks to him, but he does not make the first move to communicate – he shows some development in communication skills, but he is a *passive recipient* rather than an *active participant*. He is not good at making the first move and depends on others to approach him first. Some children who are considered good communicators are, in fact, passive recipients. Their responses are pleasing and they can show obvious enjoyment when in the company of others, but closer examination will show the communication to be very one-sided, highly dependent on the adult and limited in range.

The development of two-way communication enables the tiny, enclosed world of the person with profound multiple learning disabilities to be extended to include other people. The more active a part children can play in communication, the greater the opportunity to expand their horizons.

Nonverbal features

There are many nonverbal features which could be illustrated and discussed. However the purpose of this part of the chapter is not to survey and discuss the extensive literature available on nonverbal communication but to draw attention to the multitude of features, i.e. channels, through which nonverbal communication can be expressed, and to give some insight into their role in successful interactions. Nonverbal features include posture, gesture, gaze, facial expression, touch, proximity and tone of voice, among others. All can be subdivided into smaller units of behaviour, e.g. gesture could mean a hand movement or an expansive movement involving the whole arm. These, in turn, can be further subdivided, e.g. Birdwhistell (1971) has 57 different symbols for the face.

Areas of nonverbal communication which have been found to be particularly relevant and useful when working with people with learning disabilities will now be considered in more detail, but their presentation here is not exhaustive.

Proxemics

The term 'proxemics' was first used by Hall (1966) to describe the space between and around people. It is concerned with the distance maintained by people during interactions and the body orientation they adopt in relation to each other.

Interpersonal distance is the distance maintained by participants during interactions. This is not dictated so much by the amount of available space but more by the cultural, social and emotional aspects of the encounter. If someone places himself closer than we feel the depth of our acquaintance allows, we adjust the distance until we feel more comfortable. The distance between friends is likely to be less than that between people meeting for the first time. This distance is a fluctuating measurement: during interactions we monitor and adjust the interpersonal distance according to the social relationship we have with the other people involved in the communication.

Interpersonal distance also varies between cultures. One example is the difference found by Watson & Graves (1966) when comparing Arab and American male students during conversations. The Arab students preferred a greater degree of closeness than the American students, with a more direct eye contact and a more direct body orientation to others. Hall (1966) first described Arab-American differences from his observations, noting the discomfort Americans felt at the intensity of the encounter, while the Arabs felt alienated by the lack of intensity from their American counterparts.

People with learning disabilities do not always manage to adjust the interpersonal distance successfully to suit cultural and social norms. There are some who approach everyone from complete strangers to close relatives with the same degree of closeness and physical contact. Many people, when visiting a residential or educational unit for people with learning disabilities, will have experienced being greeted as if they were close, intimate and lifelong friends. In this context the intention of such a greeting is understood. However, if a stranger were to approach us in the street in this manner we would have a less pleasant reaction, perhaps anger or a feeling of anxiety and fear. Similarly, if an adult with learning disabilities, especially a man, were to approach strangers in the street, particularly children, in this intimate manner, it could be misinterpreted. People with learning disabilities should be helped to adapt to their nonverbal culture as part of their preparation for independent living and greater integration with their local communities. Opinions about the positive and negative values of the nonverbal rules we impose on our culture is a separate issue. Some people believe that more frequent and closer physical contact as a normal part of public communication would be more beneficial; others believe such contact should be kept to a minimum. People with learning disabilities need help to adapt to the nonverbal customs currently practised in their community.

Not all people with learning disabilities seek or enjoy the close company of others. There are those who maintain a large distance between themselves and others, immediately reestablishing this distance if someone attempts to decrease it. Where the physical confines of the room or space make this impossible the person is likely to become anxious and upset. Such people, although aware of others, are withdrawn and unwilling to communicate. They may appear oblivious to others but, in fact, they often maintain a very sensitive monitoring of the whereabouts of those around them and adjust any changes to keep the status quo.

Physical contact

In some cultures, physical contact forms a part of public communication. In the United Kingdom, touching is a very limited part of everyday communication and there are strict, although unwritten, rules about touching behaviour. When accidental touching occurs we apologize and move back; if it is unavoidable – as when sharing a seat on a crowded bus – we may tense the side in contact and adjust our position to make the contact as minimal as possible. There are occasional signs that these rules about public behaviour are now being relaxed a little, but any slight changes in trend make little difference to the overall pattern of limited physical contact when compared with cultures who incorporate touch into their daily communication.

The cultural differences are not necessarily confined to those countries separated by great geographical distances. This is illustrated in a study by Jourard (1966) in which he observed the frequency of contact of couples in city cafés in different countries. For example, Paris was compared to London and the frequency of contact was: Paris – 110 contacts per hour, London – 0 contacts per hour. The other cities were San Juan in Puerto Rico – 180 contacts and Gainsville in Florida – 2 contacts.

Recently, when I put forward the view that the United Kingdom was a nontouching culture to a Japanese colleague, his immediate reaction was one of surprise. In comparison to Japan he considered that the United Kingdom was a touching culture. In Japan British customs are considered very intimate behaviour; the Japanese do not shake hands; they do not embrace in public, even when greeting friends and relatives at places such as airports; touching is permissible in public mainly between parent and child, although it may sometimes be observed between young couples or married couples (Negayama 1991). Japanese people bow as a way of greeting and acknowledging each other instead of shaking hands, the depth of the bow depending on the seniority of the other person. It is used far more extensively than the handshake, being used even between close friends whenever they meet and part.

In the early 1980s, a television travel documentary showed a group of Japanese tourists being welcomed aboard their cruise ship by the British captain who greeted them by shaking hands. The tourists, unused to shaking hands, had to immediately adopt a set of movements which were not a usual part of their everyday behaviour. The difficulty and awkwardness they experienced with this form of greeting was obvious, yet in the United Kingdom a simple handshake is not seen as a source of difficulty. It would be interesting to observe tourists from the United Kingdom coping with a typical Japanese greeting.

Touch is not affected by cultural factors alone. Touch can play a part in communicating emotional warmth, e.g. a parent stroking a baby and can also convey status and power, e.g. a boss may place a hand on an employee's arm as he chats to him at the end of a staff meeting, but a reversal of touching roles is much less likely. Individual differences also have to be taken into account. Some people use touch more than others and are comfortable with being touched; some rarely touch others and dislike being touched.

Some people with learning disabilities do not like being touched. The more severe their learning disability the more distressing it may be for them since they will require much more physical handling and contact during their daily care. Sometimes it is *handling* rather than *touching* that the person finds distressing. Observation will show that some can tolerate touching that is gentle and restrained but, for example, they might protest during physical handling when being dressed. Handling is quite a different experience from touching. The person who becomes readily upset with any form of physical contact is more likely to display a general aversion to involvement with other people.

Looking

Looking has an important function in regulating the turns people take in speaking and listening during conversations. This function will be discussed later in the chapter.

We do not look at each other all the time while talking. Besides mutual direct eye contact, there are times when one person is looking while the other looks away, and there can also be mutual gaze avoidance. As with other nonverbal features, emotional, social and cultural factors affect looking behaviour.

Attention has been drawn to looking to emphasize a point about encouraging eye contact in people with learning disabilities. Some avoid eye contact, or even looking in the general direction of another person, while others do not appear to be aware of the need or purpose of looking at others.

Those who find communicating with others stressful usually find it difficult to look at people. It is a small effort to move one's head and direct the eyes at another person, but the emotional journey can be a long one. Such people may find it less difficult to make contact through some other nonverbal channel first, e.g. hand or foot. For example, finger games might develop that give an opportunity for the person to become involved on terms that he finds able to tolerate. As trust develops, the person might begin to give glances in the direction of the other person, eventually leading to moments of direct eye contact. It should be emphasized that this is likely to be a long process, slowly building on a nonverbal conversation through hands or whatever means has been found to work best. The prime focus is on developing a relationship, rather than increasing the frequency of eye contact for some other purpose.

Gesture

The use of gesture by different cultures varies, e.g. an Italian is likely to gesture more often than a Scot. There can also be variation in meaning, with the same nonverbal signal having different meanings or with different signals having the same meaning. This could lead to possible misunderstanding and confusion when people from different cultures meet.

LaBarre (1947) tells of such a misunderstanding, which arose while he was working alongside an American Indian woman who was in her 80s. He asked her where something was and, although he knew she must have heard him, she carried on working, apparently ignoring his request. He repeated his request several times until, with mutually shared puzzlement and exasperation, she stopped working and fetched it for him – it had been clearly in sight all the time. The elderly woman had indeed heard him and had replied to his request repeatedly, but by pointing with her lips. This particular example may now seem dated and describes a situation we are unlikely to encounter, but it does illustrate the kind of misunderstanding that can still arise today. Even with modern communication systems and travel enabling greater mixing with and awareness of other cultures, differences can still occur.

Of course, gestures are not just a series of signs. Some gestures are precise and have specific meanings, e.g. the 'thumbs up' sign, but most gestures consist of more general movements which serve to emphasize and punctuate speech and help to describe and colour what is being said. Gestures are generally considered to be movements of the hands and arms that accompany speech, with other forms of gesture, e.g. head nods, being grouped separately.

However, not all movements are gestures and we do not have to be speaking when we use movement to communicate or to convey emotions and attitudes. We can communicate and express ourselves through movement in many ways and the movement does not have to be expansive. Imagine, for example, a previously outgoing person who, after months of withdrawal and total lack of movement (apart from the functional to get from A to B), begins to respond to others with microscopic movements. These tiny movements are meaningful far in excess of the happy extrovert who flings her arms out in greeting to a friend.

Posture

Posture refers to the static position of the body as opposed to the active nature of gestures and expressive movements. The postures we adopt are influenced by various factors, such as emotional state, relationship to and feelings about the others present, and culture. It is less well controlled than the face and voice (Ekman & Friesen 1966) and could inadvertently reveal information about how we are feeling in a situation.

Posture is especially affected in terms of relaxation and tension. In a meeting the high status person is likely to have a more relaxed posture than the low status individual. The differences in posture in the meeting are caused by how people are feeling in response to the situation in which they find themselves – there is no explicit rule which determines their postures. However, some cultures have careful distinctions in posture based on sex, others on age and status (Hewes 1955). These are seen as an integral part of the rules of etiquette and strictly enforced. In the United Kingdom we do not have such strict rules

but if we are visiting a culture which does we would have to beware of misunderstandings.

Cultural differences in nonverbal communication are not only of interest as examples of the diversity of cultures. Nonverbal communication is central to the way in which a person experiences and perceives a culture, e.g. most United Kingdom residents would believe themselves to be a distant, nontouching culture whereas Japanese visitors might have a rather different view. My conversation with Koichi Negayama, reported earlier, gave me a forceful reminder that very real differences in nonverbal behaviour still exist between cultures. Mistakes can lead to misunderstandings and it takes time to adapt to and feel at ease with a dissimilar cultural style. Nonverbal communication is an ubiquitous part of human life. It is not usually foremost in our thoughts, but it soon makes its presence felt when we meet someone who uses a different style of nonverbal communication.

Nonverbal leakage

We are likely to become more aware than usual of our nonverbal communication when we are exposed to a new culture and are unsure of how to behave or respond. This awareness is normally less in evidence in the day-to-day encounters we have with people. However, awareness can become heightened when we are in a situation where we want to deceive other people by presenting a certain appearance or hiding our true feelings. In these circumstances what we are really feeling can filter through the performance or mask we have put on. This filtering is called nonverbal leakage (Ekman & Friesen 1966).

Imagine you are at an important interview for a job which carries responsibility and requires leadership qualities. You wish to present yourself as knowledgeable, confident and well-suited to the task, although at this moment you are extremely nervous, particularly as the other candidates seem confident and very able. During the interview you strive to hide your nervousness and verbally you succeed, managing to keep your voice steady and giving good answers. However, your body tells another story – your posture is tense, you constantly rub your thumb against a finger and your smile is fixed.

Some people are better at controlling nonverbal leakage than others, especially if they are aware of its likelihood. The degree of success also depends on the nonverbal behaviours that a person is trying to control. It is probably easier to tell lies with the face than it is with hands, legs and feet (Ekman & Friesen 1969). Ekman and Friesen describe legs and feet as being the chief source of nonverbal leakage.

Conflicting messages can arise from nonverbal leakage. For example, a mother greets her child with open arms as he runs up to her and then hugs him, but her body remains rigid. She wants to hug her child, but generally she keeps her distance from others and, unused to such contact, finds hugging awkward. Another mother greets her child in a similar way, but envelops him as she hugs him so that mother and child are moulded. This child is likely to feel more emotional warmth from his mother's greeting.

It can be useful to look for signs of nonverbal leakage. I worked with one young woman with learning disabilities whose whole body gave a strong message that she was totally uninterested in my presence. She sat immobile, huddled in with her head down low and impervious to any attempt to involve her in communication. The message was loud and clear, except for her eyes which almost swivelled out of their sockets in her efforts to track my movements about the room. It is worth remembering though, that the observer can also be the observed. We should be aware of our own nonverbal behaviour and the possibility of giving adverse messages to those we are trying to help.

Regulatory function

The nonverbal components also have a regulatory function during conversation. They provide people with much of the feedback they need in order to maintain the fluency of the conversation. In the course of a conversation a person will at different times have the roles of speaker and listener. There needs to be some way of allocating these roles.

Kendon (1967) found differences in gaze direction between the same person when speaker and listener. Person A in the role of speaker tends to look away as she is about to speak. During the time she speaks she alternates between looking at and looking away from B her listener. Person B, meanwhile, has been looking at A for longer and more steadily. As A is about to finish speaking she looks up. Now B, if he wishes, can take his cue and begin speaking. Person A now becomes the listener and looks more steadily and for longer at B than she did while she was speaking to him. This regulation provides a framework which enables the conversation to run smoothly.

Of course, we do not always play our parts exactly as we should! Someone who wants to continue speaking and 'hold the floor' might do so by not looking at the others in the conversation, removing an important cue from the regulatory framework. To achieve a smooth flow of conversation, each person must monitor the actions of the others. This information helps each person to regulate his or her contribution and to maintain the interchangeability necessary for successful interaction.

There is obviously more than gaze direction involved in the regulation of conversations. Other nonverbal features, e.g. head nods, also have a role in directing and allocating listener and speaker roles, and in providing feedback to the speaker of the effects on the listener of what is being said. If someone's reaction to an idea or suggestion you are outlining is very important, you will scrutinize that person's nonverbal behaviour as you put forward your proposals, trying to assess how your ideas are being received.

MOVEMENT

It is difficult to interact with someone who has a blank face and who does not look at you or turn her body even slightly towards your direction. Such a person is unable to participate effectively in reciprocal communication. Attempts to encourage communication with those people with learning disabilities who have poor interactive skills are enhanced by careful observation of the nonverbal aspects of their behaviour and their body movements. It is important to note how the person moves as well as noting which *part* is moving. This should then be extended to observing how the whole body is moving, not just the part on which the main attention might be focused, e.g. the hands.

Studies in nonverbal communication select specific aspects from the whole spectrum, e.g. smiling, as a quick search through the literature in nonverbal communication will show. In contrast, when studying expressive movements we pay attention to the whole body, the movement of one part in relation to another and the manner in which the person moves, e.g. with force, gently, quickly. If I am encouraging communication with someone who is only moving his fingers then I concentrate on his fingers, using this movement as a starting point for building communication. At the same time I will observe the rest of his body and posture, ready to incorporate any further movements into the improvisation if it seems this would help. Observations should take account of total body movements, how the person moves in the space around him or her, and the nonverbal features used to communicate.

Movement is a complex subject for study. Its ubiquitous nature and its wide variety of purposes lead to people using the same word with a different meaning and emphasis, depending on the context in which the word is used. Movement plays many roles in our lives – it is found in many contexts and in widely varying forms. For example, its purposes can be functional, recreational, educational, artistic or therapeutic. Each of these functions has different objectives and benefits and their application requires different skills from the 'teacher' and the 'performer'. Some contexts require specific skills and training before the movement can fulfil its purpose effectively, e.g. athletes. This chapter focuses on communicating *with* and *through* movement arising spontaneously at the time of the communication. The social context helps give meaning to what is being expressed and communicated and, most importantly, to the relationship between the actions of those involved in the communication.

Observing and interpreting movement

The patterns of our everyday movements are moulded by many factors. Some patterns of movement are transitory, affected by momentary moods and reactions, whereas others are a more permanent feature moulded by the type of person we have become. Sometimes the patterns are controlled by the environment, e.g. it is unlikely that we would display the same movement behaviour in a relaxed and informal situation as we would at a crucial meeting at work. Movements are also affected by emotional states, e.g. the person who is depressed will not display the same style of movement as the same person in a happy, energetic mood.

As we can see, our movements are subject to a variety of influences. This emphasizes the need for careful and consistent observation of an individual over a period, before any interpretation of the observations is attempted. When making observations it should be kept in mind that communication needs more than one person and that the actions of one person will have an effect on others. It is insufficient to observe a person's nonverbal behaviour and movements in isolation – they need to be examined in relation to the actions of the other people involved.

It is impossible to observe movement without some system of observation; even an informal system built up from personal experience will give help in sifting through the maze of activity, helping to select what is relevant. It is very difficult to observe with the naked eye, with only one chance to note what is happening. We cannot check the accuracy of our observations, nor can we see everything at once so we lose a lot of information. Sometimes it is only possible to notice behaviours when they are recorded on video and replayed at slower or faster than normal speeds. Nowadays, most people have access to video equipment, and camcorders have made video recording easier to set up and less intrusive. Video gives *all* participants (parents, care staff and people with learning disabilities) an opportunity to observe themselves and what they are doing.

When observing movements it is important to note *how* the movements are performed. When observations of different people performing the same movement are broken down into smaller parts we usually find many individual differences. These differences will often hold the key to working effectively with someone. For example, when observing someone making a rocking action some of the questions that might be asked are:

- Is the rocking fast or slow?
- What is the direction – forwards and backwards, or side-to-side?
- Is the action expansive or restricted, i.e. uses a lot or little of the space around the person?
- Is the person tense or relaxed?
- What parts of the body are involved, e.g. whole body, upper body?
- What is the rhythm of the rocking action?

Sometimes a rocking action serves as a barrier to interpersonal contact, shutting people out. It can sometimes help to sit beside the person and join in with the rocking action. This way of making contact uses actions that have meaning for the performer. Gradually, variations can be introduced to the movements which are more conducive to working in partnership with others, e.g. facing each other and joining hands, each following the other's lead in changing the speed of rocking. Variations in speed and rhythm, and using different parts of the body, give different movement experiences so it is particularly important to join in initially with *how* actions are performed. However, there are pitfalls – it should not simply be a mechanical imitation but should capitalize on what the person is doing at the time.

Observing movement and interpreting its meaning should not been seen as one and the same thing. It is possible to achieve objective observation with good inter-rater reliability for movements which have been clearly defined and described. Interpretation of the meaning and purpose of the observed movements is much more open to question and differing opinions. Interpretation should be approached with caution and should take all the factors which might have influenced the movement into account. For example, cultural influences play an important part in how we use and interpret movement. As mentioned earlier in the chapter, someone visiting a foreign culture can find major and confusing differences in nonverbal communication. This is not to suggest that we should not interpret movement – we do this constantly – but we should always keep in mind the subjective nature of the interpretations. This is especially important when we use this information in planning therapy and educational programmes for people with learning disabilities.

Movement provides a common link

People with learning disabilities do not always find it easy to assimilate cultural and social rules and styles. Those with profound learning disabilities , and very isolated and withdrawn individuals, are not readily influenced by culture. An approach sympathetic to their individual styles of communicating seems best suited to their needs. Some do not conform to our culture or to our ideas of what is 'normal' or 'correct' movement in a social situation, e.g. a person may constantly move her hands in a repetitive pattern close to her face. Although the ingredients that make up this movement are a normal part of movement, it is the way in which they are put together that makes the overall pattern look so different, e.g. the way the person uses the space around her and the timing of her movements.

This sharing of ingredients means that movement can provide a common factor between those who cannot communicate effectively and those who wish to find a way of making links with them, thus opening up opportunities for developing communication and expression.

Communication requires the involvement of at least two people, with the actions of each person having an effect on the other. It is important to take into account what the other people in the communication are doing when considering the implications of our observations of a particular individual with learning disabilities. This might yield helpful clues about how best to encourage communication. For example, a child with learning disabilities might be observed to smile more often or have a more relaxed posture when with a particular adult. It would help to find out what the adult does to promote this response, e.g. the speed of his movements, the way he uses eye contact or the distance he maintains when talking to the child. Once identified, these helpful strategies can be adopted by all those wishing to communicate with the child.

There are also intangible factors from within a person which can both prompt and influence the way in which he or she moves. Movement provides a link between inner self and the outside world. When we are with people who have difficulty in communicating verbally, then a link can be established through the medium of movement. This link can provide a channel for communicating and expressing feelings, moods and needs, and the means for forming relationships through which personal growth and development can occur. This nonverbal link allows us to develop our early relationships, as we shall see later in the chapter.

COMMUNICATION AND EXPRESSION

The nonverbal channels are particularly well suited for communicating and expressing ourselves. Communication and expression are interrelated, but they do not share the exact same meaning. If one person is transmitting factual information to another the communicative purpose is obvious: the focus is functional rather than emotional. However, if A is angry with B, he might not feel satisfied until B has received and understood the message. On the other hand, A might feel better for venting his anger, whether or not B or anyone else understood or responded to this. We have a need to express inner states, but it is difficult to draw the line between the need for this to be understood and the need for expression, regardless of response (Parry 1967). Not all nonverbal behaviour is intentional communication.

Another factor affecting communication and expression is the decoding of meaning. For example, frowning can convey disapproval, but if the person to whom the frown is directed does not understand what a frown means then the disapproval is not conveyed. Posture may indicate something about a person's emotional state, but if this cannot be interpreted correctly by others then nothing can be communicated through this posture (Danziger 1976).

In this chapter, 'communication' refers to the conveyance of emotional information to others for their acknowledgment, while 'expression' is used to indicate an expression of inner feelings, irrespective of whether this is understood by others. Expression without communication can be of value.

EARLY COMMUNICATION

Communication through nonverbal channels plays a crucial role in helping infants to join in social interactions with other people. It is through nonverbal channels that the baby's first relationships are formed. Through their encounters with other people babies begin to learn about the world around them so other people are very important in providing necessary social experiences. Bullowa (1979) aptly describes this importance: 'At first an infant's world is almost exclusively a world of people and what they do with and to and for him.' This has parallels with communication with people who have profound learning disabilities. This is not advocating that they should be treated like babies, but other people, especially caregivers, have an extremely important role in encouraging them to join the social world through 'what they do with and to and for them'. The quote from Bullowa seems just as relevant in this context.

During early interactions in the first 6 months of life nonhandicapped babies learn about cues and regulations in responding to, initiating and ending interactions with their caregivers and acquire the skills necessary in coping with social interaction (Stern 1977). They develop conversational skills long before they are able to speak. There is strong evidence to suggest babies are, in fact, preprogrammed to react to social communication (Trevarthen et al 1981) – babies are 'biologically tuned' as Newson (1979) describes it. At a very early age they are able to respond to and influence the communication of others (Trevarthen et al 1981).

Language has its beginnings in the preverbal communication patterns established between caregiver and baby in the early months of life rather than at the beginning of the 2nd year (Schaffer 1977a). It is believed that the development of verbal communication is related to the baby's ability to participate in interactions during the first year (Bruner 1974). Thus, language acquisition has been firmly placed within a social setting (Schaffer 1977b).

Adults adopt a conversational style with babies who are too young to make even a vocal response (Snow 1977). The caregiver treats the smallest behaviour as if it were meaningful (Snow 1977). The adult provides the responses for the baby until gradually the baby is able to take a more active part in the communication. For example, the baby sneezes or hiccups and the adult builds a conversation round this, playing both parts. Gradually, within the first few months, an interactive structure begins to develop. Through these many conversations the baby begins to realize that other people pay attention to his or her movements and vocalizations and that these produce certain responses. In time, the baby begins to use these movements and vocalizations with purpose, anticipating that others will respond in certain specific ways (Schaffer 1977b). Even at the age of 2 months babies can stop and start communicative activity, an essential requirement for two-way exchanges (Trevarthen 1979).

Babies show sensitive responses to the communication movements of their caregivers and initiate many communication movements themselves (Stern 1985, Trevarthen 1985). Spontaneous rhythms of movement and nonverbal behaviours, such as eye contact, facial movements and hand gestures, form the foundations for these movements. The ability to perceive and respond to the signals, cues and sequences of movement which are part of social interaction, provide

the child with some necessary prerequisites for forming relationships. All our early relationships are formed nonverbally, the first being the important relationship between primary caregiver and baby.

The child with profound learning disabilities is often denied the experience of these early relationships and the learning and development arising from them. The children may not give out the crucial cues and responses necessary for successful two-way interaction nor do they readily respond to them in others. Attempts to interact with them remain one-sided and, given no feedback, caregivers have great difficulty in establishing communication.

If a child does not interact with others then these early relationships cannot be formed. If the child does not perceive meaning in other people's movements a most important mode of communication remains unavailable and he is at a distinct disadvantage. The child's limited interactive experience further limits experience of self and others.

Before the onset of speech, nonhandicapped babies are able to communicate effectively and in a varied expressive way through nonverbal channels. Speech – when it comes – is an addition to the now familiar process of interaction. Without speech modern-day living would be extremely difficult but, as we have seen, the nonverbal components of interaction do not disappear when talking begins. They continue to add to the meaning of what is being said and at times are more valuable than the spoken word. People with profound learning disabilities may not develop speech, but they are able to take part in nonverbal 'conversations'. These conversations can be built up through consistent contact with an adult who has a perceptive, flexible and adaptable approach similar to that used by caregivers with their nonhandicapped babies. The person with profound learning disabilities will not necessarily develop the skill, variety and effectiveness of the baby who follows the normal path of development, but can develop enough to allow him or her to join the social world. No speech does not mean no communication.

INTERACTIONAL SYNCHRONY

When people communicate with each other their actions are precisely coordinated – a coordination which is a fundamental feature of social interaction (Kendon 1970). In filmed sequences of interactions – adult-to-adult as well as adult-to-child – the coordination of people's movements often resembles a dance. This dance refers to the synchronization of the participants during conversation and also to the individual's synchronization with his or her own speech patterns. As with limited nonverbal and interactive skills the impairment of interactional synchrony can have an effect on the quality of interactions.

During conversation, a person's words are accompanied by body movements which are in precise synchrony with his or her speech and the people listening also move in synchrony with the pattern of the speaker's speech (Condon 1979). Interactional synchrony can be observed even when individuals are not looking at each other but where the flow of speech can be heard (Danziger 1976). Cultural differences can affect synchrony. Although people from different cultures may be able to speak to each other in the same language their different movement styles may disturb interactional synchrony and hinder attempts to communicate fluently.

Babies also move synchronously with adult speech and this has very early beginnings indeed. Condon and Sander (1974) found that 1-day-old infants synchronized their movements with live and tape-recorded human speech, but not with isolated vowel sounds and regular tapping sounds. This synchrony was subsequently observed as early as 20 minutes after birth (Condon 1979). Trevarthen (1979) says that it is possible that the newborn baby does become locked into adult speech, with the speech sounds acting as pacemakers for the baby's limb movements, but believes that much of the timing of these movements comes from the baby's own motor pacemakers.

The baby's behaviour is temporally patterned from the very beginning of life. During interactions the caregiver fits in with this already organized behaviour, establishing a tempo suited to keeping the baby's attention. Microanalysis of interactions shows that the baby and caregiver coordinate with timing precise to a fraction of a second (Trevarthen 1984). Trevarthen (1984) also says that the tempo and organization of adult communication, especially when talking to babies, is very similar to the spontaneous tempo and organization of the movements of infants.

Von Raffler-Engel (1981) states that an adult or older child wishing to join a group conversation will establish interactional synchrony with the group members before beginning to speak, unless wishing to take over leadership. In contrast, a toddler will dyssynchronize to gain attention. Von Raffler-Engel (1981) suggests three distinct periods – the infant synchronizes, the toddler dyssynchronizes and the older child synchronizes once again.

Bower (1977) describes the movement synchrony of babies as distinctively social behaviour. The synchrony of the 1-day-old babies observed by Condon and Sanders was elicited only by human speech and not by other sounds. This synchrony, when it occurs between care giver and baby, is very important in conveying a feeling that the baby is responding (Bower 1977) and that they are both on the same wavelength. Where a baby does not display interactional synchrony, caregivers find it difficult to get on the same wavelength. There can be a serious breakdown of communication when brain damage or severe mental illness affects a person's ability to synchronize his or her movements with other people. Research has shown that a wide range of children with learning disabilities experience difficulty in moving synchronously with human speech and sound (Condon 1979). In relation to those who show an autistic-like isolation, the degree of disturbed synchrony increases with the degree of isolation (Condon 1979).

Synchronizing with others is not something we normally observe during communication in the way that we are aware of facial expressions and gestures. It is only when film or video recordings are available, allowing repeated observations at slow speeds and observing one frame at a time, that we have an opportunity to observe how people synchronize and dovetail their communicative behaviours. However, we do *feel* the effects of problems with synchrony and these problems can seriously disrupt the effectiveness of the communication. It is possible to overcome difficulties by adapting to the movements of the person with difficulties. Lewis (1978) cites as an example a mother who was unable to form a bond with her baby who suffered from cerebral palsy and whose jerky movements made it difficult for her to synchronize with him. When shown how to move in the same way as her baby, copying his abrupt actions, it is reported that she was able to achieve the synchronization needed to help form the bond.

Adapting one's movement to accommodate the movement patterns of others is not easy. It can feel strange and uncomfortable, the more so if the person's movement is odd in comparison to more usual ways of moving. However, the discomfort of adapting to an awkward movement pattern diminishes after the initial encounters. It is a very helpful approach to adopt, especially with very isolated people unaware of and unable to adapt to the movements of others. By adapting to a person's manner of moving and developing a degree of synchrony, it is possible to convey a feeling of sharing, which helps to alleviate some of the person's isolation. Through time it might be possible to encourage some adaptability from both participants.

So far, we have seen that there is more than an exchange of verbal messages during interactions; the nonverbal features of communication have been described and their purpose explained. Now the synchrony of movements during interactions can be added to this understanding. People are engaged daily in countless interactions, usually with no awareness of the complexities involved in helping the interactions to run smoothly and effectively. People may not be conscious of interactional synchrony, but it is a powerful dance; poor synchrony can seriously diminish interactive effectiveness.

COMMUNICATION THROUGH MOVEMENT – GENERAL POINTS

There are many factors to be taken into account when attempting to develop communication and relationships through movement. One chapter in a book cannot cover all the possibilities, developments and pitfalls which might be encountered. Human communication and all its variables cannot be condensed in this way. This section is intended to provide some very general guidelines. Much depends on the quality of input and sensitive awareness of the caregiver.

We have to be continually aware of the effect our activities could have on participants. If they experience anxiety or discomfort they may withdraw or fail to respond. We have to be aware of the effect on someone when we approach him closely or engage him in activity which may have no meaning for him. We should also beware of misinterpreting unconventional attempts to communicate with us. Neither should we assume that all movement feels the same to everyone. Amongst any group of people personal experience of the same movement can vary greatly. Some movement may feel pleasant to one person but be uncomfortable for another, depending on the person's usual manner of moving and the way he is feeling at the time. If a group of people were asked to run across a large open space and leap into the air with body stretched out wide, some would enjoy doing so while others would dislike the exposed feeling it gives. The person who enjoys the experience on one occasion might find it less enjoyable on another, perhaps on a day when beset by personal problems and disappointments – she just does not feel like taking a joyous leap into the air.

The pleasant or uncomfortable experience of a certain way of moving does not necessarily remain static. Moods can have an effect on this experience. We might find that a child who enjoyed rocking, bouncing and swinging in a play session the previous day does not feel like these activities the following day. She may be in a quieter mood, seeking close physical contact and gentle rocking. It helps if caregivers accommodate these fluctuations, rather than following a prescribed plan of activities which does not match up with the child's responses. The aim in this kind of approach is to open up channels of communication and develop relationships, rather than focusing on the performance of specific activities. The movement should be adapted to meet the needs of the individual.

People with profound learning disabilities who enjoy activities such as swinging and rocking may, through time, develop nonverbal 'signs' which they use to 'ask' for the activity. For example, imagine a child who particularly enjoys being given a swing. In the course of play sessions the swinging is repeated many times and the person begins to anticipate what comes next. As the caregiver bends to pick him up and swing him round, he shows his readiness by raising an arm. Once this is an established pattern the caregiver can begin waiting until the child raises his arm before repeating the swing. In time he may raise his arm out-of-the-blue to show that he wants a swing: thus his homemade sign has become a clear way of communicating choice, independent of actions by the caregiver. Having found a way of making a choice known, many children begin to develop other nonverbal ways of asking for other activities they especially enjoy.

The key word is 'enjoyment'. As we have seen, not everyone enjoys close physical contact with others or lots of movement activity. A person is unlikely to develop a homemade sign to initiate something he dislikes. The person who thoroughly enjoys a rough and tumble play session is more likely to develop some way of asking for these activities.

These signs, or cues, are idiosyncratic and their beginnings lie in the person's spontaneous actions. Different people may have different ways of indicating a wish for the same activity. The cues often arise from random movements which eventually develop into intentional actions with specific meanings. This happens because the adult consistently acts on the movement as if it had meaning. Some children will signal clearly and with intention that they want something to be repeated. Other children will develop cues that are less easy to recognize and will be difficult for strangers and those less familiar with the child to detect. Care givers are the most likely to be aware of the person's ways of communicating and what they signify and can help

greatly by making this information available to others.

The success of this approach will depend on how much the child enjoys the activities and on how well we observe her actions and are able to pick up her cues. As the child grows older and bigger she may lose interest in a particular activity and stop using the sign she has devised for it, but she will retain the lesson she has learned about communicating. This way of communicating can be viewed in practical and theoretical terms:

- *Practical* B will lift his arms when he wants to be swung round. C will hold her hand out in a certain way when she wants to be rocked. E will lie on the floor and raise his arm when he wants to be rolled along the floor.
- *Theoretical* B, C and E have all found a way of exerting some control over events in their world. They have gained an understanding that their actions have meaning and can have an effect on others. They can make choices and initiate events and are able to have a say in directing a play session. It is very difficult to encourage people with profound learning disabilities to initiate activity and this kind of approach provides opportunities for this to develop.

The communication of those with profound learning disabilities is presymbolic. The ways in which they develop these forms of requests arise from a personal desire. They are not derived from imitating the actions of caregivers. It does not follow that a person who communicates in this way will then be able to progress to copying and using a formal system of signing, e.g. Makaton.

Communication is best encouraged by working in partnership with the person with learning disabilities. Play activities should be done with the person rather than to her. Through working with the person, the caregiver will gain a sense of the force and speed of the action the person prefers. Two people using the same activities with the same person can produce very different results. In one case the person with learning disabilities might express her usual enjoyment, whereas in the other she is very quiet and sub-dued. This does not mean that the action should always be fast and furious. Sometimes a slow, gentle pace might be the most suitable approach.

Subtle differences in the pace of actions used by caregivers to encourage communication in people with profound learning disabilities can have an important effect. Caregivers frequently use repetitive actions to stimulate responses and to keep the communication going, e.g. patting a hand, stroking a person's head, playfully shaking an arm, bouncing and rocking. In a study of communication in children and young people with profound multiple learning disabilities such actions were observed to be performed by caregivers at precisely the same speed for the same purposes (Burford 1988). The pace of the movements was seen to play a critical role in the success of the communication, e.g. a timid child might only respond positively to a slow pace of movement, withdrawing from contact if it was too fast for him. Mothers were also observed using similar actions with the same precise timings with their nonhandicapped infants and, interestingly, similar actions and identical speeds were observed being used by the children and young people with profound learning disabilities (Burford 1988). This suggests that there is a biological timing for communicative movements that is a very set part of human behaviour.

Appropriate stimulation

Those with learning disabilities should be offered stimulation which is appropriate to their needs. Surrounding the person with noises, voices, activity, musical sounds and a multitude of games might have a detrimental rather than a positive effect if the person experiences it as a confusing and meaningless buzz. Some thrive on being surrounded by a variety of stimuli, while others find such bombardment difficult to tolerate. The flood of stimuli causes them distress and they find ways of withdrawing into themselves and shutting it out. With some it is more appropriate to present one thing at a time with an unhurried pace in a quiet atmosphere.

The same applies to our manner. A loud voice and animated movements may be the best approach with one person, whereas with another we may need to speak softly and minimize our movements. Sometimes it is more effective to remain silent, especially with those who are very withdrawn and wary of being near others. Using the tone of voice and speaking to a person with learning disabilities is very important, but there are times when it is best not to speak and we should be sensitive to this. In quiet moments the sound of a voice can be an intrusion, spoiling the atmosphere and having a disrupting effect on the communication. There are no set rules about when to speak and when to keep silent, but the person's responses and mood will be a helpful guide. Often doing what feels right rather than what we think we ought to be doing helps us to match the mood of the moment aptly.

Adaptable approach

The aim of this style of communication is to forge and develop personal relationships. A key word in this approach is 'adaptability'. We readily lapse into ways of moving that feel comfortable. In day-to-day activities this need not necessarily be of any consequence, unless faulty movement habits place undue stress on our bodies. However, when we use movement as a way of encouraging communication in others then our own movements do become very important and we should monitor our movements to ensure that we do not lapse into our own comfortable patterns. Rocking a child can be comforting and soothing but, as illustrated earlier, many movement factors are involved in the rocking action. An adult who prefers fast, vigorous movement will need to take care not to lapse into this way of moving when rocking a child who prefers a slow rocking action. Otherwise it can be an unpleasant experience, discouraging the child from cooperating.

Not all differences are obvious. Someone who enjoys having his hand tapped might show his interest by stopping his stereotyped mannerisms, ceasing to grind his teeth, turning his head towards the adult and holding his hand in anticipation of a repeat. It might be that he enjoys having his hand tapped in any way, but it is also possible that he prefers a certain amount of force and a certain timing. Perhaps he likes the sensation of bursts of tapping, or maybe he enjoys having his palm tapped but not the back of his hand. It takes a bit of detective work to gain a full picture of what will be most effective.

Microscopic details

It was said at the beginning of the chapter that when we enter the world of nonverbal communication we enter a world of microscopic detail. This also applies when using nonverbal communication and movement with people with profound learning disabilities. Tiny details, often idiosyncratic, can mean the difference between success or failure in eliciting and sustaining communicative responses. When these are viewed in isolation and out of context, and are judged by the standards of the world at large, their relevance seems negligible. Stating that A likes having his hand tapped does not convey the full significance of this information: that it might lead to other ways of communicating, expand A's horizons and bring him into communicative contact with a greater number of people. In the restricted world of the person with profound learning disabilities tiny details, which would usually seem very trivial, can assume great importance.

People with learning disabilities, as with any group of people, vary tremendously both in the manner in which they move and the amount of movement they use. For example, some seem to be always on the move, never being still for a moment. Others rarely move, even when unrestricted by physical disabilities. One person may move as much as the limits of her physical disabilities allow, whereas another similarly disabled person moves much less.

Observation of someone who appears to move around continuously may show that the movement is limited and repetitive. The manner of moving and the actions are always the same. By using the person's present form of movement as a starting point, it is often possible to channel this slowly into a wider range of movement, in-creasing the possibilities for responding. Many encounters will be needed to give this time to develop.

Of course, not all participants cooperate when we try to involve them in communication. Some people appear unaware of their surroundings, showing no curiosity or inclination to explore. Some, if left to their own devices, lie on the floor or sit apart, while others roam about with no purpose. There are those who deliberately block out their surroundings and withdraw from other people. With others we may have to run a gauntlet of nips, scratches and spits in our attempts to encourage positive communication. Whatever the problem, we have to work hard to find a starting point, experimenting with different ways of moving with the person and of approaching at different distances and spatial orientations. Sometimes we need to react to any movement, however slight and however random it may seem, and see where this leads.

Often, barriers are caused by stereotyped movement or the dislike of intrusion in the personal space. There are those who exhibit stereotyped activity throughout most of their waking day. For example, some move their arms, hands and fingers in a repetitive pattern, focusing on this movement to the exclusion of the people and events around them. They will carry on with this movement regardless of surroundings – a crowded shop or empty room makes no difference to them. Others might pace about the room following an unvarying fixed route. Stereotyped movements are often performed to the virtual exclusion of everything else. This type of movement can stimulate, relieve boredom, soothe and provide a secure barrier. It very effectively blocks out the outside world, making communication attempts extremely difficult. Even where we can approach someone closely without adverse effects, her postural and movement barriers can still shut us out.

We must also be careful not to intervene too quickly and for too long. As an example, someone who paces around following an unvarying pathway and constantly taps one hand with the other, with both hands held close to her face, presents strong barriers. It might be too much to pace alongside her, remain close and join in with the hand movements all at the same time. It is more likely to be successful if the process is broken down into smaller parts. For example, we might find that the person can tolerate someone pacing alongside her if a distance is maintained. Through time we can aim to get closer then begin reaching out occasionally to touch the outside of her hand, gradually becoming involved in the repetitive hand movements. Now we are in a position to encourage other hand movements that can more readily include other people. If stereotyped actions serve as a barrier to contact with others it is likely that initially they will increase in intensity, but carefully paced intervention helps to overcome this. As with any approach with people who find social contact difficult the process is slow and painstaking and has to be repeated many times.

Many different obstacles may be encountered and a flexible and adaptable use of movement will be needed to help overcome them. A very agile, active and easily distracted child will require a different approach to the child who prefers to remain huddled in a corner on his own. However, there is a shared theme running through any approach which might be used – the communication is built around the child's actions and sounds. The adult reacts to whatever the child does and elaborates on this, creating a nonverbal conversation which, at first, may be very one-sided. Gradually, the child becomes aware of the part he is playing and its effects, so that the conversation begins to have some meaning for him. He may begin to use certain actions and vocalizations for intended purposes and two-way communication begins to develop. In this way idiosyncratic actions take on a more amenable form and meaning, enabling other people to communicate with the child, opening up the possibilities for forming a variety of relationships.

Two-way communication does not require equal amounts of input from each participant. When communicating with a person with profound learning disabilities the caregiver might have a greater input both verbally and nonverbally, but the other person may well be responding equally intensely within his or her limitations. The communication is not about facts or events, rather it is a way of acknowledging each other, sharing feelings and enjoying each other's company.

Caregivers should tailor what they do and say to suit the individual's needs and style of responding. They need to give the person with learning disabilities time to respond in his own way and at his own pace, allowing him to play his part in directing the communication. In time he may become more able to adapt to what others are doing, sharing in interactions which do not need to be so focused and dependent on what he does. Thus a more genuine partnership can evolve.

Of course, it is not possible to develop the same degree of communication with everyone. For example, some people may become more responsive to others, perhaps being able to tolerate the contact for a brief time whereas before they would withdraw from any attempts to communicate. They might even initiate communication occasionally. Others may form deeper relationships and, where this is the case, students and others who will only be in a ward or unit on a temporary basis should take great care when establishing and developing relationships with residents. When temporary staff leave, the person with learning disabilities loses someone to whom he or she has become deeply attached. The pain of such a loss is compounded by the lack of understanding about why the familiar figure is no longer there. All too often those in residential care have many experiences of this type of loss – experiences that are painful for any human being. It is important for transitory staff to bear this in mind when encouraging communication and developing relationships. This is not to say that in these circumstances communication should not be attempted but that it should be tempered accordingly.

Similarly, if a caregiver is successful in building up a relationship with someone who, previously noncommunicating, now relates to the caregiver and no one else, the responsibility is enormous. It will be more beneficial for the person with learning disabilities to be able to respond to a variety of people. Other people may not be able to communicate so richly or fluently but it does relieve the burden of being the sole communicator. Each will bring something different to the communication, providing opportunities for new developments. Therefore, it is important to ensure that any information about the ways in which the person with learning disabilities responds, and the form of approach which is most effective in encouraging communication, is shared with others involved in his or her care and education.

Caregivers encounter many similar problems within the population with profound learning disabilities, but each person is also unique and a blueprint for successful communication cannot be applied mechanically in an unvarying form. This is also true for the development of early communication in nonhandicapped babies – the style of communication which, as we have seen, is relevant for people with profound learning disabilities. Stern (1977) describes the caregiver's part in the development of interactions with her baby as a lonely one, based on continual improvisation in which the 'steps and notes' have never been written down. Although there are similarities between caregivers, each mother and baby will also show differences. Learning to interact is a creative and personal process for both mother and baby. This is just as true for people with profound learning disabilities and their caregivers.

Caregivers of people with profound learning disabilities have to work very hard to establish interactions. Nonhandicapped babies come into the world primed to take part in interactions with others (Newson 1979). The person with profound learning disabilities is also primed, but their communicative ingredients have been scrambled and not all are in working order. The caregiver has to unscramble the ingredients, find out what is working and use this as a starting point for building communication and relationships. Once we have found a starting point in nonverbal interaction the way is open to establishing and developing a dialogue – we have achieved communication through movement.

SUMMARY

People can communicate through nonverbal channels whether or not they are talking to each other and this can be more powerful than the spoken word. People with learning disabilities may have a limited range of nonverbal channels through which they can communicate and express themselves, but with careful observation and sensitive adaptability the caregiver can use the remaining channels effectively.

Some of the features of nonverbal communication which can be of particular relevance to people with learning disabilities are interpersonal distance, personal space, orientation, physical contact and looking at others. These features need to be especially considered when encouraging communication in those who distance and protect themselves from communicative contact with other people.

Cultural, social and emotional factors all influence the ways in which we communicate and express ourselves nonverbally. We need to acknowledge these factors when we are developing communication through these channels and when using observations of nonverbal behaviour to provide information about a person. For example, gestures and postures can provide us with information, but the variety of factors which affect the gestures or postures should be taken into account.

From an examination of the detailed world of nonverbal communication we proceeded to look at human movement and its complex nature. The context in which the movement takes place gives it its meaning and defines its purpose. Movement, as described here, is used to develop communication with those who have little or no verbal language, whose overall ability to communicate is very restricted. We are concerned with developing communication with and *through* movement set within a social context.

It is not only the external environment that affects movement. Intangible factors from within the person also have an effect and movement can provide a link between inner self and outside world, and between one person and another. The ingredients of expressive movement are the same whether or not the movement looks strange or normally acceptable and this provides a common factor for forming a link between people.

It is important to look at *how* a person is moving as well as the action itself. Observed actions can be broken down into smaller parts and in doing this we usually discover many differences between individuals performing the same movement. It is these differences which often hold the key to success in developing some form of communication. Care should be taken in interpreting someone's movement and this should not be confused with objective observation. The subjective nature of interpretation should always be acknowledged.

Communication and expression do not share the same meaning. There is sometimes a need to express oneself regardless of whether or not it is understood by others, and sometimes a need to communicate something clearly. The person with learning disabilities should have an opportunity for both communication and expression, and where speech does not exist or is very limited, nonverbal channels can provide the means to do this.

The beginnings of communication are found very early in life. Through interactions with the caregiver and others in his or her world, the baby is able to join the social world and to form relationships. The baby is practised in conversation well before the onset of speech. Overcoming difficulties which arise when this process does not proceed smoothly demands hard work and sensitivity from the caregiver. It is important

for care givers to find a starting point in the child's behaviour through which they can form the initial link.

Interactional synchrony is another important feature for successful interaction. When people talk to each other their movements are coordinated and resemble a dance routine. Poor interactional synchrony can lead to difficulties in communicating and forming relationships.

The final section outlines general points which need to be considered by caregivers when communicating through movement. No blueprint can be offered for human communication, only general guidelines and hints. All the hints are centred on the caregiver's ability to adapt to the actions and timing of others, to monitor her or his own actions and their effects and to be sensitive to the cues, reactions and moods of the person with learning disabilities. Stimulation does not necessarily require lots of hustle and bustle and should be appropriate to the needs of the person with learning disabilities.

It is essential to use movement in an adaptable way. The end product is to develop better communication using movement, rather than developing specific movement skills. Effective communication opens up the way to form and consolidate relationships with people who have learning disabilities, allowing them to express something of themselves which may be impossible through speech. Communication through movement can be a richly varied and expressive experience.

REFERENCES

Argyle M 1972 Nonverbal communication in human social interaction. In: Hinde R (ed) Nonverbal communication. Cambridge University Press, Cambridge
Argyle M 1973 Social interaction. Tavistock, London
Birdwhistell R L 1968 Kinesics. In: Argyle M (ed) Social encounters. Penguin, Harmondsworth
Birdwhistell R L 1971 Kinesics and context. Essays on body-motion communication. Penguin, Harmondsworth
Bower T G R 1977 A primer of infant development. Freeman, San Francisco
Bruner J 1974 From communication to language – a psychological perspective. In: Lee V (ed) Language development. The Open University, London
Buck R 1984 Spontaneous and symbolic nonverbal behavior

and the ontogeny of communication. In: Feldman R S (ed) Development of nonverbal behavior in children. Springer-Verlag, Cambridge
Bullowa M 1979 Prelinguistic communication: a field for scientific research. In: Bullowa M (ed) Before speech: the beginning of interpersonal communication. Cambridge University Press, Cambridge
Burford B 1988 Action cycles: rhythmic actions for engagement with children and young adults with profound mental handicap. European Journal of Special Needs Education 3(4): 189–206
Condon W S 1979 Neonatal entrainment and enculturation. In: Bullowa M (ed) Before speech: the beginning of interpersonal communication. Cambridge University

Press, Cambridge

Condon W S, Sanders L W 1974 Neonate movement is synchronized with adult speech; interactional participation and language acquisition. Science 183, 99–101.

Danziger K 1976 Interpersonal communication. Pergamon Press, Oxford

Ekman P, Friesen W V 1966 Non-verbal leakage and clues to deception. In: Argyle M (ed) Social encounters. Penguin, Harmondsworth

Farb P 1977 Word play. Coronet, London

Firth R 1970 Postures and gestures of respect. In: Polhemus T (ed) Social aspects of the human body. Penguin, Harmondsworth

Hall E T 1966 The hidden dimension. Doubleday, New York

Hewes G 1955 World distribution of certain postural habits. In: Polhemus T (ed) Social aspects of the human body. Penguin, Harmondsworth

Jourard S M 1966 An exploratory study of body-accessibility. British Journal of Social and Clinical Psychology, 5: 221–231

Kendon A 1967 Some functions of gaze-direction in social interaction. In: Argyle M (ed) Social encounters. Penguin, Harmondsworth

Kendon A 1970 Movement coordination in dance therapy and conversation. In: Proceedings of workshop in dance therapy: its research potentials. Committee on Research in Dance, New York

LaBarre W 1947 The cultural basis of emotions and gestures. In: Polhemus T (ed) Social aspects of the human body. Penguin, Harmondsworth

Lewis D 1978 The secret language of your child. Pan Books, London

Negayama K 1991 Personal communication.

Newson J 1979 Growth of shared understanding between infant and care givers. In: Bullowa M (ed) Before speech: the beginning of interpersonal communication.

Cambridge University Press, Cambridge

Parry J 1967 The psychology of human communication. University of London Press, London

Schaffer R 1977a Mothering. Fontana/Open Books, Glasgow

Schaffer R 1977b Early interactive development. In: Oates J (ed) Early cognitive development. The Open University, London

Snow C 1977 The development of conversation between mothers and babies. In: Lee V (ed) Language development. The Open University, London

Stern D 1977 The first relationship: infant and mother. Fontana/Open Books, Glasgow

Stern D 1985 The interpersonal world of the infant. Basic Books, New York

Strube M J, Werner C 1982 Interpersonal distance and personal space: a conceptual and methodological note. Journal of Nonverbal Behaviour 6: 163–170

Trevarthen C 1979 Communication and cooperation in early infancy: a description of primary intersubjectivity. In: Bullowa M (ed) Before speech: The beginning of interpersonal communication. Cambridge University Press, Cambridge

Trevarthen C, Murray L, Hubley P 1981 Psychology of infants. In: Davies J A, Dobbing J (ed) Scientific foundations of paediatrics. Heinemann, London

Trevarthen C 1984 How control of movement develops. In: Whiting H T A (ed) Human motor actions – Bernstein reassessed. Elsevier Science Publishers B V, North Holland

Trevarthen C 1985 Facial expressions of emotion in mother-infant interaction. Human Neurobiology, 4: 21–32

Von Raffler-Engel W 1981 Developmental kinesics: how children acquire communication and non-communication. Infant Mental Health Journal 2: 84–94

Watson O M, Graves T D 1966 Quantitative research in proxemic behaviour. In: Argyle M (ed) Social encounters. Penguin, Harmondsworth

Context for decision-making

SECTION CONTENTS

13. Ethical issues   293

14. Helping agencies   307

The third section examines factors that affect the judgement of service providers, whether directly (as in day-to-day decisions taken by care staff) or indirectly (as in decisions taken by managers, civil servants and politicians).

Individuals within the services are constantly facing decisions that have a strong moral dimension. Guidelines for such decisions include social role valorization, professional codes of conduct and statutory legislation. However, many of the decisions are made without the help of clearly stated guidelines. In such cases, the individuals must depend on their own set of values. In addition, a chapter in the section examines the consequences of decisions taken in terms of resources and facilities allocated to services for those with learning disabilities.

CHAPTER CONTENTS

Introduction 293

Morals and ethics 296

Development of personal values 297

Duty of care/duty to care 297

Ethical issues 299
Personhood 299
Autonomy versus paternalism 300
Competence 301

Day-to-day dilemmas 302

Coping with ethical dilemmas 302
Philosophical models and approaches 302
   Consequentialist 302
   Motivist 302
   Deontological 302
   Naturalistic 303
   Emotivistic 303
   Utilitarian 303
A systematic approach 303

13

Ethical issues

I. Hessler   B. Kay

Key points

- While codes of ethics offer guidance for professional carers' behaviour, a conflict of values can arise within the individual carer and result in the experience of a moral dilemma
- Being aware of one's own values and beliefs is a prerequisite for coping with ethical dilemmas
- The prescribed set of values in caring for those with learning disabilities is contained in the principles of normalization
- Professional carers may experience conflict between meeting their obligations to their clients and to their employers, particularly where facilities are considered inadequate
- Acknowledgment of the right to personhood demands a client-centred holistic approach to care
- Well-intentioned, paternalistic actions aimed at protecting the individual can deprive the person of his autonomy
- Playing safe in assuming that the person has not got the competence to carry out activities that might involve a small degree of risk can be seen as depriving him or her of rights accorded to those with no learning disabilities
- Knowledge of various approaches used in dealing with ethical dilemmas can help the carer cope with situations encountered

INTRODUCTION

This chapter examines the rights of people with disabilities to exercise basic human rights and the duties of society to see that provisions are available and accessible for them to do so. Considerable responsibility for ensuring these rights are exercised rests with professional carers. Some of these rights and duties have been enshrined in codes and laws, beginning with the Hippocratic oath, drawn up in Greece, in the 5th century BC. A form of this oath is taken by doctors, binding them to observe the code of medical ethics (see Box 13.1).

Box 13.1 OATH OF HIPPOCRATES

'At the time of being admitted as a member of the medical profession I solemnly pledge myself to consecrate my life to the service of humanity; I will give to my teachers the respect and gratitude which is their due; I will practise my profession with conscience and dignity; the health of my patient will be my first consideration; I will respect the secrets which are confided in me; I will maintain by all means in my power, the honour and the noble traditions of the medical profession; my colleagues will be my brothers; I will not permit considerations of religion, nationality, race, party politics or social standing to intervene between my duty and my patient; I will maintain the utmost respect for human life, from the time of conception, even under threat; I will not use medical knowledge contrary to the laws of humanity. I make these promises solemnly, freely and upon my honour.'

Dunkerley (1975) states that:

It is necessary for a professional group to develop a code of ethics to guide the conduct of the members of the group and to provide them with the approval from society to pursue their profession. pp 55–56.

Lord Cohen, in a lecture on medical ethics cited in Phoon Wai (1971), said that the essence of a profession is that though men enter it for the sake of their livelihood, the measure of success is the service they perform and not the gains they amass.

Nursing subscribes to a Code of Professional Conduct (see Box 13.2) produced by the United Kingdom Central Council for Nursing, Midwifery and Health Visiting (UKCC 1992). The code states that:

Each registered nurse, midwife and health visitor shall act, at all times, in such a manner as to:

- safeguard and promote the interests of individual patients and clients;
- serve the interests of society;
- justify public trust and confidence and
- uphold and enhance the good standing and reputation of the professions.

Other professional groups produce their own codes. The challenge of these codes is that they must be stringent enough to give clear guidelines and yet flexible enough to allow creative decisions to be made, both in extraordinary situations and in the face of advances in care. Despite the existence of the code of conduct conflicts will occur and give rise to ethical dilemmas. Being aware of one's own values and beliefs is an important start to coping with ethical problems. Understanding the philosophies which underpin the provision of care is also important. A code of ethics of a professional group, especially in the caring professions, gives useful guidelines for behaviour and provides the people being cared for with reassurance that their interests come first, and that the highest possible standards of care will be given.

Human rights (and corresponding duties in others) are described as the universal, inviolable and inalienable rights which are due to a human being as a rational person endowed with free will. Rights are his or hers by nature because of being a person. It may be necessary at times to safeguard those with disabilities against individuals, the state, and society, and even against the institution, the Church, or parents from impinging on or denying their rights. Modern awareness of and sensitivity to human rights is associated with the Virginia Bill of Rights (1776) and the United States Declaration of Independence (1776). These could be said to have a Christian basis, but the 1789 National Assembly of the French Revolution, in defining human rights, relied on 'Reason' and explicitly rejected God. The culmination of this evolving agreement was the Universal Declaration of Human Rights (1948) by the United Nations (UN) and later the Declaration of the UN to the General Assembly of the United Nations on the Rights of the Handicapped. An outline of the rights of people with a handicap is set out in Box 13.3. Details of the rights of those who are mentally handicapped are given in Box 13.4.

Box 13.2   Code of Professional Conduct UKCC 1992

Each registered nurse, midwife and health visitor shall act, at all times, in such a manner as to:

- safeguard and promote the interests of individual patients and clients;
- serve the interests of society;
- justify public trust and confidence and
- uphold and enhance the good standing and reputation of the professions.

As a registered nurse, midwife or health visitor, you are personally accountable for your practice and, in the exercise of your professional accountability, must:

1. act always in a such a manner as to promote and safeguard the interests and well-being of patients and clients;
2. ensure that no action or omission on your part, or within your sphere of responsibility, is detrimental to interest, condition or safety of patients and clients;
3. maintain and improve your professional knowledge and competence;
4. acknowledge any limitations in your knowledge and competence and decline any duties or responsibilities unless able to perform them in a safe and skilled manner;
5. work in an open and cooperative manner with patients, clients and their families, foster their independence and recognise and respect their involvement in the planning and delivery of care;
6. work in a collaborative and co-operative manner with health care professionals and others involved in providing care, and recognise and respect their particular contributions within the care team;
7. recognise and respect the uniqueness and dignity of each patient and client, and respond to their need for care, irrespective of their ethnic origin, religious beliefs, personal attributes, the nature of their health problems or any other factor;
8. report to an appropriate person or authority, at the earliest possible time, any conscientious objection which may be relevant to your professional practice;
9. avoid any abuse of your privileged relationship with patients and clients and of the privileged access allowed to their person, property, residence or workplace;
10. protect all confidential information concerning patients and clients, obtained in the course of professional practice and make disclosures only with consent, where required by the order of a court or where you can justify disclosure in the wider public interest;
11. report to an appropriate person or authority, having regard to the physical, psychological and social effects on patients and clients, any circumstances in the environment of care which could jeopardise standard of practice;
12. report to an appropriate person or authority any circumstances in which safe and appropriate care for patients and clients cannot be provided;
13. report to an appropriate person or authority where it appears that the health or safety of colleagues is at risk, as such circumstances may compromise standards of practice and care;
14. assist professional colleagues, in the context of your own knowledge, experience and sphere of responsibility, to develop their professional competence, and assist others in the care team, including informal carers, to contribute safely and to a degree appropriate to their roles;
15. refuse any gift, favour or hospitality from patients or clients currently in your care which might be interpreted as seeking to exert influence to obtain preferential consideration and
16. ensure that your registration status is not used in the promotion of commercial products or services, declare any financial or other interests in relevant organisations providing such goods or services and ensure that your professional judgement is not influenced by any commercial considerations.

These rights are set in the wider context of civil liberties which operate within the United Kingdom and the European Convention for the Protection of Human Rights. Seighart (1988) states:

An enterprise culture of the kind which is in current fashion here and increasingly in other parts of the world brings benefits for many: it clearly promotes material prosperity, efficiency, and other economic indicators of a strong nation. But a strong nation is not enough: the only ultimate value of strength is to make it – and keep it – civilized. It is not the strong who need protection for their human rights: they have ample power to protect them, for themselves. But in return, they owe a concomitant duty to use their strength to protect those of the weak, who do not have the power to achieve this on their own.

And however little a government may wish to interfere in the lives of its inhabitants, one of its primary duties – now underpinned by International Law – is to ensure that all of them can enjoy all their human rights and fundamental freedoms.

In the United Kingdom the philosophy adopted to facilitate this duty for care for those with learning disabilities is that of normalization. In essence, what this advocated is that people who have a disability have the same rights as those without disability: to live conventional lives but with special provision being made to help them to minimize the effect of their disability or disabilities.

Box 13.3 Declaration of the UN to the General Assembly of the United Nations on the Rights of the Handicapped 1968

1. The term handicapped designates each person as unable to procure for himself all or part of the necessities of an individual or social life because of deficiency, congenital or otherwise, in his mental or physical capacities.
2. The handicapped has an essential right to respect for his human dignity whatever may be the origin, nature, and the gravity of his troubles and deficiencies; the handicapped has the same basic rights as his fellow citizens of the same age which implies in the first place the enjoyment of a decent life as normal and fulfilled as possible.
3. The handicapped has the right to medical, psychological and functional treatments, including artificial limbs and appliances, to medical and social rehabilitation, to education, to professional training and rehabilitation, to aids, counsel and services which could ensure the maximum use of his capacities and aptitudes, and would hasten the process of his social integration or reintegration.
4. The handicapped has the right to social and economic security and a decent standard of living. He has the right, according to his possibilities, to obtain and keep an employment or to carry on useful, productive and remunerative occupation and to join a trade union.
5. The handicapped has the right to have his particular needs taken into account at every stage of social and economic planning.
6. The handicapped has the right to live with his family or in a substantive home, and to take part in all social, creative or recreative activities. No handicapped should be submitted in the way of residence, to distinctive treatment which is not required by his condition or by the relief which might be procured for him. If it is necessary for him to stay in a special establishment, the surroundings and lifestyle should be as much as possible those of the normal life of people of his age group.
7. The handicapped must be protected against all exploitation, all regimentation, or discriminatory, abusive or degrading treatments.
8. Organizations for the handicapped could be usefully consulted on all questions concerning the rights of the handicapped.
9. The handicapped, his family and his community should be fully informed by all appropriate means, of the common rights contained in this declaration.

Box 13.4 Scots law and the rights of the mentally handicapped (Ward 1984)

Article I The mentally retarded person has the same basic rights as other citizens of the same country and same age.
Article II The mentally retarded person has the right to proper medical care and physical restoration and to such education, training, habilitation and guidance as will enable him to develop his ability and potential to the fullest extent, no matter how severe his degree of disability. No mentally handicapped person should be deprived of such services by reason of the costs involved.
Article III The mentally retarded person has the right to economic security and to a decent standard of living. He has a right to productive work or to other meaningful occupation.
Article IV The mentally retarded person has the right to live with his own family or with foster parents; to participate in all aspects of community life, and to be provided with appropriate leisure time activities. If care in an institution becomes necessary, it should be in surroundings and under circumstances as close to normal living as possible.

Article V The mentally retarded person has a right to a qualified guardian when this is required to protect his personal well-being and interest. No person rendering direct services to the mentally retarded person should also serve as his guardian.
Article VI The mentally retarded person has the right to protection from exploitation, abuse and degrading treatment. If accused, he has the right to a fair trial with full recognition being given to his degree of responsibility.
Article VII Some mentally retarded persons may be unable, due to the severity of their handicap to exercise for themselves all of their rights in a meaningful way. For others, modification of some or all of these rights is appropriate. The procedure used for modification or denial of rights must contain proper legal safeguards against every form of abuse, must be based on an evaluation of the social capability of the mentally retarded person by qualified experts and must be subject to periodic reviews and to the right of appeal to higher authorities.

MORALS AND ETHICS

Moral acts are social in nature, i.e. they involve people and the ways in which they behave toward each other. However, not all social acts are moral. Social acts may range from polite and courteous behaviours to highly moral behaviours. Wright (1971) sees moral behaviour as consisting of all the various things people do in connection with moral rules. He identifies moral rules as those concerned with keeping promises, honesty, respect for the rights of individuals, sympathy for those in need, and of maintaining trust, mutual help and justice in human relationships.

In any society some human actions are deemed wrong and society incorporates rules for these into the laws of the country. Breaking these rules is an illegal act and the offender is usually punished. Professional groups have more specific rules of conduct. These rules are embodied in codes of ethics and are not necessarily enshrined in the laws of the country. However, breaking these rules constitutes an unacceptable act and the group's governing body, e.g. the UKCC, may inflict a punishment on the perpetrator. Other sets of rules are part of the norm of social groups. The breach of a rule may involve formal retribution through disapproval by other members of the group, which may elicit more conforming behaviour in the transgressor.

Sometimes, individuals may experience the dilemma of having to decide on a course of action that conforms with one set of rules while breaking another set. Consider the group of people you feel closest to in your work situation. Your work colleague acts in a way you feel is wrong in the care of those you are both responsible for. Where do your loyalties lie? Which rules do you follow – those of your group, or the regulations or rules which state such action is wrong? Codes of ethics may depend on those who formulate them fully understanding the complexities and boundaries of the moral climate. Moral boundaries can change as new values emerge, e.g. the current enabling of the rights of people with an intellectual disability makes a significant shift in the moral boundaries of care.

DEVELOPMENT OF PERSONAL VALUES

A report carried out into children and their primary schools (HMSO 1967) stated that moral development was closely associated with social and emotional development:

The child forms his sense of personal worth and his moral sense from early approval and disapproval. Out of an externally imposed rule of what is permitted arises a sense of what ought to be done

and an internal sense of control – a conscience. The very young child, limited in understanding, acts according to strict rules, even though he often breaks them. What is right and wrong relates closely to what his parents say and to the situations arising in the home. Later as the child develops intellectually and lives with others his sense of right and wrong derives from a wider circle and becomes more qualified: the rules of the game are arrived at by consensus and are therefore modifiable by common agreement. p 25.

Wright (1978) describes the work of Kohlberg, who developed a theory of how moral values develop. Children move through the stages of moral development at varying speeds and not all reach the final stage even in adulthood. In his studies he set up situations which required children of varying ages to think through moral dilemmas, e.g. is a man whose wife is dying of cancer and who has failed to obtain a drug by legal means entitled to resort to stealing? In other words, in any situation what should prevail: the rule of law or the needs of the individual?

An interpretation of Kohlberg's formulation is that it is three levels, with each level having two stages. In level one the first stage is carrying out an act to avoid punishment. The second stage is carrying out an act to gain a reward. In level two, stage one is where the act is carried out in order to please others within the family or social group and stage two is performed in obedience to the law. Finally, in level three, the first stage is where an action is carried out because of agreement in society of the individual rights involved, even though the action may be contrary to the law. In stage two, an action is carried out because of ethical principles – rules based on the fundamental truths of justice and the rights of human beings. Codes of ethics attempt to prescribe behaviours that reflect this final stage.

DUTY OF CARE/DUTY TO CARE

When someone offers a service for payment to others and this offer is accepted then they enter into an agreement, forming a contract which is legally binding. This contract exists within the context of a health authority offering services to the public which are then taken up. In this situation the health authority has a duty of care.

Take, for example, the services in Britain in relation to public transport – people can travel on a bus with the assurance that the machine is serviceable, is not about to break down and is driven by a competent driver who holds a special licence to drive a heavy vehicle and follows the regulations regarding the hours he or she is permitted to drive before having a rest. In buying a ticket the customer enters into a legal contract with certain expectations.

Contracts involving the provision of a service can be more complex. Health boards and social service departments employ people to deliver the service. They, as suppliers are ultimately responsible to the customer for the service supplied. The employee may have difficulty in deciding to whom he or she is accountable – to the employer or to the patient/client who pays for the service, albeit in most cases indirectly. The relationship between the bus driver and the employer is much more straightforward in that the driver's prime commitment is to the company.

When the health service being provided is poor and the 'customer' is not able or willing to complain, the employee, e.g. a nurse, may experience considerable conflict. The relationship between the bus driver, the disgruntled passenger and the company is less likely to cause the driver to experience similar levels of conflict.

Before going on to look at a duty *to* care we can look at one example in nursing where the 1992 UKCC Code and the 1992 UKCC Standards for the Administration of Medicines give clear guidance to the nurse as to her conduct in carrying out her duty *of* care (see Box 13.5).

Guidance from the 1992 UKCC Code is clear. It states that:

As a registered nurse, midwife or health visitor, you are personally accountable for your practice and, in the exercise of your professional accountability, must ensure that no act or omission on your part or within your sphere of responsibility is detrimental to the interests, condition or safety of patients and clients.

Further guidance in this situation comes from the 1992 UKCC Standards for the Administra-

---

Box 13.5   A duty of care

Jane works as a registered nurse who has a duty of care for 15 young people with learning disabilities. She is the responsible staff member answerable for this care over an afternoon and evening. Two residents ask to go out for a walk in the fresh air. One of the residents has status epilepsy and always needs a registered nurse to accompany him. Jane has no other registered nurse on duty.

- Is there an ethical issue here?
- What constitutes Jane's duty of care?

---

tion of Medicines, Paragraphs 8–11 and 13–16, which give specific guidance on administration within the hospital setting.

Jane considers her duty *of* care is clear, she cannot accompany the resident and she has no one else available who can be held accountable to administer medication if necessary. She considers, therefore, that she is unable to offer the opportunity for this resident to go out for a walk. Jane is ensuring the safety of the resident for whom she has a duty of care.

This may appear a fairly simple decision to make but of course in practice it is not. A duty to care does not rely on a legal contract, it relies more on morally binding rules where it is the conscience of the individual which gives the impetus for action. People learn to care for each other through loving relationships. When a child is loved and is helped to learn to love himself or herself, he or she is enabled to show love to others. Caring then becomes not so much a duty but a pleasure – not something which must be done for reasons of quietening one's conscience but because it is the right and good thing to do.

However, an uneasy conscience is a strong motivating force for action. Look again at the example of Jane, the registered nurse. It may appear that her action within her duty *of* care was clear. Less clear is what action she would require to take within her duty *to* care. Jane wishes to enable two of the residents to go for a walk. However, she considers she is unable to accede to their request. She has no code or law or list of rights which specifically states that going out for a walk is something she must provide. She will not be legally held to account for being unable to facilitate this on one afternoon. Yet she knows that this activity is very important for the two residents. This example of the dilemmas facing care staff illustrates the type of situation nurses are faced with regularly in conditions where there is a low level of staffing.

This situation identifies some basic concepts that warrant closer examination, namely the concepts of personhood, competence and autonomy versus paternalism.

ETHICAL ISSUES

A multitude of issues in the care of people with learning disabilities have strong ethical implications. Many of these are underpinned by one or more of three major issues: the concepts of personhood, autonomy versus paternalism and competence. Before we look at some day-to-day dilemmas in caring relationships, we need to examine these three concepts in detail. In a sense, these three issues are themselves interrelated because it is not easy to separate them. However, we will try and explore them individually.

Personhood

The concept of personhood invites us to explore what we mean by a 'person' and what criteria we can use to define a 'person'. We also have to consider when personhood might begin and end, when we might not regard an adult human being as a person and what the effects of so depriving an individual of their personhood might be. Perhaps this issue is most familiar within the context of the debate about the ethical aspects of abortion, but it has an equal relevance in relation to the care of people with an intellectual disability.

Most service provision to people with learning disabilities is based upon the concept of social role valorization rooted in the principles of normalization. Philosophies of care tend to be introduced in statements expounding that people with learning disabilities have the same rights and obligations as any other person within their society. This is emphasized by the insistence upon referring to 'people with a mental handicap' rather than 'the mentally handicapped'. We

do not believe that anyone would now seriously want to argue that an individual with a mental handicap is anything other than a person but when we try to examine the criteria for personhood we find some complexities. For many, the criteria for personhood start with the fact that all human beings are persons and that human beings can be defined on a genetic basis, i.e. an identifiable species. In the past, this has presented problems; for instance, some more extreme members of the Eugenics groups at the turn of the century expressed concern about the consequences of people with learning disabilities and severe mental health problems being 'allowed' to procreate and the implications upon the 'national gene pool'. However, we believe we have moved beyond that type of debate now. When we identify personhood now we are more inclined to consider issues which identify human beings as different from other species in terms of intellectual functioning, autonomy and personality – those features which make human beings unique individuals. Much of this, indirectly, relates to skills of communication and social interaction. Unfortunately, these tend to be the very areas where many people with learning disabilities experience the most difficulty.

One of the most significant criticisms of the institutional patterns of care which have characterized the provision of services to people with a mental handicap throughout the first half of this century has been the view that they were 'depersonalizing'. Not only did they not promote or recognize the individuality of the person but they specifically (and deliberately) reduced it. The ability of the individual to demand respect, dignity and recognition depended upon their skill in resisting this process. Much care, while being well intentioned and responsive, was custodial and collectivist in nature. Where individuals are limited in their ability to form and project (and communicate) their personality their personhood may come to be questioned – this is not only true in relation to those with learning disabilities. Many men and women caring for their ageing spouse or partner who suffers from dementia or such conditions as Alzheimer's disease describe their partners as having lost their personhood – 'This is not the person I married but only their shell' or 'I care for them on the basis of my memory and my obligation to the person they were'. Nevertheless, there would, quite rightly, be a strong resistance by most of us to not regarding this individual as a person. We are conscious that once we allow any suggestion of a loss of personhood we enter the slippery slope towards inhuman behaviour, such as the genocide that we have seen practised at different times during this and past centuries. Part of the basis of our move from institutional and custodial care for people with intellectual disabilities to a client-centred, individual approach to care is founded upon our desire to recognize and promote the personhood of this group of citizens. Thus, one of the prime objectives of care is to encourage, assist and enable the individual to function as independently as possible, that is, for him to exercise as much autonomy as possible. This brings us to our second issue: autonomy versus paternalism.

Autonomy versus paternalism

By autonomy, in this context, we mean the right or state of self-government and the freedom (and ability) of an individual to determine his or her actions and behaviour. Alternatively, by paternalism we mean a tendency or system in which provident fostering of care is apt to pass into (unwelcome) interference or where the freedom of the individual is subject to (well-meant) regulations. Literally, paternalism may be 'fatherly care'. (We have chosen to use the term 'paternalism' here as this is the term most commonly used in philosophical and ethical debate in this context, although one may wish to argue that 'maternalism' is at least equally relevant or appropriate when looking at the caring professions.)

There is a tendency in common usage now to imply that a paternalistic approach in care provision is wrong or undesirable. We would suggest that this may not necessarily be the case – that some paternalism in health and social care provision is not only acceptable but, in the case of vulnerable and dependent groups, may even be desirable. However, it is clearly undesirable in the context of preventing either the development or exercising of autonomy in those individuals who have both the desire and the potential ability to do so. The principles of normalization emphasize the importance of individuals being able to exercise informed choice and being enabled, or empowered, to make decisions about their own lives; and the concept of risk-taking has to be considered in this context. Carers are often in the dilemma of balancing the desire to encourage the individual to exercise his or her skills (and rights) with concern about their duty to and of care, and their personal and professional accountability for any consequences. Clearly, any decisions made in this situation are affected by the motivation of the carers in relation to this concept and how they exercise their role in caring for the individual. Nevertheless, the difficulty with paternalism is that however well intentioned the carer may be their actions can still be restrictive and thus morally wrong.

Let us take a simple example to examine this. Archie Jones is a young man with moderate learning disabilities living in a group home where student nurse Chloe McPherson is undertaking a training placement. Mr Jones has decided to go to the local shop (he has done this on numerous occasions in the past) to buy some items. It is raining heavily and he is only wearing a tee-shirt and jeans. Chloe suggests to Mr Young that he wears a raincoat but he refuses, saying that he will only be gone for a few minutes. Chloe tells him that unless he puts his raincoat on she will not 'allow' him to go. Mr Jones is annoyed. In this instance, there is little doubt that he regards Chloe McPherson's intervention as unwelcome interference and unnecessarily restrictive, and he resents it. Chloe has a dilemma. She is concerned firstly with Archie's health – he may get wet and become ill. She may also be concerned about her position as a student – what will the home leader say if she lets Archie out in these conditions without proper clothing? What will the local community say? She has a dilemma both in her duty *to* care and her duty *of* care. Archie is questioning not only the fairness of her decision but also her right to make it. There seems little doubt here that however well intentioned Chloe's act may be it is clearly paternalistic in nature. However, whether she is right or wrong depends upon the emphasis we place upon Archie's right to autonomy and the role of the carer to intervene in what may be regarded as unwise actions.

In such a case, however, there are a number of possible compromises which Chloe and Archie should be able to reach amicably. Part of Chloe's dilemma may be based upon whether she views Archie as being able to make informed decisions in this context – in other words, upon her view of Archie's competence.

Competence

In this context, we are exploring an individual's ability to undertake a course of action or even to decide about whether to embark upon a course of action. We are obliged to explore the criteria upon which we decide whether a person is competent and to consider the effects of declaring someone incompetent. Obviously, this is an issue of particular relevance in caring for people with cognitive or mental health problems. We are well aware that there are legal statutes which may allow us to restrict or remove an individual's freedom to exercise his right if we feel he is not competent to do so. The criteria for deciding this can set ethical dilemmas. Equally, the basis of all service provision is founded upon a comprehensive assessment of the individual's skills, abilities and needs so all carers find themselves involved in identifying competence at some level.

The assessments are often complex. On what basis do we assess competence? Often we assess the ability of a person to carry out a piece of behaviour in a defined way. If they do this accurately for a set number of times without prompting or assistance we are inclined to say that they are competent at it. However, we may demand more than this – we may require some level of understanding beyond the physical behaviour, some assessment of the consequences of different actions. But this can present prob-

lems. What about complex decisions – voting in an election, or getting married? We can teach an individual the physical behaviours involved in casting a vote or going through the marriage ceremony, but how do we assess his or her competence to decide to undertake such an action? It would be interesting to speculate how many elections or marriages would take place if we applied strict criteria to the knowledge and understanding of the implications of these actions in the same way that we often do to empowering people with learning difficulties! Equally, what allowances do we make for error, mistakes or poor judgement? If someone makes an error do we question whether they were ever competent?

Let us return to Archie and Chloe. Suppose they resolve their disagreement about the raincoat and Archie sets off on his expedition. What if he gets knocked down by a car on his way to the shop? Suppose he walked into the road without looking? His records show that he had learned to cross the road and has been going out successfully on his own for 2 years now without any mishap. He was felt to be competent to cross the road yet now he has been knocked down – do we say he was never competent or do we say he is competent but made an error?

The implications of this are obvious – if we do not allow for errors no one is ever competent. For some, there is the tendency to regard people with learning disabilities as incompetent by definition (by virtue of their condition or label). For most of us, we would not want to be that restrictive but, as we can see, the process of deciding competence can be fraught with ethical dilemmas. It is apparent that these three issues (personhood, autonomy and competence) are interrelated and all have considerable implications in caring for people with learning disabilities.

DAY-TO-DAY DILEMMAS

Within Europe at present there is clear recognition that systems of care for many people with learning disabilities are unsatisfactory. In Britain, government White Papers propose structures which aim to improve care. One of these is

Caring for People, Community Care in the Next Decade and Beyond (HMSO 1989) which has a stated aim of 'Helping people to lead, as far as possible, full and independent lives'. This policy is currently being implemented and people who have lived for many years within institutions are now being rehabilitated in ordinary housing within local communities.

Changes of this nature do present day-to-day ethical dilemmas of different magnitude, across all levels:

- At senior management levels there are questions of hospital closures, staff redeployment and in some cases possible staff redundancies. Finite resources mean making difficult decisions as to priorities for use.
- At middle management levels there are the many changes which have to be planned for, implemented and evaluated, many of them involving major changes in lifestyle for the residents in their care, and also changes for themselves and their staff.
- At junior management levels there are the requirements of ensuring standards of care which are safe and improving within a rapidly changing situation.

For those people with cognitive disabilities who are being rehabilitated there are the challenges of learning how to relate in new roles. There are expectations also that societies will be accepting and caring of those people coming among them who are less able to deal with the complexities of everyday living. People who are disabled may be given adequate physical and economic support but have less help in gaining skill in demanding respect and preservation of their dignity. There are also dilemmas which face parents and guardians, especially where their child or ward has previously been cared for in an institutional setting.

COPING WITH ETHICAL DILEMMAS

Philosophical models and approaches

There are a number of schools of philosophical

thought whose approaches may be helpful in finding an inroad into addressing ethical dilemmas.

Consequentialist

One approach is to test the dilemma in terms of the outcomes of taking (or not taking) a particular course of action. Are the outcomes desirable, effective and do they achieve the required result?

Motivist

Here it may be more important to look at why we should act in a certain way. This approach, balanced against the consequentialist approach, often produces the means and ends dilemma, i.e. does the end justify the means? In some cases, we would feel that an end, however desirable, may not justify the means of attaining it. For example, some ethical dilemmas about the use of behavioural techniques may rest on just this kind of dilemma – we know that the technique will achieve the desired change in behaviour but are we happy that the technique itself is ethically acceptable? We come across dilemmas where an undesirable solution may be accepted if the motivation was acceptable, i.e. the individual was 'acting in good faith'.

Deontological

In this approach we are dealing with concepts such as 'duty' and 'obligation'. This is an approach with which nurses may often find themselves particularly comfortable; for example, they rationalize many actions on the basis of 'a duty to care'. Here we need to examine what obligations or duties may indicate a particular course of action – for example, is there a 'duty' to always tell the truth? For some there is such a duty and their dilemma is thus partially resolved already.

Naturalistic

This approach can be a trifle more complex. Firstly, using this approach we 'reduce' everything almost to a science, i.e. as in physics or chemistry where there are laws which govern the course of events. Thus, we look for the 'natural' laws which are 'universal' and will govern our action to resolve our dilemma. This may include concepts such as a law of natural justice or a concept that right and wrong is clearcut – it is a natural law as to what is right! This may take as a basis God's laws for humankind and thus, for example, it would be the Ten Commandments which identify what would be right or wrong.

Emotivistic

In this approach we may question the naturalistic approach, and the belief that the concepts of right and wrong are absolutes. In emotivism we may argue that right or wrong is merely a subjective expression of feeling and that it is our own feelings and responses to our actions which should dictate how we resolve our dilemma. This is clearly an approach that many nurses may find contrary to their professional culture.

Utilitarian

This is the approach that is popular both with many governments in relation to the health service. This approach is based upon the conviction that, that which is right is that which satisfies (makes happy) the largest number of people. Thus, dilemmas can be resolved by doing that which will make the largest number of people happy. (A superb example of this for those who enjoy the cut and thrust of philosophical debate is John Harris' *The Survival Lottery* (1975) which is quoted in many books on nursing and medical ethics.)

There are, of course, many other models, theories and approaches which can be used as a starting point to exploring or endeavouring to resolve an ethical dilemma and these six are only offered as examples. Nevertheless, if we ask ourselves some of the questions which they suggest when we are confronted with an ethical

dilemma we can at least start to explore solutions to our dilemma. For example:

- What would be the outcomes of taking or not taking this action?
- Why would I take this action?
- Is there an overriding duty or obligation to be met here?
- Is there a 'natural' law or process which prevails here?
- Do I have some strong feeling or intuition about this?
- What would benefit the most people in this case?

A systematic approach

Having established that there might be some applicable models to use in approaching an ethical dilemma, we can suggest that there might be a systematic approach which might prove useful, which involves tackling the dilemma in stages, sometimes by asking specific questions (see Box 13.6).

Let us, briefly, test these approaches out on a simple example. Cathy Jenning is a health and social care worker (nurse, nursing/care assistant, residential social worker) caring for Jeremy Campbell in a residential setting. Jeremy informs Cathy that he intends to run away (either abscond or discharge himself) but asks her not to tell anyone. What questions must Cathy ask herself here? Firstly, what would be the consequences of telling her line manager or colleagues – breach of confidentiality or loss of confidence in her from Jeremy? What if she does not tell anyone – lack of trust by her colleagues or culpability if anything should happen to Jeremy?

What are Cathy's motives in passing on or not passing on this information? Is she trying to protect herself? Would she like to spoil Jeremy's plans or cause him problems? Does she have a duty to pass this knowledge on? Does she have an obligation to Jeremy? To her employers? What if someone asks her before or after Jeremy goes – does she have a duty to tell the truth? What is her duty of care to Jeremy? Is there a clear rule or law of conduct here? Would it be

---

Box 13.6 A systematic approach

1. Analyse the issue/problem. What is the real issue involved? What is it that makes it ethical in nature? Is there really a dilemma or is there a more simple solution? (For example, agonizing over a particular problem may be counterproductive if, in the final analysis, there is an acceptable policy laid down by the organization which specifies what must be done in this particular situation.)

2. What factors surround the issue? In what context is it set? Is it only a dilemma in that context? In answering this we may see what type of decision has to be made, if we have taken the dilemma out of context or if we have got it out of perspective.

3. Is any one of the models/theoretical approaches we have considered more appropriate in this case? (For example, a solution where the outcome may result in death or injury suggests that a consequentialist approach may be useful.)

4. What is the objective of solving the dilemma? Thus we may discover what type of decision we are trying to make. Exploring this question may suggest where a compromise may lie. Is it solvable or is it intractable, i.e. can a solution really be found?

5. What personal difficulty do I have here? Does this issue impinge upon certain beliefs or values which I hold? What exactly are these values? Why do they apply in this issue?

6. Who's problem is it? Who owns the problem – is it really mine? This is a key aspect to explore. Often we agonize over problems that are really not ours at all. Sometimes in health care we are being unnecessarily paternalistic.

7. Who can help me? This is another crucial question to ask. Many staff wrestle with problems alone which other people could willingly and effectively help them with. It is useful to ask: Am I really on my own with this? Are there not other people with whom I could discuss this, even in principle, without necessarily breaching confidentiality? Is there an ethics committee which could be looking at this?

8. What precautions need to be taken? Are there particular aspects of this issue which require special consideration? Are there legal implications, for instance? What effect will these have on how a solution is reached?

9. How is the solution to be reached and announced? Is this a dilemma which is purely mine or does it have implications for other people? Who should I inform when I have reached my solution and how should they be informed? Again, we would not wish to argue that this process will exclusively resolve all dilemmas but it does offer a means of beginning to cope with a dilemma.

---

wrong for Jeremy to go without permission or at least discussion?

Is it wrong to stop Jeremy from doing what he wants to? How does Cathy feel about the issue? Would she be distressed to see Jeremy go without proper advice and support? How many people would be made happy by knowing about Jeremy's intentions? In terms of a systematic approach, what is the actual issue here? Is the issue whether Jeremy leaves or not or is it about rules and regulations? Is it about Jeremy's current ability to make such decisions? Is this an ethical dilemma? Would it be wrong of Cathy to break a confidence or would she be right to protect Jeremy from the consequences of his decisions? Is it fair to stop Jeremy from leaving? Is there a policy that says such disclosures must be reported? What is the context here? Is Jeremy free to make his own decisions? Is the decision whether to report Jeremy or whether to stop him? Is any particular model relevant here? Would the consequences of letting Jeremy go and something untoward befalling him outweigh other considerations?

What is the objective of informing or not on Jeremy? Is it to protect him from possible injury? Is there a compromise – must he go now or can he be persuaded to wait and give more thought to his decision?

Does Jeremy have pressing reasons for going which could be ameliorated? Does this present a personal dilemma for Cathy? Does she believe one should never break a confidence? Is this really Cathy's dilemma or is this something that can only be dealt with by her line manager? Does Cathy have a friend or colleague with whom she can discuss this problem? Would her line manager allow her to discuss the issue in general terms without pressing her? Are there legal implications here – is Jeremy a detained patient? Is he of an age to make his own decisions? Have special restrictions been applied to him? Would it be illegal to prevent him from leaving? If Cathy decides she must report Jeremy's intentions who should she report them to? Should she warn Jeremy first? Should she have warned Jeremy before he told her?

As we can see, even in this rather simplistic

example, neither the models nor the process gives us a solution to the dilemma – this is not the intention and as we have already seen ethical dilemmas are by definition difficult to resolve – but they do give us a strategy for beginning to address the dilemma and to at least get into a way of looking for a solution. For example, if Jeremy was a detained patient then the laws governing his care would give guidance as to how Cathy ought to act.

REFERENCES

Dunkerley D 1975 Occupations and society. Students Library of Sociology, Mosby, St Louis

Harris J 1975 The survival lottery. In: Campbell R and Collinson D 1988 Ending lives. Basil Blackwell, Oxford

HMSO 1967 Children and their primary schools. A report of the central advisory council for education, vol 1. HMSO, London

HMSO 1989 Caring for people: community care in the next decade and beyond. HMSO, London

Phoon Wai 1971 The role of professions in a changing world. Occasional Papers, Commonwealth Foundation

Seighart P 1988 Human rights in the United Kingdom: foreword. Pinter, London

UKCC 1992 Code of professional conduct for the nurse, midwife and health visitor, 3rd edn. UKCC, London

UKCC 1992 Standards for the administration of medicines. UKCC, London

Ward A 1984 Scots law and the mentally handicapped, Scottish Society for the Mentally Handicapped, Glasgow

Wright D 1971 The psychology of moral behaviour. Penguin, Harmondsworth

Wright A, Taylor D S 1978 Introductory psychology: an experimental approach, Penguin, Harmondsworth p. 588

FURTHER READING

Callahan J C 1988 Ethical issues in professional life. Oxford University Press, Oxford

Campbell A V, Higg R 1982 In that case. Darton, Longman & Todd, London

Evans J D G 1987 Moral philosophy and contemporary problems. Cambridge University Press, Cambridge

Faulder C 1985 Whose body is it? Virago, London

Fromer M J 1981 Ethical issues in health care. Mosby, St. Louis

Foot P 1986 Theories of ethics. Oxford University Press, Oxford

Glover J 1984 Causing death and saving lives. Penguin, Harmondsworth

Gillon R 1986 Philosophical medical ethics. John Wiley, Chichester

Griffiths N 1983 Mentally handicapped children and adults: welfare rights guide. Area 5 Action Group, Edinburgh p 2–9

Harris J 1985 The value of life. Routledge & Kegan Paul, London

Mill J S 1986 Utilitarianism. Fontana, London

Popkin R H, Stroll A, Kelly A V 1952 Philosophy made simple. Heinemann, London

Singer P 1988 Applied ethics. Oxford University Press, Oxford

Smart J T C, Williams B 1987 Utilitarianism: for and against. Cambridge University Press, Cambridge

White A R 1984 Rights. Clarendon Press, Oxford

Wolfensberger W 1982 The principle of normalization in human services. National Institute on Mental Retardation. Ontario, Canada

CHAPTER CONTENTS

The development of parents' societies   307

Pressure for education   308

Other organizations   310

The Disabled Persons' Act   311

The Griffiths Report and beyond   312

14

Helping agencies

H. Stewart

Key points
- Parents' groups are the driving force behind change
- Professional values don't always equate with what is needed
- Legislation alone is insufficient to bring about change

THE DEVELOPMENT OF PARENTS' SOCIETIES

In the late 1940s the pattern of institutional care for mentally handicapped people in Britain was well established. In Scotland there were one or two day centres, run by volunteers, which offered some occupation and care for mentally handicapped children but, in general, the only form of care offered to families was that of the residential institution. It was about that time, spurred on, perhaps, by the significant medical advances of the late 1940s, that the phenomenon of the parents' organization occurred.

The Scottish Society for the Mentally Handicapped (SSMH) is probably typical of parents' organizations. It was formed in 1954, shortly after its English counterpart, but at very much the same time as similar organizations were coming into existence, apparently spontaneously, throughout the world. Over a period of about 10 years, parents' organizations appeared in 76 countries throughout the world.

In Scotland, the Society originated from a meeting called by five parents of mentally handicapped children. They booked a hall and advertised a meeting, and were astonished when several hundred people turned up. Probably most parents who have experienced the birth of a handicapped child feel, at some point, that they are the only people to whom it has occurred. The numbers present at the meeting showed how untrue this was. Parents spoke of their feelings of isolation and even today, many still find that the fact that their child is handicapped excludes them from many normal aspects of community life, especially if they experience active hostility.

The Society found that such professional advice as there was, was often very negative and limited to the suggestion that parents should place their child in institutional care. The nature of handicap was (and often still is) described in terms of what the child was unable to do, and support and help was often nonexistent. Handicapped children were excluded from the right to education, and were in other ways often last in the queue to receive services. The attitude that professionals should only spend their valuable time helping people with handicaps after 'normal' people's needs had been satisfied was prevalent.

Thus, the Society was established by parents for parents. Its aims were to provide mutual support for parents (there is a special quality of help which can only be provided by somebody who has experienced the problem himself), to provide information, and to campaign for better attitudes to and services for mentally handicapped people. A fundamental belief was that it was the duty of the state to provide services for people with mental handicap, although there were often cases when it was appropriate for voluntary organizations to provide services.

PRESSURE FOR EDUCATION

Education was an early concern of the Society and it can serve as an example of the way in which change can be effected. Although reference will be made to the Scottish situation, the position in England and Wales was very similar at that time.

In Scotland, mildly and moderately mentally handicapped children were entitled to education

and the special schools which they attended were part of the mainstream education system. Severely mentally handicapped children were assessed as being 'ineducable but trainable', while profoundly handicapped children were regarded as being 'ineducable and untrainable'. Children who had been assessed as trainable but ineducable attended Junior Occupation Centres which were run by education authorities but in a number of ways provided what parents considered a second-rate service. In Scotland, teachers had to have at least 3 years' training, followed by 2 years' practical work, before being approved as teachers. If they wanted to do the special qualification for work in special schools they had to undertake a further year of study at a College of Education. Staff in Junior Occupation Centres were not teachers: most were untrained although some had undertaken the brief course provided for them. The curriculum within centres reflected the title, and in many centres the emphasis was simply on keeping the children amused, with little developmental work taking place.

This situation reflected public and professional attitudes. Rooted in an academic tradition, many educationists were simply unable to comprehend the value of education for children who were below that level. It might be argued that the main function of an education system is to provide suitably qualified members of the workforce, and thus there was no economic incentive to provide education for people who were unlikely to be employable. The fact that the Occupation Centres existed at all was probably due to the fact that voluntary organizations had demonstrated the value of providing some sort of service for families, and it was clear from the resources allocated to them that education authorities did not see the Junior Occupation Centres as being a real part of their system.

Perhaps because of this fundamental lack of belief in the value of education, early calls for a change to the system by parents met with little response. The situation was clearly impossible, particularly for families with profoundly handicapped children, and local branches of the SSMH and other organizations responded by setting up their own day centres to provide some care for those children who had been excluded from the education system. Typically, a centre would be run by volunteers on a part-time basis in buildings begged or borrowed from another organization. However, having established the worth of the service, it became easier to get some sort of financial support from local authorities, and limited grants enabled some centres to get bigger premises and to employ staff. Gradually, they were able to demonstrate the value of such a service and to show that, no matter how severe their handicap, all children could be and should be provided with an education.

In some cases, local authorities gradually assumed the whole responsibility for these local centres. In one instance, the local branch of the SSMH insisted that a proper, purpose-built centre must be provided before the service was taken over.

Gradually, professional perceptions began to change, although by no means universally. National pressure led to the setting up of a committee to look at the education and training of staff working in centres for mentally handicapped people, and this report made the clear recommendation that no child should be regarded as ineducable and that education for mentally handicapped children should be incorporated within the main system (HMSO 1973). Logically, this would mean that schools would require qualified teachers and, understandably, there was considerable resistance to this recommendation from staff working within the centres. There was still very little enthusiasm among most education authorities – or indeed among most teachers – for this area of education; nevertheless, continued pressure began to lead to change. The national press were persuaded to take an interest in the issue and eventually an MP took up a private member's bill to bring about change. Although a general election intervened, another MP took up the cause and Hamish Gray, then the MP for Dingwall, put forward the bill. Although there was considerable pressure for change there was still a great deal of resistance, and there were some anxious moments when the bill eventually appeared

before parliament, as its low status in the draw meant that a single objection would have had the effect of defeating it. No such objection was voiced, however, and the Education (Mentally Handicapped Children) (Scotland) Act of 1974 came into being. Quite simply, the Act ended the ability of education authorities to exclude children from the right to education. Although not much enthusiasm had been evidenced by those in authority, once given the task most set about the change willingly. Many were surprised to find that there were teachers who actually welcomed the challenge of working with mentally handicapped children. Within a comparatively few years the quality of education had improved beyond the dreams of parents and had been matched by the achievements of children.

It is an interesting reflection on change that, looking back 16 years after the event, it is difficult to imagine that the change would ever have happened if it had not been for the pressure from a parents' organization. Many of the changes that have happened since then, such as the move to integration after the Warnock Report (HMSO 1978), can be traced to this event that shortly before had been discounted by many as impossible or unnecessary.

In the context of education, a single bit of legislation towards community care was able to achieve profound change. In most other areas changes have been slower and more gradual but equally profound. The gradual shift to community care has been led by parents' organizations and in most cases they were not seeing their demands as an alternative to institutional care but rather to services that would allow them to lead an ordinary life. Most parents probably to lead saw institutional care as being appropriate for some people but usually for others rather than their own family members.

Parents wanted services that would allow them the same opportunities to enjoy their families as anybody else, and this meant services which were local to them and which could be understood by users and by the community. Sometimes, changes could be achieved by straightforward lobbying; sometimes just to be able to quantify the demand and express the need was what was needed for the authorities to get something under way. In the early 1970s the only forms of residential care available for adults were hospitals, three residential communities, and three community hostels with a grand total of 40 beds in Scotland. The SSMH set up a working party to look at good practice at home and abroad. The working party identified the type of community hostel which seemed suitable, both for residents and as a model of care, and offered a financial incentive to 'get things moving'. The offer of a loan to selected authorities amounting to approximately half the cost of a community hostel was an irresistible bait and within 5 years there were 20 hostels in operation. The principle of community residential care for mentally handicapped adults had been established and acknowledged.

The SSMH is probably typical of the various national parents' organizations which have influenced change over the last 30 years. The greatest change has been the increased confidence that parents have given to each other and which has itself influenced public attitudes. Visitors to countries where there has been no such movement, such as those in Eastern Europe, are often struck by the fact that no handicapped people are visible. It is common to see mentally handicapped people in the West nowadays, whether by themselves or with their families: 30 years ago they would have been hidden from all but those who were paid to care for them.

OTHER ORGANIZATIONS

Before national parents' organizations came into existence there were organizations with an interest in the welfare of mentally handicapped people. However, most of them were benevolent or philanthropic, and their intention was to make life more tolerable for people with a mental handicap rather than bring about a change in services and attitudes. The development of parents' organizations as self-help groups was something new and different, at least at that time. In recent years, other organizations have developed. Some have been concerned with a particular condition, others have a particular local identity, and others are concerned with the promotion of a particular philosophy or belief. Most recently self-advocacy organizations have also developed.

The emergence of organizations concerned with specific conditions probably reflects the difficulty of any general organization concerned with a large number of people with many similar, but different, needs. In that case, the advice they give is often limited by the fact that it must be acceptable to all. What is appropriate for people with one particular handicap may be inappropriate, and sometimes even dangerous, for those with another. The most common type of mental handicap is Down syndrome and in Britain the first organization concerned with a specific condition was, not surprisingly, concerned with that condition.

A psychologist called Rex Brinkworth, who was himself the father of a girl with Down syndrome, wrote a book entitled *Improving Mongol Babies (1969)*. This offered specific advice to assist the development of babies with that condition and it demonstrated the value of such advice. Before long, a Down's Babies Association had been formed to bring together parents who knew the value of sharing their experiences. This group eventually became the Down Syndrome Association, now a national organization with branches throughout Britain. Since then, quite a number of other associations have been formed, sometimes because a condition is rare rather than because it is common, and often because the advice people need simply isn't available from professionals. (For example, the Tuberous Sclerosis Association and, more recently, the establishment of the Rett Syndrome Association founded by Isobel Allan, whose experience is described in Chapter 1.)

These are examples of national organizations but, in some cases, parents and others felt that their strengths would rely on the development of their local identity. There are many cases of active and vigorous local associations concerned with developing services in particular communities, from isolated rural communities with scattered populations to those in densely populated cities.

Over the years, national parents' organizations pressed for a gradual move to community care. This meant that they accepted that some mentally handicapped people might require institutional care but that others might not and that most could benefit from much less restricted lives than had been the case in the past. This middle of the road view was, inevitably, not acceptable to everyone. On the one hand, there were those who felt that the move was too gradual, while others felt that community care was inappropriate for many. Organizations grew up to promote both these views. For example, Campaign for the Mentally Handicapped (CMH) was originally established by a journalist with an interest in the subject, and it developed into an organization which campaigned for a change in attitudes as well as improved services. Among the attitudes that CMH wanted to promote was one that avoided labelling people because of their handicap. They felt that labelling devalued the human worth of people with that condition. This led them to change their own name and they are now called Values Into Action (VIA). VIA has become a pioneer among organizations whose purpose is to express the views of people with a mental handicap rather than the views of their parents.

The self-advocacy movement is probably best developed in Canada, where its effects have been considerable. The People First organization has encouraged a widespread rethink by parents' organizations about their attitudes. In Britain, this has exposed a number of conflicts but not resolved them. Not only have the conflicts been those between the needs of the parents and of their mentally handicapped children seeking to gain independence, but also between organizational and individual needs. Organizations need money to exist and the practicalities of doing this may hinder their ultimate purpose. Images of pity produce a response from the donating public, but many feel that they do not promote a dignified image for people with a mental handicap. These conflicts are by no means unique to mental handicap and such differences are common to many organizations concerned with disability.

THE DISABLED PERSONS' ACT 1986

In 1985, Tom Clarke, the MP for Monklands West, came top in the ballot for a private member's bill. Private members' bills offer individual MPs an opportunity to try to introduce legislation that will promote their own particular cause and, while there are many restrictions on what can be done, the leader in the ballot has an unrivalled opportunity to further this cause. Tom Clarke had an interest in mental handicap so he decided to use the opportunity to do something to improve opportunities in the field.

Tom Clarke contacted, or was contacted by, almost every organization with an interest in disability and from their demands he began to draw up a bill that was intended to give new rights to disabled people. It sought to establish that disabled people have the right to be consulted about decisions that affect their lives, and sought to give status to carers, and to improve the quality of information available to and about people with disabilities. It also sought to establish the means to ensure that different agencies responsible for different aspects of the lives of disabled people had to *communicate* with each other to ensure that people did not 'fall between the gaps'.

None of this sounds very radical now, but it did highlight a significant stage in the evolution of attitudes, whereby the focus had shifted to disabled people demanding rights and to carers seeking formal recognition of their services.

That compromises were necessary can be illustrated by one or two of the arguments that took place among organizations promoting the bill. Some of the organizations which thought of themselves as being of, rather than for, disabled people wanted to insist that any organization concerned with disabled people should have a majority of disabled people on their board. This was resisted strongly by most other organizations, however sympathetic they were to the ideals of the aims of this clause, because it was virtually impossible for some organizations concerned with the needs of people who are mentally ill or mentally handicapped to implement. For example, the Rett Syndrome Association is concerned with people who are mentally handicapped, but the nature of the handicap makes it virtually impossible for those suffering from the condition to run the Association. Similarily, organizations of disabled people were concerned by the use of the term 'carer' which they felt did not emphasize the priority of disabled people themselves, and they wished to see such people regarded as 'assistants' to disabled people. This view was resisted very strongly by organizations concerned with carers, who felt that they had taken on the caring role and were working as unpaid and unvalued suppliers of services to the state, relieving the state of the burden of providing residential or day services. They were therefore anxious to see their role being given the recognition that it deserved. This meant the right not to be taken for granted, as well as realistic allowances and services.

Reference was made earlier to the growing self-advocacy movement. This had led to mentally handicapped people expressing very clearly the view that they wanted to be involved in decisions that were made concerning them. In the past, mentally handicapped people were often not considered capable of having views about their own future. Pressure from parents' organizations had meant that usually parents would be involved in a discussion about whether a mentally handicapped person should move to a hostel or a home, or go to an adult training centre, or be encouraged to find employment, but this would take place without the client being consulted about their views. Administratively, this is often easier, and mentally handicapped people can have great difficulty in expressing their views. Not only may they have language difficulties but also they will often feel inhibited by the presence of people who are more articulate than them and who control the resources which affect them.

An important aspect of the Disabled Persons' Act was to recognize this fact and to seek to provide not only a statutory right of handicapped people to be consulted about such decisions but also to take positive steps to help them express their views. Clauses 1 and 2 of the Act provide for the statutory appointment of representatives. In most countries, these people would have been referred to as 'citizen advocates', but in Scotland the word advocate means a type of lawyer, similar to the English barrister. The representative is not meant to have any view of his own but rather is meant to help the mentally handicapped person form his own view and then help him express it when important decisions are taken. This may lead to considerable difficulties for the representatives; for example, it means that their duty should be to express the wish of the handicapped person even if they themselves feel it to be wrong, e.g. a mentally handicapped person might want a home of his own when it is quite obvious that he would not be able to cope with such independence. However, it must be argued that most people, at some time in their lives, wish to undertake some action that their elders and betters feel is wrong, and that mentally handicapped people ought to be assisted at least to demand the same right.

There is still a great deal of work to be done and this may be part of the reason that, at the time of writing, these clauses have not been implemented. However, a commitment to implement these clauses would do much to allow the important work to continue. There is a long way to go before mentally handicapped people will have as much power over their own lives as other citizens, and a commitment to representation would do much to develop this.

THE GRIFFITHS REPORT AND BEYOND

Parents' organizations and other groups had been pressing for the development of community care since their formation. They wanted to see an alternative to institutional care for mentally handicapped people and also support for them to live as an ordinary family. Governments have for many years acknowledged the need for proper programmes of community care for people with a mental handicap, although frequently their actions have spoken considerably less loudly than their words.

While changes were taking place in the field

of mental handicap another change occurred which focused the attention of government on the need for change – the elderly population in Britain increased quite dramatically over a fairly short period of time. A series of allowances had been introduced in the early 1980s which had not recognized this. Provision had been made for the payment of a substantial allowance to anyone who was in residential care run by a private or voluntary organization. The allowance was payable regardless of the individual's need for this type of care, or of its suitability, but simply by virtue of the fact that somebody was in a home that had the appropriate registration. This had obvious cost implications and the bill for the allowances increased from £10m in 1979 to over £1000m in 1987–88 (HMSO 1990) which caused considerable alarm to the government. Sir Roy Griffiths, a successful businessman, was commissioned to write a report making recommendations for the development of policy. His report *Community Care – an Agenda for Action* (HMSO 1988) is a model of its kind: lucid, clearly written, and produced in a very short period of time. The report made a number of significant recommendations, including:

- that services should be based on individual needs rather than fitting needy individuals into existing services
- that local authorities should have the main responsibility for community care, but their role would be that of enabler rather than provider
- that strategy agencies should cooperate in the development of clear plans for the development of community care
- the organization of the package of service to meet the assessed needs of individuals should be the responsibility of a case (or care) manager.

In his report, Griffiths laid stress on the need for cost-effectiveness, but no one suggested that community care would be cheap. In fact, community care is inevitably going to cost society, because it recognizes that there are an increasing number of individuals in society who require some form of care. Probably, for that reason, at the date of writing most of the proposals in the

report remain unimplemented. However, there are some significant points that are worthy of comment.

Before the Griffiths report, it could be argued that the provision of care was seen as a matter of fitting an individual into one sort of service or another. Mentally handicapped people leaving school often went to the local adult training centre simply because that was where all mentally handicapped school leavers went. People went to stay in long-stay hospitals because that was the most suitable of a limited number of options, or possibly they lived in some form of a community home with the addition of some type of day care or improvement. This suggested that, rather than simply fitting people into existing services, the aim should be to provide services that responded to an assessment of the needs of the individual. Such an assessment should be thorough, i.e. not simply confined to a bed here or a day place there but rather to an identification of the whole needs of the individual. It is difficult to object to such a simple principle, but it does open up the issue for much wider thinking about how such needs might be met.

Adult training centres came into existence largely to provide relief for parents by occupying mentally handicapped people during the day. While they have altered and expanded, and many provide very interesting and exciting programmes, it can be argued that there is a need for much more imaginative thinking. Many mentally handicapped people already attend some form of facility run by further education departments, and many benefit from what is a much more normal experience in that it is not one exclusive to those with a mental handicap. However, there is a danger that these too will become simply another box into which to place mentally handicapped people, and there is a need to develop centres and FE colleges as a base to develop more exciting services.

Many mentally handicapped people would like some form of employment, not only because it is the normal thing for most people but also for the equally normal reason that they would like to earn money. Britain has a very poor record of promoting the employment of people with disability, and much could be done to improve matters. Many people with mental handicaps may find it very difficult to compete in a restricted labour market and this has meant that it has often been easy to assume that employment is impossible. However, even when things are very hard, imaginative programmes have demonstrated that it is possible to help people into employment. MENCAP's 'Pathway' scheme in South Wales demonstrated many years ago that, even in areas of high unemployment, a dedicated employment scheme recognizing the need for very special training and support to mentally handicapped people in employment, as well as encouragement to employers, could open up new opportunities for many people. The government's own 'Sheltered Placement' scheme could do a great deal more if more resources were given to it and it is useful to look at this in more detail.

Miss S works in a department store as a canteen assistant. She is mentally handicapped and because of this her ability to do the full amount of work required of canteen assistants is limited – about 50% of what would normally be expected. Despite this, she is able to hold down the job. She is employed not by the store but by the SSMH. They pay her the normal wage for a canteen assistant and receive from the company 50% of her salary. The other 50%, with a small administration charge, is paid by government. This means that Miss S has the satisfaction and the income that comes from being in employment – as significant to her as it would be to any other individual. Her workmates are happy, because they like her and recognize that she has a contribution to make. The company is happy, not only because it is part of their policy to be concerned with social and community needs, but because they are getting a good job done by a reliable employee at the right cost. Finally, the tax payer, if he or she knew it, would also be happy, because the cost of the subsidy for this position is considerably less than the cost of a place in a day centre and the range of benefits that would be necessary to support Miss S would be if she did not have this opportunity.

Not all mentally handicapped people will be able to achieve employment, and indeed not all will want to. There are other ways in which people might be able to enjoy more fulfilled lives by way of an individually tailored programme, rather than by fulltime attendance at a centre. Many centres already provide their clients with periods at sports centres, or other community facilities, such as libraries and community centres, and many people would much prefer a programme that allowed them to spend their time in services that were not labelled as being those for mentally handicapped people. Many people feel that by the time they have been in an adult training centre for 20 years they are ready for something other than training, and there is a great deal of scope for constructing programmes which have as their starting point the individual's needs rather than the existence of a particular building and its staff.

Looking more widely at individual needs is going to present a new challenge for many professionals. Many professionals dealing with mentally handicapped people will have been trained in a discipline where mental handicap is but a small part. For example, the trend towards generic social work means that, in a comparatively short training period, social workers must attempt to receive the skills and knowledge necessary to help children, elderly people, physically handicapped people and mentally ill people, undertake statutory work with offenders, help families coping with stress and poverty, as well as work with mentally handicapped people and their families.

The task of preparing a package of services and assistance that will help mentally handicapped people have more fulfilled lives socially, emotionally, and economically is a very new challenge. Some might argue that it requires a whole new approach and a different philosophy. Just as we have tried to move services for mentally handicapped people away from a medical model that focuses on illness so social workers may have to move away from the problem-oriented philosophy to one that focuses on development.

For all the caring professions, the emphasis on

value for money is going to present real difficulties. Naturally, there are concerns that value for money just means a cheap alternative, but it would be a mistake to think of the concept as unimportant for that reason. Many services for mentally handicapped people are very expensive and it will only be possible to provide them if they are properly targeted to those who need them. At present, in a typical centre, some service users will be receiving a much higher level of service than they require, and others not enough. Providing services for individual needs will mean not just meeting the average but concentrating resources where they can be most effective.

The changes may make it increasingly difficult for many professionals to decide who they really serve. Take the hypothetical case of a 25-year-old mentally handicapped man, currently living with his family. His family would like him to move to a village community for mentally handicapped people about 50 miles away where he would be safe, cared for by dedicated staff and his future assured. The local authority, who would have to meet the cost of this rather expensive service, would rather he stayed at home. They are happy to provide day care for him, and his family receives allowances from social security to help support him. The young man himself probably does not know what he wants, but judging by the fact that he enjoys the company of his friends in the neighbourhood, and that he would really like to get a job in the factory down the road, it is probable that given a real opportunity for choice he would prefer to move to a tenancy in the supported accommodation provided by a specialist housing association just up the road.

For professionals, deciding who they must help is going to be increasingly difficult. At present, the choice is often the 'best available' rather than the 'best possible'. However, a system that requires constant assessment and review will lead to the 'best possible' as an option and this will mean decision-making will be more difficult.

A major difficulty is the proliferation of agencies who see their role as being different. For example, the Sheltered Placement scheme is the responsibility of the Department of Employment, and the fact that expenditure by them leads to a saving by the Department of Social Security cannot seem of much significance. Bureaucrats are always concerned with their own patch and what goes on elsewhere is often of little interest. It is often easy to make things appear better at first sight without really solving the problem, and a new approach is needed. Some people would argue that this lies in such schemes as service brokerage, where the resources are allocated to the individual with special needs who can then buy services to meet these needs. Others would argue that the solution is for the government to take a more coordinated approach, and to recognize that the care of its handicapped citizens is a responsibility for all departments and agencies, and not just one.

Over the past 30 years, there have been a great many improvements. Mentally handicapped people live longer and the majority may now expect to lead most of their lives in comparatively normal settings. However, there is a long way to go before these settings are really normal, where people are placed there because they want to be there or because their needs are best met there, not because they are mentally handicapped. As things are at present, a mentally handicapped person born today can expect quite a high standard of care in many respects, but he cannot expect the same opportunities of fulfilment or enjoyment of his life as a contemporary born without a handicap. His chances of employment, of an individual home of his own choice, of relationships, and of dignity and respect, are much less than other people's, and there is much to be done before this will change.

Some of these changes may happen through education and improved resources. Many of the changes involved in the community care proposals can occur through the reallocation of resources rather through additional resources. Nevertheless, there are difficult questions ahead. There is no avoiding the fact that care for people with profound needs is very expensive and there are few signs that this has been recognized. The concern of most governments about the increasing elderly population and the resources needed to provide for them, often obscures the need for additional resources for mentally handicapped citizens.

As long as services remain inadequate to provide for people with mental handicap families with mentally handicapped dependents will be unable to lead normal lives. They will also need additional recognition to be able to lead such lives. As well as services such as education and day care, they will also need special services for families which we have not referred to in any depth in this chapter. These include, first of all, information, not only the type of information about their child's handicap that must derive from early assessment but also information about the services and help that they may need. Respite care, help with holidays and, above all, financial allowances, are important. Although financial allowances to handicapped people and their families have improved, a great deal of information suggests that they are still inadequate. Not only do we know that many mentally handicapped people living in fairly independent settings are extremely poor, but allowances to families have consistently failed to recognize the extra cost of disability.

There are a number of other interesting and difficult questions that may have to be tackled over the next few years. There are ethical issues that have been exposed by other developments. The Swedish Society for Mentally Handicapped People recently declared itself opposed to prenatal screening, involving such techniques as amniocentesis. They did so because the voice of mentally handicapped people is increasingly heard in their society and they felt that the use of such techniques to prevent handicap contradicted a stand for mentally handicapped people to be valued equally in society. At present, it is likely that most parents of mentally handicapped children in Scotland would support, and even demand, the provision of such services in Scotland.

A number of attempts to establish legislation that would make the discrimination against people on the grounds of their handicap illegal have been defeated by government. In America, such legislation has recently come into force and it will be interesting to see whether it actually produces improved status for handicapped people and, if so, whether it will be followed by similar action elsewhere. There are exciting times ahead.

This chapter has tried to relate some of the changes in services from the point of view of one particular voluntary organization. It is typical of its kind: throughout the world similar organizations have adapted in similar ways to meet national needs. It has been said that there is no advance in the social, education or health services that was not at first initiated by an individual or an organization founded on concern, rather than by statute. Whether or not this is the case there is a continuing challenge for voluntary organizations to lead the changes that will help make the lives of mentally handicapped people and their families more fulfilled.

REFERENCES

Brinkworth R 1969 Improving mongol babies. National Society for Mentally Handicapped Children, N. Ireland

Griffiths R (Chairman) 1988 Community care: agenda for action – a report to the Secretary of State for Social Services. HMSO, London

The training of staff for centres for the mentally handicapped – the report of the committee appointed by the Secretary of State for Scotland. The way ahead – benefits for disabled people. HMSO, London

Warnock M (Chairman) 1978 Special educational needs – the report of the committee of enquiry into the education of handicapped children and young people. HMSO, London

Index

A

Abbreviated progressive relaxation (APR), 184
ABC (Antecedents: Behaviour: Consequences) analysis in behaviour therapy, 156–7
Accidents
  brain damage caused by, 78
  danger of: persons with profound multiple handicaps, 264–5
Accommodation: persons with learning difficulties, 49–51
Acne, 248
Acquired immune deficiency syndrome, 109 (Table 6.1), 110, 113–15, 115
Adenoma sebaceum, 69
  see also Tuberous sclerosis
Standards for the Administration of Medicines: UKCC (1992), 298
Adult training centres, 130, 313, 314
Affective psychoses, 103–6, 115
  depression, 103, 103–5, 112
  mania, 103, 105–6
Aggressiveness, 112, 189, 197
  adjusting antecedents, 189
  clear and extended descriptions required for assessment, 155, 157
  gentle teaching, 197
  hyperkinetic syndrome, 99, 100, 115
  mania, 106
  medication for, 193
  schizophrenia, 107, 108
AIDS (acquired immune deficiency syndrome), 109 (Table 6.1), 110, 113–15, 115
Alcohol
  consumption in pregnancy, effect on fetus, 76–7
  dementia related to, 109 (Table 6.1)
All-Wales Strategy for people with a mental handicap (AWS): (1990), 222
Alpha-fetoprotein levels in maternal serum: use in prenatal diagnosis, 79 (Box 4.4), 81
Alzheimer's disease, 109–12 including Table 6.1
  link with Down syndrome, 109, 110
Amitriptyline, 104, 105
Amniocentesis, 72, 79 (Box 4.4), 81
Amphetamines: hyperkinetic syndrome treatment; and precautions, 100
Amsterdam dwarfism (Cornelia de Lange syndrome), 73–4, 76 (Box 4.3)
Analogue studies in behaviour analysis, 161
Anxiety, 112, 115
APR (abbreviated progressive relaxation), 184
Asylums: historical aspects, 24, 25
Asymmetrical tonic neck reflex (ATNR), 237, 256
Ataxia in cerebral palsy, 95
Athetosis, 76, 95, 98

Autism, 101–2, 115, 151
Autonomy versus paternalism in provison of care, 299, 300–1
Autosomal dominant inheritance, conditions caused by, 67–8, 69
Autosomal recessive inheritance, conditions caused by, 68, 69–73
Autosomes, 62, 80
  abnormalities, 63–4, 64–6
  numerical, 64
  structural, 64

B

Bacterial infections, maternal, affecting fetus, 75
Bar charts: data display in behaviour analysis and therapy, 168, 168–69
Barnardo's, 31
Basic ID schedule, for functional analysis of behaviour, 157
Batten's disease, 72
Battered baby syndrome, 78
Bean bags: people with multiple handicaps, 242
Behavioural Interview and Analysis Schedule (BIAS), 157
Behavioural problems, 112, 115, 150, 201–3
  assessment, 155–6, 172–3
    defining a problem, 152–3
    functional analysis, 156
    location of therapy, 154
    measuring, recording and analysing, 161
    organizational issues, 153–4
    potential pitfalls and problems in, 202, (Box 9.2)
    resources, use of, 153–4, 202
    setting priorities, 153
    skills assessment, 170–2
  behavioural approach in therapy for, 151–5
    ethics of, 197–201
  carers, training of, 201–2
  causative factors, 150–1
  decreasing inappropriate behaviours, 172, 176, 188–9
    antecedents, adjustment of, 189
    consequences, adjustment of, 189–93
    medication, 193
    punitive consequences, presentation of, 192–3
    reflective approach, 189
    reinforcing consequences: presentation, prevention, and removal, 190–2
    visual screening, 197
  ethics of behavioural approach, 197–201
    applying specialist knowledge, 201
    consent, 198
    rationale, 198–200
    use of reinforcement, 200–1

    using the least intrusive methods, 200
  increasing appropriate behaviours, 172
    antecedent control, 176
    consequence control, 176
    reinforcement, 177, 182, 183
    skills teaching methods, 180
  measuring, recording and analysing, 161
    baseline measurement, 161–2
    checklists, 165
    duration recording, 162
    frequency or event recording, 161
    interval recording, 162
    latency recording, 162
    logbooks, 165
    permanent product of behaviour, measurement by, 165
    presentation of data, 167–70
    rating scales, 165
    record charts, 165
    reliability of data, measurement of, 170
    skills assessment, 170–2
    special equipment, 166–7, 277–8, 281–2
    time sampling recording, 163–4
  nursing process in therapy for, 154–5
  prevalence, 150
  profoundly multiply handicapped persons, 239–40
  reinforcement, 177, 182, 183
  resources, provision of, 153–4, 202
  treatment planning, 174–5
    deciding on appropriate treatment methods, 175
    setting treatment goals, 173–4
    strengths and needs of person with behaviour problems, 172–3, 174 (Fig. 9.12)
    treatment programme design, 194–6, 202 (Box 9.2)
  treatment implementation
    decreasing of inappropriate behaviour, 172, 176, 188–9
    gentle teaching, 197, 216
    increasing of appropriate behaviour, 172
    potential pitfalls and problems in, 202 (Box 9.2)
  treatment evaluation, 195–7
    action if treatment results are satisfactory, 195
    action if treatment results are unsatisfactory, 196–7
    problems in, 202, (Box 9.2)
Behavioural relaxation training (BRT), 184–5
Benzhexol in cerebral palsy management, 98
Benzodiazepine group: neurotic disorders, treatment of, 112
Bereweeke Skills Teaching System, 175
Bernstein's theory of social structure, language and learning, 88
Bethlehem Hospital (Bedlam), 21, 24

BIAS (Behavioural Interview and Analysis Schedule), 157
Birth injury, 77–8
Bite reflex in people with profound handicaps, 250, 253, 256
Blindness, 135, 136, 138–41, 233
  see also Deaf-blindness; Visual impairments
Bonding (in behaviour therapy), 197
Braces, orthopaedic, 242, 248
Braille tactile system, 139, 142
Brain damage
  cerebral palsy, 95
  prenatal problems leading to, 74–8
    infections, 74–6
    maternal-fetal incompatibility, 76
    maternal nutrition insufficiency, 76
    physical factors, 77–8
    toxic agents, 76–7
  postnatal and developmental factors, 78–9
British Epilepsy Association (BEA), 94
British Sign Language (BSL), 138
BRT (behavioural relaxation training), 184–5
Bruxism (tooth grinding), 248
Butler Report (1975), 113
Butyrophenones, treatment by
  hyperkinetic syndrome, 100
  mania, 106
  neurotic disorders, 112
  schizophrenia, 108

C

Campaign for the Mentally Handicapped (CMH), 42, 311
Care
  duty of care and duty to care, 297–299
  three dimensional model for, 62 (Box 4.1), 63 (Fig. 4.2)
Caring for People, Community Care in the Next Decade and Beyond: White Paper (1989), 216, 225, 302
Case conferences, 37–8
Cause effect analysis, 56
Causes of learning disabilities, 61–2, 63 (Fig. 4.1), 79–80
  acquired conditions, 74–9
  chromosomal abnormalities, 61, 62–7
  genetically determined conditions, 67–74
  prenatal detection and prevention, 79 (Box 4.4), 81 (Fig. 4.8)
  social causes, 83–4, 89–90
Cerebral palsy, 93, 95, 115, 230
  care and management, 96–8
  causation, 95
  classification, 95–6
  communication difficulties, 97, 115
  hand function, 243
  handling children with cerebral palsy, 245
  incontinence, 239
  interactional synchrony, 282
  malocclusion of teeth, 248
  Peto Institute, 35–6
  physical handicaps, 234

speech impairment, 233
underweight problem, and diet, 252
visual abnormalities association, 136, 233
Cerebromacular degeneration, 72
  see also Tay–Sachs disease
Challenging behaviour, 150
  see also Behavioural problems
Chicken pox, 75, 76, 78, 95
Chloral hydrate in sleep problems, 264
Chlorhexidine, in dental care and oral hygiene, 248, 249
Chlormethiazole treatment in delirium, 109
Chlorpromazine, treatment by
  delirium, 109
  mania, 106
  schizophrenia, 108
Clothing: profoundly handicapped persons, 256–7
Chorionic villus sampling, 79 (Box 4.4), 81
Chromosomes, 62–3, 80
  abnormalities, 61, 62
    autosomal, 63–4, 64–6
    deletions, 64, 66, 67, 80
    mosaicism, 64, 65
    sex chromosomes, 64, 67
    translocations, 64, 65, 80
  autosomes, 62, 80
    abnormalities, 63–4, 64–6
  sex chromosomes, 62, 80
    abnormalities, 64, 67
Class differences and learning disabilities, 83–4, 89–90
Classification of mental handicap, 83–4
Code of Professional Conduct, United Kingdom Central Council for Nursing, Midwifery and Health Visiting (1992), 294, 295 (Box 13.2), 298
Codes of ethics, 293–98
Communication, development of, in thought and learning, 125
Communication difficulties, 128–9, 129
  autism, 101–2, 115
  case conference and review system, use in handling problems, 37–8
  cerebral palsy, 97, 115
  dementia, 111
  depression, 104
  movement as means of helping with communication difficulties, 269–70, 276–7, 282–8
    adapatable approach, 284–5
    appropriate stimulation, 284
    channels and codes, 271–2
    early communication (infants), 279–80, 287
    expression and communication, 279
    gesture, 274–5
    interactional synchrony, 281–2
    interpersonal distance, 272–3
    link provided by movement, 278–9
    looking, 274, 276

nonverbal communication, role of, 270–6
nonverbal leakage, 275–6
observing and interpreting movement, 277–8
physical contact, 261, 273–4
posture, 275
proxemics, 272–3
regulatory function of nonverbal communication, 276
signs by persons with disabilities, 283
stereotyped movement, 285–6
summary of above discussions, 287–8
profoundly multiply handicapped persons, 234, 248, 260–2
  see also cerebral palsy
sensory multiple impairments, 142–4
  deaf-blindness, 142, 143–6 including Box 8.1
  see also Hearing impairments; Sign languages; Speech impairments; Speech therapy
Community and Mental Handicap Education and Research Association, 42
Community, persons with learning disabilities to have place and role in, 46, 47, 48, 49
Community care, 27–8, 212, 224–7
  Caring for People, Community Care in the Next Decade and Beyond: White Paper (1989), 216, 225, 302
  Community Mental Handicap Teams, 37, 220–1
  community nurse's perspective ('Anne-Marie'), 220–1
  ethical dilemmas presented by changes from institutional care, 302
  Griffiths Report (1988), 212, 313
  Making a reality of community care: Audit Commission Report (1986), 212, 214
  move from institutional care, 27, 30, 302, 309–10, 310–11, 312–16
  National Health Service and Community Care Act (1990), 212, 225, 241
  see also Social issues
Community Care – an Agenda for Action (Griffiths Report) (1988), 212, 313
Community Mental Handicap Teams, 37, 220–1
Competence of handicapped persons, ethical considerations in assessment, 299, 301–2
Computer-assisted learning, 44, 130
Computers in behaviour analysis, 167
Conduct disorders, see Behavioural problems
Conductive education (Peto system), 35–6, 265–6, 296
Constipation: people with profound multiple handicaps, 258
Contingency factor in reinforcement, 178–9
contingency contracting, 180
Contractures: profoundly multiply handicapped persons, 235, 263

Cornelia de Lange syndrome (Amsterdam dwarfism), 73–4, 76 (Box 4.3)
Corporate statement of intent, and quality of service, 53
Cretinism, 74
Cri-du-chat syndrome, 64, 66–7, 76 (Box 4.3)
Criminality, 108, 112–3, 115
Crosby Report (1985), 9
Cytomegalovirus disease, 76, 95

D

Day centres, 307, 309, 314
de Lange syndrome, 73–4, 76 (Box 4.3)
Deaf-Blind Helpers' League, 142
Deaf-blind manual, 138, 141, 142
Deaf-blindness, 139, 141, 142–3
    bringing meaning to the world of 'John Grant' – a deaf-blind person (case study), 144–6 *including* Box 8.1, 147
    definition of, 142, 143
Deafness, 135–6, 136–7
    conductive, 137, 232
    degrees of, 137
    sensorineural, 137, 232
    time of onset, 137
    types of, 137–8
    see also Hearing impairments
Decanoate treatment in schizophrenia, 108
Decibel scales, and hearing impairment, 137
Declaration of the UN to the General Assembly of the United Nations on the Rights of the Handicapped, 294, 296 (Box 13.3)
Dehydration, 255, 258
Deletion of chromosomes, 64, 66, 67, 80
Delirium, 108–9, 115
Delusions
    in mania, 106
    in schizophrenia, 106, 107, 108
Dementia, 108, 109–12, 115
Demonic possession, 21, 22
Dental care: people with profound multiple handicaps, 248–9
Depression, 103, 103–5, 112
Destructiveness, 112, 192
    clear and extended descriptions required for assessment, 155
    hyperkinetic syndrome, 99, 100
    schizophrenia, 107
Diarrhoea: people with profound multiple handicaps, 259
Diazepam
    cerebral palsy management, 98
    neurotic disorders, treatment of, 112
Differential reinforcement of incompatible behaviour (DRI), 190
Differential reinforcement of other behaviour (DRO), 190
Diplegia, 95, 236
Disabled Persons Act (1986), 311–2

Disruptive behaviour: clear and extended descriptions required for assessment, 155
Distractibility, 99–100, 115
Doman–Delacato progressive patterning, 266
Down syndrome, 62, 64, 64–6, 73, 220, 221
    alpha-fetoprotein levels in maternal serum, 79 (Box 4.4)
    Alzheimer's disease association, 109, 110
    types, 65 (Table 4.1)
    visual limitations, 136
Down's Syndrome Association, 310
Dressing problems: people with profound multiple handicaps, 256–7
DRI (differential reinforcement of incompatible behaviour), 190
Drinking patterns
    infants and children, 251
    people with profound multiple handicaps, management of problems, 254–5
DRO (differential reinforcement of other behaviour), 190
Drug ingestion in pregnancy, effect on fetus, 76, 77
Duchenne muscular dystrophy, 69
Dwarfism
    Amsterdam (Cornelia de Lange syndrome), 73–4, 76 (Box 4.3)
    bird headed, 76 (Box 4.3)

E

Education Act (1944), 87
Education Act (1981), 121–2, 131–2
Education Act (Defective and Epileptic Children) (1914), 27
Education Acts (1870s), 119, 120
Education (Handicapped Children) Act (1970), 121
Education (Mentally Handicapped Children) (Scotland) Act (1974), 309
Education (Scotland) Act (1945), 120–1
Education (Scotland) Act (1981), 121–2, 131–2
Educational provision for children with learning difficulties, 25, 30–1, 119–20, 122
    educational integration, 132–3
    effective teaching and learning, 126–7
        administrative procedures, 131–2
        adult/child interaction, 128–9
        applied learning theory, 127–8
        curriculum, 129–31
    history of development of, 120–2
        early classification of children, 120
        extension of provision to all pupils with learning difficulties, 120–1
        Warnock Report and after, 121–2
    pressure for, 308–10
    special schools, 25, 27, 31, 120, 131, 308
    educational integration, 132

thought and learning, development of, 122–6
    sensorimotor stage, 122–4
    preoperational stage, 124–5
    concrete operations stage, 125–6
    formal operations stage, 126
Warnock Report (1978), 13, 121–2, 127
    educational integration, 132, 309
Edward syndrome, 64
Electroconvulsive therapy (ECT) in treatment of depression, 105
Elementary Education Act (Defective and Epileptic Children) (1899), 25
Employment, for mentally handicapped people, 46, 47–8, 313–14, 315
Encephalitis as cause of brain damage, 78, 95
Epilepsy, 93, 93–5, 115
    autism, association with, 101
    control of, 94
    'epileptic personality', 94–5
    profoundly multiply handicapped persons, 239
Epiloia (tuberous sclerosis), 68, 69
    autism as feature of, 101
    Tuberous Sclerosis Association, 310
Ethical issues, 293–6
    autonomy versus paternalism, 299, 300–1
    behavioural problems, ethics of behavioural approach, 197–201
    codes of ethics, 293–8
    community care: ethical dilemmas presented by changes from institutional care, 302
    competence of handicapped persons, assessment of, 299, 301–2
    duty of care and duty to care, 297–9
    ethical dilemmas, approaches for coping with, 302–5
        consequentialist, 302
        deontological, 302
        emotivistic, 303
        motivist, 302
        naturalistic, 303
        systematic, 303–5 *including* Box 13.6
        utilitarian, 303
    morals and ethics, 296–7
    personal values, development of 297
    personhood concept, 299–300
Eugenics movement, 25, 26, 299
European Convention for the Protection of Human Rights, 295
Event recorders in behaviour analysis, 166
Evolution of services *see* Service provision, evolution of

F

Families
    coping with cerebral palsy, 98
    Elaine's story (experiences with daughter with learning disabilities), 3–4
        first year of life, 4–5
        family life with Elaine, 5–7

Families (*contd*)
 Elaine's story (experiences with daughter
  with learning disabilities), (*contd*)
  Elaine in hospital care, 7–10
 future problems, 316
 living with Susan (experiences with
  daughter with learning disabilities),
  3–4
 awareness of handicap, 10–12
 living with handicap, 12–17
 parent's perspective on social well-being
  of brain-damaged son ('Margaret',
  mother of 'Derek'), 222–3
 parent's societies, development of,
  307–10
'Feebleminded' persons (in early
 classifications), 26
Feeding problems
 cerebral palsy, 96, 252
 profoundly multiply handicapped people,
  249–56
  deaf-blind person with mental handicap
   (case study – 'John Grant'), 144–6
 therapists' involvement, 256
Fetal alcohol syndrome, 77
Flupenthixol treatment in schizophrenia, 108
Fluphenazine treatment in schizophrenia, 108
Forensic psychiatry, and criminality, 108,
 112–13, 115
Fragile X syndrome, 69, 73, 151
 autism as feature of, 101
Functional analysis in behaviour therapy,
 156
 antecedents, 156, 156–7, 158, 161
  nonperformance of behaviour, 161
  performance of behaviour, 161
 behaviour, 156, 157
 consequences, 156, 157, 158–9, 161
  nonperformance of behaviour, 161
  performance of behaviour, 161
 methods of obtaining, 157
  direct observation methods, 160–1
  interviewing methods, 157–9
  recording methods, 159–60

G

Galactosaemia, 68, 70, 72
Gametes, 64, 80
Gargoylism, 69, 70, 72, 73
Gastroenteritis as cause of brain damage, 78
General paralysis of the insane, 109 (Table
 6.1)
Genes, 61, 62, 80
 autosomal dominant inheritance,
  conditions caused by, 67–8, 69
 autosomal recessive inheritance,
  conditions caused by, 68, 69–73
 polygenetic inheritance, conditions caused
  by, 69, 73–4
 sex-linked (X-linked) recessive inheritance,
  conditions caused by, 68–9, 73
Genetic counselling, 26, 75 (Box 4.2), 81

Genetic engineering, 26, 83, 89
Genetic theories
 Eugenics movement, 25
 service provision influenced by, 25–6
 social classes differences; and learning
  disabilities, 84, 85–6, 89–90
Gentle teaching in behaviour therapy, 197,
 216
German measles (rubella) *see* Rubella
Gilles de la Tourette syndrome, 151
Glue ear, 232
Graphs: data display in behaviour analysis
 and therapy, 167–70
Griffiths Reports
 Report of the NHS Management Enquiry
  (1983), 52
 Community Care – an Agenda for Action
  (1988), 212, 313
Guide Dogs for the Blind: deaf-blind people,
 143
Guthrie test, 71

H

Hallucinations
 delirium, 109
 depression, 103
 mania, 106
 schizophrenia, 106–8
Haloperidol treatment
 hyperkinetic syndrome, 100
 mania, 106
 neurotic disorders, 112
Hand function in people with profound
 multiple handicaps, 243–4
Handling of people with profound multiple
 handicaps
 see Positioning and handling of people
  with profound multiple handicaps
'Hands on' technique, 138, 142, 143 (*two
 references*)
 deaf-blind person with mental handicap
  (case study – 'John Grant'), 144–6
  including Box 8.1
Hasicom telephone system, 143
Hearing aids, 137, 138
Hearing impairments, 135–8
 acquired hearing and visual impairments,
  143
 acquired hearing impairment with
  congenital visual impairment,
  142
 characteristics of, 137–8
 communication, 138, 301
 conductive, 137, 232
 congenital hearing impairment with
  acquired visual loss, 142–3
 hearing aids, 137, 138
 hearing and multiple impairments, 143
 profound multiple handicaps, effects of,
  232–3
 sensorineural, 137, 232
 sign languages, 138, 142, 143

 see also Deaf-blindness
Heimlich manoevre in treatment of choking,
 254
Hemiplegia, 95, 236
Hepatolenticular degeneration (Wilson's
 disease), 70, 72–3, 109 (Table 6.1)
High probability behaviour (HPB), 180
Hip dislocation in cerebral palsy, 98
Hippocratic oath, 310 *including* Box 14.1
Hirschspring's disease, 69
Historical review of services *see under*
 Service provision, evolution of
HIV (human immunodeficiency virus), 93,
 113–14
 see also AIDS (acquired immune deficiency
  syndrome)
Holy wells, 20
Hospital, historical aspects, 21, 24, 27, 30
Human immunodeficiency virus (HIV), 93,
 113–14
 see also AIDS (acquired immune deficiency
  syndrome)
Hunter syndrome, 69, 73
Huntington's chorea, 68
Hurler syndrome, 70, 72
Hydrocephalus, 74
 normal pressure, 109 (Table 6.1)
 X(sex)-linked, 69, 73
Hyperactivity, 99 *see also* hyperkinetic
 syndrome
Hyperkinetic syndrome, 93, 99–101, 115
 dietary factors as potential causes, 101
 treatment, 100–1
Hypertonia, 96, 234
Hypothyroidism, 70, 74
Hypotonia, 66, 96, 234, 250

I

'Idiots' (in early classifications), 25, 26,
 120
Idiots Act (1886), 25
Image and competency concepts: and
 dilemma arising from, 51
'Imbeciles' (in early classifications), 26,
 120
Imipramine, 104
 depression, treatment, 105
 hyperkinetic syndrome, treatment, 100
Impulsiveness
 hyperkinetic syndrome, 99, 100, 115
 mania, 106
 schizophrenia, 107
Incontinence
 pressure sores, association, 247, 258
 profoundly handicapped people, 239, 247,
  257–8, 260
  deaf-blind person with mental handicap
   (case study – 'John Grant'), 144
Independent Review of Residential Care
 (Wagner Report) (1988), 219–20
Individual Programme Plans process (IPP),
 56 *including* Figs. 3.5 and 3.6

Infections
  as cause of brain damage
    maternal infections affecting fetus, 74–6
    childhood infections, 78
  people with multiple handicaps
    chest infection, 238–9, 247
    urinary tract infection, 258
  see also specifically named infections
Influenza, 76
Informed consent to assessment and
    treatment, 153, 175, 198
Inhalation pneumonia, 250, 252
'Insanity': historical aspects, 20–4
Intelligence quotient (IQ) and mental
    handicap, 231
  genetic and sociological factors, 83–7,
    89–90
Interactional synchrony in communication,
    281–2
IPP (Individual Programme Plans process),
    56 including Figs. 3.5 and 3.6

J

Junior Occupation Centres/occupation
    centres/occupational centres, 120,
    121, 308

K

Karyotype, 62, 64, 80
Kayser–Fleischer rings, 73
Kernicterus, 76
King's Fund Report (1987), 198
Klinefelter syndrome, 64, 67
Kypho-scoliosis, 235, 236 (Fig. 11.3)
Kyphosis, 235, 236 (Fig. 11.3), 238

L

Large print publications for visually impaired
    people, 139, 142
Laurence–Moon–Biedl syndrome, 70
Lead intoxication causing brain damage, 78
Legal issues see Ethical issues; and named
    statutes
Lesch–Nyhan syndrome, 69, 151
Lithium therapy
  behaviour problems, 193
  hyperkinetic syndrome (lithium
    carbonate), 100
  mania (lithium carbonate), 106
Lordosis, 235, 236 (Fig. 11.3), 238
Low probability behaviour (LPB), 180
'Lunacy': historical aspects, 20–5
Lunacy Act (1890), 24–5
Lunatic Asylum Regulation Act (1828), 24

M

Madhouses: historical aspects, 21–4

Makaton communication system, 97, 138,
    283
Making a reality of community care: Audit
    Commission Report (1986), 212,
    214
Malnutrition, effect on mental development,
    79
Mania, 103, 105–6
Manic depressive psychoses, 103–6
Maple syrup disease, 69
Maternal-fetal incompatibility causing fetal
    brain damage, 76
Meiosis, 61, 64, 80
MENCAP (Royal Society for Mentally
    Handicapped Children & Adults, 31
  'Pathway' employment scheme (South
    Wales), 314
Meningitis as cause of brain damage, 78, 95
Mental Deficiency Acts (1913), 26–7, 120
Mental Health Act (1959), 27
Mental Health Act (1983), 27, 198
Mental illness, 20, 93, 102–8, 115, 151
Microcephaly, 76 (Box 4.3)
  alcohol consumption in pregnancy, 77
  Cornelia de Lange syndrome, 74, 76 (Box
    4.3)
  Cri-du-chat syndrome, 66, 76 (Box 4.3)
  radiation damage during pregnancy, 76
    (Box 4.3), 77
  rubella as cause of, 76, 95
  true microcephaly, 70, 76 (Box 4.3)
Mitosis, 61, 64, 80
Mobility see Movement therapy in handicap
Monasteries: role in medical history, 20–1
Mono-amine oxidase inhibitors (MAOI),
    105
  phenelzine, 104, 112
Monoplegia, 95, 236
Moon tactile system for visual impairment,
    139, 141
'Morally defective' persons (in early
    classifications), 26–7
Mosaicism, 64, 65
Motivation, 295
  assessment of, in behaviour analysis,
    158–9
  deaf-blind person with mental handicap
    (case study – 'John Grant'), 144–7
    including Box 8.1
Movement therapy in handicap, 128, 131,
    245–7, 262
  deaf-blind person with mental handicap
    (case study – 'John Grant'), 144–7
    including Box 8.1
  movement as means of helping with
    communication difficulties
    see under Communication difficulties
Multi-infarct dementia, 109 (Table 6.1
Multiple handicap
    see Profound multiple handicaps; see under
    Sensory impairments
Multiple sclerosis, dementia in, 109 (Table
    6.1)
Mumps, 75, 78

Music therapy in handicap, 97, 128, 131,
    246
  autism, 102
Mutations, genetic, 68, 80

N

Naevoid amentia, 73
Naltrexone hydorchloride: behaviour
    problems therapy, 193
National Health Service, 29, 29–30, 32
  Report of the NHS Management Enquiry
    (1983), 52
National Health Service and Community
    Care Act (1990), 212, 225, 241
National Rett Syndrome Association, 11, 18,
    310, 311
Neurofibromatosis (Von Recklinghausen's
    disease), 68, 69
Neurotic disorders, 112, 115
Niemann–Pick disease, 70
Nitrazepam (Mogadon) in sleep problems,
    264
Nondisjunction of chromosomes, 64, 80
Normalization, 41–2, 149, 215–16, 295, 299,
    300
  application of principles of, 46–51
    accommodation, 49–51
    individuals in the service, 46–7
    service as it seeks to support users,
      47–8
    social life, 48–9
    work, 47–8
  image and competency concepts: and
    dilemma arising from, 51
  misunderstandings about, 51–2
  role of values in, 42–5
    consciousness and unconsciousness in
      services, 42–3
    conservatism corollary, 43
    developmental model, 44
    imitation, power of, 44
    role expectancy and role circularity,
      relevance of, 43
    social imagery, dynamics and power of,
      44
    social integration and participation,
      importance of, 44–5
    sexuality, 114
  see also Sociual role valorization
Nursing
  behaviour therapy, nursing process in,
    154–5
  quality assurance, 53–6
  style of response of nurses to problems of
    mental handicap, 34–5

O

Occupation centres/occupational centres, for
    children with learning difficulties,
    120, 121, 308

Operant conditioning/operant learning, 115, 121, 127
  autism, 102
  hyperkinesis, 100–1
  tongue thrust, 97
  see also Reinforcement in behavioural problems therapy: Reinforcement in education
Oral hygiene: people with profound multiple handicaps, 248–9
Organic reactions, 108–12
Organizations for welfare of mentally handicapped people, 27, 31, 32, 310–11, 316
  parents' societies, 307–10
  see also specifically named organizations
Otitis media, 232
Overactivity, 99–101 *see also* Hyperkinetic syndrome
Overcorrection in behaviour therapy, 192
Oxygen deprivation, and brain damage, 77, 78

P

Paget–Gorman sign system, 138
Pain and distress: detection of, in profoundly multiply handicapped people, 261
Paraplegia, 95, 236
Parents' societies, development of, 307–10
PASS (Program Analysis of Service Systems), 42, 51
PASSING (Program Analysis of Service Systems Implementation of Normalization Goals), 42, 51
Patau's syndrome, 64
Paternalism in provision of care, 300–1
'Pathway' employment scheme (by MENCAP), 314
People First organization, 311
Personal hygiene maintenance: multiply handicapped persons, 259–260
Personhood concept, 299–300
Peto Institute, 35–6, 265–6
Phenelzine treatment of depression, 104, 112
Phenothiazines, treatment by
  hyperkinetic syndrome, 100
  mania, 106
  schizophrenia, 108
Phenotype, 64, 80
Phenylalanine–reduced diet, 70, 71–2
Phenylketonuria, 68, 69, 70 (Fig. 4.6), 71.2, 76 (Box 4.3)
  recombinant DNA technology in diagnosis, 79 (Box 4.4)
Phobic disorders, 112
Physiotherapy
  cerebral palsy, 97–8
  profound multiple handicaps, 241, 246, 256, 258

Piaget's principles of development of thought and learning, 122–6
Pie charts: data display in behaviour analysis and therapy, 168–70
Play
  communication problems: play therapy, 283
  development of, 123–4, 125
  multiple handicapped persons, 264
Pneumonia, inhalation, 250, 252
Police and Criminal Evidence Act (1984) (PACE), 113
Poliomyelitis virus, 75
Polygenetic inheritance, conditions caused by, 69, 73–4
Port wine stain, 73
Positioning and handling of people with profound multiple handicaps, 241–4, 262
  correcting asymmetries, 244
  feeding, 250–1, 251–2
  hand function, 243–4
  handling, 244–5
  lying, 243
  night-time, 263–4
  sitting, 241–2
  standing, 242–3
Premack principle in reinforcement, 180
Pressure sores, 247–8, 258
Prevalence of mental handicap, 83–4
Private sector, provision of care by, 31–2, 32
Professionals as service providers, 34–6
  new challenges for, 313–16
  style of response to problems of mental handicap, 34–5
  training requirements relative to mental handicap, 35–6
Profound multiple handicaps, 229–30
  effects of, 232
    behavioural disorders, 239–40
    mental handicap, 240–1
    physical handicaps, 234–9
    sensory handicaps, 232–4
  management, 241
    attaining mobility, 262
    beyond basic care, 262–5
    conductive education, 265–6
    developing a communication system, 234, 248, 260–2
    developing functional self-help skills, 249–60
    electic approach, 266
    preventing further deterioration, 241–9
    progressive patterning (Doman–Delacato), 266
    promoting rest, 262–4
    recreation and play, 264
    safety, 264–5
    Snoezelen concept, 265
  nature of, 230–1
Program Analysis of Service Systems (PASS), 42, 51

Program Analysis of Service Systems Implementation of Normalization Goals (Passing), 42, 51
Progressive patterning treatment (Doman–Delacato), 266
Protozoal infections, maternal, affecting fetus, 76
Proxemics, in communication, 272–3

Q

Quadriplegia, 95, 98, 236
Quality assurance, 41, 52
  audits, 56
  dimensions of quality, 53
  frameworks for, in nursing, 53–6
  meaning of 'quality', 53
  PASS and PASSING (quality assurance tools), 42, 51
  total quality management (TQM), 41, 56–8

R

Radiation during pregnancy, effect on fetus, 77
Reality orientation (RO): management of Alzheimer's disease, 111
Recombinant DNA technology in fetal cells analysis, 79 (Box 4.4)
Recording in behavioural therapy
  see measuring, recording and analysing *under* Behavioural problems
Records of Needs and Statements of Needs, 13, 14, 122, 131–2, 133
Recreation and play *see* Play
Reflexes in people with profound multiple handicaps, 236–8, 250, 253, 256
Registrar General's socioeconomic classifications, 84 *including* Table 5.3
Reinforcement in behavioural problems therapy, 176, 182
  back-up reinforcement, 177, 179, 182
  conditioned reinforcers, 178–9
  contingency, 178–9
    contingency contracting, 180
  continuous reinforcement, 179
  differential reinforcement of incompatible behaviour (DRI), 190
  differential reinforcement of other behaviour (DRO), 190
  ethical considerations, 200–1
  extinction of reinforcement, 179, 191
  natural reinforcement, 178
  negative reinforcement, 177
  positive reinforcement, 177
  Premack principle, 180
  presentation of reinforcing consequences, 190
  prevention of reinforcing consequences, 190–1

Reinforcement in behavioural problems therapy (*contd*)
  primary reinforcement, 177
  satiation, 179–80
  scheduling of reinforcement, 179
    interval schedule, fixed and variable, 179
    ratio schedule, fixed and variable, 179
  secondary reinforcement, 177
  selection of reinforcement, 178
  self–reinforcement, 186, 187
  social reinforcement, 177, 178, 183–4
  stimulating reinforcement, 177
  types of reinforcement, 177–8
  see also Skills teaching methods in behavioural problems
Reinforcement in education, 127–8
Reminiscence (management method in Alzheimer's disease), 111
Respiratory tract difficulties in persons with multiple handicap, 238–9, 247
Response cost procedure in behaviour therapy, 192
Retinitis pigmentosa, 138
Rett syndrome, 11, 14, 18, 128
  National Rett Syndrome Association, 11, 18, 310, 311
Reviews by professionals of individual cases, in mental handicap, 38
Rhesus factor incompatibility causing fetal brain damage, 76
Rights of people with disabilities
  see Ethical issues
Rocking movements by handicapped persons, 278, 282, 283
Role play, 183, 186, 194, 196
Royal Commission on the Care of the Feebleminded (1904–1908), 26
Rubella
  behavioural problems resulting from, 151
  cerebral palsy resulting from, 95
  encephalitis resulting from 78
  maternal, effect on fetus, 75–6, 95
  SENSE (National Deaf-Blind and Rubella Association), 142
  methods, 142

S

Safety of profoundly multiply handicapped persons, 264–5
Scatter plot in behaviour analysis, 160
Schizophrenia, 99, 106–8, 115
Scoliosis, 98, 235, 236 (Fig. 11.3), 243
Scots law and the rights of the mentally handicapped, 296 (Box 13.4)
Scottish Society for the Mentally Handicapped (SSMH), 31, 307–10, 314
Self-advocacy movement among mentally handicapped people, 224, 310, 311, 312

Self-injury, 160, 171, 188, 197, 199, 239
  adjusting antecedents, 189
  gentle teaching, 197
  medication, 193–4
Self-management skills in behaviour therapy, 185–7
SENSE (National Deaf-Blind and Rubella Association), 142
  methods, 142
Sensory impairments, 135–6, 147, 232–4
  assessment, 143–4
  bringing meaning to the world of 'John Grant' – deaf-blind person (case study), 144–6 *including* Box 8.1, 146
  communication, 138
  hearing impairments, 135–8, 142–3, 143, 232–3
  sensory multiple impairments, 141–3
    communication, 141, 142–3, 144–6 *including* Box 8.1
    deaf-blindness, 139, 142, 142–3, 144–6 *including* Box 8.1, 146
    sensory and multiple impairments, 143
  total approach, 145–6
  visual impairments, 135, 136, 138–41, 142–3, 233
Service brokerage, 226, 331
Service providers, 29–32
  effects of multiplicity of, 32–4
    coordination and planning of services, difficulties in, 33–4
    route of entry into services, 32–3
  new challengers for, 313–16
  professionals, 34–6
  new challenges for, 313–16
Service provision, evolution of, 19–20, 38–9
  historical review of services
    early treatment methods, 20–4
    legislative approaches up to 20th century, 24–5
    legislative approaches during 20th century, 25–8
    social changes during the 20th century, 28–9
  need for better coordinated services, 36–8
    case conferences and review system, 37–8
    Community Mental Handicap Teams, 37
  see also Service providers
Service Responses (British Institute of Mental Handicap document), 198
Sex chromosomes, 62, 80
  abnormalities, 64, 67
Sex education, 115, 130–1
Sex-linked (X-linked) recessive inheritance, conditions caused by, 68–9, 73
Sexuality: and normalization: and AIDS, 114–15
'Sheltered Placement' employment scheme, 330, 331
Short attention span, 99, 100

Sign languages, 138
  deaf-blind people, 142
  see also British Sign Language (BSL); Deaf-blind manual; 'Hands on' technique; Makaton communication system; Paget–Gorman sign system; Signed English
Signed English, 138
Skills assessment in behaviour analysis and therapy, 170–2
  assessment schedules, 171
  direct interview method, 171–2
  observation method, 172
  testing, 172
Skills teaching methods in behavioural problems, 180
  chaining, 182–3
    backward (reverse) 182–3
    forward, 182
  discrimination, 187–8
  fading of prompts, 181, 182
  generalization, 187–8
  modelling, 183
  prompting, 181, 182
  relaxation training, 184–5
  role play, 183, 186, 194, 196
  self-management skills, 185–8
  shaping, 181–2
  social skills training, 183–4
Skin care: people with profound multiple handicaps, 247–8, 258
Sleep problems; profoundly handicapped persons, 262–4
Smell, use of, in helping with sensory impairments, 145
Smoking during pregnancy, effect on fetus, 76, 77
Snoezelen treatment method for profoundly multiply handicapped people, 265
Social causes of learning disabilities, 83–4, 89–90
  identification of cultural differences, 87–9
    child/parent interaction, patterns of, 87
    locus of control, 87–8
    self-fulfilling prophecy (teacher's expectations influencing child's performance), 88–9
    sociolinguistics, 88
  social classes, 84–7
    genetic perspective, 84, 85–6, 89–90
    social environment perspective, 86–7, 89–90
Social issues, 211–12
  'mental handicap' interpretation of, 212
  social well-being of people with mental handicap, 48–9, 214–17
    community nurse's perspective ('Ann-Marie'), 220–1, 224, 225–6, 226
    interpretation of 'social well-being', 212–14
    parent's perspective ('Margaret', mother of 'Derek'), 222–3, 224, 226

Social issues (*contd*)
  social well-being of people with mental
      handicap (*contd*)
    policies which can facilitate promotion
        of, 223–7
    residential carer's perspective
        ('Patricia'), 218–20, 224
    service users' perspective ('Pat and
        Davy'), 217–18, 224, 226
    social worker's perspective ('Jennifer'),
        221–2, 224
    see also Normalization; Social causes of
        learning disabilities; Social learning
        theory; Social role valorization;
        Social work services
Social learning theory, 183
Social role valorization, 41, 133, 149, 215,
    299
  development of, 41–2
  identical with 'normalization', 52, 149
  see also Normalization
Social work services
  philosophy and role
    present day, 30, 32
    new challenges, 314
  social worker's perspective on social
      issues ('Jennifer'), 221–2
  style of response of professionals to
      problems of mental handicap, 34–5
Sociolinguistics, 88
Sociological theory on social class
    differences, and learning disabilities,
    84–5, 86–90
Solution effect analysis, 56 *including* Fig. 3.7
Spasticity, 246, 250
  cerebral palsy, 95
Special schools, 25, 27, 31, 120, 131, 308
  educational integration, 132
Speech impairments
  profoundly multiply handicapped persons,
      233–4
Speech therapy
  autism, 102
  cerebral palsy, 97
  deafness, acquired, 137
  feeding and eating problems,
      management, 256
Spina bifida, 74
  alpha-fetoprotein levels in maternal serum,
      79 (Box 4.4)
Standing frames, 243
Statements of Needs and Records of Needs,
    13, 14, 122, 131–2, 133
Stereotyped behaviour, 98–9, 115, 240,
    285–6
  behavioural approaches in management,
      99
Stopwatches in behaviour analysis, 166
Sturge–Weber syndrome, 73
Suicide and attempted suicide in depression,
    104
Swimming pool activities: people with
    handicaps, 246
Symmetrical tonic neck reflex (STNR), 237

Synchrony, interactional, in communication,
    281–2
Syphilis
  congenital, 75
  general paralysis of the insane, 109 (Table
      6.1)

T

Tally counters in behavioural analysis, 166
Tape recorders in behavioural analysis, 166
Tardive dyskinesia, drug-induced, 108
Task analysis, 182 (Box 9.1)
Taste, sense of: handicapped people, 145,
    253
Tay–Sachs disease, 68, 70, 72, 109 (Table
    6.1)
Temper tantrums in hyperkinetic syndrome,
    99, 100, 115
Temple Fay patterning, 97–8
Thioridazine, treatment by
  hyperkinetic syndrome, 100
  schizophrenia, 108
Time out in behaviour therapy, 191–2
Timers in behaviour analysis, 166
Toileting: people with profound multiple
    handicaps, 257–9
Tongue thrust, 96–7, 250, 253, 256
Tonic labyrinthine reflex (TLR), 237–8
Tooth grinding (bruxism), 248
Total quality management (TQM), 41,
    56–8
Touch as means of communication, 261,
    273–4
  deaf-blind person with mental handicap
      (case study – 'John Grant'),
      144–6
Tourette syndrome, 151
Toxic agents causing brain damage
  alcohol, 76–7, 109 (Table 6.1)
  prenatal damage, 76–7
  postnatal damage, 78–9
  smoking during pregnancy, 76, 77
Toxoplasmosis, 95
Tranquillizers, treatment by
  delirium, 109
  hyperkinetic syndrome, 100
  mania, 106
  schizophrenia, 108
Translocation of chromosomes, 64, 65,
    80
Tricyclic antidepressants, 100, 104, 105
Triple X syndrome, 64, 67
Triplegia, 95
Trisomy, 64, 80
  trisomy 13 (Patau syndrome), 64
  trisomy 18 (Edward syndrome), 64
  trisomy 21 (Down syndrome), 64, 65
Tuberous sclerosis (epiloia), 68, 69
  autism as feature of, 101
  Tuberous Sclerosis Association, 310
Tunnel vision, 136, 138
Turner syndrome, 64, 67

U

Ultrasound, 79 (Box 4.4), 81
United Nations Declaration on the Rights of
    Mentally Retarded Persons (1971),
    198
Universal Declaration of Human Rights
    (United Nations) (1948), 294
Useful addresses (listed), 18, 268
Usher syndrome, 142

V

Validation therapy in Alzheimer's disease,
    111
Values into Action (VIA), 42, 327
Vicious circle (incorporation of stereotypes
    into a value system), 45–6
Video equipment in behaviour analysis,
    166–7, 277–8, 281–2
Viral infections, maternal, affecting fetus,
    75–6
Visual impairments, 135, 136, 138–41
  acquired visual and hearing impairments,
      143
  acquired visual loss with congenital
      hearing impairment, 142
  congenital visual impairment with an
      acquired hearing impairment, 142
  persons with additional multiple
      impairments, 143, 233
  see also Deaf-blindness
Visual screening in behaviour therapy, 197
Voluntary organizations, 27, 310–11, 316
  parents' societies, 307–10
  philosophy and practice of, 31, 32
  see also specifically named organizations
Von Reckinghausen's disease, 68, 69

W

Wagner Report (1988), 219–20
Warnock Report (1978), 13, 121–2, 127
  education integration, 132, 325
Wedges, 243, 244
Wheelchairs: people with profound multiple
    handicaps, 242 (*two references*), 244,
    262, 264
Whooping cough vaccination, and
    encephalitis, 78
Wilson's disease (hepatolenticular
    degeneration), 70, 72–3, 109 (Table
    6.1)
Windswept hips, 235, 243
Witchcraft: relationship to madness, 22
Wolf syndrome, 64, 67
Work, engagement in, by people with
    learning difficulties, 46, 47–8,
    313–14, 315
Workhouses, 24, 25, 27
World Health Organization, definitions on
    health and mental handicap, 211,
    212, 214

X

X-linked recessive inheritance, conditions
        caused by, 68–9, 73
XYY syndrome, 64, 67

Y

York Retreat, 23–4, 24

Z

Zangwill Report (1980), 198
Zygote, 63, 80